D0948886

The Papers of
George Washington

The Papers of
George Washington

Dorothy Twohig, *Editor*

Philander D. Chase, *Senior Associate Editor*

Beverly H. Runge, *Associate Editor*

Frank E. Grizzard, Jr., Beverly S. Kirsch, Mark A. Mastromarino,
Elizabeth B. Mercer, and Jack D. Warren, *Assistant Editors*

Presidential Series
5

January–June 1790

*Dorothy Twohig, Mark A. Mastromarino,
and Jack D. Warren*, Editors

UNIVERSITY PRESS OF VIRGINIA

CHARLOTTESVILLE AND LONDON

This edition has been prepared by the staff of
The Papers of George Washington
sponsored by
The Mount Vernon Ladies' Association of the Union
and the University of Virginia
with the support of
the National Endowment for the Humanities and
the National Historical Publications and Records Commission.
The publication of this volume
has been supported by a grant from
the National Historical Publications
and Records Commission.

THE UNIVERSITY PRESS OF VIRGINIA

First published 1996

Library of Congress Cataloging-in-Publication Data
(Revised for vol. 5)

Washington, George, 1732–1799.
   The papers of George Washington, Dorothy Twohig, ed.

Presidential series vol. 5 edited by Dorothy Twohig.
   Includes indexes.
   Contents: 1. September 1788–March 1789—[etc.]—
5. January 1790–June 1790.
   1. Washington, George, 1732–1799—Correspondence.   2. Presidents—United States—Correspondence.   3. United States—Politics and government—1789–1797.   I. Twohig, Dorothy.   II. Abbot,
W. W. (William Wright), 1922–   .   III. Presidential series.   IV. Title.
E312.72   1987b   973.4'1'092   87-410017
ISBN 0-8139-1103-6 (v. 1)
ISBN 0-8139-1619-4 (v. 5)

Printed in the United States of America

This volume is dedicated
to the memory of
John A. Castellani, 1944–1993
Resident Director of Mount Vernon, 1979–1984

Contents

Editorial Apparatus

Transcription of the documents in the volumes of *The Papers of George Washington* has remained as close to a literal reproduction of the manuscript as possible. Punctuation, capitalization, paragraphing, and spelling of all words are retained as they appear in the original document. Dashes used as punctuation have been retained except when a period and a dash and another mark of punctuation appear together. The appropriate marks of punctuation have always been added at the end of a paragraph. When a tilde is used in the manuscript to indicate a double letter, the letter has been doubled. Washington and some of his correspondents occasionally used a tilde above an incorrectly spelled word to indicate an error in orthography. When this device is used the editors have corrected the word. In cases where a tilde has been inserted above an abbreviation or contraction, usually in letter-book copies, the word has been expanded. Otherwise, contractions and abbreviations have been retained as written except that a period has been inserted after an abbreviation when needed. Superscripts have been lowered. Editorial insertions or corrections in the text apppear in square brackets. Angle brackets ⟨ ⟩ are used to indicate illegible or mutilated material. A space left blank in a manuscript by the writer is indicated by a square-bracketed gap in the text [   ]. Deletion of material by the author of a manuscript is ignored unless it contains substantive material, and then it appears in a footnote. If the intended location of marginal notations is clear from the text, they are inserted without comment; otherwise they are recorded in the notes. The ampersand has been retained and the thorn transcribed as "th". The symbol for per (℞) is used when it appears in the manuscript. The dateline has been placed at the head of a document regardless of where it occurs in the manuscript. All of the documents printed in this volume, as well as other ancillary material usually cited in the notes, may be found in the electronic edition of the Washington Papers (CD-ROM:GW).

During both of Washington's administrations, but particularly in the period shortly before and after his inauguration, he was besieged with applications for public office. Many of the applicants continued to seek appointment or promotion. The editors have usually printed only one of these letters in full and cited other letters both from the applicant and in support of his application in notes to the initial letter. When GW replied to these requests at all, the replies were generally pro forma reiterations of his policy of noncommitment until the appointment to a post was made. In such cases his replies have been included only in the notes to the original application and do not appear in their chronological sequence. Letters to or from GW that, in whole or in part, are printed out of their chronological sequence are listed in the table of contents with an indication of where they may be found in the volumes.

Since GW read no language other than English, incoming letters written to him in foreign languages were generally translated for him. Where this contemporary translation has survived, it has been used as the text of the document, rather than the original which Washington did not read. If no translation has been found, the text in the original foreign language will be used. Both the original and the contemporary translation will appear in the CD-ROM edition of the Washington Papers.

During the early years of the new government, the executive sent out large numbers of circular letters, either under Washington's name or that of one of his secretaries. Circular letters covered copies of laws passed by Congress and sent to the governors of the states. They also covered commissions and announcements of appointment for public offices sent to individuals after their nominations had been approved by the Senate. In both instances, the circulars requested recipients to acknowledge receipt of the documents. The circulars and the routine acknowledgments of these circulars, usually addressed to Washington but sometimes to one of his secretaries, have been omitted unless they contain material of other interest or significance. In such cases the letters are either calendared or printed in full. The entire text of the documents is available in the CD-ROM edition.

Individuals mentioned in the text are identified usually at their first substantive mention and are not identified at length in subsequent volumes. The index to each volume indicates where an identification appears in an earlier volume of the Presidential Series.

During the early part of Washington's first administration, he had the services of several secretaries: Tobias Lear and David Humphreys, who had been in his service at Mount Vernon, went with him to New York, and his nephew Robert Lewis of Fredericksburg joined the staff at the end of May 1789. William Jackson and Thomas Nelson arrived later in the year. Relatively few drafts in Washington's hand of letters for this time have survived, and the sequence in which outgoing letters and documents were written is often difficult to determine. In Record Group 59, State Department Miscellaneous Letters, in the National Archives, there are numerous documents that appear to be the original retained copies of letters written by Washington shortly before he became president and in the first years of his first administration.

Much of this correspondence is in the hand of Lear or Humphreys. Occasionally the frequency with which the secretary's emendations and insertions appear suggests that the document was a draft prepared by him for Washington. More rarely there are changes and corrections on a document, in Washington's own writing. On other occasions the documents appear to be simply retained copies either of his original draft or of the receiver's copy. For most of the letters found in Miscellaneous Letters, there are also letter-book copies in the Washington Papers at the Library of Congress. Some of the letters for this period probably were copied into the letter books close to the time they were written, but others obviously were entered much later. Occasionally Thomas Nelson's writing appears in the letter-book copies for the summer of 1789, as does Bartholomew Dandridge's, although Nelson did not join the staff until October and Dandridge was not employed until 1791. Finally, a few are in the handwriting of Howell Lewis, Washington's nephew, who did not assume his duties until the spring of 1792. When the receiver's copy of a letter has not been found, the editors have generally assumed that the copy in Miscellaneous Letters was made from the receiver's copy or the draft and have used it, rather than the letter-book copy, as the text, describing the document either as a copy or a draft, depending on the appearance of the manuscript.

Symbols Designating Documents

AD	Autograph Document
ADS	Autograph Document Signed
ADf	Autograph Draft
ADfS	Autograph Draft Signed
AL	Autograph Letter
ALS	Autograph Letter Signed
D	Document
DS	Document Signed
Df	Draft
DfS	Draft Signed
L	Letter
LS	Letter Signed
LB	Letter-Book Copy
[S]	Signature clipped (used with other symbols: e.g., AL[S], Df[S])

Repository Symbols

CD-ROM:GW	*see* Editorial Apparatus
CLjJC	James S. Copley Library, La Jolla, Calif.
CSmH	Henry E. Huntington Library, San Marino, Calif.
CtHi	Connecticut Historical Society, Hartford
CtY	Yale University, New Haven
CtMyM	Marine Historical Association, Mystic, Conn.
DLC	Library of Congress
DLC:GW	George Washington Papers, Library of Congress
DNA	National Archives
DNA:PCC	Papers of the Continental Congress, National Archives
DSoCi	Society of the Cincinnati, Washington, D.C.
ICHi	Chicago Historical Society, Chicago
MdAA	Maryland Hall of Records, Archives, Annapolis
MdBAr	Archdiocese of Baltimore-Maryland
MdHi	Maryland Historical Society, Baltimore
MH	Harvard University, Cambridge, Mass.
MHi	Massachusetts Historical Society, Boston
MHi-A	Massachusetts Historical Society: Adams Papers, Boston
MiU-C	William L. Clements Library, University of Michigan, Ann Arbor
N	New York State Library, Albany
NAlI	Albany Institute of History and Art
Nc-Ar:	North Carolina State Department of Archives and History, Raleigh
NHi	New-York Historical Society, New York
NjP	Princeton University, Princeton, N.J.
NjR	Rutgers—The State University, New Brunswick, N.J.
NN	New York Public Library, New York
NNC	Columbia University, New York
NNGL	Gilder Lehrman Library, New York City
NNPM	Pierpont Morgan Library, New York
O	Ohio State Library, Columbus
OHi	Ohio State Historical Society, Columbus
PDoBHi	Bucks County Historical Society, Doyleston, Pa.
PEL	Lafayette College, Easton, Pa.
PHC	Haverford College, Haverford, Pa.
PHi	Historical Society of Pennsylvania, Philadelphia
PPAmP	American Philosophical Society, Philadelphia
PPRF	Rosenbach Foundation, Philadelphia

PWacD	David Library of the American Revolution, Washington Crossing, Pa.
PWW	Washington and Jefferson College, Washington, Pa.
R-Ar	Rhode Island State Library, Rhode Island State Archives, Providence
RG	Record Group (designating the location of documents in the National Archives)
RHi	Rhode Island Historical Society, Providence
RPB	Brown University Library, Providence
Vi	Library of Virginia, Richmond
ViHi	Virginia Historical Society, Richmond
ViMtV	Mount Vernon Ladies' Association of the Union
ViU	University of Virginia, Charlottesville
WHi	State Historical Society of Wisconsin, Madison

Short Title List

Akins, "History of Halifax City."   Thomas Beamish Akins. "History of Halifax City." *Collections of the Nova Scotia Historical Society,* 8 (1895–1907), 1–320.

Aldridge, *Man of Reason.*   Alfred Owen Aldridge. *Man of Reason.* Philadelphia and New York, 1959.

Allen, *Diary of John Quincy Adams.*   David Grayson Allen et al., eds. *Diary of John Quincy Adams.* 2 vols. Cambridge, Mass., and London, 1981.

Allen, *Works of Ames.*   William B. Allen, ed. *Works of Fisher Ames as Published by Seth Ames.* 2 vols. Indianapolis, 1983.

Aman, *Officiers bleus dans la marine française.*   Jacques Aman. *Les officiers bleus dans la marine française au XVIIIe siècle.* Geneva, 1976.

Andrews, *Fountain Inn Diary.*   Matthew Page Andrews. *The Fountain Inn Diary.* New York, 1948.

Annals of Congress.   Joseph Gales, Sr., comp. *The Debates and Proceedings in the Congress of the United States; with an Appendix, Containing Important State Papers and Public Documents, and All the Laws of a Public Nature.* 42 vols. Washington, D.C., 1834–56.

Archives parlementaires.   M. J. Mavidal, ed. *Archives parlementaires de 1787 à 1860.* Paris, 1877.

Armes, *Stratford Hall.*   Ethel Armes. *Stratford Hall: The Great House of the Lees.* Richmond, 1936.

Arnow, *Seedtime on the Cumberland.*   Harriette Louisa Simpson Arnow. *Seedtime on the Cumberland.* New York, 1960.

ASP.   Walter Lowrie et al., eds. *American State Papers: Documents, Leg-*

islative and Executive, of the Congress of the United States. 38 vols. Washington, D.C., 1832–61.

"Autobiography of Nathan Read." "Autobiography of Hon. Nathan Read, Who Died at Belfast, Maine, Jan. 20, 1849." *NEHGR*, 50 (1896), 434–36.

Baker, *Medallic Portraits of Washington.* William S. Baker. *Medallic Portraits of Washington, with Historical and Critical Notes and a Descriptive Catalogue of the Coins, Medals, Tokens, and Cards.* Philadelphia, 1885.

Bailey, *Bio. Dir. of the S.C. Senate, 1776–1985.* N. Louise Bailey, Mary L. Morgan, and Carolyn R. Taylor, eds. *Biographical Directory of the South Carolina Senate, 1776–1985.* 3 vols. Columbia, S.C., 1986.

Ballagh, *Letters of Richard Henry Lee.* James Curtis Ballagh, ed. *The Letters of Richard Henry Lee.* 2 vols. New York, 1911–14.

Bartlett, *R.I. Records.* John Russell Bartlett, ed. *Records of the Colony of Rhode Island and Providence Plantations in New England.* 10 vols. Providence, 1856–65.

Bathe, *Oliver Evans.* Greville Bathe. *Oliver Evans: A Chronicle of Early American Engineering.* Philadelphia, 1935.

Belote, "Scioto Speculation." Theodore Thomas Belote. "The Scioto Speculation and the French Settlement at Gallipolis." *University Studies Published by the University of Cincinnati,* 2d ser., 3 (1907), 1–81.

Bezanson, *Wholesale Prices in Philadelphia.* Anne Bezanson et al. *Wholesale Prices in Philadelphia, 1748–1861.* 2 vols. Philadelphia, 1936–37.

Biographical Cyclopedia. *The Biographical Cyclopedia of Representative Men of Rhode Island.* Providence, 1881.

Biographical Dictionary of the Maryland Legislature. Edward C. Papenfuse et al., eds. *A Biographical Dictionary of the Maryland Legislature, 1635–1789.* 2 vols. Baltimore, 1979–85.

Biog. Dir. Cong. *Biographical Directory of the United States Congress, 1774–1789.* Washington, D.C., 1989.

Bio. Dir. of the S.C. House of Representatives. J. S. R. Faunt et al., eds. *Biographical Directory of the South Carolina House of Representatives.* 4 vols. Columbia, S.C., 1974–84.

Blanton, *Medicine in Virginia.* Wyndham B. Blanton. *Medicine in Virginia in the Eighteenth Century.* Richmond, 1931.

Bowie, *Prince George's County.* Effie Gwynn Bowie. *Across the Years in Prince George's County.* Richmond, 1947.

Bowling and Veit, *Diary of William Maclay.* Kenneth R. Bowling and Helen E. Veit, eds. *The Diary of William Maclay and Other Notes on Senate Debates.* Baltimore, 1988.

Boyd, *Jefferson Papers.* Julian P. Boyd et al., eds. *The Papers of Thomas Jefferson.* 25 vols. to date. Princeton, N.J., 1950—.

Burnett, *Letters.*   Edmund C. Burnett, ed. *Letters of Members of the Continental Congress.* 8 vols. Washington, D.C., 1921–36. Reprint. Gloucester, Mass., 1963.

Butterfield, *Adams Diary and Autobiography.*   L. H. Butterfield et al., eds. *Diary and Autobiography of John Adams.* 4 vols. Cambridge, Mass., 1961.

Calendar of Virginia State Papers.   William P. Palmer et al., eds. *Calendar of Virginia State Papers and Other Manuscripts.* 11 vols. Richmond, 1875–93.

Carter, *Territorial Papers.*   Clarence E. Carter et al., eds. *The Territorial Papers of the United States.* 27 vols. Washington, D.C., 1934–69.

Caughey, *McGillivray of the Creeks.*   John Walton Caughey. *McGillivray of the Creeks.* Norman, Okla., 1938.

Chastellux, *Travels in North America.*   Howard C. Rice, Jr., ed. *Travels in North America in the Years 1780, 1781, and 1782 by the Marquis de Chastellux.* 2 vols. Chapel Hill, N.C., 1963.

Chateaubriand, *Memoirs.*   François René, vicomte de Chateaubriand. *Memoirs of the Vicomte de Chateaubriand, Sometime Ambassador to England.* 6 vols. New York, 1902.

Childs, *French Refugee Life.*   Frances Sergeant Childs. *French Refugee Life in the United States, 1790–1800.* Baltimore, 1940.

Chinard, *George Washington As the French Knew Him.*   Gilbert Chinard, ed. and trans. *George Washington As the French Knew Him: A Collection of Texts.* Princeton, N.J., 1940.

Clark, *Naval Documents.*   William Bell Clark et al., eds. *Naval Documents of the American Revolution.* 9 vols. to date. Washington, D.C., 1964—.

Clasen, *Streiks und Aufstände.*   Claus-Peter Clasen. *Streiks und Aufstände der Augsburger Weber im 17. und 18. Jahrhundert.* Augsburg, Germany, 1993.

Contenson, *La Société des Cincinnati de France.*   Baron Ludovic Guy Marie du Bessey de Contenson. *La Société des Cincinnati de France et la guerre d'Amerique, 1778–1783.* Paris, 1934.

Cope, "Bird, Savage & Bird of London."   Sydney Raymond Cope. "Bird, Savage & Bird of London: Merchants and Bankers, 1782 to 1803." *Guildhall Studies in London History,* 4 (1981), 202–17.

Cope, "Collecting Source Material about Charles Mason and Jeremiah Dixon."   Thomas D. Cope. "Collecting Source Material about Charles Mason and Jeremiah Dixon." *Proceedings of the American Philosophical Society,* 92 (1948), 111–14.

Crane, *Dependent People.*   Elaine Forman Crane. *A Dependent People: Newport, Rhode Island, in the Revolutionary Era.* New York, 1985.

Crumrine, *Washington County.*   Boyd Crumrine. *History of Washing-*

ton County, Pennsylvania, with Biographical Sketches of Many of Its Pioneers and Prominent Men.* Philadelphia, 1882.

Davis, *Earlier History of American Corporations.* Joseph Stancliffe Davis. *Essays in the Earlier History of American Corporations.* Harvard Economic Studies, vol. 16, nos. 1–4. 2 vols. Cambridge, Mass., 1917.

Decatur, *Private Affairs of George Washington.* Stephen Decatur, Jr. *Private Affairs of George Washington, from the Records and Accounts of Tobias Lear, Esquire, His Secretary.* Boston, 1933.

Delaware Archives. *Delaware Archives.* 5 vols. Wilmington, Del., 1911–19. Reprint. New York, 1974.

DenBoer, *First Federal Elections.* Gordon DenBoer, ed. *The Documentary History of the First Federal Elections, 1788–1790.* 4 vols. Madison, Wis., and London, 1976–89.

Detweiler, *George Washington's Chinaware.* Susan Gray Detweiler. *George Washington's Chinaware.* New York, 1982.

DHFC. Linda G. De Pauw et al., eds. *Documentary History of the First Federal Congress of the United States of America.* 6 vols. to date. Baltimore, 1972—.

Diaries. Donald Jackson and Dorothy Twohig, eds. *The Diaries of George Washington.* 6 vols. Charlottesville, Va., 1976–79.

Downer, *Memoir of John Durang.* Alan S. Downer, ed. *The Memoir of John Durang, American Actor, 1785–1816.* Pittsburgh, 1966.

Dulles, *The Old China Trade.* Foster Rhea Dulles. *The Old China Trade.* Boston and New York, 1930.

Eckman, "Early Silver Mining in Lancaster County." D. J. Eckman. *Historical Papers and Addresses of the Lancaster County Historical Society,* 31 (1927), 21–24.

Ely and Brown, *Legal Papers of Andrew Jackson.* James W. Ely, Jr., and Theodore Brown, Jr., eds. *Legal Papers of Andrew Jackson.* Knoxville, Tenn., 1987.

ESTC, British Library. R. C. Alston and M. J. Crump. *The Eighteenth Century Short Title Catalogue: The British Library Collections.* London, 1983.

Evans, *American Bibliography.* Charles Evans. *American Bibliography.* Chicago, 1903–59.

Everest, *Moses Hazen and the Canadian Refugees in the American Revolution.* Allan S. Everest. *Moses Hazen and the Canadian Refugees in the American Revolution.* Syracuse, N.Y., 1976.

Executive Journal. *Journal of the Executive Proceedings of the Senate of the United States of America.* Vol. 1. Washington, D.C., 1828.

Fairchild, *Francis Adrian Van der Kemp.* Helen Lincklaen Fairchild, ed. *Francis Adrian Van der Kemp, 1752–1829: An Autobiography Together with Extracts from His Correspondence.* New York and London, 1903.

Faris, *Old Churches and Meeting Houses.*   John T. Faris. *Old Churches and Meeting Houses in and around Philadelphia.* Philadelphia and London, 1926.

Ford, *Washington and the Theatre.*   Paul Leicester Ford. *Washington and the Theatre.* New York, 1899.

Ford, *Correspondence and Journals of Samuel Blachley Webb.*   Worthington Chauncey Ford, ed. *Correspondence and Journals of Samuel Blachley Webb.* 3 vols. New York, 1893–94.

Ford, *Wills of George Washington.*   Worthington Chauncey Ford, ed. *Wills of George Washington and His Immediate Ancestors.* Brooklyn, N.Y., 1891.

Gardiner, *A Study in Dissent.*   C. Harvey Gardiner, ed. *A Study in Dissent: The Warren-Gerry Correspondence, 1776–1792.* Carbondale and Edwardsville, Ill., 1968.

Gottschalk, *Lafayette between the American and the French Revolution.*   Louis Gottschalk. *Lafayette between the American and the French Revolution (1783–1789).* Chicago and London, 1950.

Gottschalk, *Letters of Lafayette to Washington.*   Louis Gottschalk. *The Letters of Lafayette to Washington, 1777–1799.* 1944. Reprint. Philadelphia, 1976.

Gottschalk and Maddox, *Lafayette in the French Revolution.*   Louis Gottschalk and Margaret Maddox. *Lafayette in the French Revolution: From the October Days through the Federation.* Chicago and London, 1973.

Griffin, *Boston Athenæum Collection.*   Appleton P. C. Griffin, comp. *A Catalogue of the Washington Collection in the Boston Athenæum.* Cambridge, Mass., 1897.

Hamilton, *Letters to Washington.*   Stanislaus Murray Hamilton, ed. *Letters to Washington and Accompanying Papers.* 5 vols. Boston and New York, 1898–1902.

Harrison, *Princetonians, 1769–1775.*   Richard A. Harrison. *Princetonians, 1769–1775, A Biographical Dictionary.* Princeton, N.J., 1980.

Heads of Families (Massachusetts).   *Heads of Families at the First Census of the United States Taken in the Year 1790* (Massachusetts). Washington, D.C., 1908. Reprint. Baltimore, Md., 1964.

Heads of Families (Pennsylvania).   *Heads of Families at the First Census of the United States Taken in the Year 1790* (Pennsylvania). Washington, D.C., 1908. Reprint. Baltimore, Md., 1970.

Heitman, *Historical Register.*   Francis B. Heitman. *Historical Register of Officers of the Continental Army during the War of the Revolution, April, 1775, to December, 1783.* Washington, D.C., 1893.

Hening.   William Waller Hening, ed. *The Statutes at Large; Being a Collection of All the Laws of Virginia from the First Session of the Legisla-*

ture, in the Year 1619. 13 vols. 1819–23. Reprint. Charlottesville, Va., 1969.

Henry, *Patrick Henry.* William Wirt Henry, ed. *Patrick Henry: Life, Correspondence and Speeches.* 3 vols. New York, 1891.

Hunt, *Calendar.* Gaillard Hunt. *Calendar of Applications and Recommendations for Office.* Washington, D.C., 1901.

JCC. Worthington C. Ford et al., eds. *Journals of the Continental Congress.* 34 vols. Washington, D.C., 1904–37.

Johnston, *Jay Papers.* Henry Phelps Johnston, ed. *The Correspondence and Public Papers of John Jay.* 4 vols. New York and London, 1891.

Journals of the Council of State of Virginia. H. R. McIlwaine, Wilmer L. Hall, and Benjamin Hillman, eds. *Journals of the Council of the State of Virginia.* 5 vols. Richmond, 1931–82.

Journal of the House of Delegates, 1789. *Journal of the House of Delegates of the Commonwealth of Virginia; Begun and Holden in the City of Richmond . . . on Monday, the Nineteenth Day of October, in the Year of Our Lord One Thousand Seven Hundred and Eighty-nine.* Richmond, 1828. Microfilm Collection of Early State Records.

Journal of the House of Delegates, 1790. *Journal of the House of Delegates of the Commonwealth of Virginia; Begun and Held at the Capitol in the City of Richmond . . . on Monday, the Eighteenth Day of October in the Year of Our Lord One Thousand Seven Hundred and Ninety.* Richmond, 1828. Microfilm Collection of Early State Records.

JPP. Dorothy Twohig, ed. *Journal of the Proceedings of the President, 1793–1797.* Charlottesville, Va., 1981.

Kelly and Burrage, *American Medical Biographies.* Howard A. Kelly and Walter L. Burrage. *American Medical Biographies.* Baltimore, 1920.

Lamb, *History of New York.* Mrs. Martha J. Lamb and Mrs. Burton Harrison. *History of the City of New York: Its Origin, Rise, and Progress.* 3 vols. New York, 1896.

Lasseray, *Les Français sous les treize étoiles.* André Lasseray. *Les Français sous les treize étoiles.* 2 vols. Paris, 1935.

Lopez, *Mon Cher Papa.* Claude-Anne Lopez. *Mon Cher Papa: Franklin and the Ladies of Paris.* New Haven and London, 1966.

McLachlan, *Princetonians.* James McLachlan. *Princetonians, 1748–1768: A Biographical Dictionary.* Princeton, N.J., 1976.

Manning, "Nootka Sound Controversy." William R. Manning, "The Nootka Sound Controversy." pp. 279–478 in *Annual Report of the American Historical Association for the Year 1904.* Washington, D.C., 1905.

Marcus, *American Jewry.*   Jacob R. Marcus, *American Jewry—Documents; Eighteenth Century.* Cincinnati, 1959.

Marcus and Perry, *Documentary History of the Supreme Court.*   Maeva Marcus, James R. Perry, et al., eds. *The Documentary History of the Supreme Court of the United States, 1789–1800.* 4 vols. to date. New York, 1985—.

Md. Archives.   *Archives of Maryland.* Baltimore, 1883—.

Miller, "Owner of West Point."   Agnes Miller. "Owner of West Point." *New York History,* 50 (1952), 303–12.

Miller, *Treaties.*   Hunter Miller, ed. *Treaties and Other International Acts of the United States of America.* Vol. 2. Washington, D.C., 1931.

Miller, *Artisans and Merchants of Alexandria.*   T. Michael Miller. *Artisans and Merchants of Alexandria, Virginia 1784–1820.* 2 vols. Bowie, Md., 1991.

Miner, *William Goddard.*   Ward L. Miner. *William Goddard, Newspaperman.* Durham, N.C., 1962.

Mitchell, *Beginning at a White Oak.*   Beth Mitchell. *Beginning at a White Oak: Patents and Northern Neck Grants of Fairfax County Virginia.* Fairfax, Va., 1977.

Mitchell, *Crèvecoeur.*   Julia Post Mitchell. *St. Jean de Crèvecoeur.* New York, 1916.

Mitchell, *Mitchell-Boulton Correspondence.*   Clarence Blair Mitchell. *Mitchell-Boulton Correspondence, 1787–1792.* Princeton, N.J., 1931.

Mitchell, *New Letters of Abigail Adams.*   Stewart Mitchell, ed. *New Letters of Abigail Adams, 1788–1801.* Boston, 1947.

Morison, *Maritime History of Massachusetts.*   Samuel Eliot Morison. *The Maritime History of Massachusetts, 1783–1860.* Boston and New York, 1921.

Morris, *Diary of the French Revolution.*   Beatrix Cary Davenport, ed. *A Diary of the French Revolution by Gouverneur Morris.* 2 vols. Boston, 1939.

Mount Vernon Gardens.   *The Mount Vernon Gardens with Notes Pertaining to the Domestic Life of George and Martha Washington.* Mount Vernon, Va., 1941.

Mulkearn, *Historic Western Pennsylvania.*   Lois Mulkearn. *A Traveler's Guide to Historic Western Pennsylvania.* Pittsburgh, 1954.

Munson, *Alexandria Hustings Court Deeds, 1783–1797.*   James D. Munson, comp. *Alexandria, Virginia: Alexandria Hustings Court Deeds, 1783–1797.* Bowie, Md., 1990.

Myers, *Liberty without Anarchy.*   Minor Myers, Jr. *Liberty without Anarchy: A History of the Society of Cincinnati.* Charlottesville, Va., 1983.

N.C. State Records.   Walter Clark, ed. *The State Records of North Carolina.* 26 vols. Raleigh and various places, 1886–1907.

NEHGR. *New-England Historical and Genealogical Register.*

Nelson, *Wayne.* Paul David Nelson. *Anthony Wayne, Soldier of the Early Republic.* Bloomington, Ind., 1985.

New York City Directory, 1790. *The New-York Directory and Register, for the Year 1790.* New York, 1790.

Niemcewicz, *Vine and Fig Tree.* Julian Ursyn Niemcewicz. *Under Their Vine and Fig Tree: Travels through America in 1797–1799, 1805, with Some Further Account of Life in New Jersey.* Elizabeth, N.J., 1965.

Palmer, *The River and the Rock.* D. R. Palmer. *The River and the Rock: The History of Fortress West Point.* New York, 1969.

Papers, Colonial Series. W. W. Abbot et al., eds. *The Papers of George Washington. Colonial Series.* Charlottesville, Va., 1983—.

Papers, Revolutionary War Series. W. W. Abbot et al., eds. *The Papers of George Washington. Revolutionary War Series.* Charlottesville, Va., 1985—.

Petitions, Memorials, and Other Documents Submitted for the Consideration of Congress. *Petitions, Memorials, and Other Documents Submitted for the Consideration of Congress, March 4, 1789, to December 14, 1795.* A Staff Study Prepared for the Use of the Committee on Energy and Commerce, U.S. House of Representatives. Washington, D.C., April 1986.

Pierson, "Records of the French in Elizabethtown." Emiline G. Pierson. "Some Records of the French in Elizabethtown." *Proceedings of the New Jersey Historical Society,* 2d ser., 13 (1895), 163–70.

Polishook, "Edes's Report." Irwin H. Polishook. "Peter Edes's Report of the Proceedings of the Rhode Island General Assembly, 1787–1790." *Rhode Island History,* 25 (1966), 33–42, 89–97, 117–129; 26 (1967), 15–31.

Polishook, *Rhode Island and the Union.* Irwin H. Polishook. *Rhode Island and the Union, 1774–1795.* Evanston, Ill., 1969.

Powell, *Dictionary of North Carolina Biography.* William S. Powell, ed. *Dictionary of North Carolina Biography.* 5 vols. to date. Chapel Hill, 1979—.

Preble, *History of Steam Navigation.* George Henry Preble. *A Chronological History of the Origin and Development of Steam Navigation.* 2d ed. Philadelphia, 1895.

Proceedings of the General Society of the Cincinnati. John C. Daves, ed. *Proceedings of the General Society of the Cincinnati.* Vol. 1, 1784–1884. Baltimore, 1925.

Quinn, *History of Fredericksburg.* S. J. Quinn. *The History of the City of Fredericksburg, Virginia.* Richmond, 1908.

Representative Men of Rhode Island. *Representative Men and Old Families of Rhode Island: Genealogical Records and Historical Sketches of Prominent and Representative Citizens and of Many Old Families.* 3 vols. Chicago, 1908.

Robertson, *Louisiana.* James Alexander Robertson. *Louisiana under the Rule of Spain, France, and the United States, 1785–1807.* 2 vols. Cleveland, 1911.

Robertson, "Miranda and the Revolutionizing of Spanish America." William Spence Robertson. "Francisco de Miranda and the Revolutionizing of Spanish America." *Annual Report of the American Historical Association for the Year 1907,* 1 (1907), 189–539.

Robinson, "A Note on Charles Mason's Ancestry and His Family." H. W. Robinson. "A Note on Charles Mason's Ancestry and His Family." *Proceedings of the American Philosophical Society,* 93 (1949), 134–36.

Roelker, "Patrol of Narragansett Bay." William G. Roelker. "The Patrol of Narragansett Bay (1774–1776)." *Rhode Island History,* 7 (1948), 12–19, 90–95; 8 (1949), 45–63, 77–83; 9 (1950), 11–23, 52–58.

Rogers, *Evolution of a Federalist.* George C. Rogers, Jr. *Evolution of a Federalist: William Loughton Smith of Charleston (1758–1812).* Columbia, S.C., 1962.

Rogers and Chesnutt, *Laurens Papers.* George C. Rogers, David R. Chesnutt, et al., eds. *The Papers of Henry Laurens.* 13 vols. to date. Columbia, S.C., 1968—.

Rush, *Autobiography.* Benjamin Rush. *The Autobiography of Benjamin Rush.* Princeton, N.J., 1948.

Rutland, *Madison Papers.* William T. Hutchinson, Robert A. Rutland, J. C. A. Stagg, et al., eds. *The Papers of James Madison.* 17 vols. to date. Chicago and Charlottesville, Va., 1962—.

Rutland, *Mason Papers.* Robert A. Rutland, ed. *The Papers of George Mason, 1725–1792.* 3 vols. Chapel Hill, N.C., 1970.

Saffell, *Records of the Revolutionary War.* W. T. R. Saffell. *Records of the Revolutionary War.* New York, 1859.

Sargent, *Trees at Mount Vernon.* Charles Sprague Sargent. *The Trees at Mount Vernon: Report of Charles Sprague Sargent, Director of the Arnold Arboretum, to the Council of the Mount Vernon Ladies Association of the Union.* Reprinted from the Annual Report, 1917.

Schultz, *Inventory of the Talbot Papers.* Charles R. Schultz, comp. *Inventory of the Silas Talbot Papers, 1767–1867.* Mystic, Conn., 1965.

Seilhamer, *American Theatre.* George O. Seilhamer. *History of the American Theatre.* 3 vols. Philadelphia, 1888–91.

Seitz, "Thomas Paine, Bridge Builder." Don C. Seitz. "Thomas Paine, Bridge Builder." *Virginia Quarterly Review,* 3 (1927), 571–84.

Sheftall, "The Sheftalls of Savannah."   John McKay Sheftall. "The Sheftalls of Savannah: Colonial Leaders and Founding Fathers of Georgia Judaism." pp. 65–78 in Samuel Proctor et al., eds. *Jews of the South.* Macon, Ga., 1984.

Shepperson, *John Paradise and Lucy Ludwell.*   Archibald Bolling Shepperson. *John Paradise and Lucy Ludwell of London and Williamsburg.* Richmond, 1942.

Showman, *Greene Papers.*   Richard K. Showman et al., eds. *The Papers of General Nathanael Greene.* 6 vols. to date. Chapel Hill, N.C., 1976—.

Slaughter, *Truro Parish.*   Philip Slaughter. *The History of Truro Parish in Virginia.* Ed. Edward L. Goodwin. Philadelphia, 1908.

Smith, *New York City in 1789.*   Thomas E. V. Smith. *The City of New York in the Year of Washington's Inauguration 1789.* 1889. Reprint. Riverside, Conn., 1972.

Smith, *St. Clair Papers.*   William Henry Smith, ed. *The St. Clair Papers.* 2 vols. Cincinnati, 1882.

Smyth, *Writings of Benjamin Franklin.*   Albert Henry Smyth, ed. *The Writings of Benjamin Franklin.* 10 vols. New York and London, 1907.

Sowerby, *Catalogue of the Library of Thomas Jefferson.*   E. Millicent Sowerby, comp. *Catalogue of the Library of Thomas Jefferson.* 5 vols. 1952–59. Reprint. Charlottesville, Va., 1983.

Sparks, *Correspondence of the American Revolution.*   Jared Sparks, ed. *Correspondence of the American Revolution: Being Letters of Eminent Men to George Washington, from the Time of His Taking Command of the Army to the End of His Presidency.* 4 vols. Boston, 1853.

Spencer, *Historical Dictionary of Morocco.*   William Spencer. *Historical Dictionary of Morocco.* Metuchen, N.J., 1980.

Stagg, *Madison Papers, Secretary of State Series.*   J. C. A. Stagg et al., eds. *The Papers of James Madison, Secretary of State Series.* 2 vols. to date. Charlottesville, Va., 1986—.

1 *Stat.*   Richard Peters, ed. *The Public Statutes at Large of the United States of America.* Vol. 1. Boston, 1845.

6 *Stat.*   Richard Peters, ed. *The Public Statutes at Large of the United States of America.* Vol. 6. Boston, 1848.

Sweig and David, *A Fairfax Friendship.*   Donald M. Sweig and Elizabeth S. David, eds. *A Fairfax Friendship: The Complete Correspondence between George Washington and Bryan Fairfax, 1754–1799.* Fairfax, Va., 1982.

Syrett, *Hamilton Papers.*   Harold C. Syrett et al., eds. *The Papers of Alexander Hamilton.* 27 vols. New York, 1961–87.

Taubman, *Making of the American Theatre.*   Hyman Howard Taubman. *The Making of the American Theatre.* New York, 1965.

Warren-Adams Letters.   *Warren-Adams Letters: Being Chiefly a Correspondence among John Adams, Samuel Adams, and James Warren.* Massachusetts Historical Society Collections, vols. 72–73. Boston, 1917–25.

Whittemore, *Memorials of the Massachusetts Soc. of the Cincinnati.*   Bradford Adams Whittemore, ed. *Memorials of the Massachusetts Society of the Cincinnati.* Boston, 1964.

Wilkins, *History of Foreign Investment in the U.S.*   Mira Wilkins. *The History of Foreign Investment in the United States to 1914.* Cambridge, Mass., 1989.

Willett, *Narrative of the Military Actions of Col. Marinus Willett.*   William M. Willett. *Narrative of the Military Actions of Colonel Marinus Willett, Taken Chiefly from His Own Manuscript.* New York, 1831.

The Papers of George Washington
Presidential Series
Volume 5
January–June 1790

From Jabez Bowen

Sir   Providence [R.I.] Jany 17 1790

Your favour of the 27th ulto came safe to hand, and if I made an impropper request in my former Letter[1] you[r] Excellency will Pardon me, as it arose from the great Anxiety I had on viewing our almost forlorn situation.

I now have the pleasure Sir of informing you that the General Assembly have passed a Resolve, Recommending The People to Choose Delegates to meet in a State Convention on the second Monday of March at South Kingston, That the Question was carrid in the Lower house by a Majority of Five There being Thirty four Yes and Twenty Nine Nos. The Vote laboured much in the Upper house, being twice sent back with a Non concurrance, but was finally carrid by the Vote of Govr Collins. This Question being determined in our favour I can almost assure your Excellency of its being finally Adopted by a Respectable Majority.[2]

a Resolve passed the Genl Assembly requesting Congress to renew The Indulgence before granted to the Navigation of This State,[3] and which it was the intention of the Assembly should be sent forward, but was omitted Thro hurry, which Resolve I do my self the Honour of inclosing.[4] I doubt not but you will chearfully forward this Business, when I tell you, it will be highly pleasing to every Citizen of this State but in a particular manner to the Federalists.

We shall continue our Exertions to get the best men chosen to Represent The Freemen in Convention and in due time shall anounce to you the good tidings.[5] I Remain Sir with sentiments of the highest Esteeme Your Excellencys most Obedient and verry Humb. Servant

Jabez Bowen

ALS, DNA: RG 59, Miscellaneous Letters.

1. See Bowen to GW, 15 Dec. 1789. Bowen currently represented Providence in the Rhode Island general assembly.

2. Rhode Island's lower house passed two bills on 15 and 16 Jan. appointing a state convention to ratify the federal Constitution; both bills were defeated in the upper house. After adjourning to 17 Jan., a Sunday, the lower house passed a third bill calling for a convention, which became law only upon Gov. John Collins casting the tie-breaking vote in the upper house (Polishook, "Edes's Report," 26:29–30).

3. A bill requesting Collins to write to the president concerning suspension of the federal tonnage and impost acts in Rhode Island also passed on the last day of the session (Bartlett, *R.I. Records*, 10:373–74).

4. The enclosed resolution reads: "Whereas the Operation of the Federal Government, according to the existing Laws of Congress, will prove greatly injurious to the Commercial Interests of this State, unless a further Suspension of the same can be obtained: And whereas this General Assembly, at the present Session, have passed an Act recommending a State Convention, in Conformity to the Recommendation of the General Convention held at Philadelphia, and of the Congress of the United States and there is every Reason to hope that the Accession of this State to the Federal Union will, in a short Time, entitle the Citizens thereof to all the Benefits of the Federal Governmen⟨t⟩ And whereas it is necessary that Application be made in the mean Time, for a Suspension of the Acts of Congress subjecting the Citizens of this State to foreign Tonnage, and foreign Duties:

"It is therefore Voted and Resolved, That His Excellency the Governor be, and he is hereby, requested to make Application, in the Name of this State, to the Congress of the United States, for reviving the Indulgence granted to the Citizens of this State, by an Act of Congress of their last Session, during the good Pleasure of Congress" (DNA: RG 59, Miscellaneous Letters).

5. GW's secretary Tobias Lear replied for the president, on 4 Feb. 1790, noting: "The Congress of the United States have taken the matter into consideration, and it is to be hoped that the adoption of the Constitution by the State of Rhode Island will, after this instance, render similar applications unnecessary from that State" (DNA: RG 59, Miscellaneous Letters). See also John Collins to GW, 18 Jan. 1790; GW to the U.S. Senate and House of Representatives, 28 Jan. 1790.

From La Luzerne

Sir,   London January 17th 1790.

I dare to flatter myself that your Excellency does justice to the very tender and respectful attachment which I have long entertained towards you—and that you will be persuaded of the great pleasure with which I have learned the success that has followed the first movements of your administration. After having given freedom to your country it was worthy of the virtues and great character of your Excellency to establish her happiness on a solid and permanent basis, which is assuredly the result of the new federal constitution, in framing which you assisted by your counsel, and which you now support as much by the splendor of your talents and patriotism as by the eminent situation confided to you by your fellow-citizens—They possess the advantage of enjoying more particularly your beneficence, and the honor of having you born among them: but I dare to assure you that the consideration which you enjoy throughout Europe, and particularly in my country, yields not even to that which you have obtained in your native land—and notwithstanding the prejudices of the people with whom I live here there is not one among them who does not pronounce your name with sentiments of respect and veneration. All are acquainted with the services you have rendered to your country as their General in the course of the war, and with those, perhaps still greater, which you now render as a Statesman in peace.

The love of glory and of freedom, which led the Americans to surmount such great difficulties, must still prevail, after surmounting them, to establish the principles of justice towards those of their fellow citizens and strangers who assisted them in their distress; and I have seen with great pleasure that from the first moment in which you have appeared at the head of the federal government, the credit of the american nation has been established in every country of Europe, and that the confidence in her resources and mean⟨s⟩ are infinitely better founded than in many of the older Powers.

It is beyond doubt that it will take still greater consistency, and that the freest country in the world, ought also to be that which should enjoy the most extensive public credit.

I am too well acquainted with your sentiments for France not to be convinced of the interest which you take in her present position—The vices of an ancient and vitiated administration could not be reformed even by the virtues of a King who loves his people, and who has many qualities to make them happy— Some revolution was required in the form of the monarchy, and above all in setting bounds to the ministerial authority in matters of finance—it was likewise necessary that the liberty of the citizen should be assured by a conclusive law of which we were totally destitute. It is this which induced the King to assemble the States-General, who might easily have made some useful reforms, leaving the monarchy to subsist, or at least reforming it but slowly and partially: But the love of liberty, and still more the exaltation of opinions has carried us too far—they have overturned every thing without rebuilding any thing, which has reduced us to a very disagreeable situation for the moment—I hope that time will a little moderate opinions, and that we shall recur to true principles, and that, in assuring the liberty of the citizen, they will restore the authority of the executive power, which is the soul of a great Empire. If we can arrive at that state of things I am persuaded the subject will have gained infinitely, and that even the position of the King will be more happy than it formerly was. But unfortunately to attain this situation we must reiterate a very thorny career, and our french heads are little fitted for such proofs.

Your ancient friend *the Marquis de la Fayette* finds himself at the head of the revolution, it is indeed a very fortunate circumstance for the State that he is, but very little so for himself.[1] Never has any man been placed in a more critical situation—Good citizen, faithful subject, he is embarrassed by a thousand difficulties in making many people sensible of what is proper, who very often feel it not, and who sometimes will not understand what it is.

He has occasion for all the aid of that wisdom and prudence which he acquired under your tuition⟨; and⟩ assuredly he has hitherto proved himself worthy of his Master—having supported the most difficult s⟨ituation with⟩ the rarest talents, and most astonishing foresight. I have the honor to be with a very sincere and very respectful attachment Your Excellency's most humble and most obedient Servant.

Translation, DLC:GW; AL, in French, DLC:GW. The text is taken from a translation prepared for GW; the receiver's copy, in French, appears in CD-ROM:GW.

Anne César, marquis de La Luzerne, was in London as French minister to Great Britain, a post he held from January 1788 until his death on 14 Sept. 1791.

1. Lafayette had acquired considerable political prestige for his actions of early October 1789 when, as commander of the Paris National Guard, he rescued the royal family at Versailles from a Parisian mob. As the hero of the October Days, he became the chief mediator between the court and the revolutionaries.

From Thomas McKean

Sir,   Philadelphia January 17th 1790.
It appears, that Congress intend to erect Hospitals in the United States for the reception of sick & disabled seamen,[1] and

it is expected, that one may be established at Baltimore in Maryland.

Doctor George Buchanan, who practices physic there, wishes for the superintendence or direction of such an institution.[2] His pretensions are, that his studies & pursuits in life have led him to attain qualifications for such a station: he served an apprenticeship in this city with Doctor William Shippen, some time Director General of the Hospitals of the American Army; afterwards he attended the medical lectures in our University, and received its honors; he then went to London, Edinburgh and Paris to perfect himself in his profession.

I am interested, Sir, in his prosperity, as he is married to my second daughter; but this circumstance may incline me to be too partial to his talents & industry, I would therefore rather refer Your Excellency to Messieurs Smith, Carrol[3] &c. of Baltimore, Delegates in Congress (who I suppose know him) for further information of his character & conduct. The Doctor is the eldest son of General Buchanan sometime deceased, whose zeal in the American cause was so great, that I think, he could not be unknown to you: the family connexions are very numerous in Maryland, particularly in Baltimore county.

As a small proof of the Doctor's desire to be useful, and as it bears some relation to the present application, I beg leave to present your Excellency with a treatise on the Hospital fever, lately written by him.[4]

Your favoring Doctor Buchanan's suit will, in my humble opinion, serve the Public, and it will confer a particular obligation on him as well as upon one, who professes himself to be, Sir, with the utmost attachment and regard, Your Excellency's Most obedient And most humble servant[5]

Thos McKean

ALS, DLC:GW.

1. See Joseph Willard to GW, 1 Jan. 1790, n.1.

2. George Buchanan (1763–1808) was the son of Andrew Buchanan (1734–1786), a Baltimore merchant who served as a brigadier general in the Maryland militia during the Revolution. The younger Buchanan graduated from the University of Pennsylvania in 1785 and then studied abroad for three years. He received the university's medical degree in February 1789 and set up practice in Baltimore. In June 1789 he married Letitia McKean (Kelly and Burrage, *American Medical Biographies*, 161–62).

3. Daniel Carroll served on the committee appointed by the House of Rep-

resentatives on 20 July 1789 to prepare the hospitals and harbors bill (*DHFC*, 3:115).

4. A copy of Buchanan's *A Treatise upon the Typhus Fever: Published for the Benefit of Establishing a Lying-in-Hospital, in Baltimore* (Baltimore, 1789) was in GW's library at the time of his death (Griffin, *Boston Athenæum Collection*, 36).

5. GW replied on 24 Jan.: "I have been favored with the receipt of your letter of the 17th instant, together with its enclosure—As no determination has yet been taken respecting the erection of Hospitals for the reception of sick and disabled Seamen, the object, to which your letter relates, is not before me—and, as I have undeviatingly considered freedom of choice, in all nominations to office, essential to the public service, I am persuaded you will have the goodness to excuse an adherence to that sentiment on the present occasion, which forbids any previous engagement, however satisfactory the pretensions of the Gentleman, who wishes the appointment" (Df, DNA: RG 59, Miscellaneous Letters, dated 22 January. The letter-book copy of GW's reply is dated 24 January).

To Burgess Ball

Dear Sir,   New York, January, 18. 1790.

Your letter of the 26. of December came duly to hand, but occurences of various kinds have prevented an acknowledgement of it till this time.

I am not at all uneasy at the delay, or impatient for the settlement of the estate accounts of my deceased Mother; I am persuaded they will be rendered in due time, and to the satisfaction of all concerned—To pay all she owed is my first wish—to render unto every one their due is the next—The method which has been taken to dispose of the effects is, I presume, the best; and I am satisfied therewith—That none of the families of Negroes have been parted (where it could be avoided) is very agreeable to me.

I am well pleased that Mr Carter is inclined to take possession of my lots in Fredericksburg[1]—We shall not disagree about the price, or in the mode of payment; of which be so good as to inform him.[2]

I hope you have got through your difficulties on account of your surety-ship for Major Willis, and without loss—when you engaged in this business you neglected the advice of the wise man—than which no better I believe is to be found in his whole book—or among all his sayings "Beware of surety-ship"[3]—Offer my love and good wishes to Fanny and the family—accept the same yourself and those of Mrs Washington. I am &ca

G. Washington.

LB, DLC:GW.

This letter and the one to which it replies concern the settlement of Mary Ball Washington's estate. For background, see Burgess Ball to GW, 25 Aug. 1789, GW to Betty Washington Lewis, 13 Sept. 1789, Betty Washington Lewis to GW, 1 Oct. 1789, Burgess Ball and Charles Carter to GW, 8 Oct. 1789, GW to Ball and Carter, 18 Oct. 1789, and Burgess Ball to GW, 26 Dec. 1789.

1. See GW to Betty Washington Lewis, 13 Sept. 1789, n.9 and Burgess Ball to GW, 26 Dec. 1789.

2. Ball presented GW's terms to Charles Carter, Jr., of Culpeper on 6 Feb. 1790 (Carter to GW, 6 Feb. 1790).

3. GW is presumably referring to the comments on suretyship made by Solomon in Proverbs.

From John Collins

State of Rhode-Island & Providence Plantations

Sir,   January 18th 1790.

I have the Honor of transmitting to you an Act of the General Assembly of this State for calling a Convention, to take into Consideration the Constitution proposed for the United States, passed on the 17th of September, A.D. 1787, by the General Convention held at Philadelphia.[1]

This Event gives me the most sincere pleasure, as there is every Reason to hope that the Accession of this State will in a short Time not only entitle the Citizens thereof to all the Benefits of the Federal Government, but as it will render the Union complete, and affords a rational and pleasing prospect that the Thirteen States which by their United exertions, at the expence of their common blood and treasure obtained liberty and Independence, will be again joined in the firmest Bands of Friendship, under a Constitution calculated to secure to them the great Objects for which they fought and bled.

The Operation of the Federal Government, according to the existing Laws, will immediately prove greatly injurious to the Commercial Interests of this State, unless a further Suspension of them can be obtained:[2] I do therefore, at the Request of the General Assembly, and in Behalf of the State, make this application to the Congress of the United States, requesting a further Suspension of the Acts of Congress subjecting the Citizens of this State to the payment of foreign Tonnage, and foreign Duties, during the pleasure of Congress.[3]

At the same Time that I desire you to communicate this Application to Congress,[4] give me Leave, Sir, to hope for your favorable Influence in our Behalf.

I have the honor to be, with the greatest Respect and Esteem, Sir, Your Most Obedient, and Most Humble Servant,

John Collins

Copy, in Tobias Lear's handwriting, DNA: RG 46, First Congress, Records of Legislative Proceedings, President's Messages.

1. The enclosed act of 17 Jan. called for a state convention to be held in South Kingstown on 1 Mar. at which delegates chosen by town meetings on 8 Feb. would vote on ratification of the federal Constitution. It also requested the governor immediately to transmit a copy of the act to the president of the United States and ordered copies sent to each town clerk in the state (DNA: RG 46, First Congress, President's Messages).

2. The original tonnage and collection acts signed by the president on 20 and 31 July 1789 treated North Carolina and Rhode Island as foreign nations, imposing duties on their merchant ships at least five times higher than on other American vessels and subjecting the imports of their merchants to the same seizures and forfeitures as foreign goods. In response to petitions from citizens of those states, Congress considered and passed "An Act to suspend part of an Act intituled 'An Act to regulate the collection of the Duties imposed by Law on the Tonnage of Ships or Vessels, and on Goods, Wares, and Merchandises, imported into the United States,' and for other purposes," which postponed until 15 Jan. 1790 imposition of the higher tonnage duties on Rhode Island and North Carolina ships (1 *Stat.* 69–70 [16 Sept. 1789]; James Manning to GW, 29 Aug. 1789; *DHFC*, 3:278, 4:309, 334, 337, 368, 6:1947, 1951, 1957–63, 1964). See also GW to the U.S. Senate and House of Representatives, 28 Jan. 1790.

3. See Jabez Bowen to GW, 17 Jan. 1790, n.4.

4. See GW to the U.S. Senate and House of Representatives, 28 Jan. 1790.

From Benjamin Dubois

Mon Général   Mont-marin Le 18' Jier 1790.

Sans avoir demandé votre agrêment, j'ai pris la liberté de donner le nom de votre éxcellence à mon navire,[1] commandé par le Sr Duroutois,[2] sous lieutenant de Vaisseaux; Si j'etais assez malheureux que vous le trouvassiez mauvais, quoi que désesperé de changer un nom aussi cher dans toutes les parties du monde, je rémplirais vos ordres: j'ose esperer que vous voudrez bien m'eviter ce chagrin et vous rendre à ma priere.

Permettez moi de vous supplier en oûtre d'accepter le plan[3] d'un port que j'ai crée, en deux ans de tems, qui reunit beaucoup de ressources pour les traveaux maritimes; les atteliers en tous genres y font réunir ce qui me facilite les moyens de faire en peu de tems beaucoup de constructions. J'ai L'honneur d'être avec les sentimens les plus Respectueux Mon Général Votre très humble et très Obeissant Serviteur

Benjamin Dubois

ALS, DNA: RG 59, Miscellaneous Letters.

    Benjamin Dubois (b. 1738) was a son of Briand Dubois of Saint-Malo, a retired French naval officer (d. 1779). The younger Dubois had served in the French navy himself from the 1750s to the 1770s and in 1775 was an *officier de port* with the rank of *lieutenant*. He was probably the St. Malo shipowner who in 1788 won the French contract to provide six packet voyages a year between Bordeaux and Norfolk, Va., with stops in New York City (Aman, *Officiers bleus dans la marine française*, 68, 130–1, 181; Boyd, *Jefferson Papers*, 14:309n.; Mitchell, *Crèvecoeur*, 186).

    1. The "fast-sailing" 350-ton *Washington* was one of Dubois's packet ships from 1789 to 1793 (ibid., 188, 198, 211).

    2. Julian Jean Duroutois was later captain of Dubois's packet *Franklin*. In January 1791 the New-York Marine Society made him an honorary member for rescuing shipwrecked Americans (*Gazette of the United States* [Philadelphia], 5 Feb. 1791).

    3. The enclosure has not been identified.

Letter not found: from David Forman, 18 Jan. 1790. On 21 Jan. GW wrote to Forman "Acknowledging the receipt of your letters of the 3rd and 18th instant."[1]

    1. Tobias Lear transmitted this letter to John Jay: "By the Command of the President of the United States, I do myself the honor to enclose a letter from Genl Forman dated the 18th inst. upon the subject of those counterfeit Certificates which were contained in Genl Forman's letter of the 3d inst. to the President of the United States which was transmitted by the Presidents order to you, and by you handed to the Governor of the State of New York.

    "As the former letter passed through your hands, the President has directed this to be put into the same channel" (Lear to Jay, 20 Feb., DNA: RG Miscellaneous Letters).

Tobias Lear to Alexander Hamilton

Sir   United States [New York] January 18th 1790
By order of the President of the United States, I do myself the honor to transmit you a letter from His Excellency Thomas Jefferson The Secretary for Foreign Affairs to the United States, dated at Paris Augt 27th 1789,[1] and likewise the copy of a letter from Messrs Wilhem & Jan Willinck, N. & I. Van Stephorst & Hubbard to Mr Jefferson, dated at Amsterdam 13th Augt 1789[2]—both of which the President wishes may be returned to him, when you have duly considered those parts of them which relate to the Finances of the United States. I have the honor to be with perfect respect Sir Your most obedient Servt

Tobias Lear
Secretary to the President
of the United States

LB, DLC:GW.

1. See GW's Memoranda on Thomas Jefferson's Letters, 1789, and notes. In addition to discussing financial matters, Jefferson's communications abstracted by GW also presented the news of the capture of the schooner *Polly* of Salem, Mass., Joseph Proctor, master. See Giuseppe Chiappe to GW, 18 July 1789, and GW to Sidi Mohammed, 1 Dec. 1789; Syrett, *Hamilton Papers*, 6:186–88; and Boyd, *Jefferson Papers*, 15:340–42, 356–61.

2. The copy of Wilhem and Jan Willink, Nicholaas and Jacob Van Staphorst, and Nicholas Hubbard's letter to Jefferson was made by William Short. The receiver's copy is in DLC: Thomas Jefferson Papers (Boyd, *Jefferson Papers*, 15:342–44; Syrett, *Hamilton Papers*, 6:188–90).

From Henry Knox

Sir,   War Office [New York, 18] January, 1790.
Having submitted to your consideration a plan for the arrangement of the militia of the United States, which I had presented to the late Congress, and you having approved the general principles thereof, with certain exceptions, I now respectfully lay the same before you, modified according to the alterations you were pleased to suggest.

It has been my anxious desire to devise a national system of defence, adequate to the probable exigencies of the United States, whether arising from internal or external causes; and at the same time to erect a standard of republican magnanimity, independent of, and superior to, the powerful influences of wealth.

The convulsive events, generated by the inordinate pursuit of riches, or ambition, require that the government should possess a strong corrective arm.

The idea is therefore submitted, whether an efficient military branch of government can be invented, with safety to the great principles of liberty, unless the same shall be formed of the people themselves, and supported by their habits and manners. I have the honor to be, with the most perfect respect, your most Obedt Servant.

H. Knox, Secretary for the
Department of War.

Copy, DNA: RG 107, Records of the Office of the Secretary of War.

For background to Knox's enclosed revision of his militia plan, see *Diaries*, 5:508–9. Knox's report, a "plan for the arrangement of the militia," stated: "That a well constituted republic is more favorable to the liberties of society, and that its principles give an higher elevation to the human mind than any other form of government, has generally been acknowledged by the unprejudiced and enlightened part of mankind.

"But it is at the same time acknowledged, that unless a republic prepares itself by proper arrangements to meet those exigencies to which all states are in a degree liable, that its peace and existence are more precarious than the forms of government in which the will of one directs the conduct of the whole, for the defence of the nation.

"A government whose measures must be the result of multiplied deliberations, is seldom in a situation to produce instantly those exertions which the occasion may demand; therefore it ought to possess such energetic establishments as should enable it, by the vigor of its own citizens to control events as they arise, instead of being convulsed or subverted by them.

"It is the misfortune of modern ages, that governments have been formed by chance, and events, instead of system—that without fixed principles, they are braced or relaxed, from time to time, according to the predominating power of the rulers or the ruled. The rulers possessing separate interests from the people, excepting in some of the high toned monarchies, in which all opposition to the will of the princes seems annihilated.

"Hence we look round Europe in vain for an extensive government, rising on the power inherent in the people, and performing its operations entirely for their benefit. But we find artificial force governing every where, and the people generally made subservient to the elevation and Caprice of the few: Almost every nation appearing to be busily employed in conducting some external war; grappling with internal Commotion; or endeavoring to extricate itself from impending debts which threaten to overwhelm it with ruin. Princes and ministers seem neither to have leisure nor inclination to bring forward institutions for diffusing general strength, knowledge, and happiness: But they seem to understand well the Machiavelian maxim of politics—divide and govern.

"May the United States avoid the errors and crimes of other governments; and possess the wisdom to embrace the present invaluable opportunity of establishing such institutions as shall invigorate, exalt, and perpetuate the great principles of freedom: An opportunity pregnant with the fate of millions, but rapidly borne on the wings of time, and may never again return.

"The public mind, unbiassed by superstition or prejudice, seems happily prepared to receive the impressions of wisdom. The latent springs of human action, ascertained by the standard of experience, may be regulated and made subservient to the noble purpose of forming a dignified national character.

"The causes by which nations have ascended and declined, through the various ages of the world, may be calmly and accurately determined; and the United States may be placed in the singularly fortunate Condition of Commencing their Career of empire, with the accumulated knowledge of all the known societies and governments of the globe.

"The strength of government, like the strength of any other vast and complicated machine, will depend on a due adjustment of its several parts. Its agriculture, its Commerce, its laws, its finance, its system of *defence,* and its manners and habits, all require Consideration, and the highest exercise of political wisdom.

"It is the intention of the present attempt to suggest the most efficient system of defence which may be Compatible with the interests of a free people: A system which shall not only produce the expected effect, but which in its operations shall also produce those habits and manners which will impart strength and durability to the whole government.

"The modern practice of Europe, with respect to the employment of standing armies, has created such a mass of opinion in their favor, that even philosophers, and the advocates for liberty, have frequently confessed their use and necessity, in certain cases.

"But whoever seriously and Candidly estimates the power of discipline and the tendency of military habits, will be Constrained to Confess, that whatever may be the efficacy of a standing army in war, it cannot in peace be considered as friendly to the rights of human nature. The recent instance in France, cannot with propriety be brought to overturn the general principle, built upon the uniform experience of mankind. It may be found, on examining the causes that appear to have influenced the military of France, that while the springs of power were wound up in the nation to the highest pitch, that the discipline of the Army was proportionably relaxed. But any argument on this head, may be considered as unnecessary to the enlightened citizens of the United States.

"A small corps of well disciplined and well informed artillerists and engineers, and a legion for the protection of the frontiers, and the magazines and arsenals are all the military establishment which may be required for the present use of the United States. The privates of the Corps to be enlisted for a certain period, and after the expiration of which to return to the mass of the citizens.

"An energetic national militia is to be regarded as the *Capital security* of a free republic; and not a standing army, forming a distinct class in the community.

"It is the introduction and diffusion of vice and corruption of manners into the mass of the people, that renders a standing army necessary. It is when public spirit is despised, and avarice, indolence and effeminacy of manners predominate, and prevent the establishment of institutions which would elevate the minds of the youth in the paths of virtue and honor, that a standing army is formed and rivetted forever.

"While the human character remains unchanged, and societies and governments of considerable extent are formed; a principle ever ready to execute the laws and defend the state, must constantly exist. Without this vital principle, the government would be invaded or overturned, and trampled upon by the bold and ambitious. No community can be long held together, unless its arrangements are adequate to its probable exigencies.

"If it should be decided to reject a standing army for the military branch of the government of the United States, as possessing too fierce an aspect, and being hostile to the principles of liberty, it will follow that a well constituted militia ought to be established.

"A consideration of the subject will shew the impracticability of disciplining at once the mass of the people. All discussions on the subject of a powerful militia, will result in one or other of the following principles.

"First. Either efficient institutions must be established for the military education of the youth; and that the knowledge acquired therein shall be diffused throughout the community by the mean of rotation, or

"Secondly. That the militia must be formed of substitutes, after the manner of the militia of Great Britain.

"If the United States possess the vigor of mind to establish the first institution, it may reasonably be expected to produce the most unequivocal advantages. A glorious national spirit will be introduced, with its extensive train of political consequences. The youth will imbibe a love of their country; reverence and obedience to its laws; courage and elevation of mind; openness and liberality of Character, accompanied by a just spirit of honor: In addition to which, their bodies will acquire a robustness, greatly conducive to their personal happiness, as well as the defence of their Country: While habit, with its silent, but efficacious operations, will durably cement the system.

"Habit, that powerful and universal law, incessantly acting on the human race, well deserves the attention of legislators. Formed at first in individuals, by separate and almost imperceptible impulses, until at length it acquires a force which controuls with irresistable sway. The effects of salutary or pernicious habits, operating on a whole nation are immense, and decides its rank and Character in the world.

"Hence the science of legislation teaches to scrutinize every national institution, as it may introduce proper or improper habits; to adopt with religious zeal the former, and reject with honor the latter.

"A republic, constructed on the principles herein stated, would be uninjured by events, sufficient to overturn a government supported solely by the uncertain power of a standing army.

"The well informed members of the community, actuated by the highest motives of self-love, would form the real defence of the country. Rebellions would be prevented, or suppressed with ease. Invasions of such a government would be undertaken only by madmen; and the virtues and knowledge of the people would effectually oppose the introduction of tyranny.

"But the second principle, a militia of substitutes, is pregnant, in a degree, with the mischiefs of a standing army; as it is highly probable the substitutes from time to time, will be nearly the same men, and the most idle and worthless part of the Community. Wealthy families, proud of distinctions which riches may confer, will prevent their sons from serving in the militia of substitutes; the plan will degenerate into habitual contempt; a standing army will be introduced, and the liberties of the people subjected to all the contingencies of events.

"The expense attending an energetic establishment of militia may be strongly urged as an objection to the institution. But it is to be remembered, that this objection is levelled at both systems, whether by rotation or by substitutes: For if the numbers are equal, the expense will also be equal. The estimate of the expense will show its unimportance, when Compared with the magnitude and beneficial effects of the institution.

"But the people of the United States will cheerfully consent to the expenses of a measure calculated to serve as a *perpetual barrier* to their liberties: Especially as they well know that the disbursements will be made among the members of the same community, and therefore cannot be injurious.

"Every intelligent mind would rejoice in the establishment of an institution, under whose auspices the youth and vigor of the Constitution would be renewed with each successive generation, and which would appear to secure the great principles of freedom and happiness against the injuries of time and events.

"The following plan is formed on these general principles.

"First. That it is the indispensable duty of every nation, to establish all necessary institutions for its own perfection and defence.

"Secondly. That it is a Capital security to a free state, for the great body of the people to possess a Competent knowledge of the military art.

"Thirdly. That this knowledge cannot be attained in the present state of society, but by establishing adequate institutions for the military education of youth; and that the knowledge acquired therein should be diffused throughout the community, by the principles of rotation.

"Fourthly. That every man of the proper age and ability of body, is firmly bound by the social compact, to perform, personally, his proportion of military duty for the defence of the state.

"Fifthly. That all men of the legal military age, should be armed, enrolled, and held responsible for different degrees of military service.

"And Sixthly. That, agreeably to the Constitution, the United States are to provide for organizing, arming, and disciplining the militia; and for governing such part of them as may be employed in the service of the United States;

reserving to the States respectively, the appointment of the Officers, and the authority of training the militia according to the discipline prescribed by Congress" (DNA: RG 107, Secretary of War Letters Received, Unentered Series).

The remainder of Knox's report deals with the implementation of the plan, providing detailed suggestions for the organization of the army. The report is printed in full in *DHFC*, 5:1435–57, and appears in full on CD-ROM:GW. Francis Childs and John Swaine printed 300 copies of *A Plan for the General Arrangement of the Militia of the United States. Published by Order of the House of Representatives* (New York, 1790) prefaced by Knox's letter to GW (Evans, *American Bibliography*, 8:95 [no. 22988]).

From Michael Madden

Sir,   Alexandria [Va.] 18th Janry 1790

My present Situation is so distressing that I Begg leave to Trouble your Excelency to Inform me if there is any probability of the Bankrupt laws being Extended by Congress to all the States in union so as I with maney others in this State who are in like difficultys may have the benefite of it.[1]

I have langushied in prison bounds for upwards of three years, altho I have tendred to my Creditors all the propperty that I am posessed of in the worald for a release from Confinement to no purpose—and indeed the Insolvant law in this State is at best but a Temporary releiffe as the Creditor at the end of six months may Distress the Dr as often as he may Imagain him to have aquired aney propperty worth his nottice.[2]

I have a wife[3] and three Children Suffring with me in my present Distresed Situation allmost ready to perish if I do not obtain Some Speedy releiffe from Confinement.

Your answer to the above speedily will be a great favour done to Your very Oobedient Hume Servt[4]

M Madden

ALS, DNA: RG 59, Miscellaneous Letters.

Michael Madden left Ireland and settled in Virginia before the American Revolution. During the war he served as a private in Col. Nathaniel Gist's Additional Continental Virginia Regiment in 1777 and later in Capt. John Lucas's Montgomery County militia company. He removed to Alexandria before 1784 and set up a mercantile business in a shop on Wolfe Street. In 1785 he and GW both held pews in Christ Church (Saffell, *Records of the Revolutionary War*, 285; Miller, *Artisans and Merchants of Alexandria*, 1:313; Slaughter, *Truro Parish*, 97–99).

Madden controlled property in Alexandria, including lots his wife inherited from her father and a parcel granted her by the town in 1765. His financial difficulties probably originated with a £245 note he negotiated with William Sydebotham of Bladensburg, Md., in November 1785, which became due with interest in September 1788. In December 1786 the Maddens mortgaged their new house and lot on Prince Street to Sydebotham to secure the debt. After their default Sydebotham brought suit against Madden in Alexandria Hustings Court and won judgment for the sale of the property, payment of the note, and court costs. Sydebotham died before the decree was executed, and his executors successfully revived the suit against Madden, who again defaulted, and in August 1795 the court sold the property at auction (Munson, *Alexandria Hustings Court Deeds, 1783–1797,* 7, 17, 18, 47, 53, 77, 83, 110, 111, 138–39, 193, 206).

1. On 1 June 1789 a House committee was appointed to prepare a bill "to establish an uniform system on the subject of bankruptcies throughout the United States." Not until 5 May 1792, however, did Congress pass "An Act for the relief of persons imprisoned for Debt" (*DHFC* 3:78; 1 *Stat.* 265–66).

2. The Virginia act for the relief of insolvent debtors passed 13 Dec. 1792 eliminated such actions (13 Hening 357, 374–77).

3. Madden married Hannah Ramsay, one of five daughters of GW's cousin Ann McCarty Ball Ramsay (c.1730–1785) and William Ramsay (1716–1785), a founder and prominent citizen of Alexandria and GW's lifelong friend. Hannah's sisters were frequent guests at Mount Vernon, and GW contributed financially to the education of their eldest brother, William, Jr. (*Papers, Colonial Series,* 3:413; *Diaries,* 2:46, 52, 108, 119, 235, 3:81, 227, 238, 312, 4:164, 206, 257, 272, 274, 5:14, 131, 273, 318, 319, 327, 364; Munson, *Alexandria Hustings Court Deeds, 1783–1797,* 193).

4. On 27 Jan. Tobias Lear wrote Madden: "The President of the United States has received your letter of the 18th inst.—and directs me to inform you, that it is not in his power to give a decided Answer to your quære, viz. 'if there is a probability of the Bankrupt laws being extended by Congress to all the States in the Union'? as this is a subject which depends upon the *Legislative* body of the United States to decide upon, and therefore an opinion relating to the matter cannot be expected from the *Executive*" (DNA: RG 59, Miscellaneous Letters).

From Alexander Martin

Sir,   North Carolina Jany 18th 1790

As Brigadier General Martin of Washington District in this State, Agent of Indian Affairs has been criminated as he is informed before your Excellency and Congress, by a certain Bennet Belew[1] for some mal-practises in his Agency, more particularly for a Letter said Gen. Martin should have written to

Alexander McGilveray one of the Chiefs of the Creek Nation, to whom some particular Resolutions of Congress were said to be improperly communicated. In justification of himself he hath had that Transaction investigated by a Committee of both Houses of the General Assembly of this State, and a Report in his Favor hath been made, and concurred with by the General Assembly. At his Request I beg Leave to present the same to your Excellency,[2] he considering himself to deserve well heretofore of the public, that any unfavorable Impressions that may have been made as to his Conduct in this Business may be done away. As to any other Charges exhibited against him by Belew, they are unknown here, but when your Excellency is informed as to Belew's Character, Genl Martin flatters himself they will have little Weight without being supported by better Authority. Brigr Genl Charles McDowel of Morgan District hath certified to me the Character of Belew which is enclosed for your Excellency's perusal.[3]

Since my personal Acquaintance with Gen. Martin, which hath been for eight or nine years past, he hath been a Member of the General Assembly for Greene County in Washington District and Agent for Indian Affairs both for Virginia and North Carolina, in which Stations he hath served with Reputation, and generally conducted himself to public Satisfaction.

Should your Excellency from the above Representation, entertain with me any favorable Opinion of General Martin, he sollicits your Excellency for a Continuance of his Agency for Indian Affairs, being well versed in the same in such Departments to the Southward your Excellency will please to allot, & honour him with. I have the Honour to be with the greatest Respect your Excellencys most obedient humble Servant

Alex: Martin

ALS, DLC:GW.

For background to Joseph Martin and his controversial letter of 8 Nov. 1788 to Alexander McGillivray, see George Walton to GW, 11 Mar. 1789, Hugh Williamson to GW, 8 May 1789, and GW to Walton, 29 May 1789.

1. See the Cherokee Nation to GW, 19 May 1789, n.3, Beverley Randolph to GW, 5 Aug. 1789, and Bennet Ballew to GW, 22 Aug. 1789, for conflicting opinions of Ballew and his previous contact with Joseph Martin.

2. On 5 Dec. 1789 a committee of the North Carolina legislature was appointed to examine "sundry depositions relative to the conduct of General Joseph Martin, as Indian Agent." It reported on 15 Dec. that "It appears that

the said Joseph Martin was in the exercise of his duty, when he enclosed to the said McGilvray the resolutions of Congress mentioned in the first and second paragraphs of the said letter; and that the object of the said Martin in writing the third and last paragraphs, was merely to gain the good will of the said McGillivray, and to obtain a restoration of his horses, and not to injure the United States, or any of them.

"The said committee, to whom was also referred sundry depositions respecting the said Martin, report, that depositions of a similar nature have years past been laid before the general assembly, and that the committee do not find them to contain any matter sufficient to criminate the said Martin" (*N.C. State Records,* 21:659, 691; DLC:GW). Martin's letter to McGillivray is printed in *N.C. State Records,* 22:787–88.

3. Charles McDowell (c.1743–1815), a partisan Patriot leader on the Carolina frontier, was commissioned brigadier general by the North Carolina legislature in 1782 and was a state senator in 1778 and from 1782 to 1788. His enclosed letter of 21 Dec. 1789 to Alexander Martin reads: "At the time for raiseing the nine months Soldiers in 1778 I delivered one Bennet Below from the County of Burke as a nine month Soldier to Capt. Temple Cole, a Continental Officer and the said, Below after, receiveing a large sum of Money from the Company that hired him he deserted the service of his Country and was acused of passing Counterfeit Money, and joining the tory party and Plundering the good citisens of this State and was guilty of many acts of Vilany, that I do no think any credit ought to paid to his Information respecting Genl Joseph Martin's Conduct that from my own Knowledge and General Information the said Below is of a Very Contempable Caracter" (DLC:GW).

From Henry Sherburne

Sir,   Newport [R.I.] January 18th 1790

As the Legislature of this State did by a Resolution that passed Yesterday, direct that a Convention Should be called on the first Monday of March next, to determine on the adopting, or rejecting, the General Government of the United States;[1] the former of which those of us that have been Uniformly in favour of the Constitution (nay many of the opposers) have not a doubt, but such decision will be made by the Convention that will be pleasing to every well wisher to good Government.

Having devoted much the greater part of my Life to the public Service, either in the Military, or Civil Line, and Suffered the Loss of my House & buildings, which lay in this Town by the British Troops, whereby an Aged Mother and Two Maiden Sisters were deprived of Shelter, and otherways injured by my being opposed to the Measures which this State has pursued for several Years past; are inducements with me on presuming to address your Excellency, and requesting, that when it Shall be proper to appoint the Revenue Officers for this State, that I may be Nominated for the Office of Collector for the Port of Newport, Should I be so happy as to meet Your Excellencys Patronage, in this request & be appointed, you may rest assured, that nothing on my part Shall be wanting to fulfil with punctuality the Dutys of the Office.[2] I am, with the greatest Respect, Your Excellencys, most obedt Servt

Henry Sherburne

ALS, DLC:GW.

Henry Sherburne (b. 1748) retired from the Continental army as a colonel in 1781 and served as one of Newport's deputies to the general assembly in 1782.

1. See Jabez Bowen to GW, 17 Jan. 1790, n.2.

2. Sherburne also wrote to Henry Knox, asking to be recommended to GW for the post. On 14 June 1790 GW nominated Rhode Island's Continental loan commissioner, William Ellery (1727–1820), collector at Newport. Sherburne served as general treasurer of Rhode Island from 1792 to 1808. He received no federal appointment (Sherburne to Knox, 18 Jan. 1790, NNGL; *Executive Journal*, 1:51).

From William Tew

Sir   Newport Rhode Island January 18th 1790

The General Assembly of this State at their Session held last Week, have agreed (at last) to Call a Convention Which is to Meet the first Monday in march Next,[1] and as the matter is beyond a Doubt that they will Adopt the Constitution.

I have taken the Liberty to Address your Excellency Upon a Subject of Great Consequence to me tho very Small to your Excellency.

It is no Less than beging your Excellency to think of me When you appoint the Officers of the Customs in this State, or in other Words in this town. I do Not asspire to any Office higher than the Surveyor of this port, for fear of Interfering with Some more worthy Characters.

In the year 1775 I Was appointed a Captain in Col. Thomas Church's Regt in 1776 I Went into Col. Hitchcocks And in the year 1777 I Went into Col. Israel Angells And Serv'd in Said

Regt untill the first Day of January 1781. So that I Servd Six Campaigns a Captain Which Was Perhaps the only Instance of the kind During the War. Seeing No Prospect of Promotion and was Liable to Be Commanded By a Very Large Number of Officers Who I had Commanded. Which mortification I had undergone too often before I took the opportunity Which Presented upon the New Arrangement of the[2] on the first of January 1781, and Retird from the Service.

I have been in as many Actions as perhaps any officer that Was in the Service. Which Was No less than Six to Viz. on Long Island at Harlem heights at Princeton at Red Bank at Monmouth and at Springfield. And to prove my Attachment to your Excellency and Lady I Will Relate the following Circumstances, on the 9th of Feby 1776 Mrs Tew Was put to Bed With a fine Boy Who We had Christiand By the Name of George Washington[.] And on the 28th of October 1780 She Was again put to bed With a fine Daughter Who we had Christian'd By the name of Patty after your Excellencys Lady.

I know your Excellency is not Influenc'd in the Appointment of Officers By Such Matters as only Respect your Excellency And family, yet I know at Same time that it Does Not Make the Less Deserving of an Appointment.

I have a Large family to Support no Less than Seven Children and owing to the Mistaken Policy of the State for Some time Past the times are Bad.

I Belive my Character Stands fair. I think Col. Henry Sherburne who Lives But a few Doors from me, Will Give me the Character of an Honest Industrious Citizen. and Col. Jeremiah Olney Who Lives in Providence and Does me the Honour to Corespond With me at Least once a month, Will Say as Much or more in My favour.

If your Excellency in your Great Goodness Will take the Above into your Consideration and will Grant the Above or any Other favor of the kind that I May help Support a Most Amiable Woman And Seven fine Children, I will keep it in Everlasting Remembrance.[3] I am With the Greatest Respect your Excellencys Most Obedient And Most Humble Servt

William Tew

ALS, DLC:GW.

William Tew (1745–1808) served as a captain in the Continental army from 1775 to 1781. After the war he was a clothier in Newport and active in local politics. At his death he was a member of the Rhode Island legislature, president of the Newport town council, and an active member of the Cincinnati (*Newport Mercury,* 5 Nov. 1808). Tew renewed his application for office on 29 May 1790, following the ratification of the Constitution in Rhode Island, writing: "Our State has at last thought proper to Adopt the Constitution and God Grant that the peace and Prosperity of America May never Be Disturbed By Vicious and Designing Men again." Reminding GW of his references, Tew added that "I could get the Merchants in this town to Recommend me to your Excellency for the Office, But It Appears to me too much like making a Contract with them That if thro their means I Was to Obtain the Office, they would Expect me to wink at their Running their Cargoes for the Service they Did me. Therfore I have omitted applying to them" (DLC:GW). Tew did not receive an appointment from GW.

1. See Jabez Bowen to GW, 17 Jan. 1790, n.2.

2. Tew inadvertently dropped the following word or words.

3. GW nominated Daniel Lyman (1756–1830) as surveyor at Newport on 14 June 1790 (*Executive Journal,* 1:51; see also Daniel Lyman to GW, 12 Mar. 1790).

From Daniel Rodman

New York January 19th 1790
Cherry Street N. 70

Sir

Impressed with the most lively sentiments of your exalted character for justice and humanity, and The just attention shewn to Persons whose exertions, & sufferings were meritorious in The Revolution in which you had The honour To act so conspicuous a part: Together with the advice of a number of Friends, Hath emboldened me To lay The following statement of facts before you, praying your interposition in my behalf, so far, as is consistant with That duty you owe The Publick, and The superior claim of individuals. At the commencement of the late War, I was in easy: or what in New England would rather be called affluent circumstances. In The Spring 1775. I was one of the principle Persons consulted by the late Gouvernour Hopkins of Rhode Island in making all the arrangements respecting the first Troops that were publicly raised upon This continent, and I believe I may say without much vanity that I was one of the most active Members in May Session 1775 in preventing Gouvernour Wanton & Deputy Gov. Session from being sworn into Office, after they had been unanimously elected by the Freeman; as They had both (with three of The Gouvernours Counsel) Publicly protested (now upon record) against the act for raising Troops the preceeding April.[1] In consequence of which Sir James Wallis then commanding Three Frigates in the harbour of Newport, wrote several letters to the General Assembly calling us an illegal body of Men Assembled together without our legal Supreme Magistrate at our head and ordering us to disperse, upon pain of being declared Rebels & Traitors, I had The honour of drafting answers to those letters and at a day when many trembled to hear Them read, However Familiar the sound rebel became afterwards,[2] That was before we Knew that the God of armies had provided a Saviour to secure our necks from the Halter: and our Estates from confiscation—In The years 1775. 76. 77. & To April 1778, I loaned to the United States between Eleven & Twelve thousand pounds Lawfull money reduced by the scale, and for upward of one Thousand pounds of which I sold a real Estate, but reitterated misfortunes in trade obliged me to part with The whole of the securities for the money Thus Loaned and the most advantageous disposition I made of any was about £2600 sold Messrs Broom & Platt for dry goods @ 7/6 p. £. I was The second man That put Money into the Loan Office in Rhode Island, by placeing six hundred Dollars There The day that the office first opened, and upon West India goods turned out to different Commissaries of the Armey Two Thousand pounds Lawfull money in addition to all The pay That I ever received, would not have replaced me my goods exclusive of interest, by reason of the depreciation of The pay before I could obtain it—I had also a considerable store of dry goods burnt in The genneral conflagration at New London[3] I also lost rising one Thousand pounds Sterling first cost in Amsterdam Captured by The British in two Vessels from Thence without any Insurance, also rising Four Hundred pounds Sterling upon a Cargo of goods Shiped at Amsterdam & stoped at the Texel upon the rupture between the British and Dutch which was unladed and sold at Auction. And I believe it will not be contended where I was known, that many Persons advanced their property upon every call of Their Country with more chearfulness and liberality than I did—And at the commencement of peace, in hopes of redressing my losses I ventured what I had left in Navigation, and by a series of unbounded misfortunes lost The whole and am now reduced to The necessity of keeping a boarding House in this City to support a Wife and seven small Children—And as I hope and expect that The State of Rhode Island will adopt the confederacy this winter (which is the land of my nativity and in which State I held the Office of Clerk of The supreme Court for seven years and Then resigned it) should that event happen and upon inquiry you judge that my character & situation is deserving it, I will be very thankfull for the Collectors Office of the Port of Newport[4] (or if more convenient and agreeable any Thing else that will give my Family a decent support—I am not insensible of The delicasey of your exalted situation, and the numberless applications necessarily attendant upon it. in every event therefore my opinion of your goodness will remain the same. as I am an entire stranger to you I have taken the liberty to enclose Coppy of a certificate[5] (the original of which is now in my hands) given me upon leaving The State of Rhode Island, since which I have lived in the State of Connecticutt until the last spring, when I removed to this city, and for my genneral character of conduct since in Connecticutt; I beg leave to refer you to the Delegates in Congress from that state, particularly Benja. Huntington Esqr. & Colo. Wadsworth & Trumbull who were intimately acquainted with me during my residence there, and if necessary His Excelly Govr Huntington & Genl Huntington[6] as I lived in the same Town with them many years and was particularly intimate at their Houses & they at mine—I have the Honour to be with The greates[t] respt Sir Your Most Obdt & very Humbe Servt

Daniel Rodman

ALS, DLC:GW.

Daniel Rodman (born c.1748) of South Kingstown was a deputy in Rhode Island's general assembly from 1773 to 1778 and acted as its secretary in 1777. He served as major of the 2d Regiment of King's County militia from the summer of 1776 until he left the state in 1778. By 1780 he was living on Bean Hill in Norwich, Conn., where he was active in trade and town affairs. He was listed in the 1789 New York City directory as a merchant at 70 Cherry Street. Rodman received no federal appointment at this time (MS "[Rhode Island] Minute Book Lower House of Assembly Commencing at October Session (by adjournment) A.D. 1789" in Library of Congress Microfilm of Early States Records; Bartlett, *R.I. Records*, 7:602, 8:385).

1. On 19 April 1775, before news of the Lexington and Concord battles arrived, Rhode Island freemen had reelected conservative governor Joseph Wanton to office. On 25 April he, Deputy Gov. Darius Sessions, and two other members of the upper house signed a protest against the resolution presented by an emergency session of the lower house then meeting in Providence to raise a 1,500-man "army of observation." After Wanton had absented himself from the next general assembly session of 3 May (at which Rodman, Stephen

Hopkins of Providence, and a majority of the deputies had passed an act to recruit, supply, and pay the new army) and refused to sign commissions for its officers, the general assembly illegally forbade anyone from administering the oath of office to Wanton "unless in free and open General Assembly" and with its consent. In November that body officially replaced Governor Wanton with newly elected Deputy Gov. Nicholas Cooke (Bartlett, *R.I. Records,* 7:310–11, 317–26, 332–37).

2. James Wallace commanded the 20-gun frigate *Rose,* the 20-gun frigate *Glasgow,* and the 14-gun sloop *Swan* that threatened the inhabitants of Newport and Narragansett Bay from November 1774 to April 1776. Rodman may be referring to the correspondence between Cooke and Wallace that began with an exchange of letters on 14 and 15 June 1775, in which Wallace wrote, "I must desire to know *whether* or *not,* you, or the people on whose behalf you write, are not in open rebellion to your lawful sovereign, and the acts of the British legislature!" (Roelker, "Patrol of Narragansett Bay," 7:13, 18, 8:79–80, 9:58; Bartlett, *R.I. Records,* 7:337–38).

3. British forces under Benedict Arnold burned New London, Conn., in September 1781.

4. See Henry Sherburne to GW, 18 Jan. 1790, n.2.

5. The enclosure, dated 10 April 1778, about the time Rodman left Rhode Island, attests to his conscientious service as clerk of Rhode Island's Superior Court of Judicature and of King's County Court of Assize and General Jail Delivery and his honorable tenure as justice of the peace for King's County. The original certificate was signed by Deputy Gov. William Bradford as well as William Greene, Shearjashub Bourne, Jabez Bowen, Thomas Wells, and Paul Mumford, justices of the Rhode Island superior court, who testified that Rodman had discharged his duties "with great honour & integrity; And hath ever been a warm and steady advocate for the rights and liberties of America and a True Friend to his injured Country" (DLC:GW).

6. Gov. Samuel Huntington and Gen. Jedediah Huntington had also been residents of Bean Hill.

From Henry Knox

Sir,   War Office [New York] January 20th 1790.
I have but this moment been able to obtain two correct copies of the plan for the Militia.[1] I will have the honor if convenient to you to wait upon you at nine O Clock tomorrow morning to receive your orders respecting it. I have the honor to be Sir, with the highest respect Your Most Obedient Servant

H. Knox

LS, DLC:GW; LB, DLC:GW.
1. GW noted on 20 Jan. that Knox's report "altered agreeably to the ideas I had communicated to him was presented to me, in order to be laid before

Congress" and wrote the next day that it "was accordingly transmitted to both houses of Congress by the Secretary at War in a written message from me" (*Diaries*, 6:10; Knox to GW, 18 Jan. 1790; GW to the U.S. Senate and House of Representatives, 21 Jan. 1790).

To the Maryland Legislature

Gentlemen,   [New York, 20 January 1790]

I receive with the liveliest emotions of satisfaction, your expressions of gratitude for my having accepted the Office of President of the United States, and your congratulations on that event.[1]

From the enlightened policy of the Legislature of the Union, in conjunction with the patriotic measures of the State Assemblies, I anticipate the Blessings in reserve for these United States: and so far as my Administration may be conducive to their attainment, I dare pledge myself to co-operate with those distinguished Bodies, by constantly respecting and cherishing the rights of my fellow-Citizens.

Your mention of the place from whence you address me awakens a succession of uncommon reflections. In noticing the eventful period, since the resignation of my military command; I trace, with infinite gratitude, the agency of a Providence, which induced the People of America to substitute in the place of an inadequate confederacy, a general Government, eminently calculated to secure the safety and welfare of their Country.

The good dispositions of this People, and their increasing attachment to a Government of their own institution, with the aid of wisdom and firmness in their common Councils, afford a well founded hope, that the dangers of civil discord may be averted, and the Union established on so solid a basis that it may endure to the latest ages.

When I reflect on the critical situations to which this Country has been more than once reduced, I feel a kind of exultation in the character of my Countrymen, who have rescued it from threatened ruin by their virtue, fortitude, intelligence, and unanimity.

I thank you for the favorable sentiments which you are pleased to express of my public conduct, and for the affectionate interest which you have the goodness to take in the success of my measures and the preservation of my health. I pray for the Divine Benedictions on you, Gentlemen and on your State.

Go: Washington

LS, MdAA; LB, DLC:GW.

1. The undated address, signed by John Smith, president of the Maryland senate, and George Dent, speaker of the house of delegates, probably originated in the November 1789 session of the Maryland legislature, which adjourned on 23 December. Maryland's U.S. senator John Henry and congressmen Daniel Carroll, Joshua Seney, and William Smith presented it to GW on 12 Jan. 1790 and forwarded his reply to Annapolis on 20 January.

The address reads: "We the General Assembly of Maryland avail ourselves of the first occasion, afforded us, since your election to the office of President of the United States, of expressing to you our gratitude for accepting that truly honorable, yet arduous station, and of mingling our gratulations with those of our country, on this auspicious event.

"With pleasure we anticipate the blessings which these States will derive from the firmness and wisdom of your administration: The past proofs of your respect for the rights of your fellow-citizens amidst the din of arms and rage of war, are a sure pledge, that these rights will be equally respected and cherished by you in peace.

"In this place, from which we now address you, our Predecessors lately saw the affecting scene of their Patriot-Chief resigning his military command having fully accomplished its glorious ends.

"The lapse of a few years having proved the inadequacy of the late confederacy to the attainment of its objects, it affords subject of the most pleasing reflection that in the change which became necessary to the safety and welfare of the People of America, the President of the United States should be the same Person to whom they were indebted for a long series of the most important, glorious, and disinterested services.

"This People have unanimously called upon you to preside over their common Councils, under a well founded hope that, having asserted their Independence by your skill in war, your wisdom and firmness in peace, will avert the dangers of civil discord, and establish their union on so firm a basis that it will endure to the latest ages.

"We reflect on these things with gratitude, and that for you the singular happiness was reserved of being twice the Saviour of your country.

"May that kind Providence, whose protection you have frequently experienced in the midst of many and great dangers, direct your measures, and long preserve a life, in the preservation of which such numbers feel themselves so deeply interested" (LB, DLC:GW).

From John C. Ogden

Sir   Portsmouth New Hampshire Jany 20st 1790

Could I have introduced the book, which accompanies this,[1] to your perusal, or for the amusement, of some hour of relaxation, from the important duties, of your exalted station; in any other or a better method than this; I would have done it. But my distance from New York, a fear least I might be charged with taking too great liberty with you, or be suspected of some party designs; has led me to convey it by the post.

This work was aided to the press, by a general subscription of the members of the Legislature of New Hampshire; as well as very many of the first Patriots in America. It tends to bind Episcopalians to their mode—It removes antient prejudices against them on that head; and thus, by preserving them in uniformity and unity, it presents them, as Lovers of order; and gains them in New England, that religious liberty, which is the birth right of all, and to some almost their only treasure.

The subject appears to be of the first importance. The learned & pious writers of The Church of England, have ever complained; that the practice This author wishes to reform, has been an engine to promote sedition and rebellion.

Impartiality will shew, that it most powerfully assisted, in bringing about The Independance of America. This point being now obtained; a question arises, whether true policy, does not lead us as patriots, now to strive to remove, what may be a source of confusion, and disunion, at another day among our selves?

The Character of most nations is very generaly formed by their mode of Religion. As an individual It is my opinion that nothing will tend more, to cement the union of These States, and make it permanent; than our gradualy, affectionately, and generously, removing antient prejudices, and striving to unite the jarring interests, and opinions of religious communions.

The kind care of our civil fathers, in protecting all who are good subjects—Their generously avoiding all religious establishments, or acts of superiority; leaves all in their sphere, to seek the good of the whole; and to strive, for that unity in worship and doctrines, which is the duty and interest, of a free, enlightened, & truly pious people to adopt voluntarily & seriously.

This measure has most generaly been frustrated by the interference of civil government.

Pardon Sir, the liberty I have taken. As the office will convey the book *safely*, it will be, unnecessary to tax your goodness, to acknowledge its arrival,[2] and unpardonable in me, to hope to intrude my self, into your correspondence, upon this subject.

Presenting Your Excellency and family with the compliments of the season—Beseeching Almighty God, The fountain of all Goodness, to hear the prayer of The Church, that you may be prospered with all happiness; I subscribe my self to be with all possible respect and veneration, Your Excellency's, Most obedient, and most humble servant,

John C. Ogden
Rector of Queens Chapel

ALS, DNA: RG 59, Miscellaneous Letters.

GW had attended Ogden's Sunday service at Portsmouth, N.H., during his tour of the northern states (see Ogden to GW, 30 Oct. 1789).

1. The enclosed book has not been identified.

2. Lear acknowledged Ogden's letter on 4 Feb.: "The President of the United States has received your letter of the 20th of January, together with the book which accompanied it; and as he considers your sending the latter to him as a mark of polite attention which requires an acknowledgement, he has directed me to return you his best thanks for the same" (DNA: RG 59, Miscellaneous Letters).

To David Forman

Sir, New York January 21st 1790.

Acknowledging the receipt of your letters of the 3rd and 18th instant,[1] I desire to assure you that I have not been inattentive to your communications.

In order that the most prudential steps might be taken on the subject, to which your letters related, they were laid before the Chief-Justice of the United States,[2] who thought that a reference of them to the Executive of this State was the most adviseable measure—and the accompanying letter, from Governor Clinton to you,[3] expresses his opinions of what ought to be done. The Governor thinks that the papers which were transmitted by you, will be necessary in the further prosecution of this matter, and he has therefore retained them.[4]

This mark of your attention to public justice receives my best thanks. I am, Sir, Your most obedient Servant.

G.W.

Df, DNA: RG 59, Miscellaneous Letters; LB, DLC:GW.

1. Neither of these letters has been found, but see notes to letter-not-found entry for Forman to GW, 18 Jan. 1790.

2. On 8 and 20 Jan. 1790 GW's secretaries forwarded Forman's letters and enclosures of 3 and 18 Jan. to John Jay for his opinion (see David Humphreys to Jay, 8 Jan., and Forman to GW, 18 Jan. [letter-not-found entry], n.1).

3. George Clinton's letter to Forman has not been located.

4. Forman replied from Freehold, N.J., on 4 Feb.: "I had the Honour to receive Your Exclys letter of the 21st Ultimo, yesterday evening, Accompanyed by one from Govr Clinton. As your Excly has determined by the Advice of your Chief Justice that the business falls under the Notice of the Executive of New York, I shall follow such directions as I may receive from the Governor.

"Joh[n]ston was this Morning Committed agreeably to his wishes; I have written to the Govr, inclosed to him Copies of the Mittimuss both of Johnston and Farnham, allso lists of the Certificates that are lodged in the Hands of the Magestrates. Your Exclys polite Notice of my attention, to what as a Citizen was only my duty, I shall ever remember with gratitude" (DNA: RG 59, Miscellaneous Letters).

To Thomas Jefferson

Dear Sir   New York Jany 21st 1790

I had the pleasure to receive duly your letter dated the 15th of Decr last;[1] but I thought proper to delay answering or mentioning the contents of it, until after the arrival of Mr Madison, who I understood had been with you. He arrived yesterday,[2] and I now take the earliest opportunity of mentioning to you the result of my reflections; and the expediency of your deciding, at as early a period as may consist with your convenience, on the important subject before you.

Previous to any remarks on the nature of the Office to which you have been recently appointed, I will premise, that I feel such delicacy & embarrassment in consequence of the footing on which you have placed your final determination, as to make it necessary for me to recur to the first ground on which I rested the matter. In confidence, therefore, I will tell you plainly that I wish not to oppose your inclinations; and that, after you shall have been made a little farther acquainted with the light in which I view the Office of Secretary of State, it must be at your option to determine relative to your acceptance of it, or continuance in your Office abroad.

I consider the successful Administration of the general Government as an object of almost infinite consequence to the present and future happiness of the Citizens of the United States. I consider the Office of Secretary for the Department of State as *very* important on many accts: and I know of no person, who, in my judgment, could better execute the Duties of it than yourself. Its duties will probably be not quite so arduous & complicated in their execution, as you might have been led at the first moment to imagine. At least, it was the opinion of Congress, that, after the division of all the business of a domestic nature between the Department of the Treasury, War and State, that those wch would be comprehended in the latter might be performed by the same Person, who should have the charge of conducting the Department of foreign Affairs.[3] The experiment was to be made; and if it shall be found that the fact is different, I have little doubt that a farther arrangement or division of the business in the Office of the Department of State will be made, in such manner as to enable it to be performed, under the superintendance of one man, with facility to himself, as well as with advantage & satisfaction to the Public. These observations, however, you will be pleased to remark are merely matters of opinion. But, in order that you may be the better prepared to make your ultimate decision on good grounds, I think it necessary to add one fact, which is this, so far as I have been able to obtain information from all quarters, your late appointment has given very extensive and very great satisfaction to the Public. My original opinion & wish may be collected from my nomination.

As to what you mention in the latter part of your letter,[4] I can only observe, I do not know that any alteration is likely to take place in the Commission from the United States to the Court of France. The necessary arrangements with regard to our intercourse with Foreign Nations have never yet been take[n] up on a great scale by the Government: because the Department which comprehended affairs of that nature has never been properly organised, so as to bring the business well and systematically before the Executive. If you shd finally determine to take upon yourself the duties of the Department of State, it would be highly requisite for you to come on immediately, as many things are required to be done while Congress is in Session rather than at any other time; and as, in that case, your presence might doubtless be much better dispensed with after a little time than at the present moment. Or, in all events, it will be essential that I should be informed of your conclusive option, so that, if you return to France, another Person may be, at as early a day as possible, nominated to fill the Department of State.[5] With sentiments of the highest regard and esteem I am, Dear Sir Your Most Obedt Hble Se⟨rvt⟩

Go: Washington

ALS, DLC: Thomas Jefferson Papers; Df, DNA: RG 59, Miscellaneous Letters; LB, DLC:GW; copy, ViU.

1. Jefferson to GW, 15 Dec. 1789.

2. Illness prevented James Madison from reaching New York until 20 Jan. 1790 to report personally on his late December meeting with Jefferson at Monticello, but on 4 Jan. he sent to GW from Georgetown his impressions of Jefferson's feelings toward his appointment as secretary of state (Rutland, *Madison Papers*, 12:466–67, 13:1).

3. On 15 Sept. 1789 the Department of Foreign Affairs, created on 27 July, became the Department of State with the addition of domestic duties that had not been assigned to any other executive department. These new responsibilities included receiving and disseminating federal laws, keeping the great seal and affixing it to all civil commissions, and preserving and protecting the papers, records, and books of Congress. A supplemental resolution of 23 Sept. made it "the duty of the Secretary of State, to procure from time to time such of the statutes of the several states as may not be in his office" (1 *Stat.*, 28–29, 68–69, 97).

4. Jefferson had asked in his 15 Dec. letter "if there is any desire to suppress the office I now hold [minister to France], or to reduce it's grade."

5. GW sent this letter under cover to Virginia governor Beverley Randolph on 22 Jan., writing: "As it is of considerable consequence to the Public that a letter which I have just written to Mr Jefferson should reach him at as early a period as may be, and as I am unacquainted with any other certain channel of conveyance, I have taken the liberty of enclosing it to your Excellency. The importance of having it delivered to him with certainty & expedition, I hope will be considered as an apology for the trouble which may be occasioned by this measure. And even for the farther favor I am about to ask, of having it dispat[c]hed by a particular Messenger; in case no opportunity (that might with safety be depended upon) should present itself, of forwarding it in a short time from Richmond to Montecello" (LS, Vi). Joseph Clarke delivered GW's letter to Jefferson on 6 Feb. (Boyd, *Jefferson Papers*, 16:118).

To the United States Senate and House of Representatives

United States [New York] January 21st 1790.
Gentlemen of the Senate and House of Representatives.

The Secretary for the Department of War, has submitted to me certain principles to serve as a plan for the general arrangement of the Militia of the United States.[1]

Conceiving the subject to be of the highest importance to the welfare of our Country, and liable to be placed in various points of view, I have directed him to lay the plan before Congress for their information, in order that they may make such use thereof as they may judge proper.

Go: Washington

LS, DNA: RG 46, First Congress, Records of Legislative Proceedings, President's Messages; LB, DLC:GW; copy, DNA: RG 233, First Congress, Records of Legislative Proceedings, Journals.

1. See Henry Knox to GW, 18 and 20 Jan. 1790.

From John David Woelpper

Philada January 21, 1790
To his Excellency the President of the United States of America

The Petition of John David Wœlpper of the City of Philadelphia in the State of Pennsylvania Most humbly sheweth.

That Your Petitioner in the late War with Great Britain took an early and Active part on behalf of the United States, and was on the 17th Day of July 1776 honoured with a Captains Commission in the German Battalion (after having served as first Lieutenant for the Space of Six Months and upwards).

That on the Appointment to a Captaincy Your Petitioner was emulous to have his Company raised and compleated, and used his utmost endeavours for that purpose, and expended in the Recruiting service, of his own Money to the amount of 681 Dollars Specie from November 1776 to May 24th 1777 as Will appear by the annexed Account.

That in the Month of June 1778 Matthew Clarkson Esquire, then Auditor of Accounts, examined & passed Your Petitioners

Account; in Consequence whereof, Your Petitioner received on the 11th Day of June, from the United States 681 Continental Dollars which (agreeably to the Depreciation Table affixed by Congress) were then worth 246 Dollars $7/90$ & $5/8$ of a Ninetieth of a Dollar, and passed his receipt for the whole Sum of 681 Dollars: being ignorant of any Depreciation and placing too great a confidence in the Money then Current.

That Your Petitioner hath served to the End of the War, and flatters himself with reputation to himself, and satisfaction to Your Excellency and the United States, but hath never been solicitous or troublesome to his Superiors or the United States for Money, as many others were; his frugality and Œconomy enabled him from Time to Time to subsist on his pay, and at the conclusion of the War received Certificates for the Depreciation of his pay and commutation of his half pay; the Interest whereof hath hitherto been his sole Support! but the payment of Interest for want of Supplies in the Treasury being often delayed, Your Petitioner is thereby often put to the utmost straights for subsistence, as by reason of his Advanced Age having now compleated the 81th Year he is not able to support himself and Family by Labour, which induced him to apply divers Times to the Honble the House of Assembly and the Supreme Executive Council of Pennsylvania for relief; but received for Answer, "That his account for Monies Expended in the recruiting Service, was against the United States, and that he must apply to Congress for relief." Your Petitioner accordingly prefered a Petition to that Honourable Body but received no answer.

Thus Situated Your Petitioner is reduced to the Utmost Distress, the Interest not being regularly paid, and when paid, paid in depreciated paper Currency, that it was not sufficient for his support, he was consequently reduced to the necessity of contracting Debts, and is now hard pressed for the payment thereof; wherewith, he knows not, and hath now no other refuge left him but to Your Excellency, he Therefore humbly prays! Your Excellency may be pleased to take his distressed Condition into Consideration, and cause such relief to be granted him in the Premises as to Your Excellency in Wisdom shall seem meet.[1] And Your Petitioner in Duty bound shall ever pray &c.

John David Woelpper

The United States of America in Acct
with John David Wœlpper

1777   Dollr

May 24. To amount of Cash advanc'd in the Recruit-
    ing Service from Novr 1776—to this Day—
    Specie—   681.

1778

June 11. To Interest from May 24. 1777—to this
    Day—is 1 Year & 17 Days—   42.51

                  Dollars   723.51

Cr.

1778

June 11. By Cash recd in Continental Money
                 Dollr   681.

    (from which deduct depreciation,
    100 Dollr Contl Money being then
    worth 36.86.1[)]—Depreciation being   434.82.3

                                     246. 7.9

          By Balce carried to new Acct   477.43.3

                                      £723.51.

To Balance brought down   477.43.3
Interest on this Sum from June 11. 1778. to Jany 11.
    1790—is 11 years & 7 months   332.19.2½
Due J. D. Wœlpper   Dollr.   809.62.5½
exclusive of Arrearages of Interest due on his Certificates which
amounts to One hundred Pounds & upwards—January 21. 1790.

                                       John David Woelpper

LS, DNA: RG 59, Miscellaneous Letters.

John David Woelpper (Wilper) was born in Germany in 1709 and had settled in Staunton, Va., by 1751. In recommending him for a captaincy in 1776,
GW noted his personal acquaintance with Woelpper, whom he had commanded during the French and Indian War. Woelpper unsuccessfully petitioned the Continental Congress in 1781, 1784, and 1785 for resettlement of
his Revolutionary War accounts (GW to John Hancock, 8 July 1776; *JCC*,
21:1149, 30:11; Woelpper to Congress, 11 Feb. 1784, DNA:PCC, item 42;
Woelpper to Congress, 8 Dec. 1785, DNA:PCC, item 41).

1. On 27 Jan. Lear wrote to Knox enclosing Woelpper's petition dated 21
Jan. and noting that the president "directs me to observe that the Petitioner
has been a good soldier and he believes him to be a deserving man—He has
therefore ordered the Petition to be laid before you that you may judge if
anything can be done for the Petitioner—& what" (DLC:GW).

Knox forwarded Woelpper's petition to Commissioner of Army Accounts
Joseph Howell, Jr., who replied on 29 Jan. that were Woelpper's "accounts to

be revised I am fully of opinion that he would have to refund a part, if not all the monies he has recieved on the settlement made by Mr Clarkson, one of the late Auditors of the Army—for it appears by his own evidence (on file with his accounts) that more monies has been recieved by him for Bounties &c. than has been credited" (DNA: RG 59, Miscellaneous Letters).

Howell's accompanying report found it improbable that "the Petitioner could be ignorant of the Currency being depreciated nearly in a four fold sense at the time of his recieving this money—the fact was so notorious particularly with the Officers of the Army who sensibly experienced it, that the Commissioner is of opinion the assertion is intirely groundless. The Commissioner is also of opinion that when the Petitioner recieved this balance that he considered it as final and conclusive, for he could not be ignorant that the Continental Bills of credit was almost the only currency in circulation & that if any demand in specie had been made, it could not have been complied with, neither does it appear that the Petitioner made any demand for depreciation on this money untill the year 1783 or 1784 when he applied to the late Commissioner of A. Accounts who informed him that no relief would be given without the express direction of Congress. . . . Altho his situation may be such as to have a claim upon the humanity of the Public, yet a compliance with his request would create a Law of partial operation or be plead in precedent for so many claims similarly situated as to materially injure the interest of the Union" (DNA: RG 59, Miscellaneous Letters).

Knox forwarded Howell's letter and report to Lear who wrote to Woelpper informing him that his letter and petition had been submitted to the commissioner of accounts and enclosing a copy of Howell's report "for your information" (Knox to Lear, 1 Feb. 1790; Lear to Woelpper, 3 Feb. 1790, both in DLC:GW).

From Gouverneur Morris

Duplicate
Sir   Paris 22d January 1790
I received from Major Hasgill who arrived here on the twenty first Instant the two Letters which you did me the Honor to write upon the thirteenth of October. I shall in Consequence set off for London as soon as I possibly can. When last in that City I saw the Duke of Leeds twice at the french Embassadors,[1] and from some slight Circumstances was induced to beleive that the british Court are better disposed towards a Connection with the United States than they were some eighteen Months ago— the principal Difficulty will I imagine arise from the personal Character of the King, which is that of Perseverance, and from the personal Dislike which he bears to his former Subjects.

Yesterday I went to dine with the Count de Montmorin[2] and exprest to him my Wish that France might seize the present Moment to establish a liberal System of Commercial Policy for her Colonies. I observed that her Interest was deeply at Stake, because America could always dispose of the Islands and would naturally wish to see them in Possession of that Power under whose Government they would be most advantageous to her. That nothing could tend much to make the United States desirous of an Alliance with Britain as to exclude them from a free trade with the french Colonies. That if the Metropolis wishes to preserve the Affection of her distant Subjects and to derive from them the greatest commercial Benefit, she ought to suffer them to draw their Subsistence from that quarter where they can obtain it most cheaply. He assured me that he was fully of my Opinion. Said that our Position rendered it proper to make in our favor an Exception from their general System respecting other Nations; and that he hoped within a fortnight Something might be done. But he lamented (as he had done before) that they have here no Chief Minister and consequently no fixed Plan nor Principles. I shall see him again before I depart and also Monsieur de la Luzerne within whose Department this Matter most regularly lies.[3] He is an adherent of the exclusive System which is unfortunate. In the national Assembly also there is a considerable Difficulty: Among the most violent of the violent Party are some Representatives of Cities on the Western Coasts of this Kingdom whose chief Commerce is with the Islands, and those who wish for the closest Union with America do not wish to offend these Gentlemen and therefore are desirous of waving the Matter at present. For my own Part, I am very desirous that the Business should be put in Train at least. If successful so much the better, but at any Rate it will give an Alarm on the other Side of the Channel. If either of these rival Nations sets the Example, the other will soon follow, and altho it is not very clear that the Actings and Doings of the Assemblee nationale in general will long endure yet whatever they grant to us in this particular Business, those who come after them will be fearful of retracting. Under these Impressions for a long Time past I have been endeavoring to smoothe the Way towards our Object and I beleive in the Success. I am Sir, very respectfully your most obedient & humble Servant

Gouv. Morris

ALS (duplicate), DLC:GW; LB, DLC: Gouverneur Morris Papers; LB, DNA: RG 59, Diplomatic Dispatches, Great Britain.

1. Francis Osborne (1751–1799) became fifth duke of Leeds in March 1789 and was British secretary of state for the foreign department from December 1783 to April 1791. Morris conversed with him on 12 and 26 Aug. 1789 at the London residence of Anne-César, marquis de La Luzerne (Morris, *Diary of the French Revolution*, 1:188, 198).

2. In his diary Morris noted that the conversation with Armand-Marc, comte de Montmorin Saint-Hérem, the French minister of foreign affairs from February 1787 to November 1791, took place on 22 Jan.: "After Dinner I speak to the Count about the Commerce with their Islands. He says that he hopes something will be done in the next fifteen Days. That in his Opinion they ought to permit a much freer Commerce with us than with any other Nation because that the Fate of those Colonies must depend upon us. I communicate to him in the most perfect Confidence the Commission with which I am charged in Part. I tell him two very great Truths: that a free Commerce with the british Islands is the Object which will chiefly operate on us to give us the Desire of a Treaty of Commerce with Britain, and that I prefer much a close Connection with France. He tells me that their great Misfortune here is to have no fixed Plan nor Principle and at present no Chief. I tell him that they ought to go to War. He says he is convinced that if they do not soon make War it will be soon made against them: but their finances! I tell him there is less Difficulty in that than he is aware of. But the great Mischief is in a Constitution without Energy. We join the Company after having discussed another Point of minor Importance, viz Ternant's intended Appointment" (ibid., 374–75).

3. César-Henri, comte de La Luzerne, served as minister of marine from December 1787 to October 1790.

From Gouverneur Morris

[Duplicate]
Private
Dear Sir   Paris 22 January 1790

In another Letter of this Date I have mentioned a Part of Yesterday's Conversation with the Count de Montmorin. That Part of it which I am now to communicate is for yourself alone. As Monsieur de la fayette had asked me some Days ago who should be sent to replace the Comte de Moustiers[1] and (upon my answering with great Indifference it might be whom he pleased) had asked my Opinion of Colonel Ternant,[2] I told the Count de Montmorin this Circumstance to which he replied that he had communicated his Intention to Monsieur de la fayette some Time since, in Consequence of the Intimacy which has long subsisted between them. I asked him if he would permit me to mention it to you. This Idea gave him Pleasure and he told me that he should consider it as a very great Kindness, and particularly if thro the same Channel he could learn whether that Appointment would be agreable to you. This is you know a Compliment which the most respectable Courts on this Side of the Atlantic usually pay to each other. It is not without Use and on the present Occasion is not a meer Compliment because Monsieur de Montmorin is sincerely desirous of cultivating a good Understanding with the United States. It is not impossible that he should retreat from his present Office; but he will I think in that Case be appointed Governor of the Children of France[3] and his opinions while about the Court will have weight for many Reasons, among others because they deserve it. In talking over the deplorable Situation to which this Kingdom is reduced, I told him that I saw no Means of establishing Peace at Home but by making War abroad. He replied that he thought with me in Part, viz. that an offensive War might be useful but that he thought a defensive War must prove ruinous, that this last seemed the more likely to happen and that in either Case the State of the Finances was alarming. I observed that Ability in that Department might restore it even during a War, that Nothing could revive Credit without the Reestablishment of an executive Authority, and that Nothing could effect that Reestablishment but a general Sense of the Necessity. Upon this he lamented the Want of a Cheif Minister who might embrace the great whole of the public Business. He owns himself unequal to the Task, and too indolent into the Bargain. Our friend, lafayette (who by the bye is trying to stir up a Revolution in the King of Prussia's Dominions) burns with Desire to be at the Head of an Army in Flanders and drive the Stadtholder into a Ditch.[4] He acts now a splendid but dangerous Part. Unluckily he has given into Measures as to the Constitution which he does not heartily approve, and he heartily approves many Things which Experience will demonstrate to be injurious. He left America you know when his Education was but half finished. What he learnt there he knows well; but he did not learn to be a Government Maker. While all is Confusion here, the Revolt of Austrian Flanders, and the Troubles excited in Poland by the Agency of Prussia give every Reason to suppose that the King of Sweden will be vigorously supported: so that provided the Turk has but a sufficient

Share of Obstinacy to bear a little more beating, the Scale (according to human Probabilities) must turn against Austria and Russia who are the Allies of France.[5] Great Britain is as yet no otherwise engaged than as an eventual Party, and according to the best Opinion which my Judgment can form upon the Information I have been able to obtain the Premier of that Country can (to use the Words of Mr Addison) "ride in the Whirlwind and direct the Storm."[6] A Person however on whose Knowlege I have some Reliance assures me that Mr Pitt engrossed by Borough-Politics, and ignorant of continental Affairs, takes no Part in them but what he is absolutely forced into; and I am inclined to beleive that there is some Truth in that Assertion.

Before I close this Letter I think it just to mention that the Degree of Intimacy I enjoy with some of the first People here is not to be set down to the account of any Merit I may be supposed to possess. It results from the Letters of Presentation given to me, and I am particularly indebted to those written by the Marquis de la luzerne—and Mr Carmichael.[7] It is this last Gentleman that placed me well with the Count de Montmorin who was some time Embassador in Spain⟨;⟩ and I mention this Circumstance the rather as it furnishes me the Occasion of repeating what I have formerly said to you upon Mr Carmichaels Subject. He is admirably well calculated for a foreign Minister, the Proof of which is that he enjoys the fullest Confidence of the Court of Madrid and is generally esteemed by all the other Ministers there. Add to this that his Hobby Horse is the Ambition of establishing a high Character in the diplomatic Line without anything mercenary about him. He is therefore valuable. Men without Passions will do nothing, interested Men will do too much, and at such a Distance from Home the Temper of a Minister is very important to the Country he represents. Excuse me I entreat you my dear Sir, mentioning what you know so much better than I do and attribute it to the proper Motive. Accept at the same Time I pray the Assurances of that sincere Esteem with which I am yours

Gouv. Morris

ALS, DLC:GW; LB, DLC: Gouverneur Morris Papers; LB, DNA: RG 59, Diplomatic Despatches from Diplomatic Officers, Great Britain.

1. Eléanor François Elie, comte de Moustier, had been recalled as French minister to the United States and departed New York in October 1789.

2. Jean-Baptiste, chevalier de Ternant (1751–1816), served under Lafayette

during the American Revolution and in 1787 was a colonel in the Dutch Republican army and an agent of Lafayette's in Holland. On 17 Jan. 1790 Morris dined with Lafayette who "asks me who I think of to go to America in the Stead of De Moustiers. I tell him I have not any fixed Opinion, shall be readily governed in that Respect by him &ca. He asks me what I think of Ternant. I tell him that I approve. Hence I conclude that he intends the Appointment to pass, in my Opinion, as of his making" (Chinard, *George Washington As the French Knew Him*, 90; Gottschalk, *Lafayette between the American and the French Revolution*, 338–39; Morris, *Diary of the French Revolution*, 1:368).

3. Morris was probably referring to the surviving children of Louis XVI and Marie Antoinette: Louis Charles (1785–1795), the dauphin of France since the death of his brother on 4 June 1789, and Marie Thérèse Charlotte, madame royale (1778–1851).

4. King Frederick William II of Prussia (1744–1797) restored his deposed brother-in-law William V (1751–1795), prince of Orange and Nassau and hereditary stadholder of the Dutch Republic of the Seven United Provinces, to his offices in 1787. In late 1789 and early 1790 Lafayette considered sending French troops into the Low Countries to support Flemish patriots and other reactionaries in Belgium, the Austrian Netherlands, and the bishopric of Liège (Gottschalk and Maddox, *Lafayette in the French Revolution*, 274–83).

5. Frederick William II also had territorial ambitions in Poland, centered around Thurn, Danzig, and Gdansk. When Catherine II of Russia, who was also interested in acquiring Polish territory, became involved in a war against Turkey from 1787 to 1792, King Gustavus III (1746–1792) launched a Swedish offensive against Russia in order to recapture his Finnish provinces.

6. Joseph Addison, *The Campaign, a Poem, to His Grace the Duke of Marlborough* (London, 1705), 14.

7. Appointed chargé d'affaires in Madrid in September 1789, William Carmichael (c.1738–1795) was never made a full minister (*Diaries*, 6:53; Morris, *Diary of the French Revolution*, 1:98).

From Henry Merttins Bird

Sir,   Charleston [S.C.] 23 Jany 1790

The public debt of the United States of America being to be taken into consideration during the present Session of Congress, it is probable that for the purpose of raising a sum of money in Europe, an Agent or Agents may be wanted to negociate a loan, or to undertake the payment of interest to the European creditors of the united States.

Conceiving that to answer this purpose it may be thought necessary that the Appointment shou'd be given to some person or persons resident in London, I presume to offer the services of the house of Henry Merttins Bird, Benjamin Savage & Robert

Bird, known under the firm of Bird, Savage, & Bird, American merchants of London, in which I am a partner.

Should it be thought that one house is not competent to an appointment of so much trust, the house of William Manning senr, William Manning junr, & Benjamin Vaughan, known under the firm of Mannings & Vaughan, merchants of London might be added.[1]

I trust that on enquiry of the most honble Ralph Izard Esqr. or the honble William Smith Esqr the competency of one or both these houses will be found equal to the undertaking, & shou'd they be thought worthy of the trust I will immediately have the honor to attend at New York to take your Excellency's commands.[2] I have the honor to be with sentiments of the most profound respect, Sir, Your Excellency's most obedient & most devoted humble Servant[3]

H. M. Bird

ALS, DNA: RG 59, Miscellaneous Letters.

Henry Merttins (Martins) Bird (1755–1818), the leading partner in the London merchant banking house of Bird, Savage & Bird, was a grandson of Sir George Merttins, lord mayor of London, and received in 1776 an extensive inheritance from his mother's cousin, John Henry Merttins. In April 1778 he married Elizabeth Ryan Manning (1756–1817), daughter of prominent West India merchant William Manning (1729–1791). Four years later Bird joined with his younger brother Robert (b. 1760) and Benjamin Savage (b. 1750), son of John Savage, a South Carolina Loyalist who had moved to London in 1776. In 1778 Benjamin's widowed father married William Manning's sister, Rebecca Sarah Manning Hamm. Since Bird, Savage & Bird was the principal London house in the Carolina rice trade, its partners were on familiar terms with the South Carolina gentry. Bird may have been in Charleston in early 1790 to speculate in the South Carolina debt (Cope, "Bird, Savage & Bird of London," 202–3; *Gentleman's Magazine*, 87 [Dec. 1817], 563, 88 [Dec. 1818], 571; Rogers and Chesnutt, *Laurens Papers*, 13:104; *NEHGR*, 67 [1913], 319–20; Rogers, *Evolution of a Federalist*, 202–3, 273–74).

1. Bird was related by marriage to each of the three partners of Mannings & Vaughan: William Manning was his father-in-law, and William Manning, Jr. (1763–1835), and Benjamin Vaughan were both brothers-in-law (Vaughan had married Bird's wife's sister Sarah [1754–1834] in 1781). Another Manning daughter, Martha (1757–1781), had earlier married John Laurens, an aide of GW's during the Revolution (Rogers and Chesnutt, *Laurens Papers*, 10:20, n.4; Cope, "Bird, Savage & Bird of London," 203).

2. Charles Cotesworth Pinckney wrote to GW on 17 April 1790: "My friend Mr Bird an English Gentleman who has some business to settle in our State, takes the opportunity of his being on this Continent to visit with his Lady the Northern & Eastern parts of federal America; and as he anxiously desires to

have the pleasure of seeing you before he returns to Europe, I have taken the Liberty to give him this Letter of introduction, assuring you that you will find him not undeserving of your Notice" (DLC:GW). Bird was in Connecticut in the summer of 1791 where he met Jeremiah Wadsworth, a future director of the Bank of the United States (Cope, "Bird, Savage & Bird of London," 210).

3. Lear's reply to Bird of 16 Feb. 1790 reads: "The President of the United States has received your letter of the 23d of January; offering the services of the Houses of Bird, Savage & Bird—and of Mannings and Vaughn, to act as agents, if such should be wanted in Europe, for the purpose of negociating a loan—or paying of interest to the European Creditors of the United States. And in obedience to his command I have now to inform you, that your letter has been laid before the Secretary of the Treasury for his information, as belonging to his department; but the subject to which it relates has not yet come under the discussion of Congress" (DNA: RG 59, Miscellaneous Letters). Lear forwarded Bird's letter the same day to Alexander Hamilton, referring to its author as "M. H. Bird" (DLC:GW).

Bird, Savage & Bird became the main London house dealing in American securities, placing in Britain several million dollars of the domestic debt of the United States in 1791, but failed in its bid to become paying agent for the Bank of the United States in 1793. Bird's Charleston connections, however, were probably at work when Thomas Pinckney, who became American minister to Britain in 1792, recommended the firm as general agent for the federal government in London in 1795. The weakened state of its chief Carolina collaborator, Smiths, DeSassure & Darrell, in the 1780s, and ship seizures and trade dislocations during the Anglo-French war in the 1790s, as well as costly Far Eastern ventures, contributed to the house's failure in early 1803 (Syrett, *Hamilton Papers,* 6:267; Wilkins, *History of Foreign Investment in the U.S.,* 35; Cope, "Bird, Savage & Bird of London," 204–14).

From Benjamin Lincoln

My dear General   Boston Jany 23 1790

Knowing that your Excellency must be greatly burdened by the weight of public affairs and that the pressure is increased by various other avocations I should hardly have been persuaded to have broken in so much upon your time as to have given any other Gentleman, going from among us, a line of introduction But when I considered your Excellencys love of science & your partiality for scientific men I thought I could justly plead them as an apology for introducing Mr Read a native of this common wealth,[1] who from great labour & close application of mind has made very valuable improvments in the construction of several machines among them are the *Still* the *steam engine* the machinery for a self moving clock &ca His productions have been fully examined by many Gentlemen of education, and all of them saving one, are good judges of them who are fully in opinion of the great merit of the author.

If your Excellency should find a leisure hour to look into his performance, I have no doubt but you will be highly pleased and you will certainly by your countenance not only promote the interest but gratify the feelings and make a good man happy. With the most perfect esteem I have the honour of being my dear General Your most obedent & humble servant

B: Lincoln

ALS, DLC:GW.

1. The bearer, Nathan Read (1759–1849), a native of Warren, Mass., graduated from Harvard in 1781, received the A.M. degree in 1784, and remained at Cambridge as a tutor until 1787 when he moved to Salem, Massachusetts. After studying medicine and opening an apothecary shop, he became interested in steam navigation. Read designed a lightweight boiler, an improved engine, and a paddle-wheeled boat in 1789 and effectively presented them in January 1790 to a special committee of the American Academy of Arts and Sciences. The endorsements of members of the academy and Salem notables encouraged him to seek federal assistance, and Read traveled to New York in February with letters of introduction to Washington, Jefferson, Adams, "and several of the most respectable and influential members of Congress." On 8 Feb. Benjamin Goodhue presented to the House of Representatives Read's petition "praying the aid of Congress, and an exclusive privilege for constructing sundry machines and engines, which he has invented for improving the art of distillation, for facilitating the operation of mills and other waterworks, and for promoting the purposes of navigation and land carriage." With a similar petition of John Stevens, Jr.'s, it was referred to Aedanus Burke, Benjamin Huntington, and Lambert Cadwalader who were then considering a bill to promote the progress of useful arts. Read later wrote: "After spending considerable time in New York without effecting the object I had in view, I returned to Salem." He did receive one of the first patents issued by the United States, on 26 Aug. 1791, for his portable-furnace tubular boiler ("Autobiography of Nathan Read," 435; Boyd, *Jefferson Papers*, 16:111–12, 289; *DHFC*, 3:288–89, 6:1624–25; Preble, *History of Steam Navigation*, 28).

From Samuel Meredith

Sir   New York Jany 23d 1790.

I have the honor of transm[it]ting to you my Accots as Treasurer of the U: States settled to the first of January 1790.[1] It is not in the same form as the one I at first rendered,[2] which was an exact transcript of my Books, but such as the Officers were desirous of having, it being of little moment to me (only in the delay) in what way it was rendered, the balances being the same, to form which in this case, a recapitulation was necessary, and was annexed to the Account previous to its settlement.

I have likewise forwarded the Bank book as a Voucher for the propriety of my conduct, this last after examination, I shall take as a particular favour to have returned. I am with perfect respect Sir Your most obliged & humble Servant

Samuel Meredith

LB, DLC:GW.

1. A copy of Meredith's accounts was presented to Congress on 29 Jan. and is in DNA: RG 233, Accounts of the Treasurer of the United States, vol. 1 (*DHFC*, 1:231, 3:279, 599–603).

2. See Meredith to GW, 3 Jan. 1790, and note 1.

From Vaudreuil

Mr President,   Paris 23d January 1790

M. le Cte d'Estaing transmitted to me the diploma, admitting me into the Society of the Cincinnati, which your Excellency had addressed to me.[1] deign, I beseech you, to receive my thanks for it. I shall always feel myself honored in being a member of a Society which was instituted to celebrate your talents, to consecrate the virtues of which you have exhibited such an example to the Universe, and to transmit them to the admiration of posterity. I shall never cease to regret that I was not able, when I was at Boston,[2] to leave the command with which I was honored, to go & pay my respects to you, and know more intimately a hero who has added lusture to every place which he has occupied. I am with Veneration Mr President, Yr Excellency's Most Obedient Humble Servant

le Mis de Vaudreuil

Translation, DNA: RG 59, Miscellaneous Letters; LS, in French, DNA: RG 59, Miscellaneous Letters. The text is taken from a translation prepared for GW; the receiver's copy, in French, appears in CD-ROM:GW.

Louis-Philippe de Rigaud, marquis de Vaudreuil (1724–1802), commanded the French squadron that sailed to Boston after de Grasse's defeat in the Battle of the Saints in 1782. After his promotion to lieutenant general that August

Vaudreuil commanded the fleet that returned Rochambeau's army to France. In 1789 he sat with the nobles when the Estates General convened in May, and he assisted Lafayette's rescue of the royal family at Versailles in October. Vaudreuil fled to England in 1791, not returning to France until after 1799 (Chastellux, *Travels in North America*, 2:616, n.2).

1. See GW to d'Estaing, 13 Oct. 1789 and notes.

2. Vaudreuil probably is referring to his 1782 tour of duty, but it is possible he accompanied the French squadron commanded by Henri-Jean-Baptiste, vicomte de Pontevès-Giens, which visited Boston in the fall of 1789 (*Diaries*, 5:459–60, 480; GW to d'Estaing, 13 Oct. 1789, n.3).

From James Gibbon

Sir   Petersburgh [Va.] Jany 24. 1790

Unwilling to become importunate or be thought dissatisfied with the situation which you have been pleas'd to appoint me to,[1] I feel a reluctance in addressing you again on the subject, but from a pursuasion that your good intentions to me have been marr'd in their effect, and from other circumstances of serious concern to me, I'm induc'd once more to tresspass on your goodness, in soliciting some situation of more eligibility than the present some openings to which I'm induc'd to belive may occur in the present session of Congress—Being successful sir in my first attempt of this kind, I gave up Every consideration of other business, thereby to be enabled to do the public business with more propriety; in doing which, I only anticipated what wou'd have been requisite as the situation I am plac'd in, tho it does not afford constant employ occupies my whole time and necessarily ⟨deprives⟩ me of any other pursuit, under those circumstances and one or two additionall ones which I am pursuaded will have weight with you sir, I feel less the necessity of an appology for thus troubling you; Having a large and increasing family dependant on myself alone, and deriving from the public employ I'm now in, not more than £20 ℔ annum will I trust be a sufficient one, for the truth of which I beg leave to refer you to the Collector of this district (Coll Heath) who will shortly be in N. York whose information will be good, as all the fees of my office are accounted for and paid by him.

The suffution of an excise law being brought forward in the present session which will give openings,[2] is the intent of the present application, for the Collection of which in the Southern district of Virga as I wou'd beg leave to offer; this failing, shou'd the *Collectorship* of this district become vacant from resignation or otherways, I shall be than[k]full for preference[3]—From an opinion of what has been necessary sir to you where you have not a particular knowledge of the character or Capacity of applicants something more than a referrence to former recommendations may become necessary in my instance to justify my pretensions—I have only to observe sir that if the interest of the mechts of this place Richmond & Norfolk, in my behalf aided by that of some of the most respectable private characters will have any weight, I can have it with ease to myself and pleasure to them.

The situation I am *now* in of which I have troubled you with so particular acct will I hope be some appology for this premature application. I'm with great respect sir Yr ⟨*illegible*⟩ Servt

J. Gibbon

ALS, DLC:GW.

1. In response to Gibbon's previous applications of 12 Feb. and 20 May 1789, GW appointed him surveyor for the port of Petersburg on 3 Aug. 1789 under Bermuda Hundred collector William Heth (see Gibbon to GW, 12 Feb. 1789, n.1, and GW to the U.S. Senate, 3 Aug. 1789).

2. Alexander Hamilton completed his "Report of the Secretary of the Treasury on the Public Credit" with its proposed duties on domestic distilled spirits on 9 Jan. 1790 and presented it to Congress on 14 January. It recommended that the president be authorized to designate collection districts and appoint as many inspectors of the revenue as necessary, with at least one office of inspection at each port of delivery (*DHFC*, 5:722, 743, 800).

3. On 16 July 1790 Gibbon again wrote to GW about the Bermuda Hundred collectorship: "Colonel Heth the Collector of this district having receivd an appointment which will induce his relinquishing the Collectorship I once more take the liberty to trouble you on the Subject and offer as a Candidate for the vacancy. . . . Should any other recommendation be necessary than those which induced my present appointment I can with ease obtain it and should now have forwarded Something to this effect from the Merchants here but that it appears to me from the nature of the duty of the Officers of the Customs, doubt whether it would opperate to promote my pretensions or not I trust however, there is nothing in my character which will Operate to discourage you from promoting my wishes⟨,⟩ my success in which will greatly contribute to my happiness as well from a further proof of your countenance" (DLC:GW).

On 6 Mar. 1792 GW asked for Senate confirmation of his earlier appointment of Gibbon to the post of inspector of the port of Petersburg, Virginia.

When Thomas Newton, Jr., resigned his position as the inspector of survey no. 4 in Virginia in the fall of 1792, GW appointed Gibbon in his place (*Executive Journal*, 1:104, 125).

Collector Heth complained of Gibbon's handwriting to Hamilton on 14 Oct. 1792 and noted that his subordinate was "not so well versed in figures as I expected, and that, it would be some time before he could conduct the business of this Office." Heth, however, favored Gibbon as his replacement over Christopher Roan, surveyor for the port of Bermuda Hundred, as being "better acquainted with the revenue laws—understands better what he reads, is a man of superior understanding, and a more respectible character, he ought really to be the Surveyor of this Port—for his pride and Ambition would induce him to be active, prying, and inquisitive, and to make himself, at least so well acquainted with the Duties of this Office, as to be able to supply my place, in case of dire necessity; and I think he would be more attentive to orders than Roane—because, he has more sense" (Syrett, *Hamilton Papers*, 12:554–55). Gibbon became collector of the Richmond district in 1800 (*Executive Journal*, 1:356).

From Daniel Grant

Sir   Baltimore [Md.] Jany 24th 1790

By tomorrow's Stage I have forwarded 4 pr white Back Ducks In a Box directed to the President of the United States. Hopeing they will arrive safe and in good Order as they are Intended for Mrs Washington. from the great Scarceity of those ducks this Season I have been deprived of the pleasure of Sending any before. those that I have Sent are the best I Could procure. as they are a fine Bird and Such they Have not to the North of this I hope they will be acceptable. that Prosperity may Attend you Sir and Lady Washington in all Your Undertakeings is the Sincere Wish of Your Humble Servant

                                                                Danl Grant

ALS, DLC:GW.

Innkeeper Daniel Grant (1733–1816) moved from Philadelphia to Baltimore, became proprietor of the popular Fountain Inn on Market Street in 1773, and served as host to the Washingtons on numerous occasions, both before and after moving his hostelry to Light Lane in 1782 (*Diaries*, 3:327, 419, 5:153; Andrews, *Fountain Inn Diary*, 14–27, 60–61).

From Gouverneur Morris

Dear Sir   Paris 24 January 1790

I have received your kind Letter of the thirteenth of October and immediately set about procuring the Articles you there mention.[1] Such of them at least as are best to be procured in this Capital. They are already on their Way to Havre[2] and you will find here enclosed the Account of the Cost (including the Packages) ⟨L⟩ 2384ℓ. The Transportation to Havre will cost 46ℓ The Charges there and the Freight I know not. For the Cost at the present Exchange of 27½ I charge you £91 Sterling. You will perhaps exclaim that I have not complied with your Directions as to the Oeconomy, but you will be of a different Opinion when you see the Articles. I would have sent you a Number of pretty Trifles for very little prime Cost, but the Transportation and the freight would have been more and you must have had an annual Supply, and your Table would have been in the Style of a petite Maitresse of this City, which most assuredly is not the Style you wish. Those now sent are of a noble Simplicity and as they have been fashionable above two thousand years, they stand a fair Chance to continue so during our Time. If well kept they will always be worth the Cost. By the bye you must be thankful that I did not run you to farther Expence, for I was violently tempted to send out two dozen Cups and Saucers with the needful Accompanyments for Mrs Washington, to whom I pray you to present my Compliments with the Assurance that I am always at her orders. 100 to 150 Guineas will procure a very hansome Set of Tea China and a very large and neat Table Set. This last by no means in the great Style which is from one to two Guineas a Plate but of Plates at about 3ℓ each. Will you excuse me my dear Sir before I quit this Subject for making one Remark on the Subject of Oeconomy and Example as taken into joint Consideration. I think it of very great Importance to fix the Taste of our Country properly, and I think your Example will go very far in that Respect. It is therefore my Wish that every Thing about you should be substantially good and majestically plain; made to endure. Nothing is so extravagant in the Event as those Buildings and Carriages and Furnitures and Dresses and Ornaments which want continual Renovation. Where a Taste of this kind prevails, each Generation has to provide for itself whereas in the other there is a vast Accumulation of real Wealth in the Space of half a Century. Something too much of this perhaps, therefore I will call a new Cause.

It gave me very sincere Pleasure to learn from *you* the good tidings which you communicate respecting our new Form of Government. I know that you are not liable to the Dupery of false Hopes and groundless Expectations; and therefore I am confirmed in the Opinion I have invariably entertained that the new Constitution is such a plain calm sensible Appeal to the Interest Feelings and Common Sense of our Countrymen that it must by its own intrinsic Weight bear down all Opposition. I have from Time to Time received very great Pleasure at the Developement of its Principles by the Legislature, which in my Opinion does them the greatest Honor. They have far very far outgone my Expectations, and even come up not only to my Hopes but my very Wishes. I have not unfrequently brought myself to share in the Pleasure you must feel in the Consciousness of your own useful agency. Certainly it is the sublimest Sentiment of the human Heart to know that we make others happy, and more especially those whom we love. You have too much Good Sense not to know that No Person but you would have obtained that full Confidence needful to the due Establishment of the executive Authority, which certainly is the Key Stone in the great Arche of Empire I doubt also whether any other could so universally have called forth into Action the Talents and Virtues of America. Let me add what I have mentioned to you on other Occasions, and which I would not have mentioned did I not know it to be true, your Knowlege of human Character is a Gift inestimable to our Country on the present Occasion. I hope in God my dear Sir, that you may long continue to preside and that not only you but all who succeed you may be assisted by Counsellors as able and as honest as those who now fill the different Seats in Congress. The Prospect of public Felicity which must be the Result swells my Bosom with Delight. Oh my Country how happy! didst thou but know thine own Blessedness.

Your Sentiments on the Revolution effecting here I beleive to be perfectly just because they perfectly accord with my own, and that is you know the only Standard which Heaven has given us by which to judge. The King is in Effect a Prisoner at Paris, and obeys entirely the national Assembly. This Assembly may be divided into three Parts. One called the Aristocrats, consists of the high Clergy, the Members of the Law (note these are not the Lawyers) and such of the Nobility as think they ought to form a seperate Order. Another which has no Name but which consists of all Sorts of People really friends to a good free Government. The third is composed of what are called here the *Enragées* That is the Madmen. These are the most numerous and—are of that Class which in America is known by the Name of petifogging Lawyers, together with a Host of Curates, and many of those Persons who in all Revolutions throng to the Standard of Change because they are not well. This last Party is in close Alliance with the Populace here, and derives from that Circumstance very great Authority. They have already unhinged every Thing, and according to Custom on such Occasions the Torrent rushes on irresistible untill it shall have wasted itself. The Aristocrats are without a Leader, and without any Plan or Councils as yet, but ready to throw themselves into the arms of any one who shall offer. The middle Party who mean well, have unfortunately acquired their Ideas of Government from Books and are admirable Fellows upon Paper; but as it happens somewhat unfortunately that the Men who live in the World are very different from those who dwell in the Heads of Philosophers it is not to be wondered at if the Systems taken out of Books are fit for Nothing but to be put into Books again. Marmontel[3] is the only Man I have met with among their Literati who seems truly to understand the Subject. For the Rest, they *discuss* Nothing in their Assembly. One large half of the Time is spent in hollowing and bawling. The Manner of speaking to a Question is as follows. Such as intend to hold forth write their Names on a Tablet kept for that Purpose, and are heard in the order that their Names are written down, if the others will hear them; which very often they refuse to do but keep up a continual uproar till the orator leaves the Pulpit. Each Man permitted to speak delivers the Result of his Lucubrations, so that the opposing Parties fire off their Cartridges, and it is a Million to one if their missile Arguments happen to meet. As to the Arguments themselves you will observe that it is an usual Compliment of the Assembly to order them printed, therefore there is as much Attention paid (at least) to make them sound well and look well as to convey Instruction or produce Conviction. But there is another Ceremony which the Arguments go through and which does not fail to affect the form at least, and perhaps the Substance. They are read before Hand in a small Society of young Men and Women, and generally the fair friend of the Speaker is one, or else the fair whom he means to make his friend, and the Society very politely give their Approbation unless the Lady who gives the Tone to that Circle chances to reprehend Something; which is of Course altered if not amended. Do not suppose that I am playing the Traveller. I have assisted at some of these Readings and will now give you an anecdote from one of them. It was at Madam de Stahls the daughter of Mr Necker.[4] She is a Woman of wonderful Wit and above vulgar Prejudices of every Kind. Her House is a Kind of Temple of Apollo where the Men of Wit and fashion are collected twice a Week at Supper and once at Dinner, and sometimes more frequently. The Count de Clermont Tonnerre (one of their greatest orators) read to us a very pathetic oration; and the Object was to shew that as Penalties are the legal Compensation for Injuries and Crimes, the Man who is hanged having by that Event paid his Debt to the Society ought not to be held in dishonor, and in like manner he who has been condemned for seven Years to be flogged in the Gallies should when he had served out his apprenticeship be received again into good Company as if Nothing had happened. You smile; but observe that the Extreme to which the Matter was carried the other Way, dishonoring thousands for the Guilt of one, has so shocked the public Sentiment as to render this Extreme fashionable. The Oration was very fine, very sentimental, very pathetic, and the Style harmonious. Shouts of Applause and full approbation. When this was pretty well over, I told him that his Speech was extremely eloquent, but that his Principles were not very solid. Universal Surprize. A very few Remarks changed the Face of Things. The Position was universally condemned, and he left the Room.[5] I need not add that as yet it has never been delivered in the Assembly—And yet it was of the Kind which produces a Decree by Acclamation; for Sometimes an orator gets up in the midst of another Deliberation, makes a fine Discourse and closes with a good snug Resolution, which is carried with a huzza. Thus in Considering a Plan for a national Bank proposed by Mr Necker, one of them took it into his Head to move that every Member should give his Silver Buckles, which was agreed to at once and the honorable Mover laid his upon the Table, after which the Business went on again.[6] It is very difficult to guess whereabouts the Flock will settle When it flys so wild but as far as it is possible to guess at present, this (late) Kingdom will be cast into a Congeries of little Democracies laid out not according to Rivers Mountains &ca but with the Square and Compass according to Latitude and Longitude; and as the Provinces had anciently different Laws (called Coutumes) and as the clippings and pairings of several different Provinces must fall together within some of the new Divisions I think such fermenting Matter must give them a Kind of political Cholic. Their Assemblee Nationale will be Something like the old Congress and the King will be *called* executive Magistrate. As yet they have been busily engaged in pillaging the present occupant of his Authority, how much they will leave him will depend upon the Chapter of Accidents, I beleive it will be very little: but little or much the Perspective of such a King and such an Assembly brings to my Mind a Saying which Shakespear has put into the Mouth of an old Soldier, upon hearing that Lepidus one of the famous Triumvirate was dead. "So the poor third is up. World thou hast but a pair of Chops, and throw between them all the Food thou mayest they needs must grind each other."[7]

At present the People are fully determined to support the Assembly and altho there are some Discontents I do not beleive that any Thing very serious as yet exists in the Style of Opposition. Indeed it would be wonderful if there should, for hitherto an Extension of Privileges and a Remission of Taxes to the lower Class has marked every Stage of their Progress. Besides, the Love of novelty is a great Sweetener in Revolutions. But the Time will come when this Novelty is over & all its Charms are gone. In Lieu of the Taxes remitted other Taxes must be laid: for the public Burthen must be borne. The elected Administrators must then either indulge their Electors which will be ruinous to the Fis⟨*illegible*⟩, or in urging the Collection of Taxes displease their Constituents. In all Probability there will be a little of both. Hence must arise Bickerings and Heartburnings among the different Districts and a great Languor throughout the Kingdom. As the Revenue must fall short of Calculation in Point of Time, if not in Amount (and that is the same Thing where Revenue is concerned) it will follow that either the Interest of the public Debt will not be regularly paid, or that the various Departments will be starved. Probably a little of both. Hence will result a Loss of public Credit, and therewith much Injury to Commerce and Manufactures, operating a farther Decrease of the Means of Revenue, and much Debility as to the Exterior Operations of the Kingdom: At this Moment the discontented Spirits will find congenial Matter in Abundance to work upon; And from that Period all the future is involved in the Mist of Conjecture. If the reigning Prince were not the small beer Character that he is, there can be but little Doubt that watching Events and making a tolerable Use of them he would regain his Authority. But what will you have from a Creature who situated as he is eats and drinks and sleeps well and laughs and is as merry a Grig as lives? The Idea that they will give him some Money which he can Œconomize, and that he will have no Trouble in governing, contents him entirely. Poor Man! he little thinks how unstable is his Situation. He is beloved, but it is not with the Sort of Love which a Monarch should inspire. It is that Kind of good natured Pity which one feels for a led Captain. There is besides no Possibility of serving him, for at the slightest shew of Opposition he gives up every Thing, and every Person.

As to his Ministers The Count de Montmorin has more understanding than People in general imagine, and he means well, very well. But he means it feebly. He is a good easy Kind of Man, one who would make an excellent Peace Minister in quiet Times, but he wants the Vigor of Mind needful for great Occasions. The Count de la luzerne is an indolent pleasant Companion. A Man of Honor and as obstinate as you please; but he has somewhat of the Creed of General Gates that the World does a great Part of it's own Business without the Aid of those who are at the Head of affairs. The Success of such Men depends very much upon the Run of the Dice. The Count De St Priest[8] is the only Man among them who has what they call *Caractere* which answers to our Idea of Firmness joined to some Activity. But a Person who knows him pretty well (which I do not) assures me that he is mercenary and false hearted. If so he cannot possess much Good Sense, whatever may be his Share of Genius or Talents. Monsieur de la Tour du Pin the Minister at War,[9] whom I am also unacquainted with, is said to be no great Things in any Respect. Mr Necker was frightened by the Enragées into the Ac-

ceptance of him instead of the Marquis de Montesquieu[10] who
has a considerable Share of Talents and a great Deal of Method.
Montesquieu is of Course at present the Enemy of Necker, having been his friend—As to Mr Necker, he is one of those People
who has obtained a much greater Reputation than he had any
Right to. His Enemies say that as a Banker he acquired his Fortune by Means which to say the least were indelicate, and they
mention Instances. But in this Country every Thing is so much
exagerated, that Nothing is more useful than a little Scepticism.
Mr Necker in his public Administration has always been honest
and disinterested, which proves well I think for his former private Conduct; or else it proves that he has more Vanity than
Cupidity. Be that as it may, an unspotted Integrity as Minister,
and serving at his own Expence in an Office which others seek
for the Purpose of enriching themselves, have acquired him very
deservedly much Confidence. Add to this that his Writings on
finance teem with that Sort of Sensibility which makes the Fortune of Modern Romance, and which is exactly suited to this
lively Nation, who love to read but hate to think. Hence his Reputation. He is a Man of Genius and his Wife is a Woman of
Sense.[11] But neither of them have Talents. Or rather *the* Talents
of a great Minister. His Education as a Banker has taught him
how to make tight Bargains, and put him upon Guard against
Projets. But tho he understands Man as a covetous Creature, he
does not understand Mankind. A Defect Which is remed⟨iless.⟩
He is utterly ignorant also of Politics, by which I mean Politics
in the great Sense, that sublime Science which embraces for its
Object the Happiness of Mankind. Consequently he neither
knows what Constitution to form, nor how to obtain the Consent
of others to such as he wishes. From the Moment of convocing
the States General, he has been afloat upon the Wide Ocean of
Incidents. But what is most extraordinary is that Mr Necker is
a very poor financier. This I know will sound like Heresy in the
Ears of most People, but it is true. The Plans he has proposed
are feeble and ineptious. Hitherto he has been supported by
borrowing from the Caisse D'escompte, which (being by Means
of what they call here an Arret de Surseance secured from all
Prosecution) has lent him a Sum in their Paper exceeding the
Totality of their Capital by about four Millions Sterling. Last Au-
tumn he came forward to the Assemblée with a dreadful Tale of
Woe, at the Fag End of which was a Tax upon every Member of

the Community of a fourth of his Revenue, and this he declared to be needful for saving the State. His Enemies adopted it (declaring what is very true that it is a wretched impracticable Expedient) in the Hope that he and his Scheme would fall together. This Assemblée, this patriotic Band, took in the Lump the Ministers Proposition, because of their Confidence & the Confidence of the People in him as they said; but in Fact because they would not risque the Unpopularity of a Tax. The Plan thus adopted, Mr Necker to escape the Snare which he had nearly got taken in, altered his Tax into what they call the Patriotic Contribution. By this every Man is to declare, if he pleases, what he pleases to estimate as his annual Income, and to pay one fourth of it in three Years. You will easily suppose that this Fund was unproductive, and notwithstanding the imminent Danger of the State, here we are without any Aid from the *Contribution patriotique*. His next Scheme was that of a national Bank, or at least an Extension of the Caisse d'escompte. It has been variously modelled since, and many capital objections removed, but at last it is good for Nothing, and so it will turn out. At present it is just begining. By Way of giving some Base to the present Operation, It is proposed and determined to sell for about ten or twelve Millions Sterling of the Crown and Church Lands both of which are by Resolution of the Assemblée declared to belong to the Nation, but as it is clear that these Lands will not sell well just now, they have appointed a Treasurer to receive what they will sell for hereafter, and they issue a Kind of Order upon this Treasurer which is to be called an *Assignat* and is to be paid (out of those Sales) one two & three Years hence. They expect that on these Assignats they can borrow Money to face the Engagements of the Caisse D'escompte, and they are at the same Time to pay some of the more pressing Debts, with the same Assignats. Now this Plan must fail as follows. First, there will be some Doubt about the Title to these Lands, at least till the Revolution is compleated. Secondly, the Representative of Land must always (for a Reason which will presently appear) sell for less than a Representative of Money, and therefore untill public Confidence is so far restored so that the five per Cents are above Par, these Assignats bearing five perCent must be below Par. Money therefore cannot be raised upon them but at a Considerable Discount. Thirdly, the Lands so to be disposed of must sell a great Deal below their Value, for there is not Money to buy them in this Country, and the Proof is that they never obtained Money on Loan at the legal Interest but always ⟨*illegible*⟩ a Premium sufficient to draw it from the Employments of Commerce and Manufactures; and as the Revolution has greatly lessened the Mass of Money the Effect of the Scarcity must be greater. But further there is a Solecism in the Plan which escapes most of them, and which is never very palpable. The Value of Lands in Europe is you know estimated by the Income. To dispose of public lands therefore is to sell public Revenue, and therefore taking the legal Interest at five PerCent, Land renting for 100₶ ought to sell for 2000₶ but they expect that these Lands will sell for 3000₶ and that thereby not only public Credit will be restored, but a great Saving will be made as the 3000₶ will redeem an Interest of 150₶. It is however an indisputable Fact that public Credit being established, the Stocks are worth more than Land of equal Income, & for three Reasons 1st that there is no trouble whatever in the management. 2ly There is no Danger of bad Crops and Taxes & 3ly They can be disposed of at a Moments Warning ⟨if⟩ the Owner wants the Money, and be as readily re-purchased when it suits his Convenience. If therefore the public Credit be restored, and there be a Surplus Sum of 10 to 12 Millions to be invested, and if such large Sales (contrary to Custom) should not from the Amount affect the Price, still the Lands must go cheaper than the Stocks, and Consequently the Interest bought will be smaller than the Revenue sold.

Having thus given you a very rude Sketch of the Men and the Measures of this Country, I see and feel that it is Time to conclude. I sincerely wish I could say that there are able Men at Hand to take the Helm, should the present Pilots abandon the Ship. But I have great Apprehensions as to those who may succeed. The present Set must wear out in the Course of the Year, and most of them would be glad to get fairly out of the Scrape at present but it is alike dangerous to stay ⟨or⟩ to go and they must patiently wait the Breath of the Assemblée, and follow as it blows. The new order of Things cannot endure. I hope it may be mended, but fear it may be changed. All Europe just now is like a Mine ready to explode, and if this Winter does not produce Peace, next Summer will behold a wider Extension of the War. I am with very sincere Esteem my dear Sir your most obedient & humble Servant

Gouv. Morris

ALS, DLC:GW; ALS (duplicate), DLC:GW; LB, DLC: Gouverneur Morris Papers. Material in angle brackets taken from the duplicate.

1. Morris probably received GW's 13 Oct. 1789 letter, asking him to purchase and send tableware, on 9 Jan. 1790 and began searching for GW's centerpiece, or *surtout*, the following Monday. On Friday, 15 Jan., Morris first visited the Angoulême porcelain manufactory for other table ornaments, made a purchase there on Monday, 18 Jan., and discussed the order with manufacturers that Wednesday and Thursday, after which he continued his search for the *surtout* (GW to Morris, 13 Oct. 1789 [first letter]; Morris, *Diary of the French Revolution*, 1:361, 363, 366, 369, 371).

2. Morris had acquired the various pieces before 24 Jan. when he wrote a second letter of this date to GW: "I expect that this Letter will accompany three Cases containing a Surtout of seven Plateaus and the ornaments in Biscuit Also three large Glass covers for the three Groups which may serve both for ornaments to the Chimney Piece of a drawing Room (in which Case the Glasses will preserve them from the Dust & Flies) or for the Surtout. The Cases must be knocked to Pieces very carefully taking off the Top first and then the Sides and Ends. The Manufacturer promised me that Instructions for unpacking should accompany the Cases. Enclosed is his Note of the Contents of the several Cases. There are in all three Groups two Vases and twelve figures. The Vases may be used as they are or when Occasion serves the Tops may be laid aside and the Vases filled with natural Flowers. When the whole Surtout is to be used for large Companies the large Group will be in the Middle the two smaller ones at the two Ends the Vases in the Spaces between the three and the Figures distributed along the Edges or rather along the Side. I shall send you the Account by another Opportunity and the other Articles I shall procure in England. . . . I have directed the Charges of Transportation from hence with the Freight &ca &ca to be paid by Messrs Wm Constable and Company to whom you will be so kind as to replace the Amount—To clean this *Biscuit* Warm Water is to be used and for any thing in little Corners a Brush such as is used for painting in Water Colours" (DLC:GW). See also GW to Morris, 13 Oct. 1789 (first letter), n.2.

Of the pieces sent by Morris in January 1790, only the *surtout* and one of the three biscuit-porcelain groups are still (1993) at Mount Vernon. Of the dozen neoclassical figurines, only two (Venus and Minerva) have survived or been positively identified (Detweiler, *George Washington's Chinaware*, 111–12, 121).

3. Poet and dramatist Jean-François Marmontel (1723–1799), secretary of the French Academy after 1792, was a moderate Parisian elector during the popular uprisings of the summer of 1789. Morris had just dined with him at Montmorin's on 22 Jan. (Morris, *Diary of the French Revolution*, 1:374–75, 2:110).

4. Anne-Louise-Germaine Necker (1766–1817), daughter of Jacques Necker, French prime minister of finance until September 1790, became baronne de Staël-Holstein when she married the Swedish ambassador to France in 1786.

5. Morris feared that his mortification of Tonnerre on 9 Dec. 1789 had made him a new enemy (ibid., 1:328–29).

6. Morris was present on 20 Nov. 1789 when the National Assembly applauded the example of Marie-François d'Ailly (1724–1800), the deputy of the *bailliage* of Chaumont-en-Vexin, who invited his colleagues to join him in sacrificing their silver shoe buckles to the state. The assembly then voted that its members would wear only copper buckles. A large majority of them delivered over their silver buckles before the following evening, and even spectators in the galleries had met d'Ailly's challenge by joining the deputies in their offering. Several members of religious orders who did not wear silver buckles instead voluntarily surrendered an equivalent sum in silver (Morris, *Diary of the French Revolution,* 1:308; *Archives parlementaires,* 10:130, 159).

7. *Antony and Cleopatra,* 3.5.11–16.

8. François-Emmanuel Guignard, comte de Saint-Priest (1735–1821), entered Louis XVI's council as minister without portfolio in December 1788, was placed in charge of the Royal Household, and became minister of the interior after the fall of the Bastille in July 1789.

9. Jean-Frédéric de La Tour du Pin de Gouvernet (1727–1794), one of the first nobles in the Estates General to support the Third Estate, served as war minister from August 1789 to November 1790.

10. Writer and general Anne-Pierre, marquis de Montesquiou-Fézénsac (1739–1798), a member of the nobility in the Estates General, was later appointed to the finance committee of the National Assembly.

11. Suzanne Curchod (1739–1794) married Necker in 1764.

From Edward Rutledge

My dear Sir   Charleston [S.C.] January 24th 1790.

Our mutual Friend General Pinckney[1] has desired me to write with him in requesting you would be so obliging as to favor him with a Letter of introduction for a youth who is his nephew,[2] and on the Eve of entering of his Travels to the Marquis de Fayette.[3] Altho I did not imagine that there was any request that the General could make you would be declined, yet I most readily complied for a variety of Reasons. There is no doubt my dear Sir that the national Gratitude of America will remain to you, and to your Memory as long as Divine Providence shall permit any Blessings to flow from Liberty. But as my affection for you is as much attached to the Man, as that of others is to the General & the President, I am anxiously desirous that the Individual should be united to the national Regard, & that both should be continued as long as possible. I wish that our young People should look up to you as the common Father of the Country, consider your Name as a Protection to them, and entitle them to the Rights of Americans in foreign Countries—When I view the Subject as a public man, I feel an anxiety in obtaining for the rising Generation a Knowledge of the politics of foreign States. In spite of our best Efforts it may be often very difficult, & some times altogether impossible to keep clear of their Politics: it is therefore a part of our general Duty to be prepared to meet them, and if we must intermingle with them, to make the best of it. And if this be true in the general it gathers new strength when applied to the Citizens of a State peculiarly weak from its local Situation, & will forever I fear continue so from its modes of Cultivation. We must therefore endeavour to counteract what I consider as natural Evils, and I know of nothing so likely to accomplish our desires as giving to our Children good Educations & extensive Knowledge—to improve them by Travel—to enable them to travel under the most favourable Circumstances. It is from these Considerations that I unite in giving you what I look upon as that kind of Trouble which receives a compensation from the Pleasure which it affords—The occasion therefore will be the apology: & I am sure you will consider it as such.[4] I am my dear Sir with every Sentiment of Friendship & Esteem your most affectionate Humble Servt

Ed: Rutledge

ALS, DLC:GW.

1. Edward Rutledge was Gen. Charles Cotesworth Pinckney's brother-in-law and business partner (see GW to Rutledge, 5 May 1789, source note). No letter from Pinckney requesting GW to write letters of introduction for his nephew has been found.

2. Daniel Huger Horry, Jr. (1769–1828), who changed his name to Charles Lucas Pinckney Horry, was the only son of Pinckney's sister Harriott Pinckney Horry (1748–1830), whose South Carolina plantation GW visited on his southern tour in the spring of 1791. In 1781 Horry went to England with his father, Col. Daniel Horry (d. 1785), and was educated at the Middle Temple in London. He settled in France after marrying the daughter of Vincent-Marie Viénot, comte de Vaublanc (1756–1845). GW invited Horry to Mount Vernon when he visited America in 1798 with his wife and mother-in-law (GW to Horry, 6 May 1798; *Diaries*, 6:126; Rogers, *Evolution of a Federalist*, 89; *Bio. Dir. of the S.C. House of Representatives*, 2:329–30; Gottschalk, *Letters of Lafayette to Washington*, 377, 379.)

3. GW's 26 April 1790 letter to Lafayette reads: "I will draw your attention from the busy and momentous scene, in which you are acting so distinguished a part, but for one moment, to introduce to your notice, Mr Horry of south Carolina, who proposes to have the satisfaction of delivering this letter to

you—He is a Nephew of General Pinckney, and a young Gentleman, whose flattering expectations induce him to travel through Europe, for the sake of completing his education. I know full well the multiplicity of business with which you are oppressed, and only suggest that such marks of your civilities as may be bestowed upon him, consistent with the discharge of your public functions, will be considered as a particular favor to me.

"You know, my dear Marquis, that all my best wishes ever attend you—May you be as successful and as happy in your great undertakings, as your own heart can desire. I am always, with sentiments of the tenderest affection and regard, My dear Marquis, Your sincere friend and humble servant" (LB, DLC:GW). GW wrote similar letters on the same day to William Carmichael, Rochambeau, and William Short (all in DLC:GW).

4. On 26 April 1790 GW wrote to Pinckney: "I comply with your wishes in giving letters introductory of your Nephew to several Gentlemen in France and Spain—They are under flying seals, but, as I mean letters of this sort shall be rare, I pray you to close them before they go out of your hands, lest the indiscretions of youth should make an improper use of them before they are delivered to their address.

"Wishing the young Gentleman success, and yourself health and happiness I remain, with sentiments of esteem and consideration, Your most obedient humble servant" (LB, DLC:GW).

GW reported to Rutledge the same day: "I have remitted under cover to General Pickney several letters introductory of his Nephew, with my sentiments thereupon. I cannot, on the occasion of acknowledging your polite and friendly letter omit to reiterate the assurances, with which I am, My dear Sir, With the highest regard & esteem Yr Most Obedt & Affecte Servt" (ALS, PHi: Dreer Collection).

To Ebenezer Tucker

Sir, New York, January 24. 1790

Captain Burnett delivered me your letter of the 18. instant[1], and is so obliging as to take charge of this answer.

It is my sincere opinion that the land mentioned in it is worth what I asked for it—to wit four dollars per acre, and once would have sold for it; but, if, in the present scarcity of cash it will not fetch that sum, let those, who are really inclinable to buy, come forward, like men that are in earnest, and say what they will give—If they, or their Agent have seen the land, (and without this it is useless to name any price) have examined its qualities and improvements,[2] they can say what they will give, and ought to act like fair and candid men—On these terms I am ready to treat with them. It is not my intention to dispose of the land for a song, nor is it my wish to higgle, or make many words to the bargain—for which reason I pray them to come to a decision at once, and that you would inform me of the result—at any rate it would be well for you to write to me, and soon, that I may not miss any other offer, should any be made to Sir, Your most obedient, humble Servant

G. Washington.

LB, DLC:GW; ALS, sold by Charles Hamilton, catalog no. 40, item 521 (n.d.), and Sotheby's (London), 5–6 Nov. 1962 (*Catalogue of Valuable Americana, Voyages, Travel and Atlases, Printed Books, Autograph Letters, and Historical Documents,* item 376).

Ebenezer Tucker (1758–1845) was a Burlington County, N.J., judge, merchant, and shipbuilder. Tucker served under GW on Long Island during the Revolution, and after receiving recommendations from the collector for the port of Little Egg Harbor, he was appointed surveyor of the port in August 1789. Tucker later served as inspector of the revenue at Little Egg Harbor, postmaster at Tuckerton, and a member of Congress (John Ross to William Paterson and Jonathan Elmer, 10 Aug. 1789, and Joseph Bloomfield to Paterson and Elmer, 11 Aug. 1789, both in DLC:GW; GW to the U.S. Senate, 3 and 18 Aug. 1789; Tucker to GW, 8 Aug. 1791, DLC:GW; *Executive Journal,* 1:213).

1. Tucker's 18 Jan. letter reads: "After my greatfull respects to you beg leave to appologize for not giving you an Answer respecting your Lands in Washington County in Pennsylvania, in November last agreeable to my promise when I last had the pleasure of seeing you, it was for want of an Opportunity it was omitted, I therefore inform you, that the People, who proposed purchaseing your Tract, thinks the Land is rated too high, at 4 Dollrs per Acre, and, Wishes to know through me, the lowest price the President will take, as they expect to moove into that County in the Spring; Shou'd you incline to make an abatement, or treat any further on the subject, the kind bearer of this, Capt. Saml Burnet can forward it to me by his coasting Pilot, who is shortly to return to this Port" (DLC:GW). Tucker's letter and GW's reply concern GW's tract on Millers Run in present-day Washington County, Pa., which he was unable to sell until 1795. For the complications GW encountered with this property, see Thomas Smith to GW, 9 Feb. 1785, editorial note; Brice McGeehon to GW, 18 Oct. 1788, source note; *Diaries,* 4:22, n.4, 26–31.

2. When GW visited the Millers Run property in September 1784 he described it as "leveller than is common to be met with in this Part of the Country, and good; the principal part of it is white oak, intermixed in many places with black oak; and is esteemed a valuable tract." At the same time he made note of the improvements carried out by squatter families on the land (*Diaries,* 4:27–28).

From William Milnor

Hond Sir   Philada January 25th 1790

Altho' I have not Words to Express the gratefull feelings of my heart, for your great condecention in recommending me to the Collector of this port,[1] I cannot any longer resist the impelling desire I feel, to inform you, how happy you have made me, from a mind almost driven to dispair with thoughts of the increaseing distress of my family, from unavoidable indolence and from every species of indigence I am happily delivered—Immediatily on the receipt of the Papers from, you[2] Mr Delany Appointed me one of the Gaugers and from the blessed 10th day of August last, I have faithfully perform'd that office to the utmost of my abilities, & I am the happier in having the Honour to inform you that I have given intire satisfaction to my superior officers in the custom house as well as to the Merchants & all others concern'd, to confirm this, I beg your pardon for the liberty I take in Mentioning the following little anecdote. Some few days a go I waited on the Collector gave him the Complimts of the Season & thank'd him for the Appointmt he had been pleased to honour me with, and hoped he had found me faithfull in the discharge of my duty, he replied, I am sorry Mr Milnor that I did not at first give you the whole of that buisness, your Conduct has pleased every body Concern'd, I must again beg your pardon for saying so much about myself—for my past & future Conduct I must now beg leave to refer you to those Gentlemen under whome I act, when I consider that should I through neglect, be found lacking, in Industry Vigilence & accuracy in my buisness, I should merit your Contempt forever, a mortification the greatest I could suffer on this side the Grave, I confess it is a ⟨Stimoler⟩ not to be resisted—Mrs Milnor desires to join me in our best respects to Mrs Washington knowing she has ever been propitious to our welefare we feel it our duty to retain a due sense of it. I have the Honour Sir, most Humbly to be and remain, Your Most Obliged & Most obedt Servt

William Milnor

ALS, DNA: RG 59, Miscellaneous Letters.

The Quaker William Milnor emigrated from New Jersey to Bucks County, Pa., and settled in Philadelphia where he became a prominent merchant. He had business dealings with GW before the Revolutionary War, acted as his

Philadelphia agent to buy arms and uniforms in 1775, and was a frequent visitor to Mount Vernon. His son and grandson later succeeded to his post of gauger of the port of Philadelphia (*Papers, Revolutionary War Series*, 1:339, n.13; William Milnor to GW, 19 Oct. 1773, n.3; *Diaries*, 3:167, 168, 204, 244, 248, 249, 308; Hamilton, *Letters to Washington*, 4:271, n.1).

1. See Milnor to GW, 3 Aug. 1789, n.2.
2. Milnor mistakenly inserted this word above the line after the comma.

To the United States Senate and House of Representatives

United States [New York], January 25th, 1790.
Gentlemen of the Senate and House of Representatives.

I have received from His Excellency John E. Howard, Governor of the State of Maryland, an Act of the Legislature of Maryland to ratify certain Articles in addition to, and amendment of the Constitution of the United States of America proposed by Congress to the Legislatures of the several States; and have directed my Secretary to lay a copy of the same before you, together with the copy of a letter accompanying the above act, from His Excellency the Governor of Maryland to the President of the United States.[1]

The originals will be deposited in the Office of the Secretary of State.[2]

Go: Washington

LS, DNA: RG 46, First Congress, Records of Legislative Proceedings, President's Messages; LB, DLC:GW; copy, DNA: RG 233, First Congress, Records of Legislative Proceedings, Journals.

GW had earlier sent copies of the first twelve amendments to the federal Constitution to each state executive for ratification (Circular to the Governors of the States, 2 Oct. 1789, and note 1).

1. Howard wrote GW from Annapolis on 15 Jan. 1790: "I have the honor to enclose a copy of an act of the Legislature of Maryland, to ratify certain articles in addition to and amendments of the constitution of the united States of America proposed by Congress to the Legislatures of the several States" (MdAA).

The ratification act forwarded by Howard was passed by the Maryland house of delegates on 17 Dec. 1789 and by the state senate on 19 December. The copy made by Lear was presented with the president's message to Congress on Monday, 25 Jan. 1790, when the House ordered they should lie on the table, and the Senate also ordered them to lie for consideration (*DHFC*, 1:226–27, 3:271–73, 585–88).

2. Lear presented the documents to Roger Alden, chief clerk at the State Department, on 25 Jan. "to be deposited in the Office of State with other public papers under your care, and to be delivered to the Secretary of State whenever he may enter upon the duties of his office" (DNA: RG 59, Correspondence with Secretaries of State).

From Henry Knox

Sir,   War Office [New York] January 26th 1790.

In consequence of the act of the United States in Congress assembled of the 29th of September 1789 for the payment of the invalid pensions,[1] the Secretary of the Treasury submits it as his opinion that the persons whose names are stated on the enclosed paper would be proper persons to pay the pensions to the said invalid pensioners under the said act—All the said persons being collectors of the customs within the states respectively excepting Colonel Jeremiah Olney of Rhode-Island[2] and [   ] of North Carolina.[3]

And the Secretary of the Treasury submits a further opinion that it would be reasonable to allow the sum of two per cent on the sums they shall pay for their trouble in making the necessary examinations and payments aforesaid.

These names and the allowance proposed are humbly submitted for your consideration and approbation.[4] I have the honor to be with the greatest respect Sir, Your most Obedient Servant

H. Knox

New Hampshire	Portsmouth	Joseph Whipple
Massachusetts	Boston	Benjamin Lincoln
Rhode Island	Providence	Jeremiah Olney
Connecticut	New London	Jedh Huntington
New York	New York	John Lamb
New Jersey	Perth Amboy	John Halsted
Pennsylvania	Philadelphia	Sharp Delany
Delaware	Wilmington	George Bush
Maryland	Baltimore	Otho H. Williams
Virginia	B. Hundred	William Heth
North Carolina	[ ]	[ ]
South Carolina	Charleston	George Abbott Hall
Georgia	Savannah	John Habersham

LS, DLC:GW; LB, DLC:GW.

1. "An Act providing for the payment of the Invalid Pensioners of the United States" stipulated: "That the military pensions which have been granted and paid by the states respectively, in pursuance of the acts of the United States in Congress assembled, to the invalids who were wounded and disabled during the late war, shall be continued and paid by the United States, from the fourth day of March last, for the space of one year, under such regulations as the President of the United States may direct" (1 *Stat.* 95).

2. Alexander Hamilton notified Olney of his appointment as an invalid pensions official on 4 Feb. 1790, and Olney received further instructions from Knox before 12 February. After Rhode Island joined the Union, GW nominated Olney collector for the port of Providence on 14 June 1790, and the Senate appointed him the same day (Olney to GW, 16 Mar. 1789 and notes, 31 May 1790; Syrett, *Hamilton Papers,* 6:246, 263–64, 458–59; *DHFC,* 2:80).

3. GW did not nominate North Carolina federal customs officials until 9 Feb. (GW to the U.S. Senate, 9 Feb. 1790).

4. Lear replied to Knox on 27 Jan.: "The President of the United States has directed me to acknowledge the receipt of your letter of yesterday to him; and to inform you that the persons stated on the paper enclosed in your letter, as being in the opinion of the Secretary of the Treasury, proper persons to pay the pensions to the invalid Pensioners in the several States, are such as meet his idea; but the President wishes to see you upon this subject before anything is finally determined respecting it" (DLC:GW). GW noted that he consulted the same day with Knox about "nominating persons (named in a list submitted to me) for paying the Military Pensionrs." (*Diaries,* 6:21).

From William West

Sir,   Baltimore-Town [Md.] Jany 26th 1790.

Sensible that Merit only should claim the Attention of one, whom Merit alone has advanced to supreme Dignity; and sensible too that an honest Recommendation will be acceptable to you—I cannot but testify, in Favour of Mr Alexander Wooddrop Davey,[1] of this Town, that I have been acquainted with him for some considerable Time, and admire him for his Integrity & upright Principles. And I scruple not to say, that in my Heart I verily believe he will faithfully discharge any Office to which he may be appointed. He wishes to obtain the Excise Office, & could he be so happy as to succeed, I am fully convinced he would acquit himself with Honour & Reputation in the Discharge of it. Less than this I cannot say tho' duly sensible of the Weakness of my Testimony, in Favour of that honest & worthy man—And I trust you will pardon me for being interested in the

Success of such a Character, who am, with the greatest Respect & Gratitude, Sir, Your obliged humble Servt

Wm West

ALS, DLC:GW.

1. William West, an Anglican minister and rector of St. Paul's Parish in Baltimore, again recommended Alexander Wooddrop Davey to GW on 1 Feb. 1791. Davey was a Baltimore merchant who supplied Maryland troops during the Revolution (*Md. Archives*, 43:90, 47:38). On 10 Feb. 1791 U.S. senator John Henry of Maryland forwarded this second letter to GW along with an undated petition written by Davey, whom he recommended "as a Man of Industry and probity" (DLC:GW).

The enclosure stated that: "your Petitioner has been regurly bred to Mercantile Business, Which he has managed with Industry and Success, Till near the close of the late War, When he became unfortunate, but still maintained an unsuspected Character for Uprightness & Integrity for the Proof of this, your Petitioner is happy in having it in his Power to refer to the enclosed Letter, As well as to the Personal Knowledge of the Honourable Robert Morris, William Smith Joshua Seney and Benjamin Contee Esqrs. for his General Character for his Capacity & Deligence in Business, Together with an Uniform Attachment to the Cause of America.

"Altho your Petitioner pretends to no other Merit to attract your Excellency's Notice, yet depending on your Excellency's wisdom and goodness, he prays that you will be pleased to appoint him The Excise officer for the Town and District of Baltimore, where he resides, and your Petitioner as in duty bound shall ever pray &c." (DLC:GW). Davey did not receive a federal appointment.

To the United States Senate and House of Representatives

United States [New York] January 28th, 1790

Gentlemen of the Senate and House of Representatives.

I have directed my Secretary to lay before you[1] the copy of an Act of the Legislature of Rhode Island and Providence Plantations, entitled "An Act for calling a Convention to take into consideration the Constitution proposed for the United States, passed on the 17th day of September A.D. 1787, by the General Convention held at Philadelphia,"—together with the copy of a letter accompanying said Act, from His Excellency John Collins Governor of the State of Rhode Island and Providence Plantations to the President of the United States.[2]

The originals of the foregoing act and letter will be deposited in the Office of the Secretary of State.[3]

Go: Washington

LS, DNA: RG 46, First Congress, Records of Legislative Proceedings, President's Messages; LB, DLC:GW; copy, DNA: RG 233, First Congress, Records of Legislative Proceedings, Journals.

1. On 28 Jan. the Senate ordered that GW's message and its accompanying papers lie for consideration. The House referred the documents on the same day to congressmen Egbert Benson, Jonathan Grout, and Isaac Coles "with instruction that they do prepare and bring in a bill or bills for granting the suspension applied for by the Governor of the state of Rhode-Island and Providence plantations, in behalf of the said State" (*DHFC*, 1:230, 3:278; see also Jabez Bowen to GW, 17 Jan. 1790, n.3).

2. See Collins to GW, 18 Jan. 1790 and notes.

3. Lear transmitted Collins's letter and the Rhode Island act calling for a ratification convention to Roger Alden for deposit in the office of the secretary of state (Lear to Alden, 28 Jan. 1790, DNA: RG 59, Miscellaneous Letters).

From Steuben

Sir   New York Jany 29th 1790.

Though sensibly imprest with the marks of confidence & freindship, you have been pleased to manifest for me, since my arrival in America.

Nothing but the most urgent necessity could induce me at this time, to divert your attention from more important Objects of National concern, to the consideration of one, which may be of a more personal nature.

Unaccustomed to suffer pecuniary distress before I came to this Country, the indigent situation to which I find myself reduced, becomes every hour more insupportable.

Seven Years have now been spent in vain solicitations for the determination of a cause, the justice of which was at all times acknowledged by a large and respectable majority of the old Congress.

Flattered from Session to Session with the hopes of a determination in my favor—I have been induced to prolong my stay in this Country untill I have incumbered myself with Debt, and every possible resource exhausted—The immediate decision of Congress on my Memorial presented at their last Sessions[1] is therefore become indispensible to my existance, and it is to solicit such Official assistance as propriety may authorise in this respect, that I now take the liberty to address you.

The peculiarity of my situation in every respect is submitted as the true reason for making the request—It is indeed peculiar— Whatever the decision may be, I shall at least be releived from all that anxiety of mind, which arises from expectations so long deferred.

In whatever quarter of the Globe I may be obliged to seek an Asylum, the reputation I established in my own Country before, I left it, will always insure me the esteem of every honest Man, nor will this sentiment be lessened by the small share I have had, in the glorious Revolution of the United States.

And as I shall have nothing to reproach myself with, I shall be able to support my situation (however reduced) without a blush.[2] With the highest respect I have the honor to be Sir Your Most Obedient & very humble Servant

Steuben

LS, DNA: RG 59, Miscellaneous Letters.

For the background to Steuben's claims against the United States, see Steuben to GW, 25 Aug. 1789; *Diaries*, 6:25; and Syrett, *Hamilton Papers*, 5:211, n.2.

GW wrote on 29 Jan.: "Received also a letter from the Baron de Steuben, declarative of his distresses; occasioned by the Non-payment, or nonfulfilment of the Contract which was made with him by the Congress under the former Confederation and requesting my Official interference in his behalf. The delicacy of this case from the nature, and long labouring of it, requires consideration" (*Diaries*, 6:24). See also GW to Thomas Jefferson, 15 Mar. 1784, n.1.

1. Steuben's 25 Aug. 1789 memorial was presented to Congress on 14 September. On 21 Sept. the House appointed a committee to study it and similar petitions, and four days later the committee referred the petitions to Secretary of the Treasury Alexander Hamilton to be reported upon at the next session of Congress. Hamilton completed his report on Steuben's case on 29 Mar. and presented it on 6 April. A new committee appointed on 19 April brought a bill on 30 April that was read for the third time and sent to the Senate on 10 May. The amended bill returned to the House and passed on 28 May. GW signed "An Act for finally adjusting and satisfying the claims of Frederick William de Steuben" on 4 June (*DHFC*, 3:205–6, 219, 233, 256, 359, 363, 372, 392, 394, 397, 403–5, 430–31, 444, 446; 6 *Stat.* 2; Syrett, *Hamilton Papers*, 6:310–27).

2. GW apparently transmitted this letter to Hamilton, for noted on its cover is: "returned from the Secy of the Treasy Feby 24th 1790."

From Peter Trenor

Newry [Ireland] 29th Jany 1790

Shortly after I had the Honour of receiving your Excellencys Letter, at portsmouth Virginia, dated Mount Vernon the 15th November 1786[1] Enclosing one for Mrs Anne Ennis,[2] of Dublin, I returned to this Country, & handed your Letter to that, *Poor distressed Lady*, whose Circumstances, has been reduced to the Lowest Ebb, owing ⟨meerely⟩ to a train of dire Misfortunes, and I do assure your Excellency was it not for the support I gave her, from time to time, that she woud have been in a most deplorable Situation—she was in daily expectation of hearing that your Excellency, had got the affairs of the late Mrs Savage finally settled, as your Letter gave her hopes that there woud be a final Issue put to the Business, in a Term or two, from that Period.[3]

By this Conveyance I have forwarded to Geo. Pollock Esqre of Newyork[4] Authenticated before the Lord Mayor of Dublin the following Papers[5] Viz.: Copy of Mrs Savages Will—(wherein she has bequeathed to your Excellency £200 V. Cy & to Bryan Fairfax Esqre ⟨£100⟩ of like Money—which two sums & the £53 B⟨*illegible*⟩ you advanced in 1772 your Excellency will please deduct from the Amount received & the remaind⟨er⟩ you'l be so good as to order into Mr Pollocks hands[.] Copys of the late Richard Ennis's Will[;] Power of Attorney from Mrs Anne Ennis Wife to said Richard Ennis to me & Power of Attorney from me to said Geo. Pollock Esqre to be proven on your side by Capt. William Chevers of the Ship Ann & Susan[;] also ⟨Mrs⟩ Savages Death & Interment, Authenticated before the Lord Mayor of Dublin.

Knowing that your Excellency will do every thing that justice or equity will admit of, to help the Distressed Mrs Ennis, I have the Honour to be Your Excellencys very obedt Servt.[6]

Peter Trenor

⟨*Mutilated*⟩ thing defficient in the Papers, forwd to Mr Pollock, your Excellency will be so obliging as to point same out to me, which shall be rectified in course.

ALS, DLC:GW.

For background to GW's involvement in Margaret Green Savage's affairs, see Henry Lee and Daniel Payne to GW, 24 April 1767, n.1; GW to Margaret Savage, 28 June 1768 and 27 Jan. 1772; Trenor to GW, 8 Nov. 1786, and note

1; GW to Anne Ennis, 15 Nov. 1786; John Dixon to GW, 5 Mar. 1789, and note 1; GW to Bryan Fairfax, 6 April 1789, n.3; and *Diaries*, 2:181–82, 228, 3:81.

1. Letter not found. Trenor later referred to it as being dated 16 Nov. 1786 (Trenor to GW, 1 Oct. 1792, Collections of Lord Fairfax of Cameron, Gays House, Holyport, Maidenhead, Berkshire, England).

2. GW to Anne Ennis, 15 Nov. 1786.

3. "We are encouraged by our Lawyers to expect a final issue of the business in a term or two more; but what reliance is to be placed on these assurances, is not for me to decide" (GW to Anne Ennis, 15 Nov. 1786).

4. George Pollock was a successful New York City merchant who owned property at 6 Nassau and 23 Water streets and was later a legal client of Alexander Hamilton's (*New York City Directory*, 1790, 80; Syrett, *Hamilton Papers*, 18:43–44).

5. The enclosures, which have not been found, were sent in response to GW's comments: "for our security, there must be an attested Copy of the Will [of Mrs. Savage], under the Seal of the Corporation where it is recorded, annexed to a regular power of attorney (to be proved in this Country) from the Executors to some person here, to receive the money from us" (GW to Anne Ennis, 15 Nov. 1786).

6. Not having received a reply, Trenor again wrote from Newry in 1792 enclosing a duplicate of his 29 Jan. 1790 letter, which he misremembered as 28 Jan., and beseeching "that your Excellency may give directions to your Law Agent or Secretary to have this matter finally adjusted & the Money paid to George Pollock Esqre of New York, which your Excellency will Perceive by the foregoing Letter that he is fully Impowerd to receive same—I do assure your Excellency that it has been an inconvenience to me, laying out of the large sum of Money so long which I advanced towards the support of the Widow Ennis—from your Excellencys Benovelent Character I am certain that it is neither y⟨ou⟩r Inclination nor wish that The Money shou'd be withheld a day after the recovery thereof—Your Honouring me with a few Lines in case the affair is not finally adjusted, will confer a favour on your Excellencys Most Obed. Servt" (Trenor to GW, 1 Oct. 1792).

Alexander Macomb to Tobias Lear

Sunday Jany 31. 1790.

Mr Macomb presents Mr Lear with his respects he has receiv'd his note of this morning and informs him that he will take pleasure in affording any assistance in his power to effect the accomplishment of the Wishes of The President of the United States.

If Mr Lear chuses, Mr M— will propose an immediate exchange of Houses there can be no impropriety in such negociation, and he ⟨*mutilated*⟩ from Mr Ottos[1] obliging disposition the

Transaction might succeed. At the same he could speak for any part of the furniture that might be wanted.[2] Mr Macomb will See Mr Lear with great pleasure at his house this evening; or if it is any ways inconvenient for Mr Lear to visit Mr M. he will with equal cheerfulness wait upon Him.[3]

AL, ViMtV.

On 30 Jan. GW agreed to pay $1,000 to lease from 1 May 1790 to 30 April 1791 the choice mansion at 39–41 Broadway that Alexander Macomb had built in 1786–87 and that the comte de Moustier, French minister to the United States, had occupied until his recall in October 1789 (*Diaries*, 6:26).

1. Louis Guillaume Otto (1754–1817), chargé d'affaires of the French embassy from 1784 to 1792 and later the comte de Mosloy, agreed to give up the lease to the French legation two and a half months early in order to accommodate GW (GW to Rochambeau, 13 Oct. 1789, n.1; Decatur, *Private Affairs of George Washington*, 118).

2. GW evidently had admired Moustier's furnishings during visits to the French legation, and on 3 Feb. he noted in his diary that he had "fixed on some furniture of the Ministers (which was to be sold & was well adapted to particular public rooms)" (*Diaries*, 6:27–28). A 4 Mar. invoice lists the articles that GW purchased from Moustier's agent, a M. Le Prince:

2 large Looking Glasses @ £46	92. 0.0	
12 damask arm chairs	77. 0.0	
6 do—small chairs with covers.	24. 0.0	
1 Sopha with Cushions	30. 0.0	
4 Green silk windw Curtains wh appts	78. 0.0	
1 Lustre Cord with Tassels	2. 0.0	
1 Chair & Stool called the Shepherdess	9. 0.0	
3 Chimney Boards	4. 0.0	
An Awning for the Gallery	40. 0.0	£356. 0. 0
2 Mah[ogan]y Buffets in the dining Room	9.10.0	
2 Presses in the House keeper's room	12. 0.0	
2 ⟨do in⟩ do small	1. 0.0	
1 Larder in the Cellar	9. 0.0	
1 Canvas door in the Cellar	1. 0.0	
Apartmt & bottle rack in the Steward's room	8. 0.0	
A dinner bell	4. 0.0	
A large fire screen for the Green Room	3. 0.0	
2 Franklin fireplaces	9. 0.0	
1 Stove in Majr Jacksons Room	7. 0.0	
2 Clothes presses in do	8. 0.0	
1 Do—in Mr Lewis's Room	4. 0.0	
1 Do—in the Children's Room	6. 0.0	
1 Stove in Mr Lear's room	10. 0.0	
1 Do—in Mr Hyde's chamber	8. 0.0	
A Leaden weight and pully for the door leadg into the middle passage	6.18.0	52.18. 0

2 Stoves in the Coach House	4. 0.0	
Flowers for the Table	4.10.0	
2 Lamps & Glasses	3.12.0	
5 do common do	2. 5.0	
16 Green Moroco Skins @ 13/6	10.16.0	
1 writing desk for Mrs Washington	18. 0.0	
1 Drissing table for the Presidt	19. 0.0	
93 Glass flower pots of dift sizes	5. 5.6	
6 Iron m*(illegible)* for stew Holes	0.18.0	
1 Bidet	2. 0.0	
1 Chair for a model	3. 0.0	73. 6. 6
Amount carrid up		529.14. 6

Save [Sèvres] China

2 Iceries compleat	4.12.0	
1 Porringer & Cover	2. 4.0	
2 Sallad dishes	1.16.0	
4 square stew dishes	3.12.0	
4 Shells	4.12.0	
15 Round dishes	10. 3.0	
4 Saucers	4.10.0	
4 butter boats	4.12.0	
4 Confection dishes	5. 4.0	
4 mustard pots	4.10.0	
4 Sugar dishes	4.12.1	
12 Ice plates	9. 1.0	
36 Ice pots	9. 0.0	
23 Pla[tters]	9. 0.0	
21 Egg dishes	4. 6.0	
8 Cocottes	1.12.0	
20 small pots	6. 0.0	
12 Chocolate cups & saucers	3.12.0	
15 Coffee—do & do	4.10.0	
17 Tea—do & do	4.19.0	
3 Sugar dishes	3. 4.0	105.11.⟨1⟩
2 Cream Pots	1. 7.0	
2 flower Pots	2. 5.0	
7½ dozn plates	27. 0.0	
		30.12. 0
		£665.14. 6

(ViMtV; see also *Diaries*, 6:26, 27, 28; Detweiler, *George Washington's Chinaware*, 119, 123, 126; Decatur, *Private Affairs of George Washington*, 123).

GW apparently encountered difficulties in carpeting his new quarters. On 10 Feb. Lear wrote to Clement Biddle in Philadelphia: "The President wishes to get a Carpet of the best kind, for a Room 32 feet by 22. A Pea-Green ground with white or light flowers or spots would suit the furniture of the Room— and Carpeting would perhaps answer better than a Carpet—as the former would be made to fit the Room exactly, when it would be difficult to find one of the latter of the precise size. The length of the Room, 32 feet, is its full extent, but at each end there is a fire-place which projects into the Room perhaps 3½ or 4 feet including the Hearths. We can get no Carpet in New York to suit the Room—nor Carpeting of the best kind—Scotch Carpeting is almost the only kind to be found here. If you will be so good as to inform me if anything of the above description can be had in Philada you will oblige me. The price is also necessary to be known" (PHi: Washington-Biddle Correspondence).

Biddle replied two weeks later: "I have made Diligent Enquiry after Carpeting and can find none in the City that is near your Description—Indeed I never found that Article so scarce." By early March Lear was able to report that they had found a carpet for the drawing room (Biddle to Lear, 23 Feb. 1790, PHi: Clement Biddle Letter Book; Lear to Biddle, 5 Mar. 1790, ViMtV). More difficulty, however, was had in carpeting the drawing room, and Lear wrote to GW on 30 Sept. 1790, as he was preparing to move the president's furnishings to Philadelphia: "A few days ago Messrs Berry & Rogers sent the Carpeting which you had ordered out last spring in addition to the Carpet bought of them for the large drawing Room. I refused to receive it, as it did not come so soon as they had given reason to expect, and as, in all probability, it will now be useless, it being intended to fit the large drawing Room of this House. But they urged it upon the ground of its having been particularly ordered, and it was of that quality and kind as to render it altogether unsaleable; and that it had (which was the fact) arrived in Captn Bunyun, the first fall ship which had been sent from London to New York, which was as soon as circumstances would admit of its coming; it having been manufactured for the purpose after the order had reached England.

"Upon inquiry of persons acquainted with things of this kind I found that it would be considered, in a mercantile light, as having arrived in a reasonable time; and shd a matter of this nature be contested it would certainly be decided in favor of them (Berry & Rogers). I, therefore⟨,⟩ thought it would be better to take it than have any dispute upon the subject; and accordingly kept it. The amount is £22.16 with duties & charges included" (DLC:GW).

3. GW sent Lear on 1 Feb. "to examine the rooms to see how my furniture cd. be adapted to the respective Apartments." Two days later GW himself "Viewed the Apartments in the Ho. of Mr. Macombe—made a disposition of the Rooms" and "directed additional Stables to be built" (*Diaries*, 6:26, 27–28).

On 4 Feb. Lear wrote to Macomb: "I have received your polite favor of to day. Your not waiting yesterday needs no apology—the circumstance sufficiently excuses it.

"The President thinks that a Stable 30 ft square, erected at the end of the brick Stable, would extend too far into the yard and obstruct the passage between the Coach House and the Stable—or, at any rate, would destroy the regularity of the buildings: however he will say nothing decisive upon the subject until the ground is again examined, which, if the weather permits, will be tomorrow about 10 o'clock when I shall be down at the House—and it is very probable that the President may walk there at the same time if he is not then particularly engaged, and if the Carpenter is at hand he can be called upon & the matter fixed" (PWacD: Feinstone Collection, on deposit at PPAmP).

GW did not visit the house again until 6 Feb. when he wrote, "Walked to my newly engaged lodgings to fix on a spot for a New Stable which I was about to build. Agreed with [James Robinson] to erect one 30 feet sqr., 16 feet pitch, to contain 12 single stalls; a hay loft, Racks, mangers &ca.—Planked floor and underpinned with Stone with Windows between each stall for 65£." GW also hired the services of mason John Stagg, who was repaving Broadway at the time, to do the stable's stonework (*Diaries*, 6:28; Decatur, *Private Affairs of George Washington*, 121, 125, 127).

From Silas Talbot

Sir,   Johnstown [N.Y.] January 31st 1790

My motives for presuming to address you at this time is to solicit your particular favor & notice so far as to take into consideration the propriety of my being again employed in some public service in case any should offer, in which I might be thought adequate to the performance of.

I have been Informed Sir by a member of Congress, that new arrangements will probably take place in some or all of the principal Harbours in the United States and that in order to carry such Laws or regulations as may be made for that purpose into effect, there will likely be a Harbourmaster appointed to each post:[1] should it be deemed necessary to make any appointment similar to what I have before described for the *Harbour of New-york*, I have the Vanity to believe from my former acquaintance, & present knowledge of Shipping, that I could do the duties of that office And if my abilities might be viewed in so favorable a light I solicit the favor of your Excelly to nominate me to that Office. Should this request be granted I pledge myself to do my best endeavours to justify the appointmt by paying all suitable attention to the duties that shall be required of me in that station I could feign hope that my former services might in some small degree recommend me at this time; And in order that they may more readily occur to your mind, I take the liberty to inclose several copies of Original papers now in my possession;[2] besides these if it were necessary, I could have forwarded copies of Three Letters from Major Genl Sullivan wrote to Congress while I was under his immediate command[3] in these Letters he is pl[e]ased to mention me to that Honorable Body in terms of high approbation of my conduct as an Officer—I could

likewise forward three other copies of Letters from Major Genl
Gates to Congress in 1779;[4] in these Letters the General was also
pleased to hold me up to them in a light very much to my Honour And was it not Sir for taking up too much of your time I
could furnish copies of Letters from other General Officers of
less rank, & particularly one from the Governor and Council of
the state of Rhode Island in the begining of the year 1780 to
Congress, stating my services to them, in a manner very flattering to me.

The inclosed Certificates &ce. I trust will be satisfactory in regard to my public character, as to that of my private or the Iden-
tity of my persn I must beg leave to refer your Excellency to
Major Generl Knox,[5] who I trust will be able to give you Satisfactory information on that head.[6] I am &ce.

AL (copy), NNGL.

Silas Talbot (1751–1813), a native of Dighton, Mass., moved to Providence,
R.I., in 1772 and served with distinction as a Continental officer during the
first years of the Revolution, reaching the rank of lieutenant colonel. Talbot
was commissioned a captain in the Continental navy in September 1779 but
put to sea as commander of the privateer *General Washington* in August 1780
after failing to obtain a ship worthy of his rank. He was soon captured by the
British and imprisoned at New York and in England until December 1781.
After his return to America, Talbot pressed his claims against the government
and speculated in Kentucky and Ohio lands. He settled on the forfeited estate
of Sir John Johnson near Johnstown in Montgomery County, N.Y., in June
1786 after completing a tour of his western properties earlier that year (Nathanael Greene to GW, 28 July 1776, n.1; Talbot to GW, 8 July 1782, DLC:GW;
Schultz, *Inventory of the Talbot Papers*, 1–6).

1. Talbot probably had in mind the legislation that the First Congress postponed on 16 Sept. 1789 until its second session, which commenced on 4 January. When a quorum was reached on 7 Jan., the house appointed a committee
to consider the unfinished business of the previous session. It reported on 11
Jan., specifically mentioning the bill "prescribing regulations for the harbors
of the United States." On 22 Jan. the joint committee appointed two days
earlier by both houses to confer on this and other bills made its report. On 25
Jan. both the Senate and the House resolved "that the business unfinished
between the two Houses at the late adjournment, ought to be regarded as if it
had not been passed upon by either" (Joseph Willard to GW, 1 Jan. 1790, n.1;
DHFC, 3:250, 251, 256–57, 268, 270, 273, 5:939).

2. The enclosed copies have not been identified but probably consisted of
certificates from Talbot's former superiors attesting to his exemplary Revolutionary War service.

3. These letters have not been positively identified but probably included
John Sullivan to Henry Laurens, 31 Aug. 1778 and 31 Oct. 1778 (DNA:PCC,
item 160).

4. These unidentified letters may have included Horatio Gates to John Jay, 20 July 1779 (not found, but referred to in Jay to Gates, 30 July 1779, DNA:PCC, item 14). See also Jay to Talbot, 18 Sept. 1779, enclosed in Jay to Gates, 18 Sept. 1779 (both in DNA:PCC, item 14).

5. Talbot sent a copy of this letter enclosing "copies of several papers" to Henry Knox on the same day, acknowledging "that the success of my present application will very much depend on your friendship being convinced that a word from you to him [GW] in due season will have a powerfull effect on his mind and in my favor, for which I shall ever feel myself under very great Obligations to you" (Talbot to Knox, 31 Jan. 1790, NNGL). No correspondence between Knox and GW concerning Talbot's application has been found.

6. GW appointed Talbot on 3 June 1794 captain of one of the six ships to be procured under "An Act to Provide a Naval Armament," which commission he accepted on 9 June. Talbot supervised construction of the 44-gun frigate *President* at New York from Aug. 1794 to June 1796 when work on it was suspended. GW then appointed him an agent to negotiate for the release of American seamen impressed by the British in the West Indies. After returning from Jamaica Talbot assumed command of the frigate *Constitution*, which he held until retiring from the navy in 1801 (Benjamin Hoyt to Talbot, 2 Feb. 1794, Talbot to Henry Knox, 9 June 1794, Knox to Talbot, 8 Aug. 1794 [first letter], all in CtMyM: Silas Talbot Papers; *Executive Journal*, 1:160–61, 213, 274, 275; 1 *Stat.* 350 [27 Mar. 1794]; Schultz, *Inventory of the Talbot Papers*, 7–11).

Henry Knox's Notes on the State of the Frontier

[January 1790]

Although I experience a reluctance in again bringing before you the subject of a treaty with the Wabash indians, yet as some recent events have happened evincing to my mind the propriety of the measure, I conceive it to be my duty to make the following communication, and to request your advice thereon.

The indians residing on the Wabash river and its branches, and the people residing on the waters of the river Ohio, have been for some years past in the practice of exercising indiscriminate hostilities on each other—It would probably be in vain at this period to endevor to ascertain the original aggressors—The facts are but too well established that the innocent on both sides suffer more frequently than the guilty.

The evils have extended themselves to the troops of the United States who are often sacrificed to the resentments of the Indians, which they have had no agency in exciting.

Several Soldiers were killed during the last year by parties of Indians and several more during the present year, and by recent intelligence, a party of six, while escorting a Surveyor near the big Sandy river has been entirely cut off.

To patiently suffer a continuance of these enormities appears to be highly improper and disgraceful—and yet in the existing confused state of affairs, and ignorance of the perpetrators, it is difficult if not impossible, to know against what tribe to direct the vengeance of the United States—This circumstance which of itself is sufficient to create a doubt of the propriety of immediate coercive measures, is rendered more conclusive by a calculation of the expence and contingencies which would attend an effectual expedition into the Indian Country.

If it is probable that a peace with the Wabash indians could be effected by a treaty, I am of opinion that it would be wise to attempt it—If the Indians should refuse to attend the invitation to a treaty the United States would be exonerated, from all imputations of injustice in taking proper measures for compelling the Indians to a peace, or to extirpate them.

The Secretary at War has infor[med] me that it is probable the treaty with the Creeks will not require more than seventeen thousand dollars of the twenty thousand appropriated by Congress on the 20th of August 1789 to the Indian Department[1]— and that the Governor of the Western territory has in his possession Goods remaining from former treaties to the amount of one thousand eight hundred dollars.

Although I conceive these sums to be very inadequate for treating in the customary manner with the Wabash tribes, yet perhaps it may be proper to make an experiment of treating with the indians on a more oeconomical plan.

On this statement of the case I request your advice on the following inquiries.

First—In the existing state of affairs between the United States, and the Wabash Indians, will it be proper to attempt an establishment of peace with the said Indians by a friendly treaty?

Second—If so shall the sum of three thousand dollars (provided that sum shall remain of the twenty thousand dollars appropriated by Congress on the 20th of August 1789, After defraying the expences of the treaty with the Creek indians) be applied to a treaty with the Wabash tribes of Indians, together with such goods as the Governor of the western territory has in his possession remaining from former treaties?[2]

The general state of the western frontiers, and of the indian department will require the serious attention of Congress.

The invitation of the United States to the Creek Nation of Indians, to treat of a peace on terms of mutual advantages has not been accepted—The report of the Commissioners which shall be laid before you will fully show the state of this business.

Notwithstanding the verbal assurances given by some Cheifs of the peaceable dispositions of the Creek nation, the United States cannot justly place any reliance thereon.[3]

The case seems to require an adequate provisional arrangement, which should be brought into active operation, if any further hostilities should be committed by the Creeks.

The United States having made a solemn offer of a treaty of peace on liberal terms, which being refused it is incumbent on them to be in a state of preparation to punish all aggressions.

In either event of peace or war with the Creeks, the establishment of a line of military posts on the southwestern frontiers, appears to be highly requisite—Although this measure will occasion an enlargement of the military establishment it seems in the present situation of affairs to be indispensibly necessary in order to prevent extensive and complicated evils.[4]

If the number of troops should be encreased, it may be worthy of your consideration whether their pay, without affecting the existing stipulations may not be diminished, so as to be more compatible with the public finances. I shall order estimates of these several objects to be laid before you for your consideration.

Independent of the Creeks, representations have been received from almost every part of the frontier extending along the south of the Ohio, stating the depredations of the indians during the summer past, and that upwards of [   ] innocent persons have fallen a sacrifice to savage barbarity—These representations are enforced by an address on the same subject from the Legislature of Virginia all forcibly claiming the protection of the United States to the places exposed to the incursions of the Indians.[5]

At the same time the United States are requested to afford security to their distant citizens, it is just Congress should be informed of the existence of an evil which requires a remedy.

It is too frequently the case in several parts of the frontiers for individuals to exercise, indiscriminate revenge against all persons bearing the name of indians, under the specious pretext of retaliation—Unless this practice be annihilated, Government in all its treaties will be liable to disgrace.

Hence the importance of the administration of indian affairs being conducted by fixed principles established by Law, and which being published should be rigidly enforced.

The obligations which the United States owe their own dignity require that while the unenlightened tribes of Indians are treated with justice and humanity, that an arrangement should exist to exact from them a correspondent conduct.

If upon mature consideration it should be thought practicable to impart some of the blessings of civilization to the Indian tribes, the attempt would be worthy of a Government founded on the principles of general happiness.

Open and liberal treaties in which their rights and territory should be well ascertained, and secured, seem to be the only equitable foundation of peace with the Indian tribes.

If after such a treaty has been made, it should be violated, or after an invitation given for that purpose which should be re-fused, and followed by acts of hostility, the United States will possess justly the right to inflict severe punishment.

I have conceived it my duty to offer my opinion generally on the State of Indian affairs not doubting, but that the result of your deliberations on the subject will reflect honor on the national character of the United States.

While on the one hand the United States ought cautiously to avoid all unnecessary expences, so on the other they cannot make too early provision for certain primary institutions on the establishment of which the national character and existence may ultimately depend.

Among such institutions may be ranked an energetic system of national militia—The establishment of Arsenals and Magazines, and manufactories of the implements and materials of War.

I am well aware that the infant state of the finances may not admit of expensive and complete institutions of this nature— My design is to point out the present period as highly favorable to the formation of such judicious institutions as will invigorate and preserve the United States.

As no circumstances of War or predominating prejudices exist to influence the judgement, arrangements may now be decided upon, demonstrative of the wisdom and energy of the public mind, and the several parts may be executed as the finances will permit.

I shall by seperate messages lay before you for your consideration plans and estimates relative to these several objects.

There is another institution of a different nature but not less important in its effects which I would recommend to our particular consideration—I mean the propriety of establishing a National University at which the youth of the United States may receive the higher and more finished parts of education.[6]

Such an institution while it assisted in diffusing light and knowledge would be attended with the best political effects in cementing the several States of this extended Republic, and preventing a practice of sending American Youth to different parts of Europe for their education.

The public possess the opportunity by means of their unlocated lands of forming an improving and perpetual fund for this object.

A View of the troops in the service of the United States.

	Non Commissioned and Privates	
On the Ohio and its communications having two years to serve	627	
Two companies of Artillery whose services principally expire in December, January and February ensuing	76	
	703	
Wanting to complete the establishment	137	840

Proposed Modification

To march t[w]o companies of 70 each from the Ohio to the Frontiers of Georgia	140
To re-inlist the two companies of Artillery which are at West Point for 3 years or recruit to complete them	140
And also to recruit for the deficiencies of the establishment after the said companies should be filled	73
The Establishment would then be in Georgia	353

On the Ohio   <u>487</u>   840

The Distance from the Miami on the Ohio to the Oconees on the frontiers of Georgia may be estimated at 500 miles, the former being in the latitude of 39° and the latter in that of 32°—If the troops march 15 Miles per day on an average the time required will be about   33 days

The time required to transport the orders to General Harmar   20

The time which will be required to prepare the pack Horses and the companies for the march   <u>15</u>
68

By this calculation the troops would arrive at the Oconees before February which would be sooner than any troops could be raised by other means and transported to that place.

The two companies of Artillery and the seventy three men might by an exertion be recruited and transported to Savannah by the 1st day of March next.

D, DLC:GW. These notes are filed in DLC:GW at the end of January 1790. An endorsement in the writing of Tobias Lear on the back of this document reads: "Notes submitted by the Secy of War to the Presidt for his speech to both Houses on the opening of the Session in Jany 1790." See GW to the U.S. Senate and House of Representatives, 8 Jan. 1790.

1. Knox is referring to "An Act providing for the Expenses which may attend Negotiations or Treaties with the Indian Tribes, and the appointment of Commissioners for managing the same" which appropriated a sum "not exceeding twenty thousand dollars" from duties on imports and tonnage to fund negotiations with the Indians (1 *Stat.* 54 [20 Aug. 1789]).

2. The first note ends at this point and a comment in the margin states: "Notes submitted to the President (—useless)."

3. For U.S. negotiations with the southern Indians in 1789, see David Humphreys to GW, 21, 26, 27 Sept., 13, 28 Oct. 1789, Alexander Hamilton to GW, 20 Oct. 1789, Knox to GW, 18 Oct., 21, 27 Nov. 1789, and GW's Memoranda on Indian Affairs, 1789.

4. For Knox's estimate of expenses for the proposed meeting with the Creek in New York, see his letter to GW, 15 Feb. 1790.

5. For the address from the Virginia legislature to GW on Indian depredations, see Harrison County, Va., Field Officers to GW, 2 Feb. 1790, n.2.

6. GW mentions the possibility of a national university in his annual address to Congress, 8 Jan. 1790.

From Gouverneur Morris

[January 1790]

Accept I pray you the Seeds sent herewith. They are from the King's Gardens and as you will observe by the within List the trees and Plants are from the Southern Provinces of this Kingdom—I think therefore they will flourish at Mount Vernon. I am always truly yours.

AL, DLC:GW.

The original of this undated note is filed at the end of January 1790 in the Washington Papers at the Library of Congress, as it was probably assumed that Morris would most likely have sent the seeds in time for spring planting at Mount Vernon. Further evidence shows that the note must have been written before 1 Feb. 1790 and probably dates to 22–24 January. On 26 Aug. 1790 Morris wrote to GW that he delivered the originals of two letters of those dates "to the wife of Mr Le Couteulx de Caumont having waited a long time and till late in the Evening [of 1 Feb. 1790] to see him. He was to have left Paris, as he had told me, the next Day but staid I beleive one or two Days longer. My other Letters by him were received by those in America to whom they were directed but Heaven knows what he did with those directed to you. There was among them a pretty large Package containing the Seeds of various Shrubs Plants and Trees from the South of France which I had obtained from the King's Gardens hoping they might have contributed some little Ornament to Mount Vernon" (DLC:GW; Morris, *Diary of the French Revolution*, 1:402). Although GW wrote Morris on 17 Dec. 1790, when he acknowledged receipt of the seeds, that he had immediately forwarded them to his gardener at Mount Vernon, no such letter to John Christian Ehlers of this period has been found (DLC:GW). See also Morris to GW, 6 July 1790, DLC:GW.

Enclosure
List of Seeds

[January 1790]

Etat Des Graines des pais meridionaux De france

Murier Blanc pour Les Elever de vers a Soye—white
    mulberry[1] (for breeding Silk worms[)]

Lentisque—Mastic-Tree.[2]

Therebinthe—Turpentine-Tree[3]

paliure—a species of the bramble or thorn.[4]

arbousier—the arbute or strawberry-Tree.[5]

micocoulier—an african tree, being a kind of lotos.[6]

mirthe—myrtle common[7]

Laurier frane. noble laurel.[8]

Erable de montpelier—The maple of montpellier[9]
genet Epineux[.] way thorn or furze.[10]
arbre de Ste Lucie. Tree of St Lucia. a species
    of Plum.
fustet—a species of olive.
fraxinelle—frapinelle—garden ginger[11]
clematite—a species of cotton—tree or shrub.[12]
Cypres piramidal—pyramidal Cypress.
pin Cultivé—cultivated pine.

D, DLC:GW; translation, interlineated in Morris's handwriting.
    Of the species appearing on this list, only the white mulberry and garden
ginger grew at Mount Vernon during GW's lifetime. These, however, had been
planted before 1790 (*Diaries*, 4:95, 96; Sargent, *Trees at Mount Vernon*, 8; *Mount
Vernon Gardens*, 17).
    1. *Morus alba.*
    2. *Pistacia lentiscus*, a resinous evergreen shrub or tree grown for its gum,
mastic.
    3. *Pistacia terebinthus*, or the cypress-turpentine.
    4. Probably *Rhamnus paliurus*, or the "thorn of Christ."
    5. *Arbutus unedo*, a broad-leaf evergreen tree bearing clusters of white or
pink flowers and fleshy, orange-red, strawberrylike fruit.
    6. Probably *Celtis australis*, or *micocoulier* (nettle tree) of Provence.
    7. *Myrtus communis.*
    8. *Laurus nobilis.*
    9. *Acer monspessulanum*, or the Montpellier maple.
    10. Probably *Genista juncea*, grown for the beauty and aroma of its flowers.
    11. *Dictamnus albus*, also known as fraxinella, burning bush, or gas plant, a
strong-smelling perennial herb grown for its white flowers.
    12. Possibly *Clematis viticella*, an ornamental plant, or any one of a large
number of other species of *Clematis.*

Letter not found: from Asher Miller, 1 Feb. 1790. On 13 Feb. Lear wrote
to Miller: "The President of the United States has received your letter
of the 1st of February."

To the United States Senate and
House of Representatives

United States [New York] February 1st 1790
Gentlemen of the Senate and House of Representatives.
    I have received from His Excellency Alexander Martin Gover-
nor of the State of North Carolina, an Act of the General Assembly of that State,[1] entitled "an Act for the purpose of ceding to

the United States of America, certain Western Lands therein described"—and have directed my Secretary to lay a Copy of the same before you, together with the copy of a Letter accompanying said Act from His Excellency Governor Martin to the President of the United States.[2]

The originals of the foregoing Act and Letter will be deposited in the Office of the Secretary of State.[3]

Go: Washington

LS, DNA: RG 46, First Congress, Records of Legislative Proceedings, President's Messages; LB, DLC:GW; copy, DNA: RG 233, First Congress, Records of Legislative Proceedings, Journals.

1. See Martin to GW, 24 Dec. 1789.

2. Tobias Lear delivered GW's message with copies of Martin's letter and enclosure to Congress on 1 Feb. 1790. On the same day the House appointed George Clymer, George Gale, James Madison, Thomas Tudor Tucker, and George Mathews a committee to consider them. The Senate, which had ordered to lie for consideration "an exemplified copy" of the state's act of cession presented earlier that day by senators Samuel Johnston and Benjamin Hawkins of North Carolina, committed the president's message to John Henry, Ralph Izard, Oliver Ellsworth, Richard Bassett, and William Few. On 17 Feb. they reported "That it will be expedient for Congress, in behalf of the United States, to accept the cession proposed by the said act, upon the conditions therein contained; and that when a deed shall be executed for the same, they express their acceptance thereof by a legislative act," and this report was accepted and sent to the House for concurrence on 22 February. The next day the Senate appointed Ellsworth, Izard, and Caleb Strong to draft that legislation. They reported a bill on 3 Mar. which was read for the third time, engrossed, and sent to the House for concurrence on 5 March. On 26 Mar. a committee of the whole House considered and amended this "act to accept a cession of the claims of the state of North-Carolina to a certain district of western territory." Three days later the Senate accepted the returned and amended North Carolina Cession Act, which GW signed on 2 April 1790 (*DHFC*, 1:233, 234–35, 243, 245, 246, 251, 252–53, 269, 270, 272, 274–75, 3:281–82, 317, 319, 345, 345–46, 352, 354; 1 *Stat.* 106–9). The ceded territory was subsequently organized as a territory of the United States under the provisions of the "Act for the Government of the Territory of the United States, South of the River Ohio," signed by GW on 26 May 1790 (*DHFC*, 6:1901–3). In June GW appointed the territorial governor, secretary, and judges (see GW to the U.S. Senate, 7 June 1790). The new government began operating in October 1790 (Carter, *Territorial Papers*, 4:37, 38, 429).

3. Lear transmitted the originals to the office of the secretary of state the following day (Lear to Roger Alden, 2 Feb. 1790, DNA: RG 59, Miscellaneous Letters).

From Anthony Wayne

Sir   Richmond[1] State of Georgia 1st Feby 1790

Since the organization of the Federal System, & the establishment of the several departments, I have not presumed to address your Excellency respecting occurrencies in this Quarter, least it shou'd be improper—being totally unacquainted with the Mode now observed, but I have occasionally wrote to the Secy at War—giving such infor[m]ation as I deemed of moment, in full confidence that it wou'd be communicated to your Excellency!

At present the Indians are quiet—but I am apprehensive that this seeming serenity, will prove to be that *calm*—which precedes a *storm*, & that they are only waiting for the leaves of the forest to put forth: the frequent incursions they have made into this State for these two years past, & the losses I have sustained by them, together with the precarious tenor by which property is at present held in Georgia, as it depends upon the whim or caprice of Mr McGilvery & the temper of the Indians, which I have ground to believe is not very placid at this moment; has at last determined me to give up every idea of becoming an inhabitant of this place, & I am making my arrangements accordingly—my family have always continued upon my paternal Estate at Waynesborough in Pennsylvania which renders this disagreeable business more easy!

Permit me now to address you upon a subject to me very interesting! from the late recommendation of your Excellency to the Senate & house of Representatives in Congress, I have not a doubt, but that there will be a Military establishment,[2] I therefore take the liberty of soliciting your Excellency for such appointment as you think my former standing in the Army, services & abilities may merit.

It's a profession of which I am fond—the tactics have been my principle study at leasure hours in this recess—which added to former experiences meliorated by time & reflection, produces a confidence, that whatever discription of troops, may be committed to my charge, either Regulars or Militia, or both—whether Legionary or in seperate Corps—will be perfected in discipline & Manoeuvre, & rendered equally fit for actual service to any in the Union in equal time—pardon this zeal—I feel what I express!

I must acknowledge that I have been much, very much deceived & disappointed in my views & expectations in this Quarter, having placed a very considerable property within reach of the Savages, altho' on the sea board, the personal part thereof is either distroyed or lost to me forever, & the land must remain a desert, until peace can be made with the Indians, & proper posts established to insure the permanency of that peace.

Under those circumstances I have a double inducement to solicit your Excellency for an appointment,[3] & shall hold myself in readiness to act in any Quarter of America where you may please to direct me, & to serve you with the best services of your Excellency's Most Obt & most devoted Hum. Sert

Anty Wayne

ALS, DLC:GW.

1. In 1782 Anthony Wayne acquired an 847-acre plantation from the Georgia legislature for his services during the Revolution. The estate, called Richmond, was on the Savannah River and eventually encompassed some 1,300 acres. In 1784–85 Wayne also received from the Georgia legislature a 1,000-acre grant on the Satilla River in southern Georgia (Nelson, *Wayne*, 170, 198–99, 201–3).

2. See GW to the U.S. Senate and House of Representatives, 8 Jan. 1790.

3. For a recommendation of Wayne by Richard Peters, see Peters to GW, 2 Aug. 1790. Wayne received no appointment until GW named him major general and commander of the U.S. Army in April 1792 (*Executive Journal*, 1:117).

From John Armstrong

Dear General   Carlisle [Pa.] 2d Feby 1790

Notwithstanding how frequently your person and Office possess my thoughts, I have studiously avoided expressing them on paper lest I should add to that attention already so amply and so much better employed. Nevertheless

I must now beg leave to present my Congratulations to your Excellency on the pleasing appearance of our publick concerns, evinced by the apparent satisfaction of the populace, with the progress of Congress thus far: producing moderation of temper general quiet and at least a lisping approbation from various of the adversaries, who had not been a little, noisey, jealouse & turbulent heretofore. with respect to your own Administration, (as I believe you never suspected me of flattery) I ass[ure] you

Sir, the plaudit may be said to be without a negative—your Several addresses to the Senate & Representatives, gave much Satisfaction, the last attracting every one as far as it is read.

These things, whatever our fate may be, are good omens, and clear ground of reverential gratitude to the great ruler of the universe especially when we take a Retrospective view of the troubles of Britain & Ireland particularly in the reign of Charles first—The present disturbences in various parts of Europe, and our own Situation not long since. may the humble prayers of all that serve God according to the Gospel of his son, be daily offered for that wisdom that is from above, and the perpetuity of his mercies to this young nation. As I do not sufficiently know the grounds of the controversie betwixt the Southern States & the Creek Indians, shall say no more than that it seems but right that such States as claim an extensive territory should prudently & gradually buy the natives out; looking on our Situation with the Indians of N. America in a very different light, from that of the Israelites & the early inhabitants of Canaan. We understand if her leaders do not soon repent, will require a Secret but watchful eye, but at this critical conjuncture (our Ally being on his back) Britain might be tempted to essay the Establishment of a Garrison there, but hope they will not.

I cannot close this letter without suggesting a few thoughts on a Subject of a private & very interesting nature to me, I hope your Excellency will bear with them. they relate wholly to my Youngest Son, whome without farther apology I would offer to your consideration for a publick employment.[1] I will say very little of his qualifications, knowing how naturally a parent may be Suspected of partiality, others are often in this case better judges & I find they have ascribed to him both talents and honor. this far I may be permited to say—that if I were not pretty well Satisfied on these points, or knew the contrary, I should be the last man that would offer him—I know enough of publick life to be convinced that together with it's incidents & appendages, it is neither the best for this life, nor that which is to come; yet as I dispair of convincing either him or his friends of this doctrine, or rather of converting them; I am left to choose between wishing him the servant of the State, or of the Continent, and cannot hesitate a moment in prefering the latter to the former, and particularly, your patronage to that of any other.

as I neither know what Offices are yet to bestow, nor indeed
what he would wish, the manner of employing him must entirely depend on your Excellency. I will only add my Assurance
that you will be pleased to consider this as the confidential letter
of an Old and very Sincere friend & humble Servant

John Armstrong

ALS, DLC:GW.

For an identification of Armstrong, see his letter to GW, 27 Jan. 1789,
source note.

1. Armstrong's youngest son was John Armstrong, Jr. (1758–1843). As an
officer in the Continental army, the younger Armstrong was closely associated
with Horatio Gates and composed the famous "Newburgh Letters" in 1783,
inciting unrest among the officers of GW's army. In 1784 he secured an appointment as secretary to the supreme executive council of Pennsylvania, and
he later served as state adjutant general and, from 1787 to 1789, as a delegate
to the Confederation Congress. He made an unsuccessful bid for the U.S.
Senate in 1789 and in January of that year married Alida Livingston, a member of the Clermont branch of New York's influential Livingston family and
the sister of Chancellor Robert R. Livingston. The couple subsequently moved
to New York where John Armstrong, Jr., established himself as a landlord and
farmer. Unsuccessful in his first attempt to secure a position for his son, the
elder Armstrong continued to seek an appointment for him, writing to GW
again on 29 Dec. 1790, reminding the president that he had written a letter
respecting "my youngest Son" which "I have been fully led to believe you
never received." GW responded on 6 Feb. 1791, explaining his determination
to remain "to the last moment free and unengaged" in regard to appointments. "I have the best disposition to serve the person whom you then recommended," GW wrote, "and in what may comport with circumstances and public propriety, I shall be happy to do so. At present I know not what offices may
be created, and applicants multiply with every new office and some of them
come forward under such fair pretensions and pressing wants that a Preference is difficult and painful in the extream. In a word, to a man who has no
ends to serve, nor friends to provide for, nominations to office is the most
irksome part of the executive trust." GW eventually offered the younger Armstrong the post of supervisor of the revenue for New York (Alexander Hamilton to Armstrong, 1 April 1793, in Syrett, *Hamilton Papers*, 14:269–70). An
entry in the *Journal of the Proceedings of the President* for 26 April 1793 states:
"The Secretary of the Treasury laid before me a letter from Mr. John Armstrong in which he resigns his late appointmt. of Supervisor of New York and
assigns as a reason therefor, the increased expense of living in the City, which
would more than swallow up the Salary & his own income" (*JPP*, 120).

From Francis Bailey

New-York, Feby 2. 1790.

To the honorable the President and the honorable the Members of the Senate, of the United States of America the Memorial and Petition of Francis Bailey of the City of Philadelphia, Printer,

Most respectfully sheweth,

That your petitioner, has invented a mode of forming Types, for printing devices, to surround, or make parts of printed papers, for any use, which cannot be counterfeited, by the most ingenious Artists in sculpture, or by any other means. That the simplicity of his invention is such, that it would be difficult to describe it; without conveying, in a very few words, the whole secret, so plainly, as to enable any artist to profit himself by the discovery. Your petitioner apprehends, that the only mode of securing to himself and his heirs, any benefit by his invention, is to disclose it, to a Committee of your honorable house, or to such heads of executive departments, as your honorable house, shall think proper to recommend, in order to obtain an exclusive right, to the use of his discovery; not doubting, but the utility of his invention, will point out the propriety of employing the petitioner, to print all such Official Papers, as may be necessary for the several Offices, within the United States, which your petitioner will undertake to execute, at the prices which you have already paid, without charging any thing, for adding these inimitable devices.

Your petitioner, respectfully prays, that your honorable house, would direct an enquiry, into the said invention, which your petitioner is ready to disclose; and thereupon, to encourage your petitioner, in such manner, as his discovery shall appear to merit. Your respectful petitioner,

Francis Bailey.

ALS, DNA: RG 46, First Congress, Petitions and Memorials, Resolutions of State Legislatures, and Related Documents.

Francis Bailey (c.1735–1815) was a printer and journalist who began publication of the *Lancaster Almanac* in Lancaster, Pa., in 1771. During the Revolution he printed an edition of the Articles of Confederation and the fourth edition of Thomas Paine's *Common Sense*. In 1778 Bailey published, with Hugh Henry Brackenridge, the *United States Magazine*, and in 1781 he became editor of the *Freeman's Journal or the North American Intelligencer.* From time to time he acted as printer for Congress and for the state of Pennsylvania.

According to GW's diary entry for 25 Jan. 1790, Bailey was introduced by congressmen Thomas Scott and Thomas Hartley of Pennsylvania and Alexander White of Virginia (*Diaries*, 6:13). Bailey's petition was presented in the Senate on 2 Feb. and referred to a committee which recommended that the petition be referred to the secretary of the treasury. The House of Representatives, to which Bailey sent the petition on 29 Jan., also referred it to Hamilton (*DHFC*, 1:235, 245, 3:279, 284, 304). Hamilton reported, 23 Feb. 1790, stressing the difficulty of deciding "to what extent that Invention will afford the Security against Counterfeiting, which is the Object of it," but stating that "nevertheless he is of opinion, it will be likely to add to the difficulty of that pernicious practice, in a sufficient degree, to merit the countenance of Government, by securing to the Petitioner an exclusive right to the use of his Invention" (Syrett, *Hamilton Papers*, 6:277). On 26 Feb. the House ordered a bill to be brought in "securing to the said Francis Bailey an exclusive privilege to the use of his invention" (*DHFC*, 1:307). The House bill—"An Act to vest in Francis Bailey, the exclusive privilege of making, using, and vending to others, punches for stamping the matrices of types, and impressing marks on plates, or any other substance, to prevent counterfeits, upon a principle by him invented, for a terms of years"—was remanded to the Senate on 2 Mar., and on 4 Mar. the Senate postponed the bill until a "bill to promote the progress of useful arts shall be taken into consideration" (ibid., 1:250, 251). Bailey would have been able to apply for a patent under the terms of "An Act to promote the progress of useful arts" (1 *Stat.* 109–12 [10 April 1790]).

From Archibald Crary

                              East Greenwich State of Rhodeisland
Sir   Feby 2 1790
   The undoubted Prospect we now [have] that this State will recognize the Federal Government at the meeting of the Convention the first Monday of March next induces me to trouble your Excellency at this time.

   I have had the honor to be imploped eithe[r] in civil or mililitary service of my Country from the commencement of the lat[e] war with Great Brittain untill the Revolution that took place in our State Government in the year 1786: since which their proceedings have not only been degrading to the State but injurious to many individuals especially those who were openly opposed to their measures; And as a number of Gentlemen must be imploped in collecting the Revenue in this State, I take the liberty to solicit the honor of your Excellency's nomination and appointment to one of the places in the District and Port of Newport. I am encoraged to make this application by nearly all the principal Charecters in this State, as your Excellency will be more fully informed.[1]

If I should be so fortunate as to meet with your Excellency's favour I will endeavour to manifest my gratitude by a strict and faithful observance of the duties of the Office to which I may be appointed.[2] Permit me to be with the greatest veneration your Excellency's most obedient and very huml. Servant

Archibald Crary

ALS, DLC:GW.

During the Revolution Archibald Crary (1748–1812) served as colonel of the 2d Rhode Island Regiment and agent for the War Department in Rhode Island. He was adjutant general of the Rhode Island militia from 1780 to the end of the war. In 1784 he was elected a deputy to the Rhode Island assembly for East Greenwich.

1. On 1 June 1790 William Greene, William Bradford, Jabez Bowen, James Manning, Enos Mitchell, Jr., Thomas Tillinghast, Peter Turner, and Gardner Mumford, all Newport residents, wrote to GW recommending Crary for his "integrity & Abilities" and as "a suitable person for an appointment in the Revenue Department in the District and Port of Newport" (DLC:GW).

2. After Rhode Island ratified the Constitution on 29 May 1790, Crary and other Rhode Island office seekers hastened to New York. There he wrote to GW on 21 June 1790: "On my Arrival in this City. I found that the Revenue Officers for the Ports of Newport and Providence were appointed, as we did not expect, that those Appointments would take place previous to the Ratification being receiv'd. therefore Letters in favor of some Appli[c]ants were delay'd.

"I had early thought of making Application for an Appointment and was so happy as to meet with the Approbation and encouragement of all the Gentlemen to whom I made it known. I did not think that it would be necessary to trouble your Excellency with Names, whose characters would be unknown, neither did I think that the Merchants were suitable Persons to Recommend any Candidate for those Appointments, altho did not doubt of their freindship, therefore apply'd, to only, a few of the first Characters in the State, from whom I hope your Excellency has receiv'd a Recommendation in my favor previous to this request.

"Theodore Foster Esqr. who has been Honor'd with the Appointment of Naval Officer, for the Port of Providence, has also been Appointed, by the State of Rhode Island, as Senator to represent them, in the General Government, therefore as He cannot perform the duties of both Appointments, one must become Vacant.

"Newport being the Capital of the State. Govern'd me in my Choice for that Port; my place of Residence is at East Greenwich about Twelve Miles from Providence.

"If an Appointment of Naval Officer, is made in Room of Mr Foster and it is your Excellency's pleasure, I should be happy to meet with your Approbation, to fill up that vacancy If any further Recommendation from Gentlemen of Rhode Island is necessary. I doubt not of the friendly assistance of as many of, those of the first Character, as could be wish'd for.

"If my past Services has merited anything from my Country, my present Circumstances urges me to claim their Attention" (DLC:GW). Instead of nominating Crary as Foster's replacement, GW appointed Ebenezer Thompson on 2 July 1790 as naval officer of the port of Providence (Ebenezer Thompson to GW, 21 May 1790; *DHFC*, 2:83).

Crary was still in the city at the end of June when he again wrote to GW: "By particular request of a Number of the Good Citizens of Rhode Island. I take the Liberty once more to trouble your Excellency.

"From many and various causes has the Unhappy divisions that has prevailed in that State arose, perhaps from no one more than that of a Jealousy that prevail'd between the Citizens of Newport and Providence, and those in the other parts of the State. Great pains have been taken to quiet the minds of the people and to reconcile those disputes, but Sir I am informed that from the Exertions that is making, to obtain all the Officers that is to be appointed in that State, under the General Government in those Towns, that Jealousies begin again to arise, as they think that each part of the State (where suitable Characters are to be found) have a Claim to their part of those Officers, and as East Greenwich is near to Center of the State, and surrounded by inhabitants of all descriptions, they think that it would give more general Satisfaction if the Marshall might be appointed there—I have ther⟨e⟩fore been advised to give up, any application, that I may have made for any other appointment, and Solicit your Excellency to be appointed Marshall" (Crary to GW, 29 June 1790, DLC:GW). On 2 July 1790 GW appointed William Peck as U.S. marshal for the Rhode Island district (William Peck to GW, 15 Feb. 1790, source note).

Crary received no federal appointment in February or in June or July 1790. On 12 Feb. 1791 he again wrote GW, from Philadelphia, this time asking to be named as an excise district inspector in Rhode Island (DLC:GW). He was not offered the post. In 1798 he unsuccessfully solicited appointment as naval agent at Newport (Crary to Theodore Foster, 21 May 1798, DNA: RG 59, Letters of Application and Recommendation during the Administration of John Adams, 1797–1801).

From Oliver Ellsworth

Sir,   [2 February 1790]

Should you think proper to nominate a person from the State of Connecticut to the office of a Judge in the Western Territory in the room of General Parsons,[1] permit me to name for your consideration Majr William Judd;[2] of whom you probably have some knowledge from his having had the honor of serving in the late American Army. The appointment would be acceptable to him, and I beleive his services would be satisfactory to the Publick. He was liberally educated and regularly bred to the profession of the law, in which he has had the advantage of near twenty years practice. He is respectable in his profession, of a fair moral character, and active in his zeal for the honor and interest of the United States.[3]

AL, DLC:GW.

1. Samuel Holden Parsons drowned in the fall of 1789. See Winthrop Sargent to GW, 27 Nov. 1789.

2. William Judd (1743–1804) served in the Connecticut militia in 1775 and as captain in the 3d Connecticut Regiment from 1777 to 1781. He received no federal appointment.

3. The sender's name and the date of this note were supplied by a contemporary endorsement on its cover.

From Harrison County, Va., Field Officers

Sir!   Virginia Harrison County february 2d 1790.

The alarming prediciment in which this County now stands as touching the State of Indian affairs and the Small prospect of protection from his Excellency Arthur St Clair, hath moved us the Subscribers to mett this day in councell in order to concert measures as far in our power to calm the minds of our Exposed fronteers, who Expects early in the Spring to be again Harrassed by the Savages.[1]

It appears to us by the address of the general Assembly of Virginia dated the 30th of october 1789 that official Information has been given to Your Excellency of the Indians wanton Barbarity on the fronteers of this State.[2] we also have the Strongest assurance, that the members of the general assembly from the Western district did apply by a Subsequent address Separate and apart from the Said address Sent by the general assembly, which we trusted would have fell into Your hands before Governor St Clair left Newyork, which now appears to us not to be the Case. therefore the fronteers is left defenceless the people who lays exposed in complaining they are neglected, that the interior parts of the United States has Enjoyed peace Since the Year 1782. that Government has got thoughtless about the lives of their citizens &c.

We would undertake to give a full detail of the various Incursions made on the fronteers of this county, but expects our County Lieutenant will hand this petition to your Excellency who we believe will better Satisfy Your Inquireys than our detail.

We presume the aforesaid address of our Legislative Body and the Separate address Sent by the members of this Western district fully takes in our Wishes, as touching the mode of present and futer Relief.

therefore in the name and behalf of our Suffering fellow Citizens over whome we preside as field Officers of the militia, pray that Your Excellency would take our distressed Situation under your Parental Care and grant us Such Releife as you in your Wisdom shall think proper and we in duty Bound shall pray &c.

Benjamin Wilson Colo.

Geo. Jackson L. colo.

William Robinson Major

Copy, DLC:GW; copy, DNA: RG 233, First Congress, Records of Legislative Proceedings, Reports and Communications Submitted to the House; copy, DNA: RG 46, First Congress, Reports and Communications Submitted to the Senate.

1. Harrison County, established in 1784, is in what is now the northwest corner of West Virginia. The 1790 population of some 2,080 people, mostly scattered along the West Fork of the Monongahela River near Clarksburg, the county seat, with a smaller number on the Ohio near the mouth of the Little Kanawha River, was particularly exposed to Indian attack. GW referred this letter to Henry Knox who reported back to the president on 26 Feb. 1790. See his letter of that date to GW.

2. This address, drawn up in the Virginia house of delegates in October 1789, reads: "It has been a great relief to our apprehensions, for the safety of our brethren on the frontiers, to learn from the communications of the Secretary at War, that their protection against the incursions of the Indians has occupied your attention.

"Knowing the power of the Federal Executive to concentrate the American force, and confiding in the wisdom of its measures, we should leave the subject unnoticed, but from a belief that time has been wanting to gain the proper intelligence, and make the necessary arrangements of defence for a country so far remote from the seat of government. Many members of the General Assembly now present, have been either witnesses of the recent murders and depredations committed by the savages, or have brought with them information, the truth of which cannot be questioned. It is unnecessary to enter into a detail of those hostilities. Permit us only to say, that those parts of Kentucky, and the southwestern and northern counties lying on the Ohio and its waters, which have generally been the scene of Indian barbarity, are now pressed by danger the most imminent.

"We have been induced to suppose it possible, that for the purpose of affording effectual relief, it may be found expedient to carry war into the country of the Indian enemy; should this be the case, we take the liberty of assuring you that this Commonwealth will cheerfully sustain her proportion of the expenses which may be incurred in such an expedition.

"The same causes which induced us thus to offer the treasure of Virginia, have occasioned another proceeding, which we think proper to communicate to you; it is indeed incumbent on us to make this communication, least in case of silence it might be interpreted into a design of passing the limits of State authority.

"Chiefs of the Chickasaw nation have solicited the General Assembly for a supply of ammunition; the advanced season of the year, and their anxiety to return home, owing to the perilous situation of their nation, who were in daily expectation that hostilities would be commenced against them by the Creeks, have determined them to stop here, and not to proceed to New York, the place of their original destination.

"The resolution which we have now the honor of enclosing you, will therefore be executed in their favor; and we trust that our conduct, from the peculiar circumstances of the case, will be acceptable to yourself and the Congress of the United States; and being approved, that we shall receive retribution for the expense we have thereby incurred" (*Journal of the House of Delegates*, 1789, 24–25). The enclosed resolution was undoubtedly one of 23 Oct. stating that the chiefs of the Chickasaw nation, who had intended presenting their case against the Creek to GW, had been deterred from their journey beyond Richmond by the distance to New York, the weather, and "the pressing exigence of their affairs." The house of delegates resolved that the Chickasaw should be furnished with powder and lead "as their necessities may require and the public can conveniently spare" (ibid., 8–9). See also Inhabitants of Kentucky to GW, 8 Sept. 1789 (entry for letter not found), n.1.

From James Craik

Dear Sir   Alexandria [Va.] Feby 3d 1790

Since the receipt of your favour of the 8th Septr nothing has occurred to justify my breaking in upon your necessary engagements by an Epistolary Communication—Tho a Correspondence with those we Esteem and adore is one of the greatest pleasures, yet have I every gratification that I can expect from the public Prints. by them am I dayly informed, how deservedly you retain that high place in the affection and admiration of your Countrymen which your Conduct on all former occasions so justly entitled you to—from your Correspondence with Majr Washington I receive frequent intelligence of your, and families health which be assured is no small gratification to me—and I flatter myself that your trip to the Eastward has furnished you with a Stock at least sufficient to last you the present Session, when your friends to the Southward fondly hope the pleasure of a Visit—I do not know that we shall not otherwise become a little jealous—I observe the pen of satire has been employed against our *second* Majestrate—It is the usual *Tax* upon power and an Elevated Station, perhaps in some instances an evidence of Virtues and merit in the persons against whom it is directed. It is the only means of attack in the power of the Enemies of the present Government, and from my own observation I find their opposition running in that Channel—They do and will attack the Government through its Officers. may the one prove as impregnable as the other has, and may their criminations, when they are unjust recoil upon them—But I had almost forgot the Apology for this Letter—The Situation of our worthy friend Colo. Harrison has claimed my Sincere Commisuration and he trusts will be fully Satisfactory to you for his finally declining the Acceptance of his Appointment tho at this *late* hour[1]—His ill state of health for a twelvemonth past, the death of a favourite Brother, by which the management of a large family and his concerns devolved upon him; The unhappy situation of Mr Dent his friend and relation on whom he could have depended on for Assistance in his absence[2] These added to an extreme sensibility of Nerve, threw him into embarrasments & difficulties upon his, Appointment to the Fœderal Chair, which perhaps few other men could have supposed or felt—Since his appointment his mind has been the constant sport of doubt and perplexity. Public Duty and a warm attachment to you, and Acknowledgement to you for your high opinion of him on the one hand, On the other private Obligations and Domestic engagements, with a Supposed incapacity to discharge the great Dutys of his office, in his present deranged State of mind and body⟨,⟩ have placed him in a Situation, which he is as ashamed to acknowledge to the Public, as he is ready to confess to his friends & intimates—Having promised a Visit to New York, he felt himself under an obligation to attempt the Journey at all Events, having a most earnest desire of a Conversation with you—He was here for Some days waiting for his health to be Somewhat restored, and set out in the Stage for New York, but finding his Head more disordered from the Exercise; returned the next day, and has gone home with a determination, to give up all thoughts of Acceptance of his Appointment, and to endeavour to Compose himself, and again fit himself for the Duties of his present Station—I believe one great sourse of uneasyness to him, is the apprehension that his Conduct on the occasion should be thought by you unworthy of a man who has the Smallest share in your regard and good opinion; could he be satisfied on this head I think it might Conduce much to his peace and recovery—A Letter from you to that purpose would I am convinced act more powerfully upon him than all the Anodynes in an Apothecarys Shop—I do assure you his head is very much disordered, he is sensible of it and wishes his Situation, to be as much as possible a Secret—I wish he could have gone on to New York. I think the Journey and the Company of his old friends would have very much relieved him.

your Nephews George and Lawrence have left Mr McWhirr, and are now attending Mr Harrow Teacher of the Mathematics,[3] They think they are Sufficiently acquainted with the Latin-Language for their future pursuits in life, and are desirous of employing their time in other acquirements which may be more useful to them. I should be glad to know your wishes on the Subject that they may be complied with—Mrs Craik has been confined to her bed for some days very much indisposed—She and the rest of my family join me very affectionate & Respectful Compliments to Mrs Washington the Children and our other friends in your family—And I am very affectionately & Sincerely Dear Sir Your devoted Sert

Jas Craik

ALS, DLC:GW.

1. For Robert Hanson Harrison's protracted deliberations on his appointment to the Supreme Court, see GW to Harrison, 28 Sept. 1789, and notes.

2. Craik is referring to Harrison's younger brother, William, who died on 21 July 1789, leaving a young family to his brother's care. Mr. Dent is Warren Dent (1744–1794), a Charles County, Md., merchant and Harrison's brother-in-law, who was gravely ill in the fall and winter of 1789–90.

3. GW boarded his nephews George Steptoe and Lawrence Washington with Craik after the discipline of the boys became too much for Samuel Hanson. See Hanson to GW, 19 Feb. 1789, and GW to George Steptoe Washington, 23 Mar. 1789. For Craik's comments on their conduct and progress, see Craik to GW, 24 Aug. 1789, and GW to Craik, 8 Sept. 1789. For William McWhir, see Hanson to GW, 19 Feb. 1789, n.2. Gilbert Harrow, formerly a Pennsylvania

surveyor, conducted a school in Alexandria that emphasized mathematics, natural science, and the practical skills of bookkeeping and surveying (*Virginia Gazette and Alexandria Advertiser* [Alexandria], 13 Jan. 1791).

Letter not found: from Edmund Randolph, 5 Feb. 1790. GW mentions in his 13 Feb. 1790 letter to Randolph "your letter to me of the 5th inst."

From Hugh Williamson

Friday P.M. 5th Feby 1790

Mr Williamson has taken the Liberty, in the enclosed Paper to mention the Names of Gentlemen who as he conceives would discharge the Duties of the Offices affixed to their several Names with Reputation.

In Wilmington. Col: Read is now Collector & Jno. Walker is Naval Officer.

In Newbern Capt: Daves is now Collector

at Beaufort Col. Easton has long been Collecter or Naval Officer.

In Washington Capt. Keis is now Collector.

In Edenton. Thos Benbury is now Collector & Michl Payne is Naval Officer.

It appears strange that neither Navl Officer nor Surveyor are to be appointed in so considerable a Port of Entry. 330 Vessels entered there in 1787. No other Person offering who is better qualifyed to discharge the various Duties of that Office (Collector) perhaps it might be given at present to me one or 'tother of the Officers named.

Cambden is a new Port.

Genl Isaac Gregory is recommended as a Gentleman whose Character as Soldier and Citizen stands high in the universal Esteem of his fellow Citizens. He is a Man of respectable Property; has the full Confidence of his Country and is the constant Enemy to public Officers suspected of corrupt Practices.

The Gentlemen mentioned for Surveyors in the Ports of Delivery belonging to Edenton and Cambden Districts are the most respectable Characters in the Vicinity not concerned in Trade who would probably be willing to accept of such an Office.

There are two or three Blanks either because Mr Williamson does not at present recollect the Name of any Person living near the Port or does not know any Person there whom he can recommend according to his Ideas of Propriety.

AL, DLC:GW.

Hugh Williamson had been elected to the First Congress from North Carolina. He took his seat on 19 March. GW received Williamson's letter on 5 Feb. and on the same day submitted his list to North Carolina senators Benjamin Hawkins and Samuel Johnston, who had taken their seats in January, "for their Inspection and alteration" (*Diaries*, 6:28).

Enclosure
Recommendations for North Carolina Federal Revenue Officers

[5 February 1790]

For the several Ports in North Carolina the following Officers are humbly submitted.

	Wilmington	
James Read—	Collector	
John Walker	Naval Officer	
Thomas Callender	Surveyor	
Swansbro'		
	Newbern	
John Daves	Collector	
Beaufort	John Easton	Surveyor
	Washington	
Nathan Keais	Collector	
	Edenton	
Murfreesborough	Hardy Murfree.	Surveyor
Windsor	Benson	Do
Skewa[r]key	Henry Hunter	Do
Wynton	Thomas Wynns	Do
Bennetts Creek	John Baker	Do
Hertford	Joshua Skinner Jnr	
Plymouth	Levi Blount	
	Cambden	
Isaac Gregory	Collector	
Nixonton	John Lane	Surveyor
Indian Town	Saml Ferebee	
Newbiggen Creek	Edward Evenegin	
Currituck Inlet		
Pasquetank River Bridge	Edmond Sawyer	

AD, DLC:GW.

From d'Anterroches

Sir   Newyork Fabruary 6th 1790
    if I take the liberty to address myself to your Excellency, also
I never yet had the honor of being introduced to you, believe
that necessity alone can force me to do it, and not the want of
delicacy. My own interest and of course that of my wife and children, obliges me to become troublesome to you; but your well
known goodness gives me leave to hope that you will excuse me.
If you will condessend Sir to peruse the letters here inclosed,[1]
of Mr *le* duke *de* Harcourt, of Mr *le Marquis* and *la* Marquise de
Lafayette and of my Uncle the Bishop of Condom, one of the
deputy's to the general assembly of france, who hath taken care
of me since I was seven years old, and by his kindness hath enabled me to become a naturalized citizen of the United States,
If you condessend Sir, to peruse the above mentioned Letters,
your Excellency will easely perceive that I have in france, friends
and Relations who endeavour to make me confortable, and the
hope of success ought to make me avoid all occasions that may
create Jealousys which may be detrimental to me. you are Sir,
the Marquis de Lafayette⟨'s⟩ friend, and I flatter myself of having the honor of his friendship likewise; every assistance I receive from my family is sent by his means, and his goodness to
me hath made him long since one of my protectors. I shall have
the honor of relating to your Excellency the Subject on which I
write. I have bought in Elizabeth Town (the place of my resi-
dance for these seven years passed) a farm Two years ago, and
made the payment wanting few pounds only, But I owe elsewhere Two Hundred and fifty pounds york currency, which sum
I must pay before I leave this City; the want of that Money obliging my creditor to prosecute me for the same if I do not comply.
my Note of Hand is now in the Hands of an Attorney at law, and
if not redeamed, hath orders to arrest me. That Idea alone, Sir,
distress me. I have visited last year my Native Country and have
returned much pleased with the treatment I received there; my
father 78 years old hath pass'd his words to me that in a very
short time, he should send me (instigated by my friends) part of
his property which the law grants me after he is no more. on his
promise to me, on that of a Sister nominated last year abbess by
the king, and on the assistance I receive from Time to Time,

from my uncle the Bishop, I Can I believe borrow the above mentioned sum with confidancy, of paying the same very soon. I know very few persons able to assist me in so precarious a moment, and I should be affrid that if the favour was granted to me by them they should relate my present situation, in Europe, to my detriment. I shall consider myself very happy if, your Excellency desire some of your Aids to inquire into my private character, be convinced without flattery that it will turn out to my advantage, and will procure me the kindness which my Mother the Countess D'anterroches desired of you for me by letters, the Marquis delafayette is to have the honor of writing to you on the same subject, if not yet wrote, and now I ask your protection, and assistance Sir, convinced that my interest, character abroad, and futur credit shall suffer if denied to me. Be pleased to honor me with a line of answer, that I may know my fate; I shall waite for the same with the greatest impatience, and if the greatest favor asked by me is granted I shall follow the plan that you will be so good as to prescribe to me.[2] I have the honor to be with the greatest respect your Excellency Most obedient and most humble servant

Le Chr D'Anterroches
at the widow Winants Elizabeth
Town farry House white Hall.

ALS, DLC:GW.

Joseph-Louis, chevalier d'Anterroches (1753–1814) was the son of Jean-Pierre, comte d'Anterroches, and a kinsman of Lafayette. He came to the United States in 1777 and settled in Elizabethtown, N.J., about 1783, where his financial difficulties apparently began. In 1780 he married Mary Vanderpoel, daughter of David Vanderpoel of Elizabethtown, New Jersey. His mother, Jeanne-Françoise Tessier de Chaunac, comtesse d'Anterroches, wrote to GW twice in 1786, asking him to help her son (see d'Anterroches to GW, 18 Sept. 1786, and notes) and wrote similar pleas to Lafayette, Benjamin Franklin, and Thomas Jefferson (Pierson, "Records of the French in Elizabethtown," 163–70).

1. The enclosures have not been found.

2. GW apparently made some contribution to d'Anterroches. On 13 Feb. d'Anterroches wrote to William Jackson: "I went into the Jerseys wednesday after Noon last, and returned on the day following. I did myself the honor to address you in french, immediately after my arrival in the City; to acquaint you that I was to accept, with the greatest gratitude, the offer which his Excellency was Soo good as to make me by your favor; and that I expected that before long I Should have it in my power to return it. I was begging your

intercession at the Same Time for his Excellencys protection in france, concerning the office my friends, there, are asking for me, from the governement; convinced that it will produce the best of consequences twards it, and by that mean, place me in a Situation to bring up my children in a decent manner in this country my fondness for them not suffering me to trust them abroad under my parents care. They are Born in a free country and in a free Country I wish them to be Brought up, to die for it if necessity requires it, and my ambition is to make good cityzens of them and not wealthy ones. be So kind as to honor me with your answer as Soon as convenient of this letter. Do not meet the Same fate of my former one" (DLC:GW). Jackson's letter to d'Anterroches, containing GW's "offer," has not been found.

From Charles Carter, Jr.

Dear Sir   Fredericksburg February 6th 1790
I am this moment acquainted by Colo: Ball with yr answer respe[c]ting the proposals he made you on my behalf for yr house & ⟨Lotts⟩ in this place—I have for some time had it in contemplation to write you on this subject, but consider'd my self in some measure precluded by the valuation, the particulars of which were communicated to you in a letter from Colo: Ball & myself—It appears to be the general ⟨sentiment⟩ to which the valuers themselves now subscribe, that their valuation far exceeded the real worth of the property—It was under this impression that I presumed to offer the terms Colo: Ball communicated to you in his last letter. Should my proposals be agreable to you I shall be very well pleased, tho' I shall be equally well pleased to submit the terms wholly to yourself—The business, you were so obliging as to consign to the joint management of Mrs Lewis Colo. Ball & myself, being nearly compleated; we shall in the course of a few weeks forward you an account of our administration—we endeavoured to conform as nearly as possible to yr directions & trust that the parties concerned are not dissatisfied with our conduct[1]—Mrs Carter desires me to present her most respectful complements to Mrs Washington & yrself to which be pleased to add mine. I am with every sentiment of respect yrs &c.

                                                    Chas Carter Junr

ALS, DLC:GW.

For background to this letter, see Betty Washington Lewis to GW, 13 Sept. 1789, n.9, Burgess Ball to GW, 26 Dec. 1789, and GW to Ball, 18 Jan. 1790.

1. GW's reply to Carter of 8 Mar. 1790 reads: "Re-examining some letters, which in the hurry of business had been laid by, I find your favor of the 6 ultimo among them, and not being able to recollect whether I gave it an answer in the order of its date, I now inform you that it will be quite agreeable to me that you should have my lots in Fredericksburg for the sum, and on the terms of payment communicated by you through Colo. Ball. and I hope according to the intimation, there given, that they are now in your occupancy.

"I will at any time make deeds of transfer. Present my love to Mrs Carter and my Sister, in which Mrs Washington joins me. With great esteem and regard, I am, dear Sir, Your most obedient and affectionate humble Servant" (LB, DLC:GW).

From Bryan Fairfax

May it please Your Excellency   Feb. the 7th 1790.

According to your desire I have written to Mrs Bomford and have informed her of the State of the Suit against Doctor Savage.[1] The delays have been such that I don't wonder at her Surprise in not yet having heard of the Issue of it. The Day I left Mt Vernon last Winter I spoke to the Lawyer (who had the Management of the Cause after I had taken it out of the hands of the other who had done Nothing in it and who had mislaid the Papers) and desired him to proceed on with it as he had postponed it a few months on Account of what Mr Mason wrote to me about it. But tho' I spoke to him since about it, yet from what Enquiries I have made I doubt whether it is in a greater Forwardness than it was some years ago.

I have moved down to my late Purchase, and it is no small Satisfaction to me that it is not far from Mt Vernon and much more flattering that your Friendship should continue unshaken, and that I can still hope for the Pleasure of your Company once more.[2] Yet I should think it must be very uncertain, as the same desire as heretofore of yeilding to the Public Wish may again prolong Your Stay and overpower Your other Wish for Retirement—At least I think you will be reduced to a great Dilemma. We have an excellent Constitution, yet I am sorry to find some Opinions prevailing that tend gradually to weaken even good Government. As I can deliver my Sentimts freely to You I will just mention my Thoughts on some points. If Men were perfect in Love they could live happily in Society wthout Government, because they would do to all Men as they would they should do unto them, and would therefore need no Restraint nor Compulsion. But in proportion as they fall short of this perfect Love they require a Government more or less coercive. This cannot be maintained without Subordination, and this requires different Ranks, and these must be many or few in proportion as a stricter or milder Government is requisite. Of this the Army is a Proof, where a gradual Subordination preserves that order which otherwise could not be kept. Civil Society does not require such strict discipline. Yet still the Principle holds good, that in proportion to the Virtue of the People there must be a greater or less Restraint, & this should be supported by a proper Subordination. To this End many different Officers are appointed; but if these are not in some degree respectable in their own Persons their Authority becomes too weak when they derive it only from their Office. For which Reason a perfect Equality amongst Citizens if it could be had would tend to weaken the hands of Government in every State, except where there was perfect Love.

An equal Distribution of Property which some think desireable would be improper for the same Reason. And the Idea of it's Benefit seems to be entertained from that Propensity in the World to run from one extreme to another. Because a very great Inequality of wealth has been found hurtful thro' that Oppression which the poor is subject to from those that are very rich, it is concluded that the nearer it is reduced to an equal division, the better it is for the State. But this seems to be a wrong conclusion, and makes this Evil the extreme of the other. The right conclusion in this case appears to be, that a greater Equality would be better, and not an entire one. For the proper Medium if attainable would be such a division of Property as that the richest should not have it in their Power thro' their Influence to oppress, and yet that there should be so much Influence, as that the different Officers chosen from the different Classes, shall have some weight in exercising their Authority. For Men unless very virtuous are not generally to be ruled by the Laws alone and the Authority derived from them.

Hence we see how hurtful in the End it must be to lessen that Respect which Magistrates ought to possess, or to omit those accustomary honours which tend to promote it. If Experience proves that a Veneration for Magistrates is increased among the Bulk of Mankind by such Usages, it must be impolitic to lay them aside, as it would moreover be better that they had never been, than to discontinue them now that they have been long in Use. A good Government ought to be strengthend and not weakened; and where the Laws are good no Injury can arise from a proper Enforcement of them, but much Evil will follow from it's Neglect.

The Subject of Slavery too has been spoken of in such a Manner as tends to render those who are under it more dissaffected than they would have been. It does not appear that either Xst [Christ] or his Apostles ever said any thing that could have such a tendency—The Peace & Quiet of Society is what they aimed at![3]

These and some other points have given me some Uneasiness lest the Seeds of future discord should be sowing whilst we have otherwise a good Hope from the Establishment of a Government as good as any if not superior to most.

If these Errors should not increase the Evil will not be great—old opinions are not soon eradicated; but the danger arises from their spreading & continuance—which is to be feared, because Error is more easily and more readily propagated than the Truth.

I know you will pardon me for troubling you w⟨th⟩ these thoughts because you have heretofore done it when I knew they were unhappily different from your own, and that because of that Justice you shew to all Men, as well as that Friendship with which you have honored me.

Mrs Fairfax & myself present our Respects to Mrs Washington & I remain Yr Excellency's Obliged & obedt Servt

Bryan Fairfax

My Friends have often asked me to give this Spot a Name—& they have proposed so many that I am at a Loss to choose—or how to refuse ⟨Upfield, Upton⟩ Prospect Hall, Clear View—Clermont &c. have been mentioned. If the Request were not too trifling I would beg You to honour me so far as to na⟨m⟩e it. But if the name should sound too high You'l allow me to say who gave it.[4]

ALS, DLC:GW.
    1. For background on GW's involvement with Margaret Green Savage and the settlement of the estate of the Rev. Charles Green, see Henry Lee and

Daniel Payne to GW, 24 April 1767, John Dixon to GW, 5 Mar. 1789, n.1, GW to Bryan Fairfax, 6 April 1789, n.3, and GW to Sarah Bomford, 6 Jan. 1790.

2. Since the late 1760s Fairfax had lived at Towlston, built on the estate of over five thousand acres left to him by his father, William Fairfax. In January 1790 he purchased 329 acres overlooking Hunting Creek near Mount Vernon, on which he built his new house (Sweig and David, *A Fairfax Friendship*, 44, 127).

3. Fairfax may be referring to the numerous Quaker petitions against slavery that had lately been presented to Congress (see Warner Mifflin to GW, 12 Mar. 1790, n.1). More likely, the reference is to the opinions of his 16-year-old son, Ferdinando Fairfax, who had recently published an article opposing slavery in the *American Museum or Universal Magazine* for December 1790.

4. Fairfax's new house was eventually christened Mount Eagle.

Tobias Lear to James Madison

Sir,   Sunday Morning Feby 7th 1790

In obedience to the command of the President of the United States, I have the honor to enclose you a Letter from Peyton Short Esquire[1] resigning his Commission of Collecter of the Port of Louisville in Kentucky, & to request that you will be so good as to consult with Mr Brown, and any other Gentlemen from Virginia who are acquainted with characters in that part of the Country, upon a suitable person to supply the place of Mr Short and let the President know the result of your consultation this evening as he intends to give in the nominations to the Senate tomorrow.[2] I have the honor to be very respectfully Sir, Yr mot Obedt Sert

              Tobias Lear
              S.P.U.S.

ADfS, DNA: RG 59, Miscellaneous Letters; LB, DLC:GW.

1. The enclosed letter has not been found.

2. Madison wrote back to Lear the same day, noting: "I have consulted with Mr [John] Brown on the subject of a Successor to Mr Short. He is apprehensive that the reasons which induced Mr S. to decline his appointment will have the same weight with any other person who could be recommended. He names Col: Richard Taylor as worthy of the appointment, and as not more likely to follow the example of Mr Short than other fit person within his knowledge. I am acquainted with this gentleman and consider him as perfectly trustworthy. He held formerly a similar office on the Ohio when the trade of that Country was regulated by the State of Virginia" (DLC:GW). GW appointed Richard Taylor (1744–1826) collector of customs at Louisville on 9 Feb. 1790 (*DHFC*, 2:59, 62; Lear to Taylor, 11 Feb. 1790, DLC:GW). Taylor, the father

of President Zachary Taylor, had formerly served as customs officer at the Falls
of the Ohio under the state government.

To William Craik

Dear Sir,   New-York, February 8. 1790.

I have duly received your letter of the 25 of last month, and
return you my thanks for your attention to my dispute with
Stromat respecting the Proclamation warrant.[1]

If Mr Stromat will fulfil the offer of compromise in the manner he has proposed to you—or in such a manner as you, under
the aid of Mr Dunnington's information, (who is perfectly acquainted with all the land to which Stromat lays claim by virtue
of his warrants) shall think will subserve my purposes, I would
prefer it to a suit at law; by which I might *gain* or *lose* all. To
prevent the injury which my tract would sustain by the intersection of it by the slipes Stromat was endeavoring to obtain, was
my primary object—to attain which will satisfy me. If you could
make it convenient to attend the survey it would enable you to
decide on the *spot* with more propriety, and such a service would
be very agreeable to me—Bind firmly whatever agreement you
may make with Stromat without delay—that he is not punctilious in observing his word *I* know—and that he would deceive
you, if he can gain any thing by it I have very little doubt.

For your services in this business, and the ejectment of Perry,
with the expences that have been incurred, I again pray you to
apply to my Nephew, G. A. Washington, for payment. With very
great esteem and regard I am &ca

           G. Washington.

LB, DLC:GW.

For background to this letter, see GW to William Craik, 19 Mar. 1789, and
notes.

1. For this letter, see GW to Craik, 19 Mar. 1789, n.4.

From John Hamilton

Sir   Edenton [N.C.] 8 Febry 1790

Your surprise in hearing from a person altogether unknown,
cannot be surpassed by the difficulty & embarrassment which I

feel in the attempt to write; urged by my freinds, it is a task that has given me much pain and disquietude—being well assured however, that you desire only to preside over the hearts of a free people, & to be their parent & protector; altho', not the first in an honorable profession, I am emboldened to lay before you my wish to become a Servant of the fœderal government under your administration.

Having now become a Link in the Band of Union, the necessary departments are to be filled up for this State. Should you from information or Inquiry, find me worthy of the Office of Fœderal Attorney, for this District, I shall esteem it an high honor to act under your Auspices. at the same time, should my own, & the application of my freinds, be unsuccessful, I shall rest satisfyed that in the roll of Applicants, your Excellency has found one, whose qualifications & pretensions better entitle him to expect the Nomination—for my own part, I shall be convinced, that wisdom & impartial justice hath attended your Choice, & shall at once admire the hand, that gives or refuses.

If it can afford your Excellency a moments pleasure, allow me to assure you, that notwithstanding our late backwardness, a greater degree of affection for your person, and a stronger attachment to the fœderal government, does not prevail in any part of America than in this State and in this little Corner in particular; and I am proud to say, that a few to the Westward excepted (whose minds have either been deluded by false Insinuation, captivated with the Harlot Charms of an inefficient government, or actuated by Motives of Ambition to be all important in the small Circle) the general body of the people are well affected to the government and ambitious in their zeal for its Support. Being an eye Witness at the late Convention & Assembly, I am fully persuaded of the truth & justice of my Observation.

Hope now elevates, joy brightens the Countenance, and with grateful Veneration to the Disposer of Event⟨s⟩, we look forward with gladdened heart, to the efficacy of our new government, and behold in the Supreme Magistrate, a Father a Freind, & Fellow-Citizen.[1]

That Heaven may guide & protect you, is the sollicitous Wish & prayer of Sir Your most devoted & Obedt hue Sert

J. Hamilton

John Hamilton

LS, DLC:GW.

John Hamilton (d. 1833), a native of Philadelphia, studied law at Edinburgh and was at this time practicing law in Edenton. He received no federal appointment at this time. In April 1797 Hamilton was licensed to practice law in Tennessee and admitted to practice in July 1797. He was appointed state's attorney for the Mero District in September 1797 (Ely and Brown, *Legal Papers of Andrew Jackson*, 370–71). Hamilton's application was supported by letters from his uncle William Cumming to Samuel Johnston, 17 Oct. 1789 and 10 Feb. 1790 (DLC:GW).

1. Hamilton again wrote to GW from Edenton on 10 April 1790, restating almost word for word his letter of 8 Feb. 1790 (DLC:GW).

From David Humphreys

My dear General.   Hartford [Conn.] Feby 8th 1790.

I take the liberty to put under cover to you a letter for Mr Manley the Engraver in Philadelphia, who is about to strike the Medal containing your likeness.[1] At the moment when I was leaving New York he asked me for my opinion on the subject, and requested that I would write to him as soon as I might find it convenient—which I promised. In case there should be any thing erroneous in the Model, or (according to your judgment) improper, I must ask the favor, for the sake of the Public which is much interested, that you will be pleased to retain it in your hands, or make any alterations whatsoever. If otherwise, the Artist will be much obliged by your having the letter sealed & placed in the Post Office for transmission.

I arrived here only the day before yesterday, and shall probably be detained somewhat longer on my journey than I expected. Especially, as, upon the Application of the Person in New York who is publishing a Map & account of the Post Roads, I gave him encouragement to furnish him with some information for his Notes on them through Connecticut. This may retard me a few days at the Towns in the Western parts of the State, while I shall be on my return. I beg you, however, to be persuaded that I shall hasten to receive & execute your Commands with all that zeal & fidelity, with which I have the honor to be, My dear General, With perfect devotion Your Most obliged & Most humble Servant[2]

D. Humphreys

ALS, DLC:GW.

1. The enclosed letter has not been found. The "Manley Medal" was the first medal issued in the United States bearing GW's portrait. It was designed by James Manley, a portrait painter, silhouette maker, and engraver of New York and Philadelphia, and produced by Samuel Brooks, a Philadelphia goldsmith and seal cutter. The medal was advertised for sale by subscription in the *Pennsylvania Packet and Daily Advertiser* (Philadelphia) on 3 Mar. 1790. The advertisement describes the medallic portrait as "a strong and expressive likeness." Subscribers were offered copies in white metal, gold-colored metal, silver, and gold. The obverse side of the medal bears a bust of GW in uniform, his name, and date of birth. The reverse carries the legend "General of the American Armies 1775. Resigned 1783. President of the United States 1789." Many known examples are marked "J. Manley & C. 1790" (Baker, *Medallic Portraits of Washington*, 39–44). One of the medals is in the collections of the Mount Vernon Ladies' Association.

2. Manley wrote to GW from "No. 1 Carters Ally Philadelphia" on 13 Feb. 1790: "Herewith I have done Myself the Honr to transmit an Impression on Lead, taken from the Die, in its unfinished state; the likeness I hope will be Honrd by the Intire approbation of you, Mrs Washington, and friends, you will please to observe, that the Die Not being finished—dose Not give that Compleat releif, or sharpness, it will do, when Compleat which it Shall be; as soon as I am favoured, by Collnl Humphys, with the proper Inscription, for the reverse Side; I wrote Majr Jackson a few days since on that Subject; & wait the favr of his ansr: if there is any alteration or Correction you wd wish, I wil Esteem it an Honr to be Info[r]med of it" (DLC:GW).

Lear's reply to Manly of 22 Feb. 1790 reads: "The President of the United States has directed me to acknowledge the receipt of your letter to him of the 13th instant, enclosing an impression on lead, taken from the unfinished die.

"A Letter from Colo. Humphreys to you was lodged in the Post-Office last Monday, and has undoubtedly reached your hands before this time" (PHi: Society Collection).

From Robert Morris

Sir,   New York Feby 8th 1790.

The Memorial which you will find inclosed herewith,[1] Speaks so plain a Language as not to stand in need of Explanation, and the occasion such as not to require appology. The request which it contains being supported by considerations of public Justice, will I am sure from that Motive, meet your favour.[2] With Sentiments of the most perfect Esteem and respect. I have the Honor to be Sir Your most obedient and Most humble Servant

Robt Morris

LS, DNA: RG 59, Miscellaneous Letters.

1. Morris's enclosure of the same date reads: "To the President, The Senate, and House of Representatives, of the United States of America.

"The Memorial of Robert Morris late Superintendant of the Finances of the said United States.

"Humbly Sheweth.

"That, on the twentieth Day of June in the Year One thousand Seven hundred and Eighty five, and subsequent to your Memorialists resignation of his Office of Superintendant, The Congress passed a Resolution in the Words following 'Resolved that three Commissioners be appointed to enquire into the Receipts and Expenditures of public Monies during the Administration of the late Superintendant of Finance, and to Examine and Adjust the Accounts of the United States with that Department during his Administration and to Report a State thereof to Congress' which Resolution to Persons unacquainted with the Nature of the Office, and the Mode of Conducting the Business of the Department, gave occasion to the Supposition, that your Memorialist had Accounts both difficult and important to Settle with the United States in Respect to his Official Transactions. That though your Memorialist foresaw the disagreable Consequences which might result to himself, from the Diffusion of such an Opinion, He notwithstanding, not only forbore any Representation on the Subject, but Scrupulously avoided every Species of interference direct or indirect, lest it should be imagined eitheir that He was actuated by the Desire of obtaining from Congress, those marks of Approbation which had in repeated Instances been bestowed on the Servants of the Public, or that He feared to meet the proposed Investigation. Respect for the Sovereign of the United States, concurring with Motives of delicacy, to forbid even the appearance of Asking what if merited it was to be presumed would be conferred, (as being the proper Reward of Services not of Solicitation) and a firm Confidence in the Rectitude of his Conduct, leaving your Memorialist no inducement to evade any enquiry into it which it might be thought fit to Institute.

"That your Memorialist taking it for granted, that the reasons which had produced a Determination to Establish a mode of Inquiry into the Transactions of the most Important office under the Government, would have ensured a prosecution of the object till it had been carried into effect; long remained in silent Expectation of the Appointment of Commissioners, according to the Resolution which had been entered into for that purpose. But it has so happened, from what cause your Memorialist will not undertake to explain, that no further Steps has ever been taken in relation to it. And your Memorialist has remained exposed to the Surmises, which the appearance of an Intention to enquire into His Conduct, had a Tendency to excite, without having been afforded an opportunity of obviating them.

"That the unsettled condition of certain Accounts of a Commercial nature between the United States and the late House of Willing Morris & Company and your Memorialist prior to his appointment as Superintendant of the Finances, having been confounded with his Transactions in that Capacity, Your Memorialist has in various ways, been subjected to injurious Imputations on his official Conduct, the only Fruits of Services, which at the time they were rendered, he trusts he may without incurring the charge of presumption, affirm, were generally esteemed both Important and Meritorious, and were at least rendered with ardor and Zeal, with u[n]remitted attention, and unwearied application.

"That your Memorialist desirous of rescuing his reputation from the Aspersions thrown upon it, came in the Month of October 1788 to the City of New York as well for the purpose of urging the appointment of Commissioners, to Inspect His official Transactions, as for that of procuring an Adjustment of the Accounts which existed previous to his Administration. But the first object was frustrated by the want of a sufficient Number of Members to make a Congress, and the last was unavoidably delayed by the Preliminary investigations requisite on the part of the Commissioner named by the late Board of Treasury towards a competent Knowledge of the Business. That in the Month of February 1789 Your Memorialist returned to New York for the same purposes, but the obstacles which he had before experienced still operated, to put it out of his Power to present the Memorial which had been prepared by him in October, praying for an Appointment of Commissioners. That He was therefore obliged to confine himself to measures for the Settlement of his Accounts respecting the Transactions antecedent to his Appointment as Superintendant, which he entered upon accordingly with the Commissioner appointed by the Board of Treasury, and in which as much progress as time and circumstances would permit was made, untill the fourth of March last, when that Commissioner conceiving His authority, by the Organization of the New Government to have ceased declined further Proceedings, and of course your Memorialist was obliged to wait the Establishment of the New Treasury Department for the further prosecution of that Settlement, which has been accordingly Resumed, and He hopes will speedily be accomplished. But in as much as no mode of enquiry into his Official Conduct has hitherto been put into operation, and as doubts of its propriety have been raised by an act of the Government, Your Memorialist conceives himself to have a Claim upon the Public Justice for some method of Vindicating himself which will be u[n]equivocal, and definitive; Wherefore, and encouraged by a consciousness of the Integrity of his Administration, your Memorialist is desirous that a Strict Examination should be had into his Conduct while in Office, in order that if he has been guilty of Maladministration it may be detected and Punished, if otherwise, that his Innocence may be manifested, and acknowledged.

"Unwilling from this motive that longer Delay should attend the object of the Resolution which has been recited, Your Memorialist humbly Prays, that an Appointment of Commissioners may take place to carry the said Resolution into Effect. And your Memorialist as in Duty bound will Pray &ca" (DNA: RG 59, Miscellaneous Letters).

2. Morris had been plagued by congressional investigations even before his resignation as superintendent of finance in 1784. The widely held belief that he engaged in speculation in his own notes, his commercial activities during the war, and his connection with the Bank of North America led many Americans to view his administration of finances with suspicion, although during the Revolution he had apparently left much of his vast financial empire to the

management of his partners. On 20 June 1785 Congress adopted a resolution calling for an investigation of Morris's conduct as superintendent. No such investigation was pursued, but the resolution left Morris under a cloud of suspicion that he was anxious to dispel. His petition was received by the House of Representatives on 8 Feb. 1790 and referred to a committee composed of James Madison, Theodore Sedgwick, and Roger Sherman on 10 February. The next day the Senate agreed to a resolution calling for the appointment of three commissioners by the president to inquire into Morris's conduct, but the House declined to act on the resolution (*DHFC*, 3:288, 291–93, 294). As chairman of the House committee, Madison reported on 9 Mar. that "regular official examination has been already made into the transactions of Mr. Morris, as Superintendent of the Finances of the United States; and that it is inexpedient to incur the expense of a re-examination by Commissioners, as proposed by the resolution of the Senate on that Subject." The report was discussed on 19 Mar. and a committee of five, consisting of Madison, Sedgwick, Sherman, John Laurance, and William Loughton Smith was appointed to conduct a fuller inquiry ("Report on Robert Morris's Petition," [9 Mar. 1790], in Rutland, *Madison Papers*, 13:95–96). This committee did not report until 16 Feb. 1791. Madison, as chairman, reported: "That it being evidently impossible for the Committee to examine in detail, the public accounts under the administration, and unnecessary, as the same have been examined and passed in the proper offices, they have thought their duty would best be discharged by obtaining from the Register, the statements of receipts and expenditures, and other extracts from public records, herewith submitted, along with a more particular statement of the public Accounts, during the same period, made out in the year 1784, in such a number of printed copies of both, as will furnish to each member of Congress, the best practicable means of appreciating the Services of the Superintendant, and the utility of his administration" ("Report on the Financial Administration of Robert Morris," [16 Feb. 1791], in Rutland, *Madison Papers*, 13: 392–93). The first of these printed reports was published as *Statements of the Receipts and Expenditures of Public Monies, during the Administration of the Finances by Robert Morris* (Philadelphia, 1791). Although the committee did not find evidence of maladministration, critics continued to charge that Morris had made improper use of public funds.

From Bernard Hubley, Jr.

Northumberland [Pa.]
My much loved Genl and President   February 9th, 1790
     Praying your Excellency to Confer upon me a Commission or such Office, as in your Wisdom may be thought proper if upon perusal of this I may be thought Worthy to deserve one; I beleive if your Excellency would think worth Notice to enquire into my Character you would find what I mention litterally true;

At the Commencement of the late War I was but a Young Lad, my Heart then panted for the Welfare of our Country, & was Wishing to take an Active part therein, when early Appointment for Officers in the Army took place an Elder Brother of mine was Appointed Lieut. in Captn Ross's Compy of Riflemen under the Command of Col. Thompson; nothing but the ⟨re⟩straint of my Parents on account of my Youth prevented me from Marching along, when the Militia were Ordered for Elizabeth Point (in the Jersey) I then gaind Approbation to go with them and Joind the Light Infantry Compy of our County Viz. Lancaster, after the expiration of the Term of the Militia, when they March'd Home, I went to Long Island Joined Genl then Col. Hands Regt as a Volunteer after a few days there I received a Letter from my Captn & wherein was enclosed a First Lieuts. Commission for me in the German Regt, from Long Island agreeable to my Instructions I set out for Lancaster to Recruit Soldiers. I then Obtain'd the consent of my Father to continue in the Army, he Accordingly purchas'd a Sword presented me therewith giving at the same time the best Advice in the conduct of a Young Soldier, after Recruiting I Join'd my Regt at Philada under Houssecker, from thence we proceeded up the River Delaware Join'd your Excellency; I have been in the Battles of Trenton, Prince Town, Brandy Wine, German Town, Monmouth, and several skirmishes, and with Genl Sullivans Expedition to the W⟨est,⟩ I was ever trying to distinguish myself, and by every Means to become useful to our Country; in February 1778 I was Appointed a Captn to sd Regt agreeable to Rotation, all which time I served in the Army I think I may add with Honor, excepting there should be no honor without ever being Wounded, which I never was, I was ever beloved and in high estimation among such Brother Officers with whom I had Acquaintance; Agreeable to a Resolve of Congress of October 1780, for diminishing the Number of Officers, and to retire on half pay, I came under that Description, and with the Utmost reluctance owing to the situation of our Country, I went to my Native home Lancaster, out of Four Brothers there was Three of us in service, and the One of a Weak and sickly Constitution, was One of the Assistant Clothiers & Commissaries at Lancaster—Immediately after the conclusion of the War, I was Offer'd Goods on Credit, by some Merchants of Philada with a persuasion that this Place would be suitable for Business, Accordingly I took to the Amt of Twelve Hundred Pounds, and was attentive to business, I had to the Amt of above Fourteen Hundred Pounds Certificates, in the care of a Brother Resident at Philada, on the Night of the 17th November 1786, his House was enter'd by some Villains, who broke open his Desk plunder'd it of every Thing Valuable and with my Certificates, My Brother Immediately atvertizd the same, the Fellows Three in Number some time after were Apprehended in Boston, they broke Open a House there and were caught in the deed, upon examination there was a small Certificate of mine Amounting to £99.4.2 found with them, and when the Advertizement was produc'd they confess'd the whole to the Magistrate, but declar'd, they had no more of them, that they sold them all but that One, some in the Jersey, some at New York, some at Boston, and they beleived that some they sold were taken to Baltimore, the Magistrate Wrote to my Brother that for the Offence committed at Boston the Villains were sentenc'd to Work Seven Years at the Castle; My Brother took the Opinion of the Honbl. Chief Justice Mr McKean, and the Advice of some of the most Eminent Lawyers in the City, and they all agreed that those Persons who Bought not knowing them to be Stole, came honestly by them and must be paid what they gave for them (if I would recover them) being a particular kind of Property different from others as they are Negociable; and I have been Inform'd (by Men of Knowledge) the State cannot refund them to me, as they cannot be proven to be destroyd; I received Two Hundred and Thirty odd Pounds of them again that were collected in and about Boston, but had to repay those Persons there Money which was at the rate of 3s/9 in the Pound; soon after this Affair happen'd my Creditors got Alarm'd (as is ever the case with Timorous Merchts upon similar occasions) those who were timorous commenc'd immediately suits against me; the Goods were seiz'd by the Sheriff and sold at Public sale, a quantity of which sold 200 P. Cent under prime Cost, and by which Means I fell short near upon Four Hundred Pounds which I am honestly Indebted to this day, some of the Creditors more humane have shewn me every lenity, I have try'd every honest & honorable Means ever since thinking to discharge it, but still find myself baffled, and have experienced that it comes pretty hard for a Virtuous Character to surmount many Obstacles when Fortune of the Vicissitudes of Human Affairs once seems to frown upon him.

The last Summer I had an Excursion to Lake Erie, the particulars of which on my return and at the Arrival of Fort Pitt, I sent to your Excellency[1]—I think the Honbl. William McClay Esqr. can give a sketch of my Character since my retirement from service and Incorporation with the Mass of Citizens; The Honbl. Speaker Frederick A. Muhlenberg Esqr. his Brother the Genl and the Honbl. Thomas Hartley Esqr. are Acquainted with me & Connexion; The Honbl. Supreme Executive Council of Pennsylvania have lately honoured me with the Commission of Lieutenant of the County of Northumberland[;] the Pay of this Office is adequate to the Duties, but under the present form of Militia Laws, my Duty is seldom required—If your Excellency may think me Worthy and giving preference to those who ever study to be serviceable to their Country, or have been so, Your Excellency will find that I ever had and will ever have mine at Heart and Wish to see its Welfare; I have not Enter'd into the Matrimonial State yet, wherefore a Local Station with me in the United States, would be a Matter Immaterial in which part it was, as I am not bound to any particular spot, I would Wish to be in a station wherein I could really be of benefit to our Country, in being a Useless Drone I could never reconcile to myself; I Pray your Excellency to put favourable construction upon these Lines, they flow from a Heart which always ⟨*mutilated*⟩ from your first Appointment to Generallissimo, and which will ever be devoted entirely by your Directions. I take the liberty to subscribe myself Your Most Obdt & ever Humbl. servt

                                        Bernard Hubley Jnr

ALS, DLC:GW.

For an identification of Bernard Hubley, Jr., see his letter to GW, 28 July 1789.

1. Hubley transmitted this information in his letter to GW of 28 July 1789.

To the United States Senate

United States [New York]

Gentlemen of the Senate, February 9th 1790

You will perceive from the papers herewith delivered,[1] and which are enumerated in the annexed list,[2] that a difference subsists between Great Britain and the United States relative to the boundary line between our Eastern, and their Territories. A plan for deciding this difference, was laid before the late Congress;[3] and whether that, or some other plan of a like kind, would not now be elegible, is submitted to your consideration.

In my opinion it is desireable that all questions between this and other nations, be speedily and amicably settled; and in this instance I think it advisable to postpone any negociations on the subject, until I shall be informed of the result of your deliberations, and receive your advice as to the propositions most proper to be offered on the part of the United States.

As I am taking measures for learning the intentions of Great Britain respecting the further detention of our Posts &c.[4] I am the more sollicitous that the business now submitted to you, may be prepared for negociation, as soon as the other important affairs which engage your attention will permit.[5]

Go: Washington

LS, DNA: RG 46, First Congress, Records of Executive Proceedings, President's Messages—Foreign Relations; LB, DLC:GW.

This communication to the Senate concerned the northeastern boundary with Canada. The British and American negotiators at the Treaty of Paris in 1782 had used John Mitchell's 1755 map to determine which of the two large streams that flow into Passamaquoddy Bay formed the boundary between the United States and Canada. The fact that Mitchell's map designated the eastern stream as the St. Croix placed the boundary at that river, a point that remained in dispute between the United States and Great Britain. A mixed commission appointed under the terms of the Jay Treaty defined the boundary in 1798 as the western stream, known locally as the Schoodic. As early as 1785, in a report to the Confederation Congress of 21 April, Secretary for Foreign Affairs John Jay contended that "effectual Measures should be immediately taken" to settle the dispute over the line, suggesting that commissioners should be appointed to consider the boundary (*JCC*, 28:287–90). By the late 1780s settlers from Nova Scotia were moving into the disputed area, "pretending," as Jefferson noted in a letter to Benjamin Franklin "that it is the Western, and not the Eastern River of the Bay of Passamaquoddy, which was designated by the Name of St. Croix in the Treaty of Peace with that Nation." Jefferson requested that Franklin communicate "any Facts which your Memory or Papers may enable you to recollect, and which may indicate the true River the Commissioners on both sides had in their View, to establish as the Boundary between the two Nations. It will be of some Consequence to be informed by what Map they traced the Boundary" (Jefferson to Franklin, 31 Mar. 1790, in Boyd, *Jefferson Papers*, 16:283). In his reply to Jefferson, 8 April, Franklin assured him that "I am perfectly clear in the Remembrance that the Map we used in tracing the Boundary was brought to the Treaty by the Commissioners from England, and that it was the same that was published by Mitchell above 20 Years before. Having a Copy of that Map by me in loose Sheets I send you that Sheet which contains the Bay of Passamaquoddy, where you will see that Part of the Boundary traced.—I remember too that in that Part of the Boundary, we relied much on the Opinion of Mr Adams, who had been concerned in some former Disputes concerning those Territories" (ibid., 326). Jefferson sent similar letters to Henry Laurens, John Adams, and John Jay (ibid., 283). That the movement of settlers was widely known is indicated not only by the enclosures to GW's letter to the Senate but also by articles appearing in a number of newspapers. One article reprinted from a Boston newspaper stated that "Since the peace, the subjects of the British King have taken possession of all the lands between the St. Croix and Shooduck rivers, a tract nearly as large as the state of New-Hampshire, and now hold possession of the same under the pretence that the Shooduck is the true river St. Croix. They also claim all the islands in the Bay of Passamaquoddy, although many of them lay several miles to the westward even of the river which they call the boundary. They have offered many insults to the inhabitants of these islands, taken several vessels, and committed other outrages that must oblige us speedily to adopt measures to prevent such insults in future" (*Daily Advertiser* [New York], 29 Mar. 1790).

GW's letter was delivered to the Senate on 9 Feb. by Tobias Lear and was "postponed for consideration." On 10 Feb. GW's letter was sent to a committee consisting of Caleb Strong, Pierce Butler, William Paterson, Benjamin Hawkins, and William S. Johnson, and on 18 Feb. the letter and accompanying messages concerning the boundary that GW sent to the Senate that day were also remanded to the committee (*DHFC*, 2:59, 62, 63). The committee presented its report for the consideration of the Senate on 10 Mar., and on 24 Mar. the Senate resolved that "effectual Measures should be taken as soon as conveniently may be to settle all Disputes with the Crown of Great Britain relative to that Line. That it would be proper to cause a Representation of the Case to be made to the Court of Great Britain, and if the said disputes cannot be otherwise amicably adjusted, to propose that Commissioners be appointed to hear and finally decide those disputes, in the manner pointed out in the report of the late Secretary of the United States for the Department of foreign Affairs of the 21st of April 1785, a Copy of which Report accompanied the first of the said Messages" (ibid., 65–66).

1. Copies of these documents appear in *DHFC*, 2:359–87.

2. As the original list has not been found, the text of the enclosure printed below is taken from the letterbook copy.

3. GW is probably referring to the Confederation Congress's resolution of 13 Oct. 1785 to transmit to John Adams, American ambassador to the Court

of St. James, copies of papers detailing British encroachments in Maine, forwarded by Gov. James Bowdoin of Massachusetts, so that "effectual Measures should be immediately taken to settle all Disputes with the Crown of Great Britain relative to that Line" and to instruct Adams to represent the case to the king and obtain an adjustment consistent with the Paris peace treaty. Failing that, he was instructed to propose a settlement of the dispute "by Commissaries mutually appointed for that Purpose . . . conformable to the Laws of Nations" (*DHFC*, 2:381–82).

4. GW instructed Gouverneur Morris to proceed to London as an unofficial envoy to inquire into British intentions concerning their treaty violations as well as the possibility of negotiating a new commercial treaty (GW to Morris, 13 Oct. 1789 [second letter], and note 1; Morris to GW, 22 Jan. 1790 [first letter]).

Enclosure

[9 February 1790]
A List of the papers deliver'd to the Senate with the foregoing Message

In the Bundle marked A.

No. 1. Resolve of the Legislature of Massachusetts dated June 6th & 7th 1784.[1]

2. Report of Generals Lincoln and Knox to the Governor of Massachusetts dated October 15th 1786.[2]

3. Deposition of John Mitchell dated October 9th 1784.

4. Extract of a letter from the honorable John Adams to Lieut. Governor Cushing dated October 25th 1784.

5. Letter from Governor Hancock to Governor Parr of Nova-Scotia—dated November 12th 1784.

No. 6. Letter from Governor Parr to Governor Hancock dated December 7th 1784.

7. Letter from Rufus Putnam to the Committee of Massachusetts dated December 27th 1784.

8. Report of the Secretary for foreign Affairs respecting Eastern Boundary.[3]

9. Deposition of Nathan Jones dated March 17th 1785.

10. Copy of a Letter from Governor Carlton[4] to Governor Hancock dated June 21th 1785.

11. Letter from James Avery to Governor Bowdoin dated August 23d 1785.

12. Advice of the Council of the Commonwealth of Massachusetts to the Governor dated Septr 9th 1785.

13. Letter from Governor Bowdoin to Governor Carlton dated September 9th 1785.

14. Report of the Secretary of foreign affairs dated September 22d 1785.

15. Resolution of Congress dated October 13th 1785.

16. Copy of a Letter from the honorable John Jay to the honorable John Adams dated 1st November 1785.

Papers in the bundle marked B.

No. 1. The Petition of James Boyd to the President, the Senate and House of Representatives of the United States of America.[5]

No. 2. Copy of the proceedings of the Legislature of the Commonwealth of Massachusetts on the petition of James Boyd,[6] and a letter of instruction to the Delegates of that Commonwealth in Congress dated Novr 10th 1786.

3. Copy of a Declaration of John Mitchell relative to a Survey made by him in the year 1764 to ascertain the River, known by the name of St Cro[i]x.[7]

4. Copy of a Declaration of Nathan Jones to the same effect as the preceding.[8]

5. Copy of a plan delivered to Captn John Mitchell Surveyor, by his Excellency Francis Barnard Esqr. then Governor of the Province of the Massachusetts Bay, for the direction of the said Surveyor.[9]

6. Copy of remarks drawn up by C. Morris S. General respecting the western limits of New-Brunswick, and the property of the Islands in the Bay of Passamaquody.[10]

7. Extract of a Letter from his Excellency John Adams Esquire, to his Honor Lieutenant Governor Cushing—Dated Antewell near Paris October 25th 1784.[11]

8. Extract from the Journals of Congress May 20th 1785.

9. Extracts from sundry publications respecting the boundaries of Nova Scotia.[12]

LB, DLC:GW.

All of these enclosures are printed in *DHFC*, 2:362–87.

1. The actual resolve is dated 6–7 July 1784 (ibid., 363–64).

2. The report of commissioners Benjamin Lincoln and Henry Knox is dated 19 Oct. 1784 (ibid., 365–66).

3. John Jay delivered this report to the Confederation Congress on 21 April 1785 (ibid., 373–76).

4. Thomas Carleton was governor of New Brunswick.

5. See James Boyd to GW, 27 Nov. 1789.

6. The Massachusetts legislative proceedings are dated 20–22 Jan. 1785 (*DHFC*, 383–84).

7. This is probably another copy of the deposition labeled as no. 3 in bundle A.

8. This is most likely another copy of item 9 in Bundle A.

9. The copy of this plan in DNA: RG 59, Miscellaneous Manuscripts, was transcribed by John Vinall, a teacher of mathematics in Boston, on 16 Nov. 1789 (ibid., 361).

10. Charles Morris, Jr., assumed the office of surveyor general of Nova Scotia after the death of his father in 1781. His observations were probably recorded sometime in 1789 (Akins, "History of Halifax City," 229; *DHFC*, 2:385–86).

11. Adams's letter to Thomas Cushing, lieutenant governor of Massachusetts, was sent from Auteuil near Paris (ibid., 367).

12. These extracts included William Douglass, *A Summary, Historical and Political, of the First Planting, Progressive Improvements, and Present State of the British Settlements in North-America*, 1:320, 332, a Boston serial of the 1740s and 1750s reprinted in London in 1760, and unidentified pages from *The Begin[n]ing, Progress, and Conclusion of the Late War, with Other Interesting Matters Considered; and a Map of the Lands, Islands, Gulphs, Seas, and Fishing-Banks, Comprising the Cod Fishery in America Annexed, for the Better Explanation of Several Proceedings Relative to It* (London, 1770) (Evans, *American Bibliography*, 2:329, 377; *ESTC, British Library*; *DHFC*, 2:362–63).

To the United States Senate

Gentlemen of the Senate,
United States [New York]
February 9th 1790.

Among the persons appointed during your late Session, to offices under the national Government, there were some who declined serving. Their names and offices are specified in the first column of the annexed list. I supplied these Vacancies, agreeably to the Constitution, by temporary appointments; which you will find mentioned in the second column of the list. These appointments will expire with your present session, and indeed ought not to endure longer than until others can be regularly made—for that purpose I now nominate to you the persons named in the third column of the list, as being in my opinion qualified to fill the Offices opposite to their names in the first.

Go: Washington

A List of Vacancies and appointments which have taken place in the national Offices, during the late recess of the Senate, and of persons nominated for them by the President of the United States on the 8th day of February 1790.

First Column. *Resignations.*	Second Column. *Temporary Appointmt*	Third Column. *Nominations.*
Robert H. Harrison—one of the Associate Judges of the Supreme Court		James Iredell[1] of North Carolina.
Thomas Johnson—District Judge of Maryland	William Paca[2]	William Paca
Edmund Pendleton—District Judge of Virginia	Cyrus Griffin[3]	Cyrus Griffin.
John Marshall—Attorney for the District of Virginia	William Nelson Junr[4]	William Nelson Junr
Thomas Pinckney—District Judge of South Carolina	William Drayton[5]	William Drayton.
George Handley—Collector of the Port of Brunswick, in Georgia		Christopher Hillary[6]
Peyton Short—Collector of the Port of Louisville in Kentuckey		Richard Taylor[7]
Asher Miller[8]—Surveyor of the Port of Middletown in Connecticut		Comfort Sage[9]

Go: Washington

LS, DNA: RG 46, First Congress, Records of Executive Proceedings, President's Messages—Executive Nominations; LB, DLC:GW.

Lear delivered this message to the Senate on 9 Feb. 1790. The Senate considered it the next day, confirmed all the appointments, and laid a certified copy of its "advice and consent" before the president (*DHFC*, 2:61–62). An "a" following each name on the list was probably added later to indicate the Senate concurred in the appointment.

1. GW sent Iredell his commission on 13 Feb. 1790, and Iredell acknowledged its receipt on 3 Mar. (Hugh Williamson to GW, 19 Sept. 1789, n.1).

2. GW wrote to Paca on 13 Feb. 1790, notifying him that "The appointment which you now hold as Judge of the United States in and for the district of Maryland, having been made during the Recess of the Senate of the United States, can endure no longer than to the end of their present Session; and a new Commission, specifying your appointment by and with the advice and consent of the Senate, will become necessary for your continuance in the discharge of the duties of that Office. This Commission I have now the pleasure to enclose, requesting that you will acknowledge the receipt of it as soon as it gets to your hands" (LS, MdHi: Vertical File Papers; Df, in Tobias Lear's handwriting, DNA: RG 59, Miscellaneous Letters; LB, DLC:GW). Lear sent this letter to John White, the Baltimore postmaster, the same day, requesting him to forward it by a safe conveyance in a reasonable time (DNA: RG 59, Miscellaneous Letters). Paca's 6 Mar. reply from Wye Island in Queen Anne's County, Md., noted that he received GW's letter on 2 Mar., as "it lay some Time in the Post Office in Baltimore" (DNA: RG 59, State Department).

3. A note appended to the letter-book copy of GW to Paca, 13 Feb. 1790, indicates that copies of that letter were also transmitted to "the Judges of the Districts of Virginia [Cyrus Griffin] and South Carolina [William Drayton], and to Wm Nelson Junr Attorney for the District of Virginia" (DLC:GW). Griffin responded from Williamsburg, Va., on 16 Mar.: "After discharging the business of the last special Court I paid a visit to a Brother who lives at some considerable distance from the post road, and over two pretty wide Rivers, which prevented me the honor of receiving your letter of February the 13th untill this day, enclosing a second Commission for the Judge of the Virginia district" (DNA: RG 59, Acceptances and Orders for Commissions, 1789–1893, State Department).

4. Nelson acknowledged the receipt of his commission on 2 Mar. (GW to John Page, 23 Sept. 1789, n.2).

5. Drayton wrote to GW on 16 Mar. 1790 that GW's letter of 13 Feb. enclosing his commission arrived on 14 Mar. (DNA: RG 59, Acceptances and Orders for Commissions, 1789–1893).

6. Lear sent Hillary his commission on 11 Feb. 1790 and requested acknowledgment of its receipt (DNA: RG 59, Miscellaneous Letters).

7. Lear sent Taylor his commission on 11 Feb. 1790 and requested acknowledgment of its receipt (DNA: RG 59, Miscellaneous Letters).

8. Lear wrote to Miller on 13 Feb. 1790, acknowledging receipt of his 1 Feb. 1790 letter of resignation and requesting return of Miller's commission to the president (DNA: RG 59, Miscellaneous Letters).

9. Lear sent Sage his commission on 11 Feb. 1790 and requested acknowledgment of its receipt (DNA: RG 59, Miscellaneous Letters).

To the United States Senate

United States [New York]

Gentlemen of the Senate,   February 9th 1790

I nominate as Collectors, Naval Officer, and Surveyors for the Ports of the several Districts in the State of North Carolina, the persons whose names are respectively annexed to the Offices in the following list.

Districts.	*Ports.*	*Officers.*	*Nominations*
		Collector	James Read
	Wilmington	Naval Officer	John Walker
Wilmington.		Surveyor	Thomas Callender
	Swansborough	Surveyor	
Newbern	Newbern	Collector	John Daves
	Beaufort	Surveyor	John Easton
Washington	Washington	Collector	Nathan Keais
	Edenton	Collector	Thomas Benbury
	Hartford	Surveyor	Joshua Skinner Junr (Son of William)
	Murpheysborough	Do	Hardy Murfree
Edenton.	Plymouth	Do	Levi Blount
	Win[d]sor	Do	
	Skewarkey	Do	Henry Hunter
	Winton	Do	William Wynne
	Bennits Creek	Do	John Baker
	Plankbridge on Sawyers Creek	Collector	Isaac Gregory
	Nixinton	Surveyor	Hugh Knox
Cambden	Indian-town	Do	Thomas Williams
	Currituck Inlet	Do	
	Pasquotank		Edmund Sawyer
	River Bridge	Do	
	Newbiggen Creek	Do	Elias Albertson[1]

I likewise nominate Samuel Shaw to fill the Office of Consul of the United States of America at Canton in China.[2]

Go: Washington

LS, in Tobias Lear's handwriting, with later annotations; copy, DNA: RG 46, First Congress, Records of Executive Proceedings, President's Messages—Executive Nominations; LB, DLC:GW.

Upon receiving GW's message, the Senate "ORDERED, that the Rules be so far dispensed with, as to proceed to consider," it immediately and passed in the affirmative "on the question to advise and consent to" each individual appointment in North Carolina. It postponed until the next day, however, consideration of Samuel Shaw's nomination as consul at Canton. On 10 Feb. 1790 Shaw's successful appointment was the first order of business. An "a" following each name on the list was probably added later to note that the nominee was appointed by the Senate (*DHFC*, 2:60–61).

On 11 Feb. 1790 Lear supplied Alexander Hamilton with an identical list of the president's appointments to the revenue department in North Carolina, adding: "The President of the U. States has likewise appointed the following persons to fill the Offices mentioned with their names which had become vacant by resignation.

"Comfort Sage to be Surveyor of the Port of Middletown in the State of Connecticut in place of Asher Miller.

"Christopher Hillary to be Collector of the Port of Brunswick in the State of Georgia in place of George Handley.

"Richard Taylor to be Collector of Louisville in Kentuckey in place of Peyton Short" (Lear to Hamilton, 11 Feb. 1790, DLC:GW).

1. After Senate confirmation of the North Carolina revenue officers on 9 Feb. 1790, Lear wrote to Roger Alden: "In obedience to the Command of the President of the United States, I have to request that you will provide Twenty Copies of each of the Acts mentioned in the enclosed Lists, that they may accompany the Commissions which are to be transmitted to the Officers appointed for the Collection of the Revenue of the United States in the State of North Carolina.

"As the Commissions will be ready to transmit by the mail tomorrow Evening it is necessary that the above mentioned Acts should be provided in time for that purpose.

"It is not probable that the last Act mentioned in the enclosed list has yet been printed—in that case it will be necessary that an early attention shou'd be paid thereto in the morning" (DNA: RG 59, Miscellaneous Letters). The enclosed list, entitled "Sundry acts to be transmitted to the Revenue Officers of North Carolina with their commissions," reads: "An act for laying a duty on goods, wares, and merchandise imported into the United States.

"An act imposing duties on tonnage.

"An act to regulate the collection of duties imposed by law on the tonnage of ships and vessels, and on goods, wares and merchandizes imported into the United States.

"An act for registering and clearing vessels, regulating the coasting trade, and for other purposes.

"An act to suspend part of an act Entitled 'an act to regulate the collection of duties imposed by law on the tonnage of ships or vessels, and on goods, wares, and merchandizes imported into the United States, and for other purposes.[']

"An act to Explain and amend an act Entitled 'an act for registering and clearing vessels, regulating the coasting trade and for other purposes.'

"An act for giving effect to certain acts therein mentioned with respect to North Carolina, and for other purposes" (DLC:GW). This last act, which repealed the suspended discriminatory provisions of the original tonnage and collection acts of 20 and 31 July 1789, imposed the same customs establishment on North Carolina as on the other American states, excepting Rhode Island, and established five collection districts and four ports of entry, was signed by GW only the day before, 8 Feb. (John Collins to GW, 18 Jan. 1790, n.2; *DHFC*, 3:289; 1 *Stat.* 99–101).

2. For Samuel Shaw's application, see Shaw to GW, 2 Jan. 1790. Lear sent Shaw's commission to Boston on 13 Feb. 1790 (DNA: RG 59, Miscellaneous Letters), receipt of which Shaw acknowledged on 21 Feb. 1790 (DNA: RG 59, Consular Dispatches). On that latter date Shaw wrote to his "best friend" Henry Knox, thanking him for "the care you have taken to have my appointment of Consul at Canton renewed. The commission arrived by last night's post, in a letter from Mr Secretary Lear, the receipt of which I have acknowledged. It does not differ materially from the former one—and indeed I did not expect it would—though it would have read more handsomely with the addition of—'and for all places east of the Cape of Good Hope.' Had such an addition, and a decent salary into bargain, depended on you, I am sure they would have been granted with more pleasure than they could be received. However, the commission is valuable as it is—and I receive it with gratitude" (NNGL).

From Louis Le Bègue de Presle Duportail

dear general   paris 10 february 1790
   new Connexions which I have formed with america make me take the liberty of writing to your excellency. twenty three persons and myself we have acquired some lands on the ohio and we propose to make a setlement there. for that purpose we agreed to Carry or send over a certain number of Cultivators. this is a kind of experiment, which if successful, will be followed by a much greater one, so that a large french Colony may rise florishing in a few years. two members of our society mr bart and mr thiebaut are the vanguard, they go to america immediately and are to land in alessandria the Country of your excellency. I have great hopes that you will look upon our project as advantageous to the united States and deserving to be protected; besides the bounty and favour which you honored me with when in america encorrage me to beg your recommandation for those gentlemen in alessandria and in any other part where you will think it proper.
   I don't propose to follow their example in this moment and Cross the atlantic. the critical situation of our affairs at home

does not permit it. but when they will be quieted, (if god grants us that favour) I intend to visit our Colony. it will be a great pleasure for me to see our people live in an abondance and happinesse which they could never hope in this country. besides I am impatient to see again america and persons (permit me, dear general to mention you at the head) for whom I shall keep always the greatest interest and attachement.

probably your Excellency knows the extraordinary events which have taken place here. we are also struggling for liberty. but I do not know if our success will be as Compleat and perfect as that of the american. there is a very great difference between a young nation and an old one divided almost in two Classes, the one Corrupted by extreme luxury, the other by extreme misery.

I must finish this letter by making an apologie for my bad english but I depend, dear general, upon your indulgence. Since I left america I passed almost all my time in germania, prussia, itali, and have been obliged to learn other languages, which made [me] forget the english. but nothing may alterate the sentiments of veneration and attachement with which I have the honor to be yours exellency the most humble and obedient Servant

·Duportail

ALS, DNA: RG 59, Miscellaneous Letters.

Louis Le Bègue Duportail (1743–1802) had served in the French army as an officer of engineers since 1762 when he was sent to America by Franklin in 1777 as "Colonel in Chief of Engineers" of the Continental army and promoted to brigadier general in November 1777. When the French army arrived in the United States in 1780, he was attached to it with the rank of lieutenant colonel and directed work on the trenches at Yorktown. Returning to France, he remained in the army and, through the influence of Lafayette, was made minister of war in November 1790. He resigned after Lafayette's fall. He fled to the United States in 1794 and died at sea in 1802.

Duportail's letter to GW concerns the affairs of the Scioto Company, the largest single enterprise of speculator and assistant secretary of the Treasury William Duer. In 1787 Duer, at the time a member of the Board of Treasury, secured a tract of land that later surveys showed to be over four million acres north and west of the purchase of the Ohio Company of Associates and bounded on the west by the Scioto River. Thirty shares were issued to a group of American businessmen including Duer, Andrew Cragie, Royal Flint, and Richard Platt. Payment was to be made to the Ohio Company in six installments at 66⅔ cents an acre after the survey of the land was completed ("Copy of Transfer of Land from [Manasseh] Cutler and [Winthrop] Sargent to Colonel William Duer in November 1787," in Belote, "Scioto Speculation," 65–66). In mid-1788 Duer and his partners sent the young Connecticut poet Joel Barlow to France to sell land to French investors. In Paris Barlow soon found an ally and business partner in William Playfair, an unscrupulous English speculator, and the two formed the Compaignie du Scioto, designed to peddle the company's western lands to unwary French investors. An inflated *Prospectus* was issued promising prospective settlers a veritable paradise, with cleared land and thriving cities. A group of French investors in the company, calling themselves the "Twenty-Four," was formed in Paris in January 1790, and some of the members, including the marquis de Lézay-Marnésia, the comte de Bärth (Barthe), and François Adrien Thiebaud. Some members of the "Twenty-Four" actually emigrated to the United States. The majority of the emigrants, however, were Parisian shopkeepers and other small investors, and over five hundred of them came to America in reponse to the Scioto Company's alluring promises. For their unfortunate fate when they reached the frontier, see Belote, "Scioto Speculation," 48–60. Congress continued to maintain the position that negotiations on the Scioto lands were between that company and the Ohio Company, and by the spring of 1790 it was evident that the Ohio Company was unable to make its own payments to Congress and the Scioto Company itself was bankrupt. The remains of the company disappeared in the wake of the 1792 financial panic. Eventually some restitution was made to the settlers. See Belote, "Scioto Speculation," 37–43; Davis, *Earlier History of American Corporations*, 1:213–53.

From Samuel Goodwin

Pownalborough [District of Maine]

Sir   February 10th 1790

there is A Great Crye for bread in thease parts; by the Drought, the last summer, the Crops was Cut Very Short and even Potatoes, som did not Get as many: as the Seed they planted as I have been in formed (& Repeated Complaints;): and but Little money in Circulation, in thease Parts, I Cant, Tell what many will do; and when any Neceassory: is in Demand, nothing but Cash, will fetch it; Except somthing that which will fetch Double: the Callamities is Great; God often brings thinge about; that mankind dont foresee nor think of: for their Good; I hope and Pray God: to appear for us all according to his Grace and Great marcy and when we are A suffering to whome Should wee apply too but to God: our heavenly father, and to our Temporal and, Political, father which I hope, will Excuse, and Pardon all Amiss &c. therefore every thinge that Congress: Can favour us in no Dout, they, will, all which is most humbly submitted by your Excellencys Most Obedient Devoted & Very humble Serv⟨an⟩t

Samuel Goodwin

N.B. there is A Great many Poor in thease Parts: and Pinch hard; (I dont escape) A Very Cold Country.

ALS, DNA: RG 59, Miscellaneous Letters.

Samuel Goodwin had written to GW several times in 1789 on the subject of customs posts in the District of Maine. See Goodwin to GW, 17 and 25 Nov. 1789.

From John Hancock

Sir   Boston February 10th 1790

At the request of the Senate and House of Representatives of this Commonwealth, I have the honor to enclose you some papers evidential of the encroachments made by the Subjects of the King of England upon the Eastern Frontier of this Commonwealth.[1]

If the papers transmitted do not give satisfactory proof upon this point, I wish that Congress would direct a mode in which a proper and speedy enquiry may be made.

A speedy investigation of this dispute may have a tendency to prevent a disagreeable contention which is likely to take place between the people in the frontiers of the two nations. I have the honor to be with sentiments of Esteem Sir Your most obedient humble Servant

John Hancock

Copy, DNA: RG 46, First Congress, Records of Executive Proceedings, President's Messages—Foreign Relations.

For background to this letter, see GW to the U.S. Senate, 9 Feb. 1790 (first letter), source note.

1. Among the enclosures was a resolution of the Massachusetts legislature requesting the governor to "write to the President of the United States in behalf of this Commonwealth informing him that the subjects of his Britannick Majesty have made and still continue to make encroachments on the eastern boundary of this Commonwealth, in the opinion of the Legislature, contrary to the treaty of peace; and that his Excellency be further requested to forward such documents as may be necessary to substantiate the facts" (DNA: RG 46, First Congress, President's Messages, Foreign Relations). In his letter to the

Senate of 18 Feb., transmitting Hancock's letter, GW described the enclosures as "copies of some of the papers which were delivered to you with my communication of the ninth of this month." Tobias Lear listed the enclosures in his letter to Roger Alden of 19 Feb.: "I am directed by the President of the United States to transmit to you—to be deposited in the Office of the Secretary of State, a Letter from His Excellency John Hancock to the President of the United States, dated Feby 10th 1790—together with a Resolve of the Senate and House of Representatives of the Commonwealth of Massachusetts—and sundry documents respecting the eastern boundary of the United States. The documents are as follow—

Extract from a letter from His Excellency Jno. Adams Oct. 25th 1784—

Nathan Jones's deposition—March 17th 1785

John Mitchell's—do—Octr 9th 1784

Generals Lincoln & Knox report relative to the British encroachments—Octr 19th 1784.

Letter from Rufus Putnam Esqr. directed to the Committee on Eastern lands, relative to the eastern boundary of the United States" (DNA: RG 59, Miscellaneous Letters). See also *DHFC*, 2:364–66, 367, 373, 368–73.

Letter not found: from Edmund Randolph, 10 Feb. 1790. In a letter to Randolph of 10 Feb. 1790 GW refers to Randolph's letter "of this date." He again mentions "your letter of yesterday" when writing to Randolph on 11 February.

To Edmund Randolph

Sir,   United States [New York] Feby 10th 1790

I have received your letter of this date[1] and Shall give it that attention which the importance of the subject, to which it relates, demands. When I have made up my opinion on the matter you shall be informed thereof—with very gret esteem I am Sir, Yr most Obedt Sert

G.W.

Df, DNA: RG 59, Miscellaneous Letters; LB, DLC:GW.

1. Letter not found, but see GW to Randolph, 11 Feb. 1790.

From Henry Knox

(Private)   New York the 11th February 1790

From the firmest persuasion of mind that you will receive this note with the same cordiality that it is dictated, permit me my dear dear friend to felicitate you on the return of your birth day.[1]

This effusion of an heart-felt affection, as far removed from a cold compliment to your present political station, as the extreme effulgence of the sun is to utter darkness, I could not bring myself to offer in person, well knowing my own weakness on the occasion.

May you live and tread the small theatre of this globe, while your health and happiness shall continue to render life desireable—but no longer.

I do not wish you long life as the greatest blessing, beleiving Strongly the immortality of the mind, and that the next grade of existence, will present you with joys, highly superior to any attendant on the best possible situation in this. I am my dear Sir most affectionately Your friend

H. Knox

LS, DLC:GW; ADfS, NNGL.

1. GW's birthday according to the Gregorian calendar (see *Diaries*, 1:6) was 11 February. Although by the early 1790s most celebrations were held on 22 Feb., in 1791 Boston still celebrated GW's birthday on 11 Feb., and the citizens of Alexandria were celebrating the old date as late as 1798 and 1799.

To Edmund Randolph

United States [New York] February 11th 1790

I have weighed with deliberate attention the contents of your letter of yesterday;[1] and altho' that consideration may result in an approbation of the ideas the[re]in suggested; yet I do not, at present, feel myself authorized to give a sanction to the measures which you propose. For, as the Constitution of the United States, & the Laws made under it, must mark the line of my official conduct, I could not justify my taking a single step in any matter which appeared to me to require their agency, without its being first obtained; and so far as I have been able to form a judgement upon the objects held up to view in your letter, they cannot be effected without the operation of a Law.

As an act must necessarily be passed to extend the Judicial Power of the United States to the State of North Carolina, it appears to me that a clause might be there introduced to establish that uniformity & precision in the business of the United States in each district, which you observe is highly proper to be effected—and to make such other regulations as may be thought necessary. I, however, only suggest this idea to you, that you may, if you think proper, mention it to such members of the Senate & House of Representatives as are acquainted with the subject, and thereby have the matter brought to view whenever the abovementioned act shall be under consideration. I am, Sir with very great esteem, Your most Obdt Servt.

Copy, in Tobias Lear's writing, DNA: RG 59, Miscellaneous Letters; LB, DLC:GW.

Randolph had accepted GW's offer of the post of attorney general but had not yet left Virginia. See GW to Randolph, 28 Sept. 1789, n.3.

1. Randolph's letter of 10 Feb. 1790 has not been found. For Randolph's controversial views on the reorganization of the judiciary, see his report to Congress, 27 Dec. 1790 (*ASP, Miscellaneous*, 1:21–36). GW had replied to Randolph's letter of 10 Feb. on the same day, stating that he would give the letter "that attention which the importance of the subject, to which it relates, demands. When I have made up my opinion on the matter you shall be informed thereof." Some of Randolph's criticisms may have been mitigated by the passage of "An Act to prescribe the mode in which the public Acts, Records, and judicial Proceedings in each State, shall be authenticated so as to take effect in every other State" (1 *Stat.* 122 [26 May 1790]).

From John Beckley

Sir,   12th feby 1790.

The subject of supplying certified copies of the Acts of Congress in the mode prescribed by a Resolution of the last Session,[1] has been mentioned to the House by the Speaker at my request, but no Order taken therein: I therefore do not consider myself authorized to furnish the Copies of the Act you require in that mode: but if the requisite number of printed copies, as the same are published, will suffice, they will be delivered to you on application to Messrs Childs and Swaine.[2] I am, Sir, Your most Obedient servant,

John Beckley.

LS, DNA: RG 59, Miscellaneous Letters.

1. In June 1789 the House had resolved that within ten days after the passage of each act of Congress, "twenty-two printed copies thereof, signed by the

Secretary of the Senate, and Clerk of the House of Representatives, and certified by them to be true copies of the original acts, be lodged with the President of the United States; and that he be requested to cause to be transmitted, two of the said copies, so attested as aforesaid, to each of the Supreme Executives in the several States" (*DHFC*, 3:82).

2. Francis Childs and John Swaine were the publishers of the New York *Daily Advertiser.* In May 1789 Childs and Swaine were chosen by Beckley and Samuel A. Otis, secretary of the Senate, to print the laws of Congress (*DHFC*, 3:75–76).

From Samuel Carleton

Salem: Mass: 12th February 1790

May it Please your Highness

It was my great Misfortune, not to be in a Condition to see you when you honourd this our town with a Visit.[1]

My Situation is, & has been for upwards of Twelve months, Confined to my bed, having lost the use of my Limbs, all which the Honorable B: Goodhue Esqr. can Verify; who I Expect will be Kind Enough to hand this to your Highness.

The purport hereof is to lay my Grievances & present unhappy Circumstances before you—Vizt—

At the time I quited the Army in April 1779, I was Intitled to a years pay as a Supernumery officer, my being confined by Sickness in an Hospital, put it out of my power to Claim or demand it at the proper time, & therefore the Commissr for Setling the Army Accots wrote me that he Could not pay me, but by being Subject to a Depreciation during the time it lay in the paymasters hands & before he returnd it back to the Millitary Chest.

At the time I was ordered to March with the troops & Bagage from this Town to Ticonderoga, to Suport the army under General Montgomery, I paid & Expended on the army, & Transporting the Bagage, the Sum of £150.16, besides Sundry Stores, Such as rum, Suggar, Coffee &c. which were Consumed on our March, & which Cost me £45.3.02d. out of which Colo. Brewer paid me £120—so that the remainder is Still due to me.

when I set out with the army for Ticonderoga I suplyd myself with all necessary Clothing, Implements of War &c., to fit me for the Service, which Cost me £106.1.2, all which were taken by the Enemy at Ticonderoga—all these demands put together would now under my dismal Circumstances, relieve myself, wife and Seven Children.

I have no Connections or Acquaintance with the Gentlemen in Public Service, and therefore hope your Highness will be pleased to take my Situation into Consideration, & order such relief as to your Highness Shall Seem meet.

with these hopes I ventured to address myself to your Highness with all Due Defference to your Exalted Station, Humbly to Implore your Condesention to notice me thus far as to order me payment or So much thereof as may afford me Some Support.

May God long preserve you Highness a Saviour to this Country in as Illustrious a manner as you have been its Deliverer is the prayer, of your Highnesses most, Obedient & most Humble Servant[2]

Saml Carleton

ALS, DNA: RG 59, Miscellaneous Letters.

Samuel Carleton (Carlton; 1731–1804) was appointed lieutenant colonel of the 12th Massachusetts Regiment on 6 Nov. 1776. According to Francis Heitman's *Register*, he was "deranged" from the army in September 1778 (Heitman, 116). After the war Carleton returned to Salem where he spent the remainder of his life as a semi-invalid.

1. GW visited Salem on 28 and 29 Oct. 1789 during his New England tour. See *Diaries*, 5:483, 484–85.

2. Lear replied to Carleton on 6 Mar. 1790: "The President of the United States has received your letter of the 12th of February; and in obedience to his command I have to inform you that it is out of the line of his official duty to take any part in the settlement of Accounts—and altho' he sympathizes with those who still feel the distresses occasioned by the late War; particularly where they were brought on by their exertions in behalf of their Country—and would experience a singular happiness in knowing that their losses were retrieved & sufferings were at an end—yet the impropriety of his interfering in any degree with the claims of Individuals upon the public is too obvious to escape observation, to say nothing of the impractacability of his attending to all the applications which would appear equally meritorious" (DNA: RG 59, Miscellaneous Letters).

On 17 Mar. 1790 a petition from Carleton was presented in the House of Representatives "Praying relief in consideration of losses or injuries sustained in the service of the United States during the late war." The House referred the petition to Secretary of War Henry Knox who reported on 18 May. The House ordered the report to "lie on the table" (*DHFC*, 3:333, 415).

Letter not found: to William Drayton, 13 Feb. 1790. In a 16 Mar. 1790 letter to GW, Drayton refers to GW's letter "dated Feby 13th." See also GW to U.S. Senate, 9 Feb. 1790 (second letter), n.3.

Letter not found: to Cyrus Griffin, 13 Feb. 1790. In his letter to GW of 16 Mar. 1790 Griffin mentions GW's letter of "February the 13th." See also GW to U.S. Senate, 9 Feb. 1790 (second letter), n.3.

Letter not found: to William Nelson, Jr., 13 Feb. 1790. In a letter of 2 Mar. 1790 to GW, William Nelson, Jr., refers to GW's letter of "13th of last month." See also GW to U.S. Senate, 9 Feb. 1790 (second letter), n.3.

From James Nicholson

Sir   Febry 13th 1790

pursuant to the request of Doctr Morrow I take the liberty of inclosing to your Excellency this Petition[1] and will at any time with pleasure if needed give you any information that has come to my Knowledge Relative to his Character, integrity, and abilities.[2] I remain with the greatest respect your Excellency⟨'s⟩ most Obedient Humbe servt &ca.

James Nicholson

ALS, DLC:GW.

1. David Morrow was apparently a native of Maryland. In the summer of 1776 Morrow sought appointment as a surgeon for Maryland troops, but before receiving word of his appointment, he accepted the post of naval surgeon under James Nicholson (*Md. Archives*, 12:132, 245, 289). Morrow served with the army in the winter of 1776–77 when Nicholson's crew formed an artillery unit while awaiting the completion of the frigate *Virginia*. Morrow was captured along with that ship and most of her crew in 1778 and after his parole served under Nicholson aboard the frigate *Trumbull*. He was captured along with the *Trumbull* and her crew in 1781. After the war Morrow settled in Port Royal, Virginia. His undated petition, enclosed by Nicholson, reads: "The Memorial of David Morrow late Surgeon in the Continental Navy—at present an Inhabitant of the Town of Port Royal in Virginia.

"Most Respectfully sheweth, that He the said David Morrow served in the Winter 1776–77 as a Volunteer Surgen to a Core of Artillery composed of the Officers and Men belonging to the Navy, under the Command of Captains Nicholson, Read, Alexander, &c.

"In Aprile 1777 He was appointed to the Virgini⟨a⟩ Frigate commanded by Capt. James Nicholson, He continued in said Ship, until she was taken. after which He was Prisoner on Parole Nine Months.

"In 1779 He was appointed to the Trumbull Frigate, under the same Commander continued aborard said Ship, until she was taken, after which He was detain'd a Prisoner aboard the Prison Ship, and on Long Island, five Months for the Veracity of which he begs leave to appeal to Capt. James Nicho⟨lson⟩.

"your Memorialist takes the liberty further to mention that He has been constantly engaged in His profession, for Twenty four years.

"your Memorialist encouraged by the before recited Pretensions and hopeing He can give satisfaction as to His moral Conduct—most respectfully offers Himself as Physician, or Surgeon, (which ever it may be call'd in the appointment) to the Virginia Marine Hospital.

"Hopeing for the Appointment (if ⟨no⟩ Person better qualifyed should offer) your Memorialist as in duty bound shall ever Pray and so forth" (DLC:GW). Morrow apparently was prompted to apply for the position by the recent completion of the marine hospital building at Norfolk. On 20 Dec. 1787 the Virginia legislature had passed "an Act for establishing a marine hospital for the reception of aged and disabled seamen," appropriating money for the building of the hospital at Norfolk (12 Hening 494–95). Commissioners appointed to superintend the construction contracted for the completion of the hospital by the end of November 1789 (*Calendar of Virginia State Papers*, 5:130). Meanwhile Congress considered the establishment of federal marine hospitals. On 20 July 1789 the House appointed a committee "to bring in a bill or bills, providing for the establishment of sick and disabled seamen, and for the regulation of harbours." The committee brought in a bill on 27 Aug. 1789, but the House postponed action on the bill until the next session (*DHFC*, 3:171, 172). Virginia authorities apparently believed that the federal government would soon pass a hospital bill and purchase the new hospital building from the state (see Edward Archer to GW, 21 Sept. 1789). The last session of the First Congress failed to take up the matter, however, and the establishment of federal marine hospitals was not fully authorized until the passage of "An Act for the relief of sick and disabled Seamen" in July 1798 (1 *Stat.*, 605–7). Morrow received no appointment from GW.

2. A letter to Edmund Pendleton dated at Port Royal, Va., on 20 Jan. 1790 and signed by a group of Port Royal citizens also supported Morrow's application: "Doctor David Morrow of this town informs me he understands no person is yet appointed to the Office of Doctor of the Marine Hospital at Norfolk, and that he wishes to be recommended to the Honorable the President of the United States as a person qualifyed for that Office. Doctor Morrow has applyed to us (as well acquanted with him for several years past) to recommend him to our worthy representative John Page Esquire, But as some of us have not the least personal acquantance with that Honorable and much respected Gentleman, Will you be so obliging as to vouch for us to him? You know us well, & we flatter our selves you can certify to Mr Page that he may put confidence in what we put our names to.

"We are Informed Doctor Morrow served his Country during the war as Surgeon in the Continental Navy, that he can make appear. We know he has lived in Port Royal about five years, in which time he has practised physick & surgery with much reputation: He has also behaved in other respects like a Gentleman & we believe him a worthy member of society" (DLC:GW).

Letter not found: from Edmund Randolph, 13 Feb. 1790. In a letter to Randolph of 13 Feb. 1790, GW states "I have received your letter of this morning."

To Edmund Randolph

Sir,   United States [New York] February 13th, 1790

I have received your letter of this morning,[1] and in consideration of the reasons urged in that, & a former letter I consent to your returning to Virginia; but hope that your absence from the Seat of Government will not exceed the time mentioned in your letter to me of the 5th inst.[2] With very great esteem, I am Sir, Your most Obedt Servt.

Df, in Tobias Lear's writing, DNA: RG 59, Miscellaneous Letters; LB, DLC:GW.

1. Randolph's letter has not been found.
2. Randolph's letter of 5 Feb. 1790 has not been found.

Tobias Lear to Clement Biddle

Dear Sir,   New York, February 14th 1790.

I have been duly favoured with your letters of the 9th and 10th inst.[1]—the latter enclosing the President's acct as it then stood with you.

In reply to your wish to know the President's birth day, it will be sufficient to observe that it is on the 11th of February *Old Style;* but the Almanack-makers have generally set it down opposite to the 11th day of the present Style. How far this may go towards establishing of it on that day I dont know; but I could never consider it any otherwise than as stealing so many days from his valuable life as is the difference between the old & the new Style.[2] with very Sincere esteem, I am, Dear Sir, Your most Obedt Servt

                                        Tobias Lear

ALS, PHi: Washington-Biddle Correspondence; ADfS, ViMtV; LB, DLC:GW.

1. Biddle's 9 Feb. 1790 letter to Lear reads: "I have sent the Bags to Trenton for the Buckwheat and expect them down when the River Opens & shall at same time expect a Vessel to be up for Potowmack by which I may forward it.

"Colo. Procter who Commands our City Artillery requests to know whether the 21 or 22nd Instant is the President's Birth Day as they propose a field Day and are not Certain some Doubts having been mentioned" (PHi: Clement Biddle Letter Book).

Biddle wrote to Lear on 10 Feb.: "After I had wrote you last Evening I recieved your favour of 7th instant and have procured the Boulting Cloth from Mr Lewis agreeably to the last Directions & it will go by Tomorrow's post to Major Washington at Mount Vernon as the Post Master will free it by the Mail.

"Inclosed is the Presidents Account Current to this Time—the Buckwheat not being delivered is not yet paid for" (PHi: Clement Biddle Letter Book).

2. Biddle wrote to Lear in his reply of 23 Feb. 1790: "Our River is Open and the Trenton shallop hourly Expected down by which I look for the Buckwheat and there is a vessel which will put up in a few Days on freight for Alexandria by which I propose to send it—Am I to Call on Mr Meredith for the seed Potatoes for this Conveyance.

"I am much Obliged by Your Answer to my Enquiry after the Presidents Birth Day we had Celebrated it here the 11th which I think was premature" (PHi: Clement Biddle Letter Book).

From Thomas Jefferson

Sir   Monticello [Albemarle County, Va.] Feb. 14. 1790

I have duly received the letter of the 21st of January[1] with which you have honored me, and no longer hesitate to undertake the office to which you are pleased to call me. your desire that I should come on as quickly as possible is a sufficient reason for me to postpone every matter of business, however pressing, which admits postponement. still it will be the close of the ensuing week before I can get away, & then I shall have to go by the way of Richmond, which will lengthen my road. I shall not fail however to go on with all the dispatch possible nor to satisfy you, I hope, when I shall have the honor of seeing you at New York, that the circumstances which prevent my immediate departure, are not under my controul. I have now that of being with sentiments of the most perfect respect & attachment, Sir Your most obedient & most humble servant

Th: Jefferson

ALS, DNA: RG 59, Miscellaneous Letters; ALS, letterpress copy, DLC: Thomas Jefferson Papers.

1. GW's letter of 21 Jan. had taken sixteen days to reach Jefferson. See GW to James Madison, 20 Feb. 1790, n.1.

From Wakelin Welch & Son

London the 14 Feb. 1790

Since ours of the 8th Oct. to your Excellency, we recd the Bag by the Packet & prior to our forwarding it, to Mr Young, we found that a Gentleman one Mr John Symonds a Neighbour of his, had during Mr Youngs absence who was then in France, the sole transaction of his Affairs, we therefore wrote him, he observd that he had receivd the Letters we had the hon⟨r⟩ of sending from You, & desird we woud forward him the Bag, which we accordingly did.[1]

On the r[e]ceipt of your Excellencys of the 25 Augt, directing Mesr Fenwick & Co. not to put up the Champaign we immediately wrote them, but as they so soon after drew on us for £49–3 without taking Notice of ours, are fearfull the Wine might have been shipt prior to the draft.

In the New York Capt. Dominick we have sent the Globe the Charge £28.19. with the Bill of Lading is enclosed[2]—Mr Adams presumes, as no Care on his part, has been wanting in the making the Globe in the most accurate manner, that it will be found to answer your Expectation. We are yr Excellencys Most Obed. Servt

Wake. Welch & Son

LS, DLC:GW.

1. John Symonds (1730–1807) was a professor of modern history at Cambridge and contributed numerous articles to Arthur Young's *Annals of Agriculture.*

2. For GW's terrestrial globe, see Wakelin Welch & Co. to GW, 8 Oct. 1789, n.1. The enclosure reads:

"Messrs Wakelin Welch & Son London Bought of George Adams, Mathematical Instrument Maker, to His Majesty, At Tycho Brahe's Head, No. 60 Fleet Street.

A 28 inch Terrestrial Globe	25:—.—
Quadt of Altitude	—:10.6
Adams on Astronomy	—:10.6
2 Large Packing cases	1:11.6
	£27:12.6

Shiping Charges & Bills of Lading Settled & paid" (DLC:GW). On the MS the sum for the two large packing cases was inadvertently written 11.11.6.

From Henry Knox

Sir, War Office [New York] February 15th 1790

The serious crisis of affairs, in which the United States are involved with the Creeks requires that every honorable and probable expedient that can be devised should be used to avert a War with that tribe—The untoward circumstances of the case are such, that no degree of success, could render a War either honorable or profitable to the United States.[1]

Events may be expected soon to arise which will interrupt the present tranquillity. The headlong passions of the young Creek Warriors are too impetuous to be restrained by the feeble advice of the Cheifs even supposing their authority exerted to that end.

But were the dispositions of the Creeks generally favorable to peace, the corrosive conduct of the lawless Whites inhabiting the frontiers may be supposed to bring on partial quarrels—These may be easily fomented, and the flame of War suddenly lighted up without a possibility of extinguishing it, but by the most powerful exertions.

A War with the Creeks besides being attended with its own embarrassments may lead to extensive and complicated evils— Part of the lower Creeks or Semanolies reside within the territory of Spain—and a strong connection appears to subsist between the Creeks generally and the Colonies of east and west Florida belonging to that power.

In case of a War with the Creeks, and they should be pushed to take refuge within the limits of either of the aforesaid Colonies, the United States would be reduced to a most embarrassed predicament—For they must either follow the Creeks in order to extinguish the War; establish posts in their country; or retire: In the first case, they would seriously be embroiled with Spain— In the second, the operation would be extremely hazardous and expensive—In the third the impression made would not be attended with adequate or permanent effects to the expence incurred by the expedition.

This subject therefore in every point of view in which it can be placed, has an unfavorable aspect to the interests of the United States—Acting under this impression my mind has been anxiously employed in endevoring to avoid if possible so injurious an event.

In examining the proposition of the late Commissioners to send the draft of a treaty for the Creeks to sign and in case of their refusal to declare War against them[2] it appears as if the measure proposed would inevitably precipitate an event which it is the interest of the United States to avoid—For if such treaty should be transmitted to the Creeks, with a declaration that they must receive and sign it, or War should ensue, it is highly probable that the latter event would take place by an irruption of the Creeks, long before the Messenger could reach the seat of Government.

In search of expedients to avert the evils impending on this subject, I have been led into repeated conversations with the Honorable Benjamin Hawkins Senator for North Carolina who is well acquainted with the influential characters among the Creeks—He appears to entertain the opinion pretty strongly that the designs and character of Alexander McGillivray the influential Creek Chief are opposed to a War with the United States, and that he would at this time gladly embrace any rational mean that could be offered to avoid that event—It seems probable to Mr Hawkins, arising from some former intimations of Mr McGillivray that he might at this time be influenced to repair to the seat of the general Government, provided that every facility and security should be offered for that purpose.[3]

In maturely contemplating this idea of Mr Hawkins, and confiding in his knowledge and judgement of the character alluded to, I am inclined to conclude that it is an expedient deserving of experiment—and that let its success be what it may, the result cannot fail of being honorable to the United States.

For although it is proposed the overture shall have the aspect of a private transaction, yet that it shall have so much of the collateral countenance of government as to convince Mr McGillivray, that he may safely confide in the proposition as it relates to his own and the other cheifs personal security until their return to their own Country.

I have shown Mr Hawkins the enclosed draft of a letter to Alexander McGillivray, it has received his approbation, and he is willing to copy and sign the same, adding thereto some circumstances relative to a former correspondence on some philosophical enquiries.[4]

The bearer of the letter ought to be a man of real talents and judgement—Although the ostensible object of his mission should be the charge of the letter, yet the real object should be much more extensive—He should be capable of observing the effects of the proposition, on the mind of Mr McGillivray and the other chiefs—He should be of such character and manners as to insinuate himself into their confidence—of obviating their objections to the proposition—of exhibiting in still stronger colours than the letter the ruinous effects of a War to the Creeks—In the prosecution of his designs he should not be in a hurry—but wait with attention and patience the symptoms of compliance—confirm them in such dispositions—and be calm and firm when opposed—And if after all his labor and exertions he should fail of success, he should be capable of giving a clear narrative of the means he used, and the obstacles which prevented his success.[5]

On this persons negociation, would depend much blood and treasure and in any event the reputation of the United States.

The objects therefore of the mission would require an important character who although not invested with any apparently dignified public commission ought to have such private powers and compensation as would be a sufficient inducement to a performance of the intended service.

The time which the proposed negociation would require might be four months or one hundred and twenty days—If the compensation should be eight dollars per day the amount would be nine hundred & sixty dollars—The expences would probably amount to four hundred dollars in addition—Should several of the Chiefs repair to New York, the expences for that purpose would amount at least to 1000 dollars—so that the expence of one thousand three hundred and sixty dollars at least; and perhaps 2360, would be incurred by the proposed measure—and this sum would be independent of the probable expences of presents and returning the Chiefs to their own Country which would require a much larger sum—But there cannot be any doubt of the oeconomy of the proposed application of the money herein required when compared with the expence which must attend a War.

The proposed experiment would probably be attended with either one or the other of the following consequences.

1st That it would be successful, and thereby prevent a War—

For most probably if Mr McGillivray and the other influential chiefs should embrace the measure, and repair to the seat of Government their dispositions would be sufficiently pacific to conclude a treaty, especially as no terms inconsistent with the principles of justice or humanity would be imposed on them.

2dly In case the proposition should be unsuccessful—The fair and honorable dispositions of the United States would be highly illustrated, and however great the evils which might afterwards result from hostilities, the executive government would not in any degree be responsible for them.

But as this transaction may be liable to the most unworthy imputations arising from some former local prejudices against Mr Hawkins in consequence of his services and zeal for the honor and justice of the United States while a Commissioner of Indian Affairs, it seems fair and reasonable that his conduct in this instance should receive its just approbation, and be shielded from all malevolence and misrepresentations.

I have the honor therefore humbly to submit the measure herein proposed to your consideration—If you should be pleased to approve the principal parts thereof, your direction appears to be essential on the following points.

1st Your approbation of my request to Mr Hawkins in writing, to copy and sign the letter to Alexander McGillivray.

2dly An ample passport for the protection of Mr McGillivray and such chiefs as shall accompany him from the time of their entering the limits of the United States to their return to their own Country.

3dly A direction to me to make the necessary expenditures of money in pursuance of the plan proposed, and to appoint a suitable person to conduct the business.[6] I have the honor to be Sir, With the greatest respect Your Most Obedient Servant

H. Knox
Secretary of War

LS, DLC:GW; LB, DLC:GW.

1. For the unsuccessful negotiations between Creek chief Alexander McGillivray and the commissioners sent by GW in the administration's attempt to avoid a war with the Creek, see GW to the Commissioners to the Southern Indians, 29 Aug. 1789, David Humphreys to GW, 21, 26, 27 Sept., 13, 28 Oct. 1789, Alexander Hamilton to GW, 20 Oct. 1789, and Knox to GW, 18 Oct., 21, 27 Nov. 1789. See also GW's Memoranda on Indian Affairs, 1789, printed

above. By early 1790 the three-way relationship between the United States, the state of Georgia, and the Creek and allied tribes was in a state of crisis. The raids by Georgia frontiersmen on Native American villages on the Georgia and Tennessee frontier and retaliation by the tribes brought the southern frontier to the point of war. The situation was further exacerbated by the Georgia legislature's 1789 sale of over 15 million acres of land to three land companies—the Virginia Yazoo Company, the South Carolina Yazoo Company, and the Tennessee Company. The land, portions of which were claimed by the United States, by Georgia as part of its colonial territory, by the Indians, and by the Spanish, and extending over much of what is now Alabama and Mississippi, cost the companies approximately $200,000 ("An Act for disposing of certain vacant lands or territory within this State," 21 Dec. 1789, *ASP, Indian Affairs*, 1:114). In early 1790, in an attempt to gain Indian support for the companies' ambitions, "Rambling Agents" of the Yazoo companies made an unsuccessful attempt to persuade McGillivray to accept shares in the speculation (McGillivray to William Panton, 8 May 1790, in Caughey, *McGillivray of the Creeks*, 259–63). Settlers had already begun moving into the area during the Confederation, under the authority of "An Act for laying out a district of Land situated on the river Mississippi and within the Limits of this State to be called Bourbon," 7 Feb. 1785 (MS "Journal of the General Assembly of the State of Georgia" in Library of Congress Microfilm of Early State Records, 212). In March 1790, as a result of Indian depredations evoked by increasing Georgian encroachment on Indian lands, the government sent three companies of federal troops to Georgia to maintain order on the frontier (Knox to Anthony Wayne, 10 April 1790, NNGL). The federal government took as strong an action as possible during the summer of 1790 to prevent the Yazoo companies from putting their plans into operation, offering assurances to Alexander McGillivray during the negotiations for the Treaty of New York that the companies would be disbanded (McGillivray to Carlos Howard, 11 Aug. 1790, in Caughey, *McGillivray of the Creeks*, 273–76). "An Act to regulate trade and intercourse with the Indian tribes," passed by Congress in July, provided that "no sale of lands made by any Indians, or any nation or tribe of Indians within the United States, shall be valid to any person or persons, or to any state, whether having the right of pre-emption to such lands or not, unless the same shall be made and duly executed at some public treaty, held under the authority of the United States" (1 *Stat.* 137–38 [22 July 1790]). For GW's warnings to U.S. citizens not to encroach on Indian lands, see his proclamations of 14 and 26 Aug. 1790, printed below.

2. Benjamin Lincoln, Cyrus Griffin, and David Humphreys, the U.S. commissioners to the southern Indians, concluded their report to Knox, 17 Nov. 1789, with the advice that "some Person should be dispatched to the said Nation with the ultimate Draught of a Treaty, to establish perpetual Peace and Amity, That when such a Draught of a Treaty shall be properly executed by the leading Men of the Nation, all the Presents intended for the Indians, and now in the State of Georgia should be distributed among them. That if the Indians shall refuse to execute such Draught of a Treaty The Commissioners humbly submit That the Arms of the Union should be called forth for the

Protection of the People of Georgia, in the peaceable and just possession of their Lands; and in case the Creeks shall commit further hostilities and depredations upon the Citizens of the United States, that the Creek Nation ought to be deemed the Enemies of the United States and punished accordingly" (*DHFC*, 2:236). The Creek policy adopted by the administration was considerably less bellicose.

3. Benjamin Hawkins (1754–1818), at this time U.S. senator from North Carolina, had served in the Confederation Congress from 1781 to 1784 and in 1786–87. His extensive experience on the frontier as an Indian commissioner and his correspondence with Alexander McGillivray during the 1780s made him a frequent source of information on Indian affairs on the southern frontier for the Washington administration.

4. The letter to McGillivray, signed by Hawkins, indicates the Washington administration's views on the treaty with the Creek. Hawkins expressed his "Surprise when I learned that the mission of three uninterested dignified Characters Commissioned by the President of the U. States to enquire into & adjust the disputes between the State of Georgia & Creeks have proved abortive! That the cause of the disappointment appears principally to be a disinclination on your part & the other Chiefs to form any Treaty with the U. States & that your Conduct on the occasion fully Supported this opinion. By your thus refusing to treat with the U. States when so solemnly invited thereto you have placed yourself & Nation in a new & Critical Situation. The U. States have offered to interpose & settle the disputes on terms of mutual advantage which had arisen between part of their Citizens & your nation the Creeks, & you have apparently refused to Submit the disputes to a fair hearing & decision.

"The main purport of this Letter is to place before you and the Creek Nation in Strong Colours, the exigence in which the Nation is involved, & to endeavour if possible to point out those evils which are impending & which you & the other Chiefs seem only to have power to Avert.

"The U. States cannot advance one Step further, they have already proceeded to the utmost lengths that could be required of them either by the principle of Justice or humanity, and they will not be responsible for any Consequences that may ensue however dreadfull.

"You and the other Chiefs seem desireous to preserve the peace. But you understand too well the feeble restraints your people are under to believe Seriously you can prevent partial hostillities, hence arises the extreme danger to which the Creek Nation is exposed. If you Strike, the U. States *must punish*, it will then become a Contest of power the events of which may be dissagreable and expensive to the United States, but the result must be ruin to the Creeks. . . .

"The U. States have the means of estimating properly the value of your Character. They are disposed to be favorable and friendly to You, but they Cannot Sacrifice their national Dignity and Justice. If then You Should be Seriously desireous of extricating the Creek Nation from their present embarrassed Situation, Manifest Candidly your disposition for that purpose, Come forward Yourself with a few of the principal Chiefs of the Upper & Lower Creeks to the President of the U. States, lay before him a real State of the

Case, & I will answer with my Honour & my life that you will be received & treated with, on the footing of Justice & humanity. . . .

"Receive this Letter with the Candour it is written & let your Conduct thereon be open & undisguised. Artifices of which your Enemies accuse you would at this time be ill advised and immediately detected, & the result would be as pernicious as the most bitter Enemies of the Creeks could devise. . . .

"Remember that the United States are disposed to be favorable and friendly to you and that I shall rejoice if my efforts Should prove Serviceable to your Nation" (Hawkins to McGillivray, 6 Mar. 1790, in Caughey, *McGillivray and the Creeks*, 256–59).

5. The agent employed by the federal government to carry Hawkins's letter to McGillivray and to observe its effect on the Creek was Marinus Willett (1740–1830), a New York merchant and a veteran of the French and Indian War and the American Revolution. According to an account based on Willett's papers, "the day after the arrival of the commissioners from Georgia, with an account of the failure of the negociation, General Knox called upon Colonel Willett, informed him of the circumstance, and the desire of the president to see him, which was complied with. By the president, Colonel Willett was given to understand, that suspicions were entertained that the people of Georgia were not friendly to a peace, but anxious to procure from Congress a force sufficient to subdue them; that by the statement of the secretary of war, it would require fifteen millions of dollars to effect this, and that a considerable portion of the troops were to be furnished from the northern strates. The president, at the same time, mentioned it as his opinion, that if a person acquainted with Indians, could enter the country, with such instructions as he would furnish, without the knowledge of the people of Georgia, a war might be prevented, and proper treaties entered into between the United States and the Creek Indians. The president closed with requesting Colonel Willett to undertake the mission" (Willett, *Narrative of the Military Actions of Col. Marinus Willett*, 96). On 10 Mar. 1790 GW entered a similar version of the conversation in his diary, noting that he had "a long conversation with Colo. Willet, who was engaged to go as a private Agent, but for public purposes, to Mr. McGillivray principal chief of the Creek Nation. In this conversation he was impressed with the critical situation of our Affairs with that Nation—the importance of getting him & some other chiefs to this City—the arguments justifiable for him to use to effect this—with such lures as respected McGillivray personally & might be held out to him. His (Colo. Willits) going, was not to have the appearance of a Governmental act. He & the business he went upon, would be introduced to McGillivray by Colo. Hawkins of the Senate (from No. Carolina) who was a corrispondant of McGillivrays—but he would be provided with a Passport for him and other Indian chiefs if they inclined to make use of it; but not to part with it if they did not. The letter from Colo. Hawkins to McGillivray was calculated to bring to his, & the view of the Crk. Nation the direful consequences of a rupture with the United States. The disposition of the General government to deal justly and honorably by them and the means by which they, the Creeks, may avert the calamities of War which must be brought on

by the disorderly people of both nations, if a Treaty is not made & observed. His instructions relative to the principal points to be negotiated would be given to Colo. Willet in writing by the Secretary of War" (*Diaries*, 6:41–42). Willett left New York on 15 Mar. and met with McGillivray at the house of an Indian trader "living at the Killebees" (Willett, *Narrative of the Military Actions of Col. Marinus Willett,* 96, 101). Willett was warmly received by the Creek, McGillivray finding him "a Candid and Benevolent Character, possessing abilitys but without Show or parade" (McGillivray to William Panton, 8 May 1790, in Caughey, *McGillivray of the Creeks,* 260). For Willett's own account of his journey and his negotiations with McGillivray, see Willett, *Narrative of the Military Actions of Col. Marinus Willett,* 96–113. The manuscript diary of his mission is in NN: Tomlinson Collection. In the course of his conversations with McGillivray, Willett assured the Creek chief that the administration had not credited reports that McGillivray himself was implicated in the Yazoo schemes "& it was recommended to the Georgians to revoke the Grants as it would farther embroil Matters & it appeared there was a view by that measure to drag the U. States into an Indian War, which if successfull after much loss of Blood and Treasure Georgia would reap the whole advantage. . . . After arguing the foregoing & adding further Encouragement he pressed much on the Necessity of my Accompanying him to N. York with a few Chiefs. Such a measure would certainly give us peace and Security; for a Treaty concluded on at N. York ratified with the signature of Washington and McGillivray would be the bond of Long Peace and revered by Americans to a very distant period" (McGillivray to William Panton, 8 May 1790, in Caughey, *McGillivray of the Creeks,* 259–63). On 1 June Willett set out "from Colonel M'Gillivray's house, at Little Tallasee, on my return for New York, accompanied by Colonel M'Gillivray, his nephew and two servants, with eight warriors belonging to the Upper Creeks, my man John, and several bow, and some spare horses" (Willett, *Narrative of the Military Actions of Col. Marinus Willett,* 110).

6. GW addressed each of these requests in his letter to Knox of 8 Mar. 1790.

From George Olney

State of Rhode-Island &c.
Providence 15th February 1790.

The period at length apparantly drawing near when it will be expedient to appoint the Officers of the Customs at this Port, permit, Great Sir! a most Respectful Applicant to approach you with the Hope of obtaining a Birth therein, which may prove a permanent Establishment for the decent support of a Family, rendered Dear to him by the tender Ties of Nature and Affection.

You may, perhaps, recollect the Person and Character of the

Auditor of Accounts in the Quarter Master General's Department at Head Quarters, who, in the Years 1779 and 1780, resided in the Family of the late, much regretted, General Greene; and who, and his little Wife, you condescendingly honored with a short Visit, at their Lodging in this Town, in the Spring of 1781: But should he have been forgotten, he flatters himself, that those Circumstances will recall him to your Memory; and that the knowledge you had of his Character then will not prove unfavorable to this, his present, Application. For my present standing in Society, I humbly beg leave to refer you to Mr Strong, Mr Wingate, and Mr Dalton, of the Senate, and to Mr Baldwin, Mr Foster, and Mr Ames, of the House of Representatives, who have severally been written to in my behalf. I have also the honor of being personally known to Doctr Johnson and Royal Flint Esquire, to whom and to Mr Morris, I have, some time since, addressed Letters upon this Subject; the two former are acquainted with my private Character, and the latter, I have reason to believe, will give you satisfactory information respecting my Conduct as Receiver of Continental Taxes within this State, while he presided at the Head of the public Treasury.

Besides an aged and infirm Parent to maintain, I have a Son and a Daughter who look up to me for Education, present Support, and future Establishment in Life. To be enabled to effect these desirable purposes, I have made two or three attempts at Trade, but for want of a Capital, they have proved unsuccessful; and I am discouraged from making another. Could I obtain, from your Benevolent and Impartial Hand, the Naval Office at this Place, it would, by a affording a moderate Competency, relieve me from my present parental Anxiety. If therefore most Revered Sir, your own knowledge of my Character and Abilities, added to the Recommendations above referred to, should be of sufficient weight to warrant my Nomination to that Office, you will, by doing it, confer a great and lasting Obligation upon an admiring and a Grateful Family, and excite in me the utmost attention to an impartial, upright and faithful execution of its Duties.

Necessity compels me to make this Application; but Deference and Respect induce me to give you the least possible trouble, and therefore admonish me to detain you no longer from the

Duties of your, justly merited, high and Important Station. With the most perfect Veneration, Respect and Esteem I have the honor to be, Sir, Your Most Obedient and Most Humble Servant

Geo. Olney

ALS, DLC:GW.

George Olney (1745–1831), a member of a prominent Providence mercantile family, served as auditor in the army quartermaster department under Nathanael Greene (Green to Ephraim Bowen, 21 Nov. 1778, Showman, *Greene Papers*, 3:79). In October 1786 the Rhode Island legislature appointed him agent to supervise the accounts of the state against the United States. He was later appointed receiver of Continental taxes for Rhode Island. In October 1789 the state legislature appointed him commissioner to receive claims of Rhode Islanders against the United States (Bartlett, *R.I. Records*, 9:256, 661, 10:364).

From William Peck

Sir,   Providence [R.I.] Feby 15th 1790

A Convention being at length Ordered and Delegates appointed for deciding on the New Federal Constitution, there are many reasons to hope that the Accession of this State will compleat the Union in a short time. That event will probably induce the Appointment of Sundry Officers for Collecting the Federal Revenue in this State. The Note[1] accompanying this letter will more fully disclose the particular object of it, and point out to your Excellency the Grounds of my present Application for the Appointment of Naval Officer of this Port.[2] With great deference and the Most perfect Esteem & Veneration I am your Excellency's Most Obedient Servant

William Peck

ALS, DLC:GW.

William Peck (1755–1832) describes his military career in the enclosure to this letter. He did not receive the post of naval officer for the port of Providence, which he requests in this letter. It went instead to Ebenezer Thompson. Peck received the appointment of federal marshal for the Rhode Island district on 2 July 1790 (*DHFC*, 2:83).

1. The enclosed "Resumé of Affairs," dated at Providence, R.I., on 15 Feb. 1790, reads: "Mr Peck joined the Continental Army in December 1775, as first Lieutenant and Adjutant in the Seventeenth or Colo. Jedediah Huntingtons Regt. In Feby 1776 he was Appointed a Captain—in the July following, he

was presented with a Commission of Major and was sent to Rhode Island as Aid de Camp to the Honble Major General Spencer the ensuing December. In August 1777 he was by a Resolution of Congress, appointed a Deputy Adjutant General, in the Rhode Island, or Eastern Department, with the Rank of Lieutenant Colonel—he held said appointment during the Commands of the several Generals Spencer, Sullivan, Gates & Heath untill the Arrangment of the American Army in December 1781, at which period he retired from service, his Compensation for the Depreciation of the Continental Money was paid him by a Note from the Treasurer of the State of Rhode Island, which Note by Act of Government was now forfeited instead of having real Estate as the other officers had set off to them. Upon peace being proclaimed he entered into a Mercantile pursuit in the Town of Providence—at the unhappy Establishment of the present paper Money Administration of this state, he judged it prudent to withdraw the small Stock which he possessed, from Trade, lest the fate of the Currency should Materially affect the property. A continuation of the same State politics, has obliged him to remain in the same inactive situation. The support of a family for four Years without business has nearly consumed the property he possessed. Soliciting an Appointment among the Revenue Officers he is Happy in having Assurances of support from almost every Gentleman of the Town of Providence who can claim any right to influence with your Excellency" (DLC:GW).

2. Peck also wrote from Providence to Henry Knox on 15 Feb. 1790, incorrectly predicting that the state convention meeting on 1 Mar. might ratify the Constitution and noting: "The Consequence of an adoption of the Constitution by this State will probably induce the appointment of Revenue-Officers for the Port of Providence—I have Already addressed the President of the United States upon the Subject; and have requested the honor of being appointed Naval Officer of this Port—I now take the liberty of Asking such assistance from you, Sir, in obtaining the appointment, as your knowledge of, or friendship for me, may suggest, at the same time assuring you that I believe there is no gentleman in the United States, to whose recommendation the President will pay more attention than to yours—I do not make this application without assurances of support from almost every Gentleman of this place who can presume upon having any influence with the President. I am happy to find the Gentlemen of this Town are Generally in favor of the Appointments in the Revenue, being given to the Officers of the late Army" (NNGL).

After Rhode Island's acceptance of the Constitution on 29 May 1790, Peck traveled to New York and presented to GW a letter of recommendation from Ezekiel Cornell of Scituate, R.I., 8 June 1790, and probably also those of William Greene, 7 June 1790, Joseph and William Russell, 8 June 1790, Welcome Arnold, 10 June 1790, and the firm of Clarke & Nightingale, 14 June 1790, all of Providence. These documents are all in DLC:GW.

To the United States Senate and House of Representatives

United States [New York] February 15th 1790.
Gentlemen of the Senate and House of Representatives.

I have directed my Secretary to lay before you[1] the copy of a vote of the Legislature of the State of New Hampshire, to accept the Articles proposed in addition to, and amendment of, the Constitution of the United States of America, except the second Article—At the same time, will be delivered to you, the copy of a letter from His Excellency the President of the State of New Hampshire to the President of the United States.[2]

The originals of the above-mentioned vote and letter will be lodged in the Office of the Secretary of State.[3]

Go: Washington

LS, DNA: RG 46, First Congress, Records of Legislative Proceedings, President's Messages; LB, DLC:GW; copy, DNA: RG 233, First Congress, Records of Legislative Proceedings, Journals.

1. Tobias Lear delivered GW's message with its enclosures to Congress on 15 Feb. 1790. The House read the papers after Lear withdrew and ordered them to lie on the table. The Senate also read the president's message on 15 Feb. but did not report it in its journal of proceedings under that date (*DHFC*, 1:348–49, 3:297–99).

2. John Sullivan wrote to GW from Durham, N.H., on 29 Jan. 1790: "I have the honor to enclose you for the Information of Congress a vote of the Assembly of this State to Accept, all the Articles of Amendments to the Constitution of the United States Except the Second, which was rejected!" The enclosed 25 Jan. vote of the New Hampshire legislature is signed by Speaker of the House of Representatives Thomas Bartlett and Secretary Joseph Pearson (DNA: RG 46, First Congress, President's Messages).

On 3 Feb. Sullivan again wrote to GW: "In a former Letter I informed you that, this State had agreed to the amendments proposed by Congress to the Constitution of the United States except the Second Article—I now have the honor to inclose a copy of the vote." The new enclosure has only minor differences from the one Sullivan apparently forgot he had already sent (DNA: RG 59, Miscellaneous Letters).

3. Lear transmitted the originals to the office of the secretary of state the next day (Lear to Alden, 16 Feb. 1790, DLC:GW).

From Theodore Foster

Sir,   State of Rhode Island: Providence Feby 18th 1790

Knowing your Excellency to possess that Benevolence of Disposition which so much contributes to the General Happiness of the United States, and in which all the Citizens of the Union so much confide, I cannot refrain from soliciting your Attention to a Matter, which though more especially interesting to Me personally, is yet attended with such Circumstances connected with the Public, as will I hope serve to apologize for the Application.

At the Session of the General Assembly of this State holden, at Newport, in September Last an Act was passed for levying and collecting, within this State the same Duties, and in the same Manner as in the United States, a copy of which Act for your Excellency's Information I shall forward by one of the first Packets bound from this Place to New York. By this Act the state was divided into two Districts for the purpose of collecting the Revenue Viz. those of Newport and Providence and it is probable that the same Districts will be continued in future.[1]

At the same Session of the General Assembly I was appointed by Unanimous Consent Naval Officer for the District of Providence. The Honorable Ebenezer Thompson Esqr. was appointed Collector and William Tyler Esqr. Surveyor for the same District which offices we now respectively hold. The object of this Address is therefore to interceede with your Excellency for our Continuance in the same Offices after the New Constitution shall have taken place here which we expect will be in the Course of a few Weeks.[2]

I am not insensible of what was once remarked, in the Reign of the Emperor Theodosius, by Symmachus the Prefect of Rome in a Letter to the Emperor Valentinian 2d *"That men of Honor could always be found to supply the Offices of State: that in order to discover them the first Step was to reject all Solicitors for Places and among the Rest would certainly be found people who deserved them"*. But as we are already in Office, by appointment of the Representatives of the People at large, and expect to remain under our appointments respectively until the Adoption of the New Constitution by this State, We cannot but hope that we stand on a Footing a little better than common Seekers of Office referred to in the above mentioned Quotation, more especially as it has been remarked that your Excellency in the Appointments to Offices, under the New Government has generally favoured those Elected by the States, where similiar Offices had been established under the State Governments. And as we hope that our Appointments from the state will be considered at least as a Recommendatory Nomination, having more Weight inasmuch as the Act before mentioned, which we were appointed to carry into Execution, was passed purposely to pave the Way for the Adoption of the Constitution by this State, and which has been faithfully executed in the District of Providence to universal Satisfaction, so far as I know, and in such a Manner as to bear the most scrupelous Enquiry.

I have been informed that Representations unfavourable to us, or to some of us, have been made to your Excellency you will therefore the more readily pardon the present Address or any parts of it which otherwise might appear as indelicate in being too lengthy, too particular or too personal, especially as relating to myself.

My Appointment to the Naval Office for this District which I now hold arose not by any Means from my having advocated or in any Respect adhered to the Measures of the prevalent Party in the Legislature of th⟨is⟩ State for Several Years past. It is universally known th[r]oughout this State that I have ever been considered since the introduction of the paper Money here as belonging to that Description of the Citizens, who have been called the Menority, As a Proof of this I beg leave to mention to your Excellency that the office of First Assistant, who is the Third officer in the Government of this State, became vacant, at the Election in May 1787, by reason of the Non-Acceptance of William Waterman Esqr. who was chosen by the People, in which Cases it falls upon the Assembly to fill up the Vacances, and as Mr Waterman lived in Providence, the Assembly informed the Gentlemen who represented this Town that the Persons whom they should nominate from the Menority should be chosen. I had the Honor of being nominated by Mr John Brown who was then a Representative for Providence and of being unanimously elected and on the Persuasion of the Representatives I accepted the Office with Reluctance knowing that my Political sentiments differed from those of a Majority of the Members. It had been a Question at the same Session of Assembly whether Delegates

should be sent to the Convention then about meeting at Philadelphia. It was voted by the lower House to send them, but negatived by a Majority of one in the Upper House before I took
my Seat as a Member which was the Day but one before the close
of the Session. At the Session in June following I introduced a
Bill in the Upper House for Sending Members to the Convention and was happy enough to obtain a Vote for it there, but
such was the Effect of Party Spirit and Party Measures that the
Lower House in their Turn then negatived it and no Delegates
were sent from this State—After the Proceedings of the Convention were published I was pleased with the General Tenor of the
Government, and did all in my Power to obtain a Convention of
the People for considering and adopting it. This induced the
Leaders of the opposition to the Adoption of the Government
here to counteract my Election with the People at large at the
next choic[e]. They succeeded on the Idea of my being too much
attached to the New Constitution of which I have been assured
by the Present Deputy Governor and other Members of the Legislature. Many of them however have since expressed Regret for
the opposition made against Me then, and I have the satisfaction
of beleiving that I now have the Good Opinion of the State at
Large having as a Proof of it received my present Appointment
to this Naval Office.

I was educated at, and had the Honors of the College of this
State conferred on Me in the Year 1770—I married and Settled
in the Town of Providence where I now have a Family. During
the most gloomy Periods of the Late War and the whole of the
Time that the Enemy had Possession of Rhode Island I was a
Member of the General Assembly for Providence and after having Served Six Years as a Representative on my Resignation received from the Town a Vote of Thanks of which I shall take the
Liberty of forwarding a Copy being the only vote of the Kind
on the Records of the Town.

Mr Thompson was appointed Collector at the same Time I
was appointed Naval officer of the District and with Respect to
Morality and integrity of Conduct is a Gentleman of most irreproachable Character. He was for a Number of Years a Merchant of Eminence in this Town before the War. He has served
with Satisfaction to the Public in a Number of important Offices
in this State Civil and Military. He was sometime a Representa-

tive for the Town in the General Assembly and during the War one of the Upper House a Number of Years. He is now Cheif Justice of the Court of Common Pleas in the County of Providence and President of the Town Council which offices he hath sustained with Reputation; His Loses by the War were great occasioned by his Property having been vested in the Continental Securities which depreciated to that Degree that he has been a great Sufferer and as he has a la[r]ge Dependent Family and is otherwise out of Business he seems to have some Claim for his Continuance in the office unless a more worthy Competitor appears which I do not expect will be the Case not to disparage any one.

Mr Tyler is a Gentleman Younger in Life than Mr Thompson—is married and Settled in this Town, he does now and for sometime past has sustained the office of a Justice of the Peace. From his Abilities, Vigilance, Activity, independent Principles of Conduct and agreeable Manners I have no Doubt of his Serving the Public with Reputation and Strict attention to the Duties of the office should he be continued under your Excellencys Administration.

The only objection to the Continuance of these Two Gentlemen in their respective offices here of which I have heard is that they have not been in Sentiment with those who were for immediately adopting the New Constitution without Amendments and in this respect have favoured some of the Measures of this State in procrastinating the calling a Convention—This I beleive will have little weight in your Excellencys Mind when it is considered that so large a Part of the People of this State have been opposed to the New Government—It is rather an Argument in Point of Federal Policy in Favour of their being continued in their offices as they now have the Confidence and Friendship of the State at large. To Continue them would therefore have a Tendency to concilliate the Mind of the State to the New Government and to obtain the Confidence of the People at large when they see that the officers whom they have elected and confided in are continued under the New Administration—On the contrary the appointment of any Persons to these offices who might Reasonably be supposed to be under the immediate Influence of some of the principal Mercantile Characters from their personal intimate friendships and Connexions would excite uneasiness and give occasion for Distrust. With respect to their Fidelity to the United States and to Congress in the Strict unremitted and uninfluenced Execution of the Duties of their respective offices should they be continued there is not in my opinion any Doubt.

I feel happy that amidst all the Difficulties attendant on the Supreme Executive Power of the Nation arising from Misrepresentations formed from interested Motives Deception can have no Place and that whatever may be the Event of this Application the offices will not be conferred on the unworthy or those who do not deserve Confidence. That this Address may appear to your Excellency in a favourable Point of View: That the Cares and Perplexities ever attendant on the Government of a Great Nation may be alleviated by that Just Return of Gratitude and Confidence due to him who employs his Life and his Talents in promoting the Public Good and that you may long be inabled to dispense to a widely extended and flourishing empire the Blessings of a Mild Just and Equitable Government enjoying the best of all earthly Treasures the Hearts of the People and that you may ever be happy here and hereafter and the Sincere Prayers of him who begs leave to Subscribe himself with the highest Sentiments of Esteem & Respect Your Excellency's most Obedient Servant

Theodore Foster.

ALS, DLC:GW.

Theodore Foster (1752–1828) was born in Massachusetts, graduated from Rhode Island College in 1770, and established himself in Providence as a lawyer. In 1771 he married Lydia Fenner, sister of Gov. Arthur Fenner. Foster served as town clerk of Providence from 1775 to 1787, and as a member of the Rhode Island general assembly from 1776 to 1782. Foster was appointed naval officer at Providence by the Rhode Island general assembly in the September 1789 session. GW gave him the same post on 14 June 1790 (see GW to the U. S. Senate, 14 June 1790). Foster declined the post, having been elected to the United States Senate on 12 June (see Joseph Stanton and Theodore Foster to GW, 29 June 1790).

1. "An Act for levying and collecting certain duties and imposts within this state" was adopted by the Rhode Island legislature in September 1789 (Bartlett, *R.I. Records*, 10:340–55).

2. GW received similar recommendations to continue Foster, Thompson, and Tyler following the ratification of the Constitution by Rhode Island on 29 May 1790 (see Arthur Fenner, et al. to GW, 9 June 1790).

To the United States Senate

United States [New York]
Gentlemen of the Senate, February 18th, 1790.

By the mail of last evening I received a Letter from His Excellency John Hancock Governor of the Commonwealth of Massachusetts, enclosing a Resolve of the Senate and House of Representatives of that Commonwealth, and sundry documents relative to the eastern boundary of the United States.[1]

I have directed a copy of the Letter and Resolve to be laid before you. The documents which accompanied them being but copies of some of the papers which were delivered to you with my communication of the ninth of this month, I have thought it unnecessary to lay them before you at this time.[2] They will be deposited in the Office of the Secretary of State, together with the originals of the above-mentioned Letter and Resolve.

Go: Washington

LS, DNA: RG 46, First Congress, Records of Executive Proceedings, President's Messages—Foreign Relations; LB, DLC:GW.

For background to the northeastern boundary dispute, see GW to the U.S. Senate, 9 Feb. 1790 (first letter), source note.

1. See John Hancock to GW, 10 Feb. 1790.
2. See Hancock to GW, 10 Feb. 1790, n.1.

From Joshua Clayton

Sir, Delaware Feb: 19. 1790

Agreeably to the Directions of the General assembly of this State, I do myself the Honor to enclose your Excellency their Ratification of the Articles proposed by Congress to be added to the Constitution of the United States,[1] and am, with every sentiment of Esteem, Sir, Your Excellency's Most Obedient Humble Servt[2]

Joshua Clayton

Copy, DNA: RG 46, First Congress, Records of Legislative Proceedings, President's Messages; copy, DNA: RG 233, First Congress, Records of Legislative Proceedings, Journals.

Joshua Clayton (1744–1798) was president of Delaware from 1789 to 1793 and after the adoption of a new state constitution in 1792 served as governor from 1793 to 1796. Trained in Philadelphia as a physician, Clayton served briefly as a surgeon during the Revolution and saw combat as an aide to GW at the Battle of Brandywine. In 1778 he was appointed a justice of the peace for New Castle County, and he served thereafter as a member of the Delaware assembly and state treasurer before being elected president of the state. Clayton was a member of the circle of conservative Delaware Federalists associated with Bassett and George Read. He was elected to the U.S. Senate in January 1798 but died after contracting yellow fever in the Philadelphia epidemic of that year.

1. GW had submitted the amendments to the Constitution proposed by Congress to the governors in October 1789. For the text of the amendments, see GW to the Governors of the States, 2 Oct. 1789, n.1. Although there had not been a significant Antifederalist movement in Delaware nor any extensive popular clamor for amendments to the Constitution, the Delaware assembly approved the remaining eleven articles proposed by Congress, including the ten amendments that ultimately formed the Bill of Rights.

2. Lear transmitted these documents to Roger Alden, chief clerk of the domestic section of the State Department (Lear to Alden, 8 Mar. 1790, DLC:GW).

Tobias Lear to Gerard Bancker

Sir.   United States [New York] Februy 20th 1790

I have been favored with your Letter of th⟨is⟩ date,[1] accompanying a Sett of the Laws of the St⟨ate⟩ of New York, as lately revised, which you sent for ⟨the use⟩ of the President of the United States, in pursuan⟨ce of⟩ concurrent Resolutions of the Senate & Assembly of ⟨the⟩ State of New York.

The Sett of Laws has been delivered to th⟨e President⟩ of the United States, who requests that his th⟨anks may be⟩ presented to the Honorable the Senate & ⟨Assembly of the⟩ State of New York, for this M⟨ark of their attention to⟩ him; and at the same tim⟨e he desires that you⟩ will receive his acknow⟨ldgements for your⟩ politeness in trans⟨mitting them.⟩ I have ⟨the honor to be with due consideration Sir Yr Most Obedt Servt

Tobias Lear
Secry to the Presid. of the U. S.⟩

AL⟨S⟩, N; ADfS, DNA: RG 59, Miscellaneous Letters; LB, DLC:GW. Material in angle brackets is taken from the draft in DNA.

1. The letter from Gerard Bancker, treasurer for the state of New York, transmitting the laws on behalf of the New York legislature, 20 Feb. 1790, is in DLC:GW.

From William Gordon

My dear Sir   St Neots [England] Feby 20. 1790

Though I anticipated the pleasure of hearing you would be chosen President; yet it was confirmed & increased by the actual news of an event, which expressed the gratitude & wisdom of the United States, in conferring their executive power & confidence on the person, who had never deceived nor abused it— no; not when he was tempted to it. The knowledge of *this* remains to be known by them in some future period. I wished for liberty to have divulged it, in a way that might have prevented all harm, & promoted real good by attaching the public voice still more to your Excellency. For though you may plead—your being *conscious of only having* done your duty; & may from thence with a profusion of modesty infer—that *no particular credit is due to you,* I am persuaded the world of mankind will join me in rejecting the inference. There are circumstances, wherein the discharge of duty deserves the greatest credit, excites astonishment, & is entitled to the heartiest commendations: or why does the general praise the valor, the fidelity, & the patient hardiness of his troops. As it is to be hoped, that you being the younger may survive me, you may restrain me, much against my inclination, from a publication that would shew—there are scarce any among the moderns or ancients who can compare with yourself in genuine patriotism: but I have taken care (as far as I can) that when you have made your exit, your reputation shall be exalted. However when that period arrives, may you hear the plaudit of our final judge in a—well done, good & faithful servant enter into the joy of thy Lord.

Your very obliging letter of Decr 23, dated 1789 instead of 1788, was recd the 16th of the following April, while I was at Ringwood in Hampshire. Immediately on my publishing the History,[1] I withdrew with Mrs Gordon from London to her brothers country house at that place for the winter season & to notice whether any opening offered for my settling again in the ministry.[2] On the 27th of that month we set off on our return for the capital, where I was busily & constantly employed in attending to the affairs of a London Annuity Society (for the benefit of wives when we leave them widows) of which I was a director. This detained me in town till the 3d of June. While thus detained⟨,⟩ I had an unexpected invitation to preach in this place as a candidate, & with a view of settling, if agreeable to all parties. The time for my preaching not being till the first Lord's day in July, we went upon a visit to Ipswich where we settled after marriage & lived for thirteen years. Such were the regards of my former people, that when I returned from America, had they been vacant, they would have urged me to a renewal of my connexion. When the time came for my preaching, I proved acceptable, & an invitation followed, with which I thought my duty to comply. In August we crossed the country thro' Bury & Cambridge (from the last we are 18 miles) to St Neots. The getting a house, the procuring furniture, making alterations & public services, have kept me so employed as to have almost worn me down. After the fatigue I had undergone, spirits & strength were well nigh exhausted. But we are now pritty well settled, tho' far from having finished, & I find myself capable of recommencing my epistolary correspondence. I trust your Excellency's goodness will admit of this account of myself as an apology, for my not writing sooner & hope the length of it will not offend. Your avocations being so many, & important, I cannot in reason expect that your answers will be either regular or lengthy; but when you have a leisure moment, I shall rejoice to hear in a few words, of the health & happiness of self & family, & that my letters are acceptable to you. Last year I sent a quantity of the seed of the true Turkey Rhubarb to Mr Hazard with directions for the cultivation of it. If he recd it safe doubt not his having mentioned it. I apprehended it might be raised with advantage in some parts of the United States.

I have charmed many of your admirers male & female, by shewing them your letter of Decr 23. Yours of Feby 23. 1789 was recd in May, & afforded me real pleasure among other particulars, by informing me of the then tranquil state of the country. I congratulate you on its continuance, & the prospect of its doing so; & hope that France will establish their revolution shortly on so solid & liberal a basis, as to enjoy similar tranquility. The marquis de la Fayette must feel himself extremely happy on the occasion. On the 16th of Feby I wrote you a letter from Ringwood, which I suppose Mr Field carefully forwarded by the ship Eleanor Capt. Magruder for Alexandria; who had the care of a case marked GW No. 1. Mount Vernon, containing forty two sets of the History for the several subscribers. The freight was paid. Mr Field was directed to send a set of the best wove paper, most elegantly bound, of which I begged your acceptance as a token of genuine affection; & to enclose in the letter the bill of lading. Your absence, engagements with Congress, & tour to Hampshire State, has prevented, I apprehend, my hearing of their arrival. It will give me peculiar pleasure to learn, that the History meets with your approbation for the impartiality of the writer, & the goodness of the materials communicated to the public. Lest I should trespass too much upon your time⟨,⟩ shall close with mentioning that Mrs Gordon joins me in most sincere wishes for the present & future happiness of your Excellency & Lady, & for your being spared & enabled long to preside in the chair of Congress, to your own growing credit, the increasing advantage of the United States (among whom I rejoice to find North Carolina is now included) & as an instructive pattern to European princes. I remain Your Excellency's most hearty friend & humble servant

William Gordon

⟨Be⟩ pleased to direct as before ⟨to⟩ Mr Thomas Field's No. 11 Cornhill.

ALS, DLC:GW.

1. For information on William Gordon, his *History,* and GW's involvement with the Virginia subscriptions for it, see Gordon's letters to GW, 24 Sept. 1788, and notes, and 16 Feb. 1789, n.7.

2. Elizabeth Field Gordon's brother was John Field, a prominent London bookseller.

From Maria Hammond

New York Febry 20th 1790

The Memorial of Maria Hammond of the City of New York— humbly sheweth

That in October 1789 Your Memorialist's husband Thomas Hammond of said City Mariner was captured by the British frigate Pomona commanded by one Captn Savage, near the Island of Bonavista on the Coast of Africa, his Vessel and Cargo seized and sold, and himself and pilot put in Irons and in that situation deliverd to the portugueze Governor of the Island of St Jago—

where they are now closely confin'd, and in the most deplorable situation—as more fully appears by a memorial from themselves inclosed.[1]

Your Memst conceiving that the imprisonment of the free Subjects of the United States and the destruction of their property by a foreign power, without any crime, to be a national insult—and therefore humbly prays that Your Excellency will be pleased to order such methods to be used, as may procure the said Thomas Hammond & Pilot their liberties—and a restoration of the property so unjustly taken from them.[2] And in Your Memorialist as in Duty bound will pray

Maria Hammond

LS, DNA: RG 59, Miscellaneous Letters.

1. Thomas Hammond's memorial was forwarded by John Duffy of St. Eustatius to Hammond's brother Edward in Philadelphia. The memorial, dated 27 Dec. 1789, signed by Thomas Hammond and John Hillard (Hilliard), and written from "Prisson St Augo," states that they "On the 28 of October 1789 about 3 leagues S.W. from the Island Bonevest Wass fired at Severall times by the Brithish Frigate Pomono Capt. Savage wass Brought too altho We Showed Our American Collours they Sent their Boat Emedetley on board & in a Moste Hostile Manner Obligd me & the Crew of my Sloop in their Boat With the Names of Damd Rebbell Rarskalls & on Our Cuming on board Recd the Same Usage On the 31 Instant I wass Put in Irons On the 1 Day of Novemr wass Set on Shoar in Irons with all my Peopple but One[.] the Sloop Wass brought to anker Near the Ship and wass thier Sold to a Mr Jackson we where Deliverd to a Portugeas Guard and Marchd three Leagues and than Put in Prison and bought Pilot and Self put in Irons where we Remaind Untill the 10 Instant without a Hearing from the Governer Or aney Other Offecer Altho Ofting Made Suplication we where then put on board a Brig. And Sent Down to this Island & thier Put in Prison & Should have Starved had It not bin for the Charitey of Sum American that Stopt hear for we are Confined and not alowed aney Provision Not Even Watter we hope that Your Honnor Will Consider Our Misirabell Situation and Relieve Us from Our Sterving State And Dema⟨nd⟩ Us from the Portugeas for We are boat Natives of New York and have bin Good Subjects to America the Vessall wass bought of a Capt. Todd of Vergina and formerley the Propertey of Mr Sinclair and Com⟨py⟩ Near Norfolk in Vergina wass Called the Brothe⟨rs⟩ Burden thirty Six Tons I had the Regester with ⟨me⟩ Granted by Governer Randolph the Crime for whi⟨ch⟩ we So Crewley Suffer Is that they found Dollars on Board Us takeing Up in four fathoms watter of ⟨the⟩ Reef four Leagues from the Island Bonnevest where the hartwell English East Indiman wass Cast away Near three Years ago there wass a Dutch East Indey Man Lost On the Same Reef Verrey Richley Laden Sum time before the Other Ship we hear Remain in Prisson and Most Humbley Beg of Your Honnours to have Compassion On Our Distresed Situation

and Relieve Us for we are to be hear Imprisond Untill May and than Sent to Lisbon" (DNA: RG 59, Miscellaneous Letters).

2. GW received Maria Hammond's letter the day it was written since on that date he had Tobias Lear send the petition to Acting Secretary of State John Jay, requesting his opinion as to what procedures should be followed and noting: "As the wife and friends of Captain Hammond are in great distress, a speedy operation, if any thing is to be done in the case, will be peculiarly grateful to them" (DNA: RG 59, Miscellaneous Letters). Jay evidently advised GW to make inquiries of Anseto Antone Freatz, the governor of St. Jago, Cape Verde Islands, since the president noted in his diary on 2 Mar. that he "Caused a letter to be written to the Govr. of St. Jago respecting the Imprisonment of a Captn. Hammond" (*Diaries*, 6:38–39). Tobias Lear's letter of 1 Mar. to Freatz states: "In obedience to the orders of the President of the United States of America, I have the honor of informing your Excellency, that the President has received a petition from Thomas Hammond Master, and John Hilliard Pilot of the American Sloop Brothers.

"They complain that on the 28th day of October last, about three leagues from the Island of Bonavista, they were seized by the Bristish Frigate Pomona Captain Savage—That their Sloop was sold, and they and their crew imprisoned for some time at Bonavista—That from thence they have been sent to your Island and detained in prison—That the reason assigned for this seizure was, that dollars were found on board the Sloop, which dollars, they say, were taken from wrecks on a Reef near the first mentioned Island.

"The protection which is due from the United States to all their citizens entitles these petitioners to the attention of Government. The justice of her most faithful Majesty, and her friendship for the United States leave no room to doubt but that every thing that may be proper on the occasion, would, on application to her be done.

"The President is desireous to be informed of the reasons which gave occasion to the treatment which these people have received; and in case your Excellency should not think it consistant with your duty to release them from Confinement, that you would direct them to be treated with such a degree of benevolence as the nature of the Offences with which they stand charged may permit" (DNA: RG 59, Miscellaneous Letters). The memorial was also submitted to Secretary of the Treasury Alexander Hamilton (Lear to Hamilton, 25 Feb. 1790, DLC:GW).

From Joseph Lawrence

Sir   Providence [R.I.] Febuary 20th 1790

As Officiers for the collection of the Public revenue in this State will (probably) soon become necessary, the object of this address is to solicit the appointment of Surveyor in the Customs for this Port.

For information relative to my charecter, and pretentions to this appointment, I beg leave to refer your Excellency to the inclosed paper, and shall only add, that as it has always been my study to promote the Liberty and Happiness of my country, so it is my ambition to be ranked among her servants tho' in an Inferior station. With the most cordial attachment to your Excellencys Person and the most profound veneration, I am your Excellencys most obedient & most faithful servt

Joseph Lawrence

ALS, DLC:GW.

Joseph Lawrence (c.1728–1811) was a Providence merchant and insurance broker. During the Revolution he served as a barracks master and invested in privateering ventures. His application for the office of surveyor was supported by a letter signed by 119 citizens of Providence, including many merchants. The letter described Lawrence as "desended from a reputable family on the west end of Long Island, and in the former part of life was in trade as a Merchant, and is well acquainted with seafaring business. His occupation, since the War, has been that of an Insurance Broker in this Town; which, since the decline of business, has yeilded but little for the support of a numerous Family" (Providence Citizens to GW, 20 Feb. 1790, DLC:GW). Following the ratification of the Constitution by Rhode Island, Lemuel Wyatt (c.1723–1807) of Rehobeth, Mass., wrote to GW recommending Lawrence for the post of surveyor at Providence, noting his "early Attachment to the Liberties of his Country and Steady perseverance thro the late war together with his Violent opposition to the paper money system" (Wyatt to GW, 1 June 1790, DLC:GW). After news reached Providence that GW had appointed Daniel Lyman surveyor at Providence, Lawrence wrote to GW asking to be considered for the post of U.S. marshal, describing himself as "intirely Destitute of Business" for the "support of a numerous Family" (Lawrence to GW, 18 June 1790, DLC:GW). The next year he sought an excise appointment (Lawrence to GW, 26 Feb. 1791). Both of these letters are in DLC:GW. In spite of these repeated efforts, Lawrence received no appointment from GW.

To James Madison

My dear Sir   Sunday Morning [20 February 1790]

I return Mr Jefferson's letter with thanks for the perusal of it.[1] I am glad he has resolved to accept the appointment of Secretary of State, but sorry it is so repugnant to his own inclinations that it is done. Sincerely & Affectly I am—Yrs

Go: Washington

ALS, NjP: Straus Autograph Collection.

1. Madison had undoubtedly shown GW the letter Jefferson had written to him from Monticello on 14 Feb. 1790. The letter reads in part: "I received your favor of Jan. 24. the day before yesterday; the President's of the 21st. was 16 days getting to my hands. I write him by this occasion my acceptance, and shall endeavor to subdue the reluctance I have to that office which has increased so as to oppress me extremely. The President pressed my coming on immediately, and I have only said to him in general that circumstances, uncontroulable by me, will not let me set out till the last of next week, say the last day of the month. I meant to ask you to explain to him the particular reason. My daughter is to be married on the 25th. to mr Randolph whom you saw here. His father will come only a day or two before that to arrange the provision we mean to make for the young couple, & that this may be perfectly valid it's execution must take place before the marriage. Thus you see that the happiness of a child, for life, would be hazarded were I to go away before this arrangement is made" (Rutland, *Madison Papers*, 13:41–42).

To Samuel Powel

Dear Sir,   New York, February 21st 1790.

I have the pleasure to acknowledge the receipt of a letter, which you have been so good as to write to me by the direction of the Philadelphia Society for promoting agriculture—and I beg leave to request your communication of my thanks to the Society for their polite attention, in the present which accompanied it.[1]

Among the advantages resulting from this Institution, it is particularly pleasing to observe that a spirit of emulation has been excited by the rewards offered to excellence in the several branches of rural oeconomy—and I think there is every reason to hope the continuance of those beneficial consequences from such well judged liberality.

As no one delights more than I do in the objects of your Institution, so no one experiences more real pleasure from every proof of their progress—among which it marks the discernment of the Society to have distinguished Mr Matthewson's improvement in the useful art of making cheese. With sincere wishes for the advancement of our agricultural interests—and, with great regard, I am dear Sir, Your most obedient Servant

Go: Washington

LS, ViMtV; copy, DNA: RG 59 Miscellaneous Letters; LB, DLC:GW.

1. The letter from Samuel Powel is dated February, but the day of the month has been omitted. It reads: "By the Direction of the Philadelphia Society for promoting Agriculture, I am now, in their Name, to request your Acceptance of an american made cheese, being one selected from the Parcell offered to the Society by John Matthewson Esquire of Rhode Island, with a View of obtaining the Prœmium offered by the said Society, & which was adjudged to him at a meeting on Tuesday Evening last.

"From the Number of Candidates for different Prœmiums who have lately laid their different claims before the Board, the Society has the Satisfaction to find that an attention has been excited towards some of the objects which they have held up as matters of public Utility.

"Not doubting that every Proof of the advancement of our Country in Agriculture and the usefull arts, will afford you Pleasure" (DLC:GW).

The cheese was produced by Joseph rather than John Matthewson. On 30 April 1790 Joseph Matthewson wrote to GW from Providence: "Emboldened by your known patronage of American productions, together with the late flattering preference given to my Cheese by the Agricultural society of Philadelphia, I take the liberty of presenting you one, as a testimonial of the great esteem which I have for your Excellencys character. I hope it may prove worthy a place on your table. Dr [James] Manning has been polite enough to engage to see it delivered" (DLC:GW). There were several Joseph Matthewsons living in Rhode Island at this time. GW's correspondent may have been the Joseph Mathewson of Coventry who served as a member of the Coventry town council and as a deputy to the Rhode Island general assembly (Bartlett, *R.I. Records*, 8:154, 530).

Letter not found: to George Augustine Washington, 21 Feb. 1790. On 5 Mar. George Augustine Washington wrote GW referring to "your letter of the 21st Ulto."

From John Carter

Sir,   Providence [R.I.] February 22, 1790.

On a Presumption that this truly distressed State is at length on the Point of joining the Union, and that a new Arrangement of Officers will in Consequence take Place, permit me, with all Deference, to ask of your Excellency a Nomination to the Naval Office for this District.

My Object, in the first Instance, *was* the Collectorship, and I had endeavoured to make some little Interest: But learning that a Friend, and a very meritorious Officer of the late Army (Col. Olney) had applied, I readily withdrew all Pretension.[1]

I have, for more than twenty years past, *served the Public* in the Capacity of Postmaster for this Town; to which Appointment I was introduced by my venerable Friend Dr Franklin, under whose Direction, in my youth, I became a humble Typographer.

The Business of the Post-Office here was never large, and of late years has proved so unproductive to myself, that I have been obliged to pay considerable Sums to the General Post-Office more than I have *yet* received, owing to the peculiar Embarrassments our Inhabitants laboured under, and an absolute Dearth of Coin, which was banished by the abominable Trash of this State, *called* Money. True, my Accounts *have been* backward; but, on adverting to our wretched and forlorn Condition, I persuade myself, from some Knowledge of your Excellency's Character, that this Circumstance will be viewed as proceeding rather from Misfortune, than Remisness of Duty. In more than one Instance, I have been reduced to the mortifying Necessity of borrowing from a friend in an adjacent State, to remit the General Post-Office; while a considerable Part of the Postage to this Moment remains uncollected of late, I have declined delivering Letters without Postage; this has injured my printing Concern, by giving Offence, and eventually served an antifederal Competitor in Business, to the Prejudice of my numerous Family.

Should this Application prove successful, I have it in Contemplation to resign my Commission in the Post-Office—as also to relinquish my typographical Business in Favour of a Son, for whose Principles and Conduct I can answer.

I mean not to trespass on your Excellency's Patience by a lengthy Epistle—well knowing that a Variety of Applications will be made. If, among that Variety, I should be so fortunate as to meet your Excellency's Approbation, an almost fruitless Toil of 23 Years on this seemingly devoted Spot will be considered as amply compensated—and during this Period I trust that I have merited well of my Country.

With the highest Consideration for your Excellency's many Virtues, and sincere Attachment to the Government over which you so worthily preside, I have the Honour to be Your Excellency's obedient and devoted humble Servant,

Jno. Carter.

ALS, DLC:GW.

John Carter (1745–1814) was born in Philadelphia and served an apprenticeship in printing with Benjamin Franklin and David Hall. He went to Providence around 1767 and worked with Sarah Goddard on the *Providence Gazette*. When Goddard moved to Philadelphia in 1768 (see Mary Katherine Goddard to GW, 23 Dec. 1789, source note), Carter became editor of the paper, a position he held until his death, and also proprietor of Goddard's print shop. He was distinguished not only as editor but as a master printer, assisting Isaiah Thomas in 1810 with his *History of Printing in America*. Carter's opposition to Rhode Island's paper money party is evident, but more equivocal was the support of his paper for Rhode Island's ratification of the Constitution (Miner, *William Goddard*, 84, 202). He had already served as Providence postmaster since July 1772. Carter did not receive the appointment of naval officer, but in February 1790 Samuel Osgood appointed him postmaster for Providence under the new government. He served until June 1792 (DNA: RG 28, Records of Appointments of Postmasters, 1789–1832).

1. Jeremiah Olney had applied for the collectorship at Providence as early as March 1789 and renewed his application in 1790 when it seemed certain that Rhode Island would ratify the Constitution. See his letter to GW, 16 Mar. 1789, and source note. He was appointed collector in June 1790. See GW to the U.S. Senate, 14 June 1790.

To John Hancock

Sir,   United States [New York] February 22d 1790
    I have been honored with your Excellencys letter of the 10th inst. enclosing a Resolve of the Senate & House of Representatives of the Commonwealth of Massachusetts, and sundry documents relative to the Eastern boundary of the United States. Previous to the receipt of your Excellency's letter I had laid this subject before the Senate of the United States for their consideration, with such documents respecting it as had been transmitted to the former Congress from the State of Massachusetts: to these I added your letter & the Resolve immediately upon their getting to my hands.[1] I have the honor to be Your Excellency's most Obedt Servt

                                            G. Washington

Df, DNA: RG 59, Miscellaneous Letters; LB, DLC:GW.
    1. See GW to the U.S. Senate, 18 Feb. 1790.

From Patrick Lemmon

Dear Sir   New york Febry 23rd 1790

I have came from beauretout County, in the State of Virginia to recieve pay fir my Service while in the american army under Capt. Thomas Price from Frederick Town in Mireland[1] and have made application to the board of War and my name not being found in the meriland Register, they have refused to pay my demand. my distress is great for I am advanced in years, Cripled by War and stand in great need of my Right. if you thirefore Sir would interfere in my behalf with board of War I will give the most convincing proofs of my Fidelity. I am Sir your old fellow Soldier and Faithful Servt

                              Patrick Lemmon

ALS, DNA:PCC, item 78.

1. In addition to his service with Capt. Thomas Price in the Maryland Rifle Company, Lemmon's name appears as enlisted in Moses Rawlings's regiment "for & during the War" and as serving as a private enlisted for three years with Capt. Philip Griffith's company in the 4th Maryland Regiment. He was "on Detachment with General [William] Woodford" as a waiter from April to September 1778 (*Calendar of Maryland State Papers*, the Red Books [Annapolis, 1955], no. 4, pt. 3, pp. 61–62; *Archives of Maryland, Muster Rolls and Other Records of Service of Maryland Troops in the American Revolution* [Baltimore, 1900], 302).

From Beverley Randolph

Sir.   Richmond [Va.] February 23d 1790

I received a letter from the Attorney General for the United States, informing me, that a question had been officially submitted to him, respecting certain Bills of Exchange, drawn by Oliver Pollock in favour of Beauregard and Cadet Sardet; and that these Bills had been taken up by Mr Daniel Clarke, agent for Mr Pollock, in the paper money of New Orleans, at a certain depreciation.

As I conceive the State of Virginia to be interested in this transaction, I take the liberty to request the favour of you, to direct copies of the Bills, and of any other papers relative to them, to be forwarded to me.

Should there be no impropriety in communicating to me the

nature of the question which has been refered to the Attorney General on this subject, I shall be much obliged to you for information respecting it. I have the honour to be with the highest respect yr Obent Servt

Beverley Randolph

LS, DNA: RG 59, Miscellaneous Letters; Vi: Executive Letter Book.
 For background to this letter, see Beauregard and Bourgeois to GW, 14 Oct. 1789, source note.

From Moses Stebbins

Wilbraham [Mass.] Febr. 23—1790

The Humble Petetion of Moses Stebbins of Wilbraham Originally Part of Springfield County of Hampshire and Commonwealth of Massachusetts

To yr Excellency George Washington Esqr. Presidant of the United States of America

Hond Sr, Being Inform'd of yr Excellencys Generous Dispsition—I Presume ask a Favour of yr Excellency—and that your Excellency May Not Be Impos'd Upon, I Will Give yr Excellency a True account of My Circumstances, I am a Man of a Small Interest, and a Large Family—I owe one Hundred Pounds of Money—and How I Came to Owe So Much, I Will Relate to yr Excellency, Which is as Follows—(viz.) In the Year 1773, I With Two of My Neighbours, Bought Some Land, of Mr Wm Burnet Brown of Vergenia[1]—My Part of Which Was a Little upward Fifty Pounds—the War Soon Commenc'd, Which Engros'd all Our attention—My Sons Which Were Seven, Were Early Call'd into the War—one to Roxbury—one at Tycontaroga—one at West Point—one to the White Plains—one To Providence—two to Guard Stores at Springfield &c. &c. all this While the Bond Was out of the Way—the Payment of My Sons Wages Postpon'd, the Money So Deprciated that it Came to Little—one Instance as a Specimen I Will Give—one of My Sons Had four Months Wages Due Which Was £20, Continental Money, Which When Consolidated Was But Twenty two Shillings and Eight Pence— thus was I Disapointed—Now the Bond is Brought up With Compound Interest for 8—or, 9 year Which Has Doubled the Sum—Money is Exceeding Scarce, Nothing Will Be accepted

But Hard Money—⟨*illegible*⟩ Still (If any thing Can Be worse) ⟨*illegible*⟩.

To Evince the truth of the foregoing (Since I am a Stranger to you, Tho' My sons Have Seen yr Excellency often) I Will Produce the Testimony of Two Captins Bolonging to the Same Town and Parish that I Do Which is as follows. We the Subscrbers Inhabitants of the Town of Wilbraham, and Neighbours to yr above Petetioner—Do Testify that the above Representation is True, and a man of Honesty and Industry.

Phinihas Stebbins
Paul Langdon[2]

I Could Have the Testimony of Numbers More If Need Be If yr Excellency Should See Meat to Exercise any Charity Toward Me under My Difficulty and Distress, Be Pleas'd to Commit it to the Care of Mr James Warner Conducter of the Mail[3]—and yr Excellency Will Relieve one in Great Distress—and Much Oblige yr Faithful Subject and Humble Sert

Moses Stebbins

ALS, DNA: RG 59, Miscellaneous Letters.

This is probably Moses Stebbins, Sr. (b. 1718), of Wilbraham or Moses Stebbins (1750–1825), perhaps the former's son, who served with Massachusetts forces during the Revolution.

1. William Burnet Browne (Brown; 1738–1784) moved to Virginia at the time of his marriage to Judith Walker Carter, daughter of Charles Carter of Cleve in King George County. Browne and his family lived at Elsing Green in King William County, Va., and in the early 1790s the Brownes' daughter Judith Carter Browne married GW's nephew Robert Lewis.

2. Both signatures are inserted in the manuscript.

3. A letter from Stebbins to James Warner of Springfield, Mass., 23 Feb. 1790, asking that he take charge of any communications from the president to Stebbins, is in DNA: RG 59, Miscellaneous Letters.

From John Glover

(Private)

Dear General   Marblehead [Mass.] Feby 24 1790

when I had the pleasure of spending a Little Time with you in Boston, I mentiond my particular Circumstances; the Loss of property, in pursueing the fishing business since peace, took place, to the amount of twenty five hundred pounds at least;

and my wishes to return again to Some public employment, but as there did not appear to be any opening at that Time, our Conversation ceased on the Subject.

By report from the Secretary of the Treasury, I cannot but hope if it Should pass, I might find imploy as an inspector of the revenue, for the District in my neighbourhood.[1]

If there should be an appointment, of Such an officer, will, your Excellency, permit me, to offer my Self as a Candidate, and if my pretentions to enjoy the office Should be found equal, to any others, that I might be indulged with a Commission, if in your Excellencys opinion it Should on finishing the Law, be Such an one, as I could hold with honor to my Self, & with advantage to the publice—I am Dear General with every Consideration & respect your Excellencys Obdt Hbl. Sert

Jno. Glover

P.S. Should the secretarys report, not be accepted, no inspectors will be appointed—any thing else your Excellency may think my abillities equal to will be acceptable.

ALS, DLC:GW.

After his service during the early years of the American Revolution in command of the Marblehead mariners and later with the Continental army, John Glover (1732–1797) retired from the army in 1782 because of ill health and returned to Marblehead where he served as a selectman, as a member of the Massachusetts Ratifying Convention, and as a representative to the Massachusetts General Court. On 15 July 1790 Glover again wrote to GW from Marblehead about the possibility of employment: "I took the liberty to write your Excellency of the 24th of February, last, when I flattered myself, by a report from the Secretary of the Treasury, I might find employ as an Inspector of the Revenue for the District in my Neighborhood, at the same time observed, that should the Secretary's report not be accepted; any thing else your Excellency might think my Abilities equal to would be acceptable.

"Yesterday God, in his Providence was pleased to remove, by Death, Mr Richard Harris, the Collector of Impost, for the port of Marblehead. That Office being now vacant, will your Excellency permit me to offer myself a Candidate, and if my pretentions to enjoy it Should be found equal to any others that may apply, that I might be indulged with a Commission, which should I be so fortunate as to obtain your Excellency may, with the greatest confidence, rest assured that the strictest Fidelity & Punctuality, in the Duties of the Office, shall be observed, and the favor greatfully acknoledged" (DLC:GW). Glover's application was supported by a brief letter from John Langdon to GW, referring to Glover as "a worthy honest man" (DLC:GW). Glover did not succeed Harris as collector at Marblehead, the appointment going instead to Samuel Russell Gerry (*DHFC*, 2:84).

1. Glover is referring to Hamilton's "Report Relative to a Provision for the Support of Public Credit," presented to the House of Representatives on 14 Jan. 1790 (Syrett, *Hamilton Papers*, 6:51–181). In his report Hamilton had suggested that the president appoint inspectors of the revenue to superintend collection of the duties on distilled spirits (ibid., 139–40).

From Christian Senf

Sir,   Rocky Mount So. Carolina Febry 24th 1790

Your benevolent and best Disposition gives me hopes you will with Kindness and Indulgment read this Paper. To make my Mind easy is the Motive of this freedom—How contented was I. And how much did I think myself rewarded for the Endeavours I have made, to serve to the Satisfaction of this, my adopted Country, when I recd so much friendly and hospitable attention from you, and your most worthiest of families, at your House. With Pleasure did I think of the Opportunity, you had so kindly given me, to shew You, that I was not superficial in the Business I professed. Happy did I finish my fatiguing Journey. But, I can not describe to you, what Effect Your Proposition, in Respect to the Inland Navigations, had on me, wherein my Name was not even mentioned—I found then, to my Sorrow, I did not possess your favorable opinion of my Abilities.[1] I believe, that good Man, General Moultrie, observed my Emotion[2]—My feelings would, after that, not permit me, to presume to write to You about a Business, wherein, I supposed, you only indulged me with Your kind Permission—your polite and condescending answer of last Octr to my Proposition to the United Goverment, has animated me to take this freedom to address you again. With a Man of your Penetration it would be Vanity, nay Presumption to disimulate—I will be candid—I blush at my Behaviour—I depend on the greatness of your Soul; and hope you will forgive me.

In the last War, it was my Disappointment, that, besides the Disadvantage, under which I entered the American Service, I never could have the Satisfaction to serve under your immediate Orders, to give You Proofs, that I was the Man in reality, what I professed myself—I did not recieve my Military Education in a Royal Corps; But I have had very able Instructors and many opportunities, as to give me both Theorie and practice. It was often painful to me, when Brethern officiers of our Corps assumed a Superiority of Knowledge, which was not founded on any thing else, but a National Prejudice, and mixed with too much Envy and Jealousy.

On a nice Examination there is an Impropriety in the Manner, I entered the American Service; but, it can not be called dishonest. It is now above twelve Years—At that time a very young Man—A Prisoner of War—Compelled, through Necessity, to enter into a Service of Mercenaries, which I heartily despised[3]—Not bound by the one; and left at Liberty to act, as I pleased by the other—Anxious for Promotion in a Military Life—The Capacity, in which I served, being well known to the generous Conqueror—He made me such kind offers and flattering Promises, which overcame all Scruples, which arose in my young Breast—I could no longer look on Him as my Enemy, but as my friend—I resigned my Mercenary Employment—Left the Rest to Generous Minds to forgive me for it—And became One in Support of Freedom; without acting against the Country, where I was born and educated. During these twelve Years, I may mention, I believe, I have done my Duty as a Citizen and as a Soldier.

In the year 1779 the State of So. Carolina honored me with a generous appointment, as Engineer of the State, for Life. Ever since that time I did not draw any Emoluments from the United States; although I allways served under the immediate orders of the Continental Generals with the army.

The Emolument of So. Carolina I found fully sufficient for my Support. Concieving it inconsistent to recieve two Emoluments. The funds were different—The Service was but one— After the War I never have asked for those Benefits Native and foreign officers are intitled to by the different Resolves of Congress. I had no Intention to demand them; as this State had provided for me for Life. But, after my Return from Europe, the Civil List of this State seemed very burthensome to the People; almost every where I heard Complaints of; Being one of the Number, whose Emoluments amounted to near five hundred pounds Sterling pr year, tired of the Complaints; and not wishing to be considered so soon as a Pensioner, I thought, I acted becoming a Citizen to retain my Commission, but resign my Emoluments, untill the State should want my Services: Having at the same time several flattering Views in the Inland Navigation Business to make a suitable Provision.

Since that, my only (but half) Brother, who followed me through brotherly affection, served as a Surgeon for Six Years in the American Army, and settled since the War on Mohak River, paid me a Visit the Summer before last on the Catawba River, where he took sick and died—He has left me now to my sole Care an aged Parent, a Widow and four very young Orphans, without any Property. I have used my utmost Endeavour to raise the Means for their Support; But, such is the Scarcity of Money and Distress in this State, that I can scarce obtain as much to carry on the Works of this Navigation in a very languid Manner, much less to obtain any thing for myself nor for my poor family.

I am sure, you feel for the poor Orphans—you feel for the aged Parent—A compassionate Heart like yours will readily protect me to obtain to what I may be intitled to as an officer of the United States. I make so free, to enclose three Papers.[4] They may be of Service—I have requested two of my friends at New York (one of them will have the Honor to hand this Letter to you), to recieve, what ever I may obtain from the United States like other officers, and apply it for the best Purposes for my poor family—Till I may be able to add to it by my Industry. I have wrote to the Secretary of the War Office on the same Business, and enclosed the like Papers—I hope, I have not forfeited my Right by not demanding it sooner—I pray to God for Success for the Sake of the poor orphans—For my Part, I shal allways think myself happy, to be honored with your good opinion; and of your Confidence, whenever my Country should intrust me with its Commands. I have the Honor to be with the highest Respect Sir, Your very humble and faithful Servant

Ch. Senf

ALS, DNA: RG 59, Miscellaneous Letters; ADfS, NN: Stauffer Collection.

In May 1789 Christian Senf had sent GW his proposals for a navigation scheme "from the State of New York to East Florida." See his letter to GW, 20 May 1789.

1. GW told Senf in a letter of 12 Oct. 1789 that while his suggestions on inland navigation appeared useful, there had been "during the past session, such a multiplicity of business of a pressing nature before Congress that they had no opportunity of attending to any matter which could admit of delay—and your proposition being of such a nature as not to demand an *immediate* attention to the exclusion of more urgent affairs, it can be laid before congress at a future period when they will take such measures thereon as their Judgment may direct" (DNA: RG 59, Miscellaneous Letters).

2. Senf had known William Moultrie (1730–1805) when the latter served in the South Carolina legislature while Senf was state engineer of South Carolina and during Moultrie's military service in command of the 2d South Carolina Regiment.

3. Senf was serving with the Hessians when he was captured at Saratoga and recruited into the American service by Henry Laurens.

4. The enclosures to this letter include a letter, 14 Oct. 1780, from Horatio Gates to Senf conveying Gov. Thomas Jefferson's instructions to survey the southern Virginia coast; an order from Lafayette, 8 May 1781, facilitating Senf's travel to North Carolina on business for Lafayette; and a certificate from Gates, 20 May 1784, certifying that Senf "did receive a Commission as Captain of Engineers in the Service of the United States of North America dated the 20th of October 1777. . . . And I do also Certify that the said Colonel Senf Continued in the Army of the United States from the 20th of October 1777 'till the close of the War, in the Course of which he has rendered Eminent Services by his Abilities as an Engineer, and maintained the Character of a brave faithful and Meritorious Officer." These enclosures are in DNA: RG 59, Miscellaneous Letters.

From John Fitch and Henry Voigt

[c.26 February 1790]

His Excellency the President of the United States the Petition of John Fitch and Henry Voigt humbly beg leave to represent

That being convinced of the Necessity of Establishing a mint for Coining of money in the United States and the necessity of Coining Copper Cents being so obvious we doubt not but Congress will Immediately order a mint to be established Should that take place we humbly beg leave to represent that each of us have been Educated and have followed the business of workers in mettles John Fitch as a Gold and Silver Smith & Henry Voigt as a Clock and Watch maker that their Forturnes during the War were Very similer than in easy Circumstances in life they both ingaged in the Gunsmith business altho unknown to each other and shared nearly similer the same fate being drove from their abodes by the Enemy and almost every thing destroyed by them and reduced by that means to penury which by industry since has been in a small degree repaired but by being over anxious to promote Useful arts into the World they have now expended nearly four years of the Pri[m]e[1] of their days to bring one of the Greatest impro⟨ve⟩ments into common Use, Viz. (Vessels to be propelled by the force of Steam) which they are fully convinced will be of the first Magnitude to the United States but they are not so sanguine as to expect immediate profits such as which they now need.[2]

This may further inform your Excellency that Henry Voight in his younger years worked in a Mint in Germany and is fully acquainted with every process reletive to Coinage. We doubt not Sir but the recommendations accompanying this will Satisfy your Excellency that we are capable of the Task and that our best indeavours will be exerted to give you and our Country Satisfaction—Should your Excellency be satisfied that the sacrifices which we have made will recommend us to the patronage of yourself & Country and would give us an appo[i]ntment to superintend Said Business your Petitioners as in duty Bound shall ever pray.

AL, in the hand of John Fitch, DLC: John Fitch Papers.

1. Fitch wrote "Prine."

2. John Fitch (1743–1798), a metalworker, was experimenting with applying steam power to river navigation. He was assisted, particularly in the construction of the engine, by Henry Voigt (Voight), a watchmaker. Fitch had sought financial assistance for the project from the Continental Congress in 1785, without success. The pair was not employed in minting copper coins (on copper coinage, see John Bailey to GW, 17 April 1790, n.1). On 5 Jan. 1791 Fitch and Voight again petitioned GW stating: "your Petitioners from an honest Zeal to serve their Country in her Distress, have reduced themselves to straitened Circumstances, from a State of Contentment & easy Living.

"That when they saw the Extent of their Wishes gratified by the Success of your Excellency's Arms in the Establishment of Peace they turned their Attention to the Completion of their Invention of a Steam Boat, by which they hoped to render an essential Service to the internal Navigation of the United States, and flatter themselves with the Idea that they have carried their Invention to such a degree of Perfection as to merit the Countenance and Encouragement of their Country.

"These Circumstances have emboldened your Petitioners to solicit your Excellency's Appointment of them as Officers of the Mint which they hear is to be soon established in the United States; yet they would not rely on these Circumstances so far as to solicit for an Appointment in which they could not do Justice to their Country in the Execution.

"One of your Petitioners (John Fitch) is a Gold-Smith by Trade and flatters himself that he could render essential Service to his Country as Assay Master & Superintendant of the Workmen in the Mint: The other (Henry Voigt) is perfectly acquainted with the whole Process of Coining and all the Machinery for the Business, & can make the Instruments himself; having worked in a Mint in Germany in his younger years, in which he flatters himself, that he had introduced some valuable Improveme⟨nts⟩.

"If these things are sufficient to claim your Excellency's Attention we hope to be able to give the most unquestionable Security for our Honesty and Fidelity in the Execution of the Business and as in Duty bound shall ever pray" (DLC: John Fitch Papers). Neither man was employed in the mint.

From Marx Christoph Graf

Augsburg (the Capital in Suebia)

Mylord!   febry the 26th[–20 March] 1790

The worthy Speech of Your Lordship of 8th Jany to the Congress, containing among other matters—accordg to the News Paper of Leyden No. 14 "mais je ne saurois m'empecher de Vous faire sentir l'avantage qu'il y auroit a donner de l'encouragement effectif tantal introduction d'Inventions nouvelles & utiles de l'Etranger, qu'aux efforts del'habileté and du genie, pour les faire naitre dans nôtre Patrie meme["]¹—give me encouragement, humbly to offer to your Lordship spinning Machines of my own inventions, not only of the Plan, which, accordg to the below Coppy I offer'd the 8th of this Month to my late worthy Masters Messrs Wilson Coram Wayne & Co. in Charlestown (where in the year 1769—I was Book Keeper) but also of another one, since invented, different from the former in the form, yet tending to the same purpose & service, either one of 'em spinning one hunderd threads of Cottun.² Besides those I can also provide Machines that spinn but fifty threads of Cotton, very compendious, & can be both managed & attended by single one person.

Not doubting but my inventions will answer the good intents and purposes of Your Lordship, I flatter myself with His most gracious reflexions, & ambitioning the condescending Commands of Your Lordship, I beg leave to remain with th'utmost veneration Your Lordship's most humble & most obedient

Mark Christopher Graf

The 20th of March the present came bak again from Holland with th'observation on th'outside to address it to London, no Paquetboat wenting as yet from Holland to America wch in his way could touch in England—as I suppos'd and wish for the benefit of the trade in generall.

As I since heard, there are Machines in England that spinn 4,

5, 6, to 1[,]ooo threads of Cottun & goes by Water wheeles, yet being exceeding precious & requiring the Situation of a falling Water, 'tis not anywhere applicable, besides that in proportion to mine, they'll require still superior expences, as many or more people, are untransportable, & mine are transportable & applicable in any house, storage, room, situated wheresoever, and can be made use of by people that could never afford the others— Besides that whoever is possessor in England of such large Machines, I dare say, will not part with the secret upon any Consideration, & if one of 'em does it, 'twill surely be for extorsional reward.

Copy, DNA: RG 59, Miscellaneous Letters.

Marx Christoph Graf (1740–1812) was an Augsburg textile manufacturer and merchant who frequently shipped fabrics to Charleston, S.C., merchants. Graf's attempts to expand his business activities outside Augsburg did not always fare well. Between 1792 and 1794 he was engaged in an extensive controversy with Augsburg authorities over a collusive transfer of shipments of cloth that a factory owner, J. H. Schule, had shipped to Graf to evade the Augsburg ban on imports (Clasen, *Streiks und Aufstände*, 229, 286).

1. See GW to the U.S. Senate and House of Representatives, 8 Jan. 1790.

2. Graf enclosed a copy of his letter of 8 May to the Charleston firm of Wilson, Coram, Wayne & Co. stating that Graf had just "finished inventing a Machine quit of my own invention, spinning one hundred threads of Cottun at once. Two of 'em want but three people, viz: one for turning each & one for attending both in order to mend a thread that breaks, and if four Machines are placed in form of a square, one person will do for attending 'em all, so that four Machines (that spinn together 400 threads) require but five people in all. The manegment thereof is very easy, & can be comprehended in less than an hour, and they can be imitated with few expences by any exact Cabinetmaker. The great benefit that can be rip'd by on every respect, you may judge yourself, and they'll still prouve more beneficial to you than to us, since you can employ negroes for attending 'em.

"If six Machines are bespoken at once, than the price of every one will be but fifty Pounds sterling, being three hunderd Pounds Sterlg for all six, half the amount thereof to be remitted with the order in Bills of short sight on London or Amsterdam, and th'other half or £150 Stg to be paid at their arrival in Amsterdam to my friend there such inventions not being subjected to inspections ⟨illegible⟩. . . . I remember a large Tree of berrys at Mr Gibson's School in ⟨Canhoye⟩. Those berrys are like those of Avignon in france, (but which is not, for, originally, they grew in the piranneous mountains of Spain) & others of Persi⟨a—⟩Now I must tell you Gentlemen, that those berrys are made the yellow & green colours of in all Chints manufactures of England, Germany for I deal'd in that article myself—It gives me therefore the greatest pleasure in the world to inform you that those berrys are such a great advantage for your Countrys & perhaps till yet as unknown as not car'd for by its inhabitants, at least it'll prouve an advantageous branche of trade for your goodself" (DNA: RG 59, Miscellaneous Letters).

From Henry Knox

Sir.   War-Office [New York] February 26th 1790.

In obedience to your orders, I have received the communications of Colonel John Pierce Duval Lieutenant of Harrison County in Virginia; the result of which I have the honor to submit to you.

The paper Number 1 is a representation from the field officers of the said county, on the subject of their exposed situation.[1]

Colonel Duval states, that there are five counties of Virginia lying on the Western waters exposed to the incursions of the indians, all of which are to the East of the Kentucky line—to wit—Monongahalia, Ohio, Randolph, Harrison, Kanhawa—That these counties have been permitted to keep out, for their immediate protection at the expence of Virginia, certain parties of scouts and rangers.

That during the last year the Governor of Virginia directed the said scouts and rangers to be discharged, in consequence of a letter from the President of the United States; a copy of which, with the letter from the said Governor, is herewith submitted—Number 2.

That since the discharge of the said scouts and rangers, the said counties have suffered great injury from the indians, and that Harrison county in particular has had fifteen persons killed, besides houses burnt, and horses stolen.

That the object of the said Col. Duval is that he should be permitted to call into service again, the said scouts and rangers; at the expence of the United States.

That the expence of the said scouts and rangers would according to his information, for the ensuing season and for Harrison County only, amount to three thousand, four hundred and fifty-one dollars agreeably to the estimate herewith submitted—Numbr 3.[3]

That this arrangement would give perfect satisfaction to the inhabitants of said county.

On this information it may be observed, that an arrangement

of this nature for one county involves a similar arrangement not only for the other four counties of Virginia, but for the nine counties of the district of Kentucky—all of which are exposed in a greater or less degree as Harrison county.

That it would be proper, that this representation, from Harrison county, together with the memorial of the representatives of the counties of the district of Kentucky, dated the 28th November 1789, requesting a post to be established at Great-bone-lick,[4] and the petition from the inhabitants of Miro settlement, dated the 30th of November 1789,[5] should be laid before the Congress for their information in addition to other papers of the same nature which you were pleased to lay before them on the 4th of January last.[6] I have the honor to be Sir, With the most perfect respect, Your very humble servt

H. Knox

LS, DLC:GW; copy, DNA: RG 46, First Congress, 1789–1791, Records of Legislative Proceedings, President's Messages.

1. See Harrison County, Va., Field Officers to GW, 2 Feb. 1790.

2. See GW to Beverley Randolph, 16 May 1789. For Governor Randolph's letter to the county lieutenants, informing them that scouts and rangers could be discharged, see Representatives of Ohio, Monongahela, Harrison, and Randolph Counties, Virginia, to GW, 12 Dec. 1789, n.2.

3. This enclosure, signed by Knox, reads: "An Estimate of the Expence of a guard of one Captain and 30 Rangers, and eight men termed Scouts for the period of seven months, required by the Lieutenant of Harrison County for the protection of the same against the depredations of parties of Indians—the Estimate being formed from information given to the Subscriber by Colonel Duval, the Lieutenant of said County.

40 rations	@ 6d. per day	£ 214.
The pay of 1 Captain for 7 months at 35 dollars per month		73.10.
The pay of 2 Serjeants for 7 Months at 6 dollars per month		25. 4.
The pay of 28 privates for the same period at 4½ dollars per month		264.12.
The pay of 8 Scouts for 7 Months say 214 days @ 5/ per day		428.
Powder & lead furnished by Government suppose		30.
		£1035. 6.
		or 3451 Dollars

"If protection be given to the other four Counties of Virginia, and the nine Counties of the district of Kentuckey, and the same be estimated on the above scale—the expence would amount to 48,314 Dollars" (DLC:GW).

4. See David Ross to GW, 28 Nov. 1789, n.2.

5. See Citizens of Mero District, North Carolina, to GW, 30 Nov. 1789.

6. Knox is probably referring to GW's letter to the Senate and House of Representatives of 11 Jan. 1790.

To Beverley Randolph

Sir,   United States [New York] Feby 26th 1790.

I have received your Excellency's letter of the 13th inst.[1] enclosing the duplicate of an act of the General Assembly of Virginia, authorizing the Governor to convey certain lands to the United States for the purpose of building a Light-House.

Upon receiving your letter of the 18th of December, covering the first copy of the above act, I immediately transmitted it to the Secretary of the Treasury of the United States for his information.[2] This is the cause of its not having been regularly acknowledged. with very great esteem I have the honor to be Your Excellency's most Obedt Servt.

Df, DNA: RG 59, Miscellaneous Letters; LB, DLC:GW.

1. Randolph wrote from Richmond, Va., on 13 Feb. 1790: "I have had the honor to receive Your favour of the 29th of January.

"As you have mentioned in none of your Communications the receipt of my letter of the 18th of December, covering an act of the General Assembly of Virginia, authorizing the Governor to convey certain lands to the United States for the purpose of building a Light-House, I take the liberty now to inclose you a duplicate of the act. Whenever the particular spot shall be marked on which the Light-House is to be erected I shall agreeable to the abovementioned Act, be ready to execute the Deed of Cession" (DNA: RG 59, Miscellaneous Letters). The act of the Virginia assembly enclosed by Randolph was "An Act authorizing the Governor of this Commonwealth, to convey certain land to the United States, for the purpose of building a Light-House" (13 Hening 3–4; *Journals of the Council of State of Virginia*, 5:144–45).

2. The act was forwarded to Hamilton in a letter from Tobias Lear, 5 Jan. 1790 (DNA: RG 26, "Segregated" Lighthouse Records).

From Josef Ignacio de Viar

Sir.   New York Febry 26th 1790

I have just now Receiv'd three letters for your Excellency under Cover of the Post-master General of St Augustin at East Florida, which I have the honor of sending to your Excellency herein enclosed without losing the least time.[1] Sir I am with great Regard and esteem Your Exellency's most obt and humble Servt

Joseph Ignat[iu]s Viar

ALS, DNA: RG 59, Notes from Foreign Missions.

1. These letters have not been identified, but one of the letters was addressed to Joseph Barrell, a New York merchant. Tobias Lear wrote Barrell on 27 Feb. that the letter transmitted by the Spanish chargé d'affaires "was under a cover directed to the President of Congress of the United States, and accompanied by a letter addressed in the same manner, which I herewith enclose that you may see the cause of your letter being conveyed through this channel" (DLC:GW).

From Edward Hand

Sir   Philad[elphi]a 27th Feby 1790
I hope your Excelly will excuse the liberty I take in sending you the inclosed,[1] and believe me to be, with every Sentiment of respect your Excellencies most obedient and most humble Servant

Edwd Hand

ALS, DNA: RG 59, Miscellaneous Letters.

Edward Hand (1744–1802) came to America from Ireland in 1767 as surgeon's mate of Col. William Thompson's regiment of riflemen. In 1772 he resigned from the British army to practice medicine in Lancaster, Pennsylvania. He served in the Continental army throughout the war, becoming a brigadier general in 1777 and adjutant general in January 1781. After the war Hand returned to the practice of medicine in Lancaster and served in the Confederation Congress in 1784 and 1785. Under the new government he was active in Federalist politics both in Pennsylvania and on a national level.

1. The enclosures have not been identified. On 3 Mar. GW replied to Hand's letter: "I have received your letter of the 27th Ulto with its enclosures; and must request you to accept my thanks for your trouble in transmitting the same to me" (DNA: RG 59, Miscellaneous Letters).

From Alexander Martin

Sir,   North Carolina Rockingham Feby 27th 1790
Permit me to call your attention a moment from the weighty Concerns of the United States to the appointment of officers of the federal Court of this State, a Business I had determined not to interfere in, as the Senators and Representatives were generally acquainted with the several Law Characters among us who might be Candidates for offices in the same, making no doubt

but these Gentlemen will recommend proper men to your Notice on this occasion; but I am sollicited by two young Gentlemen
and their Friends to introduce them to you for the appointment
of attorney-general; Mr John Hamilton of Edenton,[1] and Mr
John Hay of Fayette Ville.[2] Mr Hamilton I have but little acquaintance with, but am informed he is a man of Learning and
abilities, and has been in the practice of the Law for some Time
past with tolerable Success.

Mr Hay I have been acquainted with for some years past, and
know him to be a man of Learning, to be possessed of considerable Law Knowledge for the Time of his practice, and appears
to be a rising Character. As it would be very agreeable to our
Citizens, late a very divided people as to the new federal government, to have the federal officers distributed through the State
for the sake of Convenience, as well as public Information to be
derived from them, the Residence of Mr Hay at Fayette Ville
where our late assemblies have convened, would well answer the
Wishes of the Western Inhabitants of this State, that he should
hold that appointment. This I expect will accord with the arrangements of the Court not doubting but two places will be
appointed for that purpose, perhaps Edenton, or Newbern on
the Sea-Board, though Newbern is the more central on that
Quarter, and Fayette Ville to the Westward.

I have declined to mention first the Judge, as I flatter myself
the Senators and Representatives of the State will unanimously
recommend Mr James Iredell of Edenton for that office, who I
am sensible will fill it with Reputation, and give general Satisfaction.[3]

While I am on this Subject, if the Register be in your appointment, not having the Law I am uncertain, I beg Leave to mention Mr William Hooper Junr of Hillsborough for that office, a
respectable young Man Son of Mr Hooper member of Congress
in 1775[4]—and Mr William Barry Grove of Fayette Ville for marshall, a young man of considerable Merit.[5]

I shall not intrude further on the great Duties of your important Station, having nothing more to communicate, but with
Sentiments of the highest Respect, I have the Honour to be Sir,
your most obedient humble Servant

Alex: Martin

ALS, DLC:GW.

1. For John C. Hamilton's application for office, see his letter to GW, 8 Feb. 1790.

2. John Hay (c.1757–1809) came to America from Ireland in 1779 after purchasing almost three thousand acres of land in Duplin County, North Carolina. Already educated in the law in Ireland, Hay was admitted to the North Carolina bar in 1783. During the 1780s he held a number of local offices and from 1784 to 1805 served intermittently as a member of the North Carolina general assembly. He received no federal appointment (Powell, *Dictionary of North Carolina Biography*, 3:81–82).

3. For an earlier recommendation of Iredell, see Hugh Williamson to GW, 19 Sept. 1789.

4. William Hooper (1742–1790) was one of North Carolina's most prominent Revolutionary War politicians and a signer of the Declaration of Independence (see Powell, *Dictionary of North Carolina Biography*, 3:199–202). His son, William Hooper, Jr., received no federal appointment and later became a North Carolina merchant.

5. William Barry Grove (1764–1818) became register for Fayette County in 1784 and served in the North Carolina House of Commons in 1786, 1788, and 1789. In 1791 he was elected to Congress and served until 1803. He received no appointment from GW (ibid., 2:381–82).

Tobias Lear to Daniel Grant

Sir,   New York, February 28th 1790.

About 3 or 4 weeks ago I wrote to Philadelphia to know if a good Cook could be had from that City for the family of the President of the United States—I received for answer that a complete one could not be found there at that time,[1] but that it was probable one might be obtained from Baltimore, and Mr Moyston had accordingly written to Baltimore for one who had lately gone thither from Philada. As I have received no information since upon the subject, and it being necessary that we should have a complete Cook established in the family (being now obliged to employ a temporary one) the President has directed me to write to you upon the subject—requesting that you will be so obliging as to inform me whether a person could be obtained from Baltimore, who perfectly understands the business of cookery in all its branches and is in other respects qualified to come into this family. The qualifications necessary, besides skill in the business, are honesty, sobriety, and good dispositions—The person who may come in this capacity will be wholly confined to the duties of a Cook—If you know any person of the above description, and who, from your own judgment, you may think competent to this place, you will oblige me by giving immediate information thereof,[2] and at the same time let me know precisely the terms upon which he would engage.[3] I am Sir, your most obedt Servt

T. Lear

S. P. U. S.

LB, DLC:GW.

1. In a postscript to a letter of 7 Feb. 1790, Lear wrote to Clement Biddle: "I will thank you, if it is not giving too much trouble, to let me know if a compleat Cook can be had in Philadelphia, for the President—a competent & compleat knowledge of *Cookery* is all that is requisite in such a person—we have a Steward—&c. Mr [Edward] Moyston would probably be able to give information on this subject—The wages that will be expected by a Cook would be proper to be known also" (PHi: Washington-Biddle Correspondence). Biddle replied to Lear's query on 10 Feb. 1790: "I enqu[i]red of Mr Moysten for a Cook he Knows of none at present that will Answer, but will make Enquiry & I shall do the same" (PHi: Clement Biddle Letterbook). A Mrs. Read had been employed as cook for the presidential household shortly before GW's arrival in New York (see CtY: Household Accounts, passim), but because her services were unsatisfactory and there was apparently some question as to her honesty (see GW to Tobias Lear, 19 June 1791), advertisements appeared in the newspapers between December 1789 and February 1790 for a new cook, stating that "No one need apply who is not perfect in the business, and can bring indubitable testimonials of sobriety, honesty, and attention to the duties of the station" (Decatur, *Private Affairs of George Washington*, 93–94).

2. On 8 April 1790 Lear wrote again to Grant, stating "I have been duly favored with your letter of the 7th of March, and should have given it an earlier acknowledgment had I received an answer from Mr Moyston of Philada to whom I wrote upon receiving your letter to know the character and qualifications of the Cook whom you mentioned—as you informed me that he had lived with him several years—Not having received the information of which I expected from Mr Moyston—and daily experiencing the inconvenience of wanting an established and good Cook in the family—the President has again directed me to write to you upon the subject—requesting that you will be so good as to learn from the Man whom you mentioned the precise terms upon which he would engage to come into this family—what he expects or wishes to do with his wife and Children if he should come—and to let me know your opinion respecting the mans qualifications as a Cook, and his dispositions as a domestic—for the great confidence will be placed in your character of him.

"The highest wages we have given for the best Cook (and I am informed that none higher have been given in this place) is twelve dollars per month with his washing, lodging &ca. I mention this circumstance that if the man should think of making an extravagant demand to serve in the *President's* family, he may know what has been given. Your attention to this matter, as soon as convenient, will oblige the President—and upon receiving your letter, an immediate and decisive answer will be given thereto with my best thanks for your trouble in this business." Lear added a postscript stating that "The duties of a Cook are far from being hard or complicated—for we entertain company but seldom, and that regularly" (DLC:GW).

3. The difficulties in finding a new cook continued into the spring of 1791 after the household had moved to Philadelphia. Rachel Lewis, one of the kitchen maids, filled in for a time. Auguste Lamuir, a French cook, was hired for a period of one month but apparently proved unsatisfactory. In May 1790 John Vicar of Baltimore was employed at a salary of fifteen dollars per month. When the capital moved to Philadelphia, Vicar and his wife accompanied the household to Philadelphia where he remained until May 1791 (see Decatur, *Private Affairs of George Washington*, 121, 152, 234).

Letters not found: to George Augustine Washington, 28 Feb. 1790. In a 19 Mar. 1790 letter to GW, George Augustine Washington refers to "Your two favors of the 28th Ulto."

From Henrich Wilmans

Most Honorable Sir! Bremen 28 febr. 1790

Your Exellence Letter dated Nw York the 12th October last, I have well receivd, and it gives me Pleasure to see that You are Pleasd with me sending the Gardiner, who I hope will behave him selff to Your Exellencys satisfaction.[1]

The linnen Weaver I had formerly engaged declined to go, and it was obmitted in mention it in my last letter, however I have since endeavourd to git one, tho not as yet Succeeded, because I would wisch to have one who could make Diaper and Tabel linnen likewises, and Your Exellency may depend that in the Cours of this year I shall send one of those abilities intirely to Your liking—either for the Potomack or Baltimore as ships Opportunity best offers.[2]

the Gardeners Wife is determined to follow her husband, and she is a Woman who can be of great service to Your Exellence Lady as she is capable in every respect.[3]

The Emperor Died the 20 of this month, and probably a general War on this Continent may take Place. I have the Honour to remain with due regard Most Honorble Sir Your Exellence most hbe and Obd. servt

                                                    Henrich Wilmans

ALS, DLC:GW.

    1. See John Christian Ehlers to GW, 24 June 1789, source note.

    2. In his letter of 12 Oct. 1789, GW had asked Wilmans to procure a linen weaver for him.

    3. In November 1788, when GW asked Wilmans to engage a gardener for him, he specified that the gardener's wife "if one comes is to be a Spinner, dairy Woman—or something of that usefulness" (*Diaries*, 5:422).

To Charleston, S.C., Officials

Gentlemen,   [New York, February 1790]

I receive your congratulations on my unanimous appointment to the first magistracy of a free People with that grateful sensibility which is due to the occasion, and which your flattering expressions of regard could not fail to awaken.[1]

Persuaded that the candor of my countrymen will do justice to the rectitude of my intentions, I am happy under the assurance that their active support of the constitution and disposition to maintain the dignity of our free and equal government will ensure facility and success to the administration of its laws—and if the result of my anxious endeavors in some measure, to justify the too partial sentiments of my fellow-citizens, should, in any degree approach to the wish which I entertain for their happiness, I shall not regret the domestic enjoyment and personal repose which may have been yielded to this superior consideration.

As Magistrates of a commercial city deeply interested in the measures of the federal government you must have beheld with satisfaction the equal and salutary influence of its regulations on the trade of america—As citizens of a State whose sufferings and services possess a distinguished rank in the history of our revolution, you must rejoice in the completion of our toils and the reward which awaits them, and as members of the great family of the union, connected by the closest ties of interest and endearment, the confidence which you justly cherish of sharing in all the benefits of the national compact, must be strengthened by the experience already received of the justice, wisdom, and prudence of its measures—a candid review of which will establish a conviction of liberal policy, and justify the most favorable anticipation of future advantage.

I desire to assure you, Gentlemen, of my gratitude for the tender interest you are pleased to take in my personal felicity, and I entreat the almighty Ruler of the universe to crown your wishes with deserved prosperity.

G. Washington

LB, DLC:GW.

1. The address "of the Intendant and Wardens of the city of Charleston, South Carolina," dated 18 Feb. 1790, reads: "Though among the latest, yet not among the least zealous of the Citizens of America, we take the liberty to intrude for a moment on your time, which is so precious to the people over whom you preside, to offer our congratulations on your unanimous appointment to the most honorable station amongst men, the first magistrate of the freest people on the Earth.

"United with our eastern and northern Brethren in our ardent attachment to the principles of a free government, equally remote from tyranny and anarchy, we rejoice with them that you have been prevailed upon by the voice of your country to relinquish your private walks of domestic life, for the toils of an untried Government, where your wisdom, moderation, and firmness would be requisite to the discharge of its various and intricate duties—with grateful hearts we add this to the catalogue of eminent sacrifices and services, by which you have so compleatly endeared yourself to the people of America.

"As Magistrates of a commercial city deeply interested in the measures of the federal government, we feel peculiar pleasure in finding it introduced into action under the auspices of an administration every way qualified to correct those errors or supply those defects, which are alledged by its enemies, or apprehended by its friends; and as in its first operations it will receive from you a tone correspondent to the spirit in which it was framed, we felicitate ourselves in the happy omens of a firm government acting by wholesome laws, through the medium of mild and equal administration.

"Possessing the fullest confidence that our distance from the seat of Government will not deprive us of any of its essential benefits, we beg leave to tender you our assurances of a cheerful submission to, and active support of the constitution—and the laws which may be framed in conformity thereto by the wisdom of Congress.

"We cherish the confidence from whence spring these assurances, because we remember that we were not neglected or deserted during the late glorious struggle for independency, but were substantially aided by the policy of your counsels, the wisdom of your appointments and the vigor of the exertions of our northern friends, who shared and lessened our severest toils.

"It is our earnest prayer to the almighty ruler of the universe that he will take you into his holy keeping, and suffer no incident to arise, which may disturb the felicity of your private life, and that he will make your public administration honorable to yourself, and happy to the people who have so unanimously confided themselves to your care" (DLC:GW). The address is signed by Thomas Jones, intendant of the city of Charleston, "by desire of and for the whole."

From South Carolina Line Officers

State of South Carolina [February-March 1790]
To the President of the United States.

The Memorial of the underwritten, late Officers of the South Carolina Line, on the Continental Establishment Sheweth

That in the year 1781, the honorable the Congress made arrangements, whereby every Officer in the American Army, was to have received four months Pay in Specie. That in the year 1782 they again made arrangements for two months more Pay.

That in pursuance thereof, all the Officers received Six months pay in Specie, except those of *this,* and one or two other States.

That, from Causes unknown to your Memorialists, they were unfortunately deprived of that Relief, which was intended for them, and for the Want of which, they were deprived of many *Necessaries* of Life. That Congress having some time ago taken the hardship of their Case into consideration, and with all the Injustice done them, recommended by their Resolve of the [   ] day of 178[   ] that this State, should compleat to the several Officers, the said six months Pay, amounting in the whole to about Ten thousand Dollars. to be deducted out of the Requisitions of Congress.

That in pursuance of such Resolve, the Commissioners of the Board of Treasury furnished each of your Memorialists, with an Order on the Commissioner of the Loan Office of this State ⟨for⟩ the amount of his demand. That the said Commissioner ⟨*mutilated*⟩ declared, that he is without funds for the satisfaction of the⟨m⟩ and they are given to understand, that no provision has been made for these their just claims. Your Memorialists, then can not but feel themselves hurt, under the Reflection, th⟨at⟩ this is *now* the only State, whose Officers are not *yet* paid ⟨the⟩ said six months *pay:* And they are still more mortified, when they find no provision made for the payment of that which ought to have been paid, seven or eight years ago; And that the order has, during that whole period, been lying dormant in their hands, without bearing the least Interest. They are however persuaded, that upon their Grievance being represented, full and ample justice will be done them, and that they will receive such Relief, as will seem just & equitable.

LS, DNA: RG 59, Miscellaneous Letters. This petition was signed by Brig. Gen. Isaac Huger and fifteen other officers or their representatives "for themselves & others of the ⟨South⟩ Carolina Line." The memorial is endorsed "recd March 5th. 1790."

The officers of the South Carolina line sought back pay for 1782 and 1783 as early as 19 July 1786 when the Continental Congress discussed the matter and passed it on to the Board of Treasury for investigation. The board reported on 26 July 1786 that the officers of South Carolina, Maryland, Virginia, and North Carolina were entitled to $37,066⁵⁶⁄₉₀ but had not been paid because of the state of the finances. It was suggested that the amount be deducted from future South Carolina specie payments (*JCC,* 30:417, 444–45). See also ibid., 31:465–66, 761.

The officers of the South Carolina line also presented a petition on 5 Mar. 1790 to the House of Representatives seeking payment of their Revolutionary War claims (PHi: Pierce Butler Papers). The petition was referred to the secretary of the treasury and Hamilton reported to the House on 18 Mar., substantiating the officers' claims but arguing that they were not entitled to the interest (*DHFC,* 3:316, 335; Syrett, *Hamilton Papers,* 6:305–6). On 17 May 1790 the House resolved to request GW to transmit to the executives of Virginia, North Carolina, and South Carolina a list of all officers to whom pay was still owed, notifying claimants that they could be paid upon proper application (*DHFC,* 3:414).

From François Crouin

Sir   Richmond [Va.] 1 March 1790

In the momentous occupations of your Excellency for the general happiness of America I fear to intrude the voice of an old Soldier who claims the compensations of his Services, but as the compassionate Soul of your Excellency unbends itself by particular acts of benevolence & justice, I am emboldened to recall to his mind that I had the honor to present myself at his lodgings in his passage thro' this town in the year 1786[1] when your Excellency had the goodness to read my Commission given under the hand of Governor Rutledge of So. Carolina specifying that I was Captain Bombardier & also a Certificate of good Conduct from General Lincoln as well as a permission on parole from Genl Clinton to go to Williamsburg as prisoner of war with other officers taken at Charlestown,[2] but your Excellency told me that tho' you wish'd it were in your power to procure me my pay as Captn, yet at the same time being yourself a single individual without power put it beyond your reach; But now your Excellency is in a Station to follow his just & beneficient inclinations I am coming to supplicate him to give necessary orders so that I may receive some compensation for my Services for which I never have received a single penny ⟨, &⟩ my age & the modicity of my fortune hinders m⟨e⟩ from making a Journey in order to obtain my just dues⟨,⟩ I have only to hope in your Excellency for whom I make the best wishes to heaven. I am with the most profound Respect Your Excellency's Most obedt & most humble Servant

François Crouin

ALS, DNA: RG 59, Miscellaneous Letters.

No further identification of Crouin has been found.

1. GW visited Richmond in April 1786 on business connected with George Mercer's estate (*Diaries*, 4:317–19).

2. Williamsburg District in South Carolina was a settlement some 60 miles north of Charleston.

To Gouverneur Morris

Dear Sir,   New York, March 1st 1790.

Since my last to you, dated the 13 of October, I have removed to a larger house (the one lately occupied by the Count de Moustier)[1]—enlarged my table, and of course my Guests—let me therefore request the favor of you to add two pieces to the number of plateaux required in the above letter,[2] and ornaments equivalent—for it will take these *in addition* to what I before asked, to decorate the present Table.

I would thank you also for sending to me at the same time fourteen (of what I believe are called) Patent lamps, similar to those used at Mr R. Morris's, but less costly—two or at most three guineas a piece, will fully answer my purposes—along with these, but of a more ordinary sort (say at about one guinea each)—I should be glad to receive a dozen other patent lamps for the Hall, Entries, and Stairs of my house—These lamps, it is said, consume their own smoke—do no injury to furniture—give more light—and are cheaper than candles. Order a sufficiency of spare glasses and an abundance of wicks.

If I had not in my former letter on this subject offered reasons accompanied with an apology for giving you so much trouble, I would, to keep up the custom, do it now, although I persuade myself you had rather comply with my request than be troubled with the best apology I could make for giving it.

Being well persuaded that you are regularly informed of the proceedings of the second Session of Congress—the disposition of that body—so far as it has been developed—and of the general complexion of our public affairs, I shall not trouble you with a repetition; but shall with much truth assure you that I am Your affectionate friend and obedient humble Servant

G. Washington.

P.S. The enclosed requests Messrs Welch and Son to pay the cost of these articles.[3]

LB, DLC:GW.

1. For GW's move to the residence formerly occupied by the comte de Moustier, see *Diaries*, 6:26, and Alexander Macomb to Tobias Lear, 31 Jan. 1790, notes.

2. See GW to Morris, 13 Oct. 1789 (first letter), Morris to GW, 24 Jan. 1790, and notes. GW cancelled this request in his letter to Morris of 15 April 1790.

3. The enclosure was GW's letter of 1 Mar. to Wakelin Welch & Son, asking the firm to extend credit to cover Morris's purchases. For the text of the letter, and for Welch's reluctance to extend credit, see GW to Morris, 13 Oct. 1789 (first letter), n.2.

From Philip Pendleton

Sir   Virginia Berkeley Co: March 1st 1790

I am informed that a vacancy has happened in the Supreme Court, for the Western Territory by the Death of General Parsons.[1] It is with great diffidence I now take the Liberty to Solicit the appointment to that vacancy, if it is not as yet filled—From a Steady and uniform attachment to the Goverment of the United States from my situation And from a long and Labourious attention to the practice of the Bar I cannot help flattering myself that I am not altogether unqualified to fill that office—I will beg leave to assure you Sir, that should you think proper to Honour me with the appointment, a Strict and regular attention to and a faithfull discharge of its duties shall not be wanting on my part. I have the Honour to be with the most perfect respect Sir, Yr Obt Hble servt

Phil. Pendleton

ALS, DLC:GW.

Philip Pendleton (1752–1802), a Berkeley County, Va., attorney, was the son of Nathaniel Pendleton of Culpeper County and the brother of Nathaniel Pendleton who had served as Nathanael Greene's aide-de-camp during the Revolution. GW sold Pendleton a portion of his Bullskin plantation in 1771 (*Diaries*, 3:37). He received no appointment from GW.

1. Samuel Holden Parsons was appointed a judge in the Northwest Territory in 1787 and confirmed in that position under the new government in August 1789. He drowned in the rapids of Big Beaver Creek in November 1789. See Winthrop Sargent to GW, 27 Nov. 1789, and notes.

From Benjamin Stelle

Providence [R.I.] 1st March 1790.

May it please the President of the United States

Before this will reach your Hands it is confidently expected that this State will become a member of the federal Union.

Having spent the chief of my time since the beginning of the late War in the public Service, I feel an ambition to receive an appointment under the new Government, as well to promote the public Service, as to find Imployment for myself & Subsistance for a dependant Family. The Credentials accompanying this will more fully explain that it is my wish to obtain an appointment among the officers for collecting the federal Revenue.

Should the President deem me worthy of his Confidence and appoint me to the Place of naval officer for the Port of Providence I should not fail to exert the best efforts in my Power to discharge the Duties of it, with Integrity & Impartiality. With great Deference & Respect I have the Honour to be your most Obedient and very Humble Servant

Benja. Stelle

ALS, DLC:GW.

Benjamin Stelle (1746–1819), a native of New Jersey, graduated from the College of New Jersey (Princeton) in 1766 and moved to Providence where, with the support of James Manning, a friend of his family and president of the College of Rhode Island (Brown), he established a Latin school in the city. During the Revolution Stelle served as adjutant of two Rhode Island regiments and as deputy paymaster from June 1779 to April 1781. By 1790 he had become a prominent Providence businessman, holding a number of offices in local organizations and establishing, with Benjamin Bowen, a chocolate mill and an apothecary shop (McLachlan, *Princetonians,* 595–97; Heitman, *Historical Register,* 381).

On 1 Mar. Dr. James Manning wrote GW a letter of recommendation for Stelle, stating that if "capacity and attention to business, and tried integrity in the discharge of the duties of public offices may be considered as founding any claim to this appointment, he stands, I believe second to none in this competition. From a long and intimate acquaintance I conceive him to be a Gentleman of an independent spirit; and as free from Mercantile influence as any man in Providence He has not sought to come forward supported by a long Catalogue of names, judging that Gentlemen in Trade might be supposed to be biassed by views to future Interest; the two only Gentlemen in this line Messrs Nicholas Brown and John Jenckes from whom he has asked and taken Testimonials, though men of large business have ever borne an open testimony against illicit Trade; and are peculiarly desirous that the officers of the Customs should be men beyond the reach of influence to warp them from their duty; and, I am in sentiment with them, that the man who has sustained the offices which they have mentioned; and, who has yet to receive almost the whole of the compensation for his faithful and approved services, notwithstanding he, for so long a time, had the sole command of the Military Chest for the Eastern department, may with safety be entrusted with the office which he solicits" (DLC:GW). The letter of recommendation from Nicholas Brown and John Jenckes, 25 Feb. 1790, is in DLC:GW. Stelle did not receive the appointment as Providence naval officer, the post going to Ebenezer Thompson. Anticipating a vacancy in the Providence customs office, Stelle again wrote GW on 19 June requesting the post. A letter of 22 June 1790 from John Henry to GW, recommended Stelle and enclosed another supporting letter of 7 June 1790 from James Manning. Stelle again wrote GW on 14 July, this time asking for the appointment as commissioner of loans for Rhode Island. All of these letters are in DLC:GW. The applications were unsuccessful.

From Samuel Whittemore

Sr   Port of Glouster [Mass.] March 1st 1790
    You will Excuse my Troubleing you with a few Lines, as I have been Naval officer for the Port of Glouster ever since the appointment of such an Office, (except one year) and knowing I

had discharged my Duty, and that to the Sattisfaction of the Publick, I thought it sufficient to Recommend me without making any applycation to any of the Members of Congress for that Purpose, but as I find that as Interest was made by others it was not, and I was superceded, and as I am the only Instance in this Commonwealth where a Naval Officer hath been put under the Controle of one that hath not been in Publick office during the Warr,[1] and as by the Report of the Secratary of the Treasury if accepted there will be a new arrangement of officers, I hope you will not be unmindfull of one who hath served the Publick ever since the Commencement of the late Warr, and in many Instances to the Prejudice of his own Interest, and who can appeal to the Treasurer and Controler for his Fidelity and Punctuallity, if that should not be the Case, as I doubt not that Congress mean to Reward their officers Adequate to their Services, they will Consider the Duty required of a Surveyor on whose Vigelance the Revenue so much depends (and who is under Bonds) that it is much less than that of a Weigher and Guager or that of an Inspector, who he hath the oversight off (and are not under Bonds) as you may See by the Return of Fees made to the Secratary and the Pay Received by such officers, as the Surveyor is obliged to attend so as to ascertain the Prooff of Spirits &c. to see that those officers do their Duty, he must Spend nearly as much Time as to Do the Duty himself whether he might not do it and Receive the same pay when He was not otherways Engaged, with the Right of appointing a Deputy when He is not able to Attend. I am with much Esteem your most Obedient Humle Servant.

Samel Whittemore

ALS, DLC:GW.

Samuel Whittemore (1733–1806) of Gloucester, Mass., was the son of Samuel and Margaret Hicks Whittemore. Whittemore graduated from Harvard in 1751, was a member of three Massachusetts provincial congresses, and served in the General Court in 1776 and from 1783 to 1784. He was justice of the peace at Gloucester from 1776 to 1795. GW appointed Whittemore, a Federalist, surveyor of the port of Gloucester in August 1789 and inspector of the port in 1792 (*Executive Journal*, 1:9, 103).

1. Whittemore was originally appointed naval officer at Gloucester by the state in 1776. Under the appointments made by GW in August 1789, Epes Sargent replaced him.

From Michael Payne

Sir　　　　　　　　　　　Edenton [N.C.] March 2d 1790

Having ever since the year 1777 been Naval officer of Port Roanoke and being the oldest officer by many years standing in the Custom House department, in which I trust I have executed my duty in a manner irreproachable, but being by the late arrangement (in which it has been Judged expedient to abolish the Naval office) thrown out of an employment in which I in a great measure depended for the support of my family, I hope sir you will, from the necessity which compells me. excuse the liberty I take of troubling you with this address, to sollicit you to take the hardness of my situation into your consideration. fully confiding, that, from your Excellencys well known humanity and inviolable regard to Justice, you will please to grant me such Relief as the Necessity of my case requires, And as it is most probable there will be an Inspector of the Duties, appointed for the District, I entreat your Excellency to pardon the liberty I take of Requesting the appointment to that office or any other you may be pleased to bestow on me. should your Excellency entertain any doubts of my character or my conduct in my former office, I beg leave to refer your Excellency to the Representatives of this State. I have the Honor to be most Respectfully your Excellencys most Obedient Hume Servt

Michl Payne

ALS, DLC:GW.

Michael Payne served as an officer in the 2d North Carolina Regiment during the Revolution. He was appointed naval officer at Edenton in 1777 and in addition held several local offices. Payne did not immediately receive an appointment under the new government, but when John Skinner, the marshal for North Carolina, declined reappointment in late 1794, he recommended Payne in a letter of 9 July, unaddressed but probably sent to GW, as a "Gentleman of this Town Who has for some time acted under me as a Deputy with whose Conduct I have found no fault. . . . I think Colo. Payne fully equal to the Task & wou'd transact the business of the Office as well as any person with whom I have an acquaintance" (DLC:GW). GW appointed Payne to the office on 10 December. Payne's letter of acceptance, 19 Aug. 1794, is in DLC:GW.

From Samuel Smith

Sir   Baltimore [Md.] 2d March 1790
Mr Philip Walsh of Cadix will have the Honor to present this
to your Excellency, that Gentlem⟨e⟩n Vis[i]ts America with a view
of forming Connexions for the very respectable House of Dom-
nick Terry & Co. of Cadix. He has the advantage of being introduced by the most respectable Mercantile Houses of Europe
Who all agree that the House he represents is considered of the
first Consequence. Mr Walsh's Views extends farther he proposes the services of his Brother Mr John Walsh (the principal
of that House) Gratis, in the Character of Consul for the United
States at Cadix. I therefore take the liberty to introduce him to
your Excellencys Attention[1] & with the highest respect Have the
Honor to be Your Excellency's Most Obdt Servt

Sam. Smith

LS, DLC:GW.

After serving with considerable distinction in the Revolution, Samuel Smith
(1752–1839) returned to Baltimore in 1779 and set about reviving his father's
ailing mercantile firm. Smith soon became one of the city's foremost entrepreneurs, with widespread interests in privateering and government contracts.
After the war he acted as Robert Morris's agent in Maryland to collect tobacco
to fill Morris's contract with the French farmers-general and built up his own
impressive shipping fleet. After serving in the Maryland house of delegates,
Smith was elected to the House of Representatives in 1792, serving there until
1803. Elected to the Senate in 1802, he served in that body until 1815. During
the War of 1812, he served as a major general of militia in the defense of
Baltimore. He served again in the House of Representatives from 1816 to
1822 and in the Senate once more from 1822 to 1833. At the time Smith was
advising GW on Maryland appointments in 1789–90, he was a Federalist, but
by the mid-1790s he had moved into the Democratic Republican camp.

1. Philip Walsh was also recommended by Bordeaux merchant Jacob
Vernes in a letter to Jefferson, 3 Nov. 1789: "I have taken the liberty to give a
letter of recommendation for you to Mr. Walsh of Cadiz, brother to the Senior
of the House of Domque. Terry & Ce. one of the more respectable houses in
Spain, and the most active in the trade of the United States." In another letter
to Jefferson of the same date, Vernes stated that Walsh's "travels in America
are intended for increasing the trade of the United States with Spain. The
instructions and the favours of your Excellency will enable him to fulfill his
design with more facility and success. . . . Mr. Walsh will collect the best informations about lumber, and . . . will give me of the knowledge he'll acquire in
that branch, and of the means of procuring a consumption of timber in this
Kingdom" (Boyd, *Jefferson Papers*, 15:538–45). John Walsh, Philip Walsh's
brother, received no consular appointment under GW.

From William Graves

sir   New York March 3rd 1790

I now beg the liberty of addressing you on the Subject of an appointment under the General Government, I was a Soldier in the late American Armey as Soon as I was capable of bearing armes & continued untill the peace was Established, after that I was appointed by the Executive of Virginia, Searcher for the Port of Norfolk, and continued in the Execution of that office untill the General Government took place which will appear from the recommendation of the Executive of Virginia and which I took the liberty of Inclosing to you in Augt last. this is further confirmed by the recommendation now Inclosed. I have the Honour to be sir your Humble Servant

Wm Graves

ALS, DLC:GW.

William Graves had sent an earlier application to retain his post as searcher at Norfolk. See his letter to GW, 28 Aug. 1789, printed above. Failing to receive a post in 1789 and 1790, he again applied for the position of searcher in a letter to GW, 12 April 1791 (DLC:GW). His application was again unsuccessful.

From William Irvine

Sir   New york 4th March 1790

I take the liberty to inclose you a copy of the proposed Constitution for Pennsylvania, which was transmitted to me, by a member of the Convention for that purpose.[1] I have the honor to be most respectfully Sir your most obedient & Most humble Servant

Wm Irvine

ALS, DNA: RG 59, Miscellaneous Letters.

1. In November 1789 a constitutional convention convened in Philadelphia to replace the Pennsylvania Constitution of 1776. The first session, November 1789 to February 1790, formulated a preliminary draft of a constitution. It was undoubtedly a copy of this document that Irvine sent to GW. The second session of the convention, August to September 1790, produced a new constitution modeled on the federal Constitution. Irvine was a member of the convention.

Tobias Lear to Clement Biddle

Sir,   New York March 5th 1790.

I have been favored with your letters of the 16th & 23d ultimo. We are furnished with a Carpet for the room which I had
described to you; but are therefore no less obliged to you for the
trouble you have had in making inquiries respecting it.[1] The
President will thank you to make an addition of two hundred
bushels to the quantity of Buckwheat you have procured for
him. It is probable that it can be carred to Virginia in bulk,
which will save the expense of bags or barrels. Major Washington informed the President that Captain Elwood had told him
that for the freight of a quantity, he would make bulk heads &
carry it free from expense of bags or barrels. If this can be done
it will be agreeable to the President, as the number of bags which
you have already are as many as will be useful—and barrels are
of little or no use at Mount Vernon where they have always a
number on hand. with very great esteem, I am, Dear Sir, Your
most Obedt Servt

Tobias Lear

ALS, PHi: Washington-Biddle Correspondence; ADfS, ViMtV; LB, DLC:GW.
    1. See Alexander Macomb to Lear, 31 Jan. 1790.

To Warner Lewis

Dear Sir,   New York March 5th 1790.

Your letter of the 18 of last month, enclosing the copy of one
dated the 26 of October came duly to hand[1]—The best, indeed
the only apology I can make for suffering the latter to remain
so long unacknowledged, is, that on my return from a tour
through the eastern States in november, I found such a multiplicity of public letters and other papers, which required to be
acted upon, that those of private concern were laid aside, and
in a manner forgotten before they could again be brought into
view.

I shall now, though I feel myself unable to give such answers
to the queries of Mr Nicholson, with respect to my land in
Gloucester county, as will be perfectly satisfactory to myself, say
enough to enable *him* to decide for *himself.*

The Gentleman of whom it was bought valued it (as I believe you have been informed) at £1000; but for particular reasons to take £800.[2] Whether from any favorable change of circumstances it would sell for more now I know not—Less than £800 with interest thereon from the time it ceased to produce it to me in consequence of the transfer, together with the taxes which have arisen since, and the charges of alienation, I would not take even if the whole sum should be paid down, which indeed would be by far the most pleasing mode of disposing of it—but as a purchase on these terms does not appear to be the intention of Mr Nicholson I will, in the next place, propose £400 in hand, with the incidental expences as before, and interest on the £800 during its suspension—and £500 payable at the expiration of 4 years without interest, provided it be paid within one month after it shall become due; if not, then with interest from the date of the bond—Or, lastly, I will take £1000 payable at the expiration of 4 years, without interest, if the whole of the purchase money be then punctually paid, otherwise to carry interest as above from the date—In this case, as in the last, the interest of the £800, with the charges, is to be paid up, the intention being not to *lose* by receiving *land* in place of *money* that was lent and bearing interest.

As there are no buildings on the premises, I had rather sell than rent, Indeed I prefer the former at any rate having found, from experience, that estates at a distance plague more than they profit the Proprietors of them. With very great esteem and regard, I am dear Sir, your most obedient and obliged humble servant

G. Washington

LB, DLC:GW.

1. For background to Lewis's transmittal of John Nicholson's inquiries concerning GW's Gloucester County land, see Lewis to GW, 26 Oct. 1789. Lewis's letter of 18 Feb. is printed in note 2 to that letter.

2. For GW's acquisition of the Gloucester County land, see John Dandridge to GW, 27 Oct. 1788, source note.

From John Van Sice

Sir   Schenectady [N.Y.] March 5th 1790

Am Sensible of my presumption—when I trouble So great a personage with my little concerns, but the distressed circumstances of my family urges the necessity of craving your Interposition—I have from the commencement of the American War Served in Schenectady as a gun Smith for the Indians, for which I received no recompence, & of which I had the honor of informing your Excellency when last in Schenectady[1]—you was then pleased to express your Surprise at General Schuyler's not paying me, Since he cou'd draw from Congress what Sums he pleased for the Use of the Indians, yet I must despair of ever reaping any benefit from my Services unless recommended by your Excellency; on whom rests my only dependance arising from the Christian disposition & great Qualities asscribed to your Excellency by all the World—I doubt not Sir of your being disposed to help me, but fear Multiplicity of matters of high importance will prevent your attending to it—⟨*mutilated*⟩ great Sir dreading to use the freedom of craving an answer—with the utmost respect your Excellency's most Obedient Servt

John Van Sice Indain Interperter
During the late war, at Schonectendy

ALS, DNA: RG 59, Miscellaneous Letters.

In addition to his services as gunsmith, John Van Sice (b. 1726) also served during the war in Col. Cornelius Wynkoop's regiment and in the Albany militia.

1. Van Sice is referring to GW's ceremonial trip to Albany, Saratoga, and Schenectady in June 1782 in the company of Gov. George Clinton. He visited Schenectady on 30 June.

From George Augustine Washington

Honord Uncle   Mount Vernon March 5th 1790.

I sent on Saturday the usual day of your Letters reaching Alexandria, but your favor of the 21st Ulto had not arrived, and did not come to my hands untill yesturday.[1]

I have informed Fairfax that it was your opinion and that I was directed to communicate it to him that £25. pr ann. is very ample wages for his Brother, or any untried man, and that it was your determination not to encrease *his* wages, and that if he did not think proper to continue, he might at the end of his year go which he has determin'd to do. as I consider his wages very sufficient[2] I said nothing to urge his continuance but confess that I am sorry to part with him, not knowing how he is to be replaced, for to get a man that can be relied on in that line of life is a mere lottery⟨.⟩ from his long continuance he has acquired that knowledge of your business which renders him very useful. I have no expectation of geting Fairfaxes Brother, nor do I know of any person that would probably answer from any information I have been able to obtain; but must extend my enquiries for this part of the County will not I fear furnish one that can be depended on.

I always thought the wages you allow'd Mr Bloxham greatly beyond what his services merited, and in no other point of view do I consider him preferable to the Overseers of this Country but in the business of seeding.[3] You were well convinced I believe long before you left home that he had no capacity for the management of Negroes; tho I am not an advocate for changes of this kind yet in this instance it would in my opinion be perfectly well to do it—for I cannot suppose but by the expiration of his time, that for less than £40. a man may be procured who will render you as essential services—Fairfax has several times expressed an inclination to be placed at the Ferry in case of the Removal of Mr Bloxham on the same wages he (Fairfax) now has[4]—but I gave no encouragement and said little in reply as I thought it too much and believed he would be more useful where he is—the impeachment of fraud is a disagreeable thing, but the embezzlement of Ferriages is suspicious from the diminution of them the year 1787—produced a profit of £55.12.1¼—88 but £32.8.10d. & 89—but £21.19.6. I have endeavourd by unseeming enquiries to make discoveries, but have not—but will continue my attempts.

I was well aware that inconveniences would attend the removeal of James from the Carpentering business,[5] but was induced to make the proposition from an œconomising principle, believing that he might answer as well as an Overser as any white man that might probably be got—*tho'* his services as a Carpenter are extremely essential yet the expence and frequently the perplexity of white Overseers is a great bar to the employg of them—I cannot see that anything better can be done than the removeal of Davy to D: Run & Will to Muddy hole and must if I can meet with a white Overseer engage one to manage the gang here[6] Will and Davy shall be moved immediately on my return from Berkley which will be in about a week as I shall set out in the morning. I have not communicated the intention to them or shall I to the Farmer untill I return as no inconvenience can attend so short a delay. There are now five hog'sheads of Tobacco prized which will go to Town for inspection on Monday and the rest will be got ready without loss of time—the whole of the wheat has been sent to the mill as appears by the Report except abt 200 B: from the R: plantn and abt 30. or 40 from M: Hole—a short crop indeed.

There is now ready in the mill about 120 Bl Common Flour and abt 70 of Ship Stuff & midlings for the former 40/ pr Bl can be had—for the Ship stuff 14/ pr hundred and midlings 16/— which prices are in my opinion so high that I should have been induced to dispose of all on hand had I not recd your Letter having frequently known a good market lost by waiting in expectation for a better—I shall wait your further advise respecting the sale of it—having fixed the new Bolting Cloth shall have the balance of the wheat manufacterd into Superfine flour.

Mr Wilson is ready at any time to comply with his contract and will send the Corn to the mill on my return[7]—Corn in Alexandria has not been altogether so high and in so great demand for a fortnight past—the scarcity of money it is thought will affect the prices of grain & Flour—it certainly is as you observe to be apprehended that the great prices will induce people to sell so near as to involve serious consequences—I have endeavourd to have provision and provender used with all possible œconomy and as you desire it will encrease the Crop of Carrots potatoes pease & Scarcity—the pease and Potatoes I think may answer better than the former or latter but we have no great encouragement to go much on any of them from the production of either heretofore.

I have informed Ehler that you would provide seeds &c. agreeable to his list[8]—He appears industrious & contented to possess knowledge and taste—at first, to converse with him was difficult but he has made such progress as to be tolerably well understood—the ground has been in such order that not much could be done—George is now with him and I hope their

labours will soon be discoverd—I have replaced in the Shrub-
beries the Dog-wood Red-bud Sas'afrass—Laurel and Crab-
apple—the Ivy have almost entirely died under both walls—
among the shrubs some of these shall be intersperced—you will
observe by the cash acct transmited what has been recd from
Muse[9]—the last letter from him enclosing a draft for 50£ on the
house of Robinson Sanderson & Co. inform'd me that he was a
little in advance but that I should the last of this or the begining
of the next month recieve his accts but gives no encouragement
for any more very shortly for he expects to be obliged to have
recourse to Law for the most of the arrearages.

For two days and nights past the weather has been very cold
the wind very high and the ground very hard froze very unfavorable for the grain—the accounts I last gave you of the grain
were not unfavorable but the thaugh which took place about the
time has given that which lay much exposed to the wet a much
more unfavorable complexion—the earth subsiding (which had
been raised by the frost) has exposed the roots and caused much
of it to put on a deadly appearance—the Barley has I think sufferd very much—if indisposition or something very unexpected
should not prevent—I shall return on or before Monday
week—with the most tender regard for Yourself my Aunt & the
Children I am Honord Uncle your truely affectionate Nephew

Geo: A. Washington

ALS, ViMtV.

1. Letter not found.

2. George Augustine Washington is probably referring to John Fairfax's half brother Hezekiah Fairfax, the son of William Fairfax of Charles County, Md., and his first wife, Benedicta Blanchard Fairfax. Fairfax was in GW's employ at least as early as 1786 (Cash Accounts, May 1786, DLC:GW).

3. Bloxham's original agreement provided for a salary of 50 guineas for the first year and 60 guineas for the second year. See Agreement with James Bloxham, 31 May 1786.

4. See GW to George Augustine Washington, 29 July 1787.

5. James was a slave carpenter at the Home House. See the slave list in *Diaries*, 4:278.

6. Davy was overseer at River Plantation; Doll's Will was overseer at Muddy Hole.

7. This is probably William Wilson, an Alexandria merchant. See Thomas Montgomerie to GW, 24 Oct. 1788, n.2.

8. For John Christian Ehlers, see his letter to GW, 24 June 1789, source note.

9. Battaile Muse was GW's agent for collecting rents on his property in

Berkeley, Frederick, and Fauquier counties. See Muse to GW, 1 Nov. 1788, source note.

Tobias Lear to William Goddard & James Angell

Gentlemen,   New York, March 6th 1790

You will be pleased to insert the enclosed advertisement in your paper for six weeks successively and charge the same in your annual account with the President of the United States— which account you will be good enough to present whenever it becomes due.[1] I am, Gentlemen, Your most obedient Servant

Tobias Lear.

LB, DLC:GW.

William Goddard and James Angell were the publishers of the *Maryland Journal*. For Goddard, see Mary Katherine Goddard to GW, 23 Dec. 1789, source note. Angell, the younger brother of Goddard's wife Abigail, came to Baltimore from Providence in 1786, briefly operated a printing shop, and in August 1789 joined his brother-in-law as a partner in publishing the *Maryland Journal*.

1. The enclosure was an advertisement "of Royal Gift and the Knight of Malta standing at Mount Vernon this season." On 8 April Lear wrote Goddard and Angell stating that he had sent them the advertisement on 6 Mar. "with a request that you would insert it in your paper—As I have not seen said advertisement published, I presume it did not get to your hands—and will be much obliged by your informing me if that was the case. The letter was franked by the President of the United States, and put into the Post-Office" (DLC:GW).

From Hans Alexander Siegfried von Steuben

Monseigneur!   A nelam le 6 Mars 1790

Votre Excellence aura la Grace de me pardonner la Liberte que jose prendre de vous adresser ce peut de Ligne. Au Sujet d'un Frere unique qui a L'honneur de Servir sous votre Commandement dans le Prowince ùnie de l'amerique. Je lui ai Ecrit plussieurs fois, mais je n'ai jamais eu le Bonheur de recevoir une reponse que jai attendu avec Ardeur. N'etant pas Connu dans se⟨e⟩ Contrée et ne Sachant la Ville et la Prowince de son Commandement. La Grace et la Bonté de votre Excellence qui est connù a tout le Monde Mohnorera de faire passer cette Lettre a son Adresse,[1] ne pouwant faire autre Chose Monseigneur pour cette Grace d'etre avec le Cour le plus Sensible et avoir l'honneur de me ranger au Nombre de ceux qui ont l'honneur de se dira avec le plus profond respect. Monseigneur, votre tres hùmble et tres Obeissante Serviteur

H. S. de Steuben
Capit. des Hussards de l'armée du Roi de Prusse

ALS, DNA: RG 59, Miscellaneous Letters.

Hans Alexander Siegfried von Steuben (b. 1743), born in Breslau in Silesia, was the only surviving brother of Gen. Friedrich Wilhelm von Steuben. The younger Steuben served as an officer in the Prussian cavalry (John M. Palmer, *General Von Steuben* [New Haven, Conn., 1937], 26).

1. The enclosed letter has not been found. Hans von Steuben had been attempting to contact his brother for several years. He had written to Benjamin Franklin on 15 Aug. 1781 and 13 Feb. 1782 in an effort to reach his brother, apparently without success (Steuben Papers, microfilm edition, reel 5, pages 279, 383). No letter from Hans Alexander Siegfried Steuben to his brother is among the more than 4,000 items collected in the microfilm edition of *The Papers of General Friedrich Wilhelm von Steuben* (Edith von Zemenszky, ed., *Guide and Index to the Microfilm Edition: The Papers of General Friedrich Wilhelm von Steuben, 1777–1794* [Millwood, N.Y., 1984], 144). During his last years General von Steuben divided his time between New York City and his estate in the Mohawk Valley, where he died on 28 Nov. 1794. Hans von Steuben wrote again to GW from Treptow in Pomerania on 1 Sept. 1796 mentioning that he had learned of his brother's death and inquiring whether his brother had made any provision for Hans in his will (DLC:GW). GW replied on 3 Mar. 1797 that upon inquiry he had learned that General von Steuben's debts would consume most of his estate, and that whatever remained had been bequeathed to American friends (DLC:GW).

Letter not found: to George Augustine Washington, 7 Mar. 1790. In a 19 Mar. 1790 letter to GW, George Augustine Washington refers to letters "of the 28th Ulto & 7th Inst."

To Henry Knox

Sir,   United States [New York] March 8th 1790

I have taken into consideration your letter of the 15th of last month, and I approve of the proposals therein suggested, of endeavoring to avoid a War with the Creek nation of Indians.

I approve particularly of your requesting Mr Hawkins to send the letter to Alexander McGillivray a copy of which you have enclosed—and I authorize you to employ a suitable person to conduct the business, and to pay him, and the expenditures proposed.[1]

I will sign a Passport for such of the Chiefs of the Creek Nation as may desire to repair to the seat of the General Government on the business of their Nation.[2] I am &c.

G. Washington

LB, DLC:GW; copy, DLC:GW.

1. See Knox to GW, 15 Feb. 1790, nn.2 and 3.

2. On 11 Mar. GW signed a passport for Marinus Willett and Alexander McGillivray for their journey to New York. It reads: "Whereas it has been represented to me that Colonel Alexander McGillivray and several other principal Cheifs, Head Men, and Warriors of the Creek Nation of Indians, may be desirous of repairing to the residence of the General Government for the purpose of forming treaties of amity with the United States. Now therefore know ye, that to facilitate so humane an object, I have granted this Passport for the protection and security of said Cheifs who shall accompany the bearer Colonel Marinus Willet or such persons as he in case of sickness may authorize for the purposes herein specified—And I require all officers civil, and military of the United States, or of the respective States, and all good citizens thereof, to protect and assist such Cheifs aforesaid as shall accompany the said Colonel Marinus Willet, or the person authorized by him as aforesaid—And I do hereby forbid, any officers civil or military, or any of the Citizens aforesaid from attempting or performing any injury of any sort to the said Cheifs, Head Men, and Warriors protected as aforesaid, as they would answer the same at their peril" (LS, PPRF).

Adamson Tannehill to Tobias Lear

Sir   Pittsburgh 8th March 1790

From the small acquaintance I had of you while at this place, have taken the liberty of requesting you, that if there should be any public appointment in this Country that may be the Gift of his Excellency the Presidt of the U. States, you would be pleased to mention me to him to that effect; Should address his Excellency on the subject, but a becoming modesty forbids it.

Therefore if any thing of the kind (that I may be thought Competent to) should offer, would esteem it a particular favor to make mention of me. His Excellency has some acquantance of me, which may probably have some weight.

Your granting me this favour, and leting me know the first

convenient oporty will be gratefully acknowledged by Your Mo. Hble Servt

Adamson Tannehill

N.B. you lodged with me when at this place, which I recite as a memorandum to remember me by[1]

A.T.

ALS, DLC:GW.

Adamson Tannehill (1750–1820), a native of Frederick, Md., served during the American Revolution as a captain of riflemen and after the war settled in Pittsburgh. Until the mid-1780s Tannehill lived on Water Street between Market and Wood streets where he apparently operated a tavern, but around 1786 he moved to Grove Hill, a house on Grant's Hill close to Pittsburgh. Tannehill was active in Democratic Republican politics, and "The Bowery," a building on his Grove Hill property, became a center for political meetings (*Biog. Dir. Cong.*; Mulkearn, *Historic Western Pennsylvania*, 28). He received no federal appointment from GW's administration.

1. Lear visited Pittsburgh in late 1786 on business for GW. See GW's instructions to Lear, 30 Nov. 1786.

To the United States Senate and House of Representatives

United States [New York] March 8th 1790

Gentlemen of the Senate and House of Representatives

I have received from his Excellency Joshua Clayton President of the State of Delaware the articles proposed by Congress to the Legislatures of the several States as amendments to the Constitution of the United States;[1] which articles were transmitted to him for the consideration of the Legislature of Delaware,[2] and are now returned with the following Resolutions annexed to them—viz.

The General Assembly of Delaware

"Having taken into their consideration the above amendments proposed by Congress to the respective Legislatures of the several States,

Resolved that the first article be postponed—

Resolved that the General Assembly do agree to the Second, Third, Fourth, Fifth, Sixth, Seventh, Eighth, Ninth, Tenth, Eleventh and Twelfth articles; and We do hereby assent to, ratify, and confirm, the same as part of the Constitution of the United States.

In testimony whereof We have caused the great Seal of the State to be hereunto affixed this twenty eighth day of January in the year of our Lord one thousand seven hundred and ninety and in the fourteenth year of the Independence of the Delaware State. Signed by order of Council

Geo. Mitchell Speaker

Signed by order of the house of Assembly

John Davis Speaker"

I have directed a copy of the Letter which accompanied the said articles, from his Excellency Joshua Clayton to the President of the United States, to be laid before you.

The before-mentioned articles and the original of the Letter will be lodged in the office of the Secretary of State.[3]

Go: Washington

LS, DNA: RG 46, First Congress, Records of Legislative Proceedings, President's Messages; LB, DLC:GW; copy, DNA: RG 233, First Congress, Records of Legislative Proceedings, Journals.

1. See Clayton to GW, 19 Feb. 1790.

2. GW had submitted the amendments to the Constitution proposed by Congress to the governors of the states on 2 Oct. 1789. For the text of the amendments, see note 1 to that document. The first of these twelve amendments proposed by Congress was intended to prevent the membership of the House of Representatives from becoming unmanageably large as the national population increased, but its political tendency, if adopted, would have been to increase the relative representation of the more populous, faster-growing states at the expense of the less populous, slower-growing ones. In 1790 Delaware had the smallest population among the states. The Delaware council opposed the amendment, and the assembly concurred without debate.

3. Tobias Lear transmitted these documents to Roger Alden, chief clerk of the domestic section of the Department of State (Lear to Alden, 8 Mar. 1790, DLC:GW).

From Samuel Meredith

Tuesday [9 March 1790]

Mr Merediths respectful Compliments wait on the President of the United States, he should be happy (if it meets with his approbation) to leave this Town tomorrow for Philadelphia,

where, some private buisiness requires his immediate attendance for a few days, having made arrangements with Mr Hamilton for every thing necessary to be done in his absence—He
shall think himself honoured by the Presidents or Mrs Washingtons Commands.

AL, DNA: RG 59, Miscellaneous Letters.

To Beverley Randolph

Sir,   United States [New York] March 9th 1790.
   In compliance with the request signified in your Excellency's
letter of the 23d ultimo, I now inclose copies of all the papers in
my possession relative to the dispute between Messrs Beauregard and Bourgeois of New Orleans and Oliver Pollock Esquire agent for the State of Virginia; and have the honor to be,
with very great esteem, Your Excellency's most Obedt Servt
                                        Go: Washington

LS, PHi: Dreer Collection; copy, DNA: RG 59, Miscellaneous Letters; LB,
DLC:GW.
   For background to this letter, see Beauregard and Bourgeois to GW, 14 Oct.
1789, source note.

From Solomon Halling

                    Newbern—North Carolina 10th March 1790
   To the President of the United States, The Petition of Solomon Halling Most humbly sheweth,
   That your Petitioner is a native of the United States, has been
a Citizen of the State of North Carolina and a resident in the
town of Newbern for seven years past.
   That, He has served in the General Continental Hospitals of
the United States, as a Mate, a Junior, and a Senior Surgeon.
   That, his character as an officer and a Citizen have ever been
unimpeachable, And,
   That having been always attached to the interests of his Country He is induced to make this application to the President of
the United States for the appointment to the office of Marshal
of the Federal Court, for the State of North Carolina.

Should he be deemed worthy of this trust—his utmost abilities shall be exerted, to render every satisfaction in the discharge of the duties thereto annexed. And your Petitioner as in duty bound Shall ever pray &c.

Solomon Halling

ALS, DLC:GW.

Solomon Halling (c.1754–1813), a native of Pennsylvania, was a surgeon in the Continental army and settled in New Bern in 1783 or 1784, where he practiced medicine and taught in the local academy. He received no appointment from GW. In 1792 Halling was ordained an Episcopal priest and served thereafter as a parish rector in New Bern and later in Georgetown, S.C. (Powell, *Dictionary of North Carolina Biography,* 3:12–13). The appointment Halling sought went to John Skinner (*DHFC,* 2:78–79).

From Thomas Mifflin

Sir   In Council Philadelphia March 10th 1790
I have the Honor of transmitting to your Excellency a Letter which has been addressed to the Executive of this State by several very respectable Inhabitants of the County of Washington in Pennsylvania; in which they represent "that many mischiefs have taken place in that County for several years past from the hostile incursions of the Indians, and that from the present aspect of Indian affairs in the western and South western Countries, the same are likely to continue," and request "the interposition of Council with the President of the United States in behalf of the Inhabitants of Washington County."[1]

Mr Ryerson a Member of our Legislature who has subscribed that letter will have the Honor of waiting on your Excellency and will give, if it should be thought proper, full information on the Subject.[2] I have the Honor to be with the greatest respect Your Excellencys most obedient and most humble Servant

Thomas Mifflin

LS, DLC:GW.

1. The letter from the Washington County citizens to Mifflin, 25 Jan. 1790, also stated: "Among many other murders and robberies practised by the Savages on the inhabitants of Ohio and Monongahela Counties in Virginia, and Washington County in Pensylvania, we shall only particularize those which happened in the latter, in the Course of the last year. We name Mr Thomas and two of his neighbours, whose names we do not at this time recollect, and One Crow, that were killed. The former three, lived on Dunkard Creek and

were killed last Spring, the latter lived on the head waters of Wheeling Creek and was killed in the month of Septemr 1789. while hunting a little way from home. Besides thes⟨e⟩ there were two other persons, (brothers to the last mentioned one killed) wounded at the same time⟨.⟩ Crow was buried by some of Mr Ryersons people⟨.⟩ In addition to the foregoeing we shall only add that the frontier Inhabitants of Washington County have been broke up, and were obliged to Shelter themselves in Block houses, or oth⟨er⟩ places of security, at one season or another, almost every year for ten years past or up⟨wards⟩.

"We therefore 'request the interposition of Council with the President of the United States in behalf of the frontier Inhabitants of our County to protect them against further depredations' from the Indians which we apprehend will take place in the spring if some means of defence is not provided for them." The letter is signed by Alexander Addison, James Ross, Thomas Ryerson, and Henry Taylor (DLC:GW). The victims were probably Captain William Thomas and Joseph Cornbridge and his wife and two children who were killed on Dunkard's Creek on 23 April 1789 (John Evans to Beverly Randolph, 25 April 1789, in *ASP, Indian Affairs,* 1:84). GW replied to Mifflin's letter on 15 Mar. 1790.

2. Thomas Ryerson, a longtime resident of Washington County, was appointed associate judge in the Washington County Court in April 1789 and was again elected to the Pennsylvania general assembly in 1790 (Crumrine, *Washington County,* 242, 249, 471). On 15 Mar. 1790 GW noted in his diary that Ryerson had presented Mifflin's letter and its enclosure to him. "This letter I sent to the Secretary of War to be laid before Congress" (*Diaries,* 6:46). The letters were transmitted to the House of Representatives on 16 Mar. (*DHFC,* 3:329; Knox to U.S. House of Representatives, 16 Mar. 1790, DLC:GW).

As a result of a deluge of complaints similar to those of the residents of Washington County from other frontier counties, on 13 April Henry Knox informed the county lieutenants of Washington County in Pennsylvania and Harrison, Randolph, Ohio, Monongahela, and Kanawha counties in Virginia that the president had authorized the lieutenants "in certain cases of imminent danger, to call out, for the protection of the county, certain species of patrols, denominated scouts, at the expense of the United States." This authority continued until mid-July 1790 when, by GW's order, it was withdrawn because of the expense and because the administration was in the process of reorganizing the army on the frontier in preparation for Josiah Harmar's campaign against the northern tribes. See Knox to the county lieutenants, 17 July 1790, *ASP, Indian Affairs,* 1:102–3).

From Beverley Randolph

Sir, Richmond [Va.] March 10th 17[9]0.[1]

I do myself the honor to forward to you, a letter, lately received, from Colonel Arthur Campbell⟨.⟩ The Executive of this state did not think themselves authorized to take any other step in this business, than the one recommended in the inclosed letter to Colonel Campbell. I have the honor to be with the highest respect your obt Servt

Beverley Randolph

LS, DNA: RG 59, Miscellaneous Letters; Vi: Executive Letter Book.
   1. Randolph inadvertently dated this letter 1770.

Enclosure
Arthur Campbell to Beverley Randolph

Sir   Washington Feb. 20. 1790

By different communications particularly a letter from one of the Kentucky Delegates of which an extract is inclosed I am informed that the unfriendly Southren Indians have notice of the ammunition intended for the Chickasaws and are preparing a force to try to take it.[1]

Piamingo when he set out from Holstein for the Chickasaws Towns, assured us, he would if possible, be back by the first of February, with a strong detachment of his own Warriors to escort the ammunition out: He reached the Cumberland Settlements, not far distant from which, he had a skirmish with a small party of Creeks, who he got the better of. Since he left Cumberland going homeward not a syllable from him. What may be the cause of this delay is uncertain; but it will be fatal, to part of our frontier Settlements, if the impatience of the enemy should prompt them to push forward, (before a Guard arrives), to destroy the powder where it now lies. The Inhabitants in Virginia adjoining are alarmed, being now apprehensive of such an event. Sometime ago I wrote the Commanding officer of the Holstein District in Carolina advising him to place a small guard at Kings, where the ammunition now lies, and that I did not doubt, but that the Executive of the United States, would sanction the measure. This is not yet done, nor can well be accomplished, without first receiving orders for the purpose. Thus, Sir, is a valuable public property, not only, in a way to be lost; but the lives of a number of defenceless Citizens in imminent danger.

Had we Orders from the Executive, or from the President of the United States, we would proceed with confidence, as we might be instructed to secure the stores.

It is a mortifying consideration the lax regulations respecting egress, and regress, between the Settlements of the white-people in Carolina and that of the Indians. It is more than probable that McGillivray has emissaries—passing and repassing, particularly a certain Bennet Bellew, (an old Tory) this man is blamed for carrying the account of the arrival of the ammunition to the enemy.[2]

It would be a happy circumstance if we had martial law on the frontiers for some time, and a rigid officer with Troops that would see it executed. I am Sir your most obedient servant

Arthur Campbell

Copy, DNA: RG 59, Miscellaneous Letters.

1. In the fall of 1789 Piomingo, or the Mountain Leader (see Piomingo to GW, 30 Oct. 1789), was on his way to New York City with several other Chickasaw chiefs to request aid from GW for the Chickasaw in their disputes with the Creek. While Piomingo was in Virginia, the legislature, on 23 Oct., resolved that "Whereas, some of the chiefs of the Chickasaw Indians have represented, that the Creek Indians have committed many insults and depredations on their nation, and have attacked them in a hostile manner and unprovoked, that they intended to make application to the President of the United States for assistance to repel those violences, but are prevented from executing that intention by the great distance to New York, the advanced season of the year, and the pressing exigence of their affairs. And the General Assembly calling to remembrance the long and uninterrupted friendship which hath subsisted between the said Indians and the people of this State, who have received constant proofs of their affectionate regards, and at the same time pitying the defenceless condition of the said Chickasaws, who are exposed to the fury of their enemies from the want of ammunition;

"*It is therefore resolved,* That the Executive be desired to furnish to the Chickasaw nation, such a quantity of gunpowder, not exceeding 2,000 weight, and lead proportioned thereto, as their necessities may require, and the public can conveniently spare, and furnish such of the said Indians as are in this city, with such articles as may be proper for them, and also make suitable compensation to the two white men who accompany the said Indians." The General Assembly, the journal indicates, acted in anticipation of approval by the federal executive (*Journal of the House of Delegates,* 1789, 8–9). On 30 Oct. Piomingo wrote GW that because of "the delays he had met with and the temporary aid he had obtained from the State of Virga," he had decided to return home (Washington's Memoranda on Indian Affairs, 1789, printed above). As Campbell indicates later in his letter, the ammunition was left behind at "Kings." This site was possibly Kings Mill, on Holston River at the mouth of Reedy Creek, a large structure built of heavy stone in 1774 by Col. James King. It stood in the area of present-day Kingsport, Tennessee. By March 1790 Piomingo was assisting Maj. John Doughty on the Tennessee River after an attack on his small force by the Cherokee. See GW to the Chiefs of the Choctaw Nation, 17 Dec. 1789, source note. Doughty requested that the powder and lead deposited at Kings Mill be sent to the Falls of the Ohio at a place designated by Doughty and Piomingo. "It is of the utmost consequence to the United States that this powder & lead should get to the nation. The present made by the State of Virginia last fall has never reached these people, and they are on the eve of a war with the Creeks" (Doughty to Josiah Harmar, 17 April 1790, WHi: Draper Collection, Harmar Papers).

Campbell's enclosure was an extract of a letter from "a Member of the Legislature of Virginia, dated Holstein-Iron Works 16th Febr. 1790," stating that "the Indians of the South have got information of the Mountain-Leaders Ammunition, and are from every intelligence I am able to get, determined to intercept it, let it go by either rout except prevented by a strong Guard" (DNA: RG 59, Miscellaneous Letters).

2. For Bennet Ballew, see the Cherokee Nation to GW, 19 May 1789, n.3. In the summer and fall of 1789 Ballew was in Virginia and in New York with a delegation of Cherokee chiefs.

Enclosure
Beverley Randolph to Arthur Campbell

Sir,   Richmond March 8th 1790

Yours of the 20th of February, by Express, has been submitted to the Council. The Executive do not conceive themselves authorized to order a Guard for the Ammunition of the chickasaw Indians, more especially as the place, where it is deposited; is not within the limits of the state. They will therefore forward your letter to the president of the United States.

As the safety of this ammunition is considered of great importance to the United states, we cannot avoid recommending it to the good citizens in its neighbourhood, upon the approach of an Enemy, to embody themselves as Volunteers for the protection of the property of our allies. There can be no doubt, but the General Government will sanction such a measure, should it be necessary. I am Sir, your obt Servt

Beverley Randolph

Copy, DNA: RG 59, Miscellaneous Letters.

From the United States Senate

United States [New York] March 10. 1790
The Senate agreed that the President of the United States direct the word "Junior" to be annexed to the name of Jonathan Palmer, appointed Surveyor of Stonington in the State of Connecticut August 3d 1790.[1] Attest

Sam. A. Otis Secy

LB, DLC:GW.

1. See GW to the U.S. Senate, 3 Aug. 1790.

From the Pennsylvania Legislature

[(]Copy)

Sir   In Assembly of Pennsylvania March 11. 1790
I have the honour to transmit an exemplified copy of the act declaring the assent of this State to certain amendments to the Constitution of the United States that you may be pleased to lay it before Congress.[1] With the greatest respect I have the honour to be Your obedt Servt

Richard Peters. Speaker

Copy, DNA: RG 46, First Congress, 1789–91, Records of Legislative Proceedings, President's Messages.

1. The enclosure was a copy of "An act declaring the assent of this State to certain amendments to the Constitution of the United States" passed by the Pennsylvania legislature on 10 Mar. 1790. The legislature ratified the third through the twelfth articles proposed by Congress as amendments to the federal Constitution, including all of those that formed the Bill of Rights (for the complete text of the proposed amendments, see *DHFC*, 4:1–3). It voted not to approve the first two proposed amendments. The second of these specified that "No law, varying the compensation for the services of the Senators and Representatives, shall take effect, until an election of Representatives shall have intervened" (ibid., 1). Pennsylvania was not among the states that subsequently ratified this article, which became the twenty-seventh amendment to the Constitution in 1992. Lear presented the Pennsylvania act to Congress on 16 Mar. 1790 (see GW to the U.S. Senate and House of Representatives, 16 Mar. 1790). For the complete text of the act and related documents, see *DHFC*, 3:330–32.

From David Stuart

Dear Sir,   11th March 1790—Abingdon [Va.]

As I have at length made an agreement with Mr Alexander, which will be binding, if it meets with your approbation, I shall endeavour to give you every information in my power, to enable you to judge of the propriety or impropriety of it[1]—I informed you in my last, that I had little expectation of effecting any with him, as he had receded so far from his original proposals, as to demand a thousand pounds, besides rents[2]—Finding soon after, that all his friends except Mr Massey, dissuaded him strongly from accepting even these terms; influenced by the importance of the suit which might issue in the total ruin of the estate, I made him the offer of six hundred pounds exclusive of the rents—He rejected it at the time, and I really believe would have continued to do so still, but for some heavy judgements which have lately been obtained against him—I can only say, I have done for the best, and have had as much trouble, as I believe any one ever had; for he is the most trifling, undecided character that ever I met with—As it may seem odd, that I never before attempted a compromise; I must observe that when I first undertook the business of the estate, besides being influenced by Mr Dandridge having never offered it; I found the Lawyers of opinion that the tender would be considered as good—About two years ago, understanding that some had been rejected, as not made in the proper kind of money, I mentioned to Mr Marshall, the propriety of inspecting the money which had been tendered to Mr Alexander, and he advised it—To my astonishment it turned out improper. After this discovery however, it was the opinion of Baker & Marshall, that the twelve thousand pounds would be scaled at six for one[3]—Considering two thousand pounds as no bad bargain for the Estate, I still remained satisfied, and pressed for a trial—When this came on last Summer, these gentlemen changed their sentiments, and gave it as their opinion, that the 48.600£ would be scaled. This circumstance induced me to put off the trial, and offer a compromise—But there is a difference of opinion between my Council, and Mr Alexanders, even with respect to the scale—Mine found their opinion of it's being fixed at six, from the date of the deeds, the 25th of December 78—while Mr Alexander's are sanguine in their expectations, of establishing it at five, the time at which the agreement afterwards confirmed was first entered into—Coll Simms whom I have consulted, agrees with Alexander's Lawyers. Tho' this difference is important, Coll Tailor thinks Alexander's chance for the 48.600£ very good—The consideration of this contrariety of opinions, with the ruin which would be entailed on an infant family, if my Lawyers were disappointed in their most sanguine expectations, (and these not very favourable) determine me in my offer—Tho' the terms are not so advantageous as those of the last year, I cannot for my part but think it better to close with them, than to remain any longer in such a dreadfull state of suspence. I have now informed you of every circumstance I am possessed of, and given you a full detail of my conduct in this disagreeable business, with the motives which have influenced me—Inclosed you have a copy of the agreement, with Messrs Randolph's, Marshall's, & Innis's opinions respecting the tender—I forgot to inform you last fall, that by the advice of all my Lawyers, I petitioned the Assembly to be empowered to make any compromise in this affair, which should recieve your approbation, and succeeded—I thought this necessary, to secure us both from any future injury or censure—I have waited from the date of the agreement, 'till now, hoping to get the law, to send to you, but I have been disappointed[4]—The time I have to prepare for the first payment, if the agreement meets with your approbation, is so short as not to permit me to use further delay. The purport of the law as I am informed by Mr Lee & Randolph, is empowering me to make any compromise, which shall recieve your approbation, expressed under your hand & seal—It will therefore be necessary I presume, that this should be done on a seperate instrument of writing, in order that it may be recorded, and have the appearance of more authenticity, than the mere signification of your consent by letter. As I shall set out for Williamsburg early in April, to prepare for the trial with Coll Basset, I must beg to hear from you as quickly as possible. The persons I mean to appoint on my part, one Coll Macarty, and Mr Wm Herbert[5]—My reasons are these—M'Cartys estimation of the land two years ago, when I appointed several for that purpose, was much the lowest—Besides, he rents out as I am informed, seven or eight hundred acres of good land, with ten negroes in Prince William, for 90£

a year—Herbert has a very unprofitable plantation near me—
If you however can think of any more proper, I beg you will
mention them.

We had last night, as heavy a fall of snow as I allmost ever
saw—it is nearly knee deep—the wheat has I fear suffered much
from the previous frosts—I have no news, except a little bustle
which Coll Forrests politicks have just excited in G[eorg]e-
town[6]—He has had influence enough with the Corporation in
that town, to get a duty laid on all imported goods for the benefit
of that place alone—It is certainly a most extraordinary measure and must if followed by other towns, produce infinitely
more variety in the duties than existed under the States. Mrs
Stuart & the family went a fiew days ago to Mt Vernon—Begging my best respects to Mrs Washington I am Dr Sir Your Affecte Serv:

Dd Stuart

ALS, DLC:GW.

1. For background on Stuart's protracted negotiations with Robert Alexander, see Stuart to GW, 14 July 1789, n.7, 12 Sept., 3 Dec. 1789, GW to Stuart,
21 Sept. 1789, Edmund Randolph to GW, 23 Dec. 1789.

2. See Stuart to GW, 3 Dec. 1789.

3. Jerman Baker (d. 1799), a prominent Chesterfield County attorney, practiced law in Richmond and often acted in cases with John Marshall.

4. Stuart sent GW a copy of the law on 15 Mar. 1790.

5. It is unlikely that Stuart is referring to Daniel McCarty (d. 1792), a friend
and relative of GW and one of Virginia's wealthiest planters, who lived at
Mount Air on Accotink Creek, a few miles from Mount Vernon, although he
was frequently referred to as "colonel." More likely it was one of the many
other McCartys who lived in the neighborhood. William Herbert (1743–1818)
was an Alexandria merchant and a frequent visitor to Mount Vernon.

6. Uriah Forrest (1756–1805) served with Maryland forces during the Revolution and as a member of the Confederation Congress in 1787. In 1793 he
was elected to the U.S. Congress and served until his resignation in November
1794. Forrest lived near Georgetown, D.C., was very active in Georgetown
business affairs, and in 1792 served as the town's mayor. From 1800 to 1805
he was clerk of the circuit court of the District of Columbia.

From Daniel Lyman

Sir　　　　　　　　　　　　　　Newport [R.I.] March 12th 1790

For some time past I have had it in contemplation to apply to
your Excellency for an appointment in the Revennue Establishment when this State shall accede to the Union. This intention

has been intimated to some of my Friends, who have favored me with the enclosed letters on the subject, which would have been forwarded at an earlier date had not the conduct of this State rendered their decission respecting our Union too uncertain to justify my troubleing your Excellency in a matter which appeared so distant.[1] But at this time our hopes begin to revive, & we immagin we discover the ⟨dawn⟩ of a brighter day. I therefore now take the liberty to forward the enclosed, and to offer myself a Candidate for any appointment of which your Excellency may think me deserveing. If there are other Persons whose abilities, past services & sacrefices give them a better claim to your Excellency's notice, I chearfully resign my pretensions. But should Your Excellency judge me worthy your notice, my unremiting endeav[ors] will be exerted to discharge the trust with honor to myself, justice to my Country & your Excellencys approbation. I take the liberty to refer your Excellency for any further information to Mr Baldwin a member from Georgia. I have the honor to be with every sentiment of respect Your Excellency's most Obedient humble Servant

Daniel Lyman

ALS, DLC:GW.

Daniel Lyman (1756–1830) served as aide-de-camp to Maj. Gen. William Heath during the Revolution. For an account of his wartime career, see General Orders, 17 Oct. 1776, n.2. After the war Lyman took up the practice of law in Newport, becoming an active Federalist and a member of the Society of the Cincinnati.

1. William Heath, noting that Lyman was likely to apply for a position in the customs, stated that "from my personal acquaintance with Colonel Lyman, and knowledge of his abilities, permit me to join in recommendation of him should others more immediately concerned in the State introduce him to notice. Colonel Humphries who is probably near you is acquainted with Colonel Lyman and his abilities" (Heath to GW, 5 Feb. 1790, DLC:GW). Lyman was described by Isaac Senter as "a faithful officer, a good citizen, a friend to the Constitution & on all occasions a firm supporter of the principles of a literal, enlightened and sound policy" (Senter to GW, 27 Feb. 1790, DLC:GW). In May 1790 Lyman again applied for a position, recapitulating his military service and noting that his "conduct dureing this period, and the confidential appointments I received, will evince to your Excellency how far I merited the approbation of my Country. Since the war, the expence of an encreasing family, and almost total loss by depreciation of seven years service have prevailed upon me to offer myself to your Excellencys notice. My Family, my Friends, my property are in Newport, and I believe I can say with truth that the Friends to the late decission of our Convention in this Town & that State in general would feel themselves gratifyed in seeing my wishes realized" (Lyman to GW,

31 May 1790, DLC:GW). On 14 June 1790 Lyman was appointed surveyor for the port of Newport (*DHFC,* 2:80).

From Warner Mifflin

Respected Friend   William shotwells, 12th of 3rd 1790

Majestracy being an ordinance of God, I desire to revere it as such, and where the sword thereof is held up for a Terror to evil doers, and a Praise, to those who do well, Then is goverment a blessing to mankind, and no doubt but the blessing, Protection, and Preservation of the Almighty, by whom Kings reign and Princes only are enabled to decree justice will be witnessed— And a hope is with me that thou as the first Majestrate of this Nation art sensable thereof and desirous to be thus guided, May thou be earnest in solisitation, for renew'd supplies of his superior wisdom to guide thee aright, I see thou hast abundant need thereof indeed, even so much that it appears to me the safety of this Nation depends greatly thereon—Surely I doubt not but the Almighty is able to do more than we can forsee, or concieve, Yet in all human Probability were he in the dispensation of his Providence to call thee hence at this time it looks to me that our Situation might be deplorable—That I concieve we as a people are under strong obligations to pray for thee, as this is the weapon we must use of to thy aid, and by our influence endeavour in our neighbourhoods to attach the People to thee, and the Goverment, and promote Harmony and concord, thus much I believe thou may be assured of from the People called Quakers.

And as our society so lately presented thee an Address agreed on when perhaps there were between 8 & 10 hundred Members present which Address I believe was resulted in the fear of the supream Ruler of the Universe & I have faith to believe receiv'd the Approbation of his Holy spirit in our Hearts—And there was no doubt but thou would receive it in the manner intended by us and not a thing of course or a mear form.

This having been the case we thought it less necessary to wait on thee on our coming to this City on a deputation from same body to present, an address to the senate, and house of representatives respecting the Oppressed Affricans, tho I was some uneasy in not doing it, and should not have continued here so long without had it not been for the short interview we had with thee, when I a little oppen'd the Nature of our embassy.[1]

And notwithstanding I cannot say I feel it as a duty incumbant on me or I should have proceeded therein, yet I feel a strong desire to have a private interview with thee—but I feel a care on this head least making such Visits too cheap might in any sort lesson the Authority of the Majestrate which I desire to pre-serve—And I wish thy table may in no⟨wise⟩ tend to this; a word to the wise is sufficient—I therefore just hint in the freedom now felt this much and if thou saw cause to open the way thereto should I believe freely imbrace the oppertunity as I have a strong inclination there⟨fore⟩ yet should not think hard if it did appear in thy view best not to give it—If thou thought well a line handed next door; to the french consuls would come readily to me, or any way that was agreeable to thee—Under an Affection-ate regard that I feel toward thee and thy consort also at this time I conclude thy real Friend

                                             Warner Mifflin

ALS, DNA: RG 59, Miscellaneous Letters.

Warner Mifflin (1745–1798), a prominent Quaker abolitionist, was origi-nally from Accomack County, Va., from a slaveholding family. Although Mifflin generally refrained from political action, refusing to vote on the grounds that such participation in government might be considered support of slavehold-ing interests, he was instrumental in presenting a number of antislavery peti-tions to the Confederation Congress.

1. An entry in the journal of the House of Representatives indicates that on 11 Feb. 1790, memorials drawn up by the Quakers at their meetings in Philadelphia and New York in 1789 "praying the attention of Congress in adopting measures for the abolition of the slave trade, and in particular in restraining vessels from being entered and cleared out, for the purposes of that trade" were read and referred to a special committee of the House; on 23 Mar. the committee of the whole House to which the findings of the special committee had been referred reported that Congress had no authority to in-terfere with the slave trade until 1808 when the Constitution provided that the trade would be abolished. The Quakers' petition met the fate of most other memorials against slavery and committee reports concerning the institution. Congress ordered this petition "to lie on the table" (*DHFC*, 3:294–96, 316, 333–37, 340–41). See also GW to the Society of Quakers, October 1789, n.1. GW recorded in his diary that on Tuesday, 16 Mar.: "I was visited (having given permisn.) by a Mr. Warner Mifflin, one of the People called Quakers; active in pursuit of the Measures laid before Congress for emancipating the Slaves. After much general conversation, and an endeavor to remove the prej-udices which he said had been entertained of the motives by which the at-

tending deputation from their Society were actuated, he used Arguments to shew the immorality—injustice and impolicy of keeping these people in a state of Slavery; with declarations, however, that he did not wish for more than a graduel abolition, or to see any infraction of the Constitution to effect it. To these I replied, that as it was a matter which might come before me for official decision I was not inclined to express any sentimts. on the merits of the question before this should happen" (*Diaries*, 6:47). On 28 Mar. GW wrote David Stuart that the "memorial of the Quakers (and a very mal-apropos one it was) has at length been put to sleep, and will scarcely awake before the year 1808."

From Samuel A. Otis

Sir,   New York March 12th 1790.

Permit me to state a few facts relative to the Impost for the District of Barnstable for your consideration.

First. the District, comprehending all the towns in the County except one, is sixty miles in length and wholly maritime, abounding in harbours and inlets on all sides, and requires the constant vigilance of the Collector; For in no district can smuggling be effected with more facility.

Second—Most of the navigation of this district is in part owned in *that* of Boston, and the Masters of Vessels take their papers from thence principally—The emoluments of the District of Barnstable to the impost officer are therefore, scarce sufficient to pay Horse hire and exertion, altho attention to the revenue requires much of the time and exertion of a Collector.

I beg leave therefore to suggest that as there will probably be a Collector of Excise necessary for the district, that the emoluments of that office in addition to those of the Collector of Impost might in some measure enable the person to subsist without additional expense to government; and as there is a natural connexion in the business, tho both in the small districts will hardly employ an active officer, it may be thought expedient to vest the same person with both appointments.

The collection of Impost and Excise were blended under the State Laws and the execution of the business effected with great facility in this mode and by the present Collector of impost.

Upon these considerations I take the liberty to recommend to your favorable regard and appointment Joseph Otis, the present Collector of Impost for the district of Barnstable, as the most eligible person also for Collector of excise; In whose fidelity and exertion I have good reason to suppose you may place confidence.[1] I have the honor to be with the utmost respect your most obedient Humble Servant

Sam. A. Otis

I took the liberty to suggest my Ideas on this subject to the Secretary of the Treasury.

ALS, DLC:GW.

1. Joseph Otis (1726–1809), Samuel Allyne Otis's older brother and a member of the prominent Otis family of Massachusetts, served as colonel of the 1st Barnstable County Regiment of militia in August 1775 and in 1776 became brigadier general in the Massachusetts militia. At various times Otis served as clerk of the court of common pleas and as a member of the General Court. GW appointed Otis collector of customs at Barnstable, Mass., on 3 Aug. 1789 and in 1792 named him inspector of the excise for Barnstable.

From Michael Ryan

Sir   Richmond [Va.] March 12th 1790
    Some unforeseen accidents and a tedious indisposition have so derang'd my affairs that I am totally out of business, I would therefore willingly accept of any place in which I may be useful. Your former approbation of my conduct in a military line emboldens me to make this direct application. Should I be call'd forward on the arrangement of the militia or in any other Station it shall be my constant study to merit the confidence that may be repos'd in me. I am With every sentiment of respect, attachment, and esteem, Sir, your faithfull Humble Servt

M. Ryan

ALS, DLC:GW.

Michael Ryan (d. 1791) of Pennsylvania served in various Pennsylvania regiments during the Revolution, rising from the rank of second lieutenant in the 4th Pennsylvania Battalion in 1776 to captain in the 5th Pennsylvania at the time of his resignation in June 1779. In 1780 he served as inspector general of the Pennsylvania militia with the rank of lieutenant colonel and in the same year was brigade major of the First City Brigade of Philadelphia (*Pennsylvania Magazine of History and Biography*, 46 [1922], 167). At some point after the Revolution, Ryan, in partnership with "Mr Whitecroft of Annapolis," acquired a substantial grant of land adjacent to GW's holdings on the Great Kanawha River in what is now West Virginia. Ryan's partner was probably William Whetcroft (d. 1791), an Annapolis clockmaker and merchant. By the mid-

1780s Ryan and Whetcroft concocted an ambitious plan for laying out two towns in the area and attracting European farmers to settle the grant, which they, perhaps overenthusiastically, estimated at two hundred thousand acres. By late 1787, however, the partners, finding that the scheme was "too arduous an undertaking for us unconnected," proposed forming a company and selling shares in the grant for expenses and to fund marketing the land in Europe. In December 1787 Ryan tried unsuccessfully to interest GW in the scheme. See Ryan to GW, 23 Dec. 1787 and GW to Ryan, 9 Jan. 1788. GW gave Ryan no federal appointment.

From Robert Morris

(private)
Dear Sir					New York 13th March 1790
	The letters sent herewith are from Madam De Miralles, after you have had them translated so that you can be informed of her wishes I will do myself the Honor to wait upon you in order to Converse on the Subject[1]—with perfect respect your obedient & hble servt

					Robt Morris

ALS, DLC:GW.
	1. Maria Josepha Elirio de la Puente Miralles was the widow of Juan de Miralles (1705–1780), first Spanish agent to the United States who died while visiting GW's headquarters at Morristown on 28 April 1780. Miralles's death left his wife, who had remained in Havana, with the care of their eight children. See GW to Diego Jose de Navarro, 30 April 1780, Maria de la Puente Miralles to GW, 6 July 1780, and GW to Maria de la Puente Miralles, 13 Oct. 1780. The letters enclosed by Morris have not been found, but they may have concerned private finances. In July 1781 Morris instructed Robert Smith, U.S. agent in Havana, to ask Madame de Miralles to allow him to invest money left by her husband in the Bank of North America (Morris to Smith, 17 July 1781, DNA:PCC, item 137).

From La Luzerne

Monsieur,					A Londres le 14 Mars 1790
	M. Dowdall qui remettra cette Lettre à vôtre Excellence est un Gentilhomme anglois qui m'est Recommandé par plusieurs personnes de ce pays cy pour lesquelles j'ai une grande Considération.[1] Sa famille lui laisse des Droits à réclamer sur des possessions très Considérables dans les Etats unis qui le déter-

minent à y passer. Si ces Droits sont fondés, je supplie vôtre Excellence de l'honnorer de sa protection dans les démarches qu'il fera pour obtenir la Justice qui lui seroit düe. Si ces demandes méritoient vôtre approbation, ce seroit un préjugé bien avantageux pour lui; et-il seroit sûr de trouver dans le Gouvernement, dans les Magistrats et dans les Loix tout ce qui peut favoriser le bon droit et contribuer à la conservation des proprietés. Je vous supplie d'être bien persuadé que je serai très Reconnoissant des bontés que vous voudrés bien avoir pour M. Dowdall: Celles que vous aves pour moi depuis longtems, me donnent Lieu d'Esperer que vous voudrés bien lui accorder votre appui.

Je proffitte avec Empressemens de cette occasion de vous Renouveller l'assurance du respectueux attachemens avec lequel j'ai L'honneur d'être, De vôtre Excellence Le très humble et très obéissant Serviteur,

le Mqs de la Luzerne

LS, DLC: Riggs Family Papers.
   1. Dowdall has not been further identified.

Letter not found: to George Augustine Washington, 14 Mar. 1790. In a letter to GW, 26 Mar. 1790, George Augustine Washington refers to a letter of "the 14th."

From Claude-Boniface Collignon

Castel near Boquenon in Lorroain—March 15. 1790.
My Lord.

I have had the honor to write you a letter in date April 28th 1780, which accompanied a work of my composition that I presented to you, "Respecting clearing all the uncultivated lands of the United States of America," particularly those which might belong to you as proprietor: I have learned that the uncultivated lands in the extent of the Provinces & United States have since been cleared in an immense degree.[1] I hope that the homage which I had the honor to render you by that production, as well as that which I have paid to Congress will be perfectly agreeable to both it & you. Here are, my Lord, two Copies of another work of my own composition, "for rendering all the weights & measures in America uniform."[2] I pray you will please to present it on my part to the illustrious Congress of the U.S., agreeably to the desire & conformably to my annexed letter, to which I refer.

I know not, my Lord, whether it has come to your knowledge, what was the principal & veritable first cause, which produced the Independence of the U.S. of America: it is not unknown to me how much you conducted yourself at the Head of the armies of the U.S. with valeur, wisdom & experience; and how great obligations they are under to you on this account—but, considering the great superiority of forces of England, undoubtedly you could not, my Lord, have accomplished what was impossible; the diversion of France & its allies, and their successes against England, are generally considered as the principal cause of the Independence of the U.S.

If then there exists a Citizen, who, when the arms of France & its allies against England were wavering, and they began to be [defeated] (& which must infallibly have been the consequence) has instructed & enlightened the Government of France, in such sort, that, by following his counsel, it has obtained that marked preponderance which forced England to subscribe to the Independence of the United States & to make the Peace of 1783. It will, without contradiction, be that Citizen, to whom the U.S. have the principal obligation for their Independence & their actual Constitution. Now, I ought to make known to you, my Lord, that it is *I*, who have given to France that Counsel & that salutary advice; and that it was by *me* that it has been enlightened on that occasion. I will not indulge myself here in any farther detail with respect to this matter, since the circumstances & the event are developed in the Memoir hereunto annexed, addressed to you & Congress, supported by justificative peices.[3] I pray you, in consequence, to be pleased to place it, jointly with my work on the uniformity of weights & measures, before the eyes of the illustrious Congress. I hope that I shall not always remain the victim of the ingratitude which I have experienced on the part of the Government of France; and that the Congress of the U.S. more grateful & more just will deign to consider it a duty & a conscientious mission to recompence a man to whom the U.S. owe so much, and who has been truly the principal Spring & Primum [Premiere] mobile of their Independence & of their present Liberty. I hope also, that you will be pleased, on your side to engage the illustrious Congress to this. I entreat you, my

Lord, consequently to advise me of the receipt of this, & to give me satisfactory news; which, it seems, you may do, by sending the answer here, through the means of M. le Chargè des Affairs of the U.S. at Paris.[4] I am, with the most profound respect, my Lord your most humble & most obedt Servant

Collignon Advocate.

Translation, DNA: RG 59, Miscellaneous Letters; ALS, in French, DNA: RG 59, Miscellaneous Letters. The text is taken from a translation prepared for GW by David Humphreys. The original letter, in French, may be found in CD-ROM:GW.

Claude-Boniface Collignon (d. 1819), a French attorney, minor government official, and member of numerous European academies, was a proponent of a wide range of sweeping legal and social reforms.

1. Letter not found. Collignon is probably referring to his *Essai de bien public, ou Mémoire raisonné pour lever, à coup sûr, tous les obstacles qui s'opposent à l'exécution des défrichements et dessèchements* (Neuchatel, 1776), which called for the removal of legal impediments to the clearing and draining of land.

2. Collignon, *Découverte d'étalons justes, naturels, invariables, et universels pour la réduction à une parfaite uniformité de tous les poids et mesures partout, par des moyens simples, advantageux à tout le monde, et faciles á executer* (Strasbourg, 1788). In this work Collignon called for the universal adoption of a system of weights and measures based on decimals. He even proposed applying the decimal system to the measurement of time, dividing a day into ten hours, an hour into one hundred minutes, and a minute into one thousand seconds.

3. Collignon's extraordinary claim to credit for American independence is elaborated in a lengthy manuscript memorial to Congress. In it Collignon claimed that in 1780, when the continuation of French support for the Revolution was in doubt, he had written six letters to the king in support of the American cause. As justification for his claim, Collignon included copies of the six letters with the memorial. No contemporary translation of this document has been found among GW's papers, and it seems unlikely that one was made.

4. The translation made by Humphreys of the second letter sent by Collignon on 15 Mar. reads: "I have the honor to inform you, that I have composed a Work, 'for rendering all weights & measures uniform every where.' Since this uniformity has been a Consideratum for a long time throughout the extent of the U.S. of A.; & for effecting which, I understand Congress is invested with special powers by its Constituents, I have judged that Body would be happy to see simple & enlightened means for that purpose. In consequence, I have the honor, my Lord, to address to you the two annexed copies, one destined for yourself & which I pray you will be pleased to accept on my part—the other, I entreat you will be pleased to submit, with this letter, to the Congress of the U.S. of A. I submit it to your & their profound wisdoms. I hope that the homage which I have the honor to render both, will be acceptable.

"As I do not doubt at all but that Congress, according to custom, will appoint Commissioners to examine & report concerning this Work, I hope by the account which will be rendered that Body will perceive easily the advantages which may result from the execution of my plan throughout the extent of the territory of the U.S. of A. These will consist among others, first, in having their weights & measures made perfectly uniform, & the inconveniencies of their diversity ceasing⟨,⟩ which will produce the re-establishment of order, & which may avoid in future a great many complicated calculations, errors, & unprofitable loss of time as it regards commerce, navigation, agriculture, the administration of the country, all sciences, arts, trades & professions. secondly, by suppressing all measures of grain, or what is called dry-measure, and by substituting weights & ballances in their stead (as I have proposed in the 120th ⟨&⟩ following pages) an infinite number of prevailing abuses, cheats & disorders of every kind will be cut up by the roots. thirdly. The new weights & measures, which are founded upon mathematical principles & upon nature, to which we must sooner or later recur, will be infinitely more simple than those in use, since by means of three new standards, the functions of perhaps more than 2000 now in use throughout the extent of the territory of the U.S. can be better performed. fourthly. The result will be, that, notwithstanding the more exact construction of the new weights & measures, they will not be dearer than heretofore—though much more perfect. fifthly, in fine, this object can produce a new annual revenue of at least 2 or 3,000,000 of Livres for the United States. I will not make mention of an infinite number of other advantages.

"As the method to be pursued for the execution of this project has appeared to me an object of the greatest importance, I have thought, my Lord, I ought to have the honor of mentioning it.

"In conformity to the preface of my book, it seems to me in the first place, that it would be very necessary for the Chiefs & most enlightened People of the U.S. to become acquainted & instructed by a considerate perusal of the book, in order that the law to be passed on this subject should be preceded by the public confidence & opinion: and I do not advise Congress, seconded by all their powers, to act otherwise, but after they shall have dissipated popular prejudice, & left a conviction derived from the good & solid reasons to be found in my book. Upon these principles, here is what I believe the manner of managing the subject.

"Congress should buy about 3 or 400 copies of my book, which I sell for two livres each. Having received them, a distribution should be made, not only to each one of its members or deputies, but to the principal Heads or officers of every Corporation, District or County in the extent of the Provinces of the U.S.; as well as to enlightened men & professors of arts, for the purpose of asking their advice, or, in every event, for the purpose of learning their manner of thinking on this subject, & of giving to their Representatives of Provinces the necessary instructions.

"After the investigation which shall have been made by every one of my book, either the sentiments of these persons will be conformable to what I have proposed, or they will not—in the first case there will be no more obstacle or inconveniency respecting the execution of my plan—in the second case, it will only require to have the principal objections inserted in a News Paper circulated through the 13 Provinces, & to send it to me free of expence—then

I engage to answer them, through the same channel, at all points. In this last case, Congress, the Ministry, the Heads & Representatives of Provinces & Towns, Men of information, & the Public, seeing what can be said on both sides of my plan, & being in condition to appreciate its value by the concession of opinions, it is to be presumed they will perceive its goodness & that a law for the execution of my plan throughout the extent of the territory of the U.S. will not fail to be regarded by all the Citizens as a real benefit, & to be received with the greatest gratitude.

"Perhaps the expence which this object will cost may be objected to me; but I will answer, that it is so moderate, that it is, as one may say, imperceptible for a great State, when compared with the advantages to be derived from it. If the illustrious Congress, judges proper to accept the proposal I have the honor to make it here of purchasing the Copies in question, you can, my Lord, give me the necessary orders, in pointing out the channel of conveyance for them: but in case that, contrary to all expectation, the purchase should not be made, I hope Congress will be pleased to transmit to me, with your answer, an honorable Present to indemnify me as well for these copies as for my trouble & expences—which indemnification, nevertheless, I do not demand, if I receive its orders for the purchase of the copies before alluded to" (DNA: RG 59, Miscellaneous Letters, translation by David Humphreys; a transcription of the ALS, in French, of this letter is in CD-ROM:GW).

As Collignon requested, GW kept one copy of *Découverte d'étalons justes;* this copy, signed by GW, was among the Washington books acquired by the Boston Athenaeum in 1848 and cataloged in Griffin, *Boston Athenæum Collection*, 50–51. GW had Lear send the memorial, along with Collignon's two letters of 15 Mar. 1790 and one copy of *Découverte d'étalons justes,* to Jefferson, who was then at work on his "Report on Weights and Measures" (Lear to Jefferson, 23 June 1790, DNA: RG 59, Miscellaneous Letters). Jefferson apparently ignored the suggestions in Collignon's letters and seems to have made no use of the book in writing his report, which was completed by 4 July 1790 (see "Report on Weights and Measures" in Boyd, *Jefferson Papers*, 16:602–75). Apparently Jefferson did not keep the book, since it was not among the works he sold to Congress in 1815 (Sowerby, *Catalogue of the Library of Thomas Jefferson*). A second copy, bearing GW's signature and that of F. M. Etting, is in the library of the Historical Society of Pennsylvania. This is probably the copy sent to Jefferson. Jefferson seems to have dismissed Collignon's claims to compensation for having supported American liberty. The memorial was apparently not presented to Congress.

Household Expenses

[15–22 March 1790]
⟨*illegible*⟩kles and the Quantity Consumed weekly in the family of the President of the United States Exclusive of marketing & Ctr. from 15th of March to 22 1790

		£	s.	d.
Madr. Wine	30 Btls. @ 3/6	5.	5.	0
Champaine	4 @ 6/	1.	4.	0
Claret	2 @ 6/	0.12.		0
Sweet wine	1 @ 2/	0.	2.	0
Common wine for Cook & Ctr.	14 @ /1od.	0.12.		0
Spirits	3 @ 2/	0.	6.	0
Rum	2 @ 1/6	0.	3.	0
Brandy	3 @ 1/8	0.	5.	0
Porter	30 @ 14/ pr doz.	1.15.		0
Cyder	54 qts @ 32/ pr bbl	0.15.		0
Vinegar	2 @ 6d.	0.	1.	0
Fine Tea	1½ ⟨℔d.⟩ @ 16/	1.	4.	0
Common Dto	1 @ 3/	0.	3.	0
Lump Sugar	46 @ 1/8	3.16.		8
Brown Dto	28 @ 8o/ pr cwt	1.	0.	
Coffee	12 @ 2/	1.	4.	0
Butter	40 @ ⟨illeg.⟩	⟨illeg.⟩		
Tallow Candles	10 @ 1/⟨2⟩	0.11.		8
Spermacity & Wax	14 @ 3/6	2.	9.	0
Lamp oill	2 G. @ 5/	0.10.		0
Table Dto	1 flask @ 3/	0.	3.	0
Mustard	1 Bttl. @ 1/3	0.	1.	3
Salt	½ Bsl ⎫			
	⎬	0.	3.	0
Dto	½ Bus. ⎭			

		£24.	8.11	
pepper	½ ⟨℔d.⟩ @ 3/6	⟨illeg.⟩		
allspice	2 oz. @ 4/ pr ⟨lb.⟩	⟨illeg.⟩		
Nut-megs	2 Dto @ 8o/ pr lb.	0.10.⟨0⟩		
Ginger	2 Dto @ 1o/ Do	0.	1.	4
Cinamon	2 Dto @ 48/ Do	0.	6.	0
Clovs	1 oz. @ 24/ Do	0.	1.⟨0⟩	
Mace	2 Dto @ 6.6/ Do	0.12.		
Flour	30 lb. @ /6d.	0.12.		6
Indian Meal		0.	0.	6
Buck wheat		0.	2.	
Raisens	7 ⟨℔d.⟩ @ 6d.	0.	3.	6
Currans	7 @ 8	0.	4.	8
Almonds	4 @ 1/6	0.	6.	0
Bitter Dto	½ @ 2/	0.	2.	0
Starch	6 ⟨℔d.⟩ @ /9d.	0.	4.	6
Blue	1 oz. @ 4/ pr lb.	0.	0.	3
Soap	14 ℔d. @ 1/4	0.18.		8
Soft Dto	17 @ 8d.	0.11.		4

Rice	7 @ 6d.	o. 3.	6
Citron	1 lb. @ 4/6	o. 4.	6
		£29.14.	11

Jno. Hyde

⟨*illegible*⟩ of weekly expenditures exclusive of
   marketing &c.   £29.14.11

Weekly Marketing—with amount of Butcher's,
   Baker's Brewer's, Fruit, Milk bills &c. as rendered in by Mr Hyde, on an average, since his
   entering service—   40.00. 0

Total amt of weekly consumption   £69.14.11

Estimate of yearly expenditures.

	Dollars	
Consumption of 52 weeks say @ 80£ or 200 Dolls.	10,400	
House Rent	1,000	
Wood—(say 8 Cords per week at 4 Dollars)	624	
16 Horses including keeping, Shoeing &c. @ 50		
Dols. ea.	800	

Salaries & Wages

	Dollars	
1	@ 800	
3 @ 600 Dolls. each	1800	
1 @ 300 Dolls.	300	
Mr Hyde	300	
Val. de Chambre @ 30 Guins.	140	
Cook (say at 12 Dollars)	144	
5 Servants @ 7 Dolls. per mo.	420	
6 Women @ 5 Dollars per mo.	360	
		4,264
	Carred over—	17,088

Austin, Giles & Paris @ 5 Dols. ea.		
per mo.	180	
Christopher, Moll & Oney @ 4 Do.		
ea. per mo.	144	
		324

6 Suits of Livery	@ 34 Dolls. each	204	
6 Hatts	@ 4 Dolls.	24	
6 Surtouts	@ 12 Dolls.	72	
3 pr boots	@ 6 Dolls.	18	
Livery &ca as above for Giles, Paris, &			
Christopher @ 40 Dolls. ea.		120	
			438
		Dollars	17,850

Annual Compensation[1]	25,000 Dollars
Estimate as above	17.850 Do
remains for other Exps.	7.150
Overcharge of £10 per week in 52 weeks is	1.300
remains for Contgt exps.	8.450 Dollars

D, N: Miscellaneous Manuscripts, vol. 2.
 1. This is a reference to GW's annual salary as president.

To Thomas Mifflin

Sir,   United States [New York] March 15th 1790.
 I have had the honor to receive your Excellency's letter of the
10th inst enclosing "a letter addressed to the Executive of the
State of Pennsylvania by several very respectable Inhabitants of
the County of Washington" representing the mischiefs which
have been done for several years past in that County, by the
Indians—expressing their apprehensions of further interruption—and requesting the Interposition of Council with the President of the United States in behalf of the Inhabitants of Washington County. I have already laid before Congress all such
papers and official information as have come to my hands,
respecting depredations which have been committed on the
Southern & Western frontiers of the United States[1]—In a word,
I have exhibited to them everything in my possession, that can
bring to their view the situation of our affairs in those parts. This
communication from your Excellency shall be added thereto.
And when Congress have duly considered the situation of our
frontier settlements, and shall make such provision for their Defence & protection as the nature of the case seems to require—
and circumstances will permit; there will be no delay in carrying
such measures into effect as shall operate in a general & systa-
matical manner. I have the Honor to be with due consideration
Yr Excellency's most Obedt Sert

G.W.

Df, in writing of Tobias Lear, DNA: RG 59, Miscellaneous Letters; LB,
DLC:GW.
 1. See GW to the U.S. Senate and House of Representatives, 7 Aug. and 16
Sept. 1789. Both of these letters covered reports on Indian depredations. GW

had already made at least some conservative provisions for the protection of the frontier counties south of the Ohio. On 3 Mar. Henry Knox informed Arthur St. Clair, governor of the Northwest Territory, and Brig. Gen. Josiah Harmar, commander of the U.S. Army on the frontier, that in "pursuance of powers vested in the President of the United States, by the act of Congress, passed the 29th day of September, 1789, he authorized you, by his instructions, dated the 6th of October following, in certain cases, and in the proportions therein specified, to call forth the militia of Virginia and Pennsylvania, for the protection of the frontiers against the depredations of the Indians.

"Since transmitting you the aforesaid instructions, he has received several applications for protection, from the inhabitants of the frontier counties of Virginia, lying along the south side of the Ohio. These applications are founded on the depredations of small parties of Indians during the last year, who, it seems, have murdered many of the unguarded inhabitants, stolen their horses, and burned their houses.

"Until the last year, an arrangement of the following nature existed at the expense of Virginia. The lieutenants of the exposed counties, under certain restrictions, were permitted to call forth a number of active men as patrols or scouts, as they are generally termed, and parties of rangers; but the government of that State thought proper to discontinue that arrangement of the organization of the General Government, to which the inhabitants of the said counties now apply for protection." All such applications had been laid before Congress, but until Congress should take measures to protect the frontier, GW authorized St. Clair and Harmar to permit county lieutenants in the counties south of the Ohio to call out scouts in case of renewed Indian raids, "In proportion to the danger of the said counties, not, however, exceeding, for one county, the number of eight men" (*ASP, Indian Affairs*, 1:101). GW also authorized Harry Innes, district judge of Kentucky, to order out the scouts (Knox to Innes, 13 April 1790, ibid., 101–2). Similar authority was given to the county lieutenant for Washington County on 13 April (see Knox to the County Lieutenants, 17 July 1790, ibid., 102). The authority was rescinded in July 1790 when preparations began for the Harmar expedition against the western tribes.

From David Stuart

Dear Sir,   March 15th 1790—Abing[do]n [Va.]

I have just recieved the laws, and therefore embrace the earliest opportunity of sending you a copy of the one, which I have mentioned to you in my letter.[1]

Coll Grayson died on Saturday last—as his death has been expected for some time, I am informed the Executive have been endeavouring to fix on someone to fill up his place—Mr Henry has been applied to, it is said, but will not serve. It is said, he is about to remove off to a territory, he has purchased in partnership from the State of Georgia.[2]

A spirit of jealousy which may become dangerous to the Union, towards the Eastern States, seems to be growing fast among us—It is represented, that the Northern phalanx is so firmly united, as to bear down all opposition, while Virginia is unsupported, even by those whose interests are similar with her's—It is the language of all, I have seen on their return from New York—Coll Lee tells me, that many who were warm Supporters of the government, are changing their sentiments, from a conviction of the impracticability of Union with States, whose interests are so dissimilar from those of Virginia[3]—I fear the Coll is one of the number—The late applications to Congress, respecting the slaves, will certainly tend to promote this spirit—It gives particular umbrage, that the Quakers should be so busy in this business[4]—That they will raise up a storm against themselves, appears to me very certain—Mr Maddison's sentiments are variously spoke of—so much so; that it is impossible to ascertain whether they are approved of by a majority or not—The Commercial and most noisy part, is certainly against them—It appears to me, to be such a deviation from the plain and beaten track, as must make every Creditor of the Public tremble—His plan of discrimination, is founded too much on principles of equity, to please even those who have advocated allways a discrimination—If the Public was to gain, what the original holders lost in their sales, I believe it would have pleased this description of Citizens better.[5] I am Dr Sir with great respect Your affecte Servt:

Dd Stuart

ALS, DLC:GW.

1. Stuart enclosed an act of the Virginia legislature concerning the protracted dispute between Robert Alexander and the Custis estate. For background, see Stuart to GW, 14 July 1789, n.7, 12 Sept., 3 Dec. 1789, 11 Mar. 1790; GW to Stuart, 21 Sept, 1789; and Edmund Randolph to GW, 23 Dec. 1789. The enclosure was a copy of "An act to enable David Stuart to re-convey a tract of land purchased by John Parke Custis, of Robert Alexander," which reads: "Whereas it is represented to the present General Assembly, that John Parke Custis departed this life in the year one thousand seven hundred and eighty-one, leaving Eleanor Custis his widow with four small children, and that the said Eleanor hath since intermarried with a certain David Stuart; And whereas it is also represented, that previous to the death of the said John Parke Custis, he purchased of a certain Robert Alexander, a tract of land lying

in the County of Fairfax, for which he was to pay a considerable sum of money, but since the death of the said John Parke Custis, a dispute hath arisen respecting the said contract, and the said Alexander hath agreed to take back the said land upon being paid a reasonable compensation for the use thereof, which will be greatly to the interest of the children of the said John Parke Custis; but as the heir at law is an infant of tender years, no contract can be made to bind him, without the interposition of this Assembly, to whom application hath been made for that purpose: *Be it therefore enacted by the Genl Assembly,* that any agreement or contract which the said David Stuart, by and with the consent of George Washington, esquire, to be expressed under the hand and seal of the said George Washington Esquire, shall make or enter into, respecting the surrendering the said lands to the said Robert Alexander, shall be deemed and taken to be valid and effectual to all intents and purposes" (13 Hening 99–100). The act was passed on 17 Nov. 1789. A copy is in DLC:GW.

2. William Grayson of Prince William County, U.S. senator from Virginia, died at Dumfries, Va., on Friday, 23 Mar. 1790, after a lengthy illness. Stuart probably learned of his death from Henry Lee, who had passed through Dumfries on 12 Mar. on his way to Alexandria (Henry Lee to James Madison, 13 Mar. 1790, in Rutland, *Madison Papers,* 13:102–3). Stuart later reported to GW that a member of the Virginia council had written privately to Patrick Henry asking him if he would accept an appointment to Grayson's seat in the Senate, but that Henry had declined (Stuart to GW, 2 June 1790). Henry was a leading investor in the Virginia Yazoo Company, one of the three companies that had arranged to purchase western land from Georgia (see Henry Knox to GW, 15 Feb. 1790, n.1), and Henry wrote to Richard Henry Lee on 29 Jan. 1790 that he was considering moving to Georgia (Henry, *Patrick Henry,* 3:412–15). On 25 Mar. Gov. Beverley Randolph offered Grayson's Senate seat to George Mason, who immediately declined (Randolph to Mason, 25 Mar. 1790; Mason to Randolph, 27 Mar. 1790, in Rutland, *Mason Papers,* 3:1191–92). The appointment then went to John Walker (1744–1809), an Albemarle County planter who had served briefly as an aide to Washington during the Revolutionary War (see *Diaries,* 6:68–69).

3. Henry Lee represented Westmoreland County in the Virginia assembly in 1789–90. A staunch supporter of the Constitution at the Virginia Ratification Convention, Lee was disturbed by developments in the First Congress and had emerged as a leading opponent of Hamilton's financial program in the Virginia legislature. On the opening day of the spring session, he delivered an impassioned speech opposing a rumored federal tax on land and was equally critical of northern congressmen's efforts to avoid placing the new seat of the federal government on the Potomac.

4. In the spring of 1790, Congress read and discussed Quaker petitions from the Philadelphia Yearly Meeting and the New York Yearly Meeting calling for the abolition of the slave trade and a petition from the Pennsylvania Society for Promoting the Abolition of Slavery calling for Congress to abolish the institution of slavery (*DHFC,* 3:294, 295–96, 316, 321, 332, 334–35, 336, 337, 338–41). See also GW to the Society of Quakers, October 1789 and notes; Warner Mifflin to GW, 12 Mar. 1790, n.1.

5. Stuart is referring to James Madison's proposal to discriminate between

the original holders of Continental securities and subsequent purchasers in discharging the Continental debt, presented in a speech to the committee of the whole House considering Hamilton's proposals for funding the national debt on 11 Feb. 1790 (see Rutland, *Madison Papers*, 13:34–39). Madison argued that justice required the compensation of the original holders of Continental securities, who included Continental soldiers and others who had been given securities in lieu of pay during the Revolution, as well as the subsequent purchasers, who had bought their securities at depreciated prices. Speculation in securities had increased dramatically after Hamilton's proposal to redeem them at full value became known in January 1790. To reward these speculators at the expense of the original holders, Madison argued, would be a travesty of justice. Madison proposed to pay original creditors still holding their securities the principal plus 6 percent interest. Subsequent purchasers, under Madison's plan, were to receive the highest market value (about 50 percent of face value) for their securities; the remaining 50 percent was to be paid to the original holders. The proposal was offered as a substitute for the second of eight resolutions presented by Thomas Fitzsimons on 8 Feb. to the committee of the whole House considering Hamilton's report on public credit, which specifically recommended against any such discrimination. Madison's resolution was debated between 15 and 19 Feb. and was rejected on 22 Feb. by a vote of 36 to 13 (see Rutland, *Madison Papers*, 13:47–59; *DHFC*, 5:839–40). Nine out of the ten Virginia representatives voted for the resolution.

From James Mathers

New York March 16 1790.
To His Excellency the President, and the Honble Members of the Senate of the United States

The Petition of James Mathers, Doorkeeper, Humbly sheweth,

That during the Recess of your Honble House, your Petitioner was usefully, and constantly, employed in attending the Secretary's Office, procuring Fuel and Stoves and in keeping your Chamber, and its Furniture clean.

That no provision hath been made by Law, on which your Petitioner can obtain any Compensation for the above Services.

Your Petitioner therefore humbly prays that your Honble House will be pleased to take his case into consideration, and grant such compensation as you in your wi[s]dom may think just and reasonable.

James Mathers

LS, DNA: RG 46, First Congress, Records of Legislative Proceedings, Petitions and Memorials, Resolutions of State Legislatures, and Related Documents.

James Mathers (1750–1811), a native of Dublin, Ireland, came to America before the Revolution and settled in New York City. He became assistant door-keeper for the Confederation Congress in 1785 and was promoted to door-keeper in 1788. On 7 April 1789 he was appointed doorkeeper for the Senate (*DHFC*, 1:11; Bowling and Veit, *Diary of William Maclay,* 116). On 26 Mar. 1790 Congress awarded Mathers the sum of $96 "for services during the late recess of Congress" under section 6 of "An Act making appropriations for the sup-port of government for the year one thousand seven hundred and ninety" (1 *Stat.* 104–5). Mathers remained Senate doorkeeper until his death.

To the United States Senate and House of Representatives

United States [New York] March 16th 1790.
Gentlemen of the Senate and House of Representatives.

I have directed my Secretary to lay before you the copy of an act and the form of ratification, of certain articles of amendment to the Constitution of the United States, by the Legislature of the State of Pennsylvania; together with the copy of a letter which accompanied the said act, from the Speaker of the House of Assembly of Pennsylvania to the the President of the United States.[1]

The originals of the above will be lodged in the Office of the Secretary of State.

Go: Washington

LS, DNA: RG 46, First Congress, Records of Legislative Proceedings, Presi-dent's Messages; LB, DLC:GW; copy, DNA: RG 233, First Congress, Records of Legislative Proceedings, Journals.

1. See Pennsylvania Legislature to GW, 11 Mar. 1790.

From Stephen Higginson

Sir   Boston [Mass.] March 17th 1790
I am induced, by various considerations of a personal nature, to offer myself as a Candidate for some office in the treasury department. that of Inspector, as proposed by the Secretary in his report, would be very agreable.[1]

persuaded, that proper qualifications can alone recommend me, I shall only observe, that I have too high a veneration for you, & too much regard to my own reputation, to solicit an appointment, was I very doubtful of being useful to the public in such an office. the enclosed letter from mr Bowdoin, will evidence to you his opinion upon that point.[2]

Should you think proper to honour me with your confidence, it will certainly command my utmost exertions to merit its continuance by a right conduct in office; & I shall ever retain a grateful Sense of the obligation conferred.

With a proper respect to your exalted Station & character, I have the honour to subscribe myself your very humble & most obedient Servant

Stephen Higginson

ALS, DLC:GW.

Stephen Higginson (1743–1828), a prominent Boston merchant, made a fortune in privateering during the American Revolution and served in the Massachusetts legislature in 1782 and in the Continental Congress in 1783. Higginson did not receive a post in the customs service at this time, although he was active in Federalist circles throughout the 1790s.

1. In January 1790 the administration publicly opened negotiations to deal with what was perhaps the most important problem facing Washington's new administration—the establishment of public credit for the new republic. On 21 Sept. 1789 the House of Representatives had stated that "this House consider an adequate provision for the support of the public credit, as a matter of high importance to the national honor and prosperity," and resolved "That the secretary of the treasury be directed to apply to the supreme executives of the several states, for statements of their public debts; of the funds provided for the payment, in whole or in part of the principal and interest thereof; and of the amount of the loan-office certificates, or other public securities of the United States, in the state treasuries respectively; and that he report to the House such of the said documents as he may obtain, at the next session of Congress" (*DHFC*, 3:220). Hamilton's "Report Relative to a Provision for the Support of Public Credit," delivered to the House on 14 Jan. 1790, went far beyond the expectations of most congressmen in establishing a blueprint for the political economy of both of GW's administrations. (For the report, and an introductory note discussing the economic precedents upon which Hamilton relied in its composition, see Syrett, *Hamilton Papers*, 6:51–168). There is virtually no documentary evidence of discussions between Hamilton and GW on the preparation of his controversial report and its implications for the administration. GW indeed probably found the intricacies of the report on public credit as abstruse as did many of Hamilton's contemporaries. However, there is no doubt that the president agreed completely with the implied objectives of the secretary of the treasury's fiscal program to create economic policies designed to produce a strong centralized federal government. The acrimonious debate on the report continued in Congress until June 1790 when a funding bill was sent to the Senate without provision for the assumption of state debts (*DHFC*, 3:442–43).

2. The enclosure is presumably James Bowdoin's letter to GW of 13 March. Bowdoin recommended Higginson, "a gentleman of unexceptionable character," as inspector for the revenue service in Massachusetts. "His great acquaintance with trade, both in practice & theory, his general knowledge, close application to business, and strict probity, do strongly recommend him; and would enable him I conceive, to Suggest plans to Administration, for the encouragement of trade, and encreasing, at the same time, the revenue arising from it" (DLC:GW).

From Lafayette

My dear General   Paris March the 17th 1790

It is with the Utmost Concern that I Hear My letters Have Not Come to Hand, and While I lament the Miscarriage, I Hope You do Not impute it to Any fault on My part[1]—In these time of troubles, it Has Become More difficult to Know, or to Reach Opportunities, and How this Will be Carried I leave to the Care of Mr Payne Who Goes to London.[2]

Our Revolution is Getting on as Well as it Can With a Nation that Has Swalled up liberty all at once, and is still liable to Mistake licentiousness for freedom—the Assembly Have More Hatred to the Ancient System than Experience on the proper Organisation of a New, and Constitutional Governement—the Ministers are lamenting the loss of power, and Affraid to use that which they Have—and As Every thing has been destroied and Not much New Building is Yet Above Ground, there is Much Room for Critics and Calomnies.

to this May be Added that We still are Pestered By two parties, the Aristocratic that is panting for a Counter Revolution, and the factious Which Aims at the division of the Empire, and destruction of all Authority and perhaps of the lifes of the Reigning Branch, Both of which parties are fomenting troubles.

And after I Have Confessed all that, My dear General, I will tell you With the Same Candour that We Have Made an Admirable, and Almost incredible destruction of all abuses, prejudices, &c. &c. that Every thing Not directly Useful to, or Coming from the people Has been levelled—that in the topographical, Moral, political Situation of France We Have Made More changes in ten Month than the Most Sanguine patriot could

Have imagined—that our internal troubles and Anarchy are Much Exagerated—and that upon the Whole this Revolution, in which Nothing will be wanting But Energy of Governement just as it was in America, Will propagate implant liberty and Make it flourish throughout the world, while We must wait for a Convension in a few years to Mend Some defects which are not Now perceived By Men just Escaped from Aristocracy and despotism.

You know that the Assembly Have adjourned the Westindia affairs, leaving Every thing in the Actual State, Viz.—*the ports oppened* as We Hear they Have Been to American trade. But it was impossible, circumstanced as We are, to take a definitive Resolve on that Matter—the Ensuing legislature will More Easily determine, after they Have Received the demands of the Colonies who Have Been Invited to Make them, particularly on the object of *Victualling*.

Give me leave, My dear General, to present you With a picture of the Bastille just as it looked a few days after I Had ordered its demolition, with the Main Kea of that fortress of despotism[3]—it is a tribute Which I owe as A Son to My Adoptive father, as an aid de Camp to My General, as a Missionary of liberty to its patriarch.

Adieu, My Beloved General, My Most Affectionate Respects Wait on Mrs Washington, present me most affectionately to George, to Hamilton, Knox, Harrison, Jay, Humphrey and all friends Most tenderly and respectfully Your Most Affectionate and filial friend

Lafayette

ALS, PEL.

1. GW had written Lafayette on 14 Oct. 1789 that he had not received a letter from him since his own arrival in New York City in April 1789.

2. For Thomas Paine's activities at this time, see his letter to GW, 16 Oct. 1789, source note. See also Paine to GW, 1 May 1790.

3. The key sent by Lafayette to GW was the main key to the Bastille, supposedly carried from the Bastille to the Paris town hall after the fall of the prison on 14 July 1789 and there presented to Lafayette. The delivery to GW of the key and a drawing of the Bastille by Cathala was entrusted by Lafayette to Thomas Paine who was considering returning to the United States at this time. Since Paine's departure was delayed, the key and the drawing apparently were turned over to John Rutledge, Jr., who had been traveling in Europe and now planned to return home (see Paine to GW, 31 May 1790). The two gifts, to-

gether with letters from Lafayette and Paine, arrived in New York in August 1790 (GW to Paine, 10 Aug. 1790, and to Lafayette, 11 Aug. 1790). The key and the drawing apparently remained in New York and Philadelphia during GW's presidential years and were sent to Mount Vernon shortly before his retirement. Upon GW's return the key was hung in the passage in a "kind of small crystal lantern," and the drawing was hung beneath it (Niemcewicz, *Vine and Fig Tree*, 96).

GW acknowledged receipt of the two items in a letter to Lafayette of 11 Aug. 1790 as the "token of victory gained by Liberty over Despotism." That the souvenirs of the attack on the Bastille were not always viewed with such reverence is indicated by the not unbiased comments of the vicomte de Chateaubriand, who had observed the attack on 14 July 1789 and saw GW's key in Philadelphia: "The keys of the Bastille multiplied; they were sent to all the important simpletons in the four quarters of the world." These keys, Chateaubriand continued, "were rather silly toys which passed from hand to hand at that time. The consigners of locksmiths' wares might, three years later, have sent to the President of the United States the bolt of the prison of the monarch who bestowed liberty upon France and America. If Washington had seen the 'victors of the Bastille' disporting themselves in the gutters of Paris, he would have felt less respect for his relic" (Chateaubriand, *Memoirs*, 1:158, 211).

When Col. John A. Washington sold Mount Vernon to the Mount Vernon Ladies' Association in 1858, he also presented the key to the Bastille to the association, but his family retained the drawing until its sale in 1891. For many years the sketch of the Bastille was represented in its place beneath the key by a photograph of the original drawing. In 1987 the original drawing was returned to Mount Vernon where it is now (1994) on loan from the Masonic Charity Foundation of Connecticut (the Connecticut Corporation) and the Shriners Hospitals for Crippled Children (the Colorado Corporation). For the history of the drawing, see the *Annual Report* of the Mount Vernon Ladies' Association for 1987, 26–36, 49.

From Francis Adrian Van der Kemp

Sir! Kingston [Jamaica] 17 March 1790.

The eminent Station, which you adorn in this Common wealth, obliges me to trouble you few moments with letters—respecting alone me private circumstances. I flatter myself Sir! that the Liberty, which I take wil easily find an excuse, if She want it, as Soon, as I have informed your Excellency, that honour and duty entreates me to this performance to which I am encouraged be the expectation wil be crowned with a happy Success—if it depends alone of your Excellency's inclination.

Engaged Since Several years in the domestic quarrel of the People of the united Netherlands for recovering those ancients rigths, which they enjoyed—even under a Charles the 5th and Philip the Second, I was particularly interested in the fate of the Province of Utrecht, and the city of Wyck by Duurstede. In this city I was taken Prisoner together with Sir Adriaen de Nÿs then commander of the city, transported with him nothwithstandig we we⟨r⟩ nominally included in the general Amnestie—published by the pretended States, under a Strong escort to Amersfort—from there to Utrecht, after this place was evacuated by the troops of the Patriotic Party. After an imprisonment of twenty three weeks about, Liberty was offered to us upon condition, that we first and before our enlargement, must ⟨namptise⟩ the Sum of 45000 Guldens—or 7500£ New-yorks Currency—"in order, as the Resolution was, to recover of that Sum the damages, and losses, sustained by the Province of Utrecht and city of Wÿck by Duur Stede in particular, under our direction.["]

How iniquitous this exaction, to which we must Submit, to recover our Liberty, may be judged, it is not Sir! upon this point, that my grievance is founded. I know to wel, that it was a domestic transaction in that Country; that no foreign State could properly interfere in it—and that I was—to that moment—a citisen of that Province and your Excellency, I am persuded, wil do me the justice, to acquit me of the presumtuous folly of wishing your interference in this matter. But Sir! though ⟨namptised⟩, the Sum of 75000£, was ours, undoubtly the residuum of that Sum, after the recovering of the damages, which should have been judged to have been occasioned by our direction. To this residuum my friend with me though, exiled, was entitled—there our goods were not confiscated, nor this Sum forfeited, after our departure in Braband and France, and my naturalisation in this Republic wil not, I hope, afford a valuable reason to deprive me of the expectation of recovering the whole, a part of this Sum, at least of receiving an account of the States of Utrecht, if the total Sum was adjudged for Sustained damages.

I dare not Say Sir! in what manner your Excellency may afford us a Succesful adsistance, but this, I hope, wil not be rejected, if I request your Excellency's interference by your Minister, as far, as may be proper. The Sum is ⟨namptised⟩ to the Deputies of State of the Province of Utrecht—19 Dec. 1787 in the city of the Same name, with the above mentioned expressed condition. Your Protection will obliges us infinitly, afford my an occasion, to acquit me of a debt, contracted at that time to my friend, and pay a part of my obligation to his uncommon generosity.

That every day of your Excellency's Presidency may be blessed, and the remembrance of it may rejoy the heart of the latest free American, is the ardent wish of him, who remains which dutiful Sentiments of the highest respect and esteem Sir! Your Excellency's most humble and obedient Servant!

Francois Adrian Vanderkemp

ALS, DNA: RG 59, Miscellaneous Letters; copy, DNA: RG 59, Domestic Letters.

For an identification of Van der Kemp, see the source note to GW's letter to him, 27 Sept. 1788. For several years before Van der Kemp's departure for the United States in 1787, he and his colleague Adrian de Nys (d. 1830) were deeply involved in the struggle of the Dutch Patriot party against the policies of the stadtholder, Van der Kemp producing a number of antigovernment pamphlets and serving as captain of the Free Corps, a volunteer military group consisting of liberals opposed to the stadtholder. In July 1787 both Van der Kemp and de Nys were arrested after a Free Corps force was defeated by the government's provincial militia at Wyk am Dursted. Van der Kemp was released in December 1787 after the payment of some 45,000 guilders, representing "the losses incurred by the public during our usurpation, as it was termed, of the public administration" (see Van der Kemp's autobiographical account of his imprisonment, in Fairchild, *Francis Adrian Van der Kemp*, 88–95, 99–103).

After his arrival in the United States, Van der Kemp turned to John Adams for a solution to his problems, and Adams advised him to consult the president (Van der Kemp to Adams, 7 Jan., 17 Mar., 26 May, 19 June 1790, MHi: Adams Family Papers). GW turned Van der Kemp's letter over to Jefferson, who on 31 Mar. wrote Van der Kemp: "The letter has been duly received that you wrote the President of the United States, praying his interference with the government of the United Netherlands, on the subject of property you left there on your coming to America. I have it in charge to inform you that the United States have at present no minister at the Hague, and consequently no channel through which they could express their concern for your interests. However free we are to receive and protect all persons who come hither with the property they bring, perhaps it may be doubted how far it would be expedient to engage ourselves for what they leave behind, or for any other matter retrospective to their becoming Citizens. In the present instance we hope that no confiscation of the residuum of your property left in the United Netherlands having taken place, the justice of that government will leave you no occasion for that interference which you have been pleased to ask from this" (DNA: RG 59, Domestic Letters).

From Otho Holland Williams

Dear Sir   Baltimore [Md.] 17th March 1790

I assure myself that your moments of leasure are, some times, passed in the contemplation of rural concerns.

Your known attachments to subjects of domestic, as well as public, utility; and your former attention to the improvement of Stock, encourage me to mention to you that I have had, for more than two years, an order, in the hands of an American in London, to procure for me one of the finest Stud Horses of the Dray breed, that could be procured. The order was executed last Summer and the Horse arrived in perfect health, and excellent order, in the month of September last.

The enclosed advertisement describes him—and I assure you that his merits are not exaggerated.[1]

Those who have seen him, after hearing the most elaborate encomiums of him, have seen him with surprize, and pleasure— No person pretends to have seen so fine an Animal, of the kind, in this Country: and no one has told me that they have seen a finer in England. I enquired because I wished to be satisfied in that respect.

The dray and the Arabian, or runing Horse full bred, I am told, produce the Coach Horse; the Coach Horse and the Arabian, produce the Hunter; and these, promiscuously produce the best Horses for Harness, and the Saddle, that are known in Europe.

If, Sir, you think that his blood will be any advantage to your present Stock I will give particular directions respecting any Mares which you may direct to be sent to him.

I have reason to be confident that a greater number will offer than can be served, as it being his first Season I do not intend that the number shall much exceed fifty. You will have the goodness to excuse the Subject, and to believe that I am, with the greatest respect Dear Sir, Your most affectionate Servant

O. H. Williams

ALS, DLC:GW; ADfS, MdHi: Otho H. Williams Papers.

1. Williams enclosed a broadside dated 19 Mar. 1790 advertising the stud services of Nebuchadnezzar, "A full-bred Dray Horse," at Ranelagh, the country seat of Benjamin Nicholson, 17 miles from Baltimore (DLC:GW). Williams apparently did not overestimate his horse's capabilities. In mid-1793 he wrote a friend that Nebuchadnezzar had already covered sixty mares, "and I expect

he will at least have 20 or 30 more" (Williams to Cephas Beall, 28 May 1793, MdHi: Otho H. Williams Papers).

From Christian Philippe Carl Brenneysen

New York March 18th 1790

May it please your Excellency!

When I intrude upon So high a character as I have now the honor to address I feel deeply mortified that I have no other excuse to plead than the cause of misfortune & distress; nor Should I think my Self justyfiable, even by the extreems of necessity, were it not for that benevolent & humane disposition which your Excellency have often manifested towards men of my profession.

I have been an officer in the Prussian Service, in a Regiment commanded by General de Curbiere, to whom I was aid de Camp during 5 years. Being young, I grew tired of the garrison duties and resolved to take my discharge, which I obtained by the friendly interference of the Prussian Ambassador at the Haag, Baron de Tulmeyer, on whose recommendation I engaged in the dutch Squadron, which brought Mr van Berkel to America, as Capt. of the marines, with a view to enter into the Service of the united States. These circumstances are known to Baron de Steuben and General Mühlenberg.

My Idea, that these States would raise troops, has since proved a mistaken one; whereby I am reduced to a distressed Situation, leaving me no other alternative than to return to my native Country, and again to resume the Service of my sovereign.

But of this last refuge I am also deprived, for want of the money required for my passage. In Short I am driven to the disagreeable necessity to implore your Excellency for a small pecuniary assistence towards obtaining the end proposed, which doubtless will be followed by a few Gentlemen, and be the means, not only of relieving me from my present distresses, but to restore me to my former Situation in Life.

I fervently join with the multitude who pray for your Excellency's long & happy Life and remain with the most profound Respect Your Excellency's most devoted & obedt humble Servt

Christian Philippe Carl Brenneysen

LS, DNA: RG 59, Miscellaneous Letters.
Christian Philippe Carl Brenneysen has not been identified, nor has evidence been found that GW offfered him any financial assistance.

From Fraissinet & Co.

Monseigneur   Marseille [France] Le 19. mars 1790.
 Nôtre frere Consul General de LL: HH: CC. à Alger vient de nous adresser L'Incluse pour Vôtre Excellence, nous nous empréssons de vous l'acheminer et de vous présenter l'hommage des Voeux que nous adressons au tout Puissant pour la Conservation des Jours de Ve. E. à la quelle le Bonheur du Peuple Genereux que Vous gouvernés est si etroitement Lié. Nous Sommes avec un respectueux attachement Monseigneur De Vôtre Excellence Les trés humbles et trés Obeissants Serviteurs

III Jn Marc & Js
Fraissinet & Cie

LS, DNA:PCC, item 78. No further identification of Fraissinet & Cie has been found, nor has the enclosure been identified.

From George Augustine Washington

Honor'd Uncle   Mount Vernon March 19th 1790.
 On my return yesturday from Berkley I found Your two favors of the 28th Ulto & 7th Inst.[1]—when I left this my intention was to have return'd on Monday last, but the most excrutiating pain in my jaws and teeth, attended with a severe inflamation kept me in a constant state of misery—deprived me almost wholy of rest and has very much reduced me. a tooth which had been very troublesome before, and which I concieved to be the cause I had extracted from a hope of relief—but am very much afflicted yet but when the weather becomes setled & mild I hope to be relieved—I am always thankful for your advise and am well persuaded that great inconvenience frequently arises from delay in business and endeavour to avoid it, but it will some times be unavoidable from the intervention of circumstances— Your Letter of the 28th continues the advise of witholding the

sale of wheat & Flour from the expectation of an increase of price but that of the 7th Inst. leaves me at liberty to embrace a good price before I went to Berk'ly the price of wheat was 8/6 & flour (Common) was 41/ but am informed it has fallen and that wheat is now 8/ & Flour 40/—when Flour got to 40/ I felt a difficulty in resisting the price from an apprehension of its falling but your advise induced me to delay it if I am well enough shall go to Town tomorrow and shall endeavour to obtain the best information I can respecting the probability of its rising or falling, and if I cannot be well convinced of the former shall sell— for in so doubtful a case I think it would be wrong to decline so good a price, for the uncertainty of geting a better—I had delay'd the experiment of grinding 100 B: of wheat untill the arrival of the new Bolting Cloth but had a trial made sufficient to satisfy me that it would answer to manufacture the wheat. of this you shall have a statement in my next and a reply to such parts of your Letter as I must now omit not having time for I was too much indisposed on my return yesterday to inspect the reports or do any thing towards preparing for the Stage to day—Tom Davis is now on the recovery the Doctr had apprehensions of his disorder terminating in a consumption[2] it arose the Doctr said from a violent cold—the weather for a fortnight past has been very severe and disagreeable the snow that fell on Wednesday week was much the deepest we have had this year—over the ridge it was almost knee deep and on this side by all accounts there was a greater fall—that and the heavy rains that follow'd has put the earth in such a state that nothing in the way of seeding or preparing for it was practicable—I had made arrangements for begining the day after I went away⟨—⟩we shall begin tomorrow or Monday if any ground can be found sufficiently dry—Fanny joins me in tenderest regards to you, my Aunt & the Children—and good wishes to the Family. I am Hond Uncle Your truely affectionate Nephew

Geo: A. Washington

ALS, DLC:GW.

1. Neither of these letters has been found.
2. Tom Davis was a Home House dower slave.

From Joseph Barrell et al.

Boston 20th March 1790

To the President of the United States of America.

The Memorial of Joseph Barrell⟨,⟩ for himself and the other Owners⟨,⟩ of the Ship Columbia & Sloop Washington Most Respectfully Sheweth

That those Vessels were fitted at Boston, for the Pacific Ocean and sailed in the month of September in the year 1787, furnished with Sea Letters & Pass Ports from the United States, and the State of Massachusetts; together with Certificates from the Consuls of France & Holland; that they refreshed themselves at the Cape de Verd Islands, and proceeded on their Voyage around Cape Horn, but meeting with severe weather in doubling the Cape, the Ship Columbia was obliged to touch at the Island of Juan Fernandes, on the 24th May 1788, where she met with Humane treatment from His Excelcy Seignr Don Blas Gonsales, who was Governor of the Island, who suffered them to remain a few days to compleat the repairs they wanted, and to *wood* and *water;* for this act of *kindness,* it appears the said Governor has been removed from his Government, and has suffer'd many inconveniencies; the Knowledge of which has filled your memorialists with very great concern.

Your Memorialists therefore relying on your good⟨ness⟩ have presumed to present a Copy of the several papers, which by the said Governor have been forwarded to the Honble M. Le Tomb Consul of France, which papers are couched in terms that must affect the heart of an honest man; and your memorialists knowing your firm attention to Justice and Humanity, are emboldened'd to solicit your attention ⟨to⟩ the situation of the said Governor, and to request you will take such measures, and give such orders to the Minister of the United States at the Court of Madrid, that He may *feelingly* appear in the cause of Injured Innocence, and represent the truth of this transaction in such manner to His Catholic Majesty, as may induce him to reinstate the said Governor, and compensate him for the Injury he has suffered for this act of Humanity.[1]

The President of the United States, alive to every just advantage that may attend the Subjects of said States, will clearly see, if his friendly assistance had been deny'd, the Object of this first adventure from America might have been intierly frustrated; and He, will suffer the concerned in the Enterprize, to be importunate and to express their keenest feelings that they have been the innocent cause of a good man's suffering.

It would be presumeing in your memorialists, to point out anything more to the President of the United States, who will see by the documents accompanying this memorial, what is proper to be done, and the intimations of His own benevolent heart, will we trust induce Him to give as speedy orders on this matter, as His wisdom shall judge necessary.

Your memorialists beg leave to add to the papers, such parts of the General orders given to the Commander of this enterprize, as will shew there was no intention, in any wise to interfere with, or to traffick in any of the Spannish settlements in the South Seas, but only to pursue the object of their Voyage without giving offence to any power whatever.[2]

Your memorialists relying on your interferrence in this bussiness, as in duty bound will pray.

Joseph Barrell
for himself and the rest of the Concerned.[3]

ALS, DNA: Miscellaneous Letters.

Joseph Barrell (1739–1804) was a prominent Boston merchant and shipowner. The expedition to the Pacific Northwest was financed by the sale of fourteen shares of $3500 each, and among the shareholders, besides Barrell, were Samuel Brown and Crowell Hatch of Boston, Charles Bulfinch, John Derby of Salem, and the New York merchant John Pintard. The *Columbia*, with a 212-ton burthen, was eighty-three feet long; John Kendrick of Wareham, Mass., was in command of the *Columbia* and of the expedition. The *Columbia* was accompanied by the sloop *Lady Washington*, ninety tons, under the command of Capt. Robert Gray of Rhode Island. The vessels, which sailed from Boston on 30 Sept. 1787, were the first North American ships to pass Cape Horn. After a stormy passage both ships reached the northern Pacific coast nearly eleven months after they sailed from Boston (Morison, *Maritime History of Massachusetts*, 46–47; Dulles, *The Old China Trade*, 52–55).

1. Among the enclosures in Barrell's letter is a communication from the governor of Juan Fernández to Don Theodoro de Croix, 28 May 1788: "I have to inform your Excellency that on Saturday the 24th instant, at about ten in the morning, there was seen, at about a Leagues distance from this Place, a Bostonian Ship with her main & foretop gallant mast to appearance lost, which I was inform'd of by many People that I dispatch'd to reconnoitre her. With this notice & judging that it might be some Barque from the Land which had suffered some damage in a Tempest that happened some days before, I dispatched a Soldier from the Garrison in a Fishing boat to the sublieutenant

Don Nicholas Illanet to get information & see, at the same time, what might offer; which in effect the said Officer executed & at his arrival at the said Ship, he met with a novelty that of a Frigate from Boston called the *Columbia*, commanded by John Kendrick, & that making signs of Peace, they asked him to come alongside, which he did & at their request went on Board, & was confirmed in that she was a Foreign Ship from the American Republic. That some days before a furious Tempest arose which drove them within an hundred Leagues of these Islands in Company with a Sloop from the same Nation, who had seperated from them, they know not where, & that she was come to take shelter in this Port for the purpose of repairing the masts, & the tiller which was broken to peices, & to wood & water: in case I should give them my Permission; that they had not advanced nearer the Port to prevent giving me the least suspicion. That they had nothing on Board their respective Vessels but Provisions, Charts & other things proper for Navigation, for a proof of which they showed the whole Vessel & the Crew by which the Officer knew that the Relation which had been made him by the above named Captain was true in all its parts. The Crew comprehending himself & three Subaltern Officers, consisted of 40 men, including 16 Boys from 12 to 16 years of age. that they had but 12 Cannon, 6 on each side. With this information, which the above named Officer brought me, & a supplicatory message from the Bostonian Captain in which he requested me not deny him Hospitality by means of which he should be enabled to pursue his Voyage to his own Country, offering to my consideration the sincere Friendship & Peace which subsisted between our Nation & his own, I found myself greatly perplexed with respect to the part I ought to take especially as I had no orders or instructions by which to regulate my conduct in the like & unhop'd for occasion, I at last resolved to grant them what they requested for which purpose I made them the Signal which had been agreed upon between them & the Officer. Upon which they entered the Port & Anchored under the Cannon of the Battery of this place called *Santa Barbara,* where after the ship was moored, the Captain came on shore in the Boat with four men who remained there while he convers'd with me, which conversation ended by referring me to the Off(icer) Don Nicholas Illanet, & to give me thanks for the Liberty that had been granted to him. In the course of this conversation, I agreed with him upon the manner & form which his People were to observe in coming on Shore to wood & water, the days he was to stay here & other matters which military experience dictated be best for the Service of His Majesty; every thing in fine to prevent his forming the least conception of this Place & Port. I ordered them to Anchor, with the greatest expedition, a little within pistol shot of the Mole, for the purpose of observing their proceedings which in fact have not differed in the smallest instance (during the 3 days they have been here) from the agreement I made with them; On the contrary, they have given the greatest proofs of their intention to act in conformity the 3 Days which complete the time granted to them to stay. The above mentioned Ship is very differently constructed from European Ship's, because the Stern Battery is in the Round House, on a level with the Quarter Deck & the rest of the Ship to the Prow, the Cabbin which you enter by a winding staircase is below the round house & stern battery, it is very clean & the Births for the Officers very convenient, & the whole of the Vessel so clean as that she appears to be finish'd, the binnacle is at the foot of the Mizen mast uncovered & there the Helm's men stand to manage the helm; the Kitchen & Fire place are all of one peice & placed between the main mast & Quarter Deck; the apartments for the Blacksmith & Carpenters are situated between the fore & main mast. Before the seperation of the Ship, by the above said Storm, from the aforementioned Sloop, the two Captains had agreed that if they should loose sight of one another, they should form a junction in the Environs of these Islands, from whence it may be clearly inferr'd that their intention always was to come to request my permission to wood & water, besides which they wanted nothing; because they carried no Merchandize warlike stores; or other effects, which relate thereto; & for my own entire satisfaction, I agreed, previous to my giving them assistance, that there should be a search through the whole Ship, for which purpose I deputed the Lieutenant Don Gregorio Rubio, which he performed diligently & with the greatest activity, agreeing exactly with the relation given me by the Sublieutenant Don Nicholas Illanet. They requested me that if after their departure the above mentioned Sloop should arrive at this Port, that I would afford the same kindness as to themselves: that the Crew consisted of only ten men & that she had only one mast, that the services & favors I had done them would be engraved on their Hearts, & that, on their arrival at Boston their Republic, they would make known how much they were indebted to our Nation. For the purpose of verifying what they had said above, they left me three medals, one of which I send to your Excellency, another to the President & Captain General of the Kingdom of Chili, & the other I have kept for myself. On these medals are figured or engraved the said Vessels, the names of General Washington & the Captain Commandant John Kendrick.

"The account which he gave me of his voyage & expedition was as follows: That in the month of September of the last year 1787 they sailed from Boston Commissioned to make discoveries especially about those establishments which the Russians hold in & about California, that coming from the above place to this, they had crossed the Line & passed Cape Horn & had not touched at any Port but at the Cape de Verds, that shattered & put in disorder they had gained the Assylum of this Port from whence they should pursue their Voyage with all speed. . . . I hope for your Excellency's highest approbation & justification of my conduct, & to overlook my defects which may have occurred, since my intention was no other than that of rendering my best services to His Majesty my Lord & natural master" (DNA RG 59, Miscellaneous Letters).

Among the other enclosures was a letter from Capt. Gen. Don Ambrosio Higgins de Vallenar, 3 Oct. 1788, ordering Gonzalèz's removal from office, a letter from Gonzalès to Higgins de Vallenar, 2 Jan. 1789, describing his removal, and a letter from Gonzalès to Philippe-André-Joseph de Létombe, French consul general at Boston, from St. Jago, Chile, 7 Feb. 1789, writing: "though in this remote Country, to implore your Patronage & your Support, as I do by this medium begging you to have the goodness to facilitate some Recommendation from the United States to the Gentleman residing at the

Court of Madrid for his interposition with my King." All of these letters are in DNA: RG 59, Miscellaneous Letters.

2. Also enclosed in Barrell's letters was an extract from Captain Kendrick's orders: "The Ship Columbia and Sloop Washington, compleatly equipt for a Voyage to the Paciffic Ocean, & China, We place such confidence in you, as to give you the entire command of this Enterprize.

"It would be impossible, upon a Voyage of this nature to give with propriety, very binding instructions, and such is our reliance on your Honor, ⟨In⟩tegrity & good Conduct, that it would be needless at any time, you will be on the spot, and as circumstances turn up, you must improve them; but We cannot forbear to impress upon your mind, our wish, & exp⟨ectat⟩ion that the most inviolable Harmony and Friendship, may subsist, between you, & the Natives; and that no advantage may be taken of them in Trading; but that you endeavour, by Honest conduct to impress upon their minds, a Friendship, ⟨*illegible*⟩.

"You are strictly enjoined not to touch a⟨t⟩ any part of the Spanish Dominions on the West Continent of America, unless driven there by unavoidable accident in which case you will st⟨ay⟩ no longer than is necessary, & while there be c⟨are⟩full to give no offence to any of the Subjects of ⟨His⟩ Catholic Majesty—and if you meet with any Subjects of any European Prince, you are to treat them with friendship & civility.

"The Certificates you have from the Fr⟨ench⟩ & Dutch Consul, you will make use of if you meet with any Ships of those Nations, & you wi⟨ll⟩ pay them every Respect that is due to them.

"The Sea Letters from Congress & this State you will also shew upon every proper oc⟨ca⟩sion, and altho' we expect you will treat all Nations with great Respect & Civility, yet W⟨e *illegible*⟩ you will suffer Insult & Injury from no one wi⟨th⟩out shewing that Spirit which ever becomes a Free & Independent American" (DNA: RG 59, Miscellaneous Letters).

3. On 11 April 1790 Jefferson wrote to William Carmichael, U.S. minister resident in Spain, recapitulating the circumstances surrounding Gonzalèz's removal and stating that "we are satisfied it is because his case has not been able to penetrate to his majesty's ministers, at least in it's true colours. We would not chuse to be committed by a formal sollicitation. But we would wish you to avail yourself of any good opportunity of introducing the truth to the ear of the minister, and of satisfying him that a redress of this hardship on the Governor would be received here with pleasure, as a proof of respect to those laws of hospitality which we would certainly observe in a like case, as a mark of attention towards us, and of justice to an individual for whose sufferings we cannot but feel" (Boyd, *Jefferson Papers*, 16:329–30).

From James Bowdoin

Sir   Boston [Mass.] March 20. 1790

Letters of this kind would need apology, or rather would, in every view, be unwarrantable, if the writer had any reason for doubt concerning the character of the person recommended. But as I am sure no apology is needful on that score, I persuade my self your candour will induce you to think it unnecessary on any other.

I have the honour of enclosing a Letter which I have lately received from Samuel ⟨Henshaw⟩ esqr. who is the Representative in our Assembly for the Town of North Hampton.[1]

The object of his wish is to be employed in the Revenue Department under the federal government in this district. He was for a considerable time Collector of Impost & Excise for the Port of Boston & County of Suffolk: to which Office under this Commonwealth he was annually, and without interruption, chosen by the General Court for a number of years; and would probably have been continued in it to the present time, had he not removed from Boston.

On this occasion it is but an act of justice due to him to inform you, that he is a worthy sensible man, and a good friend to the federal government; that he was principally concerned in the bringing forward & framing the Impost & Excise Laws made here, after the conclusion of the war, that he has had great experience in this line of business, and that by his attention to it, methodizing it, and rendering those bra⟨nches⟩ of Revenue more productive than they had been he made an excellent officer.

Should he be appointed to office under the federal Government, his Conduct, I believe would insure to him the fullest approbation of Administration.

I am happy in this opportunity of expressing my sentiments of the character of this Gentleman, and am with all the respect due to the first Magistrate of the Union, and which public & private virtue ⟨c⟩an inspire, Sir, Yr most obedt hble Servt

James Bowdoin

ALS, DLC:GW.

1. Samuel Henshaw, who had served as collector of the customs at Boston under the state government, had applied earlier for a post in the Boston customs. See Henshaw to GW, 18 June 1789. The enclosure was a letter from Henshaw to Bowdoin, 7 Mar. 1790, requesting Bowdoin's support for his application (DLC:GW).

From d'Estaing

Sir,   Paris March 20th 1790

Permit one of the least, but one of the most zealous assistants in the great work which you began, conducted, and have completed, to join a private letter to his official answer[1]—and to commune freely with you. The small token which I take the liberty to send you begging your acceptance of (the Bust of M. Necker, and the engravings which accompany it) will better express the public opinion and my own than any dissertation could do.[2]

When a bow has been too much bent the vibrations of its cord are proportionably lasting and strong; when the wavering of ideas, and the false steps they occasion which produces diffidence, and which serve as pretexts, have caused sudden jerks and the cord which ought to have been gently relaxed is broken by the same hand with a stroke, too often unseasonably, and meets in its course an ill-timed opposition of some week branches, which it has broken without an effort, but of which it has been able, and perhaps ought, to exagerate voluntarily, the imaginary resistance; then all the data vary, and political Geometry no longer exists; supposing always that another example like that of the conduct of General Washington has been able to establish the probability of the reality of such Geometry. The duration of the movements of the cord which we draw, and the sufficient springing, and the lawfulness of the arrow of the executive power, without which there can be no active and imposing bow—appears to me to be more incalcalable, but the time is not far distant.

Thus where force is wanting there must be annihilation; or repose; the first is demonstrated impossible in my eyes, the public spirit which combines, and which unites individual forces, will not produce a dislocation of the members of the great whole. I dare to believe that repose is very near. I am going to prove to you how much I am pursuaded of it by putting into your hands wishes which may appear chemerical to others as to you. The wisest have considered it here, and in the midst of the confusion in which we are yet involved as being at least ill-timed—they imagine that I busy myself about future ages; I pursuade myself, nevertheless, that it is time to submit to you what it is possible to be actually preparing for, and that which I presume can be executed in a few months.

The goodness of your heart, which connects, in the strongest degree the indulgent simplicity of a man who regards the private virtues with the majesty of the founder—the president— and the General induces me to hope to be pardoned for the imprudence of turning your attention to so small an object as what relates to me. I have three debts to pay—Strongly attached to my nation I have rendered, such as they are, all the services in my power to her; I percieve that I am now about to cherish her—my career is terminated as to action, but my wishes yet remain with me. My zeal alone has obtained for me the favor of being adopted by two other nations. Spain and America have honored me with their best titles—I enjoy their rights of Citizenship. It is painful to me to think that there can exist, between those who have condescended to distinguish me by marks of their goodness, motives of division which France might endeavour perhaps in vain to accommodate, and that for an object which ought to increase their forces and unite them forever. I do not dissemble that I suffer myself to be more easily led to this inquietude, because heretofore I proposed the same object as a means of accomplishing the American Liberty. When Louisiana was ceded to Spain M. le Duc de Choiseul[3] had ministerial influence: he sometimes consulted me respecting distant countries; and I gave him a memorial in which I proved the honesty, the convenience and the utility of making Louisiana a free colony under its own government & its own laws, and immediately protected by France & Spain. [The] Stamp Act, and that which I learnt after being governor of St Domingo of the dispositions of the continent, made me say in that memorial, that an example so near would establish the confidence—increase the desire & that this would be to put under a hot bed a germ which has sprouted from the revolution of North America.

This America, Sir, you have; she is sufficient of herself, the injustice of the English has done more than I dared to foresee; the events which I wished to hasten have come on of themselves—and your virtues and talents have rendered them possible. The circumstance of the Island of Corsica which they had just trafficked with Geneva, and which they then laboured to subject, drew M. de Choiseul's attention, he appeared to me to be principally detered by the unimportance of which they would accuse him if he should be occupied at the same time about two objects whose principals were so diametrically opposite. The tragical mission so unfortunate to the talents of M. O'Reiley was effected at New Orleans,[4] and the only fruit of my reasonings and solicitations has been to leave to our government traces of an opinion which has been held by me in the place of talents, and which probably led to a belief that I was the most proper person to command the first forces which were united with you. This very long narration appears to me to be a suitable preface to the ideas which an irresistable sentiment for everything which can contribute to peace engages me to lay before you. I have endeavoured by it to justify the short exposition which follows.

I wish Sir for that which I have heretofore proposed. I believe it possible. The Liberty of Louisiana established upon the same basis of protection, and having nearly equal relation to the three nations, appears to me necessary for their tranquility and their accommodation. The territorial madness, and the excluding principles of the spanish nation have less influence with the Count de Florida Blanca than upon any other minister. I have been a witness of the confidence so productive with which M. le Comte de Montmorin inspired him when the French ambassador had to combat the predictions of other ministers of Spain, who, under the gloom of appearances, foresaw not only the dollars but the sovereignty of Maxico ranged under your approaching conquests. The power of Spain which I have certified to you, which I have yet in my hands, incontestably proves how far M. le Comte De Montmorin was credited; and how far the Ct de Florida Blanca is susceptable of just and great ideas. I have had the right to employ Spanish troops, vessels and money under your direction upon the continent of North America; and you have known what the forces were which sailed from Cadiz to join those at St Domingo & Porto Cavello. The credit of the Count de Florida Blanca has survived the change of the King.[5] The King of this day is less attached to Louisiana than his predecessor; he has not acquired it himself; he will moreover remain its protector; the pomp of his titles and the map of his territories cannot be lessened by it; it will secure the immensity of his other possessions. I wish by exchange they might be still augmented by participating the sovereignty of the Isles of France & Bour-

bon, and the co-sovereignty of our commercial possessions in
the East Indies. This would be a satisfactory equivalent to the
people of Spain whose particular inclinations it appears to me
the government attends to and consults more than is generally
beleived. From this arrangement mutual advantages will result
to the three nations. The solidity of the existance, and the success of the Philippine company as well as of the free commerce
of Spain in this part of the world depend upon it. The distance
between Manilla & Europe is too great to be run over without
some place to touch at. And so long as Manilla has not the means
to purchase directly from the continent of India those merchandizes of which the English have learnt them the necessity, or the
luxuries of Peru, these last will always have the art to furnish
them either by their proximity, or by the force of their new Colonies, or by their superior address in smuggling; and they will
likewise give to European Spain the merchandize of India sufficiently low for this counterband trade to be profitable & consequently it will exist.

The establishment of Pondicherry and the other French settlements justify that of the Isle of France; a colony which is
a much greater expense in proportion than any that we have
founded & supported. Things have been so arranged from the
beginning that it is all a dead weight on the finances of the metropolis. The existance, cultivation, commercial speculations,
whether profitable or unprofitable, its very faults or knaveries
of the most insignificant kind are all paid from the Treasury of
our marine. This will appear to you inconceivable, but a reform
in this Island can only be gentle and difficult. It is to be feared,
I dare say by the universe, that we are threatened with having
only one market, that of the English. It is apprehen⟨ded⟩ by every body, that our national assembly, distracted by the crowd of
great objects, will only consider the abuses and expen⟨ses⟩ without perceiving the political importance of this Island, and pass
a decree which will amount to a dereliction of it. A participation of the Sovereignty with Spain will produce a new order of
things. The expenses will no longer fall upon one. The expanded views of commerce will turn our Colonies from their
narrow circle, so burdensome for our finances. Your corn and
naval Stores in the time of distress or of war will occasion those
millions; which we there employ, to pass through better hands

than those of the Dutch at the Cape of Good Hope. The Triumvirate of the guarantee of the triple alliance will be a safe-guard
to our settlements in the East Indies. it will suffice to render
them respectable without further expense, and without increasing their forces. These commercial arrangements will be advantageous to all three. The triple pavillion of each of these modest
consular houses of the three allied people will do as much or
more than cannon badly supported.

Under your presidency, Sir, America must become what
Rome & Carthage formerly were. The terrible friendship England prepares for herself the inheritance of the commerce of
the Dutch Company; already the money, destined to the envoys
which this company actually established in season at Batavia,
goes, it is said, to pay the Prussian Soldiers. The fury of the savages on your frontiers will be one day much better paid. I will
not pretend to say but that the French of Canada may one day
be tempted to enjoy the same good fortune as those of Loisiana.
It is unnecessary to remark to you that the English tree produces branches stronger than its trunk; and that sooner or later
the vigour of the sap must seperate them from it with the fruit:
that of the East Indies will be also in this predicament; its matu-
rity must be attended to without being too much hastened. Far
from every thing that is honest, is that which accelerates a fatal
Revolution by the scourge of war, but the key of the East Indies
is the Isle of France; some feeble essays which heretofore I hazarded about this place, have proved it much more than another
would have done; this precious key belongs to the human race,
let there be three to keep it, and let us take care that it is not
delivered to those who have wished to deprive the Americans of
the right to tax themselves—who then have not offered them at
least the shadow of liberty—Representation in their parliament—and who finally have employed fire & sword to subject
them.

I have conversed too much with M. Alexr Hamilton on board
the Languedoc of your great talents and what they could effect
to doubt his opinion. He so sincerely condemned the proceedings of the English when he had the goodness to transmit me
the first letter which I received from you, that I hope he will not
disapprove my ideas.[6] He thought that agriculture and commerce ought to form the first ages of American greatness. The

conquest of the Mexican dollars, if it ever happened, would mark the epoch of corruption & depopulation. Will you have the goodness to condescend to transmit for me to M. Hamilton two of the little engravings.

Our two greatest men are ignorant of the homage which I pay them: the greatest they could wish is to have their pictures distributed by you. They are so necessary to our existence, to our tranquility, to our good fortune, to our glory, that they will be viewed with pleasure in that part of the globe which has formed for us the Marquis de la Fayette, and which has given us a double example. It would be too much to go so far as America for one of these resemblances, when we have a king who has himself opened the career of liberty—who consents & desires to be but the father as he has been the preserver of the blood of his subjects, he must be pleased to give his children repose, but shall not have attained in the second resemblance, to the perfection to which you have arrived until the modulation of our executive power shall have compleated the bow of our Government. You must certainly interest you[r]self enough to take part in the satisfaction which I feel. M. Necker is much better, we keep him at the helm of our affairs. The health of the Marquis de la Fayette resists his fatigues, his popularity increases every day, I would give my blood to cement it if it would contribute towards serving my country & my friendship; It seems to me that I esteem him more & more every day, & yet it appears to me impossible that I should.[7] I am with Respect Sir, your most obedt & very Hble St

Estaing

Translation, DLC:GW; ALS, DLC:GW. The text is taken from a translation made for GW. The original letter appears in CD-ROM:GW.

1. On 20 Mar. 1790 d'Estaing also wrote a public letter to GW. See GW to d'Estaing, 13 Oct. 1789, n.4.

2. The bust of Jacques Necker, modeled in unglazed biscuit-porcelain, was copied from a 1789 bust of Necker by Jean-Antoine Houdon by Louis-Simon Boizot, master of the biscuit-porcelain studio at Sèvres. A plaque at the base of the bust reads: "Presented to George Washington, President of the United States of America, by his most dutiful, most obedient, and most humble servant, Estaing, a citizen of the state of Georgia, by an act of 22d Feb., 1785, and a citizen of France in 1786." The bust was placed over a door in GW's study (Detweiler, *George Washington's Chinaware*, 136, 138). Bushrod Washington acquired the bust in 1802, and in 1891 it was sold to the Pennsylvania Historical

Society. It was returned to Mount Vernon in 1969. The crate containing Necker's bust and engravings of Necker and Lafayette arrived in Baltimore some weeks after d'Estaing's letter (see William Patterson to GW, 5 Aug. 1790) and created considerable confusion for GW. On 3 Oct. he wrote Lear: "When you can get at the last letter, or letters of the Count de Estaing to me, I wish you would send me a transcript of what he says, ⟨or⟩ whether any thing, of a Bust he has sent me of Mr Necker, together with a number of prints of that Gentleman and the Marquis de la Fayette which are come to my hands in a package from Baltimore" (ALS, CSmH). See also Lear to GW, 24 Oct. 1790.

3. France had ceded Louisiana to Spain at the Treaty of Paris in 1763. Although the cession was made in compensation for Spain's loss of East Florida, the duc de Choiseul, chief minister to Louis XV, had noted in 1762 that "Louisiana cost 8,000 livres annually and yielded nothing" (Robertson, *Louisiana*, 1:179).

4. Alexander O'Reilly (born c.1735–c.1788), an Irishman in the service of Spain, was appointed governor of Louisiana in 1769. His repressive policies against the residents of French extraction in Louisiana were widely criticized.

5. The conde de Floridablanca, Charles III's secretary of state, retained his position after the death of Charles in 1788 and the succession of Charles IV.

6. Alexander Hamilton visited d'Estaing on board his ship the *Languedoc* in mid-July 1778. Hamilton, who was GW's aide-de-camp at the time, probably brought to d'Estaing GW's letter of 14 July, welcoming the French admiral to the American coast. At the time d'Estaing was anchored off the New Jersey coast and was preparing to sail for Rhode Island. For Hamilton's report of his conversation with the French admiral, see Hamilton to GW, 20 July 1778.

7. GW replied to this letter on 10 Aug. 1790: "Not knowing how far I may have a secure conveyance for this letter, which is merely designed to announce the receipt of your highly esteemed favor of the 20th of March last, I forbear to enter into any discussions on the interesting and delicate subject you have unfolded. Let it be sufficient for the present to say, that I consider the plan a proof of your real patriotism and good understanding. Whether the Scheme will ever be feasible in its utmost extent, or what advantages may be drawn from it by some modification hereafter time alone must disclose. In the meantime for the tokens of your personal attachment to me, and extraordinary respect for my friend which you are pleased to manifest, I request you will have the goodness to accept my best thanks" (LB, DLC:GW).

Before he sent his private letter to GW, d'Estaing submitted it to William Short, American chargé d'affaires in Paris, for his inspection. See Short to John Jay, 4 April 1790, in Boyd, *Jefferson Papers*, 16:301–5. D'Estaing's letter to GW arrived under cover of Short's letter to Jay, on 17 June 1790. GW evidently conferred with Jefferson on d'Estaing's proposals since the secretary of state wrote Short on 10 Aug.: "You will perceive by this letter, and the papers it incloses, what part of the ideas of the Count d'Estain coincide with our views. The answer to him must be a compound of civility and reserve, expressing our thankfulness for his attentions; that we consider them as proofs of the continuance of his friendly dispositions, and that tho' it might be out of our system to implicate ourselves in trans-Atlantic guarantees, yet other parts of his plans are capable of being improved to the common benefit of the parties. Be so good as to say to him something of this kind, verbally, and so as that the matter may be ended as between him and us" (Boyd, *Jefferson Papers*, 17:121–25).

From Friedrich von Poellnitz

Sir,   New York the 20th March 1790.

   That encouragement and protection which You are pleased to grant to agriculture are my only apology for intruding on time so precious to the happiness of America: In hopes that this may plead my excuse, I humbly lay before You Sir, the following Ideas on a general improvement of this art, the plan there in sketched has a tendency to be of more effect, than the choicesd theory can be; and 'tho it differs from plans of similar views adopted for public purposes in france, England, Italy, Russia &c: &c: it will equally exhibit under Your auspices Sir, husbandry fully exemplify'd. There may be temerity in me to propose myself to execute the plan, as my skill is no doubt inferior to gentlemen's who direct those establishments in Europe, my good will only is equal to theirs and by this I will try to make amends for my small ability's. The outlines of the plan are—

   The ground in general to be workd with horned cattle; arable ground dressed in the Spring with variety of summer plants, and with winter ones in the Fall; on select spots the garden and field culture intermixed, work'd by the plough with total exclusion of the spade except for plants of running vines. If the situation is convenient for irrigated meadows, I should establish such on the plans of Italy and the Swiss country; and foreign artificial meadows of various Kinds. I would spare no trouble to discover usefull indigeneous grasses, and describe these agreable to Lineus system: This may be conducive to increase the sum of green manures, and of green food for sheep both in the fall and spring, a success in this pursuit is also likely to procure an improvement in the quality of the wool itself; as I have reason to presume that the beauty of the Spanish wool, arises more from the variation and the nature of the food, than from the Climate. I would stock the land in the propre proportion to arable, meadow, and pasture, horses only excepted, which are an expence to the farmer, and 'tho their utility for other purposes is obvious, an object of luxury to him. I would sow special useful trees in separate clumps agreable to the best rules. For the entire distribution of the ground a plain rustic stile should be observed, which is to combine usfulness, and agreableness with simplicity, and to unite continued pasture with cultivation.

The arable, meadow, and pasture grounds; I would divide in enclosures mark'd by numbers, stating the chymical analysis of soil of each number as far as it may have reference to agriculture; these numbered enclosures to be kept in account with their contents in acres, their course, the annual change of courses, their produce, and loss or profit drawn up every two years; such accounts I should be willing to publish, as I presume that in time they may become usefull to establish regular systems in farming. I should make meteorological observations, and try to compare the state of the atmosphere with some vegetable, animal or mineral body; this field is rather as yet unexplored, but the analogy exists and I believe it to be the best method to make on a simple scale meteorology serviceable to agriculture.

Sir if this plan meets Your Gracious approbation, and You should please to favor me with the execution of it, then I humbly request the grant of Three Thousand acres of land in the vicinity of the federal City near some great river, communicating with one by a creek, on which I would settle as soon as The Honble the Congress has chosen the future Residence. A smaller extent of ground would set the plan on a scale not to answer, and a too great distance from the federal City would I presume equally defeat the desired end.

I have three sons I educate to be farmers, it is probable that the one or the other will be able to follow my steps, and I will bind myself for me and my heirs, neither to sell or mortgage this land under penalty of forfeiting the Grant, as I believe that such a condition is proper to promote industry in my family, and to preserve the spirit of the institution. My domestic family consits in the whole out of Twenty three persons; my implements I thinck are equal to the undertaking; those of husband'ry and others applicable to it will be, 3 levers ready made, 2 levers not finished all differently constructed for drawing trees out of the ground. 2 hog ploughs. 1 four coultered plough. 4 Dutch ploughs. 4 horsehoe ploughs. 2 turnwrist ploughs. 2 sowing ploughs. 1 rippeling cart not finished. 1 thrashing mill. 1

mill for fattening cattle. 1 Earth augre. 1 augre for conducting water works. Phisical instruments, 2 air pumps. 1 electrical aparatus, and instruments for experiments on Air. Chymical tools, 1 burning glass able to melt metals; 1 fire thermometer ascertaining from boiling to melting heat, and from that to the greatest heat that fire can produce. 1 Essaying furnace &c. &c.

Moreover what would make this undertaking specially usefull is, that whenever desired, this ground will be open to the view of gentlemen from all quarters who on business apply to the Honble The Congress, and as I presume that a establishment Patronised by You Sir will attract particular notice those gentlemen will improve what they have seen, and diffuse agricultural intelligence over the whole extent of the Empire. Sir, I am with the greatest respect, your, most obedient, and most humble, Servant

⟨*illegible*⟩ B. Poellnitz

ALS, DLC:GW.
For Friedrich Charles Hans Bruno, Baron von Poellnitz, see his letter to GW, 26 Dec. 1789. The agricultural system Poellnitz describes in this letter is discussed at more length in his *Essay on Agriculture* (New York, 1790). GW replied to Poellnitz's letter on 23 Mar. 1790.

To Beverley Randolph

Sir,   United States [New York] March 20th 1790
Your Excellency's letter of the 10th inst. with its enclosures has been duly received.

It appears from the best information which I can obtain, that the place where Piamingo's amunition was deposited, at the time of Colo. Campbell's writing to the Executive of Virginia, is not such as to subject it to the danger which was apprehended; for the vicinity is pretty well inhabited, and the people thereof knowing that their tranquility might in a great measure depend upon the security of that amunition, would not tamely permit it to be carried off until Piamingo should return with the detachment of his own Warriors, which it seems he had gone for to guard it to the Chickasaw Towns.[1] And if this was not the case, it is highly probable that if the capture of it was premeditated it would be attempted before any communications could reach the spot from this place; The opinion, therefore, which you gave in your answer to Colo. Campbell, with respect to "the Inhabitants embodying themselves as voluntiers" for the protection of the property of our "allies" meets my approbation. If, however, it should be found, contrary to the information before stated, that the place in which the amunition is lodged, is not sufficiently secure—or if Piamingo should not arrive in season with the guard; I think it would be advisable to have it removed to the nearest settlement that could give it perfect security. I have the honor to be with very great regard Yr Excellency's most obdt Hb. Set.

Df, DNA: RG 59, Miscellaneous Letters; LB, DLC:GW.

1. See Arthur Campbell to Beverley Randolph, 20 Feb. 1790, enclosed in Randolph to GW, 10 Mar. 1790.

From Anthony Wayne

Sir   Richmond State of Georgia 20th March 1790

Nothing but the particular ⟨*illegible*⟩ of an Officer of merit which request I cou'd not refuse shou'd have induced me to intrude upon your Excellency's time at a season when I know it must be precious—but as the Object which he has ⟨in View⟩ might be lost by any delay—I take the Liberty to mention Colo. James Armstrong[1]—who wishes an Appointment in one of the Regiments which are expected to be raised he wou'd prefer Dragoons to the foot Service if any such establishment takes place, he however has been accustomed to both, & was an Officer in Canada in the Pennsa Lines early in 1776 & afterwards a Capt. of Dragoons in Colo. Lees Legion & highly esteemed by that Gallant partisan—not only for his bravery which is not to be Questioned but Conduct & continued to preserve and merit that esteem until the close of the War even after which he became a Citizen of this State & has alternately been a member of the House of Representatives or Council ever since he lately Commanded the troops raised for the protection of the Frontiers which have been members disbanded for some time.[2]

shou'd an Opening offer & that it is con⟨*illegible*⟩ with your Excellency's Opinion—to nominate him for rank he wishes it will add to the Obligations already confered upon Your Excellency's most Obt Hume Servt

Anty Wayne

ADfS, MiU-C: Anthony Wayne Papers.

1. James Armstrong had also served in Armand's Partisan Corps during the Revolution. After the war he settled in Georgia. Armstrong was not immediately given a military appointment, but during the Quasi-War he served as a major in the 5th Infantry from July 1799 to June 1800.

2. At this point Wayne wrote and crossed out "a representative in the present house assembly & one of the minority on the late Imprudent Cessions of the Western or ⟨Yazo⟩ Lands." For the Yazoo land companies, see Henry Knox to GW, 15 Feb. 1790, n.1.

From John Hazelwood

Philadelph⟨e⟩ia March 22d 1790

The Memorial & Petition of John Hazelwood respectfully Sheweth

That your Memorialist was early appointed to Command a Vessell of force in the Pennsy[lvani]a State Fleet when he was sent by the Council of Safty to New-York to Form some fire Rafts & Ships which he performed, was ordred by your Excellency to pokepsy to construct a Boom & Chain a cross the North river which was effected, that on his return to New-York was active in bringing off the troops from long Island and Governor's Island with Genls Putman & Mifflin, on his return to Philada he was Commi[ssion]ed Commodore of the State fleet & also was Commissiond by Congress to Command all the Contl Vessells then in the Deleware bay & river which he did and Exerted his utmost abillities at the Seige on the river Deleware & the Defence of mud Island & Red Bank Forts which your Excellency may possibly remember, & flatering himself that in these & other services he gave General Satisfaction, & for which he was honoured by Congress with a Sword—Since the peace being out of office & meeting with some heavy Losses in trade finds himself constrained to Solicit some Publick employment, and being Informed that a person is to be appointed to superintend & take care of the Buys Bacons & piers in the Deleware Bay & river

Your petitioner therefore prays your Excellency to appoint

him to that office as he has a thorough Knowledg of that business having been some time a Warden of the Port, or that your Excellency will give him some other appointment to assist him in supporting his family, which will be ever remembred with Gratitude by your Excellencies Most Obt & Very Humbl. Sevt[1]

John Hazelwood

I beg leave to mention the Honble Robt Morris & Mr Fitzimmons to whom I have the honor of being known.

ALS, DLC:GW.

John Hazelwood (c.1726–1800) emigrated from England at an early age and became one of the most prominent Philadelphia ship captains in the decade before the American Revolution. In 1775 and 1776 he served as superintendent of fire rafts in the Delaware River and in July 1776 was sent to New York where he performed the services described in his memorial. Appointed a commodore in the Pennsylvania navy in April 1777, he distinguished himself in the defense of the Delaware from the British fleet in the fall of that year (see Pennsylvania Council of Safety to GW, 11 July 1776). When the Pennsylvania navy was disbanded, Hazelwood returned to private business. He was appointed commissioner of purchases for the Continental army in Philadelphia in June 1780 and in December of that year became receiver of provisions for the Pennsylvania militia. On 11 April 1785 he was appointed one of the wardens of the port of Philadelphia.

1. The office of superintendent of buoys, beacons, and public piers was authorized by "An Act for the establishment and support of Lighthouses, Beacons, Buoys, and Public Piers" (*DHFC*, 5:1245–54). The Pennsylvania legislature ceded control of navigational aids in the Delaware in the fall of 1789, and shortly thereafter William Allibone, master warden of the port of Philadelphia, applied to GW for the post of superintendent (Allibone to GW, 12 Oct. 1789). Allibone acted temporarily as superintendent until his appointment was confirmed in April 1790 (Allibone to Hamilton, 29 April 1790, in Syrett, *Hamilton Papers*, 6:398–99). Hazelwood received no federal appointment from GW.

From Hugh Williamson

New York 22nd March 1790.

Mr John Skinner of North Carolina who is at present in New York has been mentioned by severals ⟨of⟩ his fellow Citizens as a Gentleman who would discharge the Duties of Marshal with great Reputation.[1]

Mr Skinner having had the Misfortune to lose his Wife a short

Time before the Sitting of our Convention had resolved to attempt the Relief of his Mind by Traveling, for this Reason Governor Johnston gave him a Certificate that is inclosed.

The Family and Connections of Mr Skinner have long been influential and much respected in the State. One of his Unkles Genl Skinner was Treasurer for many Years and has lately been Officer of Loans.[2] Mr John Skinner has been a Member of our Legislature, ever since he was eligible, either in the Commons or Senate, except when he has been of the Governors Council. He has ever been distinguished in political Life by a manly firmness as well as by a sound Understanding whence he is generally respected in the State.

The Office of Marshal would probably be the more acceptable to Mr Skinner from the Idea that it is considered as being honourable rather than profitable. He is very independent in his Circumstances.[3]

Hu. Williamson

ALS, DLC:GW.

1. John Skinner was a wealthy planter and a member of a prominent family in Edenton, North Carolina. He served in the North Carolina general assembly in 1783 and was a state senator from 1784 to 1788 and a member of the first North Carolina Ratifying Convention in 1788, in which he was an active supporter of the Constitution. GW appointed Skinner U.S. marshal for North Carolina on 7 June 1790 (see GW to U.S. Senate, 7 June 1790). Skinner declined reappointment in 1794 and recommended his deputy, Michael Payne, who received the appointment.

2. William Skinner (d. 1798), also of Edenton, was a planter and a leading North Carolina Federalist. During the Revolution he served as a brigadier general (1777–79), member of the North Carolina provincial congress (1775–79), and as state treasurer (1779), as well as in the first North Carolina Ratifying Convention in 1788, in which he supported the Constitution. He was reappointed commissioner of loans under the new government in 1790 and served until his death.

3. Enclosed in Williamson's letter was an undated testimonial from Williamson, Timothy Bloodworth, John B. Ashe, and John Steele, members of Congress from North Carolina, stating that Skinner's appointment would "give general Satisfaction to his fellow Citizens." Also enclosed was a certificate from Samuel Johnston, governor of North Carolina, dated 4 Dec. 1789, testifying that Skinner "is a Gentleman of respectable Connections & Property within the said State, and hath acquitted himself honorably in the discharge of the Publick Service, and as an honest Man, in his private concerns." Both documents are in DLC:GW.

Conversation with Thomas Jefferson

[New York] 23 March 1790. In his diary for this day GW notes that there was "A full, & very respectable Levee to day—previous to which I had a conversation with the Secretary of State on the following points, viz—

First, with respect to our Captives in Algiers,[1] in which, after detailing their situation—the measures he had taken for their relief and the train in which the business was in by means of a Genl. [   ] who is at the head of a religious society in France whose practice it is to sollicit aids for the relief of the unfortunate Christians in captivity among the Barbarians, it was concluded betwn. us, that it had better remain in that train a while longer.[2] This person had been authorised to go as far as about £150 Sterlg. each, for the ransom of our Captives; but the Algerines demanding a much larger sum it was conceived that acceding to it might establish a precedent which would always operate and be very burthensome if yielded to; and become a much stronger inducement to captivate our People than they now have, as it is more for the sake of the ransom than for the labour, that they make Slaves of the Prisoners. Mr. Short was to be written to on this Subject, and directed to make enquiry of this General [   ] what his expectations of redemption are at present.

Second—He is of opinion, that excepting the Court of France, there is no occasion to employ higher grades in the Diplomatic line than Chargé des affaires; and that these, by the respectibility of their appointments, had better be at the head of their grade, than Ministers Plenipotentiaries by low Salaries at the foot of theirs. The reason of the distinction, in favor of a Minister Plenipo at Versailles, is, that there are more Ambassdadors at that Court than any other and therefore that we ought in some measure to approximate our Representative and besides, its being a Court with which we have much to do.[3]

Third—With respect to the appointment of Consels he refers to a letter on the nature of this business—the places where necessary—and the characters best entitled to appointmts. which he had written on the Subject, while in France, to the Secretary of Foreign affairs.[4]

Fourth—That it might be advisable to direct Mr. Charmichael to Sound the Spanish Ministry with respect to the obstacles which had hitherto impeded a Commercial Treaty to see if there was any disposition in them to relax in their Territorial claims & exclusive right to the Navigation of the River Missisipi."[5]

Diaries, 6:51–52.

Jefferson arrived in New York on 21 Mar. 1790 to take up his duties as secretary of state. GW received him that afternoon and the next day "conversed for more than an hour with Mr. Jefferson on business relative to the duties of his office" (ibid., 49).

1. For background on the American captives in Algiers, see Mathew Irwin to GW, 9 July 1789, source note.

2. The Mathurins were a religious order founded in the twelfth century whose main purpose was the redemption of captives. Jefferson had suggested in early 1787 that the offices of the order might be used to effect the release of the American captives in Algiers (Jefferson to John Adams, 11 Jan. 1787, and to John Jay, 1 Feb. 1787, in Boyd, *Jefferson Papers,* 11:35–36, 101–2). By the end of 1788 Jefferson was negotiating with Père Chauvier, who held the title "Général and Grand Ministre" of the order and at the end of the year put the subsistence of the captives and negotiations for their release in Chauvier's hands (ibid., 14:395–97, 401–2, 433). William Short, who carried on negotiations with the Mathurins after Jefferson left Paris, reported in the early summer of 1790 that Chauvier had stated that he had "little hopes of any thing being done for our captives through his chanel, although he continues assurances of his zeal in case of any opportunity presenting itself" (Short to Jefferson, 14 and 25 June 1790, in Boyd, *Jefferson Papers,* 16:505, 570). On 14 May 1790 the House of Representatives referred a petition "of sundry persons, citizens of the United States, captured by the Algerines, and now in slavery in Algiers" to Jefferson and requested his report on the captives (*DHFC,* 3:412). For Jefferson's detailed account of his negotiations with the Mathurins, see his report, enclosed in his letter to GW, 28 Dec. 1790.

Information concerning the captives and their fate had continued to reach GW during the first year of his presidency. In addition to Mathew Irwin's letter, GW was approached on the matter early in 1790 by Elbridge Gerry. As Gerry informed Acting Secretary of State John Jay, a letter from James Anderson to Thomas Russell of Boston, covering a letter from the British consul at Algiers, Charles Logie, had "been communicated to the President of the United States, and relates to some american prisoners at Algiers. The President has desired that the papers may be enclosed to the Secretary of State, and is disposed to do whatever may be requisite on his part to afford relief to the unhappy sufferers adding at the same time, that by letters from Mr Jefferson dated in August last, our Bankers at Holland had given information of their having money in their hands appropriated amongst other purposes, to the one mentioned" (Gerry to John Jay, 21 Jan. 1790, with enclosures Anderson to Russell, 4 Oct. 1789, and Logie to Anderson, 24 June 1789, DNA: RG 59, Domestic Letters).

3. The subject of diplomatic appointments was of considerable concern to GW at this time because a bill for "providing the means of intercourse between

the United States and foreign nations," introduced in the House of Representatives in January 1790, had engendered extensive and occasionally acrimonious debate on the appointment of American diplomats abroad and the manner in which they were to be paid. The bill involved constitutional questions as to whether the president should determine the rank and emoluments for diplomatic appointments or whether this was to be a function of Congress as had been the case during the Confederation (*Annals of Congress,* 1:1004–5, 1113, 1118–30; Bowling and Veit, *Diary of William Maclay,* 301). On 31 Mar. 1790 "the committee to whom was re-committed the bill 'providing the means of intercourse between the United States and foreign nations,' presented an amendatory bill to the same effect, which was received, and read the first time" (*DHFC,* 3:351). Debates in the House and Senate on the amended bill dragged on until the passage of "An Act providing the means of intercourse between the United States and foreign nations" (1 *Stat.* 128 [1 July 1790]). See also GW to the U.S. Senate, 4 June 1790, n.1.

4. This is probably Jefferson's letter of 14 Nov. 1788 to John Jay, detailing Jefferson's views on a consular establishment and suggesting individuals who might fill consular posts in France (Boyd, *Jefferson Papers,* 14:56–66).

5. William Carmichael (c.1738–1795), a native of Queen's County, Md., had served in the Continental Congress from 1778 to 1779 and as John Jay's secretary in Spain in 1779. After Jay left Spain in 1782, Carmichael remained as chargé d'affaires at Madrid and other residences of the Spanish court. GW appointed him chargé under the new government in September 1789, and he remained in Spain until his death, although William Short was named as his successor at the Spanish Court in May 1794 (*DHFC,* 2:50; *Executive Journal,* 1:157). Jefferson's instructions to Carmichael on the navigation of the Mississippi River are dated 2 Aug. 1790 (Boyd, *Jefferson Papers,* 17:111–12).

From Jeremiah Jordan, Edmund Plowden, and Joshua Thomas

Sir,   Maryland St Marys County 23 March 1790

We hope we stand excused in recommending to Your Excellencys Notice Captain Henry Carbery, as nothing could induce us to do it, but a thorough conviction that he is not unworthy of it, and that he is well able to discharge with propriety the duties of any place he may be employed in.[1]

We have known him from his early Youth, and we can truly say, that we never heard, or knew any thing, either in his public or private life (the unfortunate Affair of Philadelphia excepted)[2] that he or his Friends need be ashamed of. The little patrimony left him by his Father, was sunk during the war, and his present situation is such, that he stands much in need of some assistance to screen him against Want.

If, Sir, you should think proper to employ him, either in the Civil or Military Line (the latter we believe he would prefer) we can venture to say, that so far from disgracing, he would do Honour to the appointment. He is well qualified to serve as a Clerk in any of the Departments, where writing a good hand, and a competent knowledge of figures should be required—and we are certain, if employed, he will pay every attention to the Business he may be ingaged in.

Few men among us are better acquainted with the Creek, Chacktaw, Chickesaw, and Waybash Indians than Captn Carbery is, having not long since been in their Countries, and is personally known to many of their great men. His faithful unremitted Services during the War, and the Blood he has shed in his Countrys cause, we trust has not only obliterated his unfortunate conduct, but will restore him again, to the Favor and protection of his Country. We have now only to beg Your Excellencys excuse for troubling You with this Letter, and to assure You that we have the Honor to be, Your Excellencys Most Obedt Most humble Servants

Jeremiah Jordan
Jo. A. Thomas
Edmd Plowden

LS, DLC:GW.

    Jordan, Plowden, and Thomas were St. Mary's County, Md., planters.

    1. Henry Carbery had applied for a post in the federal government in 1789. See Carbery to GW, 25 July 1789.

    2. For Carbery's involvement in a 1783 attack on the Continental Congress in Philadelphia, see Carbery's application for office, 25 July 1789, n.1.

To Friedrich von Poellnitz

Sir. New York March 23d 1790

I received, a few days ago, your letter on the subject of establishing a farm, under the public patronage, for the purpose of encreasing & extending agricultural knowledge—in answer to which, I have only leisure to make the following general observations.[1]

As I have passed a considerable portion of my life very satisfactorily in the business of agriculture, it will be understood, that I am alike fond of it, on an individual account, as on account of its public emoluments. But, however convinced I am of the great advantages to be derived to the Community from improvements in it, however susceptible of improvements I consider the present state of farming in this Country, and however desirous I am of seeing these improvements take place immediately—yet, in my public capacity, I know not whether I can with propriety do any thing more at present, than what I have already done. I have brought the subject, in my speech at the opening of the present Session of Congress, before the national Legislature.[2] It rests with them to decide what measures ought afterwards to be adopted for promoting the success of the great objects which I have recommended to their attention. I can only say farther, that whatever wise & prudent plans may be deemed most feasible & effectual (as being clearly within the functions & abilities of the general Government) will meet with my ready & hearty concurrence.

Since the Seat of Government of the United States is not yet determined, and since the subject of Finance has not yet received such a form as may justify any considerable new expenditures, it is hardly probable that Congress could enter deeply into the discussion of your meditated improvements in agriculture, during their actual Session—But, I request, Sir, you will be persuaded, that, in all events, I have a proper sense of your zeal in this matter, that I have great confidence in your ability, and ardent wishes for your success; being with due consideration Sir Your most obedt & humble Servant.

Df, DNA: RG 59, Miscellaneous Letters; LB, DLC:GW.

1. See Poellnitz to GW, 20 Mar. 1789. See also Poellnitz to GW, 26 Dec. 1789.
2. See GW to the U.S. Senate and House of Representatives, 8 Jan. 1790.

To David Stuart

Dear Sir,   New York March 23d 1790
The only answer I can give to your letter of the 11th Instt is, that under my present view of the subject, the agreement you

have entered into with Mr Robt Alexander had better be carried into effect. But I must declare to you at the sametime, that from my imperfect knowledge of the original bargain—of the proceedings which have been had under it—and of the points on which the dispute between Mr Custis & Mr Alexander have turned, that I feel an incompetency, and of course an unwillingness to give a final opinion thereon, without further information.

All I recollect of this business is, that the former was to have given the latter the sum of (I believe) £12,000 for the Mansionhouse tract; to be paid as Mr Alexander says, with compound interest at the expiration of (I think) 24 years—or, according to Mr Custis's ideas, *on* or *before* the expiration of *that* period.

This difference of opinion has given rise, it seems, to the dispute now subsisting—a highly important one indeed it is—and very interesting in its decision to both parties; but how it came to pass that there should be this difference of opinion on a point which might, I should suppose, be decided by resorting to written documents, I am at a loss to discover; nor am I better informed with respect to the kind of money in which the payment was to have been made; and yet, as in the last case, one would think this also might be determined by the plainest construction of the Instruments, or by such oral testimony as could be adduced in explanation of the words, if they are found to be ambiguous.

With respect to the first point, if it was optional in Mr Custis to pay *on* or *before* the expiration of the term, on what ground did Mr Alexander refuse to receive payment? and if the payment was not to be made in Specie (by the agreement) why was any medium that was currt at the time, refused? The great nominal sum which was to be given for the land, is, to my mind, an unequivocal proof (if nothing is expressed to the contrary) that both parties were Speculating in paper; for the one never could have had the conscience to ask or the other the folly to have given, £12,000 specie for it.

If my comprehension of this matter (as here stated) is not right, I wish to be set right—If it is, I could wish, before I give any conclusive opinion, to receive information on the following points.

First—What are the opinions of those who have been consulted, with respect to the option, claimed by Mr Custis, to pay *on* or *before* the expiration of the term of 24 years?

Second—Whether in the articles of agreement, Mortgage, bond, or other evidence, there is an exception of Paper Money, or proviso to pay in any other sort?

Third—At what period was the agreement made? How long after this agreement was the deed dated? and what was the Continental & State Scale of depreciation, at both those periods?

Fourth—In what sort of paper money was the tender made, and how long after the date of the Deed was it, before it was made? Why in the opinion of your Lawyers, was not *that* paper a legal tender? Was there any other Paper money in being at that time which would have been? and why, unless emitted by the State, and made tenderable by law? In that case, why was not such money tendered?

After the solution of these several questions I shall be able to decide with much more satisfaction to myself than at the present moment, whether it will be best to give £600 to annul the bargain—Pay rent (but this is just)—and sustain the loss of the sums which went to procure the money tendered—or hazard a decision in the high Court of Chancery; by which the whole Sum of £12,000 with interest might be decreed, if not scaled, according to the opinion of the Lawyers on the one side, or the other, agreeably to your statement thereof.

My best wishes, in which Mrs Washington & the Children unite are presented to Mrs Stuart and yourself & family—With much truth I am Dr Sir Your Obedt & Affecte Hble Servt

Go: Washington

ALS, PWacD: Sol Feinstone Collection, on deposit at PPAmP; LB, DLC:GW.

From Jacob Wray

Virginia Port Hampton

May it please your Excellency   March 24th 1790

As I, find myself groing very short in Memory & of coarse my small abillities going in the same line & find publick business if ever so profitable so great a burthen to my mind without I could controll the business according to Law & Instructions which in my Opinion makes some nice reflections.

Therefore if you will please to relieve me of a great Burthen altho of so little business to the Nation I, shall rest happy in keeping up till a successor comes to hand which is my real wishes to Resign. I am with all Duty your most Obedt Sert

Jacob Wray Collr
Port Hampton

ALS, DNA: RG 59, Resignations and Declinations, Letters of Resignation and Declination of Federal Office.

1. Jacob Wray was appointed collector of customs at Hampton, Va., in August 1789. He had been recommended for a federal post by Samuel Griffin, John Page and Miles King. See Conversation with Samuel Griffin, 9 July 1789, Page to GW, 14 July 1789, and King to GW, 19 July 1789. Wray was succeeded in the collectorship at Hampton in April 1790 by George Wray, Jr. (*DHFC*, 2:68; GW to the U.S. Senate, 28 April 1790).

To John Eager Howard

Sir,   New York March 25th 1790

You will receive with this a Medal struck by order of the late Congress in commemoration of your much approved conduct in the battle of the Cowpens—and presented to you as a mark of the high sense which your Country entertains of your services on that occasion.[1]

This Medal was put into my hands by Mr Jefferson; and it is with singular pleasure that I now transmit it to you. I am, with very great esteem, Your Excellency's most Obedt Servt

Go: Washington

LS, MdHi.

1. During the course of the Revolution, Congress authorized the presentation of fourteen gold and silver medals to specific individuals "to signalize and commemorate certain interesting events and Conspicuous Characters" (*JCC*, 33:422). A medal was to be presented to GW, commemorating the evacuation of Boston; to Horatio Gates, for the defeat of Burgoyne's army at Saratoga; to Anthony Wayne, François de Fleury, and John Stewart, for their services at Stony Point; to Henry Lee, for the victory at Paulus Hook; to John Paulding, David Williams, and Isaac Van Wart, for the capture of Major John André; to Daniel Morgan, John Eager Howard, and William Washington, for their victory at Cowpens; to Nathanael Greene, for his victory at Eutaw Springs; and to John Paul Jones, for the victory of the *Bonhomme Richard* over the *Serapis*.

See John Adams to GW, 1 April 1776, n.2. The medal commemorating the capture of André was executed in America during the war, and the one for François de Fleury was executed under Franklin's direction in Paris, but nothing was done to procure the others until after the war, when Robert Morris, as superintendent of finance, wrote to David Humphreys, secretary to the American peace commissioners, requesting him to have the medals made in Europe. When he left Paris in November 1785, Humphreys turned the business over to Jefferson, who oversaw the completion of eight of the medals in Paris (for the details of their production, along with illustrations of all of the medals executed under Jefferson's direction, see the editorial "Notes on American Medals Struck in France" and accompanying correspondence in Boyd, *Jefferson Papers*, 16:53–79). The medals for Gates and Greene were the first completed and were sent to Congress on 6 July 1787 (William Short to John Jay, 4 May 1787, in Boyd, *Jefferson Papers*, 11:345–47). Arthur St. Clair, as president of Congress, sent Greene's medal to Jeremiah Wadsworth, one of Greene's executors, on 9 Aug. 1787, and Gates was sent his medal on the same day (Burnett, *Letters*, 8:633–34). A ninth medal, for John Paul Jones, was not complete when Jefferson left for America. Morris had neglected to include the medal for Henry Lee on the list sent to Humphreys, and no subsequent provision for this medal had been made by Jefferson. Jefferson thus brought six medals with him from France—for GW, Wayne, Stewart, Morgan, Howard, and William Washington—and presented them to GW on or shortly after 21 March. GW accepted his gold medal and assumed responsibility for distributing the other five. On 25 Mar. GW wrote letters transmitting these medals to their recipients.

GW sent three of the five medals to the heroes of Cowpens—Daniel Morgan, John Eager Howard, and William Washington. GW's letter of 25 Mar. 1790 transmitting Daniel Morgan's gold medal is in NN: Myers Collection, Daniel Morgan Papers. His letter to William Washington, who commanded the American cavalry at Cowpens, has not been found. The latter wrote to GW on 7 Nov. 1790 referring to "Your Excellency's favor of March 25th accompanied with a Medal struck by order of the late Congress." The letter was probably identical to the one GW sent to Howard.

The other two medals honored heroes of Stony Point. The first was sent to Anthony Wayne, who commanded the select force that stormed the British fortifications at Stony Point on the night of 16 July 1779. Congress voted to present Wayne with a gold medal on 26 July 1779 (*JCC*, 14:890). To his letter transmitting the medal to Wayne, GW added a postscript acknowledging receipt of Wayne's letter of 1 Feb. 1790 (LS, CLjJC). Wayne replied to this letter on 7 Nov. 1790: "I have the pleasure of acknowledging the receipt of your favor of the 25th of March together with the Medal struck by order of the late Congress—in commemoration of the Assault of Stoney Point—the polite manner in which you have transmited it, adds not a little to it's value—& permit me to assure you, that I can much better feel—than express—the high sense I entertain of the honor done me by the late Congress—& by your Excellency upon that Occasion" (DLC:GW).

The letter accompanying the medal honoring John Stewart was the only one that differed significantly from the others. John Stewart joined the Continental army in 1776 as a lieutenant in John Allen Thomas's Independent Maryland Company and was promoted to major before being captured at Staten Island in 1777. On the night of 16 July 1779, Stewart and François-Louis Teissèdre, marquis de Fleury, led specially picked detachments of about a hundred and fifty men each to cut away the abatis in front of the British works at Stony Point. For this service Congress voted on 26 July 1779 to award both men silver medals (*JCC*, 14:890). Stewart died in December 1782. GW transmitted the medal honoring Stewart to his father, Stephen Stewart, a planter in Anne Arundel County, Md., on 25 Mar.: "You will receive with this a medal struck by order of the late Congress in commemoration of the much approved conduct of your Son (the late Colo. John Stewart) in the assault of Stoney Point—and was to have been presented to him as a mark of the high sense which his Country entertained of his services on that occasion. This Medal was put into my hands by Mr Jefferson, and it is with singular pleasure that I now transmit it to you, as it must afford some pleasing consolation, when reflecting upon the loss of a worthy Son" (LB, DLC:GW).

Letter not found: to William Washington, 25 Mar. 1790. William Washington wrote to GW on 7 Nov. 1790, referring to "Your Excellency's favor of March 25th."[1]

1. See GW to John Eager Howard, 25 Mar. 1790, n.1.

From George Augustine Washington

Honord Uncle   Mount Vernon March 26th 1790.
    Your Favor of the 14th did not come to hand untill the day before yesterday owing as I was informed to a delay of the Mail north of Baltimore.[1]
    Previous to my paying Messrs Porter & Ingrahams[2] Acct I satisfied myself by Mr Lears statement on the Ledger and their last acct renderd that I was right in so doing. but in all matters of the kind where I have doubts, shall delay payment and take Your directions: the last payment Mr Lear made those Gentlemen was 28 oz. 1 Qr Gold £106.13.6 at which time there was a Ball: due them as stated in their last acct of £39.8.0¾. The original accts I kept, those forwarded You were Copies.
    I did not in many instances suffer Mares or Jennets to be taken away which were sent to the Jacks without payment being made, but confess I was wrong in suffering it in any, and in future will not allow it. it is disagreeable to refuse some persons.

notwithstanding it is an indulgence that no one has a right to expect.

The 6 mares which remain to complete the 20 purchased by Mr Zantzinger arrived here on Friday night last.[3] a Copy of the discriptive list which accompanied them is enclosed, of these I do not think less favorably than the first sent—there were three of the last Blacks which with the one before discribed as black and all black are pretty well matched and are fine mares—the black and all black is the youngest and promis's to be the largest—I have enclosed Mr Zantzingers Letters—I would have setled with the Men—the bills taken by them to this place would have enabled me to have done it but could not ascertain their return expences.

I shall be making enquiry for a person to replace Fairfax (but make no engagement) in case he continues his determination of going[4]—The Son of Mr James DeNeil who Doctr Stuart was speakg to you of in such high terms he has now in his service as an Overseer on the plantn he purchased of Pain[5]—the Doctr speaks in terms of the greatest dissatisfaction of his cruelty and intolerable management and has determin'd to part with him— Mr Gwins character stands very high and I believe deservedly so—but no enducement short of setling on his own estate would tempt him to leave Mr Fitzhugh I am persuaded[6]—he has purchased Mr Fendall⟨s⟩ seat in Maryland and is very desirous of setling himself, but has been prevented by Mr Fitzhughs great aversion to parting with him—I have had an application for The Ferry & Frenches from a Mr Anthony Whiting an Englishman who says much of his knowledge as a manager and produced as a proof of it a certificate from General Dickinson and Mr Cadwalader, a copy of which I took and have enclosed[7]—he desired I would refer You to Mr Cadwalader who is in Congress for further information of his qualifications and character[8]—he says he is out of service at present and would take the management of those places—but talks of 40 Guineas the first year and signified his expectation of an encrease after from the proofs he expected to give of his good management⟨.⟩ he appeared conversant in the business he profess⟨'d⟩ he said that he had been entrusted with the entire management of General Cadwaladers estate and for some time had no assistant, but finding he was incompetent to it they allowed him I think 70 Guineas, out of which he was

to obtain assistance on the best terms he could—he applied for
the Ferry understanding a person would be wanting but seem'd
to signify that he thought himself competent to act on a larger
scale—Mr Cadwalader perhaps may be able to give you certain
information—he may perhaps be qualified to replace Fairfax
should he go—the Mans conversation so far as I am capable of
judging is much superior to what is met with among people of
that pursuit—he is now in Chester Town Maryland where he
desired I would direct to him in case You should incline to employ him—I have informed Mr Bloxham that You would continue him no longer than the end of the year—I believe it was
not an agreeable communication to him but he said that it was,
and wished to go before winter set in. if you would liberate him
I told him that this was an unseasonable time for changeing
Overseers but should mention it to you and if one could be got
I did not know of any great objection there would be to it nor
do I for He has not much to recommend him—I intended on
my return from Berkley to have removed Davy to D: Run and
Will⁹ to Muddy hole but on mentioning it to Davy he beged that
he might not, and urged that he did not think You would com-
pell him to it for that since the severe fit of the jaundice he had
before you went away that he had been very weakly and thought
himself unable to take the management at D: Run that he was
now fixed and hoped to give you satisfaction—he really appears
to conduct himself well and what he says of his health I think is
so, for he looks badly—I thought it best to communicate his dislike to removing and take your directions, for to press it on him
I fear'd not much could be expected of him—and by continuing
Will untill I heard from You no great injury could arise—tho'
not much can be said of his skill he is active and perfectly disposed to execute orders—but do not think his management
equal to conducting a plantan of its consequence—I have enclosed the No. of 8 hoggsheads of Tobacco which have been in-
spected and will the others which I expect will be 6. I have not
seen the Inspecter but understand it was much approved—I
shall be sorry if Colo. Biddle should not be able to furnish the
ballance of the Buckwheat—the 200 Bushls shiped on bord of
Capt. Elwood has arrived—the Gardner very much lamented
not recieving the Cabbage seed which was mentiond in his list,
the other seed came safe—he seems fond of flours &c. but says

he will pay strict attention to the more necessary parts of Gardning by furnishing a good supply for the Kitchen—The Posts which stood against the Barn at the Mansion house I had put within shortly after You left home—the winter has been so wet that the Fence at D: Run from the Corner of No. 7 across the swamp has not yet been done but shall not be neglected and hope to make the divisions in the Mill meadow which were directed—When Bishop and Green went away I had the house secured and attended to, so that it has sufferd no injury—they are living at a place of Colo. McCartys where Mrs Barns formerly lived.[10]

The Ground has only been in order for seeding for a few days and that in parts of the fields at D: Run Muddy hole and R: Plantn at Frenches they were plowing but the Ground too wet for sowing at the above mention'd Plantns they have been seeding for 3 or four days but the rain that fell last night and to day will I fear put a stop to it for some time and the present appearances of the weather threatens much more—the plowing at the Ferry & Frenches has and fear will for some time be much interupted by the distemper among the horses some of them are very ill 2 Peter fears will die I make him direct for them[11]—it is a violent running at the nose and some swell very much in throat it has attacked several of the horses about the house—I lost one some time ago and had another on the eve of death for near two months most of the Mules have had it and some severely—the severe frost previous to the heavy fall of snow has been a very fatal one the wheat where the ground is flat has sufferd severely and I fear very little inded will ever recover it— I delay'd the sale of Flour as long as it appeard prudent to risk it indeed before I went to Berkley I was offerd by Mr Potts 41/ which I would have taken but you appeard by Your Letters to think there was no reason to apprehend a fall therefore declined it—on my return went to Alexandria to examin the Market and found that 40 was the highest price—Mr Potts & Wilson who had been among the Principal purchasers Commission'd by Mr Donald[12] had recd orders not to exceed 36/. it appeard to me from the best information that I could obtain that a rise was very uncertain and from the fluctuating state it had been in for some time ⟨thought it⟩ advisable after a full deliberation to dispose of the whole on hand—119 Bls Comn Flour @ 40/6 d. taken from the Mill by Colo. Hoe.[13] 38 Bls of Ship Stuff @ 14/6 d. pr hundred and 1/6 d. for the Barrel—35 Bls Midlings @ 17/ pr hundred and 1/6 d. for the Bl taken at the Mill and the Cash pd by Horn & Jemmison Bakers in Alexandria—Mr Lawry offerd me 41/ deliverd at Alexandria but required a credit untill June[14]— but accident and delay taken into consideration induced me to prefer 40/6 d. Cash—Fanny joins me in sincerest affection to You my Aunt & the Children and good wishes to the Family— with the tenderest regard I am Honord Uncle Your truely affectionate Nephew

Geo: A: Washington

ALS, ViMtV.

1. Letter not found.

2. Thomas Porter and Nathaniel Ingraham operated a store near the corner of Fairfax and King streets in Alexandria, Virginia.

3. See GW to Thomas Hartley, 29 Sept. 1789, source note.

4. John Fairfax remained in GW's employ until December 1790, when he moved to Monongalia County, where in 1794 he became a justice of the peace and in 1809–10 and 1814–15 represented the county in the Virginia house of delegates. As late as November 1799 Fairfax visited GW at Mount Vernon (*Diaries*, 6:373).

5. James Deneale (d. 1806) was a planter with holdings near the intersection of the Difficult Bridge and Ox roads in Fairfax County. His son was probably James Deneale, Jr. The overseer was probably Benjamin Gwinn. In 1785 David Stuart had purchased 1,250 acres from Edward Payne, James Deneale's brother-in-law (Mitchell, *Beginning at a White Oak*, 155; Fairfax County Deed Book Q [1785–88], 145–50).

6. Presumably George Augustine Washington is referring to William Fitzhugh of Chatham in Stafford County. Mr. Fendall may be Philip Fendall who was at that time living in Alexandria.

7. GW offered Whitting the position of manager for Ferry and French's plantation in April 1790, and George Augustine Washington signed an indenture with him on 20 May. See GW to Whitting, 14 April 1790, and notes. When George Augustine Washington died in early 1793, Whiting took over the management of Mount Vernon for the few months remaining until his own death in June 1793.

8. Lambert Cadwalader (1743–1823) was elected to the House of Representatives from New Jersey in 1789 and served two terms. He was the proprietor of an extensive estate at Greenwood, N.J., near Trenton.

9. Both Davy and Will were slave overseers on GW's plantations.

10. Thomas Bishop (c.1705–1795) came to America with Edward Braddock's forces in 1755. Shortly after GW assumed command of the Virginia Regiment, he employed Bishop as a personal servant. Bishop resigned from

GW's service in early 1760 and rejoined the British army, but by the end of the year GW, at Bishop's request, sought his release so that Bishop could once more enter his employ. Bishop's daughter Sarah married Thomas Green, one of GW's overseers. For Green, see the source note to GW's letter to him, 31 Mar. 1789. By 1790 the 85-year-old Bishop was evidently living with his daughter and son-in-law at property owned by GW's friend and neighbor Col. Daniel McCarty (d. 1792), and formerly occupied by his mother Sarah Ball McCarty Barnes.

11. GW had several slaves named Peter. It is uncertain which one George Augustine Washington is referring to here.

12. John Potts, Jr. (1760–1809), operated an import store in Alexandria. Wilson is probably William Wilson of Alexandria, an agent for a Glasgow-based mercantile and shipping business, James Wilson & Sons. Donald may be Alexander Donald, a Richmond merchant who often did business with GW. For some months after 1789 Donald was in London as a partner in the firm of Donald & Burton.

13. Robert Townsend Hooe, a partner of the Alexandria mercantile firm of Hooe & Harrison.

14. Possibly John Lowrey of Elizabeth City County, Va., who engaged in business dealings with GW in the mid-1780s (*Diaries*, 4:200).

From the Earl of Buchan

Sir,   Dryburgh Abbey Scotland March 27. 1790

I have the honour to reccomend to your Excellency's Countenance a Periodical work about to be circulated in the States by Dr James Anderson, whose view of it will be handed along with this Letter for your perusal.[1]

I have long wished for a publication of this kind that should be neither a Booksellers jobb nor a stalking Horse for party and such from my confidence in Dr Anderson I expect his Journal to be and if so of great importance to literature and to usefull information wherever it may be circulated.[2] I have the Honour to be with high Esteem & Respect Sir! yr Excellencys most Humble and Obedient Servant

                                        Buchan

ALS, MH.

David Erskine, eleventh earl of Buchan (1742–1829) was a Scottish lord, literary patron, and writer. A prominent antiquarian, Buchan founded the Society of Antiquaries of Scotland in 1780 and wrote several essays on historical subjects for British periodicals. In 1787 he retired to Dryburgh Abbey, which he sought to make a center of Scottish culture. An indefatigable letter writer, he maintained correspondence with members of the British royal family, Horace Walpole, and many others and exchanged at least eighteen letters with GW between 1790 and 1798. A distant relative of the Fairfax family, Buchan was pleased to call GW his "kinsman" (Buchan to GW, 17 July 1798).

1. Enclosed with the letter was a prospectus of the *Bee, or Universal Literary Intelligencer,* now in the collection of the Boston Athenaeum (Griffin, *Boston Athenæum Collection,* 10). The prospectus was the work of James Anderson (1739–1808), a Scottish economist and promoter of commercial and agricultural reform. A farmer by background, Anderson began publishing works on trade and agriculture in 1771 and after moving to Edinburgh in 1783 became one of the leading proponents of agricultural reform in Scotland. He launched the *Bee* in December 1790 and continued it until 1794, when he stopped publication after eighteen volumes because of the "extreme tardiness" of payments from subscribers (James Anderson to GW, 6 Dec. 1794). The *Bee* included articles on literature, history, agriculture, and commerce as well as poetry and excerpts from contemporary books; the earl of Buchan was a frequent contributor. Anderson first wrote to GW on 28 Sept. 1791, initiating a correspondence on agricultural subjects that continued until GW's death. Largely at GW's suggestion, Anderson was elected a member of the American Philosophical Society (see GW to Buchan, 22 April 1793, Buchan to GW, 22 Oct. 1793, GW to Thomas Jefferson, 31 Dec. 1793). GW owned copies of at least three of Anderson's works on agriculture at the time of his death: *Essays Relating to Agriculture and Rural Affairs* (3 vols., Edinburgh, 1784–96), *A Practical Treatise on Peat Moss* (Edinburgh, 1794), and *A Practical Treatise on Draining Bogs and Swampy Grounds* (London, 1797), inscribed to GW by Anderson. GW also owned two volumes of Anderson's later periodical, *Recreations in Agriculture, Natural History, Arts, and Miscellaneous Literature* (Griffin, *Boston Anthenæum Collection,* 9–10).

2. At GW's request a notice announcing the publication of the *Bee* was printed in the *Gazette of the United States* (New York) on 14 July 1790 (see GW to Buchan, 30 June 1790). Although he did not ask to be enrolled as a subscriber, GW received the first six volumes of the *Bee* from Anderson on 10 June 1792 and wrote to him on 20 June asking "to be informed to whom, or in what manner I shall cause payment to be made for it." Anderson sent GW volumes 7 through 11 on 3 Nov. 1792. After insisting that he be regarded as a regular subscriber and repeated efforts to find out whom he should pay for the volumes, GW sent Anderson six guineas for the fifteen volumes he had received (GW to Anderson, 26 May 1794). Anderson responded that he had intended GW accept the volumes as a gift (Anderson to GW, 6 Dec. 1794). The inventory of GW's books made at his death indicates that he owned all eighteen volumes. GW's copies of the *Bee* were dispersed in the nineteenth century; volume 7 is now (1994) at Mount Vernon.

To Robert Morris

Saturday 27th March 1790

The President and Mrs W—— Compliments and thanks to Mr Morris for his politeness. They have nothing to charge Mr Morris with but their affectionate regards for Mrs Morris and the family; and to wish him a pleasanter journey than the state of the Roads promise, and a safe return to this City when his business in Philadelphia shall be accomplished.[1]

AL, PWacD: Sol Feinstone Collection, on deposit at PPAmP.

1. Robert Morris left New York for Philadelphia by Tuesday, 30 Mar., and returned by Friday, 16 April (Bowling and Veit, *Diary of William Maclay,* 231, 246).

To David Stuart

Dear Sir,   New York March 28th 1790.

Your letter of the 15th enclosing the Act of Assembly authorising an agreement with Mr Alexander came to my hand in the moment my last to you was dispatched.

I am sorry such jealousies as you relate should be gaining ground, & poisoning the minds of the Southern people. But, admit the fact which is alledged as the cause of them, and give it full scope, does it amount to more than what was known to every man of information before, at, and since the adoption of the Constitution? Was it not always believed that there are some points which peculiarly interest the Eastern States? And did any one who reads human nature, & more especially the character of the Eastern people, conceive that they would not pursue them steadily by a combination of their force? Are there not other points which equally concern the Southern States? If these States are less tenacious of their interest, or, if whilst the Eastern move in a solid phalanx to effect their purposes, the Southern are always divided, which of the two is most to be blamed? That there is diversity of interests in the Union none has denied. That this is the case also in every State is equally certain—and that it extends even to Counties, can be as readily proved. Instance the Southern & Northern parts of Virginia—the upper & lower parts of So. Carolina &ca—have not the interests of these always been at varience? Witness the County of Fairfax, has not the interests of the people thereof varied, or the Inhabitants been taught to believe so? These are well known truths, and yet it did not follow that seperation was to result from the disagreement.

To constitute a dispute there must be two parties. To understand it well both the parties & all the circumstances must be

fully understood. And to accomodate differences good temper &
mutual forbearance is requisite. Common danger brought the
States into Confederacy, and on their Union our safety & importance depend. A spirit of accomodation was the basis of the present Constitution; can it be expected then that the Southern or
the Eastern part of the Empire will succeed in all their Measures? certainly not. but I will readily grant that more points will
be carried by the latter than the former, and for the reason
which has been mentioned—namely—that in all great national
questions they move in unison, whilst the others are divided;
but I ask again which is most blameworthy, those who see & will
steadily pursue their interests, or those who cannot see, or
seeing, will not act wisely? and I will ask another question (of
the highest magnitude in my mind) and that is, if the Eastern &
Northern States are dangerous *in Union,* will they be less so *in
seperation?* If self interest is their governing principle, will it for-
sake them, or be less restrained by such an event? I hardly think
it would. Then, independent of other considerations what
would Virginia (and such other States as might be inclined to
join her) gain by a seperation? Would they not, most unquestionably, be the weaker party?

Men who go from hence without *feeling* themselves of so much
consequence as they wished to be considered—disappointed ex-
pectants—and malignant designing characters that miss no opportunity to aim a blow at the Constitution, paint highly on one
side without bringing into view the arguments which are offered
on the other. It is to be lamented that the Editors of the several
Gazettes of the Union do not more generally & more connect-
edly publish the debates in Congress on all great National questions that affect different interests instead of stuffing their papers with scurrility & malignant declamation, which few would
read if they were apprised of the contents. That they might do
this with very little trouble is certain. The principles upon which
the difference in opinion arises, as well as the decision, would,
in that case, come fully before the public, & afford the best data
for its judgment.

Mr Madison, on the question of discrimination, was actuated,
I am persuaded, by the purest motives; & most heartfelt conviction; but the Subject was delicate,[1] & perhaps had better not
have been stirred. The assumption of the State debts by the

United States is another subject that has given birth to long and laboured debates without having yet taken a final form. The Memorial of the Quakers (& a very mal-apropos one it was) has at length been put to sleep, from which it is not ⟨*illegible*⟩ it will awake before the year 1808.[2] With much truth I am ⟨Sir⟩ Yr Affecte Hble ⟨Servt⟩

Go: Washington

ALS, PHi: Gratz Collection; LB, DLC:GW.

1. See David Stuart to GW, 15 Mar. 1790, n.5.

2. The House of Representatives debated a response to Quaker petitions concerning slavery and the slave trade from 16 to 19 Mar. 1790 and on 23 Mar. adopted an amended committee report denying the authority of Congress to abolish the slave trade before 1808, to interfere in the abolition of slavery, or to "interfere in the internal regulation of particular States" relative to the regulation and conditions of slavery (*DHFC*, 3:332, 334–41). See also GW to the Society of Quakers, October 1789 and notes, Warner Mifflin to GW, 12 Mar. 1790, n.1.

From John Talbot Ashenhurst

Dame Street Dublin Ireland

May it please your Excellency   March 29th 1790

Being firmly attached to the cause of public Liberty and a zealous admirer of those virtues by the exertion of which America obtained her freedom, I take the liberty with all possible respect of introducing myself to your Excellencies notice upon the following occasion.

Denmark and Spain may it please your Excellency have severally appointed their respective Consuls here, these Consuls are natives of this Country and were and still are Merchants resident in this City—Portugal too hath her Consul resident amongst us, but I do not find that the United States of America have as yet conferred upon any person the Dignity of their Consul General for this Kingdom: Should they at any time deem such an appointment expedient may I presume to offer my best Services to your Excency and the Congress and at the same time find credit when I declare that the high honour of being thought worthy the confidence of so Illustrious a Body, divested of every Idea of pecuniary consideration, is the motive alone by which I am influenced.

I do beseech your Excellency not to accuse me of too much presumption in thus obtruding myself (a stranger) on your leisure. I am, may it please you, a native of this country, a resident of this City, allow me to say of Independent fortune and, I trust, unsullied reputation—This I intend as my humble introduction to your Excellency nor know I of any other, that I could make use of, unless you will permit me to add that I had the honour of filling the office of Principal Secretary to sixty thousand of my countrymen, the volunteers of Ireland from the origin of their institution; and that I likewise served as Principal Secretary to the National Conventions held here for the purpose of obtaining a more equal Representation of the people in Parliament, and of Inducing Great Britain to renounce all right of Enacting Laws to bind this Realm in the British Senate, which latter measure was happily effected—and in the discharge of the duties of those stations I have the happiness to think that I never incurred the imputation of faction on the one hand or of want of promptitude on the other. I have formed and am Secretary to the Irish Insurance Company for Ships, Merchandise and Lives which is composed of the first Commercial Characters of all the great trading towns of this Kingdom a circumstance which I humbly conceive places me in a situation to fill the department I have the ambition of aspiring to with some advantage: But lest other authority be deemed necessary for what I have taken the liberty of submitting to your Excellency's consideration respecting myself, I will, with all deference, suggest that having served as an Officer, in various gradations, under his Excellency the Earl of ⟨Charlemont⟩ Commander in Chief of the Volunteers of this Kingdom and President of those Conventions I have before mentioned (a nobleman whose many distinguised quallities are possibly not intirely unknown to your Excellency) I have the confidence to hope that he would vouch my probity and report me not unlikely to merit the honour I anxiously wish to obtain.

May it please your Excellency in your goodness to acquit me of vanity, charge me with ambition if you will, but let it be the ambition of being denominated the servant of the United States of America which should I have the good fortune to be constituted—to discharge the duties of my station with Caution, firmness, and fidellity shall be the first wish of my heart and the invariable rule of my conduct.[1] I have the honour to remain

May it please your Excellency with the highest veneration your Excellency's most obedient And Devoted Servant

John Talbot Ashenhurst

P.S. lest this should miscarry through the post I shall take the liberty of forwarding a Duplicate at the end of three months.

ALS, DLC:GW.

John Talbot Ashenhurst has not been otherwise identified. He was apparently a member of the political circle of James Caulfeild, fourth viscount and first earl of Charlemont (1728–1799), one of the most important figures in the Irish Parliament during the last quarter of the eighteenth century and a leading proponent of Irish legislative independence. Charlemont became commander-in-chief of the Irish volunteers in 1780 and presided over their subsequent conventions, including the convention of 1782 widely credited with forcing the British ministry to concede a large measure of home rule to Ireland. Contemporaries, according to Irish historian Owen Edwards, "very generally ascribed" this achievement "to the direct influence of the American Revolution" (Owen D. Edwards, "The Impact of the American Revolution on Ireland" in Library of Congress Symposia on the American Revolution, *The Impact of the American Revolution Abroad: Papers Presented at the Fourth Symposium, May 8 and 9, 1975* [Washington, D.C., 1976], pp. 127–59).

1. Ashenhurst did not receive the appointment. When consular appointments were made in June 1790, the post of U.S. consul at Dublin went to William Knox (see GW to U.S. Senate, 4 June 1790).

From Alexander Hamilton

Treasury Depar[t]ment [New York] March 29th 1790.

The Secretary of the Treasury begs leave respectfully to inform the President of the United States of America,

That, in order to be able to furnish in the course of the ensuing month for the compensation of the members of Congress, & the officers and Servants of the two houses, a sum of about sixty thousand dollars; for the payment of the Salaries of the Civil List to the end of the present month a sum of about forty thousand dollars; for the use of the Department of War a sum of about fifty thousand dollars; and for procuring bills to pay an arrear of interest on the Dutch Loans to the first of June next, a sum of about thirty five thousand Dollars: amounting together to about one hundred and eighty five thousand dollars, it will be requisite to obtain a Loan of one hundred thousand dollars, There being in the Treasury now a sum not exceeding fifty thousand dollars, including thirty thousand dollars which the Bank of New York stands engaged to advance on demand to complete a Loan of fifty thousand dollars stipulated for on the seventeenth day of February last, which is considered as equivalent to a sum in the Treasury.

And in as much as the payment of former Loans and other current demands, will probably call for a considerable part of the monies which may be expected in the interim from the product of the Revenues,

Wherefore the said Secretary submits to the President of the United States the propriety of authorising a Loan to be made to the extent of the said sum of one hundred thousand Dollars.

A. Hamilton
Secy of the Treasury

LB, DLC:GW.

1. GW replied to Hamilton on 31 Mar.: "The Secretary of the Treasury is hereby authorised to negotiate and agree for a Loan to the United States to an amount not exceeding one hundred thousand Dollars, bearing an Interest not exceeding six ℔ Cent ℔ annum to be applied towards carrying into effect the appropriations made by the act Entitled, 'An Act making appropriations for the support of government for the year one thousand seven hundred & ninety.' and according to the annexed representation" (LB, DLC:GW). Hamilton's efforts to obtain this loan have not been clearly identified. In the spring of 1790, Hamilton corresponded with Thomas Willing, president of the Bank of North America, about a loan of $50,000, but this may not be the loan referred to here (see Willing to Hamilton, 12 Mar. and 8 April 1790, Syrett, *Hamilton Papers*, 6:301, 359).

Letter not found: from Charles Cotesworth Pinckney, 29 March 1790. Listed in McKay 3905, item 2192.

From James Walton

Sir   New York new Goal March 29th 1790

I humbly beg liberty to present your Excellency the small ship *Pastime* which accompanies this—It is the production of Liesure hours which hard fortune deprived me the priveledge of employing to better advantage—I never studied the mechanical art for any other purpose but to pass a lingering moment, & to keep disagreeable reflections from encroaching on my mind, which my unfortunate situation was likely to excite—I have been near two years a prisoner, in the Goal of this City,[1] for debts which a variety of misfortunes has put out of my power to discharge, &

have experienced all the wretchedness common to such a situation—during this time I made the little ship and as she is not sufficient to transport me from this harbour of misery, I humbly pray your Excellency to accept of her—As I consider your Virtues a proper shrine, to which every Lover of a noble & humane soul should make an offering, and this (except my Good wishes and prayers) is all I have to make—I have myself been a soldier, & honored with a Commission, but even in that I have been unfortunate, having lost a leg, which obliges me to recruit a wooden one—But I have yet a heart left that adores your bravery in the field and wisdom in the Cabinet—and do (like all others) consider you as the protector & ornament of your Country. That you may long continue so, & final meet with endless felicity is the fervent prayer of your ever respectfull Humbl. Servt

James Walton

ALS, DLC:GW.

1. Walton undoubtedly was incarcerated in New York City's debtor's prison, "a rough stone building three stories high, surmounted by a large cupola containing a bell," located near Murray Street beside the almshouse and the Bridewell, or criminal prison (Smith, *New York City in 1789*, 13–14).

From Marinus Willett

Charleston, S.C., 29 Mar. 1790. "The sole designe of this letter is to signify to you Sir, That I have a very great desire of serving in some executive appointment under the Union—Should any office present itself for which in your opinion I am Qualified, no person shall be more carefull to do Justice to such appointment than Sir your most obedient & very humble Servant."[1]

ALS, DLC:GW.

1. For Willett's determined pursuit of a post in the Washington administration, see his letter to GW, 7 July 1789, and source note.

Bezaleel Howe to David Humphreys

Sir   New York 30 March 1790

As Congress are making an Addition to their Military Establishment, I am induced to offer myself as a Candidate for an Appointment in the same—hopeing my past Services will claim

Your influence with the President in my behalf I served in the late War almost Nine years which I hope will plead in my favor. I was a Captain in the Army, and since the Peace have been a Captain of Infantry in this City which I recruited & Disciplind for which I received the most flattering Marks of Approbation, from the Principal Officers in the State & City, many of whom have Certified, that my private as well as my Military Character stands fair—and to keep it so shall ever be my study—These are my Pretensions to the Notice of the President, and hope he may think me Worthy of an Appointment, Your Communicating my Wishes to the President will much Oblidge sir your most obedt Hbbe Servt

Bezaleel Howe

ALS, DLC:GW.

Bezaleel Howe (d. 1825), a native of New Hampshire, served as a lieutenant from 1776 to the end of the Revolution. In May 1788 GW issued a certificate stating that Howe "was an officer of a fair and respectable character, that he served some part of the last year of the war as an auxiliary Lieutenant with my own Guard, that he commanded the Escort which came with my baggage and Papers to Mount Vernon at the close of the war, and that in all my acquaintance with him I had great reason to be satisfied with his integrity, sobriety, intelligence and good dispositions" (GW to Howe, 12 May 1788, LB, DLC:GW, 9 Nov. 1783, LS, NHi: Howe Papers). After the war Howe settled in New York. In March 1791 he was appointed a lieutenant with the U.S. Infantry, served in the army's western campaigns, and retired from the army in 1796 as a major. During the Quasi-War Howe again applied for military appointment, but on a list of officers considered for appointment a notation by Hamilton next to his name comments that Howe "has been a Major in the army & looks to it again—is believed to be *not fit* for it" (Hamilton to James McHenry, 21 Aug. 1798, Syrett, *Hamilton Papers*, 22:105, 107).

From Mary Mason

SIR, March 30, 1790.

MARY MASON and family, being the widow and children of the late Charles Mason, deceased, respectfully wait on you, and solicit your friendly assistance, towards paying their passage to England. The character of Mr. Mason, as an eminently useful Astronomer, is well known in Europe and America. He was for several years assistant to Dr. Bradley, the British Astronomer Royal, at Greenwich,: From thence he was sent, in 1764, to the

Cape of Good Hope, to observe the transit of Venus. On his return to Europe, he was sent, in company with Mr. Dixon, to America, to run the boundary line between Pennsylvania and Maryland: And after being appointed to observe the second transit of Venus in Ireland, in 1769; he engaged in the correction of Mayer's Lunar Tables, and brought them to a degree of perfection, exceeding the most sanguine expectations of the best astronomer; nevertheless he began and completed a second and still more accurate set of tables, from which the British and French nautical Almanacs, for finding the Longitude at sea, are now calculated; the utility whereof is well known to every maritime nation in the world, but especially to those trading to the East-Indies. He received 800[£] from the British government for the first set of tables, but nothing for the second; as they were under consideration of the board of longitude, when he sailed with his family for Halifax, in Nova-Scotia, with an appointment to survey the lands given by the British government to the royalists; but this business, through a variety of circumstances, being delayed, whereby what little cash he had was exhausted, and there appearing no probability of being supplied in time from England, he resolved to remove with his family to Philadelphia, where he was well acquainted with Drs. Franklin, Rittenhouse, Ewing, &c. and whose friendship he had formerly experienced. But being worn out with disappointments, and laying the same much to heart, he fell sick before he reached Philadelphia, and died four weeks after his arrival there, without meeting a friend he had ever seen before, except Dr. Ewing.[1] He left behind him, in the deepest poverty and distress, the widow and eight children, the youngest two months old, and eldest scarce thirteen years; who must inevitably have perished, were it not for the benevolent interposition of Dr. Franklin, Mr. Robert Morris, Mr. Phineas Bond, Drs. Rittenhouse, Ewing, White, &c. who have raised subscriptions for their support since the time of Mr. Mason's decease, in October 1787.[2]

With an intention of returning home to her native country and friends, and with a desire of living no longer on the generosity of benevolent strangers, besides hopes of receiving some gratuity from the British government, for Mr. Mason's second set of tables, she has came to New-York to embark for England; if, through humanity, and respect for the memory of a good man, who spent his life-time in promoting useful knowledge, she should be so fortunate as to raise a sum sufficient to pay the family's passage to England. For which, Sir, your kind contribution is solicited.

MARY MASON.

P.S. Your Excelly will please to send your Subcription, to Sir John Temple Queen Street, or to Mrs Mason at her lodgings No. 17 Maiden Lane.[3]

L, DLC:GW. All of this letter, except the postscript, is taken from a printed broadside.

Mary Mason was the widow of Charles Mason (1728–1786), the English astronomer who, with the assistance of Jeremiah Dixon, surveyed the disputed boundary between Pennsylvania and Maryland. Mason returned to England in 1768 where he continued his astronomical and geodetic work. His first wife having died in 1759, Mason married again sometime between 1768 and 1770. In 1778, while working under the auspices of the Royal Observatory at Greenwich and the Board of Longitude, he published *Lunar Tables in Longitude and Latitude according to the Newtonian Laws of Gravity* and completed an improved set of the same tables in 1780. Mason arrived in Philadelphia from Nova Scotia with his second wife, Mary, and eight children in September 1786. On 27 Sept. 1786 he wrote to Franklin that financial reverses had left them in a helpless condition (Mason to Benjamin Franklin, PPAmP: Franklin Papers). Having fallen ill during the trip, Mason died on 25 Oct. 1786. No reply from GW to this letter has been found, nor any evidence that he contributed to the family's passage. Mary Mason nonetheless managed to return to England, where she sought to obtain compensation for her husband's later work. In 1791 she sent a memorial to the Board of Longitude, and in response she was awarded £50 and was paid another £50 for two manuscript books. After an interview with the commissioners of the Board of Longitude on 3 Mar. 1792, she was paid a total of £120 for other papers, but she apparently did not receive any further compensation (Robinson, "A Note on Charles Mason's Ancestry and His Family").

1. John Ewing (1732–1802) was a Presbyterian clergyman and provost of the University of Pennsylvania. Born in Maryland, Ewing was educated in a school kept by Dr. Francis Alison at New London Cross Road, Pa., and at the College of New Jersey, from which he graduated in 1754. After serving as a tutor at the college, he returned to Dr. Alison, who prepared him for the ministry. In 1759 he became pastor of the First Presbyterian Church of Philadelphia, a post he held for the rest of his life. Ewing had a particular interest in natural philosophy, astronomy, and mathematics and probably befriended Charles Mason during the latter's stay in Pennsylvania between 1763 and 1768. Their friendship evidently was resumed between 1773 and 1775, while Ewing was in England in an unsuccessful effort to solicit funds for an academy in Delaware. In 1779 Ewing was appointed provost of the University

of Pennsylvania, where he also served as professor of natural philosophy. When Charles Mason died in Philadelphia in 1786, he left all the manuscripts and scientific papers in his possession to Ewing (Cope, "Collecting Source Material about Charles Mason and Jeremiah Dixon").

2. This is undoubtedly a printer's error. Charles Mason died on 25 Oct. 1786. See the *Pennsylvania Gazette,* 8 Nov. 1786.

3. The postscript was added to the printed form by hand. Sir John Temple was British consul general at New York.

To the United States Senate

United States [New York]
Gentlemen of the Senate,   March 30th 1790.

I nominate the following persons to fill the Offices which are affixed to their respective names—viz.

Rufus Putnam, to be one of the Judges in the Western Territory, in the place of Samuel Holden Parsons deceased.

James Brown, to be Attorney for the United States in the District of Kentucky, in the place of George Nicholas who has declined his appointment.

Henry Bogart (of Albany) to be Surveyor of the Port of Albany, in the place of Jeremiah Lansingh who has resigned his office.[1]

Go: Washington

LS, DNA: RG 46, First Congress, Records of Executive Proceedings, President's Messages—Executive Nominations; LB, DLC: GW.

1. The Senate confirmed these appointments on 31 Mar. 1790 (*DHFC,* 2:66–67).

To the Society of Free Quakers

Gentlemen,   [New York, March 1790]

I desire to assure you of the sensibility with which I receive your congratulations on my appointment to the highest office and most extended trust which can be confided by a free People—and I thank you with sincerity for the obliging terms in which you express yourselves in my behalf.[1]

Ever happy in being favored with the approbation of my fellow-citizens, the time at which yours is declared does not diminish my sense of the obligation it confers.

Having always considered the conscientious scruples of religious belief as resting entirely with the sects that profess, or the individuals who entertain them, I cannot, consistent with this uniform sentiment, otherwise notice the circumstances referred to in your address, than by adding the tribute of my acknowledgement, to that of our country, for those services which the members of your particular community rendered to the common cause in the course of our revolution—and by assuring you that, as our present government was instituted with an express view to general happiness, it will be my earnest endeavor, in discharging the duties confided to me with faithful impartiality, to realise the hope of common protection which you expect from the measures of that government.

Impressed with gratitude for your supplications to the supreme Being in my favor, I entreat his gracious beneficence in your behalf.

G. Washington

LB, DLC:GW.

The Society of Free Quakers was a group of Quakers who either bore arms in or actively supported the Revolution. After the war they were disowned by the main body of Quakers and in 1781 formed their own society, consisting of about 100 members. In 1783 the society purchased land and a building on the southwest corner of Arch and Fifth streets in Philadelphia where they constructed a meetinghouse (*Pennsylvania Magazine of History and Biography*, 16 [1892], 315; Faris, *Old Churches and Meeting Houses*, 225–27).

1. The Society of Free Quakers had addressed to GW the following statement, drawn up at the society's meeting in Philadelphia on 4 Mar. 1790 and signed by Timothy Matlack, clerk: "We beg leave to join the general voice in the most respectful congratulation on thy appointment to the highest office and most extended trust which can be confided by a free People: A trust which the force of precedent in the first exercise of the supreme executive authority, at the founding of such an empire, renders infinitely important, not to its immediate citizens only, but to every part of mankind, who have an interest in the firm establishment of religious and civil liberty.

"We offer no apology for the time of this address, as decency required that the youngest religious Society in the empire should give place to those that are more numerous, and of far more ancient establishment; yet springing up with and growing out of the revolution, it is our duty on this great occasion to appear among our fellow-citizens; and we feel a dignity in declaring, that we have reason to believe there is not a member of our religious society who has at all times and on all occasions, relied on and confided in thy patriotism, prudence, and virtue.

"Many of our members having been educated Quakers, admitted the doctrine declared by that People, of a state attainable here in which a christian cannot be concerned in wars and fightings of any kind, yet they perceived the wisdom and soundness of the distinction, made by the apologist of that People, when he expressly declares that until men attain that state, they cannot be undefending themselves[.] They indeed, saw, that by discharging the great duty they were called upon to perform, in support of their own civil rights and those of our country and posterity, they would, probably, be disowned by that people; and there was no means of retaining or recovering their rights among them; but by neglecting that duty, or by publickly condemning their conduct in the discharge of it: A treachery to the cause of liberty and truth, of which they feel themselves utterly incapable.

"They were not unaware of the alienation of friendship, and many other injurious effects on temporal affairs, which too commonly attend offence given by individuals to a body so numerous as the Quakers are, and of such weight in civil society; but in the course of divine providence they were called to make so great a sacrifice, and they obeyed.

"They perceived the advantage of religious society, and being desirous of obtaining it, united together in such a body. They had felt the evil of undue restraint on the conscience of men, and determined, if possible, to leave their members free: They therefore founded our society on the enlarged and catholic principles of the Gospel, appealing to the lessons of wisdom and virtue left us by Christ and his Apostles, as the best external rule of faith and practice, and leaving every man to answer to God, to his own conscience, and to civil government for his conduct. And being formed on this ground, we ask no extraordinary or special privilege; but having discharged a common duty, and being determined to pay a due obedience to the laws, we claim the common protection of that government.

"Far from repining at our sufferings we have rejoiced in the triumph of liberty over despotism; and exulted in the praise which our fellow-citizens have bestowed on the measures which led to success: They are justly styled glorious; but it is that undeviating steadiness of mind, and invariable regard to the rights of the people, that has so honorably distinguished thy conduct on such varied and trying occasions, which lead us to a full confidence that thy administration will, indeed, tend to make liberty more secure than it ever before has been: And we feel, that it is this confidence which gives the unusual glow to congratulation from every quarter on this happy occasion.

"The prospect of an union that will embrace all that contended for the cause of freedom, is highly pleasing to us; and we beg leave to add our most cordial congratulation on the high honors so deservedly bestowed by the Nation of France on thy illustrious Pupil the Marquis de la Fayette; We trust that it will be a brilliant and lasting honor to America, that her conduct has inspired the world with the most noble emulation in support of liberty and the common cause of mankind.

"May that supreme Being which rules in Heaven and among men, continue to pour his wisdom into thy heart, and so guide thy administration as to make the government a blessing to the People, and render it free, efficient, and stable. And to whatever length of days he shall please to extend thy life to a purpose so eminently important, may thine eye never become dim, nor thy natural force abate. And finally when the great task shall be fully compleated, and thou shalt advance into that state which is the end and highest glory of our Being, may thine inheritance be among 'the Spirits of just men made perfect'" (DLC:GW).

To Roman Catholics in America

United States of America [New York]

Gentlemen, [March 1790]

While I now receive with much satisfaction your congratulations on my being called, by an unanimous vote, to the first station in my Country; I cannot but duly notice your politeness in offering an apology for the unavoidable delay.[1] As that delay has given you an opportunity of realizing, instead of anticipating, the benefits of the general Government; you will do me the justice to believe, that your testimony of the increase of the public prosperity, enhances the pleasure which I should otherwise have experienced from your affectionate address.

I feel that my conduct, in war and in peace, has met with more general approbation than could reasonably have been expected: and I find myself disposed to consider that fortunate circumstance, in a great degree, resulting from the able support and extraordinary candour of my fellow-citizens of all denominations.

The prospect of national prosperity now before us is truly animating, and ought to excite the exertions of all good men to establish and secure the happiness of their Country, in the permanent duration of its Freedom and Independence. America, under the smiles of a Divine Providence—the protection of a good Government—and the cultivation of manners, morals and piety, cannot fail of attaining an uncommon degree of eminence, in literature, commerce, agriculture, improvements at home and respectability abroad.

As mankind become more liberal they will be more apt to allow, that all those who conduct themselves as worthy members of the Community are equally entitled to the protection of civil Government. I hope ever to see America among the foremost nations in examples of justice and liberality. And I presume that your fellow-citizens will not forget the patriotic part which you took in the accomplishment of their Revolution, and the establishment of their Government: or the important assistance which they received from a nation in which the Roman Catholic faith is professed.

I thank you, Gentlemen, for your kind concern for me. While my life and my health shall continue, in whatever situation I may be, it shall be my constant endeavour to justify the favourable sentiments which you are pleased to express of my conduct. And may the members of your Society in America, animated alone by the pure spirit of Christianity, and still conducting themselves as the faithful subjects of our free Government, enjoy every temporal and spiritual felicity.

G. Washington

LS, MdBAr; LB, DLC:GW.

The address, dated 15 Mar. and signed by John Carroll on behalf of the Roman Catholic clergy and Charles Carroll of Carrollton, Daniel Carroll, Thomas Fitzsimons, and Dominick Lynch on behalf of the Roman Catholic laity, reads: "We have been long impatient to testify our joy and unbounded confidence, on your being called, by an unanimous vote, to the first station of a country, in which that unanimity could not have been obtained without the previous merit of unexampled services, of eminent wisdom, and unblemished virtue. Our congratulations have not reached you sooner, because our scattered situation prevented the communication and the collecting of those sentiments, which warmed every breast: But the delay has furnished us with the opportunity, not merely of presaging the happiness to be expected under your administration, but of bearing testimony to that which we experience already. It is your peculiar talent, in war and in peace, to afford security to those, who commit their protection into your hands. In war, you shield them from the ravages of armed hostility: in peace you establish public tranquillity by the justice and moderation, not less than by the vigour of your government. By example as well as by vigilance, you extend the influence of laws on the manners of our fellow citizens you encourage respect for religion, and inculcate, by words and actions, that principle, on which the welfare of nations so much depends, that a superintending Providence governs the events of the world, and watches over the conduct of men. Your exalted maxims and unwearied attention to the moral and physical improvement of our country have produced already the happiest effects. Under your administration, america is animated with zeal for the attainment and encouragement of useful literature; She improves her agriculture, extends her commerce, and acquires with foreign nations a dignity, unknown to her before. From these happy events, in which none can feel a warmer interest than ourselves, we derive additional pleasure by recollecting, that you, Sir, have been the principal instrument to effect so rapid a change in our political situation. This prospect of national prosperity is peculiarly pleasing to us on another account; because whilst our country preserves her freedom and independence, we shall have a well founded title to claim from her justice equal rights of citizenship, as the price of our blood spilt under your eyes, and of our common exertions for her defence, under your auspicious conduct, rights rendered more dear to us by the remembrance of former hardships. When we pray for the preservation of them, where they have been granted; and expect the full extension of them from the justice of those States, which still restrict them; when we solicit the protection of Heaven over our common country: we neither omit nor can omit recommending your preservation to the singular care of divine providence; because we conceive that no human means are so available to promote the welfare of the united States, as the prolongation of your health and life, in which are included the energy of your example, the wisdom of your counsels, and the persuasive eloquence of your virtues" (DLC:GW). John Carroll (1735–1815) was educated at Jesuit schools in Maryland and France. He returned to America as a Roman Catholic priest shortly before the Revolution and after the war was a leader in organizing the church. He was selected on 14 Nov. 1789 to be the first American Roman Catholic bishop by a convocation of clergy meeting at Whitemarsh, Md., and consecrated in England on 15 Aug. 1790. This address to GW was one of Carroll's first official acts as leader of the church in the new nation.

From Thomas Jefferson

[1 April 1790]

Th: Jefferson has the honor to inform the President that mr Madison has just delivered to him the result of his reflections on the question *How shall communications from the several states to Congress through the channel of the President be made?*[1]

"he thinks that in no case would it be proper to go by way of *letter from the Secretary of state:* that they should be delivered to the houses either by the Secretary of state in person or by mr Leir. he supposes a useful division of the office might be made between these two, by employing the one where a matter of fact alone is to be communicated, or a paper delivered &c. in the ordinary course of things and where nothing is required by the President; and using the agency of the other where the President chuses to recommend any measure to the legislature and to attract their attention to it."

The President will be pleased to order in this what he thinks best. T. Jefferson supposes that whatever may be done for the present, the final arrangement of business should be considered as open to alteration hereafter. the government is as yet so young, that cases enough have not occurred to enable a division of them into classes, and the distribution of these classes to the persons whose agency would be the properest.

He sends some letters for the President's perusal praying him to alter freely any thing in them which he thinks may need it.[2]

AL, DNA: RG 59, Miscellaneous Letters; LB, DLC:GW.

1. After his arrival in New York on 21 Mar. 1790, GW held several conferences with the secretary of state on the duties of his office and on specific questions concerning the administration. On 22 Mar. they conversed for over an hour, and on 23 Mar. they discussed American captives in Algiers, the establishment of the diplomatic service, and the possibility of a commercial treaty with Spain. See Conversation with Thomas Jefferson, 23 Mar. 1790. The two met again on 26 Mar. to discuss diplomatic appointments (*Diaries,* 6:49–54). At one of these meetings, probably that of 22 Mar., GW asked Jefferson to confer with James Madison "as to the mode of conveying *official communications from the states through the channel of the President to the two federal houses,*" and particularly whether Madison thought such messages should come from GW through Tobias Lear or through the secretary of state, communicating by letter or appearing in person (Jefferson to Madison, c.March 1790, in Boyd, *Jefferson Papers,* 16:286). Madison's reply, quoted by Jefferson in this letter, has not been found. During the first sessions of Congress, GW received several reports from state governors regarding legislative action, mostly on proposed amendments to the Constitution. See, for example, GW to the U.S. Senate and House of Representatives, 8 Mar. 1790. Before Jefferson took up his post as secretary of state, Lear delivered these messages in person to both houses of Congress. This practice was subsequently continued.

In the first year of his administration, GW was greatly concerned with establishing efficient routine procedures for dealing with political matters and handling correspondence with dispatch. His custom of requesting advice from his cabinet and from political allies was apparent from the start. The method he established for handling policy questions and paperwork is perhaps best described by Jefferson in a circular to his cabinet dated 6 Nov. 1801, at the beginning of his own administration: "Having been a member of the first administration under Genl. Washington, I can state with exactness what our course then was. Letters of business came addressed sometimes to the President, but most frequently to the heads of departments. If addressed to himself, he referred them to the proper department to be acted on: if to one of the Secretaries, the letter, if it required no answer, was communicated to the President simply for his information. If an answer was requisite, the Secretary of the department communicated the letter & his proposed answer to the President. Generally they were simply sent back, after perusal, which signified his approbation. Sometimes he returned them with an informal note, suggesting an alteration or a query. If a doubt of any importance arose, he reserved it for conference. By this means he was always in accurate possession of all facts & proceedings in every part of the Union, & to whatsoever department they related; he formed a central point for the different branches, preserved an unity of object and action among them, exercised that participation in the gestion of affairs which his office made incumbent on him, and met himself the due responsibility for whatever was done. During mr. Adams's administration, his long & habitual absences from the seat of government rendered this kind of communication impracticable, removed him from any share in the transaction of affairs, & parcelled out the government in fact among four independant heads, drawing sometimes in opposite directions. That the former is preferable to the latter course cannot be doubted. It gave indeed to the heads of departments the trouble of making up, once a day, a packet of all their communications for the perusal of the President; it commonly also retarded one day their dispatches by mail: but, in pressing cases, this injury was prevented by presenting that case singly for immediate attention; and it produced us in return the benefit of his sanction for every act we did" (Stagg, *Madison Papers, Secretary of State Series,* 2:227–29). The entries in *JPP* for 1793 through 1797 corroborate Jefferson's description.

2. The letters have not been identified.

To the United States Senate and House of Representatives

United States [New York] April 1st 1790.
Gentlemen of the Senate and House of Representatives.

I have directed my private Secretary to lay before you a copy of the adoption, by the Legislature of South Carolina, of the articles proposed by Congress to the Legislatures of the several States as amendments to the Constitution of the United States; together with the copy of a Letter from the Governor of the State of South Carolina to the President of the United States, which have lately come to my hands.[1] The originals of the foregoing will be lodged in the Office of the Secretary of State.

Go: Washington

LS, DNA: RG 46, First Congress, Records of Legislative Proceedings, President's Messages; LB, DLC:GW; copy, DNA: RG 233, First Congress, Records of Legislative Proceedings, Journals.

1. The enclosure was a letter of 28 Jan. 1790 from Gov. Charles Pinckney of South Carolina announcing the adoption by South Carolina of the amendments to the Constitution (DNA: RG 46, First Congress, Records of Legislative Proceedings, President's Messages). Pinckney enclosed copies of the 18 Jan. resolution of the South Carolina house of representatives, signed by Speaker Jacob Read, and of the 19th Jan. concurring resolution of the South Carolina senate, signed by Daniel DeSaussure, president of the senate. GW's letter and its enclosure was received by the U.S. House of Representatives on 1 April 1790 (*DHFC,* 3:353–54).

From George Clinton

Sir,   New York 2nd April 1790.

I have the honor of transmitting to your Excellency, herewith inclosed, Exemplifications of three Acts of the Legislature of this State, passed at their present Session,[1] and to be with the highest Respect Your most Obedient Servant

Geo: Clinton

Copy, DNA: RG 46, First Congress, 1789–91, Records of Legislative Proceedings, President's Messages.

1. The enclosures were copies of three acts of the New York legislature: an act adopting the articles of amendment to the federal Constitution, an act authorizing sheriffs to confine prisoners committed under the authority of the United States, and an act transferring ownership to the United States of the lighthouse at Sandy Hook (DNA: RG 46, First Congress, 1789–91, Records of Legislative Proceedings, President's Messages).

From John Paradise

Sir,   c.2 April 1790

I avail myself of the opportunity, afforded me by my friend Count Andriani, of conveying to you an ode, which Count Alfieri, the author of it, desired me long ago to convey to you. The rambling and of course unsettled condition I have been in since my return to Europe has entirely put it out of my power to comply sooner with Count Alfieri's request; and this unpleasant condition added to an apprehension of being troublesome has likewise deprived me of the satisfaction of joining my most sincere congratulations with those of my fellow citizens on the auspicious event, which has placed you, the object of our veneration, love, confidence and gratitude at the helm of our government. That you may long, Sir live to make our country prosper is, I can assure you, the most ardent wish not only of us Americans, but of all those Europeans also, who, sensible of the value of liberty, know how much indebted they are to the example which the glorious cause you have so nobly defended has given to the world, for the rapid and successful strides that are now making in a considerable part of Europe towards the attainment of that invaluable blessing. There is not a more popular man in France than our gallant Marquis, your pupil; nor indeed can popularity

be more justly merited—His actions are directed by the purest
views, and his glory consists in doing good to mankind. May his
labours, therefore, be crowned with success. Count Andriani is
a nobleman from Milan, highly distinguished by every valuable
endowment, and deserving of the honour of being presented to
you. As he is thoroughly acquainted with the affairs of Europe,
I have nothing further to say at present, than to offer my most
respectful compliments to Mrs Washington, and subscribe myself with the greatest respect, Sir, your most obliged, and most
obedient humble servant

John Paradise.

ALS, DLC:GW.

For an identification of John Paradise, see Lucy Paradise to GW, 12 May
1789, source note.

1. The enclosed work was probably *Bruto Primo, tragedia* (Parigi, 1788), by
Vittorio Alfieri (1749–1803). Three pages of this are devoted to a dedication,
"Al chiarissimo e libero uomo il generale Washington." A copy of this work is
among GW's books in the Boston Athenaeum (Griffin, *Boston Athenaeum Collection*, 5). Count Andriani, the bearer of the letter, was a young Italian friend of
John and Lucy Ludwell Paradise (Shepperson, *John Paradise and Lucy Ludwell*,
93, 420–22). In a letter to John Adams, Richard Price described Andriani as
"a respectable Nobleman from Milan . . . a friend to the liberties of mankind"
(Price to Adams, 21 Mar. 1790, quoted in Boyd, *Jefferson Papers*, 16:294). John
Paradise wrote a letter to Jefferson on 2 April 1790 to be delivered by Andriani, who apparently left for a tour of America shortly thereafter (ibid.; see also
John Rutledge, Jr., to Jefferson, 25 Mar. 1790, ibid., 266–67).

From David Stuart

Dear Sir,   Abingdon [Va.] 2nd April 1790

As it was my desire to give you the fullest information on the
subject submitted to your judgement, I have to lament that I
have failed; particularly, as I think it would have been of some
importance, to have had the rents fixed, before the plantation
was improved in its appearance, by the advance of the Spring—
However, in a matter of such moment, a clear knowledge of every circumstance is certainly superior to every other consideration—To aid the explanations I have already given, and those
I shall now attempt, I inclose a copy of the bill in Chancery,
exhibited by Mr Dandridge.[1] I wish it was in my power to furnish you with all the papers on the subject. By the agreement,

Mr Custis was not to pay 'till the expiration of the 24 years—By the mortgage however, he undoubtedly had the right to pay at any time before, he thought proper—The reason of Mr Alexander's disputing this right, is founded on the difference between the agreement, and Mortgage—As the words "on or before," are not in the agreement, as well as mortgage, he insists these words were introduced without his knowledge, and contrary to the intentions of either party—But this evasion in the opinion of my Lawyers, would have been of no avail if the money tendered had been of the proper kind. I informed you in my last, how it happened that this discovery was made—This being the case, you will observe that the object of the Bill, so far as it prays that the Mortgage should be cancelled, in consequence of the tender, is defeated—You appear to be in the same error with respect to the scaling the £12,000, that my Lawyers were in; 'till last Summer, when the trial was expected—Tho' this sum no doubt gave rise to the £48,000: You will observe, from the short recitement of the agreement & Mortgage in the Bill, that there is no mention of it—The £48,000 only is mentioned—On discovering this circumstance, the Lawyers are of opinion that the £48,000 will be scaled, as there is no foundation for the Court to enquire, how it accumulated; and every man has a right to sell his property for the most he can get—The omission of the £12,oo[o] in the writings, was no doubt asigned, to avoid all evidence of Compound interest—Had my Counsel continued in opinion, that the £12,000 would be scaled I should never have thought of a compromise; for at either of the scales of five, according to the time of the agreement or six, the time at which Alexander contends the deed and mortgage ought to have been dated, I should have thought it a good bargain to the estate—I confess I was alarmed at the sum to which the £48,000 would amount, at either of the scales, and immediately consulted you respecting the compromise—I informed you last fall, of the dispute about the time at which the deed is dated, and when Alexander contends it ought to have been dated. This I informed you, was the circumstance on which my Lawyers founded their advise to me, to suffer a nonsuit; if a compromise could not be effected—hoping that Alexander at the expiration of the 24 years would not be able to exhibit such strong proofs of its being Post-dated, as he could at present—It seems that the deed and mortgage both, are dated the 10th of April 1779. The scale at this time was sixteen—If we could have assurance in succeeding in this point, I should disapprove of a compromise. But tho' the Lawyers view it as the most favourable circumstance in the cause, they are by no means sanguine respecting it; as Alexander might obtain an order, and no doubt would, to perpetuate the testimony, proving how it happened to have this date, rather than the 25th December 1778—It is certain, Mr Custis was put into possession on the 25th of December 1778, and had his Overseer with all his hands there—I find I mentioned in my last letter to you on this subject, that the Deed was dated the 25th December 1778—This has happened, from the opinion at present entertained by my lawyers, on a consideration of all circumstances, that Alexander at present at least, would succeed in establishing it at this period—I have already mentioned, that it was the expectation of Alexander's Lawyers to have the scale fixed according to the date of the agreement, which would be five—Marshall[2] thinks according to the present adjudications, was it a suit at Common Law, that it would be regulated by the date of the deed; but that in a suit of Chancery, exhibited by us, and resting on the merits of our cause, the Chancellor would order the error to be corrected, if the testimony adduced, was strong.

I shall now proceed to answer your questions, tho' many of them are already solved; as it will be the best means of drawing the whole to a point—1st What are the opinions &c.—It has ever been the opinion of those I have consulted, that Mr Custis had the option of paying at any time, before the expiration of the 24 years—2nd Whether in the articles &c.—There is no exception or proviso whatever against paper money in any writing whatever—3rd At what period &c. The agreement was entered into the 1st of July 1778, the deed is dated on the 10th of April 1779—the Virginia scale at the first period is five, at the second sixteen—I am not acquainted with the Continental scale—On December 25th 1778, the time at which Alexander contends the deed ought to have been dated, the scale is at six—4th In what sort of paper money &c.—The inclosed description of the money certifyed by the person who tendered it, and one of the witnesses will satisfy you of the sort tendered; on which I inclosed in my former letter the opinions of Messrs Randolph,

Marshall & Innis, that it was not proper—Mr Randolph's opinion contained the reason, (if I don't forget) why it is not proper—You will see by the inclosed bill, that it was tendered in May 1781. Why the proper money was not obtained I cannot say—You have now every information which I can give you on this subject—If there is any point in which I have not succeeded, I will make any application you shall propose to my Lawyers to clear it up—I have only to add further that I saw Mr Randolph on his return from New York and mentioned the conditional agreement I had made with Alexander. He expressed much satisfaction at it, and thought it fortunate for the estate, Alexander had acceded to the compromise—As I must set out for Williamsburg, by the 10th of the month, I must beg, if you approve of the agreement, that you will inclose your approbation to Mr Lund Washington, whom I must depute to manage the fixing the rents in my absence[3]—I must also beg, you will drop me a fiew lines directed to the care of Mr Nicholson at Williamsburg, signifying your determination, one way, or the other, that I may know what directions to give to my Lawyers. I am Dr Sir with the greatest respect Your Affecte Serv:

David Stuart

ALS, DLC:GW.

This letter concerns Stuart's protracted negotiations with Robert Alexander on behalf of John Parke Custis's estate. For background, see Stuart to GW, 14 July 1789, n.7, 12 Sept., 3 Dec. 1789, 11, 15, 23 Mar. 1790, GW to Stuart, 21 Sept. 1789, 28 Mar. 1790, Edmund Randolph to GW, 23 Dec. 1789.

1. One of the enclosures was probably a bill of chancery, dated 2 April 1790, for £1,000 (DLC:GW). The agreement also enclosed and signed by David Stuart and Robert Alexander, reads: "Whereas by an act of the Assembly of the Commonwealth of Virginia entitled 'an Act to enable David Stuart to reconvey a tract of land purchased by John Parke Custis of Robert Alexander' it is declared

"'That any agreement or contract which the said David Stuart, by and with the consent of George Washington Esquire, to be expressed under the hand and seal of the said George Washington Esquire, shall make or enter into respecting the surrendering the said Lands to the said Robert Alexander, shall be deemed and taken to be valid and effectual to all intents and purposes' And whereas an agreement hath been entered into accordingly between the said David Stuart and the said Robert Alexander in the words following.

"Articles of agreement made and entered into this ninth day of February one thousand seven hundred and ninety between Robert Alexander of the County of Fairfax of the one part and David Stuart of the same County of the other part Witnesseth That whereas John Parke Custis in his life time purchased of the said Robert Alexander Two tracts of land in the County of Fairfax, one of them laying on the river Potomac, being the tract of land on which the said David Stuart now lives, the other laying between the lines commonly called North and the North six supposed to contain between two and three hundred acres. For securing the purchase money of the said first mentioned tract the said John Parke Custis made and executed a mortgage thereof unto the said Robert Alexander, and for the payment of the last mentioned tract gave his bond to the said Robert Alexander—Respecting which mortgage a suit is now depending in the High Court of Chancery—and the said David Stuart being authorized by act of assembly to compromise all disputes with the said Robert Alexander relative to the aforesaid mortgage and purchase of said lands with the consent and approbation of George Washington Esquire, President of the United States.

"The said David Stuart doth agree with the said Robert Alexander that if the said George Washington shall approve thereof he will put the said Robert Alexander in possession of the aforesaid Tracts of land on or before the 25 day of December next, and will pay him the sum of six hundred pounds on or before the 20 day of June next—and moreover will pay unto the said Robert Alexander whatsoever sum any five Gentlemen, two of them to be named by the said Robert Alexander and two of them by the said David Stuart and the other to be named by the persons so appointed shall adjudge and determine the said Alexander ought to receive for the rents of the said first mentioned tract of land from the time he has been out of possession of the said Tract, on or before the 10 day of February next ensuing. And the said Robert Alexander on his part doth agree with the said David Stuart that he will release the Heirs, Executors, and Administrators of the said John Parke Custis from all claims and demands against them or any of them in consequence of the aforesaid mortgage and bond. Provided always that this agreement shall not be binding on either of the Parties to these presents unless the said George Washington shall approve of this agreement and compromise, nor unless the Fee Simple Estate in the aforesaid Tracts of land can be vested in the said Robert Alexander or his Heirs by act of Assembly or otherwise.

"In witness whereof the Parties to these Presents have hereunto interchangeably set their hands and affixed their seals the day and year first before written" (DLC:GW).

Following Stuart's and Alexander's signatures, the following statement signed by GW appears: "Now be it known to all whom it may concern that under the best evidence I have of the circumstances, and from the fullest consideration I am able to bestow on them my opinion is that the agreement ought to be ratified, and do accordingly under my hand and seal consent to the same this 10 day of April 1790."

2. Probably John Marshall who was practicing law in Richmond at this time.

3. At the bottom of the agreement between Stuart and Alexander, GW appended and signed the following note: "The original of the enclosed was sent by Doctr Stuarts directions (who when he wrote was about to set out for Williamsburg) to Mr Lund Washington, who was authorised by him to ascertain the rents and to carry the bargain into effect."

From Harriot Washington

Mt Vernon April 2d 1790

I now set down to write to my dear Uncle as I have not wrote to him since he left this place I should have done it but I thought you had so much business that I had better write to Aunt Washington yet I am sure you would be very glad to se me improveing myself by writeing letters to my friend's.

I am a going to ask you My Dear Uncle to do something for me which I hope you will not be against but I am sure if you are it will be for my good, as all the young Ladyes are a learning musick, I will be very much obleiged to you if you will send me a gettar, there is a man here by the name of Tracy that teaches to play on the harpsicord & gettar, a gettar is so simple an instrument that five or six lessons would be sufficient for any body to learn, If you think it proper to send me a gettar I will thank you if you will send it by the first opportunity I was informed the other day that you and Aunt Washington were certainly a comeing home this Summer which gave me a great deal of pleasure for I want to se you very much.[1]

If you please to give my love to Aunt Washington Nelly & Washington. I am My Dear Uncle your Sincere Neice

Harriot Washington.

ALS, ViMtV.

Harriot (Harriet) Washington (1776–1822), GW's niece, was the daughter of GW's brother Samuel and his fourth wife, Ann Steptoe Washington. Samuel died in 1781, and Harriot was apparently taken into the household of her mother's sister Elizabeth Steptoe Fendall, wife of Philip Richard Fendall and the widow of Philip Ludwell Lee. She probably lived with the Fendalls at Stratford Hall in 1781–82 and moved with them to Alexandria in late 1782 after Elizabeth Fendall's daughter Matilda and her new husband Henry Lee took possession of the estate. GW refers to Harriot "being given over to me by Mrs Fendall" (GW to David Stuart, 21 Sept. 1794). This probably occurred in 1782 or shortly thereafter, although in 1792 GW referred to his having provided for Harriot "for seven years past" (GW to Betty Washington Lewis, 7 Oct. 1792), suggesting that Harriot came to Mount Vernon as late as 1785. She remained at Mount Vernon primarily in the care of Frances Bassett Washington, wife of George Augustine Washington, until October 1792 when GW sent her to live with Betty Washington Lewis because there would be no woman at Mount Vernon to care for her. After George Augustine Washington died, GW invited Fanny to return with her children to Mount Vernon and further invited her to bring Harriot with her, but Harriot apparently remained in Fredericksburg (GW to Frances Bassett Washington, 24 Feb. 1793). Harriot married Andrew Parks, a Fredericksburg merchant, in 1796. From the time she arrived at Mount Vernon until her marriage, GW provided Harriot with clothing and "such reasonable and proper necessaries as she may stand in need of" (GW to Betty Washington Lewis, 7 Oct. 1792).

1. Thomas Tracy, previously engaged as a music master in the household of Arthur Middleton of South Carolina, was employed by David Stuart to teach music and other subjects, including arithmetic and penmanship, to the two oldest Custis girls, Elizabeth and Martha. GW later hired him to teach music to Nelly Custis (GW's Cash Memoranda, 1 Sept. 1797–20 Feb. 1799, entry for 20 Dec. 1798, RPJCB). Tracy visited Mount Vernon periodically between April 1788 and February 1799 (*Diaries*, 5:306, 6:333). He apparently was not employed to teach Harriot the guitar. Harriot wrote to GW again on 28 May 1792, asking him to send her a "guittar," indicating that Anne Blackburn Washington, wife of Bushrod Washington, had offered to teach her. Harriot evidently learned to play other instruments, since on 5 Jan. 1793 she wrote to GW asking him to send her money for a "Lutestring."

From Alexander Johnson

Sir, G. Portland St. London April 3rd 1790.

The Complacent Attention generally granted to a Cause of Humanity makes me bold in the Liberty of bringing before You one of its Pleas, which were it not founded on the Basis of public Utility, discretion would forbid me to propose, considering the Interruption it must Cause in numerous Weighty Matters that engross Your Attention: Yet as the Subject in its Nature is analogous to a purpose, which on other Occasions, and to good Advantage often has occupied Your Thoughts, I may venture to offer it for a moments Consideration; announcing it to be that of preserving the Lives of Individuals.

The Discovery of the practice affording that great Benefit the easy Treatment by which it is obtained, and the Cheap Means by which everyone can be taught to produce it are set forth in the Papers I herewith make free to lay before You, and which at a Moment's Leisure, Sir, will shew that the practice is not of the medical Kind, as likely it might be thought from the Conduct of some Societies in England sprung from my early proposals & called Humane, composed and managed by Men professionally medical who arrogate the practice to themselves, and craftily exclude from it, that Class of Common People that performed the numerous Recoveries abroad & thereby withhold its extensive Advantage from the Nation.

This new Practice is of undeniable Value to Mankind, as its Application is unlimited to Countries and Climates; the Method of disseminating the Knowledge of it, described in these papers, must therefore be everywhere necessary—It is to be taught to the people at large, and they in speedy Return will not fail to give convincing Proofs that they understand and like it—Striking Instances of this were seen in the numerous Recoveries made by them in Holland and France, Countries whose late and present Proceedings deservedly call to them the Attention and Consideration of all Nations.

As therefore this practice can easily be learnt & exercised, and that its salutary Effects have undoubtedly been proved by the active Efforts of the People: Can a doubt be entertained of its Acceptance by judicious Rulers, while the Art of Medecine offers no effectual Method for recalling Life, when its powers are suspended, & it can be done by an unmedical Treatment that offers at the same Time a discriminate Test between Life & Death! May I not rather, in full Belief of its Adoption for the Growth of a rising nation, say with the Voice of the Nation: From whose Hands can the Diffusion of such Benefits receive the generous Sanction that will so effectually spread them thro' the United States, as from those of our Protector! from whom can the Care of the Lives of His People so naturally derive, as from him who has saved us! To whom should we owe the Blessing of lasting social Enjoyment, but to our Deliverer! Who are we to look up to for our share of this universally beneficent Discovery, but to the Eminent Preserver of our Rights! Can it then be doubtful whether a great Conductor of a rising free People, shall among other Gifts, dispense Longevity, the Means of preserving and restoring Life, to its Individuals with the consequent happy Effect of an encreased Population. These Blessings can be dispensed by no other than Your great Self! At your Command, Sir, the practice will be everywhere made known, exercised & operate its surprising Effects! Acclamations & Shouts of Gratitude will do honour to your Philanthropy! The Magistrates & persons in power, generally addressed, will follow the liberal Example; & every Family will thankfully owe to You & them thro' you, the Comforts enjoyed in the preservation of a Parent, a Child, a Relation, a Friend, or some valuable person.

That it may be Your pleasure, Sir, on this earnest Representation, to honor my proposal with a gracious Assent, is my ardent Request, which divested of Motives of sordid Interest, is animated by a zealous Expectation of ultimately procuring & ascertaining to Mankind, the particular Advantage of a long & probably a more useful Existence in this World. I have the Honor to profess myself, an Admirer of Your great Talents & Virtues & thence, with much Respect & Veneration, Sir, Your most humble and very obedient Servant

Alexr Johnson

LS, DNA: RG 59, Miscellaneous Letters.

Alexander Johnson (1716–1799) was a British physician and the author of several works on what would now be understood as the treatment of shock and conditions, such as hypothermia, that produce similar symptoms. In 1773 Johnson published *A Short Account of a Society in Amsterdam . . . for the Recovery of Drowned Persons: with Observations Shewing the . . . Advantages . . . from a Similar Institution . . . Extended to Other Accidents* (London, 1773). In an effort to popularize this system, he later published several brief summaries in pamphlet form, principally *Relief from Accidental Death: or Summary Instructions for the General Institution, Proposed in the Year 1773 . . . for Recovering Persons Who Meet with Accidents Producing Suddenly an Appearance of Death* (London, 1785). In his letter to GW, Johnson enclosed copies of at least five of these works, now among GW's books in the Boston Athenaeum (Griffin, *Boston Athenæum Collection*, 111–12). These include *Directions for an Extension of the Practice of Recovering Persons Apparently Dead* (London, c.1785), his *Circular Letter for England, Scotland, and Ireland in Regard to Saving Lives of Persons Apparently Dead* (London, 1790), two summaries of two pages each, and even a version in verse, titled *Relief from Accidental Death; or, Summary Directions, in Verse, Extracted from the Instructions at Large, Published by Alexander Johnson, M.D.* (London, 1789).

To the United States Supreme Court

Gentlemen,   United States [New York] April 3d 1790

I have always been persuaded that the stability and success of the National Government, and consequently the happiness of the People of the United States, would depend in a considerable degree on the Interpretation and Execution of its Laws. In my opinion, therefore, it is important that the Judiciary System should not only be independent in its operations, but as perfect as possible in its formation.

As you are about to commence your first Circuit, and many things may occur in such an unexplored field, which it would be useful should be known; I think it proper to acquaint you, that it will be agreeable to me to receive such Information and Remarks on this Subject, as you shall from time to time judge expedient to communicate.

Go: Washington

ALS, NNC; Df, DNA: RG 59, Miscellaneous Letters; LB, DLC:GW.

The first session of the Supreme Court convened in the Merchants Exchange on Broad Street, New York City, on 1 Feb. 1790, with justices John Jay, James Wilson, William Cushing, and John Blair (Marcus and Perry, *Documentary History of the Supreme Court*, 1:171–81, 335–40). On 4 Feb. justices Wilson, Cushing, and Blair, together with Attorney General Edmund Randolph, Secretary of War Henry Knox, and Secretary of the Treasury Alexander Hamilton, and others joined GW for dinner (*Diaries*, 6:28). The first session of the Supreme Court lasted ten days and adjourned on 10 February. The justices then prepared to hold circuit courts (see GW to the U.S. Senate, 24 Sept. 1789, source note). James Wilson and David Brearley convened the first of these circuit courts in New York on 2 April 1790. On 17 June James Iredell, who was not present at the first session of the court, wrote to GW that John Jay had shown him GW's letter of 3 April and that he would do "every thing in my power to contribute to the important purpose of it" and that he hoped "to consult with the other Judges when I have the pleasure of meeting them at New York in order that we may jointly communicate to you the observations which occur to us." In September 1790 the justices responded with a long letter arguing that the assignment of Supreme Court justices to the circuit courts was unwise, primarily because it threatened to impair the legitimacy of the appellate jurisdiction of the Supreme Court. See the Supreme Court Justices to GW, c.13 Sept. 1790.

From James McHenry

Sir.   Baltimore [Md.] 4 April 1790.

About two years ago Mr Copeley an English manufacturer did himself the honor to pay his respects to you at Mount Vernon: Being about to return to his own country he wishes to renew his homage and respects, and has intreated me to recal him to your remembrance by another introduction.[1]

I pray you to excuse this liberty, and am with the greatest and most sincere respect Sir your most devoted and humble servant

James McHenry

ALS, DLC:GW.

1. Burrow Copley of Leeds, England, was among the first manufacturers to introduce water-powered scribbling and slubbing machinery to the Yorkshire

woolen industry. He was the focus of popular discontent with laborsaving machinery in the mid-1780s and may have visited the United States to explore the possibility of establishing woolen manufacturing in this country. He visited GW at Mount Vernon on 19 Jan. 1788 (*Diaries*, 5:266).

From Thomas Jefferson

Apr. 5. 1790. a quarter before one.
Mr Jefferson has the honor of inclosing for the perusal of the President rough draughts of the letters he supposes it proper to send to the court of France on the present occasion.[1] he will have that of waiting on him in person immediately to make any changes in them the President will be so good as to direct, and to communicate to him two letters just received from mr Short.[2]

AL, DNA: RG 59, Miscellaneous Letters; LB, DLC:GW.

1. Jefferson apparently did not submit these drafts to GW until 10 April 1790. On that date GW recorded in his diary: "In the afternoon the Secretary of State submitted for my approbation Letters of credence for Mr. Short as Charges de affaires at the Court of Versailles, & his own Letter to Monsr. Montmorin taking leave of that Court both directed to that Minister—also to Mr. Short on the Subject of our Prisoners at Algiers" (*Diaries*, 6:60). Jefferson's two letters to Armand-Marc, comte de Montmorin Saint-Hérem, French minister for foreign affairs, the first presenting Short and the second announcing his own recall, are dated 6 April 1790 and are printed in Boyd, *Jefferson Papers*, 16:313–15. Jefferson's letter to Short, 6 April 1790, touching on the prisoners in Algiers is in ibid., 315–17. At the 10 April meeting, Jefferson probably also presented GW with a draft of the president's letter to Louis XVI announcing Jefferson's recall.

2. On 5 April Jefferson received a letter from William Short under cover of a letter dealing with European affairs addressed to John Jay, both dated 12 Jan. 1790 (ibid., 103–9).

To The United States Senate and House of Representatives

United States [New York] April 5th 1790.
Gentlemen of the Senate and House of Representatives,
I have directed my private Secretary to lay before you Copies of three Acts of the Legislature of the State of New York, which have been transmitted to me by the Governor thereof.[1] viz.

"An Act declaring it to be the duty of the Sheriffs of the
several Counties within this State to receive, and safe keep
such prisoners as shall be committed under the authority
of the United States."

"An Act for vesting in the United States of America the
Light-House and Lands thereunto belonging to Sandy
Hook."

and "An Act ratifying certain Articles in addition to and amendment of the Constitution of the United States of America,
proposed by Congress."

A copy of a letter, accompanying said Acts, from the Governor
of the State of New York to the President of the United States,
will, at the same time, be laid before you—and the originals deposited in the office of the Secretary of State.[2]

Go: Washington

LS, DNA: RG 46, First Congress, Records of Legislative Proceedings, President's Messages; copy, DNA: RG 233, First Congress, Records of Legislative
Proceedings, Journals.

1. See George Clinton to GW, 2 April 1790.

2. This letter and its enclosures were delivered to Congress on 5 April by
Tobias Lear where they were read and "ordered to lie on the table" (*DHFC*,
3:356–57).

From Ferdinando Fairfax

Sir   Fairfax County [Va.] April 6. 1790.

Being informed that William Vans Esq. of Salem (a friend of
mine) has received an appointmt from the General Court of
Massachusetts, as Collector of the Excise for the South District
of the County of Essex in that State, and that it is expected that
Congress will take that branch of Revenue into their own hands;
I take the Liberty of mentioning this appointmt to you, and (as
it is probable his modesty will prevent his making a *direct* application) to request, that, if upon enquiry, you shou'd think him,
as well qualified for that office under Congress, as any other
person who may apply, you wou'd confirm his appointment.[1] Or
that, if he shou'd not succeed in this, you would confer upon
him such other office at your disposal as you may think best
suited to his abilities & Situation in Life.

Sensible that nothing which may be said in his favour, will have so much weight with you, as the general Character for Probity & Integrity, which he bears in the place of his Residence, on this I rest his probability of Success; and am, with every Sentiment of unfeigned Esteem & Regard Sir your obedt servt

Ferdinando Fairfax

ALS, DLC:GW.

Ferdinando Fairfax (1769–1820) was the third son of Bryan Fairfax and the nephew of George William Fairfax, from whom he inherited the Belvoir estate in Fairfax County.

1. William Vans (c.1730–1820), a Salem merchant, represented that town in the Massachusetts General Court and was appointed collector of excise for the South District of Essex County by the General Court in March 1790. On 24 Dec. 1790 he wrote to GW asking to be considered for excise collector "should there be an Excise established by the Union." He reminded GW that he "had the honour through my late freind Genl Reed of Supplying your Excellency as a Merchant with family nescessaries on your first arrival at Cambridge" (DLC:GW). He did not receive an appointment as an excise collector.

From Henry Knox

Sir.   War Office [New York] April 6th 1790

In consequence of your instructions, I have directed Captains Burbeck's and Savage's companies of artillery, and Captain Smith's company of infantry, to be embarked, at the Garrison of West Point, on board of vessels, in order to be transported to Georgia, and I expect they will arrive at this city, and be in readiness to proceed to sea, by the 9th instant.[1]

All the said companies are to act as artillery, or infantry, as the service may require, as each of them are armed with muskets, besides two brass field-pieces, with the proper quantity of ammunition.

I beg leave to submit to your judgement, the following disposition of said companies, after their arrival in Georgia.

To wit—One company—at—The St Mary's.
        One ditto—at Beard's Bluff on the Altamaha.
        One ditto—at the Rock Landing on the Oconee.

Each company to form such detached posts, as circumstances may require, and its strength shall admit.

I beg leave also to submit the draft of instructions to be given to each Captain, varied only as to the stations to be occupied.[2] I have the honor to be, with the greatest respect, Sir, Your most obedt Servt

H. Knox
secretary of War

LS, DLC:GW; LB, DLC:GW.

1. No written instructions from GW to Knox on these companies have been found.

2. Knox's instructions to the company commanders have not been found.

To Louis XVI

[New York, 6 April 1790]

Very great and good Friend and Ally

As the Time limited for the Duration of Mr Jefferson's Residence in Quality of our Minister plenipotentiary near your Majesty will shortly expire, and the public Interests require that he should undertake other Functions, we have directed him to take Leave of your Majesty, and to assure you of our Friendship and sincere Desire to preserve and strengthen the Harmony and Confidence which so happily subsist between the two Nations. We are persuaded that he will do this in the Manner most expressive of these Sentiments, and of the Respect and Sincerity with which they are offered.[1] We pray God to keep your Majesty under his holy Protection. Written at the City of New York the 6th Day of April 1790.[2] Your good Friend and Ally.

Go: Washington
by the President
Th: Jefferson

LS, PWW; LB, DLC:GW; copy, DNA: RG 59, Ceremonial Letters, Credences; copy, DNA: RG 59, Instructions to Diplomatic Officers.

1. See Jefferson to GW, 5 April 1790.

2. Louis XVI replied on 11 Sept. 1790. GW laid this letter before the Senate on 17 Jan. 1791.

To Henry Knox

Sir,   United States [New York] April 7th 1790

The papers which you yesterday submitted to me, respecting the arrangement[1] of the three companies to be sent to Georgia and the Instructions to be given to their Captains, have been duly considered, and meet my approbation.

The proposed disposition of the said companies after their arrival in Georgia—

"To wit One company—at the St Mary's.
One do—at Beards Bluff on the } Altamaha
One do at the Rock Landing on } the Oconee,"

appears from the maps and information to be the best. In fortifying or constructing such works as may be necessary for the defence and security of the Troops, I would have it impressed upon the commanding Officer to make the area sufficiently large within the pallisadoes[2] to admit of building all the Barracks and houses of every kind; for experience has strongly shewn the utility of this mode where you have to contend with an Indian Enemy.

Go: Washington

Df, DLC:GW; LB, DLC:GW. The draft has several substitutions by GW written above the line.

1. In the draft GW substituted "arrangement" for "disposition."

2. In the draft GW substituted "to make the Area sufficiently large within the pallisadoes" for "to extend his pallisadoes far enough."

From Gouverneur Morris

Sir   London 7 April 1790

I arrived in this City on Saturday Evening the twenty eighth of March and called the next morning on the Duke of Leeds minister for foreign affairs—He was not at Home, I therefore wrote to him a note Copy whereof is enclosed as also of his answer received that Evening.[1] On Monday the twenty ninth I waited upon him at Whitehall and after the usual Compliments, presented your Letter telling him that it would explain the nature of my Business.[2] Having read it, he said with much Warmth and Gladness in his appearance "I am very happy Mr Morris to see this Letter and under the Presidents own Hand. I assure you it is very much my wish to cultivate a friendly and commercial Intercourse between the two Countries *and more,* and I can answer for the Rest of his Majesty's Servants that they are of the same opinion."

"I am happy my Lord to find that such Sentiments prevail for we are too near neighbours not to be either good friends or dangerous Enemies."

"You are perfectly right Sir and certainly it is to be desired as well for our mutual Interests as for the Peace and Happiness of mankind that we should be upon the *best* Footing"—I assured him of our sincere Disposition to be upon good Terms and then proceeded to mention those Points in the Treaty of Peace which remained to be performed: and first I observed that by the Constitution of the United States which he had certainly read all Obstacles to the Recovery of british Debts are removed, and that if any Doubts could have remained they are now done away by the organization of a federal Court which has Cognizance of Causes arising under the Treaty. He said he was very happy to receive this Information, that he had been of opinion and had written so to Mr Adams that the articles ought to be performed in the order in which they stood in the Treaty. Not chusing to enter into any Discussion of his Conduct in Relation to Mr Adams, I told his Grace that I had but one Rule or Principle both for public and private Life, in Conformity to which I had always entertained the Idea that it would consist most with the Dignity of the United States first to perform all their Stipulations and then to require such Performance from others, and that (in Effect) if each Party were on mutual Covenants to suspend his Compliance expecting that of the other all Treaties would be illusory. He agreed in this Sentiment, upon which I added that the United States had now placed themselves in the Situation just mentioned: and here I took occasion to observe that the Southern States who had been much blamed in this Country for obstructing the Recovery of british Debts, were not liable to all the Severity of Censure which had been thrown upon them— that their Negroes having been taken or seduced away, and the Payment for those Negroes having been stipulated by Treaty they had formed a Reliance on such Payment for Discharge of Debts contracted with british merchants both previously and subsequently to the war. That the Suspension of this Resource had occasioned a Deficiency of means, so that their Conduct had been dictated by an overruling necessity. Returning then to the main Business I observed that as we had now fully performed our Part it was proper to mention that two Articles remained to be fulfilled by them viz. that which related to the Posts and that regarding Compensation for the Negroes unless indeed they had sent out orders respecting the former subsequent to the writing of your Letter, and I took the Liberty to consider *that* as a very probable Circumstance.[3] He now became a little embarrassed, and told me that he could not exactly say how that matter stood. That as to the affair of the Negroes he had long wished to have it brought up and to have Something done, but Something or other had always interfered. He then changed the Conversation but I brought it back, and he changed it again. Hence it was apparent that he could go no farther than general Professions and assurances. I then told him that there was a little Circumstance which had operated very disagreably upon the Feelings of America. Here he interrupted me "I know what you are going to say—our not sending a minister— I wished to send you one but then I wished to have a man every way equal to the Task. A man of abilities and one agreable to the People of America, but it was difficult. It is a great way off—and many object on that Score." I expressed my Perswasion that this Country could not want men well qualified for every office; & he again changed the Conversation: wherefore as it was not worth while to discuss the winds and the weather I observed that as he might probably chuse to consider the matter a little and to read again the Treaty and compare it with the American Constitution. He said that he should and wished me to leave your Letter which he would have copied and return to me. I did so telling him that I should be very glad to have a speedy answer and he promised that I should—Thus Sir this matter was began but nine Days have since elapsed and I have heard nothing farther from the Duke of Leeds. It is true that Easter Hollidays have intervened and that public Business is in general suspended for that Period—I shall give them sufficient Time to shew whether they are as well disposed as he has declared and then give him a Hint. Before I saw him I communicated to the french Embassador *in Confidence* that you had directed me to ⟨call⟩ for a Performance of the Treaty—He told me at once that they would not give up the Posts. Perhaps he may be right—I thought it best to make such Communication

because the Thing itself cannot remain Secret and by mentioning it to him we are enabled to say with Truth that in every
Step relating to the Treaty of Peace we have acted confidentially
in Regard to our ally.[4] With sincere Respect I am Sir your
obedt Servant

Gouvr Morris[5]

ALS, DLC:GW; copy, DNA: RG 46, First Congress, 1789–91, Records of Executive Proceedings, President's Messages—Foreign Relations; LB, DLC: Gouverneur Morris Papers; copy, DNA: RG 59, Despatches from Diplomatic Officers.

For background to this letter, see GW to Morris, 13 Oct. 1789 (second letter), and source note, and Morris to GW, 24 Jan. 1790.

1. Morris enclosed a note to the duke of Leeds, written from Froomes Hotel, Covent Garden, and dated 28 Mar., stating that he had called upon Leeds
that morning "but had not that of seeing him. He presents most respectful
Compliments and will be happy to know the Time when it will be most convenient for his Grace to receive certain Communications which Mr M. is directed
to make to his Majesty's Ministers by the President of the United States of
America." Leeds's reply from Whitehall, also dated 28 Mar., indicated that he
would "be glad to see him at the Office ToMorrow at Half past two." Both
enclosures are in DLC:GW. Morris's diary account of the meeting with Leeds
on 29 Mar. substantially agrees with the description in his letter to GW. See
Morris, *Diary of the French Revolution*, 1:464–66.

2. Morris is referring to GW's second letter to him of 13 Oct. 1789.

3. American claims for compensation for slaves evacuated by the British
when they left the United States at the end of the Revolution were based upon
Article VII of the treaty of peace which stipulated that the British army withdraw "with all convenient speed, & without causing any Destruction or carrying away any Negroes, or other Property of the American Inhabitants"
(Miller, *Treaties*, 2:99). The British contended that the slaves' entry into British
lines had automatically manumitted them.

4. Morris's intimacy with the French minister in London no doubt contributed to the skepticism of the British ministry concerning his mission although
it was far down on the list of reasons the British did not rise to the American
bait. The two frequently exchanged visits—on 28 Mar., the day of his arrival,
Morris visited La Luzerne before he left his card at Whitehall and dined with
him that evening (Morris, *Diary of the French Revolution*, 1:460, 461). That the
connection was not lost on British observers is indicated by British agent
George Beckwith's unofficial complaints to Hamilton later in the year about
Morris's connections with La Luzerne and the rumors that he was frequently
in the company of Charles James Fox, leader of the Parliamentary opposition.
In a conversation with Beckwith, Hamilton admitted his own initial misgiving
about Morris's mission but stated that if Morris "has cultivated an intimacy
with the Ministers of any other power in Europe, or has caused suspicion on
that ground with respect to France, or elsewhere, he has had no authority, for

so doing; it occurs to me, that he was very intimate with Monsr. de La Luzerne the Ambassador of France now in London, when he was Minister in this country, possibly from that circumstance he may have been more frequently there, than prudence ought to have dictated, and the knowledge of this circumstance may have produced a greater reserve on the part of Your administration" ("Conversation with George Beckwith," 25–30 Sept. 1790, in Syrett, *Hamilton Papers,* 7:70–72). For the view that domestic criticism of Morris's supposed indiscretion was orchestrated by Alexander Hamilton, see Boyd, *Jefferson Papers,* 17:99–102. That criticism of Morris was indeed widespread in political circles in the United States is indicated by GW's letter to Morris in 1792 recounting opposition to his appointment as minister to France. "Whilst your abilities, knowledge in the affairs of this Country, & disposition to serve it were adduced, and asserted on one hand, you were charged on the other hand, with levity, and imprudence of conversation and conduct. It was urged, that your habit of expression, indicated a hauteaur disgusting to those who happen to differ from you in sentiment; and among a people who study civility and politeness more than any other nation, it must be displeasing. That in France you were considered as a favourer of Aristocracy, & unfriendly to its Revolution—(I suppose they meant Constitution). . . . That in England you indiscretely communicated the purport of your mission, in the first instance, to the Minister of France, at that Court; who, availing himself in the same moment of the occasion, gave it the appearance of a movement through his Court. This, and other circumstances of a cimilar nature, joined to a closer intercourse with the opposition member, occasioned distrust, & gave displeasure to the Ministry; which was the cause, it is said, of that reserve which you experienced in negotiating the business which had been entrusted to you" (GW to Morris, 28 Jan. 1792; see also GW to Thomas Jefferson, 28 Jan. 1792, and Thomas Jefferson to GW, 28 Jan. 1792). For Morris's defense of his actions, see his letter to GW, 10 April 1792.

5. On 13 April Morris sent GW a duplicate of his letter of 7 April, noting that "I am still waiting for Intelligence from the Ministers, who to judge by appearances slumber profoundly upon the Application made to them. Yesterday the two Houses of Parliament again entered on Business after their Recess for the Easter Holidays and Mr Pitt has announced the Budget for next Monday. Some rational Conjectures as to their Dispositions and Intentions may perhaps be formed from the Business of that Day" (DLC:GW).

Roger Alden to Tobias Lear

Sir   Office of Secy of State—April 8th 1790

The Secy of State has given directions, that six copies of the Laws, in sheets, should be delivered to the President of the United States—Agreeably to his orders I have the honor to transmit the Laws passed this session; in future they will be regularly sent from this office, as printed, and at the close of the Session, the same number bound, with marginal Notes and Index. I am—sir your most obedt h'ble servant

R: Alden

ALS, DNA: RG 59, Miscellaneous Letters; LB, DLC:GW.

Proclamation

[9 April 1790]
Whereas a Convention for defining and establishing the functions and privileges of the respective Consuls and vice-Consuls of his most Christian Majesty and of the said United States, was concluded and signed by the Plenipotentiaries of his said most Christian Majesty and of the said United States, duly and respectively authorized for that purpose, which Convention is in the form following, vizt[1]

(here the Translation of it was inserted)[2]
And whereas the said Convention has been duly ratified and confirmed by me on the one part, with the advice & Consent of the Senate, and by his most Christian Majesty on the other, and the said Ratifications were duly exchanged at Paris on the 1st Day of January in the present year. Now therefore, to the end that the said Convention may be observed and performed with good faith on the part of the United States, I have ordered the premises to be made public, and I do hereby enjoin and require all persons bearing office, civil or military within the United States, and all others, Citizens or Inhabitants thereof, or being within the same, faithfully to observe and fulfil the said Convention and every clause and article thereof.

In Testimony whereof I have caused the Seal of the United States to be affixed to these Presents and signed the same with my Hand. Given at the City of New York the ninth day of April in the year of our Lord 1790, and of the Sovereignty and Independence of the United States the fourteenth.

George Washington
by the President
Thomas Jefferson

Copy, DLC: Thomas Jefferson Papers.

1. See also Ratification of the Consular Convention with France, 9 Sept. 1789, and notes.

2. The text of the treaty was to be inserted at this point. For the text, see Miller, *Treaties*, 2:228–41.

From Noirmont de La Neuville

Sir,   St Marc april 10th 1790.

I cannot determine myself to let my Brother to return to America, without charging him with a letter for your Excellency.[1] I Beseech you to look upon it as a very inadequate testimonial of my constant and respectful gratitude for your past kind offices. they have been confered in too flattering a manner and are still too deeply imprinted into my mind to permit my heart ever to forget them. it will be the everlasting debt of my life to form vows for the continuance of your so well deserved renown; and I can assure your Excellency that your reputation never shone with a purer lustre as Since the beginning of our dear-bought revolution. how often since one year has your name been repeated with enthusiastick respect, and painful and melting remembrance, attended with comparisons absolutly redounding to the inexpressible advantage of the Restorer of american liberty! how often have we lamented that the generous, human and loyal principles upon which has been pursued and attained the Redress of your grievances have not been adhered to in france! when General Washington is still alive, when he is still the pride and glory of his grateful country, when his example, his virtuous principles, his unshaken firmness are still warming and filling with indelible veneration the breast of every french officer that has been wittness to that glorious and just war, by what fatalaty must we see our annals stained with deeds that make every human heart almost regret the dawn of liberty which begins to light upon us? excuse, Sir, the overflowing of a heart that can not think of your Excellency's and our conduct in the present contest without invoking the same tutelary genius that unhappily for our national honor has been ever deaf to my prayers. I am with every sentiment inspired by Respect and gratitude, Sir, your Excellency's The most humble and obedient Servant

                                                Noirmont

ALS, DLC:GW.

René-Hippolyte Penot Lombart (Lombard) de Noirmont de La Neuville

(1750–1792) was aide-de-camp to Lafayette until the latter's first return voyage to France in January 1779. Noirmont served under Maj. Gen. Benjamin Lincoln in the southern army and took part in action at Savannah. Promoted lieutenant colonel by Congress in October 1779, he obtained permission at the same time to return to France. He was killed in the September Massacres in Paris in 1792 (Lasseray, *Les Français sous les treize étoiles*, 356–58). For GW's comments on him, see his certificate of service, 1 Oct. 1779, DLC:GW.

1. Noirmont's elder brother, Louis-Pierre Lombart, chevalier de La Neuville (b. 1744), served as inspector of the northern army in 1778 under Horatio Gates. In August 1778 he received a controversial appointment, over GW's disapproval, as brevet brigadier general and returned to France where he participated in several campaigns with the French army (see GW to Gouverneur Morris, 24 July 1778). In early 1790 he sailed from France to Santo Domingo and to the United States, returning to France later in the year (Lasseray, *Les Français sous les treize étoiles*, 349–56).

From Rochambeau

Rochambeau near Vendome [France] april the 11th 1790.

Do you remember, my Dear general, of the first repast that we have made together at Rod island. I did you remark from the Soup the difference of the character of our two nations, the french in burning their throat, and all the americans waiting wisely of the time that it was cooled. I believe, my dear general, you have Seen Since a year that our nation has not change of character. We go very fast—God will that we come at our aims. I have had my part of the troubles of that revolution. I have passed half of the last year in my department of Picardy, they made me passed in the month of July in that of the province of alsace—I did find there Strasbourg and all the province in a terrible insurection—I have employed there six months to retreive good order. I came back here afterwards to rest myself and make Some remedies for my health which has been altered of. The natal air made me well, and the king has named me yet here commissary to have an eye to the organisations of the assemblies of department—you are you, my dear general, in a full enjoyment of a work of fourteen years, and we will in a year of time complete a work that cannot be but the fruit of the patience that I have known to you and of a complete regeneration of the manners—God make us arrive to it and make forget to the univers Some wicked Strokes that have not fouled the revolution of america—Let me hear of you my Dear General and be well persuaded of the inviolable attachment with which I have the honour to be my Dear General Your most obedient and very humble servant

le cte de rochambeau

a thousand kindness and compliments to M. Jefferson, to M. Knox and to all my ancien camarades and friends which are near you.

LS, DLC:GW.

To David Stuart

Dear Sir, New York April 11th 1790

I have given my consent in the manner the law directs, to the agreement you have made with Mr Alexander; and, agreeably to your desire, have this day forwarded it under cover to Mr Lund Washington;[1] being persuaded, under the existing circumstances, it is better to do this than hazard a decision at Law—but it is a strange affair!

I wrote to you a few days ago, and directed for you at Abingdon or Richmond;[2] and hope, as it is to Williamsburgh you are going, that the letter came to hand before you set out. The question of assumption has not been taken yet—when decided, I wish it may be for the best; it has been fully, & I think ably discussed; but the majority will be small on whichever side it happens; which, in questions of such magnitude, is to be regretted.

As this letter will have to travel to Williamsburgh, I shall take another opportunity to forward such original papers as you have transmitted to me. When you return, I should be glad to learn from you in what temper and state of politic's you found the Country—such information would be *always* satisfactory; and *may be* very useful. I am—Dear Sir Your Obedt & affecte

Go: Washington

ALS, ViMtV.

This letter concerns Stuart's protracted negotiations with Robert Alexander on behalf of John Parke Custis's estate. For background, see Stuart to GW, 14 July 1789, n.7, 12 Sept., 3 Dec. 1789, 11, 15, 23 Mar., 2 April 1790, GW to Stuart, 21 Sept. 1789, 28 Mar. 1790, Edmund Randolph to GW, 23 Dec. 1789.

1. Letter not found.

2. GW is probably referring to his letter to Stuart of 28 Mar. 1790.

Letter not found: to Lund Washington, 11 April 1790. In a letter to GW, 28 April 1790, Lund Washington refers to "Yours of the 11th."

From Joseph Wheaton

May it Please the President   April 11th 1790
Sir

Having had an oppertunity of learning that an additional force is to be aded to the present Establishment of the troops, I am constrained to mention to the President.

The office which the House of Representatives have been pleased to appoint me to, is not altogether that popular Situation nor So profitable to our Country as one would wish to fill.[1]

Having Served in the army from the begining of the war to the end, and having made the duty of a Soldier much of my Study that with the encouragement of many of my Friends in both Houses of Congress, have Considered it a duty I owe my Country to make known my wishes.

If my Services could be made acceptable in the army, it would be the pride of my Heart to perform a duty in which there was full Conviction of rendering Services eaqual to the rewards.

I have only to observe that Should the President view these with a favourable eye I would be happy to resign my present office in favor of Some disabled officer or other person whom the House of Representatives might think proper to appoint as my Successor. This with great defferance is Humbly Submitted to the President By His Most obedient and most devoted Servant

Joseph Wheaton

ALS, DLC:GW.

Joseph Wheaton (d. 1828) of Rhode Island served as a lieutenant in the Continental army during the Revolution. On 18 April 1789, at Wheaton's request, Marinus Willett wrote to John Peter Gabriel Muhlenberg, speaker of the House of Representatives, recommending Wheaton for a congressional post, and on 12 May 1789 he was appointed sergeant-at-arms of the House (DLC:GW; *DHFC*, 3:58). Wheaton did not receive an army commission from GW and continued as sergeant-at-arms until 26 Oct. 1807. In April 1813 he was commissioned a captain and deputy quartermaster general in the U.S. Army.

1. "An Act for allowing Compensation to the Members of the Senate and House of Representatives of the United States, and to the Officers of both

Houses" allowed four dollars per day "during the sessions and while employed on the business of the House" as compensation for the sergeant-at-arms (1 *Stat.* 70–72).

From Gouverneur Morris

Dear Sir   London 12 April 1790

I have ordered at a capital manufacturers the plated Coolers which you desired.[1] Nothing of this Sort has ever yet been executed here except in a coarse and clumsy manner in lacquered Ware. As far as I can judge from the Design which has been drawn consequent upon my Directions they will be very elegant, and cheaper than in a Form less beautiful. Still they will be expensive. I own that considering the Simplicity of the Workmanship I have been much tempted to have them made of Plate but upon considering well your Letter I could not venture what would have looked so much like Extravagance—It will require about six weeks from this Time to have them compleated and I expect that an opportunity will then offer for sending them out so that about the middle of July you may receive them.[2] Should the weather in America have continued as mild as our accounts to the Begining of February have anounced it these machines will be useless. I am my dear Sir very sincerely yours

Gouvr Morris

ALS, DLC:GW; ALS (duplicate), DLC:GW; LB, DLC: Gouverneur Morris Papers; LB, DNA: RG 59, Despatches from Diplomatic Officer, Great Britain.

1. In his first letter to Morris of 13 Oct. 1789, GW requested that Morris order silver-plated "handsome and useful Coolers for wine *at* and *after* dinner."

2. Morris placed the order for the wine coolers in Paris on 8 April, but by 23 June they were still not completed. On that day Morris called "at the Warehouse and see some Wine Coolers made for Genl. Washington which will I find come very high" (Morris, *Diary of the French Revolution*, 1:478, 548).

From Gouverneur Morris

private
Dear Sir   London 13 April 1790

My Letter of the seventh will have communicated what passed with the Duke of Leeds respecting the Business you committed to me. I take the Liberty to mention here that from his Countenance and Manner on the Perusal of your Letter, he seemed to derive from it that Sort of Pleasure which a Man feels at the Removal of Some thing which every now and then brings to his Mind disagreable Ideas. I do not exactly see from what Cause this Emotion was produced. By the Eagerness of his subsequent Expressions I conjectured that the critical Situation of Europe had excited some Disquietude respecting the Part which the United States might take in Case of a general War—What strengthened that Idea, and perhaps led me to form it was that in a Chamber to which I was introduced previous to the Audience there was a large Book of Maps open at that of Poland— But the Silence since observed leads to a Suspicion that his Satisfaction was derived from another Source. I am told that in a late Debate the Ministers committed themselves by throwing out in pretty clear Terms the Idea that some Sort of Treaty was on the Carpet with America; and if so, the opening now given must have releived them from the Fear of future Contradiction.

I trouble you my dear Sir with all this Conjecture because it is not impossible that Circumstances may turn up on your Side the Water with which it may be useful to compare minutely what passes here. I am always most sincerely yours

Gouvr Morris[1]

ALS, DLC:GW; ALS (duplicate), DLC:GW; LB, DLC: Gouverneur Morris Papers.

1. On 13 April Morris addressed a second letter to GW: "This will accompany the Duplicate of what I had the Honor to write on the seventh by the Packet. I am still waiting for Intelligence from the Ministers, who to judge by appearances slumber profoundly upon the Application made to them. Yesterday the two Houses of Parliament again entered on Business after their Recess for the Easter Holidays and Mr Pitt has announced the budget for next Monday. Some rational Conjectures as to their Dispositions and Intentions may perhaps be formed from the Business of that Day" (DLC:GW).

To Anthony Whitting

Sir,   New York, April 14th 1790.

By a letter which I have lately received from my nephew, Major Washington of Mount Vernon, I find you have made a tender of your services to him to overlook one of my farms, and have referred me to Colo. Cadwalader, now in Congress, for your qualifications and character.[1]

This enquiry I have made, and the result of it is that you have a competent knowledge in the business of agriculture, and understand the economy of a farm—That he believes you to be industrious, and has no distrust of your honesty—These undoubtedly are very good and essential requisites in a manager; but candor, he added, obliged him to inform me that he thought you were too much given to your pleasures—however of the impropriety of this he hoped and believed you were convinced, and of course would reform.

Under this information and persuasion I am disposed to employ you on the terms mentioned by my nephew—to wit, Forty guineas ⅌ annum—and wish you to name the time, in a letter to me, that would be convenient for you to enter on the trust— I must inform you however that the present managers are engaged till December—but Mr Bloxham (having had notice that he would be continued no longer than the term for which he is engaged, and intending it is said when he quits my employ, to return to England) wishes I am informed to embark before that period—To this I shall have no objection if his place can be supplied—but not being well enough acquainted with all the circumstances relative to this matter, I can make no arrangement relative thereto until I hear first from you, and next from my nephew with respect to Mr Bloxham—after this matters may be precisely fixed so as to place all parties on a certainty.

The reason why I write to you from hence is that a Post goes directly from this city to Chestertown in Maryland (where my nephew informs me you at present live) whereas a letter written from Mount Vernon might be long on its passage, or perhaps never get to you at all.

That there may be no delay in the business from a misconception of the terms on your part, or for want of knowing the expectations on mine, I have sketched articles of agreement declaratory of both, which my nephew will, on my behalf subscribe to, if the same is done by you.

From this communication (accompanied with an assurance that I shall make no alteration) you are enabled to say yea or nay to the proposals which I request may be done by letter addressed to me at this place—the result of which I shall communicate to my nephew that he may know what to depend upon—If it is your determination to accept that he may know at what time (under the existing circumstances) he could receive you—of which I shall delay no time in giving you notice, and shall expect you will repair to Mount Vernon accordingly.[2] I am Sir &ca

G. Washington

LB, DLC:GW.

1. For Whitting's application for employment as farm manager, see George Augustine Washington to GW, 26 Mar. 1790. On 20 May 1790 Washington completed an indenture with Whitting on GW's behalf: "Articles of Agreement made and entered into this twentieth day of May one thousand seven hundred and ninety between Anthony Whiting late Manager of the Estate of the deceased General Cadwalader (but at present of Alexandria Virginia) of the one part, and George A: Washington of Mount Vernon in Virginia in behalf of the President of the United States, of the other part; Witnesseth that the said Anthony Whiting for the wages and other considerations hereafter mentioned doth agree to serve the said President for the space of one year to commence the first day of June next as an Overlooker of his two Farms, which are united and distinguished as the Ferry & Frenches, and that he will faithfully & diligently attend to the duties thereof; using his best skill to carry into effect the present rotation system of Cropping practised on the said Farms, or such other course as shall be approved by the said President through his agent George A: Washington. That he will hold it as an incumbent duty to suggest such changes and alterations in the present system of management as to him shall appear better calculated from the soil or other circumstances to promote œconomy and to encrease the profits of the Farms, but to make no actual change therein without permission; as matters for some time have been tending to the present mode, and ought not to be departed from but under the ful'est conviction of the superior advantages of an other; and in the accomplishment of whatever plan shall be adopted that he will use every possible œconomy consistent with good management in the execution—That he will be particularly attentive to the Negroes which shall be committed to his care—to the work Oxen and Horses—to the stock of every denomination—and to all the Tools and impliments of husbandry of every sort belonging to the Farms entrusted to his care—That he will be particularly attentive to the Inclosures endeavouring as far as time and the means with which he may be furnished will admit, to substitute Ditching and Hedging to dead fences—That he will see the labourers at their work as soon as it is light in the morning, and (unless he is called of for other purposes benificial to his employer or absent with leave if for purposes of his own except on Sunday when he may occasionally go to Church, and as he will not be allow'd to keep a Horse the use of one belonging to the Farms will be granted when necessary—) that he will always be with the people while they are at their labour, as the only sure means of geting the business done and the work properly executed without punishment—That he will consider

it as an essential part of his duty—by this close attention to see that the work is carried on with diligence and propriety especially the Plowing part of it, as the goodness of all Crops depend materially upon the preparation that give birth to them—That he will pay the utmost attention to the Stocks of every kind, will use every endeavour to encrease and properly distribute the manure on the Farms, and also will improve to the best of his judgment the implements of husbandry necessary thereto—and will instruct as occasion may require, and opportunities offer the labourers therein how to Plow, Sow, Mow, Reap, Thatch, Ditch, Hedge &c., in the best manner—That he will have proper attention given to the Ferry and a regular return with the proceeds rendered once a week (Saturday) with a report of the labour of the People, the encrease and decrease of the Stock, the receipts and disbursement &c. (a form of which will be furnished with a plan of the Farms—). The retail of liquors is particularly restricted as such a practise must be attended with pernicious consequences, and to avoid enumeration it is only necessary to observe that no emolument will be allow'd but what will hereafter be specified nor no departure from this agreement, as dismission or the claim of the penalty will be resorted to—Lastly if instead of being confined to the cares of those Farms it should be found from circumstances, more expedient to remove and extend his superintendance, that he is still to be governed by the principles here mention'd, although his attention will be more divided and in either case is to consider himself under the controul of the said George A: Washington who acts agreeably to directions received from the said President, And will conduct himself soberly honestly and with the most exemplary industry. In consideration of services thus fully and faithfully performed on the part of the said Anthony Whiting the said George A: Washington for and on behalf of the said President of the United States doth agree to allow the said Anthony Whiting the sum of forty Guineas per annum, to commence the first day of June next— Will allow him three hundred weight of Pork and one hundred weight of Beef at killing time but such provision as may be furnished untill that time will be deducted therefrom, if in Bacon such a proportion as shall be deemed equivalent—also f⟨our⟩ hundred weight of Flour distinguished as midlings— the use of a Cow—the privelege of raising Fowls for his own consumption, and the use of a Boy or Girl which can be most conveniently spared to cook &c. And in case his superintendance should be extended will allow him the use of a Horse to enable him to discharge with more convenience & facility, the business which will be required of him. For the true and faithful performance of this agreement the parties each to the other doth hereby bind themselves in the penal sum of One hundred Dollars, the day & year first written" (DLC:GW).

2. For George Augustine Washington's report on Whitting's first months as farm manager, see his letter to GW, 20 Aug. 1790.

To Gouverneur Morris

Dear Sir,   New York, April 15th 1790.

Since my last to you, dated March 1st I have been favored with your letter of the 24th of January accompanied by the surtout of Plateaux &ca. These came very safe—are very elegant—much admired—and do great justice to your taste—accept my thanks for the attention.[1]

Upon trial it appears that they need no addition, the intention therefore of this letter is to counteract, if it should arrive in time, my request of the first of March of two Plateaux more and ornaments equivalent thereto—but to repeat the other wish contained therein namely "I would thank you &ca"—[2]

Your not having acknowledged the receipt of my commission of a public nature that went from hence at the same time, and was of the same date with the letter, to which yours of the 24. of January is an answer, to wit the 13th of October, gives me some pain, lest it should have been arrested on its passage. With great and sincere esteem and regard I am yours

G. Washington

LB, DLC:GW.

1. See GW to Morris (first letter), 13 Oct. 1790, and Morris to GW, 24 Jan. 1790, n.2.

2. Here GW inserted "see paragraph respecting lamps."

From John Bailey

                                    New York—Little dock Street No. 22
Sir,   April 17th 1790

I have witnessed an application made to Congress by a person residing in Great Britain who wishes to undertake the supply of a copper coinage—I shall not call in question the superiority of his apparatus and process for coining—tho' I must insist that a coinage can be executed as well in America and cheaper to the United states than if executed abroad—Had the applicant given the result of one hours work by the steam engine I should have been enabled to have drawn a comparison between his process and my own—I have actually struck at the rate of 56 coins in a minute—coins in every respect equal to the Specimens which that artist hath transmitted to Congress.[1]

I am acquainted with the whole mystery of Coining in gold in silver in Copper or in Billon[2]—I can make my tools as well as prepare the metals, and can undertake to furnish coin in a state of *as high perfection* as has yet been issued by any nation. I can not only do this but am disposed to undertake it whenever the general government shall establish a mint, if I am called upon by you for that purpose—and I have at this moment in my possession as complete an apparatus for coining as was as yet ever used in any part of Europe that I am acquainted with.

Sir, you may perhaps do me the honor of recollecting me, during the late war I resided at Fredricksburg and at Fish-kill as a Cutler and was often favored with your commands.[3]

Trusting you will bear this application in mind and if on a full enquiry into my abilities you should be pleased to consider it as advancing the interest of the United States to employ me in furnishing this country with coin, I shall, never, I trust give you a moments cause of inquietude or dissatisfaction. In the mean time I remain with respectful esteem Sir Your very humble and Most Obedient Servant

John Bailey

ALS, DLC:GW.

John Bailey, a New York metalworker, was born in England and trained in Sheffield. In the 1760s he was engaged in the cutlery trade in New York City. He left the city during the British occupation and conducted a substantial metalworking business in Fredericksburg (now Patterson) and Fishkill, N.Y., during the war. He later returned to New York City, where he operated an extensive metalworking business throughout the 1790s. He received no appointment from GW.

1. The Articles of Confederation granted Congress the authority to coin money, but Congress did not approve plans for a mint until 16 Oct. 1786. Until a mint could be established, Congress determined to contract privately for the production of copper coins. After considering various proposals Congress entered into an agreement with James Jarvis of New York, but Jarvis seems to have experienced difficulties in obtaining the necessary dies in Europe and proved unable to fulfill the terms of the contract (see James Jarvis to Congress, 1 Nov. 1786, DNA:PCC, item 139, and to the Board of Treasury, 23 Aug. 1788, DNA:PCC, item 140). The idea of contracting for copper coins was revived on 7 April 1790 when Thomas Tudor Tucker, a representative from South Carolina, "presented to the House a letter addressed to him from John H. Mitchell . . . reciting certain proposals of Matthew Boulton, of the Kingdom of Great Britain, for supplying the United States with copper coinage to any amount that government shall think fit to contract with him for, upon the terms therein mentioned" (*DHFC*, 3:360). For the text of Mitchell's letter, see

Mitchell to Tucker, 22 Mar. 1790, in Boyd, *Jefferson Papers*, 16:342–45. Boulton (1728–1809) was one of the most important entrepreneurs of the English Industrial Revolution. In partnership with James Watt, he was responsible for the perfection and widespread introduction of the steam engine to industrial production. In 1787 Boulton entered into an agreement with Jean Pierre Droz (d. 1823), a Swiss engraver living in Paris who had invented a device for minting copper coins that struck the planchet on both sides and the edge simultaneously, producing a coin that was difficult to counterfeit. The next year Boulton established several steam-driven coining presses employing Droz's methods at his Soho works near Birmingham and thereafter made large quantities of copper coins for the East India Company. John Hinckley Mitchell (b. 1765), whose letter presented Boulton's proposal to Congress, was a young Charlestonian who had met Boulton in England in the mid-1780s. Hoping to make a profit on the contract, Mitchell had discussed with Boulton the possibility of supplying copper coins to South Carolina. In 1789 Mitchell raised his sights to the new federal government. According to his correspondence with Boulton, Mitchell met with GW in September 1789 "respecting a general Coinage for the Union." GW's diary for this period is missing, and no letters between Mitchell and GW have been found. Mitchell may have claimed to have met with GW to bolster his general claim to possessing the confidence of the new government. A comparison between the letter presented to Congress by Thomas Tudor Tucker of South Carolina and Boulton's letter to Mitchell of 25 Nov. 1789 reveals that Mitchell deliberately altered or omitted passages from Boulton's letter that were based on Boulton's inference that Mitchell would again consult with GW about the coinage. Mitchell altered Boulton's assertion that "It will be necessary that you (in Conjunction with General Washington or such Persons as may be appointed) fix upon a proper Device & proper inscription" to read "It will be necessary to fix upon a proper device and inscription." He completely omitted Boulton's instruction that he be "perfectly explicit with General Washington" and the complimentary close in which Boulton asked him to present sample coins, along with "my most respectful Complts. to the truly great & Honble. General Washington" (Mitchell, *Mitchell-Boulton Correspondence*, 13, 18–20). GW referred to the proposal of Mitchell and Boulton briefly in his diary on 12 April 1790 without mentioning either man by name, noting that he read with approval Jefferson's report to Congress advising against the production of coins by any foreign manufacturer, "which report appeared to me to be sensible & proper" (*Diaries*, 6:61). No other reference to Mitchell by GW has been found, nor any evidence that he was on familiar terms with GW or had been encouraged by the president or any member of his administration. After receiving the proposals contained in Mitchell's letter to Tucker, the House referred the matter to Jefferson, who produced a "Report on Copper Coinage" within four days. Jefferson had seen Droz's invention in Paris in company with Boulton in December 1786 and recognized its merits, but he argued strongly against contracting with any foreign firm or individual for American coins (Report on Copper Coinage, 14 April 1790, in Boyd, *Jefferson Papers*, 16:345–49). See also Jefferson to Charles Thomson, 17 Dec. 1786, to John Jay, 9 Jan. 1787, ibid., 10:608–10, 11:29–33.

For a detailed treatment of Jefferson's involvement, see ibid., 16:335–42. Jefferson's report was read in the House on 15 April and tabled, apparently without debate, the House instructing the secretary of the treasury "to prepare and report to this House a proper plan or plans for the establishment of a national mint" (*DHFC*, 3:368–69). Hamilton presented his "Report on the Establishment of a Mint" to the House on 28 Jan. 1791 (ibid., 689–90; the text of the report is in Syrett, *Hamilton Papers*, 7:462–607). Bailey wrote to GW again on 5 Feb. 1791, reminding him: "Sir On the 17th of April last I had the honor to address your Excellency on the Subject of my being employed in a Mint for the United States—In My Letter I set forth that I Was well acquanted With that Business, & was possessed of a very Compleate Apparatus for the purpose—Least the Multeplicety of Business Your Excellency, is engaged in Should be the means of Your forgetting My former application, I now take the Liberty to repeat it again, as I find by a Report of the Secretary of the Treasury a Mint is likely to be established—Should Your Excellency be Pleased to employ me as Master of the Mint, I make not the Least doubt but I Will give that satisfaction required in executing the Business With the utmost Fidelity and despatch" (DLC:GW). He received no appointment from GW. For Mitchell's later plan for a mint, see Lear to Hamilton, 29 May 1791.

2. Billon is copper alloyed with a small amount of silver. Jefferson's report advocated its use in lieu of copper. In his "Report on the Mint" Hamilton argued against the use of billon on the grounds that it would lead to extensive counterfeiting (Syrett, *Hamilton Papers*, 7:603).

3. GW's headquarters was located in the vicinity of Fredericksburg and Fishkill, N.Y., between 19 Sept. and 29 Nov. 1778. No record of any communication between Bailey and GW during this period has been found, although while in camp at Fishkill GW sought to obtain a sword with chains and swivels and other equipment that Bailey would have been capable of producing (see GW to John Cox or John Mitchell, 4 Oct. 1778). Bailey moved from Fredericksburg to Fishkill in early 1778.

From Bertier & Co.

Philadelphia April 17th 1790

To the President, the Senate and House of Representatives of the United States,

The Petition of Bertier & Co. of the city of Philadelphia in the State of Pennsylvania Merchants;

Respectfully sheweth,

That your Petitioners having frequently received Goods to their address in Philadelphia, by vessels to different parts of the United States; they, on the twenty fourth day of March last received Letters from Baltimore in the State of Maryland, which had arrived there by the Ship Van Staphorst Captain Atkinson from Amsterdam, directed to your Petitioners, advising of One Package of Merchandize marked B&C no. 2; One Package of Merchandize marked AL, and one other package of Merchandize marked BC no. 1286, a Keg of Herring and a Cheese, being shipped onboard the said Ship Van Staphorst at Amsterdam, Consigned to your Petitioners;[1] that on the twenty fifth of the same month your Petitioners transmitted by Post to Adrian Valck Esqr., Consul for the United Netherlands at Baltimore, the original Bill of Lading and Invoices of the said Goods, with the Proofs required by the Laws of the United States, and directions to enter the said Goods and secure the Duties charged on them. That on the twenty seventh of the same month the said Adrian Valck Esqr. acknowledged the Receipt of the said Letter from your Petitioners, and declared that he should follow their orders respecting the said Goods, but on the thirtieth of the same Month the said Adrian Valck Esqr. wrote to your Petitioners, that he could not get the said Goods—as they had been seized by one of the Inspectors of the Port of Baltimore, before he had received the Invoices and Bill of Lading from your Petitioners, because the Captain had landed them before a permit had been obtain'd for that purpose from the Custom House.

That the said Adrian Valck Esqr. on behalf of your Petitioners, applied to the Collector of the Port of Baltimore, to secure the Payment of the Duties on the said Goods, and to have them deliverd to him, but the said Collector not conceiving himself authorised to determine on the Case, refered and wrote concerning the same, to the Secretary of the Treasury for relief, and that your Petitioners also addressed themselves to the Secretary of the Treasury, and stated the Circumstances of their Case to him, and he was pleased (as they are informed) to write to the said Collector, to shew all the Indulgence in his power to them,[2] but as your Petitioners are inform'd that a Bill is now depending in Congress, to give relief in Cases of Seizure where no frauds were intended; and as there was not any Intention of fraud on the part of your Petitioners, nor any other Person concerned in the Transaction, and they had taken (as they have in all Cases) every Precaution in their power strictly to Comply with the Laws of the United States, for securing the Duties on Goods imported, they humbly pray Congress to make such provision in the said Act now before them, for granting them relief under their present Case, or to grant them such other relief in the Premises, as

to Congress in their Wisdom shall seem just. And your Petitioners shall ever pray.

Bertier & Compne

LS, DNA: RG 46, First Congress, Records of Legislative Proceedings, Petitions
and Memorials.

C. A. Bertier (Berthier) & Company was a Philadelphia firm of merchants
and shipowners.

1. Berthier & Company enclosed with its petition a bill of lading for the *Van
Staphorst* and a statement from George P. Keeports, notary public in Baltimore
that on 1 April 1790 he had boarded the ship and demanded of Capt. William
Atkinson the merchandise listed on the bill of lading. Atkinson replied that "in
his absence his mate had sent the said Merchandise ashore, that the Permits
for landing the goods of the different shippers, did not express either Marks
or Numbers, and therefore he could not be certain thereby, which of the different shippers goods were to be landed, his Cargo being for different persons
and some of them having a like kind of packages, and the Bills of Lading being
to the order of the consignees of the shippers, a mistake had happened by the
Mate sending the said Merchandise (in the said Bill of Lading mentioned)
ashore, without a Permit for Landing thereof; that through this error, one of
the Inspectors made a Seizure of said Merchandise and had lodged them in
the Surveyors Office; he could not therefore deliver said goods" (DLC:GW).

2. Bertier & Company's petition was submitted to the House of Representatives on 26 April 1790 and ordered to lie on the table (*DHFC*, 3:378). At some
point the problem evidently was turned over to Alexander Hamilton. On 31
May 1790 Otho H. Williams, collector of customs at Baltimore, wrote Hamilton: "I am favored with a letter of the 18 Ulte from Messrs Bertier & Company
of Philadelphia . . . in which they inform me 'that the kind and favorable letter
they recd. last night from the honorable the Secretary of the Treasury gave
them the greatest hopes that I would be pleased to deliver their goods in the
manner the secretary writes it may be done'" (Syrett, *Hamilton Papers*, 6:451).
Neither Hamilton's letter to Bertier nor Bertier's letter to Williams has been
found. In his reply, 14 June, Hamilton referred Williams to recent action by
Congress to "shew you the line of proceeding to obtain relief in the case of the
Ship Van Staphorst. Messrs. Bertier & Company have had the same information" (ibid., 465). Hamilton is probably referring to "An Act to provide for
mitigating or remitting the forfeitures and penalties accruing under the revenue laws, in certain cases therein mentioned" (1 *Stat.* 122–23 [26 May 1790]),
which provided for submission of disputed cases to the district court.

William W. Morris to David Humphreys

Sir   New York April 20th 1790

I am directed by the Secretary of the Treasury, to request that
you will inform him, whether any of the States, have transmitted
to the President of the United States, Acts, ceding Territory for

the erection of Light houses upon—If any, what particular States.[1] I am Sir with Sentiments of the greatest respect your humble Servant

Wm W. Morris.

LB, DLC:GW.

    For an identification of William Walton Morris, see Morris to GW, 12 May 1789. Morris had applied unsuccessfully for the post of geographer of the United States and marshal of New York. He may have been working temporarily in the Treasury Department in early 1790.

    1. On 20 April Humphreys replied to Morris's letter: "The President of the United States has gone to Long Island; upon having recourse to his public papers, I believe that all the Acts which have been received from particular States have been communicated to Congress, and are deposited in the Office of the Secretary of State; where you will, I presume, be able to obtain all the necessary information on the subject of enquiry" (DLC:GW). GW had left New York for a five-day tour of Long Island early on the morning of Tuesday, 20 April. For his account of his journey, see *Diaries*, 6:63–67.

From Joel Barlow

Sir   Paris 24 April 1790

    The Marquis de Marnasia, who will do me the honor to wait on your Excellency with this, is a gentleman of great respectability, a member of the national Assembly, & enjoys considerable fortune.[1] He & many others are transfering their property to the United States, and are going to settle themselves on the Ohio near the Scioto. He requests me to take the liberty to announce to your Excellency their intentions, & to solicit for them your countenance & protection. I am confident of the good dispositions of these emigrants, that they will be industrious peaceable citizens & well attached to the Government under which they have chosen to reside. The Scioto Company for whom I act, has made sales of lands to a considerable number who are already gone & to many others who will soon follow them. I think it a fortunate circumstance for the interest of the United States that an agent for the sale of lands happened to be here at the time of this revolution in France. Great emigrations from this country must take place, and of consequence from many other parts of Europe, where the same spirit of emigration must inevitably extend. In governments so full of ancient & complicated abuses, &

in countries so full of inhabitants, it is in the nature of such reforms to render numbers of people of all classes uneasy with their situation. The rich cannot repair their shattered fortunes nor the poor find employment in any other country in Europe after leaving their own. There is therefore almost a physical necesity for their going to America. The United States is that part of America to which they are invited by the excellence of our government, and they are attracted to the Ohio by the excellence of the soil & climate. The vacant lands in that country offer to these people the very succour & consolation which they want, to render happy themselves & their posterity, under the administration of a government, which is regarded through Europe as the wisest & happiest in the world. It is doubtless for the interest of the United States (& I think it now in their power) to sink a considerable portion of the public debt by the sale of lands, & to introduce inhabitants, provided they are industrious. I think there can be no doubt of the good intentions of such men as purchase to go & cultivate for themselves, nor of the honest character of such hired laborers as they choose to accompany them. and none but people of these two classes will go.

I ask your Excellency's pardon for the trouble of so long a letter. As the object of it promises to be of considerable magnitude, I thought it a duty I owed to your station as the guardian of my country's welfare, as well as the dictate of personal veneration & respect, to make the communication to you in this early stage of the business. with every sentiment of gratitude & respect, I have the honor to be Sir your Excellency's obet & most humble servt

J. Barlow

ALS, DLC:GW.

For Joel Barlow's role in the Scioto Company, see Louis Le Bègue de Presle Duportail to GW, 10 Feb. 1790, and notes.

1. Claude-François-Adrien, marquis de Lézay-Marnésia (1735–1800), was a philosopher of wide-ranging interests. An advocate of legal and agricultural reform, he abolished the corvée on his own estate and wrote a number of works on natural history; he also published poetry, a novel, contributed to the *Encyclopédie*, and composed a ballet. As a member of the Estates General, he supported equal taxation and the abolition of feudal privileges. Marnésia was among the original "Twenty-four" who founded the Scioto Company in France. In late 1790 he left France, along with workingmen, farmers, and artists he had gathered to settle on land acquired from the company. This

visionary project foundered when the Scioto Company failed to fulfill its contract, although Marnésia's *Lettres écrites des rivers de l'Ohio* (Fort Pitt, 1801) indicates that the author still hoped to recoup his fortunes in America. In April 1792 Marnésia submitted a petition to Congress asking for a right of preemption to land on the Mississippi where he proposed establishing a settlement for French emigrants (*Petitions, Memorials, and Other Documents Submitted for the Consideration of Congress*, 158). The petition was submitted to a committee but apparently without result as Marnésia returned to France before the end of 1792. During his time in America, he evidently associated primarily with Royalist refugees from the regime in France, since one correspondent of Edmund Charles Genet lists him among French "gangrenous aristocrats" in Philadelphia (Childs, *French Refugee Life*, 49, 163.)

Another letter of recommendation for Marnésia came to GW from Louis Le Bègue de Presle Duportail. Duportail wrote GW on 27 April 1790 from Paris that "the revolution which takes place now in france has altered so much the situation of a certain Class of people that many of them disgusted with their native country determine to live in another. of that number is the marquis Marnesia who is to cross the atlantic and become the fellow cityzen of your excellency. his choice is a proof that he is not an ennemy to true liberty and a reasonable equality of the men. it may then seem extraordinary the marquis leaves france in this circumstance but probably he finds the french men have mistaken the liberty and is afraid that class of people who was really so much oppressed and so comptemptuously treated by the government and the nobility being reintegrated too rapidly and without degrees in their wrights will be disposed to exercise their veangeance againts the first class so that liberty justice will not be for her alone. I hope it will not be Case, but those who thinck otherwise have arguments and (we must Confess it) examples to justify their gloomy Conjectures. however it be, the marquis is a very Cleaver, sensible, good gentleman, and as I am persuaded that your excellency will find him such when you will make acquaintance with him I beg you to recommend him in virginia and in the Country of the ohio where he intends to make a settlement. if he finds himself there as well as he hopes; a great number of frenchmen Intend to follow his example. I cannot but approve of them. where can one man live more happi than under the governement of the united states. the americains seem to me to show themselves wiser than the old europeans notwistanding all their experience" (DLC:GW).

From Thomas Jefferson

New York. April 24. 1790.

The Constitution having declared that the President "shall *nominate*, & by & with the advice & consent of the Senate, shall *appoint* ambassadors other public ministers & consuls" the President desires my opinion whether the Senate has a right to negative the *grade* he may think it expedient to use in a foreign mission, as well as the *person* to be appointed?[1]

I think the Senate has no right to negative the *grade*.

The Constitution has divided the powers of government into three branches, Legislative, Executive & Judiciary, lodging each with a distinct magistracy. the Legislative it has given completely to the Senate & House of representatives: it has declared that "the Executive powers shall be vested in the President," submitting only special articles of it to a negative by the Senate; & it has vested the Judiciary power in the courts of justice, with certain exceptions also in favor of the Senate.

The transaction of business with foreign nations is Executive altogether. it belongs then to the head of that department, *except* as to such portions of it as are specially submitted to the Senate. *Exceptions* are to be construed strictly. the Constitution itself indeed has taken care to circumscribe this one within very strict limits: for it gives the *nomination* of the foreign Agent to the President, the *appointment* to him & the Senate jointly, & the *commissioning* to the President. this analysis calls our attention to the strict import of each term. to *nominate* must be to *propose: appointment* seems that act of the will which constitutes or makes the Agent: & the *Commission* is the public evidence of it. but there are still other acts previous to these, not specially enumerated in the Constitution; to wit 1. the destination of a mission to the particular country where the public service calls for it: & 2. the character, or grade to be employed in it. the natural order of all these is 1. destination. 2. grade. 3. nomination. 4. appointment. 5. commission. if *appointment* does not comprehend the neighboring acts of *nomination,* or *commission,* (& the constitution says it shall not, by giving them exclusively to the President) still less can it pretend to comprehend those previous & more remote of *destination* & *grade.* the Constitution, analysing the three last, shews they do not comprehend the two first. the 4th is the only one it submits to the Senate, shaping it into a right to say that "A. or B. is unfit to be appointed." now this cannot comprehend a right to say that "A. or B. is indeed fit to be appointed, but the grade fixed on is not the fit one to employ," or "our connections with the country of his destination are not such as to call for any mission." the Senate is not supposed by the Constitution to be acquainted with the concerns of the Executive department. it was not intended that these should be communicated to them; nor can they therefore be qualified to judge of the necessity which calls for a mission to any particular place, or of the particular grade, more or less marked, which special and secret circumstances may call for. all this is left to the President. they are only to see that no unfit person be employed.

It may be objected that the Senate may, by continual negatives on the *person,* do what amounts to a negative on the *grade;* & so indirectly defeat this right of the President. but this would be a breach of trust, an abuse of the power confided to the Senate, of which that body cannot be supposed capable. so the President has a power to convoke the legislature; & the Senate might defeat that power by refusing to come. this equally amounts to a negative on the power of convoking. yet nobody will say they possess such a negative, or would be capable of usurping it by such oblique means. if the Constitution had meant to give the Senate a negative on the grade or destination, as well as the person, it would have said so in direct terms, & not left it to be effected by a sidewind. it could never mean to give them the *use* of one power thro the *abuse* of another.

Th: Jefferson

ADS, MHi: Adams Family Papers, ADS (letterpress copy), DLC: Thomas Jefferson Papers; ADf, DLC: Thomas Jefferson Papers; LB, DLC:GW.

1. In his message to Congress of 8 Jan. 1790, GW wrote that "The interests of the United States require, that our intercourse with other nations should be facilitated by such provisions as will enable me to fulfil my duty in that respect, in the manner, which circumstances may render most conducive to the public good: And to this end, that the compensations to be made to the persons, who may be employed, should, according to the nature of their appointments, be defined by law; and a competent fund designated for defraying the expenses incident to the conduct of our foreign affairs." In response the House of Representatives appointed a committee to prepare a bill to provide compensation to members of the foreign service. This bill, designated the Foreign Intercourse Bill (HR-35), was presented on 21 January. It empowered the president to draw up to $40,000 out of the Treasury for the support of the foreign service and designated the maximum salaries to be paid to resident ministers, chargés d'affaires, and secretaries. In the ensuing debate Richard Bland Lee argued for inserting a clause requiring the president to obtain the advice and consent of the Senate before making disbursements (*DHFC*, 4:698–701). This proposal and the attendant debate raised the possibility that the Senate might attempt to use the power over disbursements to control the number, grade, and placement of American diplomats abroad. The issues at stake were crucial to the establishment of the diplomatic service, as well as to the broader division of authority over foreign affairs between Congress and

the president. Under the Articles of Confederation, the Continental Congress had control of foreign affairs, including the naming and placement of diplomats, as well as their instructions, rank, and pay. The federal Constitution had shifted most of this power to the president, acting in some situations with the "advice and consent" of the Senate. The extent of Senate authority under the "advice and consent" provision remained uncertain, however, and GW was determined to resist legislation based on this provision that might undermine executive authority over foreign affairs. The House bill was recommitted on 24 Mar., and a new bill, designated the Foreign Intercourse Act (HR-52), was presented on 31 March. On 8 April debate on the measure was postponed until 27 April (*DHFC*, 4:702–3). The new bill did not contain a provision requiring the president to obtain the advice and consent of the Senate before disbursing funds, but GW seemingly anticipated that the proposal would again be introduced, or that some other amendment might be offered that would compromise executive authority over foreign affairs. The issues at stake were crucial to the establishment of the diplomatic service, a matter to which GW devoted a great deal of time and attention during the spring of 1790. GW and Jefferson first discussed diplomatic appointments on 23 Mar., two days after Jefferson's arrival. On 26 Mar. they discussed the Foreign Intercourse Bill, which had just been recommitted, agreeing that the diplomatic service would require between $36,000 and $50,000 annually, and on 16 April they had a long discussion about the consular establishment. GW probably asked Jefferson for a written opinion on the issues raised by the Foreign Intercourse Act at this meeting or shortly after. GW was on his tour of Long Island from 20 April to 24 April and doubtless received Jefferson's written opinion immediately after his return (*Diaries*, 6:51–52, 54, 60, 64–66). In addition to Jefferson, GW consulted James Madison, John Jay, and probably John Adams about these issues. On 27 April, the day debate on the Foreign Intercourse Act resumed in the House, GW "Had some conversation with Mr. Madison on the propriety of consulting the Senate on the places to which it would be necessary to send persons in the Diplomatic line, and Consuls; and with respect to the grade of the first. His opinion coincides with Mr. Jays and Mr. Jeffersons—to wit—that they have no Constitutional right to interfere with either, & that it might be impolitic to draw it into a precedent, their powers extending no farther than to an approbation or disapprobation of the person nominated by the President all the rest being Executive and vested in the President by the Constitution" (ibid., 68). No written opinion by John Jay on this matter has been found. A copy of Jefferson's letter, in his writing and endorsed by GW "Construction of the Powers of the Senate with respect to their agency in appointg Ambassadors &c. and fixing the grade," is in MHi: Adams Papers, suggesting that GW consulted Adams about the matter as well. After debate resumed in the House, it became clear that the size of the appropriation constituted the principal challenge to executive authority over the diplomatic service. On 30 April the House set the appropriation at $30,000, which threatened to make it impossible for GW to appoint resident ministers to both France and England and to provide proper representation elsewhere (*DHFC*, 4:704–5). Debate then moved to the Senate. On 3 May the Senate referred the House bill to a committee consisting of Strong, Ellsworth, Carroll, Maclay, and Few.

The committee reported on 7 May. On that day GW recorded in his diary: "As the House of Representatives had reduced the Sum, in a Bill to provide for the expences of characters in the diplomatic line, below what would enable the Executive to employ the number which the exigencies of Government might make it necessary I thought it proper to intimate to a member or two of the Senate the places that were in contemplation to send persons to in this Line—viz to France & England (when the latter manifested a disposition to treat us with more respect than She had done upon a former occasion) Ministers Plenipotentiary and to Spain, Portugal & Holland Chargé des Affaires and having an opportunity, mentioned the matter unofficially both to Mr. [Charles] Carroll & Mr. [Ralph] Izard" (*Diaries,* 6:75). Carroll was a member of the committee to which the bill was referred by the Senate on 3 May. The Senate considered the committee report on 10 May and ordered the bill recommitted. A final committee report was delivered on 25 May. The Senate passed an amended version of the House bill on 26 May, but the House refused to agree to the changes, and the bill was referred to a conference committee on 31 May. When a compromise bill was reported in the Senate on 23 June, William Maclay recorded that the bill had been referred "to a Committee of Conferrence so long That I had forgot it. but the thing was neither dead nor sleeping. It was only dressing. and friends making. The report encreased the Salaries. and added 10,000 dollars to the Appropriations. I concluded that they had secured Friends enough to support it. before they committed it to the House. This turned out to be the case. The Whole appropriation was 40,000 Doll. and they were voted with an air of perfect indifference. by the affirmants. altho' I consider the Money as Worse than thrown away. For I know not of a Single thing, that we have for a single Minister to do at a Single Court in Europe. indeed the less We have for them to do the better. Our Business is to pay them What We owe and the less Political connection the better, with any European power. It was well spoke against. I voted against every part of it" (Bowling and Veit, *Diary of William Maclay,* 301). Both houses agreed to the compromise bill on 25 June. On 30 June GW noted in his diary the passage of the bill appropriating $40,000, which he signed on 1 July (*Diaries,* 6:78–79). While Congress was considering this legislation, the Senate took up GW's nominations for the consular service. Senate actions on these nominations in June also constituted a challenge to executive authority over foreign affairs (see GW to the U.S. Senate, 4 June 1790, note 1).

From Noailles

Dear Général   Paris April 24th 1790.

I have, tho' remote incessantly borne you that share of admiration you have filled every french man's breast with who has marched under your colours; it is not only now with a Spirit replete with freedom that I durst address you, but partaking of all the rights nature has reserved to mankind and america has reaped the first benefits of. in the french revolution which portends the greatest blessings almost all those who have beheld the foundation of liberty in the United Provinces, have brought from thence of american Spirit and have displayed it with undaunted courage as they have had a hand in preparing the revolution so are they doomed in firmly supporting its Establishment. Such a Brotherhood has been of the utmost help, and will be our greatest prop. it is in your power to contribute to its indissolubility by a deed both equitable and useful, the National dignities are the only badges we Set a value on, and are willing to preserve. the Cross of St Lewis, the Sign of military Service is going to be confered throughout all the rangs of the army; Condescend in granting the Same favour on all the officers who have been under your orders and who have contributed as well as we to the salvation of the Commonwealth, Condescend to obtain for them the right of bearing the order of Cincinnatus, we Shall hold the dearer, when we behold our brethren dignified with it.[1] fill up their Vow and our own it is in the name of the small army you had Some esteem for I durst petition the favour. it is granting us a second Reward of having our fellow at arms honoured as well as we with a benefaction that evinced that liberty has been labour'd for. Such a bounty were less pleasing and were perhaps impossible in Experiencing its influence if you were not so generous as to diffuse it over all those who are intitled to it.

the deliberation to be held on this request is that the officers of the french army who were in America at the time Mr de Rochambeau left the continent to repair to the leaward islands as also those of the legion of Lauzun be indulged with the leave of bearing the order of Cincinnatus provided they give an unexceptionable testimony of their Service and obtain a Certificate of their corps revised and signed by General Rochambeau.

Numbers of french officers have brought from the american war but scars. they will receive an healing remedy when they have an additional proof of their service. I have the honour to be with respect Dear Général Your most humble and obedient servant

Noailles
a member of the National assembly

ALS, DSoCi.

Louis-Marie, vicomte de Noailles (1756–1804), Lafayette's brother-in-law, served as colonel of the Soissonnais Regiment in Rochambeau's army and was instrumental in constructing the allied works before Yorktown. Noailles continued in the army after the war, eventually reaching the rank of *maréchal de camp* (brigadier general). In 1789 he embraced the cause of the French Revolution. As a member of the Constituent Assembly on the night of 4 Aug. 1789, Noailles proposed the redemption of feudal dues and the abolition of seigneurial corvées and all remaining personal servitude, reforms that effectively dismantled the legal foundations of the feudal regime. By 1792 Noailles was disillusioned with the excesses of the Revolutionary regime and emigrated to England. In 1793 he came to the United States and remained until 1800. For a discussion of the difficulties his presence caused for GW, see GW to Alexander Hamilton, 5 May 1793.

1. The founders of the Society of the Cincinnati, "deeply impressed with a sense of the generous assistance this country has received from France," extended the privilege of membership to the four French admirals who had served in the Revolution along with Rochambeau and "the Generals and Colonels of his army" (Myers, *Liberty without Anarchy,* 263–64). See also d'Estaing to GW, 8 Jan. 1784, Barras to GW, 23 Jan. 1784, La Bretonnière to GW, 1 Feb. 1784, n.1, Lafayette to GW, 9 Mar. 1784, Pierre-Charles L'Enfant to GW, 29 April 1784, General Meeting of the Society of the Cincinnati, 4–18 May 1784, appendix 3. Later, captains and majors were admitted to membership if they had reached the rank of colonel in the French army. Lafayette and Rochambeau were hesitant to present new candidates for membership, in part because the king, who oversaw the admission of new members, was reluctant to sponsor the extension of a society associated with a republican revolution. Louis XVI forbade admission of new members in September 1784 and, after making some exceptions, renewed the prohibition on 17 April 1785 (Meyers, *Liberty without Anarchy,* 145–76; Rochambeau to GW, 9 Sept. 1784). The progress of the French Revolution and the decline of royal authority apparently prompted Noailles, who was an active member of the French society as well as a leader of reform in the assembly, to ask GW to authorize the extension of membership to all French officers who had served in America without regard to the standing royal prohibition against new members. GW did not respond to Noailles's request. The act of the French assembly of 19 June 1790, abolishing hereditary titles, made further efforts to extend the membership of the Cincinnati unlikely, and on 18 Nov. 1793 the convention effectively suppressed the order by decreeing that "all citizens decorated with the cross of Saint Louis or other decorations" who did not turn them in would be subject to arrest (translation, Contenson, *La Société des Cincinnati de France,* 76–77).

To James Madison

Tuesday, 27th Apl 1790
If the weather will permit, & Mr Madison's health suffer him
to go out to day, the Presdt would be glad if he would give him
a call before he goes to the House.[1]

Transcript, MH: Sparks Transcripts.
 1. Madison was ill with influenza during the last week or so of April but was
well enough to consult with GW on 27 April about the Foreign Intercourse
Act (*Diaries*, 6:68). For the substance of this meeting, see Thomas Jefferson to
GW, 24 April 1790, n.1. On 2 May Madison wrote to his father that "The
influenza or something like it but less severe has revisited this quarter of the
Union. I have had an attack which has kept me at home for several days. I am
now pretty well over it, and shall resume my seat in the House tomorrow, or
at least shall be able to do it" (Rutland, *Madison Papers*, 13:183–84).

To the Virginia Legislature

United States [New York]
Gentlemen,   April 27th 1790
With a due sense of the affectionate terms in which your affection is conceived, I offer my best thanks for your congratulations on my election to the Chief Magistracy of a free and enlightened Nation.[1]
If I have been enabled to make use of whatever abilities
Heaven has been pleased to confer upon me, with any advantage to our common Country, I consider it not less owing to the
fostering encouragement I received in early life from the Citizens of the Commonwealth in which I was born, than to the
persevering support I have since experienced from my fellow-
Citizens collectively, in the course of their exertions, which, under Divine Providence, saved their Liberties and established
their Independence.
However I may have confirmed my professions by my conduct, I can claim no merit for having been involved in the duties
of a military command through necessity, or for having retired
to the state of a private citizen through inclination. But I may
be permitted to avow, that the construction you are pleased to
put upon my motives for returning to public life is peculiarly
satisfactory to me. Because I receive, from the voice of my Coun-

trymen, the only reward I wished for the sacrafice—a just interpretation of the principles by which, I am conscious, I have
been actuated.

Accustomed to have my actions viewed through a favorable
medium by my fellow-Citizens in general, and more especially
by those of my native State; I can but poorly compensate for
such indulgence, by the purest emotions of gratitude, demonstrated in an active devotion to that Republican Government,
which is so deservedly the first object of their political attachment.

In looking forward to that awful moment, when I must bid
adieu to Sublunary Scenes, I anticipate the consolation of leaving our Country in a prosperous condition. And, while the cur-
tain of seperation shall be drawing, my last breath will, I trust,
expire in a prayer for the temporal and eternal felicity of those,
who have not only endeavoured to gild the evening of my days
with unclouded serenity, but extended their desires to my happiness hereafter in a brighter world.

Go: Washington

ALS, CSmH; LB, DLC:GW.

1. The address, dated 28 Oct. 1789, was presented to GW by Richard Henry
Lee and John Walker soon after their arrival in New York to attend the second
session of Congress. GW's reply was presented to the two Virginia senators on
the same day (*Diaries*, 6:68). There was apparently some discussion among
members of the assembly concerning the address. Edmund Randolph wrote
to James Madison on 26 Sept. 1789 that "The president is supposed to have
written to Mr. Adams, while titles were in debate, that if any were given, he
would resign. Whether it be true or not, it is a popular report. However I
question if even this, added to his services will draw forth from the assembly
an address of congratulation. I will endeavour to prevent any pain to him, or
imputation on Virginia. But I fear the ardor of those, who wish to be conspicuous, will not suffer them to be prudent" (Rutland, *Madison Papers*, 12:421).

The address from the legislature reads: "The General Assembly of your
native State embrace the first moment in their power, to present the congratulations of your countrymen, on your elevation to the magistracy of a free and
enlightened nation:

"In early life you engaged the affections of your fellow citizens, by the exercise of those social virtues which have so eminently marked your conduct, and
acquired their confidence, by the display of those abilities, which afterwards
saved their liberties, and established their independence:

"That you were a citizen, was never forgotten by you whilst a soldier, and
the end of your military command confirmed the professions with which you
commenced it:

"The very toils and dangers through which you have passed for our defence, although they sanctified your claim to retirement, yet by presenting an earnest of your worth, created a title in your fellow citizens to demand your return to public action. Yes, sir, you have been called to your present high station by the unanimous voice of a free people; you have obeyed them with a peculiar greatness of mind, disdaining all scruples which could induce even a momentary pause, and renouncing that domestic tranquillity, which you sought as the reward of victory:

"Devoted as we are to republican government, we fear not to utter these truths to you, for we believe you will feel no emotions from the cordial offerings of universal praise, but those which the purest virtue inspires:

"We look forward therefore, with ardent hopes that you may long continue the instrument of general happiness, and when the awful moment shall arrive, in which, the citizen most distinguished for his piety, wisdom, valor and patriotism, must quit this sublunary scene, the people of Virginia can be consoled, only by their firm persuasion, that he is summoned to meet that well earned recompense, which gratitude itself cannot render upon earth" (*Journal of the House of Delegates*, 1789, 19).

On 30 Oct. 1789 the assembly voted to send another address to GW concerning Indian affairs, which came with a covering letter from Gov. Beverley Randolph (Vi: Executive Letter Books). No reply from GW to this address has been found. "It has been a great relief to our apprehensions for the safety of our brethren on the frontiers, to learn from the communications of the Secretary at War, that their protection against the incursions of the Indians has occupied your attention.

"Knowing the power of the Federal Executive to concentrate the American force, and confiding in the wisdom of its measures, we should leave the subject unnoticed, but from a belief that time has been wanting to gain the proper intelligence, and make the necessary arrangements of defence for a country so far remote from the seat of government. Many members of the General Assembly now present, have been either witnesses of the recent murders and depredations committed by the savages, or have brought with them information, the truth of which cannot be questioned. It is unnecessary to enter into a detail of those hostilities. Permit us only to say that those parts of Kentucky, and the southwestern and northern counties lying on the Ohio and its waters, which have generally been the scene of Indian barbarity, are now pressed by danger the most imminent.

"We have been induced to suppose it possible, that for the purpose of affording effectual relief, it may be found expedient to carry war into the country of the Indian enemy; should this be the case, we take the liberty of assuring you that this Commonwealth will cheerfully sustain her proportion of the expenses which may be incurred in such an expedition.

"The same causes which induced us thus to offer the treasure of Virginia, have occasioned another proceeding, which we think proper to communicate to you; it is indeed incumbent on us to make this communication, least in case of silence it might be interpreted into a design of passing the limits of State authority.

"Chiefs of the Chickasaw nation have solicited the General Assembly for a supply of ammunition; the advanced season of the year, and their anxiety to return home, owing to the perilous situation of their nation, who were in daily expectation that hostilities would be commenced against them by the Creeks, have determined them to stop here, and not to proceed to New York, the place of their original destination.

"The resolution which we have now the honor of enclosing you, will therefore be executed in their favor; and we trust that our conduct, from the peculiar circumstances of the case, will be acceptable to yourself and the Congress of the United States; and being approved that we shall receive retribution for the expense we have thereby incurred" (ibid., 24–25).

To the United States Senate

United States [New York]
April 28th 1790

Gentlemen of the Senate

I nominate George Wray to be Collector of the port of Hampton in the State of Virginia in the place of Jacob Wray resigned:[1] also John McCullough to be Surveyor of the port of Swansborough in the District of Wilmington and William Benson to be Surveyor of the port of Windsor in the District of Edenton, both in the State of North Carolina.

Go: Washington

LS, DNA: RG 46, First Congress, Records of Executive Proceedings, President's Messages—Executive Nominations; LB, DLC:GW.

1. This appointment was intended for George Wray, Jr., son of Jacob Wray, rather than Jacob Wray's brother, George Wray. In a letter to GW of 12 May, George Wray, Jr., attempted to explain the confusion, noting that he had received "by Mr Thos Nelson a Commission under your signature for George Wray as Collector of this Port on the 11th Inst:, the direction was to Mr George Wray surveyor of the Port of Hampton, now sir as I have acted as my Fathers deputy & all the Offices of this port being vested in one of Collr I as the acting Officer in measuring the Vessels that were to be register'd or licenced in filling up the blanks generally put my name in the certificate of registry or licence as surveyor, therefore have taken the Commission upon myself, but as my Father omited in his letters of resignation when he mentioned me as his deputy to put junior to my name & as I have an Uncle of the same name at this port (although never employed as an Officer of the Customs) am in some doubt as to the intention & Commission, but shall continue to act as D: Collr untill farther information" (DLC:GW). Jacob Wray had resigned in March. See his letter to GW, 24 Mar. 1790. He wrote on 12 May that his son was continuing as the acting office at Hampton "till a small doubt may be got over by him. . . . Law matters now a days every minutia is so fine drawed & Extended as if for controversalist only" (DLC:GW). On 23 May Tobias Lear acknowleged George

Wray's letter and informed him that the president "directed me to inform you that you were the person appointed to fill that office upon the resignation of your father—and the addition of Junior not being inserted in the commission arose from not knowing that any other person of the same name resided at Hampton" (DLC:GW).

From Lund Washington

Dr Sir   Hay Field [Va.] April 28th 1790

Yours of the 11th with your assent to Doctr Stuarts and Alexanders agreement inclosed,[1] I have received. however injurious Mr Custis's bargain with Alexander has been to his Estate, I cannot but think that it's now fortunate for the Estate that a Compromise is to take place—had Mr Custis's Tender been Made in the proper paper Money there is no doubt but the payment wou'd have been Legal, for no one Doubts his haveg a right at any time to pay £48000. his not haveg made that payment with the Legal currency of the Country it remains still to be done, and most people think with nothing less than £48000—but shoud the high Court of Chancery judge the payment to be made agreeable to the Scale of Depreciation it cannot be less than £1200 for money was at 4. for 1. at the time Mr Custis had possession, or rather made the purchase, and carry it on until the Deeds were made it will be £8000. but the great fear is the Chancellor may decree £48000 thinking it wrong to alter so possitive an agreement—and if the Currency of the Country at the End of the 21 years shoud be equal to Gold & Silver, the Estate perhaps woud not amt to more than what woud pay it, the Children born & Educated in expectation of a Fortune, left without a shilling, upon the whole I rejoice, I feel pleased, that the bargain bad as it has been & expensive to the Estate, is likely to End & the worse known. I Loved the Father, and I Love the Children and wish them every good.

I am told that Colo. Mason either was or pretended to be vexd at his appointment saying that it was a ps. of D—n'd impudence to send him a Commission to act under a Government that he never had subscribed to, but had openly opposed & condemnd, altho the expression is some thing like Mason yet I hope that a man of his good understandg, & time of life woud not make use of so rude a return for the Compliment made him, for surely he must consider it as such rather than an Insult, beside I am informd by Mr Hector Ross who is much at Gunston that he thinks Masons acrimony agnst the Constitution much abated.[2] Ross says that Mason is generally condemg the Pomp & parade that is going on at New York, and tells of a number of useless ceremonies that is now in fashion, swearing by G–d that if the President was not an uncommon Man—we shoud soon have the Devil to pay—but hoped & indeed did not fear so long as it pleased God to keep him at the Head—but it woud be out of the power of those Damnd Monarchical fellows with the Vice president, & the Women to ruin the Nation—that Mason has seen some poem in which the Vice president is much Satarised & was so pleased at it, that he took two copys of it in his own handwriteg,[3] so far as I am able to judge all that I have seen or heard speak of the Government are well pleased, it must be a Mortification to the opposers of Government in this Cty to see things turn out so different from what they told the Common people woud be the event of it—Commerse is Flourishg & every species of produce that the Farmer can raise he can sell at a high price, the port of Alexandria has seldom less than 20. Square Riggd Sale of Vessles in it and often many more—the Streets are crowded with waggons & the people all seem busy—while Commerse was regulated by the Virginia Laws, the Warfs were growg over with grass, the Houses uninhabited & the people lookd dejected.

They have obtaind a Law for moveg the Court House from Alexandria to a more centrical place, by the industry & activity of Mr Chichester, this was done, no one actg agnst him until it was too late, but the people generally who sign'd a petition for the removal seem now sorry for it, & one will be presented next session for continuing it where it is, so that it is probable it may still remain in Alexandria,[4] Mr Roger West who has twice been very honourably elected to serve in the assembly was the other Day thrown out because his conduct with respect to the Courthouse business, has not been approved of[5]—Since Last september my Eyes have been in an alarmg Situation, it was then feard I shoud lose the sight of them altogether, but I thank God it has not been the case—the one that was swelld, under it, before you left home is more so now, & I fear must ee'r long have an opperation perform'd on it, it matters much & is often very sore

though not painfull—the other is in bad condition it has generally a small inflamation in it which causes it to be very weak &
tender, the water from it, runing down my cheeks so that I am
in a Manner deprived almost of the pleasure of readg or
writeg—The weather is uncommonly cold for the Season I feard
last night a Frost that might injure the Wheat—at this Moment
it is snowing very fast & the ground almost covered the Wheat
Crops in this Neighbourhood in general are promiseg & the
growth forwarder than is common at this time of the year—I
was the other Day through yr Field at Morrises, Frenches & the
Ferry, the first is much injured by the Winters Frost—but abt
one half of the Feild layg on the side next the slipe of Meadow
is very fine looks perfectly green, & is almost knee high—the 2d
is so little injured by the Frost as not to make it worth Mentiong
and the wheat is as good ⟨*illegible*⟩ as is common—the 3d I think
will scarcely make more than 100 bushels I never see a Feild of
that extent have so little Wheat on it, I am told it was well taken
in the Fall.

We hope to have the pleasure of seeg Mrs Washington & you
on a visit to Mt Vernon in the Course of the summer, for a visit
I expect will be all that ever will be permited you, no person has
an idea but that you must remain at the head of the Government
so long as you Live—which I pray God may be with some degree of Comfort and satisfaction to yourself, for I have no doubt
but your fatigue, trouble, & vexation is very great—I have wrote
until I can scarcely read what I have writen, My most respectfull
compliments to Mrs Washington & Love to the two Dear Children, W. & N.—in which I am join'd by Mrs Washington—and
believe me Dr Sir now, as I ever have been, yr warmest Friend &
very Hbl: Servt

Lund Washington

ALS, ViMtV.

1. Letter not found, but see David Stuart to GW, 2 April 1790 and notes.
The first paragraph of Lund Washington's letter deals with the protracted
dispute between Stuart, as administrator of the Custis estate, and Robert Alex-
ander. See Stuart to GW, 14 July 1789, n.7, 12 Sept., 3 Dec. 1789, 11, 15, 23
Mar. 1790, GW to Stuart, 21 Sept. 1789, 28 Mar. 1790, Edmund Randolph to
GW, 23 Dec. 1789.

2. Washington is referring to George Mason's appointment as U.S. senator
from Virginia to replace William Grayson who died on 12 March. Gov. Beverley Randolph wrote Mason on 25 Mar., enclosing the appointment. Mason, in

a letter to Randolph of 27 Mar., declined the appointment, "my present State of Health (if I had no other Objection) rendering me unable to discharge the Duties of the Office" (Rutland, *Mason Papers*, 3:1191–92). Hector Ross was a Colcester, Va., merchant. Both Mason and GW did a considerable amount of business with him since his establishment served as a store of convenience for clothing and other necessities for GW's tenants, slaves, and white servants.

3. The "Women" probably refers to the wives and daughters of Federalist politicians who critics charged were turning GW's government into a republican court complete with the trappings of monarchy. No copy of a poem satirizing John Adams has been found among George Mason's surviving papers. Mason may have been pleased by the satirical verses aimed at Adams by "Republican," which originally appeared in the *Massachusetts Centinel*.

> Be grateful then, YE CHOSEN! mod'rate wise,
> Nor stretch your claims to such preposterous size,
> Lest your too partial country—wiser grown—
> Shou'd on your native dunghills set you down.
> Ape not the fashions of the foreign great,
> Nor make your betters at your *levees* wait—
> Resign your awkward pomp, parade and pride,
> And lay that useless *etiquette* aside;
> The unthinking laugh, but all the thinking hate
> Such vile, abortive mimickry of State;
> Those idle lackeys, saunt'ring at your door,
> But ill become *poor servants* of the POOR.

The poet further enjoined his readers to resist "the lawless lust of POW'R in embryo" and to "resist the VICE—and that contagious pride / To that o'erweening VICE—so near all'y'd" (Page Smith, *John Adams* [New York, 1962], 2:778).

4. Washington is referring to "An act for altering the place of holding courts in the county of Fairfax," passed 4 Dec. 1789, which represented that the courthouse in Alexandria was inconvenient to most of the residents of the county and provided that on or before 1 June 1790 the justices should levy "on the tithable persons within their county a sum sufficient to erect the necessary buildings, and to purchase two acres of ground whereon to place them, and that they provide for building a courthouse, prison, pillory and stocks on the lands of William Fitzhugh, gentleman, or on the lands of any other person, within one mile of the Cross Roads, at Price's ordinary, and that after such buildings shall be completed, the courts for the said county shall be held at the said place" (13 Hening 79). Mr. Chichester is probably Richard Chichester (c.1736–1796), originally of Lancaster County, Va., and a distant relative of GW. In the mid-1760s Chichester moved from Lancaster to Fauquier County but in 1774 bought land on Accotink Creek in Fairfax County and settled there with his family.

5. Roger West (c.1755–1801) was a justice of the peace for Fairfax County c.1787–99 and represented Fairfax County in the Virginia house of delegates, 1788–89, 1791–92, and 1797–99.

From Silas W. Arnett

Sir,   New York 29th April 1790.

The Judicial system being extended to North Carolina, I take the liberty of offering my services to the United States as their attorney for that district. I have practiced law in that State near seven years & feel a confidence in my abilities to discharge the duties of the office. The honorable Hugh Williamson (who represents the district wherein I live) & the other representatives from the State of North Carolina can vouch for my private Character. I have the honor to be with great esteem, sir, Your most Obedient Servant

S. W. Arnett

ALS, DLC:GW.

Silas W. Arnett (d. 1806) began his career as a printer in New Bern. He took up the practice of law about 1783 and served as a Federalist in the North Carolina Ratifying Convention in 1789 (Powell, *Dictionary of North Carolina Biography*, 1:47–8). Timothy Bloodworth suggested Arnett, along with four others, as a suitable candidate for U.S. attorney for North Carolina (Bloodworth to GW, 5 June 1790). Arnett did not receive the appointment, which went to John Sitgreaves (*DHFC*, 2:79).

From Thomas Jefferson

Thursday Apr. 29. 1790.

Mr Jefferson has the honor to submit to the President draughts of letters to mr Short and the Marquis de la Luzerne.[1] as to the former he asks his attention to the paragraph respecting the devices for the Medal.[2] he hopes he will change and accomodate the letter to M. de la Luzerne to his own ideas of the part that gentleman acted, & of the length proper to go in expressing our sense of it.[3] the President was a witness, where Th: J. had only hearsay evidence, and may therefore have formed ideas not just.[4] he will have the honor of waiting on the President tomorrow on these subjects.

AL, DNA: RG 59, Miscellaneous Letters; LB, DLC:GW.

1. The enclosures, drafts of Jefferson's letters to William Short and to Anne-César, chevalier de La Luzerne, both dated 30 April 1790, are in DNA: RG 59, Miscellaneous Letters. Final drafts of Jefferson's letters to Short and La Luzerne are in Boyd, *Jefferson Papers*, 16:394–96.

2. Jefferson called GW's attention to the following paragraph in his letter to Short: "It has become necessary to determine on a present proper to be given to Diplomatic Characters on their taking leave of us; and it is concluded that a medal and chain of Gold will be the most convenient; I am therefore to ask the favor of you to order the dies to be engraved with all the dispatch practicable. The medal must be of 30 lines diameter, with a loop on the edge to receive the chain. On one side must be the Arms of the United States, of which I send you a written description and several impressions in wax to render that more intelligible, round them as a Legend must be 'the United States of America.' The device of the other side we do not decide on. One suggestion has been a Columbia (a fine female figure) delivering the emblems of peace and commerce to a Mercury, with the Legend 'Peace and Commerce' circumscribed, and the date of our Republic, to wit, IV Jul. MDCCLXXVI. subscribed as an Exergum. But having little confidence in our own ideas in an Art not familiar here, they are only suggested to you, to be altered, or altogether postponed to such better device as you may approve on consulting with those who are in the habit and study of Medals. Duvivier and Dupré seem to be the best workmen, perhaps the last is best of the two" (Boyd, *Jefferson Papers*, 16:396).

3. Rather than make changes to Jefferson's letter, GW wrote a separate letter to La Luzerne (see GW to La Luzerne, 29 April 1790).

4. GW recorded on 29 April that he "fixed with the Secretary of State on the present which (according to the custom of other Nations) should be made to Diplomatic characters when they return from that employment in this Country and this was a gold Medal, suspended to a gold Chain—in ordinary to be of the value of about 120 or 130 Guineas. Upon enquiry into the practice of other Countries, it was found, that France generally gave a gold Snuff-box set with diamonds; & of differt. costs; to the amount, *generally,* to a Minister Plenipotentiary of 500 Louisdores—That England usually gave to the same grade 300 guineas in *Specie*—And Holld. a Medal & Chain of the value of, in common, 150 or 180 Guineas the value of which to be encreas'd by an additional weight in the chain when they wished to mark a distinguished character. The Reason why a medal & Chain was fixed upon for the American present, is, that the die being once made the Medals could at any time be struck at very little cost, & the Chain made by our own artizans, which (while the first should be retained as a memento) might be converted into Cash" (*Diaries*, 6:70–71).

To La Luzerne

Sir.   New York April 29th 1790.

Your letter of the 17th of Janry, replete with politeness to myself & useful informations respecting public affairs, has but lately been received.

In making my acknowledgments for the distinguished place I hold in your remembrance & for the obliging terms in which you allude to my conduct in war & peace; I should do injustice to conceal the favorable sentiments which were always entertained by myself & my Countrymen of your private deportment, & ministerial agency, while you resided in America. Those times, in which we always found you a sincere friend, were truly times of peril & distress. Now our situation is indeed much more eligible, & our prospects perhaps as good as could reasonably have been expected. We are recovering slowly from the calamities & burdens with which we were almost overwhelmed by a long & expensive war. Our Crops the year past have been more abundant, & our markets much better than usual. These circumstances will assist in enabling our Citizens to extricate themselves from their private & public debts. I hope a disposition will be found to prevail among us, for doing justice (as far as the nature of the case will admit) to all who afforded us their assistance in the hour of adversity. In the arrangement of such new & complicated business, as must inevitably come before our general Government, it is reasonably to be expected, that the proceedings will be slow—It is devoutly to be wished that they may terminate in such just & wise measures, as will fully establish our happiness at home & credit abroad. I am much pleased with the interest you take in our national reputation, and the information you give that our credit is becoming so respectable in Europe, under the influence of our new Government.

You are right in conceiving that nothing can be indifferent to me, which regards the welfare of the French Nation. So far removed from that great Theatre of political action, & so little acquainted with many of the minute circumstances which may induce important decisions, as I am; it would be imprudent for me to hazard opinions which might possibly be unfounded. Indeed the whole business is so extraordinary in its commencement, so wonderful in its progress & may be so stupendous in its consequences, that I am almost lost in the contemplation. Of one thing, however, you may rest perfectly assured, that nobody is more anxious for the happy issue of that business than I am; as nobody can wish more sincerely for the prosperity of the French Nation than I do. Nor is it without the most sensible pleasure I learn, that our friend the Marquis de la Fayette, has, in acting the arduous part which has fallen to his share, conducted himself with so much wisdom & apparently to such general satisfaction.

We, at this great distance from the nothern parts of Europe, hear of wars & rumours of wars—as if they were the events or reports of another Planet. What changes the death of the Emperor will occasion in the other Cabinets of Europe, time is yet to inform us. A spirit for political improvements seems to be rapidly & extensively spreading through many of the European Countries. I shall rejoice in seeing the condition of the Human Race happier than ever it has hitherto been. But I should be sorry to see, that those who are for prematurely accelerating those improvements, were making *more haste than good speed, in* their innovations. So much prudence, so much perseverance, so much disinterestedness & so much patriotism are necessary among the Leaders of a Nation, in order to promote the national felicity, that sometimes my fears nearly preponderate over my expectations. Better, however, will it be for me to leave such foreign matters to those who are more competent to manage them: and to do as much good as I can, in the little sphere where I am destined to move at present. With sentiments of the highest esteem & consideration I have the honor to be Your Excellency's &c. &c. &c.

Df, DNA: RG 59, Miscellaneous Letters; LB, DLC:GW.

From Daniel Benezet, Jr.

[April 1790]

His Excellency the President of the United States

The Petition of the Subscriber resident at Great Egg Harbour in the County of Gloucester in the State of New Jersey Humbly Sheweth that your Petitioner is informed a Port of Entry is appointed on Great Egg harbour aforesaid and that an Officer of the Customs is to be appointed at said Port, therefore your Petitioner with all Deferrence solicits the Honour of being commissioned for said Office & begs leave to refer your Excellency to the Honourable Robert Morris William Patterson & Jonothan Elmer Esquirs. of the Senate & the Honourable the Speaker of the House of Representatives & Thomas Fitzsimonds & Thomas Sinnickson Esquires of House of Representatives for his Character & your Petitioner as in Duty bound will ever Pray

Daniel Benezet Junior

ALS, DLC:GW.

Daniel Benezet, Jr. (1760–1798), was born in Philadelphia, the son of merchant Daniel Benezet and grandson of Philadelphia reformer and antislavery advocate Anthony Benezet. During the later stages of the Revolution, the younger Benezet served in the Pennsylvania militia and was made a second lieutenant in 1780. By 1790 he was established in Great Egg Harbor, where he operated a gristmill and a sawmill and was a justice of the peace for Gloucester County. Benezet sent his application to his father in Philadelphia, who enclosed it in a letter of his own to Robert Morris on 30 April 1790. Morris presented the letter and application to GW on 3 May 1790. All of these letters are in DLC:GW. GW appointed Benezet collector of customs at Great Egg Harbor on 7 Aug. 1790, and the Senate confirmed his appointment on the same day (*DHFC*, 2:90). Benezet was appointed excise inspector on 6 Mar. 1792.

From John Brown Cutting

Sir   London 1 May 1790

I take the liberty to inclose you an english newspaper wherein is inserted the copy of a treaty between the king of Prussia and the sublime Porte.[1] This copy I am informed by a foreigner of veracity who perused the original at the house of the imperial minister, is a genuine translation. The terms of it are such that a war between the respective parties to it in conjunction with the kings of Sweden and Poland against the austrian and russian empires it is believed here must immediately and inevitably ensue.

Wishing You to possess the earliest intelligence of an ⟨*illegible*⟩ that menaces the peace of Europe I make no other apology for fulfilling ⟨*illegible*⟩ish than assuring you that it originated in a belief that such a communication might be useful to the United States and wou'd not be deemed improper or obtrusive, in Your respectful and most obedt sert

John Brown Cutting

ALS, DNA: RG 59, Miscellaneous Letters.

1. On 31 Jan. 1790 the Prussian minister at Constantinople signed a treaty with the Ottoman Porte providing for Prussia to enter the ongoing Russo-Turkish war in the spring of 1791. Two months later Prussia and Poland signed a treaty promising one another aid in case of attack by a third party. Prussia then prepared for war with Austria, which was allied with Russia. A broadening of the ongoing war between Russia and Austria on the one side and Turkey and Sweden on the other was widely anticipated, particularly in

Great Britain, which had concluded an alliance with Prussia in 1788. The death of the Austrian emperor Joseph II on 20 Feb. 1790 and the accession of his brother Leopold II changed the situation. At Leopold's initiative the differences between Prussia and Austria were settled by the Convention of Reichenbach, 27 July 1790, and a broader war was averted. The enclosure, providing an English translation of the treaty between the Ottoman Porte and Prussia, was clipped from an English newspaper (DNA: RG 59, Miscellaneous Letters).

From Samuel Johnston

Sir   1st May 1790

The following is an Extract from Genl Gregory Collector of the District of Camden's Letter to me.

"Respecting a Surveyor for Currituck Inlet there is no person that lives on Crow Island but Herbert. I am told the people dont like him, Mr Samuel Jasper is the only man that I think will answer, who lives on Knot's Island, within six or seven miles of the Inlet, I have sent Mr Thomas Williams, who is Surveyor for Port Indian Town, down to the Inlet, he informs me that he can do all the Business for both Ports himself by attending at Mr Younghers lands one day in a Week there are very seldom any other than coasting Vessells which come in at that Inlet."[1]

I believe the above state of facts may be relied on. I have the Honor to be sir Your most Obedient Servant

Sam. Johnston

ALS, DLC:GW.

1. In his letter to the U.S. Senate of 9 Feb. 1790, presenting nominees for the customs service for North Carolina, GW made no nomination for surveyor at Currituck Inlet. The office eventually went to Johnston's candidate Samuel Jasper (d. 1801) of Knots Island, a merchant and justice of the peace for Currituck County, N.C., who was appointed by GW on 25 May 1790. The appointment was confirmed by the Senate the next day (*DHFC*, 2:69). General Gregory was Isaac Gregory, collector at Plankbridge in Camden District.

From Gouverneur Morris

Sir   London 1. May 1790

Herewith I have the Honor to transmit a Duplicate of my last Letter of the thirteenth of April. Not having heard from the Duke of Leeds I wrote him a Note on the nineteenth, of which a Copy is enclosed marked No. 1. To this I received no Reply,[1] wherefore on the twenty ninth I addressed him again by a Letter of which a Copy is enclosed marked No. 2.[2] This was delivered at his Office Whitehall between eleven and twelve in the Morning of the twenty ninth, and at half past ten in the Evening the Letters were sent to me of which No. 3 & 4 are Copies.[3] You will observe that his Letter No. 3 is dated the 28th and of Course takes no Notice of that to which it is in Fact the answer; but the Style and general Complection as well as the Circumstances attending the Delivery of it, clearly shew that it was not written until the Evening of the twenty ninth.

I might, in Reply, have made some Strictures upon the Information that I was in Holland &ca &ca. I might also have contrasted the *Expressions* of Good Faith with the *Conduct* of administration, and have observed upon the Idea that the *United States* were bound in the most *solemn* Manner, while from the subsequent Parts of his Letter it would seem that Great Britain is not bound at all, or at most but loosely. There is also a Confusion of Language which resembles the Stammering of one who endeavors to excuse a Misdeed which he resolves to commit. Thus on the Supposition that a Completion of the Treaty by us is impossible he insists that we shall compleat it or make Compensation. The Expressions in the last Clause are if possible more vague than all the Rest, and the Reply might have been proportionately more pointed.

My Letter of Yesterday of which No. 5 is a Copy contains Nothing of what is just stated, altho perhaps it ought to have noticed some Part.[4] I must rely on your Kindness Sir both to interpret favorably what I have done and to excuse my omissions. I thought it best to heap Coals of Fire on their Heads, and thereby either bring them into our Views or put them most eminently in the wrong. It was moreover my wish to draw forth specific Propositions, because these will admit of Discussion, or else if manifestly unjust, they can not only be repelled but they will serve to shew a predetermined Breach of Faith by them which will justify whatever Conduct we may afterwards find it proper to adopt. If as is not improbable he should give no answer or one so vague as to mean Nothing I shall pursue according to Circumstances my Object of compelling them to speak plainly or refuse absolutely.

It seems pretty clear that they wish to evade a commercial Treaty but not peremptorily to reject it, and therefore I have construed into Rejection his Graces abstruse Language leaving him the Option to give it a different Intrepretation. I do not expect that he will, tho he may perhaps write an explanatory Comment more unintelligible than the Text.

I have some Reason to beleive that the present administration intend to keep the Posts, and withhold Payment for the Negroes. If so they will color their Breach of Faith by the best Pretexts in their Power. I incline to think also that they consider a Treaty of Commerce with America as being absolutely unnecessary, and that they are perswaded they shall derive all Benefit from our Trade without Treaty. It is true that we might lay them under Restrictions in our Ports but they beleive that an attempt of that Sort would be considered by one Part of America as calculated by the other for private Emolument, & not for the general Good. The Merchants here look on it as almost impossible for us to do without them; and it must be acknowleged that past Experience and the present Situation of neighbouring Countries go far to justify that Opinion. Whether the Ministers, then, shall act according to their own Ideas, or consult mercantile People they will equally (I think) repel advances from us, & therefore it seems more prudent to lay the Foundations of future advantage, than attempt to grasp at present Benefit. I will not pretend to suggest any Measures for the adoption of Congress whose wisdom and whose Sense of national Honor will certainly lead them to act properly when the proper Moment shall present itself. It will naturally strike every Mind that while the Legislature of this Country continue to invest the executive authority with great Power respecting the American Commerce the administration here will have advantages in Treaty which can only be ballanced by similar Confidence on the Part of Congress in the executive of America. But very much will I think depend upon the Situation of France. If Appearances there should change and so much Vigor be infused into the Government as would enable it to call forth the national Efforts in Support of their Interest and Honor, a great Revolution would be produced in the Opinions here. From the Conduct of the aristocratic Hierarchy in the low Countries who are instigated and supported by Prussia I have long been thoroughly convinced that the alternative of war or the most ignominious Terms of Peace would be proposed to the imperial Courts. Counting upon the absolute Nullity of France, and supposing that this Country can at any Moment intimidate that into abject Submission Prussia and Poland will I think join themselves to Turkey and Sweden against Russia and Austria which are both exhausted and one of them dismembred. Probably the war will be commenced before this Letter reaches your Hands, and then Britain and Holland are to be the Umpires or rather Dictators of Peace.

I have taken the Liberty to touch thus far upon the general System of European Politics, as it may tend to shew that for the present Great Britain will rather keep Things in Suspense with us, being herself in a State of Suspense as to others. I will not go into Conjectures about the Events which will take Place upon the Continent. They will I beleive (as is usual) disappoint the Projectors; but be that as it may, our affairs can derive no advantage now, from what shall happen hereafter. I presume that a Dissolution of Parliament will take Place shortly, altho many of the best informed People think or at least say they think otherwise. But it is clear to my mind that administration will wish to have before them a Prospect of seven Years Stability to their System be that what it may, and they will not at the Moment of a general Election expose themselves to Criticism by any act of doubtful Construction. This forms with them a⟨n⟩ additional Reason for being evasive in Regard to us. Perhaps there never was a Moment in which this Country felt herself greater and consequently it is the most unfavorable Moment to obtain advantageous Terms from her in any Bargain. But this appearance of Greatness is extremely fallacious. Their Revenue is not yet equal to their Expenditure. Money is indeed poured in upon them from all Quarters because of the distracted Situation of affairs among their Neighbours, and hence their Stocks have risen greatly since the Peace so that they can borrow at an Interest of four per Cent: but supposing they should not be obliged to engage in the war, still there are two Events either of which would overturn the Fabric of their Prosperity. If France establishes a solid System of Finance then Capitalists will prefer five per Cent with her to four per Cent from Britain, for all other Things being equal there is no Shadow of Comp⟨arison⟩

between the real Resources of the two Countries. If France commits a Bankruptcy, the Disorders consequent thereon will doubtless be violent but the Storm once passed, she would then be able to make greater Exertions by her annual Resources than Britain could compass by every possible anticipation of Credit. There is a middle Situation between sinking & Swimming in which the french Finances may flounder on for some Time to come, but even this State of wretchedness will produce rather Evil than Good to Great Britain; for she has already reaped all the Harvest which could be gathered from the Distress of her Neighbour, and must necessarily loose the Benefit of the famous commercial Treaty in Proportion as the Resources of her Customer are cut off.

Under all the various Contingencies which present themselves to my Contemplation and there are many which I will not trouble you with the Perusal of, it appears clearly that the favorable moment for us to treat is not yet come. It is indeed the moment for this Country and they seem determined to let it pass away. I must again entreat your Indulgence Sir for this lengthy and desultory Letter. Accept I pray you the assurances of that Respect with which I have the Honor to be your most obedient & humble Servant

Gouvr Morris

ALS, DLC: GW; LB, DNA: RG 59, Despatches from Diplomatic Officers, Great Britain; LB, DLC: Gouverneur Morris Papers.

1. In his letter to the duke of Leeds, written from "Froomes Hotel Covent Garden," 19 April 1790, Morris wrote: "Mr. Morris presents respectful compliments to the Duke of Leeds, and prays leave to remind his Grace of what passed in conversation on Monday the 28th of March, in consequence of which Mr Morris flattered himself with the hope of hearing from his grace at an early period" (DNA: RG 59, Despatches from Diplomatic Officers, Great Britain). See also Morris to GW, 7 April 1790, n.1.

2. Morris's letter to Leeds, 29 April 1790, reads: "When I had the Honor of an Interview with your Grace at Whitehall on Monday the twenty ninth of last Month, I left at your Request a Letter from the President of the United States to me which you promised to return after you should have had it copied. As your Grace seemed to be particularly pleased with the Contents of that Letter, I took the Liberty to request that I might be speedily honored with the Communication of your Sentiments on the Subject of it. This you was so kind as to promise. Your subsequent Silence led me to apprehend that this affair might have been overlooked in the attention to matters of more apparent moment. I took the Liberty therefore to recall it to your Graces Recollection, by

a Note of the nineteenth Instant which was delivered at Whitehall, and to which no Reply has been received.

"Permit me now my Lord to request that the President's Letter may be returned, and excuse me for expressing at the same Time a wish that you would enable me to transmit the Evidence of those friendly Dispositions towards America which you was pleased to express. It flows from the sincere Desire that more perfect Harmony may be established between the two Countries; and a Solicitude to obviate unpleasant Circumstances" (DNA: RG 59, Despatches from Diplomatic Officers, Great Britain).

3. In his letter of 28 April Leeds stated: "I should not have so long delayed returning an answer to the Letter you received from General Washington, which you had the Goodness to communicate to me last month, had I not heard you were in Holland. I received some Time ago a Note from you which I should sooner have acknowleged, but was at first prevented by a multiplicity of Engagements and since by Illness.

"The two Subjects contained in General Washington's Letter are indisputably of the highest Importance, and I can safely assure you that it has ever been the sincere and earnest wish of this Country to fulfil her Engagements (contracted by the Treaty of Peace) with the United States in a manner consistent with the most scrupulous Fidelity.

"We cannot but lament every Circumstance which can have delayed the accomplishment of those Engagements (comprized in the Treaty) to which those States were in the most solemn manner bound and should the Delay in fulfilling them have rendered their final Completion impracticable, we have no Scruple in declaring our Object is to retard the fulfilling such subsequent Parts of the Treaty as depend entirely upon Great Britain, until Redress is granted to our Subjects upon the specific Points of the Treaty itself, or a fair and just Compensation obtained for the non Performance of those Engagements on the Part of the United States.

"With Respect to a commercial Treaty between the two Countries, I can only say, that it is the sincere wish of the british Government to cultivate a real and bona fide System of friendly Intercourse with the United States, and that every measure which can tend really and reciprocally to produce that object will be adopted with the utmost Satisfaction by Great Britain" (DNA: RG 59, Despatches from Diplomatic Officers, Great Britain).

Enclosure no. 4 is a letter of 29 April, signed by J. B. Burges, stating: "The Duke of Leeds, being prevented from coming to the office by indisposition, has directed me to convey to you the inclosed answer to your communication from General Washington, together with the letter from the General which you left with his grace, and at the same time, to express his concern, that the circumstance I have mentioned, added to a multiplicity of important business, has prevented him from sooner answering your communication and note" (DNA: RG 59, Despatches from Diplomatic Officers, Great Britain).

4. Morris's letter of 29 April (no. 5) reads: "I was honored by your Graces Letter of the twenty eighth late last Evening, and take the earliest opportunity to acknowlege it. Be assured my Lord that I regret much the Indisposition

which suspended your Answer and sincerely wish that it may be speedily removed.

"I am happy to be assured by such respectable authority 'that it has ever been the sincere and earnest wish of this Country to fulfill her Engagements with the United States in a manner consistent with the most scrupulous Fidelity.' This indeed had never admitted of question in my mind because I could not harbor a Doubt of the national Faith of Great Britain: & I have the Pleasure to observe to you my Lord that Sentiments of this Kind induced the Congress at their last Session to reject, by a considerable Majority, some Regulations which might have appeared hostile, and proved injurious to your commercial Interests. I am perfectly convinced from this, and from many other Circumstances, that the united States have a constant Determination to perform in the fullest manner every Stipulation which they have made: for this is not only in itself a moral Duty, peculiarly binding upon every Sovereign Power, but it is specially secured by that constitutional Compact which the People of America have made with each other. Since both Parties therefore have the best Dispositions, and are actuated by the purest motives, I indulge my Lord, the Hope that every Obstacle to a complete Performance will be speedily removed. And in this Hope, without going into an Enquiry as to the Causes of former Delay, which might not perhaps tend toward Conciliation, I must entreat of your Graces Goodness to be informed in what Respects and to what Degree you consider the final Completion of those Engagements to which the United States were bound as having been rendered impracticable; for I must own that the Idea is new to my Conception—The Candor with which your Grace avows the Intent to retard a Fulfilment of such Parts of the Treaty as depend upon Great Britain, meets as it merits my utmost acknowlegement. I am very far from questioning the Policy, nor will I presume to doubt the Propriety of a Caution which is I trust unnecessary, and which might indeed be unpleasant to the Feelings of America, if they could be affected with punctilious Sentiment in the Discussion of national Interest. But it becomes my Duty to ask of you my Lord, the Nature and Extent of the Redress expected for your Subjects upon the specific Points of the Treaty; and in the supposed Case that this should have become impracticable, the Kind and the measure of Compensation to be required from us as preliminary to the fulfilment of those Stipulations which remain to be performed by you.

"I trust that I am mistaken in that Part of your Graces Letter which relates to a commercial Treaty, because it really appears to me as expressive only of the wish to cultivate merely an amicable intercourse founded on commercial Good Faith, and as implying some Disinclination to the securing of that Intercourse by the Force of Treaty. I should be very unhappy to convey a false Interpretation of the Sentiments of this Government upon an Object of such Importance. This might be prejudicial to both Countries and therefore I shall indulge the Expectation that if I am wrong your Grace will have the Goodness to set me right" (DNA: RG 59, Despatches from Diplomatic Officers, Great Britain; copies of the enclosures, in Morris's hand, are in DLC:GW).

From Thomas Paine

Sir   London May 1st 1790

Our very good Friend the Marquis de la Fayette has entrusted to my care the Key of the Bastile and a drawing, handsomely framed,[1] representing the demolition of that detestible prison, as a present to your Excellency, of which his letter will more particularly inform. I feel myself happy in being the person thro' whom the Marquis has conveyed this early trophy of the Spoils of Despotism and the first ripe ⟨fru⟩its of American principles transplanted into ⟨Eur⟩ope to his great Master and Patron—when he mentioned to me the present he entended you my heart leaped with Joy—It is something so truly in character that no remarks can illustrate it, and is more happily expressive of his remembrance of his American friends than any letters can convey. That the principles of America opened the Bastile is not to be doubted, and therefore the Key comes to the right place.

I beg leave to suggest to your Excellency the propriety of congratulating the King and Queen of France (for they have been our friends) and the National assembly on the happy example they are giving to Europe. You will see by the King's Speech, which I enclose that he prides himself on being at the head of the Revolution, and I am certain that such a congratulation will be well received and have a good effect.[2]

I should rejoice to be the direct bearer of the Marquis's present to your Excellency but I doubt I shall not be able to see my much loved America till next spring. I shall therefore send it by some *American* Vessel to New York. I have permitted no drawing to be taken here, tho' it has been often requested, as I think there is a propriety that it should first be presented.

⟨But⟩ Mr West wishes Mr Trumbull to make a painting ⟨of⟩ the presentation of the Key to you.[3]

I returned from France to London about five Weeks ago—and I am engaged to return to Paris when the Constitution shall be proclaimed and to carry the American Flag in the procession—I have not the least doubt of the final and compleat success of the French Revolution—little Ebbings and flowings, for and against, the natural companions of revolutions, sometimes appear, but the full current of it, is, in my opinion, as fixed as the Gulph Stream.

I have manufactured a Bridge (a Single arch) of one hundred & ten feet Span, and five feet high from the Cord of the Arch—It is now on board a vessel coming from Yorkshire to London—where it is to be erected[4]—I see nothing yet to disappoint my hopes of its being advantageous to me—it is this only which keeps me Europe—and happy shall I be when I shall have it in my power to return to America. I have not heard of Mr Jefferson since he sailed except of his arrival. As I have always indulged the belief of having many ⟨friends⟩ in America, or rather no Enemies, I have ⟨nothing else particu⟩larly to mention—but my affectionate rem⟨embrances to⟩ all—and am, Sir, with the greatest Respect your much obliged and Obedient Humble servant

Thomas Paine

If any of my friends are disposed to favour me with a letter—it will come to hand by addressing it to the care of Benjn Vaughn Esqr. Jeffries Square London.

ALS, DLC:GW. Material in angle brackets taken from Sparks, *Correspondence of the American Revolution*, 4:328–9.

1. See Lafayette to GW, 17 Mar. 1790, Paine to GW, 31 May 1790, and GW to Paine, 10 Aug. 1790.

2. The copy of Louis XVI's speech to the National Assembly sent by Paine to GW has not been found, but the speech, in which Louis promised to defend and maintain the constitutional liberty of France, "whose principles the general will, in agreement with my own, has sanctioned," was delivered on 4 Feb. 1790 and is printed in *Archives parlementaires*, 11:429–31.

3. John Trumbull never followed the suggestion of his mentor Benjamin West in producing a painting of GW receiving the key to the Bastille.

4. After his return to Europe in 1787, Paine attempted with some success to interest the French court in the construction of a bridge across the Seine. After these plans fell through, Paine returned to England and opened negotiations with the four Walker brothers who operated a large ironworks near Sheffield. (The Walkers were mentioned but not identified in Paine's letter to GW, 16 Oct. 1789, printed above.) In June 1789 Paine proposed to the Walkers that they erect a bridge based on his plans for an arch with a 110-foot span and five or more ribs. The Walkers provided all the materials, and the bridge was to be erected across the Thames at Paine's expense and put up for sale. By May 1790 the Walkers had finished construction and shipped the bridge by water from Yorkshire to London (Aldridge, *Man of Reason*, 113–16; Seitz, "Thomas Paine, Bridge Builder," 571–84).

From Arthur St. Clair

Cahokia [Territory N.W. of River Ohio]

Sir   May 1st 1790

I have this day communicated to the Secretary of the Department of War all the Intelligence respecting the Indian Affairs that has come to my knowledge and Observation since I wrote to him before,[1] and I am very sorry to have it to remark, that they do not wear a very favorable Complexion! That the Ouabush Indians should have taken the Resolution to be guided entirely by those of the Miami Village, is nearly tantamount to a declaration that they will continue their Hostilities;[2] if Matters come to that Issue, there can certainly be no hesitation about employing force to reduce them to reason, and I hope the Legislature will not boggle at the Expense, be it what it may; for it is certainly better for a Nation in every Case, to incur Expense, whatever may be its difficulties, than to lose Reputation: and should the Savages be suffered to insult the Government, and murder and rob the People with impunity its credit would be lowered, very much, both with foreign Nations and its own Citizens. The quietly putting up with one Injury seldom fails to prepare the way for the offering another.

My Time, since my Arrival in this Country, has been chiefly taken up with the receiving & examining the Claims of the Inhabitants, which have been presented very slowly; partly from their extreme Ignorance, and partly from their total want of the English Language: The Secretary being little accquainted with the french, I had required a state of their Claims in English, but as not a fiftieth Man can either read or write any Language, I was obliged to dispense with that, and interpret between him and them myself.[3] The People are reduced to the lowest Ebb of Poverty—for four Years successively the Country has been laid under Water (for the french Settlements are all in the low Grounds or River Prairies, which are very extensive) which destroyed much the greatest part of their crops in each of those Years; and the last Season a Frost in the beginning of September destroyed nearly all the Corn—They were so much discouraged that, had my Arrival been much longer delayed, the Country would have been abandonned alltogether; perh⟨aps⟩ what had the principal Effect in preventing it was, that on the Spanish side the Lands are naturally less fertile, and had suffered nearly as much from the Innundations. The Spirit of Industry, which however they never possess ⟨in⟩ any great Degree, seems to be reviving, and as the Season advances ⟨*mutilated*⟩ happily, and they are naturally of a sanguine temper, and look fondly ⟨for⟩-ward to better times, their Misfortunes will I hope be forgotten. I have been trying to persuade some of them to quit their Villages, where as Farmers they can never thrive, and establish themselves upon on Plantations in the higher Lands for the Prariries are every where bounded by a steep and high Bank, at the foot of which it is very evident that the Missisippi has some-time run, but they have so perfect a dread of the Savages, that, tho' they are satisfied of the truth of it, it is impossible to bring them to attempt it; tho the high Lands are both fertile and Healthy, and the Indian Commerce, which was the Resource of their Villages, has entirely forsaken them: I suspect however they dread the Timber, with which it is covered, almost as much as the Savages; having never been accustomed to the clearing or cultivating timbered Lands. If some of the great number of Families that are daily descending the Missisippi, and are, for a time at least, lost to their Country, could be diverted this Way, they would find a Country which would abundantly supply them with all the Necessaries and many of the Conveniences of Life, and without a great deal of Labor; for, even in the interior Country, far from the great Rivers, there are abundance of ex-tensive Prairies, where there is nothing to do but to enclose them and put in the Plough—The Habits of Industry and the knowledge of Husbandry would from them be communicated to the ancient Inhabitants. I do not know whether the design to dispose of this Country, in small Quantities to People who would settle it, has been resumed by Congress or not; but of this I am certain that, while the rage of Emigration continues, it would be good Policy to discharge a part of it here, where the People would become good Subjects⟨,⟩ and form an effectual Barrier against future contingencies: neither is it by any means improb-able that when the Advantages which this Country offer come to be generally known, they may turn this Way of themselves, and establish themselves without Authority; if not in the face of it; which would introduce a Spirit of Licentiousness, hitherto unknown here that might not be very easily repressed.

The Judges are not yet arrived neither have I the least information about them: their Absence has embarrased me a good Deal, as many Regulations, suited to the peculiar Circumstances of this part of the Country are necessary and cannot with propriety be established but by Law; I have been obliged however, in some Instances, to take it upon myself, after waiting for them as long as possible, and direct them by Proclamation[4]—I have no doubt of a ready Obedience, for it is the mode to which the People are habituated, but I am sensible, that in so doing, I have gone beyond my proper Powers—My Excuse Sir I hope will be found in the necessity of the Case, and as the good of the People only was in View, I cannot doubt but Laws will confirm them as soon as possible. One of these Proclamations respects a County which I have erected here.[5] The Settlements are three princip⟨al *mutilated*⟩ Cahokia, the Prairie du Rochers and Kaskaskia, with some sm⟨*mutilated* o⟩nes—not one of those contain a sufficient number of People ⟨*mutilated*⟩ its being a separate County, (indeed in the whole Country taken ⟨*mutilated*⟩ have been very much put to it to find proper Subjects to fill the different Offices) and they are at too great a Distance from each other, in present Circumstances, for any two of them to have been joined, I was therefore obliged to divide the County into Districts, and to direct Sessions of each of the Courts to be held in each District, and the Records to be kept in them in the same manner as if they had been distinct Counties: It will be attended with the Inconvenience to one or two of the Magistrates to go to the different Places but it was impossible to concenter the Business of the whole, and confine the Courts to one Place, without putting an entire stop to the Administration of Justice.

In a Letter which I had the honor to address to you from the Rapids of Ohio, I mentioned the Information I had received respecting Mr Morgan in that part of the Country.[6] I found that he had been still busier here, if possible: in order to induce the Inhabitants to abandon the Country and follow him, he had a number of Sacks of Earth brought up from the Ance de la Graise, to shew them, and convince them of its very superior Quality; but his chief argument, and that which operated most powerfully, was drawn from that Article in the Constitution of the Territory which ⟨respects⟩ Slaves.[7] he assured them, most positively, that they would all be liberated without any Compensation being made to the owners—He pressed them to save them while it was yet in their Power—that the Governor was then on his way, and after his arrival it would be too late—to fly if they had any regard to themselves—they had not a moment to lose: it had the Effect to drive away many respectable Inhabitants, but not the Effect he expected, very few followed him, but they took refuge on the opposite Shore and became Subjects of Spain, which they now very heartily regret—He is now at this Moment sending away the Inhabitants of New Jersey to that Country under printed Passports directed to all civil and military Officers and requiring them to receive them as Subjects of his Catholic Majesty—Major Doughty was shewn one of those by the commanding Officer at the Ance de la Graise, who did not however very cordially accept the *Greeting*.

By the Ordinance for establ[ish]ing the Indian Department the Superintendant is empowered to appoint two Deputies and a Salary of five hundred Dollars is annexed to the Appointment—Two Deputies, should a good Understanding be brought about with the Indians, is not sufficient ⟨for⟩ this extensive District, and I believe the Salary might safely be ⟨lowe⟩red—Persons equally capable and worthy of trust might be got I think for one half the Sum; for five hundred Dollars will not call off any Persons of much consequence from their other Pursuits, whereas to a Person who has nothing but a farm to attend to, the half of it is a considerable Object—four Deputies would not be found too many, tho hitherto I have appointed but One—but it will not be long before more will be necessary.

While I am speaking of Salarys wi⟨ll yo⟩u permit me Sir to mention that of the Governor—I do assure you ⟨Sir⟩ it is a very inade⟨qu⟩ate One, and I was sensible of it before I took the Office upon me. I suppos⟨ed⟩ that a little management would have secured an increase of it at the last Session of Congress, but where Money was the Object I would never in my life make use of any on my own Account—Whoever undertakes it after me will find that it will by no means support him, in the manner that will be expected, and which the Dignity of Government requires—it is even necessary that a little Splendor should be thrown round it. This is however the most expensive Country in the World—Money they have none, and European Goods, wh⟨ich⟩ are at an excessive Price, is the Measure of that, and of every thing else—Money is the Measure of no one Thing—even Linnen cannot be got washed under three Dollars a dozen Pieces—besides the Person who will be sent to th⟨is⟩ Country in the Capacity of Governor must make some Sacrifices, for which he may reasonably expect some Indemnification, independent of the long and dangerous Journies he must necessarily make both by Land and Water. My Salary I am confident will not support me; and yet I am as careful I think as I can be without Meaness.[8]

With the most earnest Wishes for your Health and Happiness and the prosperity of the Country under your Government, and with the greatest Respect and Attachment I have the honor to be Sir Your most obedient and very humble Servant

Ar. St Clair

P.S. I have thought proper to explain the Article respecting Slaves as a prohibition to any future introduction of them, but not to extend to the liberation of those the People were already possessed of, and accquired under the Sanction of the Laws they were subject, at the same time I have given them to understand that Steps would probably be taken for the gradual Abolition of Slavery, with which they seem perfectly satisfied.[9]

ALS, DNA: RG 59, Territorial Papers, Territory Northwest of the River Ohio; Df (incomplete), OHi. Words in angle brackets taken from Carter, *Territorial Papers, Northwest Territory*, 2:244–48.

Gov. Arthur St. Clair was in Cahokia to carry out the instructions of the Confederation Congress, 20 June 1788, to confirm "in their Possessions & Titles the French & Canadian Inhabitants, & other Settlers on the Mississippi" who had accepted United States citizenship before 1783 (ibid., 3:296). (For the acquisition of this territory by the United States, see GW to St. Clair, 6 Oct. 1789, n.3). In addition his mission in the Illinois country included implementing GW's instructions to him, 6 Oct. 1789, to acquire "full information whether the Wabash and Illinois Indians are most inclined for war or peace" and to open a dialogue with the western tribes. St. Clair, who was in the east on one of his frequent absences from his post in the Northwest Territory, left for the frontier in December. On 19 Dec. Knox forwarded additional instructions to the governor: "As it is highly probable that you may before this letter can reach you be far down the Ohio it may not be prudent to be very particular in my communication.

"The people of Kentuckey are loud in their complaints of the murders that have been committed in that district during the last summer—The President of the United States has received several letters from the Principal characters in that quarter. While he has directed that they be promised all the protection that he can reasonably afford, he has stated his opinion of the effects of the desultory expeditions into the Indian Country North west of the Ohio—an extract of a letter written by his direction to Samuel McDowell Esqr Chairman of the late Convention of Kentuckey District and dated the 15th instant is as follows

"'The President of the United States has desired that it may be clearly understood to be his opinion that the best foundation for peace with the Indians is by establishing just and liberal treaties with them—which shall be rigidly observed on our parts, and if broken on theirs to be *effectually punished* by legal authority.

"[']But irregular and unauthorized expeditions involve the innocent and guilty in equal calamity—make enemies of those disposed to be friends—disgrace government and defeat its designs.

"[']And further that in future it is his just expectation that no expedition be undertaken agains the Indians North west of the Ohio, but with the approbation of the Governor of the said Territory, and the Commanding Officer of the federal troops who are particularly instructed on this subject.[']

"The President of the United States is extremely desirous of a general treaty with the Wabash Indians as the only rational foundation of peace—If a treaty of peace was once effected, any partial breaches of it by the Indians could easily be punished—He therefore requests you to use your highest exertions for that purpose" (Carter, *Territorial Papers, Northwest Territory,* 2:224–26). For GW's correspondence with McDowell, see the Kentucky Convention to GW, 25 July 1789, and Washington's Memoranda on Indian Affairs, 1789, printed above.

On 8 Jan. 1790 St. Clair reached the rapids of the Ohio, and at least by 23 Jan. the governor was at Vincennes. His somewhat halfhearted peace efforts with the western tribes were conducted mainly through intermediaries.

1. St. Clair's letter to Henry Knox is in Smith, *St. Clair Papers,* 2:136–40.

2. By the late 1780s the Miami were virtually the only tribe in the Ohio country that had not conducted negotiations, however nebulous, with the United States. Led by principal chief Le Gris and war chief Little Turtle, the Miami consolidated other tribes west of the Ohio into what was termed the Miami Confederacy, with headquarters on the Maumee River. The confederacy became the principal opponent of U.S. expansion on the northwest frontier, refusing to accept the terms of the treaties of Fort Harmar (see St. Clair to GW, 2 May 1789) and carrying on a series of raids on American settlements in Kentucky and the Northwest Territory with the support of their client tribes. As early as 1788 Maj. John Francis Hamtramck had noted that "the Nations of the Wabash are well enough disposed to be our friends; but they are menaced by the upper Indians who have ordered them to cease all connection with us" (Hamtramck to Josiah Harmar, 1 Jan. 1788, WHi: Draper Collection, Harmar Papers). In his letter to Knox of 1 May, St. Clair pointed out that "every thing seems to be referred to the Miamies, which does not promise a peaceable issue. The confidence they have in their situation, the vicinity of many other nations not very well disposed, and the pernicious counsels of the English traders, joined to the immense booty obtained by the depredations

upon the Ohio, will most probably prevent them from listening to any reasonable terms of accommodation, so that it is to be feared the United States must prepare effectually to chastise them" (Smith, *St. Clair Papers*, 2:136). Sometime in the spring or summer of 1790, St. Clair sent GW a report containing a detailed account of his activities between 5 Mar. and 11 June (see ibid., 2:164–80).

3. For examples of the petitions presented to the governor by the French residents of the Illinois country, see Carter, *Territorial Papers, Northwest Territory*, 2:241–44, 251–57, 261–62, 278–82.

4. One of the major problems in administration in the Northwest Territory was the perennial absence of the three judges from their posts. Judges George Turner, Rufus Putnam, and John Cleves Symmes were all elsewhere for varying lengths of time. Winthrop Sargent complained as early as December 1789 that "there has been but Little Attention by the Gentlemen of the Bench to the important Business of their Commission" (Sargent to Knox, 7 Dec. 1789, NNGL). On 2 Feb. 1791 GW wrote a private letter to St. Clair explaining that he understood the problem with the judges but cautioning him against exceeding his executive authority. By 1793 the problem with the judges' absences still continued, Sargent writing St. Clair on 7 Feb. that "the General Court sit only annually—the Judges thereof are almost always absent—on the morrow there will not be one in the Territory" (O: St. Clair Papers). An even more serious problem was created by St. Clair's frequent absences at which times his duties were assumed by Winthrop Sargent, the secretary of the Northwest Territory. After much public criticism of St. Clair's negligence, Jefferson wrote to him in November 1792: "The present situation of the Territory North west of the Ohio, requiring the presence of those to whom the administration of its affairs is confided, I am charged by the President to bring this circumstance to your notice, not doubting but that the public exigencies of your office will over-weigh in your mind any personal inconveniencies which might attend your repairing to that Country" (Jefferson to St. Clair, 10 Nov. 1792, DNA: RG 59, Domestic Letters).

5. See Carter, *Territorial Papers, Northwest Territory*, 3:296–303.

6. Letter not found. For George Morgan's activities at New Madrid, see James Madison to GW, 26 Mar. 1789, n.1.

7. Article 6 of "An Ordinance for the government of the territory of the United States North west of the river Ohio" (1787), establishing the Northwest Territory, provided "There shall be neither Slavery nor involuntary Servitude in the said territory otherwise than in the punishment of crimes, whereof the Party shall have been duly convicted: Provided always that any Person escaping into the same, from whom labor or service is lawfully claimed in any one of the original States, such fugitive may be lawfully reclaimed and conveyed to the person claiming his or her labor or service as aforesaid" (Carter, *Territorial Papers, Northwest Territory*, 2:39, 49).

8. The ordinance of 1787 provided that the governor, appointed for a term of three years, should have a freehold estate of 1,000 acres of land while he held his commission. His salary, as superintendent of Indian affairs for the territory, was $800 (ibid., 41, 195).

9. St. Clair's interpretation followed that of Congress. A committee report on a memorial from residents of Vincennes and the Illinois country in September 1788 held that the ordinance "shall not be construed to deprive the Inhabitants of Kaskaskias Illinois Post St Vincents and the other Villages formerly settled by the French & Canadians, of their Right and property in Negro or other Slaves which they were possessed of at the time of passing the said Ordinance, or in any manner to Manumit or Set free any such Negroes or other persons under Servitude within any part of Sd Western territory; any thing in the said Ordinance to the Contrary notwithstanding" (DNA:PCC, item 19, vol. 6).

From Gouverneur Morris

Private
Dear Sir   London 2d May 1790

You will find enclosed the Copy of what I took the Liberty to trouble you with on the thirteenth of last Month. On Saturday the seventeenth I dined in Company with Mr Fox. The State of french Politics formed of Course a large Part of the Conversation. The Situation of other Countries was then passed in Review, and it became a question how far Britain might be engaged in the Affairs of the Continent. At length I took an Opportunity to ask what System the administration had adopted respecting America. He told me that he could not tell but beleived they had none, and would in all Probability be governed by Events. That he did not beleive Mr Pitt would trouble his Head about the Matter, but would probably leave it to Lord Hawksbury & Mr Grenville who are both of them indisposed to us whereas Pitt himself is he supposes rather friendly than otherwise. Mr Fox said farther that he and Burke are now almost alone in their Opinion that we should be permitted to trade in our own Bottoms to their Islands, and that this Opinion looses Ground daily tho for his own Part he persists in it.

I find that the Ministers apply for Information respecting America, and particularly american Commerce to a Mr Irwin who long resided in America and is now here in the Customs. A mighty Sour Sort of Creature and one who seems to have a mortal Aversion for us. I met him at Dinner one Day and he took Pains to let me know that he was doing all he could to prevent any Encouragement from being given to our Exports by the Corn Bill which is now on the Carpet. He declared that he would by the Force of Starvation oblige the People of Britain to raise Corn enough for their own Consumption, and that even the Supply of the West India Islands ought to be provided in this Country.

You will readily perceive Sir from this rude Sketch of influential Characters, that there is but little Disposition for treating with us at present. With sincere Regard I am truly yours

Gouvr Morris

ALS, DLC:GW; LB, DLC: Gouverneur Morris Papers.

From Thomas Jefferson

May 3. 1790.

The state of Georgia having granted to certain companies of individuals a tract of country within their chartered limits, whereof the Indian right has never yet been acquired, with a proviso in the grant which implies that those individuals may take measures for extinguishing the Indian right under the authority of that government, it becomes a question How far this grant is good?

A society taking possession of a vacant country, & declaring they mean to occupy it, does thereby appropriate to themselves, as prime occupants, what was before common. a practice introduced since the discovery of America authorizes them to go farther, & to fix the limits which they assume to themselves; & it seems for the common good to admit this right to a moderate & reasonable extent. if the country, instead of being altogether vacant, is thinly occupied by another nation, the right of the natives forms an exception to that of the new comers; that is to say, these will only have a right against all other nations except the natives: consequently they have the exclusive privilege of acquiring the native right by purchase, or other just means. this is called the right of pre-emption; & is become a principle of the law of nations, fundamental with respect to America. there are but two means of acquiring the native title. 1. War; for even war may sometimes give a just title. 2. Contract, or treaty. the states of America, before their present union, possessed completely, each within it's own limits, the exclusive right to use these two means of acquiring the native title: & by their act of union they have as completely ceded both to the general government. Art. 2. sect. 1. "the President shall have power, by & with the advice of the Senate, to make treaties, provided two thirds of the Senators present concur." Art. 1. sect. 8. "the Congress shall have power—to declare war—to raise & support armies." sect. 10. "no state shall enter into any treaty, alliance, or confederation. no state shall, without the consent of congress, keep troops or ships of war in time of peace, enter into any agreement or compact with another state, or with a foreign power, or engage in war, unless actually invaded, or in such imminent danger as will not admit of delay." these paragraphs of the Constitution, declaring that the general government shall have, & that the particular ones shall not have, the rights of war & treaty, are so explicit that no commentary can explain them further, nor can any explain them away. cons[e]quently Georgia, possessing *the exclusive right to acquire the native title* but having relinquished the *means* of doing it to the general government, can only have put her grantee into her own condition. she could convey to them the exclusive right to acquire; but she could not convey, what she had not herself, that is, the means of acquiring. for these they must come to the general government, in whose hands they have been wisely deposited for the purposes both of peace & justice.

What is to be done? the right of the general government is, in my opinion, to be maintained. the case is sound; and the means of doing it as practicable as can ever occur. but respect & friendship should, I think mark the conduct of the general towards the particular governments; & explanations should be asked, & time & colour given them to tread back their steps, before coercion is held up to their view. I am told there is already a strong party in Georgia opposed to the act of their government. I should think it better then that the first measures, while firm, be yet so temperate as to secure their alliance & aid to the general government. might not the eclat of a proclamation revolt their pride & passion, & throw them hastily into the opposite scale? it will be proper indeed to require from the government of Georgia, in the first moment, that while the general government shall be expecting & considering her explanations, things shall remain in statu quo, & not a move be made towards carrying what they have begun into execution. perhaps it might not be superfluous to send some person to the Indians interested, to explain to them the views of government, & to watch with their aid the territory in question.

Th: Jefferson

ALS (letterpress copy), DLC: Thomas Jefferson Papers.

Jefferson's opinion concerns the sale of land to the Yazoo companies. See Henry Knox to GW, 15 Feb. 1790, n.1. On 28 April GW noted in his diary that he had received from Henry Knox "a report respecting the Sale of certain Lands by the State of Georgia; and the consequent disputes in which the United States may be involved with the Chicasaws & Choctaw Nations; part, if not the whole of whose Countries, are included within the limits of the said Sale. This report refers to the Act of the Legislature of Georgia, by which this sale is authorized and to the opinion of the Attorney General respecting the Constitutionality of the Proceeding—submitting at the same time certain opinions for the consideration of the Presidt" (*Diaries*, 6:69). Although neither Knox's nor Randolph's opinion has been found, it is likely that Knox's views were similar to those expressed in his report to GW, 22 Jan. 1791, that "although the right of Georgia to the pre-emption of said lands should be admitted in its full extent, yet it is conceived, that should the said State, or any companies or persons claiming under it, attempt to extinguish the indian claims, unless authorised thereto by the United States, that the measure would be repugnant to the aforesaid treaties, to the Constitution of the United States, and to the law regulating trade and intercourse with the indian tribes" (DNA: RG 46, First Congress, Records of Legislative Proceedings, President's Messages). As the request for opinions on the Yazoo companies indicates, GW had quickly established the procedure of requesting advice from his cabinet. See Jefferson to GW, 1 April 1790, n.1.

From Thomas Jefferson

[3 May 1790]

a letter is received from Mr Dumas, begun Dec. 4 & ending Jan. 26.[1] the only interesting passage is the following

"I have the satisfaction to be able to testify that the American funds are in great favor with the monied men of this country. I have seen them sell from one to another the obligations of the Congress of the first loan at 100.¾ per cent; those of the last of 1788. at 99 to 100. those of the Amsterdam negotiation of the Liquidated debt at 99½ to 102. per cent."

AL, DNA: RG 59, Miscellaneous Letters.

1. Dumas's letter was actually begun on 2 Dec., continued on 4 and 5 Dec. 1789, and completed on 26 Jan. 1790 (DNA:PCC, item 93).

From Gouverneur Morris

Dear Sir London 3 May 1790

The forgoing is Copy of what I wrote to you the twelfth of last month. I have since received yours of the first of March. The additional Pieces for your Surtout I cannot get untill I return to Paris⟨.⟩ I beleive no additional ornaments will be wanting and I incline to think that the Surtout as it now is will be large enough However you will have judged better upon seeing it and I shall probably hear from you on the Subject before long. I have bespoke the Lamps you desired and at about the limited Prices. They are as handsome as those Prices would admit of but in a different Style from those at Mr Morris's which cost a great Deal more. These will however be I beleive as useful tho not quite so ornamental. You are perfectly right in not offering an apology for putting it in my Power to render you this trivial Service. If you had not done it an apology might perhaps have been necessary.

you take it for granted that I am regularly informed of the Proceedings of Congress &ca but in this you are mistaken for I have had very little Information on the Subject. Even the News Papers have not reached me. I trust however that I shall get a large Budget one of these Days. All which I do learn is good and that is a great Comfort. In this Country People begin to beleive that it is possible for America to subsist under an independent Government: but that opinion is not yet general much less universal.

LB, DLC: Gouverneur Morris Papers.

From John Mitchell

Colrain Township Lancaster County & state of Pennsylvania
Honoured Sir May 4th 1790

As it is a virtue highly to be commended in every member of society to study the benefit of the body at large more than their own private interest so it is more particularly incumbent on those who are placed at the helm of affairs and are as it were the soul of the body politic to exercise this virtue in an eminent degree and I may justly say without flattery that you sir have given sufficient evidence to the inhabitants of the United States of America by your disinterested conduct since you were called to the office of Generallisimo in the contest between Great Britain and America that you possess this virtue, in proportion to your elevation in office above others And therefore no doubt you will attend to every opportunity of doing any thing that you find will tend to the advantage of the United states and impartially examine the merit of any thing that may be submitted to your judgment taking this for granted I a poor obscure farmer who never saw your face nor have had any other knowledge of you than what I have acquired by common fame make bold to offer a few thoughts to your consideration You sir are sensible that the depriciation of the Continental money has rendered the circulation of paper currency impracticable and it appears to me that we never can have a sufficient medium of circulation otherwise than by coining gold and silver unless that trade can be otherwise regulated and manifactures more attended to among ourselves than they have been heretofore And it is generally allowed that we have a sufficiency of gold and silver mines to supply us in a medium of circulation if they were opened I myself now possess a plantation through which a vein of mine runs which is supposed to be several miles in length which I am credibly informed has been proven to be silver and as I am not able to open it if you think proper to take any notice of it I shall chearfully submit it to your disposal and leave it to your generosity to allow me what you think fit for my good will of it you can have sufficient information about it by employing a man skilled in minerals to ⟨co⟩me and try it I shall take it as a great favour if you condescend to ⟨se⟩nd me a few lines the first opportunity to let me know whether or no you intend to do any thing in it which if you do I shall perhaps be able to inform you how you may conveniently bring a considerable length of the vein into your possession[1] I am Honoured sir with due respect your cordial friend & Hume Servt

John Mitchell

ALS, DNA: RG 59, Miscellaneous Letters.

1. Silver was mined in Pequea Township in western Lancaster County in the eighteenth century (see Eckman, "Early Silver Mining in Lancaster County," 21–24). Small amounts of silver have been mined elsewhere in the county, but no record of any silver mining in Colerain Township has been found. Mitchell

has not been identified, but property tax records reveal that a John Mitchell owned land in Colerain Township from 1785 to 1790—one hundred acres in 1788. The 1791 return has a line drawn through Mitchell's name, suggesting that he no longer owned the property at that date. Mitchell does not seem to have resided in Colerain Township. His efforts to have the federal government purchase the land were unsuccessful. The editors are indebted to Mr. John W. W. Loose, President Emeritus of the Lancaster County Historical Society, for assistance on this point.

From James B. Pleasants

Baltimore [Md.] May 5th 1790

As soon as the power of Granting Patents is vested by Law in the President, Angelheart Cruse intends to make application for Exclusive rights to a machine invented by me some years since, and for which he has my leave to take a Patent in his own name, The object in ⟨view⟩ is to apply Liquid force, as is apprehended, ⟨wi⟩th more simplicity, and superior power, ⟨tha⟩n has hitherto been done; particularly ⟨S⟩team, Water, and Air.[1] A perpetual Cylinder, mooving on the exterior of a piston ⟨w⟩ith equal and Continual force, constitute ⟨o⟩ne of the Essential principles of this machine; and one of its great advantages, arises from the immidiate Communication of force (without the intervention of Cogg's, Rounds or any ⟨o⟩ther Machinery) to millstones or wheels of any kind whatever. In communicating the force of Stea[m], this machine will appear in the most superior point of view in which it probably can be plac'd; the Cylinder revolv⟨in⟩g round its axis, which is also the axis of the millstones or wheels employ'd to apply the force: in a Common Steam Engine the force is communicated by the recuring movem⟨ent⟩ of a Piston; in the this, the continual revolution of the Cylinder itself around ⟨its⟩ axis, the piston being stationary; the Cy⟨linder⟩ in this Machine mooves with the same force that the piston in a common Engine does, multiplied by any number that we please under 25; the difficulty arising from the complexity of machinery necessary in ap⟨ply⟩ing a recuring force to Wheels is remoov'd: This difficulty is Threefold. 1. Expence 2. friction, 3. the loss of force apply'd to a Cra⟨*illegible*⟩.

I k⟨n⟩ow no better appology for this let⟨ter⟩ than the cause— I have observ'd an application (mention'd by the publishers of the debates of Congress) made to that bod⟨y⟩ for an exclusive right to the use of perpetual steam if it is the same with mine, the priority, and superiority, will be Questions that appear to ⟨me⟩ to justify the foregoing explanation of the prin⟨ciples⟩ my machine acts upon. I have confined my⟨self⟩ in the foregoing Explanation to general princip⟨les;⟩ the particular machine will be best Explain'd by a model that will be presented by the appl-⟨icant⟩ for a Patent—I am with the highest sentiments of Respect

James B. Pleasants

ALS, DNA: RG 59, Miscellaneous Letters.

1. Pleasants was prompted to write to GW by the passage of the Patents Act on 10 April 1790 (*DHFC*, 6:1620–42). He sent an identical letter to Jefferson, who as secretary of state was principally responsible for patent applications (Boyd, *Jefferson Papers*, 16:412–13).

Angelhart (Englehart, Englebert) Cruse (Cruze) was a Baltimore mechanic; in a letter to Jefferson of 18 April 1791, James McHenry described him as "an ingenious mechanician of this town who has made certain improvements in steam engines for which he is desirous to get a patent. His scientific attainments are not many, but his natural powers very considerable" (ibid., 413). In 1788 Cruse had published *The Projector Detected; or, Some Strictures, on the Plan of Mr. James Rumsey's Steamboat* (Baltimore, 1788). Pleasants wrote to GW again in August 1790: "I have this moment recd information that induces me to believe that some mistake has arisen on the subject on which I wrote you some time since the application of steam by means of a perpetual Cylinder the name I mentioned is not Evans, the name is Cruce, if Evans has imposed himself by the name of Cruse the Imposition appears to me to be so gross as not to admit of a doubt of detection—If there is any mistake in the business I have no doubt of its being rectified" (James B. Pleasants to GW, 6 Aug. 1790, DNA: RG 59, Miscellaneous Letters). Pleasants apparently was alarmed by the efforts of Oliver Evans (1755–1819), a Philadelphia inventor and millwright, to secure patents for his inventions. Evans was engaged in experiments with stationary steam engines for use in milling and had obtained exclusive rights to his improvements from the legislatures of Pennsylvania, Maryland, and Delaware in 1787. He applied for a patent from the new national government in 1790 (Bathe, *Oliver Evans*, 14–20). Subsequent to Pleasants's two letters, Cruse wrote to GW: "As the Patronage of Arts has ever been your Excellency's desire—Induces me to make so free as to lay the Inclosed plan of a Steam Engine before your Excellency—The great Utility of this Contrivance your Excellency must be too well accquaintd with to Riquire any Comment from me.

"The Plan I take the liberty to lay before your Excellnys consideration is now complete—and its performance I have exibited before many Respectfull Characters in this Town—and I believe has met with their approbation—Should your Excellcys Time permits to view its performance—which in a very little time could be put in Motion And should it meet with your Excellnys approbation I should think my Time happily bestow'd—in forming an Institution—that your Excellcy might approve of—and what I should hope in my time might be of useful Utility—I hope your Excellny will Pardon this Freedom" (Cruse to GW, 1 Sept. 1790, DNA: RG 59, Miscellaneous Letters). Cruse enclosed a series of drawings of the invention; these drawings are reproduced in Boyd, *Jefferson Papers,* 16: facing p. 53. He may also have included an explanation of the engine or key to the numbered figures in the drawings, but no such enclosure has been found. Cruse was issued a patent for the device on 30 Aug. 1791 (Lear to Jefferson, 30 Aug. 1791, DLC:GW).

From Alexander Hamilton

Treasury Department [New York] May 6th 1790

The Secretary of the Treasury has the honor to inform the President of the United states of America, that he has received a letter from the Governor of Virginia intimating, that it is necessary an election should be made of the particular spot upon which it may be deemed proper to erect the intended Light house on Cape Henry, after which the Cession will be completed.[1]

The said Secretary having heard the propriety of the place contemplated for that purpose by the State of Virginia, called in question, as being peculiarly exposed to accumulations of sand in its vicinity, begs leave to submit to the President the expediency of appointing a trusty and judicious person to view the ground & make the choice; with power to take with him one or two seafaring people, who may possess local information.

The said Secretary further informs the President, that by a letter received from Benjamin Lincoln Esquire, it appears, that the widow Thomas, charged under the state of Massachusetts with the care of the Light-house at Plymouth has a son named [   ] Thomas, who is of good character and deserves the consideration of the President as Keeper of that Light-house.[2]

The said Benjamin Lincoln also informs the said Secretary, that he has agreed for the supply of oil for the Light-houses in the State of Massachusetts, at the rate of one hundred & four dollars per ton, which is lower than it has of late sold for, subject to ratification by the said Secretary with the approbation of the President.

On these particulars the said Secretary request's the order of the President.[3]

Copy, DLC:GW; LB, DNA: RG 26, Light House Services Correspondence (vault material).

1. Gov. Beverley Randolph of Virginia wrote to Hamilton on 23 Feb. 1790 that he was prepared to execute a deed for land for a lighthouse on Cape Henry as soon as the "particular spot . . . shall be marked out" (Randolph to Hamilton, 23 Feb. 1790, Syrett, *Hamilton Papers,* 6:277). For the background to this transaction, see GW to Thomas Newton, Jr., 12 Oct. 1789, n.1, and Beverley Randolph to GW, 18 Dec. 1789.

2. Benjamin Lincoln wrote to Hamilton on 6 April 1790 recommending "Mr. Thomas, son of the late General Thomas" for the post of lighthouse keeper at Plymouth (Lincoln to Hamilton, 6 April 1790, Syrett, *Hamilton Papers,* 6:355). John Thomas was subsequently appointed keeper. See also Hamilton to GW, 3 Jan. 1790, n.3.

3. William Jackson replied to Hamilton on 6 May 1790: "The President of the United States authorises the Secretary of the Treasury to engage Edward Carrington Esquire to visit Cape Henry and to make a selection of the spot for the purpose of the cession within mentioned (with permission to take with him one or two seafaring persons) and to make the parties a reasonable allowance for expence and trouble out of the monies appropriated towards erecting the said Light house.

"The President also thinks fit to appoint the said [   ] Thomas, Keeper or Superintendant of the Light house at Plymouth, and authorises the said Secretary to ratify the provisional Contract for oil within mentioned" (DNA: RG 26, Lighthouse Services Correspondence).

From John Nicholson

sir,   Philad[elphi]a May 6th 1790

It is not with a view that your mind should descend to the Matters which concern an individual that I beg leave to present the inclosed for your perusal: but As the subject relates to the interests of the states over whose concerns you preside And as the public paper both here And at the seat of General Government have exhibited representations of one side of the affairs therein refered to A desire to stand Justified in the Eyes of A personage whose Judgment I so highly revere makes me wish that if you have read Any of the others you would Also Audi Alteram partem. I have the honor to be with the highest respect your Most obedient most humble servant

Jno. Nicholson

ALS, DNA: RG 59, Miscellaneous Letters.

John Nicholson (1757–1800) was the principal financial officer of Pennsylvania and a prominent speculator in public securities. After serving as clerk to the Continental Board of Treasury from 1778 to 1781, he was appointed state comptroller general in 1782 and given responsibility for settling all the accounts to which the state was a party. In 1785 he was also appointed receiver general and in 1787, escheator general, responsible for liquidating the estates of those attainted of treason. In politics Nicholson was a defender of the Pennsylvania Constitution of 1776 and a prominent Antifederalist. In the late 1780s his political leanings combined with his extensive powers to make him the object of criticism from Federalists in the state legislature. In 1790 he was charged with abuse of his authority, and an attempt was made to remove him from public office. The enclosure has not been found but may have been a copy of Nicholson's defense, *Address to the People of Pennsylvania Containing a Narrative of the Proceedings against John Nicholson* (Philadelphia, 1790). In 1793 he was impeached by the Pennsylvania house of representatives for redeeming his own state certificates instead of funding them in new federal certificates. He was acquitted in the Pennsylvania senate in 1794 but resigned all of his offices. Nicholson was later involved with Robert Morris and James Greenleaf in investing in lots in the new federal city, which along with other speculations led to the collapse of his finances in 1797 and subsequent imprisonment for debt.

From Henry Hill

Sir   Philad[elphi]a May 7th 1790
I have the honor as one of the Executors of the late Doctor Franklin to present you by the hands of Major Clarkson a token left by him in the following words—"My fine Crabtree walking stick with a gold head curiously wrought in the form of the cap of Liberty I give to my friend & the friend of Mankind General Washington—If it were a sceptre, he has merited it, & would become it."[1] I am with best Compliments to Mrs Washington, & all sincere respect and affection Sir Your most obedt hble sert
Henry Hill

ALS, DLC:GW.

1. The walking stick was a gift to Franklin from Marianne Cammasse Deux-Ponts, comtesse de Forbach, one of his many French admirers (see Chevalier de Keralie to Franklin, 20 July 1783, PPAmP: Franklin Papers; see also Lopez, *Mon Cher Papa*, 191–92). The bequest to GW was part of the codicil to Franklin's 23 June 1789 will (Smyth, *Writings of Benjamin Franklin*, 10:501–10). Franklin's will adds: "It was a present to me from that excellent woman, Madame de Forbach, the dowager Duchess of Deux-Ponts, connected with some verses which should go with it." The poem was entitled "A Mr. Franklin, En lui présentant, de la part de Madame la Comtesse Douairière de Deux Ponts,

un bâton d'épine surmonté d'une pomme d'or, figurant le chapeau de la liberté":

> Dans les plaines de Marathon,
> Où l'insolence Musulmane
> A d'éternels affronts condamne
> La postérité de Solon;
> Parmi la ronce et les épines
> Qui couvrent ces bords malheureux,
> Et cachent les cendres divines
> Des sages, des héros fameux,
> La Liberté, votre déesse,
> Avant d'abandonner la Grece,
> Arracha ce bâton noueux:
> Ou le vit aux Alpes Pennines,
> Pour terrasser l'Autrichien,
> Briller entre les javelines
> Du valeureux Helvétien;
> Elle en fit depuis une lance,
> Lorsque dans les champs de Trenton
> Elle dirigeoit la vaillance
> Et l'audace de Washington.
> Ce symbole de la victoire
> Qu'orne aujourd'hui le chapeau du grand Tell,
> Ce ferme appui que votre gloire
> Rendra désormais immortel,
> Assurera vos pas au Temple de Mémoire.

Franklin had the poem printed by the Paris printer Didot the Elder in 1783 (copies of this printing are in the collections of the Library of Congress and the University of Pennsylvania). It is not known whether a copy of the poem was delivered to GW as Franklin instructed; no such enclosure to Hill's letter has been found. GW bequeathed the walking stick to his brother Charles, who died in 1799. The walking stick passed at GW's death to Charles's son, Samuel Washington, who gave it to his son, Samuel T. Washington. The latter presented it to Congress, along with one of GW's swords, in January 1843 (Ford, *Wills of George Washington,* 101). The walking stick is now (1994) in the Smithsonian Institution, Washington, D.C.

GW acknowledged receipt of the bequest in a letter to Hill of 3 June 1790: "The severe indisposition from which I am just recovering will excuse this late acknowledgement of your letter of the 7th instant, which accompanied the cane left me by the great and invaluable Dr Franklin.

"As a token of remembrance and a mark of friendship, I receive this legacy with pleasing sensations and a grateful heart, and the words in which it was conveyed were highly flattering, as coming from a man, of whom the world justly entertained an exalted opinion, and whose favorable sentiments could not fail of being grateful to the person upon whom they were bestowed.

"To you, Sir, my best acknowledgments are due for the polite manner in which you have executed your trust" (LB, DLC:GW).

From Beverley Randolph

Sir,   Richmond [Va.] May 7th 1790.

I do myself the Honour to inclose you a Letter from Colo. Clendenen Lieutenant of Kanawha covering Letters received by him from Colonels Lewis, and Rankins, on the subject of Indian depredations,[1] and am with the highest Respect &c.

Beverley Randolph

LB, Vi: Executive Letter Book.

1. Among the enclosures was probably "a letter from Robert Rankins, of Kantuckey, directed to Col. Thomas Lewis at the mouth of Kanawa, representing many depredations lately commited by the Indians, also his letter enclosing the same to him. He says that it is unnecessary for him to mention anything respecting their situation other than they are collected in bodies, and wait the moment when the savages will make a formidable attack to depopulate our settlements on the Ohio and Kanawa." The letter was forwarded to Beverley Randolph in a letter from George Clendenin, county lieutenant of Kanawha County, 15 April 1790 (*Calendar of Virginia State Papers*, 5:138).

From Robert Brough

Hampton [Va.], May 10th 1790. "I sometime ago unsuccesfully applied to you for an Appointment in the Customs—yr reasons were such as ought to govern—I am told there will be offices of a public Nature again in yr power—having read Law I have sometime been Notary Public at this place—if any thing of that sort or any other that is like to become profiteble shou'd occur, shall be ever obliged by an Appointment—I am not so much attachd to Hampton, but wou'd remove to Norfolk or any other place. I have, Sir but few, if any Virtues & not many friends to recommend me to your Attention—but I have *a family* and a greatful Heart."

ALS, DLC:GW.

1. For Brough's earlier application for public office, see his letter to GW, 20 July 1789.

From Eliphalet Fitch

Sir   Kingston Jamaica May 10th 1790
  The Respect which the World shews to your eminent Virtues and exalted Rank, has induced me to forward the inclosed Papers, relative to the Slave-Trade; which I beg Liave to present to you, thro' the Indulgence of the Vice-President, to whom I have the Honour to be known.[1] I am with the most perfect Respect and Esteem, Sir, Yr most Obedient and Most Humble Servt

Elipht Fitch

ALS, DLC:GW.
  Eliphalet Fitch (born c.1740) was a grandson of Dr. Thomas Boylston and a distant cousin of John Adams (John Adams to John Quincy Adams, 12 June 1783, MHi: Adams Family Papers). A native of Boston, he moved to Jamaica where he owned a sugar plantation, engaged in mercantile activities, and held the post of receiver general. In 1781 he was involved with Francisco de Miranda in supplying the Spanish with naval stores (Robertson, "Miranda and the Revolutionizing of Spanish America," 235–37; see Alexander Hamilton to GW, [c.15–22 July 1790]). John Adams apparently met Fitch in Paris in 1783 and noted in his diary that Fitch was "said to be very rich." Fitch socialized with both John and John Quincy Adams in Paris, Delft, and London in 1783 (Butterfield, *Diary of John Adams*, 3:128, 134; Allen, *Diary of John Quincy Adams*, 1:175, 204). He wrote to John Adams on 7 May 1790, renewing their acquaintance, and in a separate letter of 10 May he informed Adams that he was shipping him a barrel of sugar, a dozen bottles of rum, and two dozen bottles of madeira, adding: "I have requested my Mother to send you a Packet with some Papers relative to the Slave-Trade; and if you approve of sending Copies to the President I would avail myself of your kind Attention to them; as you will see by the inclosed Copy of my Letter." Fitch enclosed a copy of his letter to GW of 10 May (Fitch to John Adams, 7 and 10 May 1790, MHi: Adams Family Papers). The original of Fitch's letter to GW, along with the pamphlets, apparently was transmitted to Adams by Fitch's mother, who lived in the United States. No letter from her to Adams has been found.
  1. Among the enclosed pamphlets was almost certainly Bryan Edwards, *A Speech Delivered at a Free Conference between the Honourable the Council and Assembly of Jamaica Held the 19th of November, 1789 on the Subject of Mr. Wilberforce's Propositions in the House of Commons, concerning the Slave Trade* (Kingston, Jamaica, 1790). What other pamphlets Fitch may have enclosed is not known. GW had the Edwards pamphlet bound with five others under the title "Tracts on Slavery." Now in the collection of the Boston Athenaeum, this volume includes five other pamphlets. One of these, *Debates in the British House of Commons, Wednesday, May 13th 1789* (Philadelphia, 1789) may have been sent by Fitch. Of the remaining four, one is not about slavery, one was published in 1791, and two

others were American imprints, unlikely to have come to Fitch's attention in Jamaica (Griffin, *Boston Athenæum Collection,* 66, 179, 561). Tobias Lear replied to Fitch on 28 Aug.: "the Pamphlets relative to the Slave trade which you have been so obliging as to present to [GW] thro' the hands of the Vice President have been received, and he requests you to accept his best thanks" (DLC:GW).

From Moustier

Sir,   Paris May 11th 1790

The desire which I have had to multiply the portraits which Mad. de Brehan has made of you, has deprived her of the original for five months, which has remained during that time in the hands of the Engraver[1]—Our citizens of all denominations are at this day more or less taken off from their habitual occupations—and their functions, civil or military, absorb the greater part of their time—employed in trying to establish liberty between depostism, which has been overturned, and licentiousness which is eager to replace it. Accept, with goodness, I pray, Sir, the homage which I have the honor to make in the accompanying proofs—Mad. de Brehan will profit of the first certain opportunity which presents to address to Madam Washington the medallion intended for her—in the mean time, She will make a copy of the original for herself.

The Country in which I dwell at this moment ought no longer to be considered as that which I knew before I went to America. If excesses procure but rarely the happiness which they hold out, the virtuous and prudent part of the french nation ought to tremble.

"Without proper men to govern the best laws are a mere dead letter" said a Sage to me a short time before my departure from the United States—who more than we ought at this day to be convinced of it. The kingdom of France has been deeply wounded, and the remedies employed in its cure may prove fatal. I fear that many of those employed in restoring us are not sincere or sufficiently enlightened—There are among the principals, men of whom I have suspended my judgment till now— we cannot sound their intentions—actions wear frequently different aspects. Time indicates what ought to fix opinion.

I experience a solace of the chagrins caused by the situation of my own country, in learning the state of yours, Sir, which has the happiness to be guided by a chief capable of giving life to the laws. No one more sincerely and feelingly interests himself than I do in the successes of the United States and particularly in yours. I avow frankly that I cannot conceive the possibility of maintaining the prosperity of a great Empire without great means, and consequently without great force in the execution. It was not necessary to be convinced of this that I should within two years become a witness of two revolutions in opposite senses. In seeing on one side a great executive Power created—on the other, one, altogether established, overturned, and which, he who was clothed with it, offered of himself to regulate by the usage of wise laws. The want of this great and indispensable re-source holds us at this day in an anarchy which cannot cease but by the establishment of this legal resource, and for which I can-not see a substitute, notwithstanding the endeavor⟨s⟩ of ambi-tious and metaphysical men. I am, with respect, Sir, your most humble and most obedient Servant

The Count de Moustier.

Translation, DLC:GW; ALS, in French, DLC:GW. The text is taken from a translation made for GW. A transcription of the ALS in French may be found in CD-ROM:GW.

1. Moustier and his sister, the marquise de Bréhan, visited GW at Mount Vernon on 2–6 Nov. 1788 (*Diaries*, 5:417–19). See also Moustier to GW, 5 Oct. 1788, source note. The marquise subsequently visited GW in New York on 3 Oct. 1789. On that date GW recorded that he "sat about two Oclock for Madam de Brehan to complete a Miniature profile of me which she had begun from Memory and which she had made exceedingly like the Original" (ibid., 451–52). She may have begun the work during her visit to Mount Vernon or in Paris, working from one of Houdon's busts (hence GW's comment that the miniature looked "like the Original"). For a photograph of one of Bréhan's miniatures of GW, see ibid., 416.

William Jackson to Clement Biddle

Editorial Note

On Sunday, 9 May 1790, GW recorded in his diary that he was "Indis-posed with a bad cold, and at home all day writing letters on private business." His condition worsened overnight, and the next day he was confined to bed, apparently suffering from a bad case of influenza that developed into pneumonia. GW described the illness as "a severe attack of the peripneumony kind." James Madison, who had himself just recovered from a bout with influenza, described GW's illness as "peripneumony, united probably with the Influenza." Maryland congressman Michael Jenifer Stone described the illness as "Influenza Pleurisy and Peripneumony all at Once."[1]

Influenza was epidemic through most of the United States in the spring of 1790 and was particularly virulent in New York City. On 12 May William Maclay reported that "The whole Town, or nearly so, is sick and many die daily." On 15 May Richard Henry Lee described the city as "a perfect Hospital—few are well & many very sick."[2]

Although no hint of illness has been found in his diaries or letters before 9 May, GW apparently contracted influenza in late March or early April. On 6 April Richard Bland Lee reported to David Stuart that "the President has been unwell for a few days past." By 11 April GW's condition had apparently deteriorated. "I do not know the exact state of GW's health for a day or two last," George Clymer wrote, "but it is observed here with a great deal of anxiety that his general health seems to be declining. For some time past he has been subject to a slow fever. Jackson seems to think that as soon as the adjournment will let him, he will begin a long journey to the southward, which will probably reinstate him."[3]

GW apparently undertook his tour of Long Island (20–24 April) in order to recover his health through exercise. Abigail Adams reported that GW "has been very unwell through all the Spring, labouring with a villious disorder but thought, contrary to the advise of his Friends that he should excercise away without medical assistance; he made a Tour upon Long Island of 8 or ten days which was a temporary rielief." Robert Morris agreed that the tour of Long Island improved GW's health. To his wife Morris reported that "the President . . . has been riding on Long Island all last week & he has regained his looks, his appetite and his Health." Abraham Baldwin wrote that "Our great and good man has been unwell again this spring. I never saw him more emaciated, he has been out for a ride on Long Island for ten days, and since his return appears manifestly better. If his health should not get confirmed soon, we must send him out to mount Vernon to farm a-while, and let the Vice manage here; his habits require so much exercise, and he is so fond of his plantation, that I have no doubt it would soon restore him. It is so important to us to keep him alive as long as he can live, that we must let him exercise as he pleases, if he will only live and let us know it. His name is always of vast importance, but any body can do the greater part of the work, that is to be done at present, he has got us well launched in the new ship." Any relief GW may have obtained from his Long Island tour did not last

long. William Maclay reported to Benjamin Rush on 7 May that GW
had "nearly lost his hearing" as a consequence of the illness.[4]

GW apparently was confined to his bed from 10 May until at least
20 May and does not seem to have resumed his regular duties before
30 May. During the illness he was attended mainly by Dr. Samuel Bard
(1742–1821), one of the most prominent physicians in New York City.
Bard graduated from King's College and studied medicine in London
and Edinburgh. In 1767–68 he established the first medical school associated with King's College, and he later succeeded to his father's
extensive practice. Bard lived in the city through the British occupation and was widely accused of Loyalist sympathies, but his practice
continued to grow after the war. Bard had attended GW in June 1789,
when he operated to remove a tumor from GW's leg.[5]

At first the illness did not seem to be life-threatening. On 12 May
Martha Washington reported to Abigail Adams that "the President is
a little better today than he was yesterday." The same day William Jackson wrote to Clement Biddle (below) enclosing a letter from Bard to
Dr. John Jones of Philadelphia. Jackson assured Biddle that GW's
symptoms were not grave and presented Bard's desire to consult with
Jones as a mere precaution. The enclosed letter from Bard to Jones
has not been found. Dr. John Jones (1729–91) was born in Jamaica
and studied medicine in Philadelphia and several European cities.
After taking his degree at Rheims, he settled in New York. He served
as a surgeon in the French and Indian War and was later involved with
Samuel Bard in establishing the first New York Hospital. Jones was
highly regarded in Philadelphia and attended Franklin during his last
illness in the spring of 1790. Benjamin Rush regarded him as the finest
surgeon in the country. On the address sheet of Jackson's letter to
Jones is a contemporary note that Jones received the letter at 10:30
A.M. on 13 May and set off for New York at 1:00 P.M. that afternoon.
Sarah Jay records that Jones was in attendance on 15 May. He subsequently was paid £75.18.4 for his services.[6]

Bard also consulted two New York physicians, Dr. John Charlton
and Dr. John McKnight. Charleton was an English surgeon who had
come to New York with the British army and remained in the city after
the war. McKnight (1750–91) was born in New Jersey, graduated from
the College of New Jersey in 1771, and studied medicine with William
Shippen in Philadelphia. He served as a surgeon in the Continental
army, ending the war as one of the three chief physicians of the army.
After the war he practiced in New York City, where he was physician
to some of the city's most prominent families, professor of surgery and
anatomy to Columbia College, and port physician. Little is known
about the treatment these doctors prescribed. Abigail Adams reported

that GW was treated with James's Powder, a favorite fever remedy of the late eighteenth century, but nothing else about his treatment has been found. Henry Wynkoop thought that GW's recovery was "owing . . . more to the natural strength of his Constitution than the Aid of Medicine."[7]

GW's condition seems to have deteriorated quickly between 12 May and 15 May, when the crisis was reached. William Maclay, himself suffering from influenza, recorded on 15 May that he "called to see the President" and found "every Eye full of Tears" and "his life despaired of. Doctor Macknight told me he would Triffle neither with his own Character nor the public Expectation, his danger was iminent, and every reason to expect, That the Event of his disorder would be unfortunate." Theodore Sedgwick reported on 16 May that "About five oclock in the afternoon yesterday, the physicians disclosed that they had no hopes of his recovery. But about six he began to sweat most profusely, which continued untill this morning and we are now told that he is entirely out of danger, if he should not relapse." The passage of this crisis was described in detail by Thomas Jefferson, who wrote to his daughter Martha Jefferson Randolph on 16 May that "On Monday last the President was taken with a peripneumony, of threatening appearance. Yesterday (which was the 5th. day) he was thought by the physicians to be dying. However about 4. oclock in the evening a copious sweat came on, his expectoration, which had been thin and ichorous, began to assume a well digested form, his articulation became distinct, and in the course of two hours it was evident he had gone thro' a favorable crisis. He continues mending to-day, and from total despair we are now in good hopes of him." John Fenno reported that GW "expectorates blood & has a very high fever." Abigail Adams wrote that "just at the crisis [GW] was Seazd with Hicups & rattling in the Throat so that Mrs Washington left his room thinking him dying. The Physicians apprehended him in a most Dangerous State. James powders had been administerd, and they produced a happy Effect by a profuse perspiration which reliefd his cough & Breathing."[8]

By 17 May GW's improvement was clear. Jackson wrote to Clement Biddle at nine o'clock that evening that "The President is much better, and, I trust, out of all danger." On 20 May he was sufficiently recovered for Jackson to report to Biddle that "You will learn with pleasure that the President's recovery is now certain—the fever has entirely left him, and there is the best prospect of a perfect restoration of his health." On 22 May, Richard Henry Lee was admitted to GW's room and found him much improved, sitting up in an easy chair. "The President is again on his legs," Philip Schuyler wrote on 23 May; "he was yesterday able to traverse his room a dozen times." James Madison recorded on 25 May that GW was "so far advanced in his recovery as to be able to ride out."[9]

In the first days of GW's confinement, efforts were made to keep his condition from the public; "it was thought prudent," Abigail Adams explained, "to say very little upon the Subject as a general allarm may have proved injurious to the present State of the government." Nonetheless, GW's condition seems to have been widely known in New York City and Philadelphia as early as 15 May, and the policy of silence seems to have been abandoned after that date. Reports on GW's condition for public consumption apparently were made by those around him as early as the evening of 15 May or the following morning. News of his illness was carried from New York in private correspondence. Newpapers soon took up the story. On 18 May the *New York Journal* reported that "The President of the United States has been exceedingly indisposed for several days past, but we are rejoiced at the authentic information of his being much relieved the last evening." Similar news appeared in the *Pennsylvania Gazette* (Philadelphia) the next day. The popular response was overwhelming; reports of concern for GW's health were received from all parts of the country and from Europe. Samuel Ogden reported "Universal Gloom throughout this Country, on Acct of the President's Illness." Edward Rutledge reported that in South Carolina people were "greatly alarmed of late at the Account of the President's ill-health." The *Pennsylvania Gazette* (Philadelphia) reported on 26 May that "the President's recovery is now certain"; GW's recovery was reported in the *Alexandria Gazette* the next day.[10]

As news of his recovery spread, expressions of relief were universal. William Short wrote from Paris that reports of GW's "narrow escape affected sincerely all the friends to America here. His re-establishment gives great pleasure." Martha Washington wrote appreciatively to Mercy Otis Warren about this outpouring of public concern for her husband: "During the President's sickness, the kindness which everybody manifested, and the interest which was universally taken in his fate, were really very affecting to me. He seemed less concerned himself as to the event, than perhaps any other person in the United states. Happily he is now perfectly recovered, and I am restored to my ordinary state of tranquility, and usually good flow of spirits."[11]

During GW's illness the daily operations of the office devolved upon William Jackson, since Tobias Lear, who was married on 22 April, was absent on his honeymoon until late in May. GW does not seem to have resumed the duties of his office until the end of May; Jefferson reported him "well enough to resume business" on 27 May. No document dated between 9 May and 31 May 1790 bearing GW's signature has been found. GW did not resume making entries in his diary until 24 June 1790, and on or about that date he noted, heading the entry 10 May, that "A severe illness with which I was seized about the 10th. of this Month and which left me in a convalescent state for several weeks after the violence of it had passed; & little inclination to do more than what duty to the public required at my hands occasioned the suspension of this Diary."[12]

Although he was able to resume most of his duties by the end of May, GW did not recover fully for several more weeks. He wrote to Lafayette on 3 June that he had recovered "except in point of strength," and in mid-June he was still experiencing chest pain, coughing, and shortness of breath. His doctors advised GW to exercise more and devote less energy to public business. GW found this advice difficult to follow, but as soon as he was able, he resumed his habit of exercising to improve his health, making a three-day fishing trip off Sandy Hook in June; his trip to Rhode Island later in the summer may also have been motivated, in part, by a desire to exercise and recover his strength. GW apparently believed that the change from an active, outdoor life to the "inactivity" of administering the government had strained his constitution and caused two severe illnesses within a year. Reflecting the common belief that each bout with disease used up the body's ability to withstand future attacks, GW confided to David Stuart that he feared his next serious illness would "put me to sleep with my fathers."[13]

1. *Diaries*, 6:76; GW to Lafayette, 3 June 1790; Madison to James Madison, Sr., 2 May 1790, Madison to Edmund Randolph, 19 May 1790, Rutland, *Madison Papers*, 13:183–84, 222; Michael Jenifer Stone to Walter Stone, 17 May 1790, MdHi: Stone Papers.

2. Maclay to Benjamin Rush, 12 May 1790, DLC: Rush Papers; Lee to [Thomas Shippen Lee], 15 May 1790, Ballagh, *Letters of Richard Henry Lee*, 2:514–15.

3. Richard Bland Lee to David Stuart, 6 April 1790, privately owned; George Clymer to Henry Hill, 11 April 1790, PHC: Roberts Autograph Collection.

4. Abigail Adams to Cotton Tufts, 30 May 1790, MHi: Adams Family Papers; Morris to Mary White Morris, 28 April 1790, CSmH: Morris Papers; Abraham Baldwin to Joel Barlow, 8 May 1790, CtY; Maclay to Benjamin Rush, 7 May 1790, DLC: Benjamin Rush Papers.

5. James McHenry to GW, 28 June 1789, n.1. For GW's comments on Bard, see his letter to James McHenry, 3 July 1789.

6. Martha Washington to Abigail Adams, [12 May 1790], MHi: Adams Family Papers; Rush, *Autobiography*, 200–201; Sarah Livingston Jay to John Jay, 15 May 1790, Johnston, *Jay Papers*, 3:399; Decatur, *Private Affairs of George Washington*, 133; Tobias Lear to Clement Biddle, 20 June 1790, PHi.

7. Sarah Livingston Jay to John Jay, 15 May 1790, Johnston, *Jay Papers,* 3:399; Lamb, *History of New York,* 2:305; Harrison, *Princetonians, 1769–1775,* 156–60; Wynkoop to Reading Beatty, 20 May 1790, PDoBHi: Wynkoop Papers.

8. Bowling and Veit, *Diary of William Maclay,* 269; Theodore Sedgwick to Pamela Sedgwick, 16 May 1790, MHi: Theodore Sedgwick Papers; Jefferson to Martha Jefferson Randolph, 16 May 1790, Boyd, *Jefferson Papers,* 16:429; Fenno to Joseph Ward, 16 May 1790, ICHi: Joseph Ward Papers; Abigail Adams to Cotton Tufts, 30 May 1790, MHi: Adams Family Papers.

9. Jackson to Biddle, 17, 20 May 1790, PHi; Richard Henry Lee to Thomas Lee Shippen, 23 May 1790, DLC: Thomas Lee Shippen Papers; Philip Schuyler to Stephen Van Rensselaer, 23 May 1790, NAlI: Schuyler Family Papers; Madison to Beverley Randolph, 25 May 1790, Rutland, *Madison Papers,* 13:227–29.

10. Abigail Adams to Cotton Tufts, 30 May 1790, MHi: Adams Family Papers; Richard Henry Lee to [Thomas Lee Shippen], 15 May 1790, Ballagh, *Letters of Richard Henry Lee,* 2:514–15; Fisher Ames to George Richard Minot, 20 May 1790, Allen, *Works of Ames,* 735–37; Samuel Ogden to Henry Knox, 22 May 1790, NNGL; Edward Rutledge to Thomas Jefferson, 20 June 1790, Boyd, *Jefferson Papers,* 16:544–45.

11. William Short to Thomas Jefferson, 7 July 1790, Boyd, *Jefferson Papers,* 17:10–14; Martha Washington to Mercy Otis Warren, 12 June 1790, *Warren-Adams Letters,* 2:319–20.

12. Jefferson to William Short, 27 May 1790, Boyd, *Jefferson Papers,* 16:443–45; Henry Wynkoop to Reading Beatty, 27 May 1790, PDoBHi: Wynkoop Papers; *Diaries,* 6:77.

13. GW to Lafayette, 3 June 1790, to David Stuart, 15 June 1790, to Clement Biddle, 20 July 1790, to James Craik, 8 Sept. 1789.

Dear Sir,   New York, wednesday noon, May 2nd 1790.

The enclosed letter, from Doctor Bard to Doctor Jones, is transmitted to you with a view to ensure *secrecy, certainty,* and *dispatch* in the delivery of it.

To relieve you from any extraordinary personal anxiety I am happy to inform you that the symptoms which attend the President's indisposition, are not threatening—but it has been thought the part of prudence to call upon Doctor Jones, in anticipation of any unfavorable change that *may* arise.

I need not repeat to you the necessity of delivering the letter with *privacy,* and keeping the object of it a secret from every person—even Mrs Biddle.

Doctor Jones may want your aid to accelerate his arrival at New York—and I am persuaded you will give him every assistance in your power—The Doctor's prudence will suggest the propriety of setting out as privately as possible—perhaps it may be well to assign a personal reason for visiting new York, or going into the Country. I am, with great regard, Dear Sir, your most obedient Servant

W. Jackson.

ALS, PHi: Washington-Biddle Correspondence.

From Giuseppe Chiappe

Mogador [Morocco] 13 May. 1790.

Since my last of the 18th of July, which joined the copy of another preceding of the 25th of April which I had the honor to dispatch by Captain Joseph Proctor of Salem, I have always flattered myself with the hope of receiving an answer—and nothing remarkable having happened since, which merited the attention of the honorable the Congress of the United States of america, I have confined myself to keeping the monarch in the continuation of his favorable dispositions towards the illustrious nation for which he has manifested so much attachment in his sovereign conduct—in fact he spoke of it frequently with distinction, and with marks of desire to maintain a mutual friendly correspondence.

His Majesty J. Sydy Mohamet Ben Abdalla having left Morrocco on the 27th of March to go to his capital of Mequinez, being on the road about three hours distance from his city of Salee, died on the 11th of last month, in his little carriage, being taken therein with a violent hemor⟨r⟩hage of blood up and down, which naturally suffocated him.[1]

The new monarch Sydy Mulay Lyasid, natural Son of the deceased Sultan⟨,⟩ and worthy successor of so great a father has already mounted the throne, and it is anticipated of him that he will not cease to follow the laudable examples of his August Predecessor.

I acquit myself of my duty in immediately communicating this intelligence to your Excellency that you may inform respectively the honorable the Congress of the United States, in order that the necessary dispositions may be made, which in similar cases tend to the continuance of good harmony. and on my part I will not fail to preserve it by the most suitable means, and which are indispensably attached to the employment with which I have been charged by the very happy nation that I serve. And always in the expectation of their approbation and venerable commands. I have the honor to be, very profoundly your Excellency's most humble and most obedt Servt

Giuseppe Chiappe

Translation, DNA: RG 59, Miscellaneous Letters; ALS, DNA:PCC, item 98. The text is taken from a translation prepared for GW. For the text of the original French document, see CD-ROM:GW.

1. Muhammed Ibn Abdallah (generally referred to as Sidi Muhammed), sultan of Morocco (1757–1790), restored order to Morocco after decades of anarchy, built the first Moroccan navy, and signed commercial treaties with several European nations. Under his rule Morocco became the second nation to recognize the independence of the United States, and the two nations concluded a commercial treaty in 1786. He died in March 1790 and was succeeded by his son, Yazid Ibn Muhammed, who died in 1792 (Spencer, *Historical Dictionary of Morocco*, xiii, 80). For the background to this letter, see Giuseppe Chiappe to GW, 18 July 1789.

From Betty Washington Lewis

My Dear Brother   May the 18th 1790

   my being absent from Home for Six weeks is the reason of my not writing to you sooner, I was on a Visit to my Son Lawrence In Essex at the time I Expect'd his wife to lyin, Pore thing it Prove'd fatal to her, she was takein with Fits and died in twelve Ours without being Deliver'd, he lost a very good wife and with her all the Fortune as she was not of age to make a Right to any Part.[1]

   We have not yet settled the accompts of my Mothers Estate Some not Prov'd, and One Hogshead of Tobacco belonging to the Estate not Sold as the Price is very low[2] I thought it better to wait as there was a Prospect of its riseing, the last Letter I Receiv'd from Robert mentions his accompany'g Mr Lear to New Hampshire I hope it was not without your approbation, I have Inclos'd a letter to him, as I Expect he is returned by this.[3] my sincar Love and Best wishes attend you and my Sister Washington and Children. I am Dear Brother your affectionate Sister

Betty Lewis

N.B. when the accpts is made out and settled I shall have them sent you.

ALS, ViMtV.

1. Lawrence Lewis (1767–1839) was the third surviving son of Fielding and Betty Lewis. He was educated at an academy in Fredericksburg and by private tutors at Kenmore. About 1789 he married Susannah Edmundson and established himself on a plantation in Essex County. In 1799 Lawrence married Nelly Custis, Martha Washington's granddaughter.

2. Mary Ball Washington died 25 Aug. 1789 (see Burgess Ball to GW, 25 Aug. 1789), making GW executor of her will. GW left responsibility for settling their mother's estate to his sister Betty (see GW to Betty Washington Lewis, 13 Sept. 1789).

3. Tobias Lear left New York about 15 April and traveled to Portsmouth, N.H., where he married Mary (Polly) Long on 22 April (*New Hampshire Gazette* [Portsmouth], 28 April 1790). Lear arrived back in New York with his bride about 21 or 22 May; he may have cut his trip short after learning of GW's illness, which was reported in the *Boston Gazette* on 18 May. No evidence has been found that Robert Lewis accompanied Lear to New Hampshire.

From Mercy Otis Warren

Sir   Plimouth [Mass.] May 18 1790

Though it is my wish to prefix the inclosed dedication to a volume prepared for the press I would not take this liberty without first asking your permission. The work contains two Tragedies and some micellaneous pieces, written several years since a subscription has been advertised & it will be commited to the press as soon as I have the honour of your reply.[1]

Most unfeignedly sir have your friends at plimouth been affected by hearing of your late severe Illness. God Grant a restoration & perfect Comfirmation of Health to a gentleman on whose life the most important Consequences may depend.[2]

Mr Warren unites with me in the most Respectful regards to yourself & lady. He has been very Ill since his return as he was during the whole of his residence at new york:[3] this circumstance prevented him the pleasure of paying that perticuler attention to Mrs Washington that both friendship & politness dictated. an apology also for myself is due to her: for introducing a son as the bearer of a letter: but an accident impeded his journy to New york & consequently the honour of a personal attendence. Give me leave sir to subscribe most respectfully & sincerly your most obedient

M. Warren

ALS, DLC:GW.

Mercy Otis Warren (1728–1814) was a leading American poet, dramatist, and historian of the Revolutionary era. Through her brother, James Otis, and her husband, James Warren (for an identification, see James Warren to GW, 2 May 1789, source note), Mercy Otis Warren was associated with some of the leading figures in Revolutionary Massachusetts. Deeply interested in politics, she corresponded with John and Abigail Adams, Samuel Adams, and Thomas Jefferson, among others, and upheld the right of women to be involved in public life. She is perhaps best known for her *History of the Rise, Progress, and Termination of the American Revolution,* published in 1805.

1. The enclosure was apparently Mercy Warren's letter to GW, 1 May 1790: "Ambitious to avoid both the stile and the sentiment of common Dedications more frequently the incense of adulation than the result of truth, I only ask the Illustrious Washington to permit a Lady of his acquaintance to introduce to the publick under his patronage a small Volume written as the amusement of solitude at a period when every active member of society was engaged either in the feild or the cabinet to resist the strong hand of foreign domination.

"The approbation of one who has united all hearts in the feild of Conquest, in the Lap of peace, and at the head of the Government of the United States must for a time give countenance to a Writer who claiming the honour of private friendship hopes for this indulgence. But it must be a bold adventurer in the paths of Literature who dreams of fame in any degree commensurate with the duration of Laurels reaped by an Hero who has led the armies of America to glory, victory and independance.

"This may perhaps be an improper Place to make many Observations on a revolution that may eventually shake the proud Systems of European despotism; yet you Sir (who have born such a distinguish'd and honorable part in the great Conflict till the nations wearied with slaughter listen'd to the voice of nature and providence & gave truce to the miseries of man) will permit me to observe, that connected by consanguinity or friendship with many of the principal Characters who asserted and defended the rights of an injur'd country, the mind has been naturally led to contemplate the magnitude both of the causes and the consequences of a convulsion that has been felt from the Eastern borders of the atlantick to the western wilds.

"Feeling much for the distresses of America in the dark days of her affliction a faithful record has been kept of the most material transactions through a period that has engag'd the attention both of the philosopher & the politician; and if Life is spar'd a just trait of the most distinguish'd Characters either for Valour, Virtue, or Patriotism, for perfidy, intritgue, inconsistency or ingratitude, shall be faithfully transmitted to posterity by one who unites in the general wish that you Sir, may continue to preside in the midst of your Brethren, until nature asks the aid of retirement and repose, to tranquillize the last stages of human Life" (DLC:GW). GW responded on 4 June 1790: "Madam, I did not receive before the last mail the letter wherein you favored me with a copy of the Dedication, which you propose affixing to a Work preparing for publication. Although I have ever wished to avoid being drawn into public view more than was essentially necessary for public purposes; yet, on the present occasion, duly sensible of the merits of the respectable & amiable writer, I shall not hesitate to accept the intended honor.

"With only leisure to thank you for your indulgent sentiments, and to wish that your Work may meet with the encouragement which I have no doubt it deserves; I hasten to present the Compliments of Mrs Washington . . . " (ALS, DSoCi).

The text of Mercy Warren's letter dated 1 May 1790, with minor deviations in capitalization, was published as the dedication to Warren's *Poems, Dramatic and Miscellaneous* (printed by I. Thomas and E. T. Andrews, Boston, 1790), under the heading "To George Washington, President of the United States of America." The published dedication was dated "Plymouth, Massachusetts, March 20, 1790." Warren may have intended that the dedication be delivered to GW by James Warren, who left for New York on 25 March. The book consisted of two dramatic works, "The Sack of Rome, a Tragedy," and "The Ladies of Castile, a Tragedy," along with eighteen miscellaneous poems. Warren wrote to GW from Plymouth on 12 Sept. 1790: "I have taken the liberty to inclose and ask your acceptance of a Volum which if you sir do the author the honour to read: much more if your taste should be pleased & your judgment approve will she be flattered with an Idea that the work has some real merit" (PHi: Gratz Collection). This copy of *Poems, Dramatic and Miscellaneous*, inscribed to GW, is among GW's books now in the Boston Athenaeum (Griffin, *Boston Athenæum Collection*, 219, 490). GW replied from Mount Vernon on 4 Nov. 1790: "My engagements since the receipt of your letter of the 12th of Septr, with which I was honored two days ago, have prevented an attentive perusal of the Book that accompanied it—but, from the reputation of its Author—from the parts I have read—and from a general idea of the pieces, I am persuaded of its gracious and distinguished reception by the friends of virtue & science" (ALS [photocopy], ViMtV).

2. On GW's illness, see William Jackson to Clement Biddle, 12 May 1790, editorial note.

3. James Warren went to New York on 25 Mar. 1790 to settle his accounts as a member of the Continental Navy Board, on which he served from 1776 to 1781 (see Gardiner, *A Study in Dissent*, esp. 238–240). On 3 April he presented a petition to Congress, seeking settlement of a claim against the United States. This petition was referred to the secretary of the treasury, who reported against paying Warren's claim (Syrett, *Hamilton Papers*, 6:309, 362–64). A motion to pay Warren $384.92 was defeated in the House of Representatives on 23 April 1790 (*DHFC*, 3:377). Shortly afterwards, Warren applied to GW for a federal appointment (see James Warren to GW, 10 June 1790).

From John Joseph de Barth and Mr. Thiebaud

Sir,   New York 19th May. 1790.

A great number of french people are arrived in this Country with an intention to settle on lands, which they have respectively acquired from the agents of the Scioto Company residing in Paris; which lands are situated between the Ohio & Scioto rivers in the Western territory of the United States, as expressed in the Contract between the United States and Messrs Sergent & Cutler.

Independent of the duty which obliges them to offer to the United States an homage of the most profound respect, and most perfect submission to all the laws of their new Country, in quality of new subjects and faithful Citizens; these emigrants determine to sacrifice their lives & property, in whatever manner it may depend on them to promote the public good. They hope therefore they may be permited to implore the protection of the supreme power of the United States for their persons and property; which they have conceived to be in great danger from the numerous accounts in the public papers, as well as from the reports of individuals respecting the depredations of the savages committed on the inhabitants in that quarter.

Under these circumstances, sir, in the name of our Countrymen & associates we have presumed to supplicate you to direct the Governor & Officers in the Western territory to afford us such military support as the nature of our situation may from time to time require; and of which we may have the more occassion as the distance between the two principal establishments we are about to form, makes it difficult to act in concert.

We most ardently supplicate the great author of all good for the speedy & perfect establishment of your precious health; & permit us sir to assure you, that in obtaining this favour, Our gratitude will be equalled only by the respect—with which we are sir Your most Obedient and most humble servants[1]

> De Barth
> thiebaud
> for ourselves and associates

Copy, PHi: Scioto Land Company Papers.

For background to this document, see Louis Le Bègue de Presle Duportail to GW, 10 Feb. 1790 and notes.

1. GW replied to the Scioto Associates' letter on 30 June 1790: "At the time when your first application arrived, my health was unfortunately in such an impaired condition as to prevent me from attending to any business whatever. My sickness at that period, also, deprived me of the pleasure of seeing several Gentlemen concerned in the Scioto Settlement, who were then in this Town. Upon my recovery, and before those Gentlemen had returned to Alexandria, I received another Address. But understanding that arrangements had been made to remove most or all of the difficulties which had occurred; and understanding likewise that the Persons best advised on the subject were well satisfied with the measures which had been taken, and in general with the prospects I omitted to acknowledge the receipt of those applications at an earlier day. The variety of objects which demanded my immediate attention, on the re-establishment of my health must be considered (as was really the case) a principal occasion of this delay on my part.

The design of this letter is particularly to acquaint you, Gentlemen, that I had not through inattention neglected taking notice of your Addresses; to wellcome you upon you⟨r⟩ arrival in this Country; and to assure you of all that *Countenance* and *protection* from the general Government of the United States which the Constitution and Laws will enable the Executive to afford under existing circumstances" (ALS, owned [1970] by Mr. Blanchard Randall, Jr., Charleston, West Virginia).

From Arthur Fenner

Sir.   State of Rhode Island. Providence May 20th 1790.

Having been lately elected, by the Freemen of this State, to the office of their first Magistrate, I therefore embrace this early oppertunity of assuring you of the sincere regard which I, in common with the Citizens in general, feel for your Excellency personally. Admist the Universal Applause and the grateful Acknowledgements of United America singular indeed would it be, if the Citizens of Rhode Island were insensible of the Obligations they are under to your Excellency for the constant Exertions and display of those Talents, and that Patriotism manifested on all Occasions, since you came into public life, and which so much contributed to the Emancipation and Independence of our Country. The Citizens of this State were among the foremost in the support of the common cause of the American Confederacy, in the late War, and they will always remember with Gratitude and pride the repeated Testimonials you was pleased to give of your Approbation of their Exertions, and of the Valour of their Troops, on Various Occasions, in the Hours of difficulty and Danger.

This State was at all times during the War anxious if possible to comply with any wish signified to them by your Excellency. And when it is considered that a large Army of the Enemy for near three years of the most gloomy and uncertain Periods of the War were, in Possession of their Capital, and of the Island of Rhode Island, and the other Islands in the Narraganset Bay. That the Towns of Warren, Bristol and Jamestown were burnt on excursions of the Enemy, and that during the whole Period of their having Possession of Rhode Island, a considerable part of the Militia of the State were necessarily kept on constant Duty, guarding the Shores of the Narraganset Bay more than sixty miles in Extent, it will be natural to conclude that no State suffered more than the State of Rhode Island in proportion to their numbers and extent, or made greater Exertions for the support of the common Cause. I Just mention these Circumstanc's to recal to your Excellency's mind those trying times when we looked to your Excellency as our common Protector, Friend, and Father endearing Appellations under which we hope yet long to consider you. It hath been published in the Newspapers that a Bill is now pending before the Senate of the United States entitled "An Act to prevent bringing goods wares and Merchandize from the State of Rhode Island and providence Plantations into the United [States] and to authorize a demand of Mony from the said State" A Copy of which Bill at large hath been published.[1]

This being a matter highly interesting to this State your Exccellency will permit me to make some observations upon it. It was natural to expect that there should be a Degree of Anxiety and impatience in the States in the Union on seeing this State not under the General Government. But after it was known to Congress that a Convention of the people of this State had been called agreeable to the Recommendation of the Convention of Philadelphia and the consequent Resolution of Congress, and that the Convention of this State was adjourned to the last Monday of this month for the purpose of Reconciling the people to an adoption of the Constitution, who had been oposed to it and when there was the greatest Probability that the New Constitution would then be adopted by the Convention of this State, a Measure of such an Hostile appearance and so degrading to this State as the one before mentioned could not be expected by us. I can account for it only by supposing that Representations un-

favourable to the Adoption of the Constitution here must have
been forwarded to Congress by Persons in this State who have
had selfish and personally interesting motives therefor. It must
be a matter known to your Excellency and to Congress that this
State hath been very unhappy for several years past, in having
been invol[v]ed in all the dificulties and Animosities of party
Spirrit. The great Exertions of the People in general in the War
caused an heavy accumulation of Debt payable from the Public
to the Individuals, who had done personal services or advanced
property. But the public having taken no seasonably effectual
measures for keeping up the Credit of their Securities, till they
greatly depreciated and had generally been parted with by the
Original Holders or Earners for very small Considerations to
the Richer, the more Speculating, and enterprising part of the
Community, who availed themselves of the then low price—
When therefore the Body of the People who had thus parted
with their securities came to be taxed for the annual Interest of
six per Cent payable on the Face of the securities which in a
short time would amount to more than the Purchasors had
given both for principel and interest it caused investigations and
discussions of the Reasonableness and Justice of the Public paying so much more than the purchasers had given for the Securities. Especially as many of the Purchasers had been instrumental
in depreciating the Securities and at the time of purchasing had
made use of the argument of the uncertainty of their ever being
paid to induce the Original Earners to part with them at a low
price. Many supposed that there ought to have been a descrimi-
nation in favour of the present original Holders and a Liquidation of those which had been transferred that the same arguments and the same principles and the same policy which led
the Congress *in 1780* to adopt the measure of sinking forty Dollars of their Currency for one Silver Dollar notwithstanding the
Bill promised forty Silver Dollars would apply with the same
Equity and Reason proportionably to the Case of the Securities
which had been purchased for less than a quarter of their nominal amount[.] Difference of opinion respecting this interesting
Subject and the Introduction of the paper mony here in 1786
and the unremitted Efforts of a part of the State to destroy its
Currency, by depreciating it, and the jarring Interests introduced by the Depreciation with some Local considerations and

personal Resentments naturally consequent thereon laid the Foundation of that party Spirrit which hath agitated the Government of this State for sometime past, and hath occasioned the unfavourable Complexion of many of its Legislative proceedings and that Torrent of obloquy and abuse of the State and its officers which hath been poured forth in the Newspapers. But I mean not to Trouble your your Excellency with an account in detail of the Circumstances which have led Step by Step, to our present unhappy Situation—Was I to undertake it, your Excellency would behold the Picture of a People, who from being respectable in themselves, by their Struggles in party, have been reduced into a Political situation so uncommon & peculiar, and of such irreconciliably varying and jarring interests, that to a benevolent and philosophic mind particularly informed of the Circumstances, they would appear rather to deserve the Mantle of Charity, than the Obloquy of Reproach, and to merit pity rather than resentment or contempt. The Conduct of the Legislature respecting the New Constitution is a proof more of Indecision of Council, than of Refractoriness of Disposition. In *May 1787* on the Question in the Lower House whether Delegates should be sent to the Convention then about meeting at Philadelphia it was, after long Debate voted in the Affirmative, by a Majority of two, and non-concurred in the upper House by the same Majority. But at the Session in June following it appearing that the other States had all agreed to a Convention, the upper House altered their opinion and by a large Majority Voted to send forward Delegates. But on sending their Vote to the Lower House they in their turn non concurred and no Delegates were sent. And since the Publication of the Constitution and the adoption of it by the other States the Various and numerous proceedings of the Legislature respecting it, from time to time, have been more influenced by party considerations than a determination finally to reject it. And as I can now assure your Excellency that all the other States having joined the New Confederacy and many important Amendments having been proposed, some of which have already been agreed to, many persons of influence who have heretofore opposed the adoption of the New Constitution here, have withdrawn their opposition, there is therefore reason to suppose that it will be very soon adopted in this State; and as measures which have the appearance of Coertion may be productive of Alienation of Affection, and will be peculiarly degrading to a State, which though small when She comes to join the Union will not be wanting in that public Spirrit and Patriotism which She hath heretofore been acknowledged to Possess Permit me therefore in behalf of a State, towards which your Exellency hath heretofore appeared friendly disposed, to solicit your Exellency to take such measures as your Wisdom shall suggest for preventing any fu[r]ther proceedings of Congress, on the before mentioned Report of the Committee of the Honorable the Senate, at least until it shall be determined, by the Convention of this State whether they will adopt the New Constitution or not of which your Excellency shall have the Earliest information immediately after their rising.

Any Communications your Excellency may wish to have made to the Legislature of this State committed to my care shall have the earliest and most respe[c]tful attention paid them by him who begs leave to subscribe himself with the highest sentiments of Esteem and the sincerest Regard Your Excellencys most Obedient Servant

Arthur Fenner.

ALS, DNA: RG 59, Miscellaneous Letters.
   Arthur Fenner (1745–1805) of Providence, R.I., served for a number of years as clerk of the court of common pleas in Providence. When Rhode Island first considered ratification of the federal Constitution in 1787, Fenner became a leader of the party opposing ratification. On 5 May 1790 the Rhode Island legislature elected him governor to replace John Collins. Fenner was reelected governor in 1791 and served successive terms until his death.
   1. Rhode Island had not yet ratified the Constitution, and on 28 April 1790 the U.S. Senate appointed a committee consisting of Charles Carroll of Carrollton, Roger Ellsworth, Robert Morris, Ralph Izard, and Pierce Butler "to consider what provisions will be proper for Congress to make, in the present session, respecting the State of Rhode-Island." On 5 May the committee presented its report, and on 11 May the Senate considered the report, resolving that "all commercial intercourse between the United States and the State of Rhode-Island, from and after the first day of July next, be prohibited under suitable penalties." The bill also authorized the president to demand an undetermined sum of money from Rhode Island (*DHFC*, 1:294–95, 303, 305–6, 307, 720; an annotated copy of the bill is in DLC: Rare Book Room). As William Maclay noted, the bill would, in effect, "put that State in a kind of Commercial Coventry. to prevent all intercourse with them in the way of Trade" (Bowling and Veit, *Diary of William Maclay*, 260). On 13 May "An Act to prevent

bringing goods, wares and merchandizes from the State of Rhode-Island and Providence Plantations, into the United States, and to authorize a demand of money from the said State" was read for the first time, on 14 May for the second time, and on 17 May read for the third time and recommitted. The bill, with amendments, was sent to the House on 18 May. The ratification of the Constitution by Rhode Island on 29 May ended deliberation on the bill (*DHFC*, 1:309, 311, 312, 720, 3:418).

From George Clinton

Sir   New York 21st May 1790.

With this I do myself the Honor to inclose You Copies of Letters from Lieut. Colonel Woolsey, Judge Platt, Justice Moor, and other Inhabitants of this State residing on the West Banks of Lake Champlain containing all the Information which I at present have on the Subject to which they relate.[1]

Your present Indisposition will not permit me personally to attend You on this Business and I have therefore thought it prudent for the present only to write to Colo. Woolsey who commands the Militia in that Quarter recommending it to the Inhabitants not to remove unless they are compelled by an armed Force and I shall also direct him and the Civil Magistrates to make farther Enquiry respecting this Aggression. His Answer and whatever other Information I may receive shall be immediately communicated to your Excellency. I have the Honor to be with the highest Respect Your most obedient Servant

                                       Geo: Clinton

LS, DNA: RG 59, Miscellaneous Letters.

1. This letter concerned land occupied by refugees from the United States' Canadian campaign during the early years of the American Revolution. Many Canadian supporters were forced to flee Canada with the Americans during their retreat and Congress eventually provided land near the Canadian border in settlement of their claims. See Clement Gosselin to GW, 18 Sept. 1789, source note. The interference by Canadian officials with the settlers described in the enclosures to Clinton's letter undoubtedly arose from disputes over the boundary of the refugee tract. See Everest, *Moses Hazen and the Canadian Refugees in the American Revolution*, 137. Among the enclosures to George Clinton's letter, was a letter to the governor, 26 April 1790, describing the challenge of Canadian officers to the settlers of Champlain, New York. It was signed "in behalf of ourselves and the Inhabitants of the Town" by William Beaumont, Elnathan Rogers, Murdock McPherson, and Jacques (James) Rous (Rouse), who, together with Pliny Moore, had all settled in the area around 1787. "We

the Subscribers beg leave to Represent to your Excellency the Peculiar Situation of ourselves and A number of the Inhabitants of this Town we are Setled in the Northermost Township in the State of New York on the West Side of Lake Champlane in the Neighbourhood of the British Garison at Point Aufair, the 24th of Inst. Apl—The officer Commanding at Point au Fair Came to A Number of our Houses With A Party of unarm'd Soldiers and informd us that he had Orders from head Quarters in Canada to Command Us the Subscribers and A number more of the Inhabitants of this Town Not to make any more Improvements on the Lands here, but to remove with our families and Effects from this Place as soon as possible our answer was that we had Setled here on land that were our own and that we Should Continue here until we were remov'd by force (Some of the Inhabitants were Commanded to remove within Eight Days) Should Those Orders be put in Execution⟨,⟩ Should we be forced to remove, our situation would be Peculiar⟨ly⟩ Distressing the most of us have Expended what Property we ⟨were⟩ Possessd of in Cultivating this New Country our dependence is therefore on the produce of our Lands, we have Suffered Every fatigue and hardship incident to Setling New Countrys and our Situation is very Critical on Account that we are so far from any Old Settlement and we have no Land roads nor any sufficient water Craft to Transport ourselves our families and Effects in Case of Necessity, all which tend to Increase the Difficulties of our Situation—We would therefore beg your Excellency to take our Circumstances into Consideration and if possible direct Some Measures for our relief should matters Come to Extremity we Expect from your Wisdom and Paternal Care Every Consistant Support and that we Shall not be Abandon'd in the hour of Distress, we would likewise Claim Some Merrit (and think ourselves Intitled to the Attention of the State) from our past Services We have the most of us Personally Servd in the American Army During the Late Unnatural War with Great Britain the Greatest number of the Inhabitants of this Town are Refugees from Canada who have left their Country and their All for the American Cause and have no Where to Look for relief Should they be driven from their habitation but in the Indulgent Care of the Suprem⟨e⟩ Authority of this State.

We beg therefore your Excellency would be pleasd to give us you⟨r⟩ advice how to Conduct in the present Crisis. . . ." (DNA: RG 59, Miscellaneous Letters).

Pliny Moore's letter to Clinton, dated Champlain, 24 April 1790, reads: "This day the officer Commanding the British Garrison at Point ofere was at my House attended by a party of unarmed Soldiers, Told me he was Commanded by the Governor of Canada to order me not to make any further improvement on the Land where I am settled but to remove from it in a short time—I gave him for answer that the Land and improvement where he saw me Settled were my property by a Grant from the Governor of the State of New York that I was determined to remain on my possession till compelled by force of arms to remove⟨.⟩ I asked him if he had orders to inforce a compliance, he told me his orders were only to deliver the message and report my answer. I requested a Copy of his orders or the purport in writing which he declined giving. He then proceded up the River to Mr Rogers's and Esquire Beaumonts and delivered the same message to them their answers were for Substance the same as mine, he requested of each of us a determinate answer—as soon as the officer has reported our refusal to Head Quarters we shall probably hear more of their determinations with respect to us, may we not expect and depend on protection in the enjoyment of our property from the Goverment to which we are subject, or are we to submit to the repeated incroachments of British Govement? was it merely a sacrifise of the property of a *few* individuals though grievous in the last degree to the sufferers it might be born with some degree of patience, but the insult to the United States to a person who feels for the Honour of his Country is intolerable—Two or thre⟨e⟩ families who lived near the Garrison have been ordered of[f] by the officer and have actually removed about three weeks ago—I Enclose your Excellency the Copy of a Letter Received by Express from Esquire McPherson who resides about Ten miles distant on the Lake Shore and about five miles South of Point ofere—this together with the Reports from Canada of the warlike preperations, the Militia ordered ⟨to⟩ hold themselves in readiness the frequent presents lately made to the Indians and an other armed Vessel to be refitted and put in Commission to be stationed on this Lake to Inhabitants so cont⟨e⟩gious as we are and so defenceless your Excellency will think somewhat alarming—In th⟨is⟩ situation we beg your Excellencys Speedy advice—Ruin to us attend our ⟨remo⟩val and for ought we know our stay may be equally dangerous if no⟨t⟩ fatal—The Loyalists settled on the other side the line near us talk much of the British Lines being extended to Split Rock and the Maria and the other armed Vessel to be refitted to be stationed there, of this and the reports I mentioned from Canada I will endeavour to gain a more certain account of and give your Excellency the earliest information." Moore added a postscript dated 27 April: "since writing the above I have been convinced of a small mistake respecting the person from whom the officer received his orders. he told me his orders were from Head Quarters I had the Idea that Head Quarters was at Quebeck and that consequently they were from the Governor I have since been informed that the Garrison of point ofere is releived from St Johns (the officer monthly) and believe he calls that post Head Quarters, probably the Governor knows nothing of those orders and that they have been influenced by interested persons.

"That they are raising and repairing the Shipping at St Johns all that will answer I believe may be depended on" (DNA: RG 59, Miscellaneous Letters).

Also enclosed was a letter from Murdock McPherson to Pliny Moore, 24 April, reporting the Canadian order that he move from his residence within eight days (DNA: RG 59, Miscellaneous Letters). A similar letter from James Rous to Melancthon Woolsey, dated 27 April, indicated that Rous had been given six days to vacate his property (DNA: RG 59, Miscellaneous Letters).

The letters were enclosed by Melancthon Woolsey and Charles Platt in a letter to George Clinton, 28 April from Plattsburg, N.Y.: "Inclosed are two letters from Pliny Moor Esqr. and Capt. Jaques Rouse, those letters will inform your Excellency of our situation—in consequence of them I have Ordered all the Militia to be in readiness for service & Capt. Rouse particularly to be prepared and in case of invasion by an armed force, to repel the same by force, but by no means to be the agressor.

"I request your Excellencys pointed Orders on this subject which untill I receive I shall govern myself by the militia law and the advice of the superior magestrates near me.

"Judge Platt who is all the friend I have here to advise with, approves of the Orders already issued & joins as your Excellency will perceive by his signature in beging for such instructions, (as spedily as may be) as will conduce most to the *Dignity* of the State and our security.

"Had it been in our power to have raised money sufficient to defray the Expences of an Express, this information would have been communicated in that way as it is, we are obliged to forward it to Albany, and from thence by Post" (DNA: RG 59, Miscellaneous Letters).

From Ebenezer Thompson

Sir   Providence [R.I.] May 21st 1790

Tho I am not insansiable that your Excellency must be troubled with many applications of this nature, Yet as it is probable that this state will in a few days adopt the Constitution and Laws of the Union, I take the liberty to request that you will be pleased to appoint me to the office of Collector of the Revenue for the port and District of Providence, an office which I now Sustain Under the Authority of this State, the duties of which I have performed to the best of my Abilities and I trust so as to bare the test of any Examination—I was bred a merchant which Occupation was my business till the commencement of the late War, when I deposited nearly the whole of my Stock in the Continental Loan Office, since which from a Combination of circumstances I have been Necessiated to dispose of my Securities at and Under 4/ on the pound from which I have lost the hard earning of my Youth—As your Excellency Ought to be made acquainted with my Abilities Integrity and the Claim I have to the notice and Confidence of my Country I rely on your Candour to Excuse my mentioning that my Character has been such with my fellow Citizens of this State that in the Arduous Years of 76–77 they appointed me an Assistant and a member of the Council of War, which Offices I sustained Under Govenor Cooke, and continued in them to the End of his Administration, Since which my Country have Noticed me by a number of appointments, and for a number of Years past have been Elected by the suffrages of the Citizens of this Town as President of the Town Council which office I now hold—should you be pleased to Acquiese with this request you may be assured that the office shall be supported with Integrity punctuality and Industry— As the punctual collection of the revenue will depend in some measure on the Vigilence of the other Officers at the port, in what ever light you may consider or determine on the propriety of my request above Mention'd I think it a du[t]y I owe to the publick to mention to your Excellency that Theodore Foster Esquire the present Naval officer, and Willm Tyler Esquire the present Sur[v]eyor for this port, that from the Knowledge I have of those Gentlemen and the Experiance I have had of their Abilities and faithfullness in the Execution of the trust committed to them I can with Confidence recommend them to your Excellency as qualified for dischargeing of their respective offices—I am with sentiments of the Greatest Respect Your Excellency's Most Obed. Humbl. Servt

Ebenezer Thompson

ALS, DLC:GW.

Ebenezer Thompson (c.1734–1805) served as a major in the Providence County regiment in 1776 and was a member of the Rhode Island general assembly in 1783–84. From 1783 to 1792 Thompson was a member of the Providence town council, and from 1786 to 1789 he was a justice of the Providence County Court of Common Pleas. He was appointed collector at Providence by the general assembly in the September 1789 session and reappointed in May 1790 (Bartlett, *R.I. Records*, 10:378). Thompson's son, Edward K. Thompson, wrote to Lear on 20 Jan. 1790 to secure his father's continuance in office (DLC:GW). Gov. Arthur Fenner, Deputy Gov. Samuel Potter, and eight of the ten members of the upper house of the legislature wrote to GW recommending Thompson be continued in office (see Arthur Fenner et al. to GW, 9 June 1790). Thompson was also recommended by Daniel Owen and by Moses Brown (Owen to GW, 5 June 1790; Moses Brown to GW, 6 June 1790, DLC: GW). The federal appointment as collector at Providence went to William Ellery (see GW to the U.S. Senate, 14 June 1790). Thompson was subsequently recommended for appointment to the post of naval officer at Providence by Rhode Island senators Theodore Foster and Joseph Stanton; this office had been vacated by Foster when he was elected to the Senate (see Joseph Stanton and Theodore Foster to GW, 29 June 1790). Thompson was appointed naval officer at Providence on 2 July 1790 (see GW to the U. S. Senate, 2 July 1790). On 3 Mar. 1791 Joseph Stanton and Theodore Foster recommended him for supervision of the revenue. All of these letters are in DLC:GW.

From Thomas Wignell

Philadelphia May 22nd 1790.

Mr Wignell, with the utmost respect and deference, has the Honor of transmitting to the President of the United States, two copies of the Contrast.[1]

AL, DLC:GW.

Thomas Wignell (d. 1803), an English actor, was a cousin of actor and theatrical manager Lewis Hallam. After performing in David Garrick's Drury Lane Company, Wignell came to America in 1774. He performed with Hallam's American Company in Jamaica during the war and returned to the United States in 1785, where he became the principal comic actor in the company as well as its treasurer and financial manager. In 1790 he left Hallam and later formed his own company (Seilhamer, *American Theatre*, 2:136, 177, 335–38).

1. The enclosures were copies of Royall Tyler's play, *The Contrast, a Comedy; in Five Acts: Written by a Citizen of the United States; Performed with Applause at the Theatres in New-York, Philadelphia, and Maryland; and Published (under an Assignment of the Copy-Right) by Thomas Wignell* (Philadelphia, 1790). One copy is now among GW's books in the Boston Athenaeum (Griffin, *Boston Athenæum Collection*, 489–90). *The Contrast* is generally regarded as the first American comedy; although modeled on Sheridan and Goldsmith, the play was set in New York, and its characters and situations were distinctly American. Celebrating republican ideals, the play focuses on the contrast between the virtues of the simple, sturdy American and the absurd pretensions of polished society. One of its heroes, Manly, invokes the example of GW when he says, "I have humbly imitated our illustrious Washington, in having exposed my health and life in the service of my country, without reaping any other reward than the glory of conquering in so arduous a contest" (Taubman, *Making of the American Theatre*, 46–50). The play was first performed at the John Street Theater in New York by Hallam's Old American Company on 16 April 1787 and was performed four more times before the close of the New York season on 8 June. It was later performed in Baltimore in 1787 and 1788 and in Philadelphia in 1790. Tyler assigned the copyright to Wignell shortly after the play was first performed; Wignell's proposal for printing the play by subscription was published in several newspapers in 1787 (Seilhamer, *American Theatre*, 2:225–39). GW subscribed to the work, and his name headed the list of 375 subscribers in the published edition when it appeared in 1790. Lear wrote to Wignell on 30 May 1790 acknowledging receipt of two copies of *The Contrast* along with Wignell's note (Lear to Wignell, 30 May 1790, DLC:GW); Lear's letter was delivered to Wignell by Clement Biddle (Biddle to Lear, 16 June 1790, PHi: Washington-Biddle Correspondence). Although GW probably never saw the play, he saw Wignell perform in Philadelphia in July 1787 (*Diaries*, 5:175, 176) and in New York in 1789 and was later acquainted with him in Philadelphia (Ford, *Washington and the Theatre*, 39–45; see also *Diaries*, 6:229). According to John Durang, an actor and contemporary of Wignell, "When Gen'l Washington visited the theatre, the east stage box was decorated with the United States coat of

arms over the box. Mr. Wignell, dress'd in black and powdered, with two silver candlesticks would wait at the box door to receive him and light him to his seat" (Downer, *Memoir of John Durang*, 27).

From Thomas Bee

Dear Sir   Columbia So. Carolina 23 May 1790

The Death of Mr Drayton having caused a Vacancy in the Fœderal Court for this State, I am induced to Offer myself as a Candidate for the Office I requested Mr Izard and Major Butler on a former Occasion to mention my Name to your Excellency, but your absence from New York, prevented them doing so in time.[1] The reason of my not writing to you then myself was that I apprehended an application through Friends would be more acceptable, I have since been informed otherwise, which is the cause of my troubling your Excellency now.

If you should think any Investigation necessary the Gentlemen above mentioned are fully informed on every Point, with every sentiment of respect and Esteem I am your Excellencys most Obt & very humble Servt

Tho. Bee

ALS, DLC:GW.

Thomas Bee (1739–1812), a South Carolina planter and lawyer, was a leader in the Revolutionary movement in South Carolina. He served in the legislature almost continuously from 1762 to 1790 and was a Federalist delegate to the South Carolina convention that ratified the Constitution in 1788. He also served as lieutenant governor, judge of the court of general sessions, and as a delegate to the state constitutional convention in 1790. GW appointed him judge of the district court of South Carolina on 11 June 1790; the appointment was confirmed on 14 June (*DHFC*, 2:79, 80). Bee held the post until his death (Bailey, *Bio. Dir. of the S.C. Senate*, 1:120–22).

1. William Drayton, appointed district court judge on 18 Nov. 1789, died 18 May 1790 (*Bio. Dir. of the S.C. House of Representatives*, 2:205–7). GW was absent from New York on his tour of New England immediately before appointing Drayton to the bench.

From William Scudder

Sir   Goshen in the State of N. york May 23d 1790

I am informed that a Body of Troops are to be Raised for the defence of the Frontiers—I would beg the liberty to mention, that during the late War, I took an active Part in the cause of the Country as early as Seventeen Hundred & Seventy five, & in the Service in July 1779 I was taken a Prisoner by the Indians at Fort Schuyler, and from a long Captivity in Canada, with a number of Misfortunes & losses having happened to Me since that Period even to this Day, Several Debts I contracted in My own name on account of Recruiting which I have had to pay from my private Interest, there being no regular system provided at the early commencement of the War, which has reduced My Circumstances—But I ever had & still retain a strong impression to Serve My Country; Should be exceeding happy (If it should meet with Your Excellencys Pleasure) to be Honoured with a Commission to raise a Company of Infantry in the Service above mentioned: as I flatter myself I could very soon complete a Company of Stout able Bodyed Men—I had a Lieutn. Commission Dated in November Seventeen Hundred & Seventy Six in the first N. York Regt Commanded by Colo. Van Schaick—but On ac[coun]t of being a Prisoner And not exchanged was absolved with the Army Occasioned My non appointment to a Company.

I Would further beg leave to mention, that I was in the light Infantry in the Regt Commanded by Colonel Richard Butler at the Monmouth Battle Major Benjamin Ledyard of the York line being in the same Regt; who can inform the President respecting my abilities; or as a soldier.

As to my Private Character as a Citizen, & my Family, General Dayton Colo. Ogden or Capt. Dayton at Elizabeth Town, I trust can give ample Sattisfaction.

I have so great a Veneration for My Beloved President, as to rest assured he will forgive the freedom I have taken, & will not neglect me consistant with his Dignity—Could I not obtain a Company I should be happy, to the appointment of a Military Post that would not be below my former Rank, or an Embassy into any part of the Continent of America, as I am in the Prime of Life & Blessed be Providence of a Sound Constitution. I am Sir with every mark of Respect your Devoted Servant

William Scudder

ALS, DLC:GW.

William Scudder was appointed ensign of the 4th New York Regiment in June 1776 and was commissioned a lieutenant of the 1st New York in November of that year. He was taken prisoner by Mohawks led by Joseph Brant at Minnisink, near Goshen, on 22 July 1779. He received no appointment from GW.

From John Collins

Sir   Newport [R.I.] May 24th 1790

In all the Vicissitudes of time, and changes of Sentiments that have taken place in the united states, I have uniformly believed that the most essential happiness of our Country, ultimately depended, upon the establishment of an efficient executive power, under one fœderal head; being the only means, to obtain that tone to government necessary, to answer the ends of its institution; the securing the general peace, promoting the general interests, establishing the National character and rendering the Union indissolubly permanent—A power to controul the selfish interests of a Single state, and to compel the sacrifice of partial view to promote the common-weal.

A government thus calculated to cultivate the principles of universal Justice, probity and honour, must be the source of national strength, as well as happiness to mankind. However I have been Uniformly Activated by these principles, and my consciousness of possessing the general confidence hath hitherto led me to a degree of caution in my conduct and open declarations on the score of political concerns; expecting to effect more from my moderation and influence in public character, than by a conduct more explicit & pointed; which is fully evinced by what has taken place in consequence of my act in the appointment of a convention to adopt the constitution; which depended solely on me; and such was the caprice of the people, that all public confidence was withdrawn from me, and was deprived of every public trust and emolument. This was a Voluntary sacrifice, the event being well known, and comparatively a small one when Just Anticipations pourtray to me the great, the general advantages arising from a Completion of the union of the states (for have no doubt of the Adoption) but altho personal sacrifices for the public good, have been long familiar to me, (and if you have any knowledge of my property or character you must be conscious they have been many and weighty) they are more easily supported by the hope of compensation—and when I reflect upn your friendship, generosity and goodness, with how much it will be in your power to gratifie me, you will give me leave to anticipate your influence and appointment to the Office of Collector for the district of Newport—your Excellency's attention to me in this shall be ever had in lasting remembrance.

Your goodness will forgive the trouble given you, by an application from him, who will obey your commands with chearfulness and Alacrity—and honour you without flattery with every sentiment of respect & Esteem Your Humble Servt

John Collins

ALS, DLC:GW.

Collins had just been replaced as governor of Rhode Island by Arthur Fenner.

To the United States Senate

United States [New York]

Gentlemen of the Senate,   May 25th 1790.

I nominate the following persons to fill the offices affixed to their names—viz.

Samuel Jasper, to be Surveyor of the Port of Currituck-Inlet in the State of North Carolina.[1]

Nathaniel Wilkins, to be Collector of the Port of Cherry Stone in the State of Virginia, in the place of George Savage, who has resigned.[2]

Henry Deering, to be Collector of the Port of Sagg Harbour in the State of New York, in the place of John Gelston, who has resigned.

Thomas Davis Freeman, to be Surveyor of the Port of Plymouth in the State of North Carolina, in the place of Levi Blount, who has resigned.

Benjamin Bartlett, to be Surveyor of the Port of Suffolk in the State of Virginia, in the place of Archibald Richardson, who has resigned.[3]

Go: Washington

LS, DNA: RG 46, First Congress, Records of Executive Proceedings—Executive Nominations; LB, DLC:GW.

1. See Samuel Johnston to GW, 1 May 1790.

2. Nathaniel Wilkins of Gloucester County, Va., served as a lieutenant dur-

ing the Revolution and was captured at Germantown. He escaped and resigned from the army in 1778, having lost a hand. In 1790 he was in indigent
circumstances (Heitman, *Historical Register*, 435; *Calendar of Virginia State Papers*,
5:164). Wilkins was recommended for the post by Josiah Parker, who described him as a "Gentleman of good Character & I know he is qualifyed for
the appointment & lives near the port. whether it will be worth his acceptance
or not I am not to determine haveing no request from him, or any other for
the appointment" (Parker to GW, 10 May 1790, DLC:GW). His appointment
as collector at Cherrystone was approved by the Senate on 27 May (*DHFC*,
2:69, 70, 555).

3. Benjamin Bartlett was recommended for the post of surveyor at Suffolk
by Josiah Parker, who wrote: "Since I had the honor of transmiting to you the
resignation of Archibald Richardson Surveyor of the Customs at Suffolk I have
received a letter from Willis Riddick Esqr. representative for Nansemond
County recommending Mr Bartlet as a proper person to fill the vacancy—as
I have the firmest reliance on Mr Riddicks honor and integrity—I can hazard
a recommendation of Mr Bartlet in preference to Mr Lawson" (Parker to GW,
25 May 1790, DLC:GW).

Letter not found: from Giuseppe Chiappe, 28 May 1790. In a letter to
GW of 18 Jan. 1791, Chiappe refers to his letter of the "28th of the
month of May."

From Alexander Hamilton

Treasury Department [New York] May 28th 1790.
The Secretary of the Treasury has the honor respectfully to
submit to the President of the United states, for his approbation,
five Contracts made by the superintendant of the Light house,
piers &c. on the river and Bay of Delaware, and the letter received with them.

After due examination in this Office, the Contracts appear advantageous to the United states. Should they be approved, immediate attention will be paid to supplying the omission of the
day of the Month in the Contract with Michael Dawson.[1]

LB, DLC:GW.
1. The enclosed contracts for supplies and services were transmitted to
Hamilton by William Allibone, superintendent of lighthouses, buoys, and beacons on the Delaware River on 22 May 1790 (Syrett, *Hamilton Papers*, 6:428).
Lear replied to Hamilton on 29 May 1790: "The President of the united states
approves of the following contracts which have been submitted to his consideration by the Secretary of the Treasury Vizt.
"Articles of Contract entered into on the 12 day of May 1790 between Wil-

liam Allibone Superintendant of the Lighthouse Beacons &c. in the Bay & river Delaware—and Hews and Anthony to supply the Lighthouse on Cape Henlopen with oil for one year from the date of said contract at the rate of 3/7 Pennsyla curry ₩ Gallon.

"Articles of Contract entered into on the 19th day of May 1790 between William Allibone aforesaid & Daniel Rodney to transport the oil and other necessaries to the Light-house on Cape Henlopen for 60 Dols. ₩ year.

"Articles of Contract entered into on the 21st day of May 1790 between William Allibone aforesaid & Henry Drinker to furnish Iron Castings for mooring the Beacons and Buoys in the Bay and river Delaware at the rate of 14/ Pa Curry per ⟨Cut.⟩ for said Castings.

"Articles of Contract enter'd into on the 11th day of May 1790 between Wm Allibone aforesaid & Mathew Van Duren to furnish mooring chains &c. for the Beacons & buoys in the Bay & river Delaware at the rate of 7d. Penna Cury per pound.

"Articles of Contract entered into between Wm Allibone aforesaid, and Michael Dawson to attend to & shift said Beacons & buoys at the rate of £200 pennsa cury per year" (DLC:GW). Accounts of payment authorized under these contracts can be found in DNA: Miscellaneous Treasury Accounts, Account no. 1233.

From Hugh Williamson

Sir   New York 28th May 1790.

While you are considering of a proper Person for Governor of the Territory ceded by North Carolina I take the Liberty of requesting that you would be so good as to enquire whether Mr William Blount would not probably discharge that Trust with Honour to himself and advantage to the Public.[1] Those People who had most of them been separated from the State for some Years, have been toren by Factions and very disorderly; Some address will be required in governing them and I think there is not any other Man who possesses the Esteem and Confidence of both Parties so fully as Mr Blount, for some of the Leaders of both Parties have assured me that they knew no Man in whom they could be so fully united.

It is true that Mr Blount has a considerable Quantity of Land within the ceded Territory, but he has none to the Southward of it, and he must be the more deeply interested in the Peace and Prosperity of the new Government. Perhaps it is because I have many Relations and some Land there, given me by the State, that I am the more anxious to see it prosper.

Mr David Campbell, who lives near Holsten and is an assistant Judge under the State of N. Carolina, of a fair Character and respectable abilities, appears to be a proper Person for a Judge.[2]

Mr Howel Tatum formerly a Continental officer, now a Lawyer in that Country whom I have ever considered as a Man of Honour and respectable abilities might be a proper Person to Discharge the Duties of Secretary.[3] I have the Honour to be With the utmost Consideration Sir your most obedient and very humble Servt

Hu. Williamson

ALS, DLC:GW.

1. William Blount (1749–1800), a prominent North Carolina merchant, planter, and politician, was born in Bertie County, North Carolina. He served as paymaster of North Carolina troops in 1777 and as a member of the North Carolina general assembly in 1780–81 and 1783–85. He represented North Carolina in the Continental Congress in 1782–83 and 1786–87, was a member of the Philadelphia Convention in 1787, and served in the state senate from 1788 to 1790. A Federalist, Blount advocated ratification of the Constitution in the second North Carolina convention in 1789. Blount was unanimously recommended for governor by the North Carolina delegation to the House of Representatives (see John Steele to GW, 4 June 1790, John B. Ashe to GW, and Timothy Bloodworth to GW, both 5 June 1790). GW nominated him for the post on 7 June 1790 (see GW to the U.S. Senate, 7 June 1790).

2. David Campbell (1750–1812) was born in Virginia and served in the Virginia militia from 1776 to 1780, rising to the rank of major. He served as clerk of the courts in Washington County, Va., from 1777 to 1780 and was admitted to the bar in 1780. Moving to western North Carolina, Campbell was elected judge of the superior court of the state of Franklin. In 1787 he represented Greene County in the North Carolina house of commons. Campbell was also recommended for territorial judge by Timothy Bloodworth (see Bloodworth to GW, 5 June 1790) and suggested for the office by John B. Ashe (see Ashe to GW, 5 June 1790). GW appointed him judge of the Southwest Territory in 1790 (see GW to the U.S. Senate, 7 June 1790). Campbell served in that office until 1797, when he was commissioned a judge of the Tennesee Superior Court of Law and Equity. He resigned in 1807 and was later appointed territorial judge for the Mississippi Territory (Ely and Brown, *Legal Papers of Andrew Jackson*, 361–62).

3. Howell Tatum (1753–1822) served as an officer in the 1st North Carolina Regiment from 1775 until 1780, rising to the rank of captain. He was captured at Charleston in May 1780 and paroled for the rest of the war (Heitman, *Historical Register*, 393). In 1787 he was an unsuccessful candidate for judge of the superior court of Davidson County, N.C. (later Tennessee). Tatum thereafter established himself at Nashville where he was admitted to practice in 1789 and later served as a judge of the Tennessee Superior Court of Law and Equity (Ely and Brown, *Legal Papers of Andrew Jackson*, 388–89). Tatum was recom-

mended for territorial judge by Timothy Bloodworth (see Bloodworth to GW, 5 June 1790) and John B. Ashe (see Ashe to GW, 5 June 1790) but did not receive the appointment. Tatum was later suggested as a candidate for federal district judge for Tennessee (see Andrew Jackson to GW, 8 Feb. 1797, DNA: RG 59, Miscellaneous Letters) but received no appointment from GW.

From Alexander Hamilton

[New York] saturday May 29th 1790

The Secretary of the Treasury presents his respects to the President of the United states and submits to his consideration some remarks on the Resolutions, which have passed the two Houses respecting the Lines of Virginia and North Carolina.[1]

The Secretary has taken this method of communication as the one best calculated to place the subject under the eye of the President with least trouble to him. If any further explanation should be desired by the President, The Secretary will have the honor of waiting upon him, at any time it shall please him to appoint.

LB, DLC:GW.

1. The enclosure was Hamilton's comments, 28 May 1790, concerning army pay that had been working its way through Congress in the spring of 1790. On 5 Mar. Thomas Tudor Tucker of South Carolina introduced a memorial from the officers of the South Carolina line, requesting payment with interest of certain arrears of pay (*DHFC*, 6:2065–66). In 1781–82 Congress had resolved to give each officer in the army six months' pay in specie, requesting the states to make these payments and deduct the total amount from the specie portion of the congressional requisition. South Carolina had not complied. In October 1786 Congress had authorized the Board of Treasury to issue warrants to each of the claimants, payable to the bearer, for the amount due him, to be redeemed in specie by the commissioner of loans for the state. Because of a shortage of specie, the commissioner was unable to comply, and many of the holders had sold their warrants to speculators for a fraction of their face value. Upon receipt of the South Carolina memorial, Congress referred the matter to Hamilton for consideration. In his report, received by the House on 19 Mar., Hamilton recommended payment of the warrants but argued that claims to interest should be disallowed (see Report on the Memorial of the Officers of the South Carolina Regiments, 18 Mar. 1790, in Syrett, *Hamilton Papers*, 6:305–7). No further action was taken until 7 May, when Theodorick Bland introduced a resolution calling for the payment of similar arrears due to Virginia and North Carolina soldiers. The Bland Resolution further stipulated that "no claim of any assignee, under any transfer or power to receive the same, be admitted as valid, to entitle any person to receive any part of the

said arrears of pay due to the officers or soldiers of the said lines" other than the widows or legal representatives of those who had died (*DHFC*, 6:2068). The intent of this provision of the Bland Resolution was to deprive speculators who had purchased warrants of any payment and ensure payment to the original holders or their legitimate heirs. The substance of this provision was embodied in the the third of three resolutions passed by the House on 17 May. This resolution provided: "the Secretary of the Treasury, in cases where the payment has not been made to the original claimant, in person, or to his representative, be directed to take order for making the payment to the original claimant, or to such person or persons as shall produce a power of attorney, duly attested by two justices of the peace, of the county in which such person or persons reside, authorizing him or them to receive a certain specified sum" (ibid., 2070). This resolution occasioned considerable debate when the legislation was taken up in the Senate on 21 May. Efforts were made to amend the resolution to facilitate payment to subsequent holders. In the final vote on this question, the Senate deadlocked, eleven to eleven. The tie was broken by Adams, who voted against the amendment (see Bowling and Veit, *Diary of William Maclay*, 272–74). The House agreed to minor Senate changes to the resolutions on 24 May, and the legislation was sent up for GW's signature the next day. No reply from GW to Hamilton in regard to these resolutions have been found. GW signed the resolutions into law on 7 June (see *DHFC*, 6:2063–65).

1. Hamilton's comments on the resolutions, 28 May, read: "The Secretary of the Treasury conceives it to be his duty most respectfully to represent to the President of the United states, that there are, in his judgment, objections of a very serious and weighty nature to the resolutions of the two houses of Congress of the twenty first instant, concerning certain arrears of pay due to the officers and soldiers of the Lines of Virginia and North Carolina.

"The third of those resolutions directs, that in cases where *payment* has not been made to the original Claimant in person, or to his representative, it shall be made to the original Claimant, or to such person or persons only, as shall produce a power of Attorney, duly attested by *two Justices* of the Peace of the County, in which such person or persons reside, authorising him or them to receive a certain specified sum.

"By the Law of most, if not all the States, claims of this kind are in their nature assignable for valuable consideration; and the assignor may constitute the assignee his attorney or agent, to receive the amount. The import of every such assignment is a Contract, express, or implied, on the part of the assignor, that the assignee shall receive the sum assigned to his own use. In making it, no precise form is necessary, but any instrument, competent to conveying with clearness and precision the sense of the parties, suffices; There is no need of the cooperation of any Justice of the Peace or other Magistrate whatever.

"The practice of the Treasury and of the public officers in other Departments, in the adjustment and satisfaction of Claims upon the united States, has uniformly corresponded with the rules of that Law.

"A regulation therefore having a retrospective operation, and prescribing, with regard to past transactions, new and unknown requisites, by which the admission of claims is to be guided, is an infraction of the rights of Individuals, acquired under preexisting Laws, and a contravention of the public faith, pledged by the course of public proceedings—It has consequently a tendency not less unfriendly to public credit, than to the security of property.

"Such is the regulation contain'd in the resolution above referred to. It defeats all previous assignments not accompanied with a *Power of Attorney* attested by *two Justices* of the peace of *the County* where the assignor resides; a formality, which for obvious reasons cannot be presumed to have attended any of them, and which does not appear to have been observed, with respect to those, upon which applications for payment have hitherto been made.

"It is to be remarked, that the assignee has no method of compelling the Assignor to perfect the transfer by a new instrument, in conformity to the rule prescribed; if even the existence of such a power, the execution of which would involve a legal controversy, could be a satisfactory cause for altering by a new Law that state of things, which antecedent law and usage had established between the parties.

"It is perhaps, too questionable, whether an assignee, however equitable his pretensions were, could, under the operation of the provision, which has been recited, have any remedy whatever for the recovery of the money or value which he may have paid to the assignor. It is not certain, that a Legislative act, decreeing payment to a different person, would not be a legal bar; but if the existence of such a remedy were certain, it would be but a very inconclusive consideration. The assig[n]ment may have been a security for a precarious or desperate Debt, which security will be wrested from the assignee; or it may have been a composition between an insolvent Debtor and his Creditor, & the only resource of the latter; or the assignor may be absent and incapable either of benefiting by the provision, or of being called to an account: and in every case the assignee would be left to the casualty of the ability of the assignor to repay; to the perplexity, trouble and expence of a suit at Law. In respect to the soldiers the presumption would be, in the greater number of cases, that the pursuit of redress would be worse than acquiescence in the loss. To vary the risks of parties; to supersede the contracts between them; to turn over a creditor; without his consent, from one *Debtor* to *another;* to take away a right to a *specific thing* leaving only the chance of a remedy for retribution are not less positive violations of property, than a direct confiscation.

"It appears from the debates in the house of representatives, and it may be inferred from the nature of the proceeding, that a suggestion of fraud has been the occasion of it—Fraud is certainly a good objection to any Contract, and where it is properly ascertained, invalidates it—But the power of ascertaining it, is the peculiar province of the Judiciary Department. The principles of good Government conspire with those of Justice, to place it there. 'Tis there only, that such an investigation of the fact can be had, as ought to precede a decision, 'Tis there only, the parties can be heard and evidence on both sides produced; without which, *surmise,* must be substituted to *Proof,* and *conjecture* to *fact.*

"This, then, is the dilemma incident to Legislative interference—Either the legislature must erect itself into a Court of Justice and determine each case upon its own merits, after a full hearing of the allegations and proofs of the parties; or it must proceed upon vague suggestions, loose reports, or at best upon partial and problematical testimony, to condemn in the gross and in the dark, the fairest and most unexceptionable claims, as well as those which may happen to be fraudulent and exceptionable—The first wou'd be an usurpation of the Judiciary authority, the last is at variance with the rules of property, the dictates of Equity and the Maxims of good government.

"All admit the truth of these positions as general rules. But when a departure from it is advocated for any particular purpose, it is usually alledged that there are exceptions to it; that there are certain extraordinary cases, in which the public good demands & justifies an extraordinary interposition of the Legislature.

"This Doctrine in relation to extraordinary cases is not to be denied; but it is highly important, that the nature of those cases shou'd be carefully distinguished.

"It is evident that every such interposition, deviating from the usual course of Law and Justice, and infringing, the established rules of property, which ought, as far as possible to be held sacred and inviolable, is an overleaping of the ordinary and regular bounds of Legislative discretion; and is in the nature of a resort to first principles. Nothing therefore but some urgent public necessity, some impending national Calamity, something that threatens direct and general mischief to the Society, for which there is no adequate redress in the established course of things, can, it is presumed, be a sufficient cause for the employment of so extraordinary a remedy: an accommodation to the interests of a small part of the community, in a case of inconsiderable magnitude, on a national scale, cannot, in the judgment of the Secretary, be entitled to that character.

"If partial inconveniencies and hardships occasion legislative interferences in private contracts, the intercourse's of business become uncertain, the security of property is lessened, the confidence in Government destroyed or weakened.

"The constitution of the United states interdicts the States individually from passing any Law impairing the obligation of contracts. This, to the more enlightened part of the community was not one of the least recommendations of that constitution. The too frequent intermeddlings of the state Legislatures, in relation to private contracts, were extensively felt and seriously lamented; and a Constitution which promises a preventative, was, by those who felt and thought in that manner, eagerly embrac'd. Precedents of similar interferences by the Legislature of the United states, cannot fail to alarm the same class of persons, and at the same time to diminish the respect of the state legislatures for the interdiction alluded to. The *example* of the national government in a matter of this kind may be expect'd to have a far more powerful influence, than the *precepts* of its Constitution.

"The present case is that of a particular class of Men, highly meritorious indeed, but inconsiderable in point of numbers, and the whole of the property in question less than fifty thousand Dollars, which when distributed among those who are principally to be benefited by the regulation, does not exceed twenty five Dollars per man. The relief of the Individuals, who may have been subjects of imposition, in so limited a case, seems a very inadequate cause for a measure which breaks in upon those great principles, that constitute the foundations of property.

"The eligibility of the measure is the more doubtful, as the courts of Justice are competent to the relief, which it is the object of the resolutions to give, as far as the fact of Fraud, or imposition, or undue advantage can be substantiated. It is true that many of the Individuals would probably not be in a condition to seek that relief, from their own resources; but the aid of government may in this respect, be afforded in a way, which will be consistent with the established order of things. The Secretary, from the information communicated to him, believing it to be probable, that undue advantages had been taken, had conceived a plan for the purpose, of the following Kind; that measures shou'd be adopted for procuring the appointment of an agent, or attorney by the original claimants, or if deceased, by their legal representatives; that payment of the money should be deferred, until this had been effected; that the amount of the sums due should then be placed in the hands of the proper officer for the purpose of payment; that a demand should be made upon him on behalf of the original claimants by their agent; and as a like demand would of course be made by the assignees, that the parties should be informed that a legal adjudication was necessary to ascertain the validity of their respective pretentions; and that in this state of things, the attorney general should be directed either to prosecute or defend for the original claimants, as should appear to him most likely to assure Justice. A step of this kind appeared to the Secretary to be warranted and dictated as well by a due regard to the defenceless situation of the parties, who may have been prejudiced, as by considerations resulting from the propriety of discouraging similar practices.

"It is with reluctance and pain, that the Secretary is induced to make this representation to the President—The respect which he entertains for the decisions of the two houses of Congress; the respect which is due to those movements of humanity, towards the supposed sufferers, and of indignation against those who are presumed to have taken an undue advantage, an unwillingness to present before the mind of the President, especially at the present juncture, considerations which may occasion perplexity or anxiety, concur in rendering the task peculiarly unwelcome: yet the principles which appear to the Secretary to have been invaded, in this instance, are, in his estimation, of such fundamental consequence to the stability, character & success of the government, and at the same time so immediately interesting to the Department entrust'd to his care, that he feels himself irresistably impelled by a sense of Duty, as well to the Chief Magistrate, as to the Community, to make a full communication of his impressions & reflections. He is sensible, that an inflexible adherence to the principles contended for must often have an air of rigor, and will sometimes be productive of particular inconveniencies. The general rules of property, & all those general rules which form the links of Society, frequently involve in their ordinary operation particular hardships and Injuries; yet the public order, and the general happiness require a steady conformity to them. It is perhaps always better, that partial evils should be submitted to, than that principles should be violated—In the infancy of our present government, peculiar strictness and circumspection are called for by the too numerous instances of relaxations, which in other quarters & on other occasions, have discredited our Public measures.

"The secretary is not unaware of the delicacy of an opposition to the resolutions in question, by the President, shou'd his view of the subject coincide with that of the Secretary: yet he begs leave on this point to remark, that such an opposition in a case, in which a small part of the community only is directly concerned, would be less likely to have disagreeable consequences, than in one which shou'd affect a very considerable portion of it: and the prevention of an ill precedent, if it be truly one, may prove a decisive obstacle to other cases of greater extent and magnitude and of a more critical tendency. If the objections are as solid as they appear to the Secretary, to be, he trusts, they cannot fail, with the sanction of the President, to engage the approbation, not only of the generality of considerate men, but of the community at large. And if momentary dissatisfaction should happen to exist in particular parts of the union, it is to be hoped, that it will be speedily removed by the measures which under the direction of the President may be pursued for obtaining the same end in an unexceptionable mode, for the success of which the Secretary will not fail to exert his most zealous endeavours.

"It is proper, that the President should be informed, that if objections should be made by him, they will, in all probability, be effectual, as the resolutions passed in the Senate with no greater majority than twelve to ten.

"The Secretary feels an unreserved confidence in the Justice and magnanimity of the President, that whatever may be his view of the subject he will at least impute the present representation to an earnest and anxious conviction, in the mind of the Secretary, of the truth and importance of the principles which he supports, & of the inauspicious tendency of the measure to which he objects, co-operating with a pure and ardent zeal for the public good, and for the honor & prosperity of the administration of the Chief Magistrate. All which is humbly submitted" (DLC:GW).

From Thomas Hughes

Newport [R.I.] May 29th 1790.

May it please your Excellency,

If long Service and great Sufferings can Supply the place of extraordinary Merit (of which I dare not boast) your Excellency will excuse me for humbly representing, that I entered the Service of the United States in May 1775, as a Commissioned Officer. That as such I was Present on Long-Island in the action that took Place there on the 27th of August 1776, under the Command of Colo. Hitchcock and there in that Action received a Gun Shot Wound. The Ball passing through both Thighs a

Little below the Hips and Shattered my right Thigh Bone from which I recovered after more than twelve Months pain and Lanquish. that upon my Recovery I immediately rejoined my Regiment under the Command of Colo. Israel Angell and was appointed and Commissioned a Captain therein upon the 27th June 1777, and as Luck Continued untill the end of the War under the Command of Colo. Jeremiah Olney at all times conducting myself irreproachably and to the Best of my skill and abillity.

Now Sir I humbly ask your Excellency In Consideration of my Services and Sufferings, that I may be Appointed Naval officer for the Port and District of Newport Which is the place of my Nativity, and this will Confer a Lasting Obligation and fully Compensate sr your Excellency much oblidge[d] and most obedient Humble Servant

Thomas Hughes

ALS, DLC:GW.

Thomas Hughes (c.1751–1821) of Newport served as an officer in the Continental army and was wounded at the Battle of Long Island. He served until the end of the war, rising to the rank of captain. Hughes did not receive a revenue appointment from GW.

From Gouverneur Morris

Sir   London 29 May 1790

I do myself the Honor to enclose a Copy of my Letter of the first Instant. On the Night of the fourth there was a hot Press here which has continued ever since, and the declared object is to compel Spain to atone for an Insult offered to Great Britain by capturing two Vessels in Nootka Sound.[1] Permit me to observe incidentally that it would not be amiss for the American Captain who was a Witness of the whole Transaction to publish a faithful Narrative.[2] The general Opinion here, is that Spain will submit, and that Spain only is the Object of this Armament. But I hold a very different Faith. If Spain submits she may as well give up her american Dominions for the Position advanced here is that Nations have a Right to take Possession of any Territory unoccupied. Now without noticing the Inconsistency between this assertion and those which preceeded the War of 1755 when France built Fort Duquesne upon Ground unoccupied by british Subjects, it cannot escape the most cursory Observation that the british sitting down in the Vicinity of Spanish Settlements will establish such a System of contraband Traffic as must ruin the Commerce of Cadiz, and the Revenue now derived from it by the spanish Monarch. In former Letters I have communicated in some Measure my Ideas upon the second opinion. I shall not therefore recapitulate them, but only in general notice that the Armament against Spain, should Spain shrink from the Contest, will undoubtedly be sent to the Baltic with decisive Effect. You will observe also that the Ministers count upon the Nullity of France, of which I shall say a Word presently.

In Consequence of the orders for impressing of Seamen a Number of Americans were taken, and the Applications made for their Releif were in some Instances ineffectual. On the Morning of the twelfth Mr Cutting called to inform me that he was appointed agent to several of the american Masters of Ships; I gave him my advice as to the best Mode of Proceeding and particularly urged him to authenticate all the Facts by Affidavits, assuring him that if he was unsuccessful I would endeavor to obtain the Assistance of such Persons as I might be acquainted with. On the seventeenth Mr Payne called to tell me that he had conversed on the same Subject with Mr Burke, who had asked him if there was any Minister Consul or other Agent of the united States who could properly make application to the Government: To which he had replied in the Negative, but said that I was here who had been a Member of congress and was therefore the fittest Person to step forward. In Consequence of what passed between them he urged me to take the Matter up, which I promised to do. On the eighteenth, I wrote to the Duke of Leeds requesting an Interview. He desired me to come at three oClock of the next Day, but his Note was delivered after the Hour was passed, & very shortly after it came another Note giving me another appointment for the twentieth.

Upon entering his Closet he apologized for not answering my Letters. I told him that I had in my Turn an apology to make for troubling him with an Affair on which I was not authorized to speak. He said I had misunderstood one Part of his Letter to me, for that he certainly meant to express a Willingness to enter into a Treaty of Commerce. I replied that as to my Letter I supposed he would answer it at his Leizure, and therefore we would wave the Discussion. That my present Object was to mention the Conduct of their Press Gangs who had taken many american Seamen and had entered American Vessels with as little Ceremony as those belonging to Britain. "I beleive my Lord this is the only Instance in which we are not treated as Aliens." He acknowleged that it was wrong, and would speak to Lord Chatham on the Subject. I told him that many disagreable Circumstances had already happened, and that there was Reason to expect many more in a general Impress thro the british Dominions. That Masters of Vessels on their Return to America would excite much Heat "and *that*⟨,⟩ my Lord, combined with other Circumstances, may perhaps occasion very disagreable Events; for you know that when a Wound is but recently healed 'tis easy to rub off the Skin." He then repeated his Assurances of Good Will, and exprest an anxious Wish to prevent all Disagreement, observing at the same Time that there was much Difficulty in distinguishing between the Seamen of the two Countries. I acknowleged the Inconveniencies to which they might be subjected by the Pretence of british Seamen to be americans, and wished therefore that ⟨some⟩ Plan might be adopted which, founded on good Faith, might at the same Time prevent the Concealment of british Sailors, and protect the Americans from Insult. As a Means of accomplishing that End, I suggested the Idea of Certificates of Citizenship, to be given by the Admiralty Courts in America to our Seamen. He seemed much pleased and willing at once to adopt it, but I desired him to consult first the Kings Servants in that particular Department, and having again reminded him that I spoke without Authority,[3] took my Leave, but at his Request promised to visit him again the next Day.

The Morning of the twenty first I found him sitting with Mr Pitt, to whom he presented me. The first Point we took up was that of the Impress. Mr Pitt exprest his Approbation of the Plan I had proposed to the Duke, but observed that it was liable to Abuse notwithstanding every Precaution which the Admiralty Offices in America could take. I acknowleged that it was, but observed that, even setting aside the great political Interests of both Countries, it was for the commercial Interest of Britain rather to wink at such Abuse; for that if they should be involved in a War *with the House of Bourbon* our Commerce with Britain must be in American Bottoms, because a War Premium of Insurance would give a decided Preference to the Manufactures of other Countries in our Markets. But that no Wages could induce American Seamen to come within the british Dominions, it they were thereby liable to be impressed. Mr Pitt replied to this, that the Degree of Risque, and consequently the Rate of Insurance, must depend upon the *Kind of War.* not taking any direct Notice of this Expression, I observed that Notwithstanding the wretched State of the *french Government* there still existed much Force in that Country, and that the Power of commanding human Labor must also exist somewhere; so that if the Government could not arm their Fleets there would still be many Privateers, & that (in Effect) the slenderest Naval Efforts must involve merchant Vessels in considerable Danger. Returning then to the Consideration of the principal Point, we discussed the Means of carrying the Plan into Effect; and for that Purpose I recommended that his Majesty's Servants should order all their marine Officers to admit as Evidence of being an american Seaman the Certificate to that Effect of the Admiralty in America, containing in it a proper Description of the Person &c., but without excluding however other Evidence; and observed that in Consequence of the Communication that such Orders were given the executive Authority in America, without the aid of the Legislature, by Directions to the several Admiralties might carry the Plan into Effect, so far as relates to those Seamen who should apply for Certificates. I am induced to beleive that this Measure if adopted, will not only answer the desired End, but be productive of other good Consequences in America, which I will not now trouble you with the Detail of.

This Affair being so far adjusted, we proceeded to new Matter, and they both assured me that I had misapprehended the Duke's Letter in Regard to a Treaty of Commerce. I answered coolly that it was easy to rectify the Mistake, but it appeared idle to form a new Treaty untill the Parties should be thoroughly satisfied with that already existing. Mr Pitt then took up the Conversation and said that the Delay of Compliance on our Part had rendered that Compliance less effectual, and that Cases must certainly exist where great Injury had been sustained by the Delay. To this I replied that Delay is always a Kind of Breach, since as long as it lasts it is the Non Performance of Stipulations.

I proceeded then to a more exact Investigation of the question. And first, as I knew them to be pestered with many Applications for Redress by those who had and those who pretended to have suffered, I attempted to shew what I verily beleive to be the Fact viz. that the Injury was much smaller than was imagined, because among the various Classes of American Debtors, those only could be considered who had the Ability and not the Will to pay at the Peace, and were now deprived of the Ability. These I supposed to be not numerous, and as to others I stated Interest as the natural Compensation for Delay of Payment, observing that it was impossible to go into an Examination of all the incidental Evils. In the second Place I desired him to consider that we in Turn complained that the british Government had not, as they ought, paid for the Slaves which were taken away. That we felt for the Situation they were in of being obliged either to break Faith with the Slaves whom they had seduced by the Offer of Freedom, or to violate the Stipulations they had made with us upon that Subject. That we were willing therefore to w⟨ave⟩ our literal Claims, but had every Right to insist upon Compensation, & that it would not be difficult for the Planters to shew that they had sustained an annual Loss from the Want of Men to cultivate their ⟨Lands⟩ and thereby produce the Means of paying their Debts. Mr Pitt exclaimed at this as if it were an exagerated Statement. I at once acknowleged ⟨my⟩ Beleif that in this, as in all similar Cases, there might be some Exageration on both Sides "but Sir what I have said tends to shew that these Complaints and Enquiries are excellent if the Parties mean to keep asunder: if they wish to come together all such Matters should be kept out of Sight, and each Side perform *now,* as well as the actual Situation of Things will permit." Mr Pitt then made many Professions of an earnest Desire to cultivate the best Understanding &ca &ca &ca. On the whole he thought it might be best to consider the Subject generally, and to see if on general Ground some Compensation could not be made mutually. I immediately replied "If I understand you, Mr Pitt, you wish to make a new Treaty instead of complying with the old one." He admitted this to be *in some Sort* his Idea. I said that even on that Ground I did not see what better could be done than to perform the old one—"as to the Compensation for Negroes taken away; it is too trifling an Object for you to dispute;

so that Nothing remains but the Posts. I suppose therefore you wish to retain those Posts." "Why perhaps we may." "They are not worth the Keeping, for it must cost you a great Deal of Money, and produce no Benefit. The only Reason you can have to desire them is to secure the Fur Trade, and that will center in this Country let who will carry it on in America" I gave him the Reasons for this Opinion, which I am sure is well founded, but I will not trouble you with them. His Answer was well turned. "If you consider these Posts as a trivial Object, there is the less Reason for requiring them." "Pardon me Sir, I only state the retaining them as *useless to you,* but this Matter is to be considered in a different Point of Light. Those who made the Peace acted wisely in seperating the Possessions of the two Countries by so wide a Water. It is essential to preserve this Boundary, if you wish to live in Amity with us. Near Neighbours are seldom good ones, for the Quarrels among Borderers frequently bring on Wars. It is therefore essential for both Parties that you should give them up; but as to us it is of particular Importance, because our national Honor is interested. You hold them with the avowed Intention of forcing us to comply with such Conditions as you may impose." "Why Sir as to the Considerations of national Honor we can retort the Observation, and say our Honor is concerned in your Delay of the Performance of the Treaty." "No Sir, Your natural and proper Course was to comply fully on your Part, and if then we have refused a Compliance, you might rightfully have issued Letters of Marque and Reprisal to such of your Subjects as were injured by our Refusal. But the Conduct you have persued naturally excites Resentment in every American Bosom. We do not think it worth while to go to War with you for these Posts, but *we know our Rights, and will avail ourselves of them when Time and Circumstances may suit.*" Mr Pitt asked me if I had Powers to treat. I told him I had not and that we could not appoint any Person as Minister, they had so much neglected the former Appointment. He asked me whether we would appoint a Minister if they did. I told him that I could almost promise that we should, but was not authorized to give any positive Assurance. The Question then was how to communicate on this Subject. I suggested, that since much time might be unnecessarily consumed by ⟨R⟩eason of the Distance and Uncertainty of Communication, it would perhaps be expedient for them to ap-

point a Minister and delay his ⟨d⟩eparture untill you should
have made a similar Appointment. Mr Pitt said they might communicate to you their Intention to appoint &ca—I told him that
his Communication might encounter some little Difficulty, because you could not properly hear any Thing from the british
Consuls, those being Characters unknown in America. His Pride
was a little touched at this. "I should suppose Mr Morris that
⟨A⟩ttention might as well be paid to what they say, as that the
Duke of Leeds and I should hold the present Conversation with
you." "By no means Sir I never should have thought of asking
a Conference with his Grace, if I had not possessed a Letter from
the President of the United States, which you know my Lord I
left with you, and which I dare say you have communicated to
Mr Pitt"—He had—Mr Pitt said they ⟨c⟩ould in like Manner
write a Letter to one of their Consuls. "Yes Sir, & the *Letter* will
be attended to, but not the Consul, who is in no Respect different from any other british Subject; and this is the Circumstance
which I wished you to attend to." He said, in Reply to this, that
Etiquette ought not to be pushed so far as to injure Business,
and keep the Countries asunder. I assured him that the Rulers
of America had too much Understanding to care for Etiquette,
but prayed him at the same Time to recollect, that they (the
british) had hitherto kept us at a Distance, instead of making
Advances. That you had gone quite as far as they had any Reason to expect, in Writing the Letter just mentioned, but that
from what had passed in Consequence of it, & which (as he
might naturally suppose) I had transmitted, we could not but
consider them as wishing to avoid an Intercourse. He took up
this Point, and exprest again his Hope that I would remove such
an Idea; assuring me that they were disposed to cultivate a Connection &ca. To this I replied, that any written Communications
which his Grace of Leeds might make, should be duly transmitted, but I did not like to recite meer Conversation, because it
might be misconceived⟨, &⟩ disagreable Questions afterwards
arise, whereas written Things remain and speak for themselves.
They agreed to the Propriety of this Sentiment. I observed farther, that our Disposition towards a good Understanding was
evidenced, not only by your Letter, but also by the Decision of a
Majority of the House of Representatives against laying extraordinary Restrictions on british Vessels in our Ports—Mr Pitt said

that, instead of Restrictions, we ought to give them particular Privileges in Return for those which we enjoy here. I assured him that I knew of none except that of being imprest, a Privilege which of all others we least wished to partake of. The Duke of Leeds observed, in the same Stile of Jocularity, that we were at least treated in that Respect as the most favored Nation, seeing that we were treated like themselves. But Mr Pitt said seriously, that they had certainly evidenced Good:Will towards us, by what they had done respecting our Commerce. I replied therefore, with like Seriousness, that their Regulations had been dictated by a View to their own Interest, and therefore as we felt no favor, we owned no Obligation. The Subject being now pretty well exhausted, they promised to consult together and give me the Result of their Deliberations. This I am yet to receive, but I learn that Mr Grenville has this Day consulted some Persons skilled in the Fur Trade, and that from his Conversation it seemed probable that they would give up the Posts. My Information is good.

I have already said, that the Ministers here count upon the Nullity of France. They do not however expect that She will violate her Treaty with Spain, and therefore they are rather I beleive in Hopes that Spain will submit to such Terms as they may impose. How far they may be bound to aid Prussia, seems as yet to be doubtful but for my own Part I beleive that a War is inevitable, and I act on that Ground. If it does not take Place, they will I think desire such things of us in a Treaty of Commerce as we shall not be disposed to grant: but if it does happen, then they will give us a good Price for our Neutrality, and Spain I think will do so too, wherefore this appears to be a favorable Moment for treating with that Court about the Mississippi.

Before I close this Letter, already too long, I must entreat Permission to make one or two explanatory Observations. It is evident that the Conduct of this Government towards us, from the Time of my first Interview with the Duke of Leeds, has depended on the Contingency of War or Peace with the neighbouring Powers; and they have kept Things in Suspense accordingly. When therefore they came a little forward, it proved to me their Apprehension of a Rupture. I have some Reason to think that they are in greater Danger than they are themselves aware of, and I have much Cause to suspect that they meditate a Blow in Flanders in which it is not improbable that they will be foiled and disappointed. Beleiving therefore that I knew their Motives, it only remained to square my Conduct and Conversation accordingly. And here you will consider, that the Characteristic of this Nation is Pride; whence it follows that if they are brought to sacrifice a little of their self Importance, they will readily add some other Sacrifices. I kept therefore a little aloof, and did not, as I might have done, obtain an assurance that they would appoint a Minister if you would. On the contrary it now stands on such Ground that they must write a Letter making the first Advance, which you of Course will be in Possession of, and to that Effect I warned them against sending *a Message* by one of their Consuls. With perfect Respect I have the Honor to be Sir your most obedient & humble Servant[4]

Gouvr Morris

ALS, DLC:GW; LB, DLC: Gouverneur Morris Papers; copy, DNA: RG 46, First Congress, 1789–91, Records of Executive Proceedings, President's Messages—Foreign Relations.

1. Nootka Sound, on the western short of Vancouver Island, was a point of contention between Great Britain, Russia, and Spain. In the spring of 1789 both Spain and Britain sent expeditions to take possession of the area and establish colonies. The Spanish arrived first and some two months later the first British ship appeared off the coast. The resident Spanish seized the British ship and sent it, and another English vessel that arrived a few days later, as prizes into Mexico. Although the vessels were eventually released, the Spanish government issued a formal complaint to Whitehall that their sovereignty over the Nootka Sound area had been violated, a complaint that was rejected by the British government. For a detailed account of the incident, see Manning, "Nootka Sound Controversy." Although both powers had been involved in negotiations for some weeks, it was not until 5 May that the British public was aware of the seriousness of the incident. On the morning of 5 May the British navy engaged in a "hot Press," involving the impressment of as many as three thousand seamen, some American, and provoking a war scare in London. For a vivid description, see John Rutledge, Jr., to Jefferson, 6 May 1790, in Boyd, *Jefferson Papers*, 16:413–15. In September 1790 William Short reported that more than three hundred American sailors had been impressed into the British navy (Short to Jefferson, 5 Sept. 1790, ibid., 17:488–93). By the summer of 1790 the United States had become peripherally embroiled in the affair, and the question of whether passage of British forces from Canada would be resisted in case of a British attack on Spanish possessions in the Southwest became foremost in cabinet discussions.

2. Both the *Columbia*, commanded by Capt. John Kendrick, and the *Lady Washington*, commanded by Capt. Robert Gray (see Joseph Barrell et al. to GW, 20 Mar. 1790, source note), observed the capture of the British vessels at

Nootka Sound. There was some suggestion that the two ships had been unwilling participants in the capture. See William Short to John Jay, 23 May 1790, in Boyd, *Jefferson Papers,* 16:436–41.

3. To this point, Morris's diary entry for 20 May is almost a verbatim copy of his letter to GW. In the diary, however, Morris continues: "I then observe to him further, that not only the political Interests of both Countries may be affected by the present Practice but that it will prove fatal to the Commerce of this Country. That in Case of War the Intercourse, if any, must be in American Bottoms because the Insurance will be so high as to give a decided Preference to the Manufactures of other Nations in the American Market over those brought from Britain in british Ships. But no Wages which the Merchant could offer would induce the American Sailor to expose himself to the Chance of being impressed into the British Service" (Morris, *Diary of the French Revolution,* 1:519).

4. At the end of the copy the following note, dated 30 May 1790, appears: "P.S. It is utterly impossible for me to copy the letters which I intended to enclose. It is now near One O'Clock in the morning, and Mr Williams sets off at Eleven."

From Daniel Owen

Sir,   State of Rhode Island Newport May 29th 1790.
    I have the pleasing satisfaction of informing your Excellency that the Constitution of the United States of America was this day ratified and adopted by the convention of the People of this State, agreeable to the recommendation of the general Convention, assembled at Philadelphia, and the consequent resolution of Congress thereon.[1]
    The lower House of the general assembly of this State at their session the former part of this month past a resolution requesting His Excellency the Governor in case the Constitution should be adopted by the Convention to call the assembly together by warrant, as soon after the adoption as might be, for the special purpose of electing the Senators, and taking measures for a representation of this State in Congress—I can therefore assure Your Excellency that in the course of a few days, not to exceed sixteen, the Legislature will be assembled, either by special warrant, or pursuant to their adjournment on the second monday of June, when I have not the least doubt, the Senators will be immediately appointed, and the State represented in Congress, agreeable to the constitution, as soon as the elections can be accomplished.

The ratification of the Constitution will be made out and forwarded by way of the Post office with all possible expedition.[2]

Colonel William Barton, who was a Member of the Convention, will have the honor of delivering this letter.[3] With the highest sentiments of esteem and respect, I have the honor of being your Excellency's most obedient Servant

Daniel Owen Presidt

Copy, DNA: RG 46, First Congress, 1789–91, Records of Legislative Proceedings, President's Messages.

Daniel Owen (1732–1812), a blacksmith and leader of the country party in Rhode Island, represented Gloucester in the Rhode Island general assembly in 1785 and served as deputy governor from 1786 to 1790. He also served as a justice of the Rhode Island Superior Court. An advocate of paper money and a leading Antifederalist, Owen was president of the Rhode Island Ratifying Convention (*Representative Men of Rhode Island*, 1983; Polishook, *Rhode Island and the Union*, 124–25, 152).

1. The Rhode Island Ratifying Convention convened on 1 Mar. 1790 but on 6 Mar. members of the Antifederalist country party forced an adjournment until after the spring elections in order to preserve the dominance of their party in state office. The convention reconvened on 25 May and ratified the Constitution by a vote of 34 to 32 on 29 May (Polishook, *Rhode Island and the Union*, 207–230).

2. Despite Owen's assurances, GW did not receive a copy of the formal instrument of ratification until 15 June 1790 (see GW to the U.S. Senate and House of Representatives, 16 June 1790). Owen apparently delayed sending a copy of the formal instrument until a special session of the legislature, dominated by the country party, could convene to appoint senators who would go to New York to recommend the continuance of state officeholders under the federal government. Federalist Jeremiah Olney explained to Alexander Hamilton on 7 June that "The president of our late Convention, with the advise of the Governor, means to Keep back the Ratification untill about the time the Senators go forward, as they Wish to have all the *Ante* Revenue officers of the State reappointed & expect the Senators will Influence the President In the nomination of these *Bitter & Uniform* opposers of the Constitution" (Syrett, *Hamilton Papers*, 6:458–59). Owen forwarded the formal instrument of ratification to GW with a letter of 9 June (see Rhode Island Constitutional Convention to GW, 9 June 1790).

3. William Barton of Providence was one of the leading Federalists in the Rhode Island convention. He had applied for a position in the customs service in September 1789 (see William Barton to GW, 3 Sept. 1789, and Michael Jenifer Stone to GW, 9 June 1790).

From Cyrus Griffin

Richmond [Va.] May 30th 1790

pardon me, Sir, that I take the freedom to disturb your anxious moments, to congratulate you and my Country on the most happy recovery from your late Indisposition. the last mail has brought to us that pleasing and most important Intelligence, the reverse of which would have thrown this Country into despair and confusion. I hope to heaven the malady may operate as the renovation of health, and will continue the blessing unto a very distant period.

as the first Circuit of the Supreme Court in my district was holden the other day I think it my duty to inform you, Sir, that the Court was complete, that an excellent charge was given by Judge Wilson to the best Grand Jury that perhaps have been assembled under the new Judiciary, and that all the people p[r]esent seemed perfectly satisfied with the proceedings throughout.[1]

may I presume to offer my respectful Compliments to mrs Washington. I am, sir, with every sense of admiration, Gratitude, and respect Your most obedient Servant

C. Griffin

ALS, DNA: RG 59, Miscellaneous Letters.

1. The first U.S. Circuit Court for the District of Virginia convened in Charlottesville on 22 May 1790 with Associate Justice of the Supreme Court James Wilson and federal judges John Blair and Cyrus Griffin present. Wilson presided and delivered a charge to the grand jury on the role of juries. Having no further business, the court adjourned to the next term (for the text of Wilson's charge, see Marcus and Perry, *Documentary History of the Supreme Court,* 2:33–45).

From Francis Nicholson

⟨Gla⟩stenbury Connecticut May 30th 1790

Notwithstanding your exalted Station, I am confident you will not turn a deaf ear to the cries of the distressed, therefore relying on your Goodness and compassion I make bold to communicate to you through this channel the causes of my calamity (as far as h⟨u⟩mane nature is able to comprehend) being fully assured if you judge me an object worthy of your attention you will assist in alleviating some of my distresses.

I had the honour of serving in the late Army under your command in the Regt Commanded by Saml B. Webb Esqr. as a Sergeant & am bold to assert I discharged my duty as a good Soldier without the least murmer under all the fatigues & hardships incident to a Military Life because I had discretion enough to know they were unavoidable—I engaged in July 1778 in good health & Constitution being 20 years of age & 3 Months & continued in good health being able to perform any kind of Military duty & was equal to any without exception (under a Commission) in instructing soldiers till 1781 at which time I had the Smallpox in April by your Excellencies Command which, together with the fatigues of that years Campaign entirely ruined my Constitution & threw me into an Astmatic disorder so that I was never after Septr of that year able to perform Military duty—I continued after that time sometim⟨es⟩ in the Contry Sometimes in the Hospital & Sometimes with the Regt till the army was Disbanded when I received an honourable Discharge on west-Point.

I have not been able to Labour or undertake any business ever since & am not able for a great part of the time to lie down, & I undergo the most excruciating pains that a man can & live through them—Consequently ⟨illegible⟩ reduced to Poveverty & do not receive any thing for my support ⟨tho⟩ugh the Puplic has made Provision for disabled soldiers &c.—I have a ⟨wi⟩fe & 5 small Children to share the effects of my misfortune⟨s⟩.

I have made application to this State for relief with the nescesary certificates but they allow no person any thing without he was wo⟨u⟩ded in Battle or was hurt by the fatigue of some Battle or ill usage while a Prisoner of war—which is contrary to the very words of the act only a rule which the Gentlemen adopted to go by that examined—which is contrary to all Law, reason or Justice & is the most ungrateful thing in my opinion that could be done—My misfortune is certainly greater than if I had lost my right hand & foot & I absolutely contracted my disorder while in actual service; I am confident I ought to receive a pension if any other person does & it is the opinion of our best Characters & their is not an Officer that servd in Colo. Webbs Regt but would Certify the truth of what I have asserted above & would contribute all in their power for my relief—I desired a Gentleman who lately had business to Newyork (which was furnished with a Letter from a Gentleman that served in the late Regular Army as a field Officer to a member of Congress which he held a correspondance with; recommending me for relief) to enquire if they thought Congress would grant me any Assistance—but they gave him so little encouragement he thout it not expedient to be at the Cost of presenting a Petition &c.—I have still some gleam of hope that your Excellency will recommend me & I am confident that one word of recommendation from your Excellency will recover to me the pension & enable me to enjoy some comfort in this Life—Genl Saml B. Webb who resides at New york is a Gentleman I trust your Excellency can confide in he can satisfy you on my behalf if you will be pleased to confer with him on the subject—I shall consider it as a singular favour if your Excellency will not censure me on account of this Letter more than a private rebuke—& desire that it may be approvd of so far that you will cause that I may be informd whether their is any hopes for me & what method I must take to recover any relief—I cannot think that my country can be so lost to all feelings of humanity as not to contribute something for me if they knew my necessaties & that the services I performd for them & the fatigues I underwent in their service was the cause—but I entirely submit myself to Providence. I am as ever I have been ready to obey your Excellencies Command

Francis Nicholson

ALS, DNA: RG 59, Miscellaneous Letters.

Francis Nicholson (b. 1758) served as a sergeant in the 3d Connecticut Regiment during the Revolution. In 1781 he apparently was inoculated with smallpox in accordance with GW's orders and developed a serious case of the disease. Several months after his recovery, Lt. Col. Ebenezer Huntington reported to Col. Samuel Blachley Webb: "Sergeant [Francis] Nicholson . . . is very thin & feeble I advised him to get to Camp a soon as he Could, tho I am sensible he is not at present fit" (Huntington to Samuel B. Webb, 3 June 1782, in Ford, *Correspondence and Journals of Samuel Blachley Webb*, 2:401–2). No evidence has been found that Nicholson was granted a pension.

From Thomas Paine

Sir　　　　　　　　　　　　　　　　London May 31. 1790

By Mr James Morris who sailed in the May Packet I transmitted you a letter from the Marquis de la Fayette, at the same time informing you that the Marquis had entrusted to my charge the Key of the Bastile and a drawing of that Prison as a present to your Excellency.[1] Mr J. Rutlege Junr had entended coming in the Ship.[2] Marquis de la Fayette and I had chosen that opportunity for the purpose of transmitting the present but the Ship not sailing at the time appointed Mr Rutledge takes his passage, in the Packet, and I have committed to his Care those trophies of Liberty which I know it will give you pleasure to receive—The french Revolution is not only compleat but triumphant & the envious disposition of this nation is compelled to own the magnanimity with which it has been conducted.

The political hemisphere is again clouded by a dispute between England and Spain—the circumstances of which you will hear before this letter can arrive—A Messenger was sent from hence the 6th Inst. to Madrid with very peremptory demands and to wait there only forty-eight hours—his return has been expected for two or three days past—I was this morning at the Marquis del Campo's but nothing is yet arrived.[3] Mr Rutledge setts off at 4 oClock this afternoon, but should any news arrive before the making up the mail on Wednesday June 2 I will forward it to you under cover.

The views of this Court, as well as of the Nation so far as they extend to South America, are not for the purpose of Freedom but Conquest—They already talk of Sending some of the young Branches to Reign over them and to pay off their national Debt with the produce of the Mines—The Bondage of those Countries will, as far as I can perceive, be prolonged by what th⟨is⟩ Court has in Contemplation.

My Bridge is arrived and I have engaged a place to erect it in—a little time will determine its fate but I yet see no cause to doubt of its Success—tho' it is very probable that a War, should it break out, will, as in all new things prevent its progress so far as regard profits.[4]

In the partition in the Box, which contain⟨s⟩ the key of the Bastile—I have put up half a dozen Razors manufactured from

Cast-Steel made at the Works where the Bridge was constructed which I request you to accept as a little token from a very grateful heart.

I received about a Week ago a letter from Mr G. Clymer—It is dated the 4th Feby—but has been travelling ever since—I request you to acknowlege it for me and that I will answer it when my Bridge is erected. With much affection to all my Friends and many wishes to see them again I am Sir your much obliged and Obedient humble Servant

Thomas Paine

ALS, DLC:GW.

   1. See Paine to GW, 1 May 1790.

   2. For John Rutledge, Jr.'s European tour, see Count d'Estaing to GW, 8 June 1789, n.5.

   3. The marquis del Campo was the Spanish ambassador to London.

   4. For Paine's proposed bridge across the Thames, see his letter to GW, 1 May 1790, n.4.

From Beverley Randolph

Sir,   Richmond [Va.] May 31st 1790.

The inclosed copy of a letter from the Spanish Governor of New Orleans to a respectable Gentleman in Kentucky was handed to me by mr Banks of this City. As the subject of this paper appears interesting to the United States I have taken the liberty to forward it to you.[1] I am with the highest respect your most obt Servt

Beverley Randolph

LS, DNA: RG 59, Miscellaneous Letters; LB, Vi: Executive Letter Books.

   1. The enclosure was a copy of letter from Esteban Miró to Benjamin Sebastian, dated New Orleans, 16 Sept. 1789: "General Wilkinson having represented it to me that you had it in contemplation to settle in this province, and that your example would have considerable influence on many good Families of your country; I think it my duty in order to forward the intentions of my royal master, to inform you, that I shall receive you and your followers, with great pleasure, and that you have liberty to settle in any part of Louisiana, or any where on the east side of the Mississippi below the Yazou river. In order to populate the province his majesty has been graciously pleased to authorize me to grant to the Emigrants free of all expence, tracts from 240 to 800 Acres, in proportion to their property, and in particular Cases of men of influence, who may aid these Views, I shall extend the grant as far as 3000 Acres To all

persons, who actually become settlers, liberty is granted to bring down their property in the produce of your Country duty free but the King does not agree to take your Tobacco and of Consequence you must depend on the Common Market of this City, as the province makes more than the quantity which the King allows me to take. I mention this particular to prevent disappointment. You will be exempt from taxation, and will be allowed the private exercise of your religion, without molestation from any person whatever, and will enjoy all the rights, privileges and immunities of his majesty's other subjects.

"In order to cultivate an amicable connection with the settlers of the Ohio, his majesty has been graciously pleased at the same time to give liberty to the inhabitants of that Country to bring down their produce to this City for sale, subject to a duty of 15 per Cent: on the value here, but to prevent imposition and to distinguish between the real Settler and the Trader, the former on entering their produce at the Custom hou⟨se⟩ will be obliged to subscribe to the Conditions mention⟨e⟩d in the proclamation, of which General Wilkinson can [make] a copy for your information.

"Though unknown to you General Wilkinson has taught me to respect your character, it is ther⟨e⟩fore I subscribe myself with great esteem . . . " (DNA: RG 59, Miscellaneous Letters).

On 14 June GW replied, thanking Randolph for the information in his 31 May letter (copy, DNA: RG 59, Miscellaneous Letters), to which Randolph replied on 22 June, assuring GW that he would "regularly communicate to you all such Information as I may receive, which will in any manner effect the Interest of the United States" (DNA: RG 59, Miscellaneous Letters).

To the United States Senate

United States [New York]
Gentlemen of the Senate,   May 31st 1790

M. de Poiery served in the American Army for several of the last years of the late war, as Secretary to Major General the Marquis de la Fayette, and might probably at that time have obtained the Commission of Captain from Congress upon application to that Body. At present he is an officer in the French National Guards, and solicits a Brevet Commission from the United States of America. I am authorised to add, that, while the compliance will involve no expense on our part, it will be particularly grateful to that friend of America, the Marquis de la Fayette.

I therefore nominate M. de Poiery to be a Captain by Brevet.
Go: Washington

LS, DNA: RG 46, First Congress, 1789–91, Records of Executive Proceedings, President's Messages—Executive Nominations; LB, DLC:GW.

For background to this document, see Lafayette to GW, 14 Jan. 1790, and notes.

From Gideon Wanton

Newport [R.I.]

May it please your Excellency.   May 31th 1790

For two years past I have been elected by the General Assembly of this State, Naval Officer for this port and District of Newport, and at present hold that Office, but as that appointment ceases by the adoption of the new Constitution, I humbly supplicate your Excellency's interposition for my continuance in the same, being altogether unacquainted with every Gent. who has a Seat in Congress I conceive that will be my excuse for an immediate Application to your Excellency.

Pardon me Sr for informing you that I am the Son of Gideon Wanton Esq; deced, many years Governor here previous to American Independency, that I am now advanced in life and my Fortune by a concourse of unfavourable Events far from splendid, and that during the time of my officiating under this State, I have discharged the trust reposed in me to the Satisfaction of the Publick, and if it shall please Your Excellency to promote my continuance in that Office, it shall be my earnest endeavour to discharge the same with all Fidelity, and ever to acknowledge, that I am with due respect Sr Your Excellys most obedient, obliged & humble Servt

Gideon Wanton

ALS, DLC:GW.

Gideon Wanton, a Newport merchant, was the son of Gideon Wanton, governor of Rhode Island in 1745–46 and 1747–48. The younger Wanton served on the council and represented Newport in the general assembly in 1776. During the Revolution he was imprisoned by the British. After the war he was appointed naval officer at Newport by the state. Wanton renewed his application with a nearly identical letter on 8 June, apparently concerned that the first letter had not reached GW. Daniel Owen recommended Wanton for the office "as a man worthy to be continued in Office, and more especially having suffered for the general Cause both with the Provost and on board the prison ship at Newport, while that place was held by a British Garrison, and as a Man whose integrity may be depended upon" (Daniel Owen to GW, 10 June 1790, DLC:GW). After news that Robert Crooke had been appointed naval officer at Newport reached Rhode Island, Wanton wrote to GW reminding him: "I lately did my self the honour to address Your Excellency. . . . I presume however my Letter did not get forward seasonably, and the Senators for this State not setting out so early for Congress as was expected, the Officers of the Customs here, have been appointed, and I find my self excluded to my great regret." Wanton repeated his summary of his own qualifications and concluded by expressing his "earnest desires to serve the public in any vacancy that is now, or, may arise, whether in the Loan Office, Excise or any other department where employment will be attended with adequate reward" (Wanton to GW, 21 June 1790, DLC:GW). Wanton received no federal appointment.

To the Savannah, Ga., Hebrew Congregation

Gentlemen,   [c.May 1790]

I thank you with great sincerity for your congratulations on my appointment to the office, which I have the honor to hold by the unanimous choice of my fellow-citizens: and especially for the expressions which you are pleased to use in testifying the confidence that is reposed in me by your congregation.

As the delay which has naturally intervened between my election and your address has afforded an opportunity for appreciating the merits of the federal-government, and for communicating your sentiments of its administration—I have rather to express my satisfaction than regret at a circumstance, which demonstrates (upon experiment) your attachment to the former as well as approbation of the latter.

I rejoice that a spirit of liberality and philanthropy is much more prevalent than it formerly was among the enlightened nations of the earth; and that your brethren will benefit thereby in proportion as it shall become still more extensive. Happily the people of the United States of America have, in many instances, exhibited examples worthy of imitation—The salutary influence of which will doubtless extend much farther, if gratefully enjoying those blessings of peace which (under favor of Heaven) have been obtained by fortitude in war, they shall conduct themselves with reverence to the Deity, and charity towards their fellow-creatures.

May the same wonder-working Deity, who long since delivering the Hebrews from their Egyptian Oppressors planted them in the promised land—whose providential agency has lately been conspicuous in establishing these United States as an independent nation—still continue to water them with the dews of Heaven and to make the inhabitants of every denomination participate in the temporal and spiritual blessings of that people whose God is Jehovah.

G. Washington

LB, DLC:GW.

The first Jewish congregation in Georgia, Mickve Israel, was established in Savannah about 1735 but discontinued services around 1740. The congregation was reorganized in 1774, only to have regular services interrupted by the Revolution. The congregation was reformed again in 1786, largely through the leadership of the brothers Mordecai and Levi Sheftall. The leaders of the congregation wrote to GW, apparently in May 1790, congratulating him on his election as president: "Sir, We have long been anxious of congratulating you on your appointment by unanimous approbation to the Presidential dignity of this country, and of testifying our unbounded confidence in your integrity and unblemished virtue: Yet, however exalted the station you now fill, it is still not equal to the merit of your heroic services through an arduous and dangerous conflict, which has embosomed you in the hearts of her citizens.

"Our eccentric situation added to a diffidence founded on the most profound respect has thus long prevented our address, yet the delay has realised anticipation, given us an opportunity of presenting our grateful acknowledgements for the benedictions of Heaven through the energy of federal influence, and the equity of your administration.

"Your unexampled liberality and extensive philanthropy have dispelled that cloud of bigotry and superstition which has long, as a veil, shaded religion—unrivetted the fetters of enthusiasm—enfranchised us with all the privileges and immunities of free citizens, and initiated us into the grand mass of legislative mechanism. By example you have taught us to endure the ravages of war with manly fortitude, and to enjoy the blessings of peace with reverence to the Deity, and benignity and love to our fellow-creatures.

"May the great Author of worlds grant you all happiness—an uninterrupted series of health—addition of years to the number of your days and a continuance of guardianship to that freedom, which, under the auspices of Heaven, your magnanimity and wisdom have given these States" (DLC:GW). The letter was signed by Levi Sheftall (Shestal; 1739–1809), the first president of the Mickve Israel congregation. Sheftall engaged in mercantile activities and operated a butchering and tanning business before the Revolution and after the war invested in farm and timber land. Along with his brother Mordecai Sheftall (1735–1797), he was among those chiefly responsible for the reformation of the Mickve Israel congregation. Levi Sheftall later held the post of U.S. agent for fortifications in Savannah (Sheftall, "The Sheftalls of Savannah," 65–78). The congregation's letter to GW may have been related to their efforts to obtain a charter of incorporation. In December 1789 the Georgia legislature passed an act authorizing the governor to grant charters to religious societies, enabling them to hold property and assume other corporate privileges. The leaders of Mickve Israel applied for incorporation under this act in August 1790 and were granted a charter by Georgia governor Edward Telfair on 30 Nov. 1790 (Marcus, *American Jewry*, 172–75).

To the Delegates of the State Societies of the Cincinnati

[May 1790]
To the Delegates of the State Societies of the Cincinnati
assembled at their triennial Meeting.

Gentlemen

Although it is easier for you to conceive, than for me to explain the pleasing sensations which have been excited in my breast, by your congratulations on my appointment to the head of this rising Republic: yet I must take the liberty to thank you sincerely for the polite manner in which you felicitate our Countrymen, and testify your regard to me on this occasion.

In addition to that reward for your Sufferings & Services which arises from the consciousness of having done your duty; you have erected monuments more expressive of your merits than even the universal applause of your Country, in the establishment of its Independence and Sovereignty. Nor should any possible circumstances of poverty or adversity compel you to give up that sweet satisfaction for the part you have acted, which ought to attend you as well through the vicissitudes of life as in the moment of dissolution.

The candour of your fellow-citizens acknowledges the patriotism of your conduct in peace, as their gratitude has declared their obligations for your fortitude and perseverence in war. A knowledge that they now do justice to the purity of your intentions ought to be your highest consolation, as the fact is demonstrative of your greatest glory.

The object for which your gallantry encountered every danger, and your virtue sustained unparalleled difficulties, has happily been attained. A Government, promising protection and prosperity to the People of the United States, is established; and its operations hitherto have been such as to justify the most sanguine expectations of further success. It was naturally to be expected, that lives which had long since been devoted on the Altar of Freedom, could never be offered at the Shrines of Anarchy or Despotism. And the offer which you make of the residue of those lives to support the Administration of this Government is not less a proof of its excellence, than an encouragemt for those concerned in its execution to use their best endeavours to make it a source of extensive and permanent blessings to their Country.

Whatever titles my military services may have given me to the regard of my Country, they are principally corroborated by the firm support of my brave and faithful Associates in the field: and, if any consideration is to be attributed to the successful exercise of my civil duties, it proceeds, in a great measure, from the wisdom of the Laws, and the facility which the Disposition of my fellow-citizens has given to their Administration.

To the most affectionate wishes for your temporal happiness, I add a fervent prayer for your eternal felicity.

Go: Washington

ALS, DSoCi; LB, DSoCi; LB, DLC:GW.

1. The fourth general meeting of the Society of the Cincinnati was held in Philadelphia on 3–4 May 1790. On 4 May the meeting adopted the following address to GW: "We the Delegates of the State Societies of the Cincinnati, assembled at our triennial general meeting congratulate you on being unanimously elected the Head of our rising republic.

"As a part of the community we felicitate our countrymen on this happy event, and we embrace the first opportunity of expressing our sentiments with no less zeal than sincerity.

"When we say we love and revere you as a Father we not only speak the language of our own hearts, but we speak the language of all, who have fought, suffered, and conquered under your command. Were poverty and consciousness of duty our only recompense still should we glory in the part we have acted For our motives, as they regarded our country, will afford us satisfaction as well through the vicissitudes of life, as in the moment of dissolution—As members of our Institution, on a former occasion, we appealed to Heaven and our own hearts for the purity of our intentions—Our fellow-citizens will witness that the conduct of the Officers and Soldiers of the late American Armies has not been less patriotic in peace than it was glorious in war.

"A good constitution was the object for which we risked our lives and experienced unparalelled difficulties—We are happy in the conviction that our views are answered in the present government of the United States—While we applaud the wisdom of our countrymen in placing you at the head of it, we pledge ourselves to support its administration with the remnants of lives long since devoted to the public service.

"We need not enumerate your titles to the gratitude of your Country; or echo in the suffrages of our particular Constituents the public sentiment But we may say that we see with exultation our Countrymen beginning to reap the fruits of independence under the auspices of the Person, who was more instrumental than any other in its establishment. May you as a reward for your services enjoy length of days and every temporal blessing, and may such blessings be a prelude to everlasting felicity!" (DLC:GW). The address was signed by Thomas Mifflin, vice-president general.

The meeting appointed a committee of nine, consisting of Gen. Henry Knox, Col. Benjamin Hawkins, Gen. Matthew Clarkson, Capt. Jonathan Dayton, Col. Jeremiah Wadsworth, Col. James Gunn, Col. William S. Smith, and Col. David Humphreys, to present the address to GW and inform him of his election as president general of the Cincinnati for the ensuing three years (*Proceedings of the General Society of the Cincinnati*, 42). GW noted in his diary for 8 May 1790: "Received from Genl. Knox Secretary Genl. of the triennial Genl. Meeting of the Cincinnati held at Philadelphia the first Monday of this Month, the Copy of an Address from that body to me to which I was to return an answer on [ ] next" (*Diaries*, 6:76).

From Joseph Mandrillon

Rue des ⟨J⟩euners no. 26.

My General,   Paris June 1. 1790.

The letter with which your Excellency has honored me of the 29. of august last, and which accompanied a copy of that excellent work, the history of the insurrection in Massachusetts, is a new favor, which I appreciate in all its extent.[1] Happy, if with the aid of your indulgence, I may be able to justify the good opinion which you have of my real and eternal devotion to the american cause.

With regard to Mr Morris, the bearer of the above mentioned letter, I have seen but few men so well instructed in the interests of his country, and in those of Europe. I regret much not to have had his acquaintance but in the moment when I was setting out for France—Some friends have undertaken to supply my place, and to offer to the worthy american all their zeal and attachment. I have employed myself since I have been in Paris in translating *the history of the insurrection*—I shall be ready in a couple of months, and I will hasten to send to your Excellency a copy of the translation, to which I shall give every attention to render it with fidelity.[2]

You know, my General, the fatal consequence⟨s⟩ of the invasion of the Prussian troops in Holland, and the abandonment in which France has been forced to leave us at that epoch. I have shared in some sort the fate of the friends of the country, by the confidence which the government then reposed in me. impatient to emancipate myself from the yoke under which the Hollanders bent, I determined to come to reside in Paris—in fine to live more free, and to trace more nearly the effects of the french revolution *in regard to us* since we can only hope for safety from their succour The Marquis de la Fayette, the worthy Emulant and friend of your Excellency, covers himself with glory in France—and if the guardian Genius of France preserves him to them, he will enjoy the sweet satisfaction of having done that for his fellow citizens, which your Excellency has done for America.

I have the honor sometimes to see this young Hero, and I should desire much to make my zeal and my services agreeable to him—but little accustomed to ask places for myself, and maladroit in soliciting, I have energy only for others—perhaps Mr la Fayette will give me some department when he knows that, without renouncing the interests of Holland, I may be of some utility in France—our Dutch refugees desire, and interest themselves in, it.

I propose publishing my memoirs relative to ⟨the⟩ negociation with which I have been charged in ⟨Prus⟩sia, in which will be developped all the secret causes which have served as the basis of the odious policy of England, Prussia, and the House of Orange.[3] This work will proscribe me from Holland while the present system subsists—but I would rather fulfil my task, by a new sacrifice, than maintain any longer a silence, from which my fellow-citizens can draw no advantage.

I recommend me, my General, to the continuance of your precious esteem—I refer to the desires, motives, in my last letters—and I have the honor to say with the most profound veneration I am, my General your most humble and most obedient Servant

Jh Mandrillon

Translation, DLC:GW; ALS, DLC:GW. The text of this document is taken from a translation prepared for GW. The original letter in French is available on CD-ROM.

1. No letter from GW to Mandrillon of 29 Aug. 1789 has been found. GW wrote to Mandrillon on 12 Oct. 1789 acknowledging receipt of a book Man-

drillon sent with a letter dated 25 Oct. 1788. The book to which Mandrillon refers may have been a copy of George Richards Minot's *The History of the Insurrections in Massachusetts in the Year 1786* (Worcester, Mass., 1788). GW received a copy of this work from the author (see Minot to GW, 28 Aug. 1788, DLC:GW) and a second copy from William Tudor (see Tudor to GW, 26 July 1788, DLC:GW). One of these copies is now among the Washington books in the Boston Athenaeum (Griffin, *Boston Athenæum Collection*, 512). GW may have sent the second copy to Mandrillon.

2. Mandrillon does not seem to have completed his translation. No contemporary French translation of Minot's history or of any other work on Shays' Rebellion has been found.

3. Mandrillon apparently did not complete such a memoir before his execution in 1794.

From Stephen Moore

New York 1st June 1790

The Memorial and Petition of Stephen Moore of the State of North Carolina Humbly Sheweth

That, at a season when it is the wish of every friend to America not to break in upon your tranquility, your Memorialist finds himself under the painful necessity of intruding a few moments on your time.

That having devoted his constant efforts and a large proportion of his property in aiding & furnishing the Army acting in the southern department; And having endured the miseries of a tedious & painful captivity in the City & harbour of Charleston; with a number of other expensive casualties in this line, his fortune is become exceedingly impaired.

That having a numerous & growing family, looking to him for tuition & support through early life, he wishes by every virtuous endeavour to occupy himself, in such way, as that his labours may tend towards making his Children useful to the society of which they are to become members.

That your memorialist has his residence near Hillsborough, one of the most central towns in the State of North Carolina, and could with general convenience to the people of the State, and he hopes with due justice to the United States execute such office as he may be thought worthy of.

With this view your memorialist humbly prays that his case may be taken into your favourable consideration, And that he may receive such marks of your attention as in your goodness may seem right. And your memorialist as in duty bound will ever pray

Stephen Moore

ALS, DLC:GW.

Stephen Moore (c.1740–1800) was the son of a wealthy New York merchant, from whom he inherited 1,795 acres of land on which the fortifications at West Point were built (see Nathanael Greene to Col. Udny Hay, 25 Dec. 1779, in Showman, *Greene Papers,* 5:208). Shortly before the Revolution he moved to Caswell County, N.C., where he established himself at his plantation Mt. Tirzah. During the war he served as a colonel in the militia and was captured at Charleston in May 1780 (see Moore to Nathanael Greene, 5 Dec. 1780, ibid., 6:528–29). Moore petitioned Congress in 1786 for compensation for the property at West Point, but Congress was unable to raise the money (Palmer, *The River and the Rock,* 355). On 4 May 1790 another petition from Moore seeking compensation was received by Congress (*DHFC,* 3:396). On 10 June Hamilton reported in favor of the purchase, which was authorized by the West Point Act, signed by GW on 5 July 1790. Moore received $11,085 for the entire property (*DHFC,* 6:2059–62; see also Miller, "Owner of West Point," 303–312). Moore was recommended for a federal appointment by Timothy Bloodworth (see Bloodworth to GW, 7 Aug. 1790). He received no appointment from GW.

From Edward Thurston

Newport [R.I.] June 1st 1790.

May it please Your Excellency,

Having been appointed by the General Assembly of this State at the two last Elections to the Office of Surveyor for the Port of Newport, and as such having discharged my duty to the Public to their intire Satisfaction, I do therefore humbly solicit your Excellency that I may be continued in that Office, and do assure You Sir that if it shall please You to continue me therein, my most earnest Endeavours shall be exerted with all Fidelity in the executing that trust reposed in me to the utmost of my skill and ability, and I humbly hope to the Satisfaction of your Excellency and advancement of the public Revenue. I am, with the utmost respect, sr Your Excellency's most obedient humble Servt

Edward Thurston

ALS, DLC:GW.

Edward Thurston, Jr., a Newport merchant, was the son of merchant Edward Thurston, who joined the British in New York and was proscribed as a

Tory (Bartlett, *R.I. Records,* 9:139, 504). The younger Thurston was surveyor at Newport under the state government. His continuation in the post under the federal government was recommended by a group of Antifederalist state leaders including Arthur Fenner, Daniel Owen, Samuel J. Potter, Benjamin Watson, Thomas Hoxie, and Thomas G. Hazard (Arthur Fenner et al. to GW, 12 June 1790). Thurston received no appointment from GW.

To the United States Senate and House of Representatives

United States [New York] June 1st 1790.
Gentlemen of the Senate and House of Representatives.

Having received official information of the accession of the State of Rhode Island and Providence Plantations to the Constitution of the United States, I take the earliest opportunity of communicating the same to you, with my Congratulations on this happy event, which unites under the general Government all the States which were originally confederated; and have directed my Secretary to lay before you a copy of the letter from the President of the Convention of the State of Rhode Island to the President of the United States.[1]

Go: Washington

LS, DNA: RG 46, First Congress, 1789–91, Records of Legislative Proceedings, President's Messages; LB, DLC:GW; copy, DLC: Alexander H. Stephens Papers.

1. For the background to this letter, see Daniel Owen to GW, 29 May 1790. Daniel Owen, president of the Rhode Island Ratifying Convention, did not send GW the formal instrument of ratification until 9 June 1790 (see Rhode Island Ratifying Convention to GW, 9 June 1790).

From Wakelin Welch & Son

Sir   London 1st June 1790

We had the honor of receiving your Excellencys favors of 13th Octr & 1st March by the hands of Mr Morris.[1]

Mr Morris has given his orders for the ornaments suitable for your dining Table, & for which, we have promised to pay, he observed that by sending some Goods, for you while he was in France⟨,⟩ he had advanced near £100, which if the Balance due to you in our hands would admit he should be glad of having it but if not, it was very immaterial as he should send an order to a friend to receive it in the country.[2]

In looking to your Excellency's account in our Books it appears that the Balance in your favor is £95.16.—agreeable to the inclosed[3] & which would have been more than to have purchasd the Goods but on a supposition you would have no objection to our paying the whole of the Balance to Mr Morris we wrote him accordingly and therefor⟨e⟩ do suppose when the Goods are ship'd and which imagine will be in the Montgomery Capt: Bunyan who sails for New York some time this Month he will draw for it.

There were Books we sent from Mr Young in Augt last as their value was to us unknown they remain unpaid.

In hopes to have the honor to receive your Excellencys farther commands we remain Your Excellencys Much Obliged and Most Obedt Ser⟨vts⟩

Wakn Welch

LS, DLC:GW; LS (duplicate), DLC:GW.

1. For these letters, see GW to Gouverneur Morris, 13 Oct. 1789 (first letter), n.2.

2. See GW to Morris, 13 Oct. 1789 (first letter), Morris to GW, 24 Jan. 1790 and notes, and GW to Morris, 1 Mar. and 15 April 1790.

3. The enclosed account, dated 1 June 1790, is in DLC:GW.

Letter not found: from John Cannon, 2 June 1790. In a letter to John Cannon of 25 June 1790, GW refers to a letter of "the 2. instant."

From James Manning

Sir   Providence [R.I.] June 2d 1790

I beg leave to congratulate your Excellency on the joyful Event, the adoption of the Constitution of the United States by the State of Rhode Island on Saturday last; and to recommend to your Notice Capt. Samuel Snow (Son of the Revd & venerable Joseph Snow of this Town) as a Candidate for the office of Surveyor of the Customs in the Port of Providence.[1] He was esteemed a good officer in the service of this State during the late War: was liberally educated, & is a man of Industry & Principle; &, in my opinion, would with ability, fidelity, & exactness, discharge the duties of that office. Among other reasons to enforce his claim is that of a young and helpless family, with other dependants wholly indebted to his Industry for their support. He is viewed as second to none of the Applicants for that appointment, yet heard of by Sir Your Excellency's Most obliged Most Humble Servt

James Manning

ALS, DLC:GW.

1. Samuel Snow was the son of Joseph Snow, a popular New Light minister in Providence. The younger Snow served as an officer in the Rhode Island militia during the Revolution, reaching the rank of captain before resigning in September 1780 (Bartlett, *R.I. Records,* 9:234–35). After the war Snow apparently engaged in mercantile activities in Providence. Benjamin Huntington wrote to GW recommending Snow for the post of U.S. marshal, noting: "from the Acquaintan⟨ce⟩ I have with him which was in the way of Business I always found him a Man of honor and Good Conduct and think him Capable of Executing the Office of Marshal for the District of Rhode Island" (Huntington to GW, 7 June 1790, DLC:GW). Huntington enclosed a letter from Theodore Rogers, Zabdeil Rogers, and Samuel Woodbridge, soliciting Huntington's assistance in obtaining the post of surveyor at Providence for Snow. The three described Snow "as a Gentleman of known Integrity and Ability and a man well Acquainted with Business" (Theodore Rogers et al. to Benjamin Huntington, 13 May 1790, DLC:GW). Snow was also recommended by Providence merchant Welcome Arnold, who wrote GW from Providence to "Recommend the Bearer Capt. Samuel Snow as a Man well qualified to do the duties of the Office of Surveyor for this district" (Arnold to GW, 10 June 1790, DLC:GW), and from David Howell, who wrote from Providence that Snow was "educated under my inspection in the College here" (David Howell "to all persons whom it may concern," 7 June 1790, DLC:GW). Snow received no appointment from GW but was appointed U.S. consul at Canton in May 1798 (*Executive Journal,* 275).

From David Stuart

Dear Sir,   Abingdon [Va.] 2nd June—1790

The accounts of your recent illness having just reached this place on my return, I delayed writing, 'till I could again congratulate you on the reestablishment, of your health; which I now do most sincerely, both on your account, and on that of your Country—I fear much, that the great change which has been unavoidably made, in your accustomed mode of living, by your office; has been the cause of both the attacks you have so unfortunately been subject to—I have understood, that you had some intention before your late illness, of visiting Virginia this Summer for your health. I hope you will now think it ind⟨i⟩spensably necessary.

Your several letters, all, came safe to hand—You have indeed reason to think the business with Alexander a strange affair— That the lawyers were completely ignorant of the real merits of the cause before it was ready for trial, may be concluded from their advise then to me, to suffer a nonsuit if I could not succeed in a compromise, which they thought most advisable—Had this advise been given earlier, I have no doubt, but it might have been accomplished on better terms—Mr Randolph is I think principally to blame, who brought the suit in Mr Custis's lifetime, and ought surely to have known, whether the money was a legal tender or not—It gives me however, much pleasure to find, that the relinquishment of the bargain is universally approved of; and considered as a fortunate event for the estate. But, I shall have much trouble with Alexander still, before all matters are completed; as he cannot prevail on himself to name any one on his part to value the rents, and objects to those I have named, tho' he has no right to do it.

The suit with Coll Basset is again continued; and I am not displeased at it, as it was set to the last of the Court; when there is but a bad chance of getting a tolerable jury, from the people being worried ⟨*illegible*⟩ by their service, in the commencement It will now come on early at the n⟨ext⟩ term, when I hope a good one may be got—The Coll and his sons, are very indefatigable in their searches after an advertisement put into the papers in the 78, by Mr Custis they say, in which he calls on all indebted to him to make payments to Posey—Admitting he did so at that time, I think he may have seen enough to have changed his mind in the 79, & 80, when the payments were made to Posey; tho he may not have been prudent enough, from his unfortunate confidence in Posey, to have revoked this power in the same public manner—His retention of the bonds notwithstanding those payments, is I think a confirmation of the opinion, that they were made either without his knowledge, or at least his approbation—Coll Innis thinks it important for our side, to know before trial, whether there ever was such an advertisement or not, and has directed me to search for that purpose—He has already searched with the Printers without success—As you have a considerable collection at Mt Vernon, of news-papers, I must beg your permission to examine them, and take it if found.

I fear from the large payment I am to make Alexander this month, I shall not have it in my power to discharge your annuity this Spring—I hope from the fine prospect for wheat below, to be able to do it either entirely, or in a great measure pretty early in the fall. Mr Macaulay, who purchased the wheat and corn of the last year, having failed to pay, has been the occasion of the ballance of the former year's annuity, not being paid up yet— As he has now given the strongest assurances that it shall be immediately paid; I shall on recieving it, pay it to the Major.

I shall now endeavour to give you, all the information I have been able to collect during my journey, respecting the present temper of mind of the people of this State; so far as I can judge, from those I mixed with, and from what I could hear—I could wish indeed, to speak more favourably of it; but it appears to me, that the late transactions of Congress, have soured the Public mind to a great degree; which was just recovering from the fever which the Slave business had occasioned, when the late much agitated question of the State debts came on[1]—With respect to the Slave business, I am informed by Mr Lomax, whom I met on his return from Pittsylvania, that great advantage⟨s⟩ had been taken of it in that distant quarter, by many who wished to purcha⟨se⟩ slaves, circulating a report that Congress were about to pass an act for their ge⟨ne⟩ral emancipation[2]—This occasioned su⟨ch⟩ an alarm, that many were sold for the merest trifle—That the sellers were of course much enraged at Congress, for taking up a subject which they were precluded by the Constitution from medling with for the present, and thus furnishing the occasion for the alar⟨m wc[h]⟩ induced them to sell— As the people ⟨of⟩ that part of the Country were before much opposed to the Government, it may naturally be supposed, that this circumstance has embittered them much more against it— as to the assumption of the State debts, I scarce think it would be a measure generally acceptable on any principles—On such as have been contended for, I hardly think it would be acquiesced in by this State—How far indeed, a certain degree of shame or obstinacy natural to the human mind, which acts as a constant check on every rising disposition to depart from a cause or side once resolutely espoused; would continue to operate, I know not—But setting this aside, I think I should not be far wrong in saying, there would be as nearly an unanimity of opi[n-i]on for an opposition, as perhaps could ever be expected on any subject—There is I think in general, in consequence of these two instances, a strong apprehension, that the predictions relative to the grasping at power by unwarrantable contructions of the Constitution will be verifyed—On these two subjects at least, it is observed by most, (for there are some who after a proper liquidation, and allowance of credit to the States, for what has been paid, approve of the Assumption) that the Constitution appeared so clear, as to be incapable of misconstruction, by tho⟨se⟩ who wished to make it a rule and guide to their conduct.

At any rate on a subject of such importance, which may be considered as doubtfull in any shape, under the Constitution, it would at least have been prudent in the Members, to have consulted the general sentiment entertained of it, in their respective States—But it really appears, as if they were so charmed with the plenitude of their powers, as to have considered this as a degrading step—a strong suspicion too is entertained, from the number of Speculators, who have been traversing the State purchasing up State Securities, that there is a good deal of selfishness mixed with the plan—and this perhaps causes it to be viewed with more particular dislike—Mr Maddison's conduct on this business has gained him great popularity, even among those, who were illiberal enough, to pass severe censures on his motives respecting his discrimination plan.

As I passed through Richmond, the news of the rejection of the motion made by Mr Lee, for opening the doors of the Senate, agreeable to his instructions from our Legislature, had just arrived—It occasioned much disgust—But the manner of the rejection seemed to be as offensive, as the rejection itself—It being said, that after speaking two days ably on the subject, without recieving an answer, the question was called for and lost; no one voting wi⟨th⟩ him but his Collegue, and Mr Ma⟨clay.⟩ It is supposed, it will be productive of an application from our Legislature, to the other States calling on them, to join them in similar instructions to their Members—It is a pity the public wish (as I believe it to be) in so trivial a matter, cannot be gratifyed[3]—The slowness with which the business is carried on, is another cause of complaint—Congress it is said, sit only four hours a day, and like School boys observe every Saturday as a Holyday. If this be true, it is certainly trifling with their Constituents in the extreme, who pay them liberally, and have therefore a right to expect more diligence from them. It is the more unfortunate as it is represented at the same time, that they generally live for two dollars a day—I have now, gone throu⟨gh⟩ the Catalogue of Public discontents, and it really pains me much, and I believe every friend to the government, to think that there should be so much cause for them; and that a spirit so subversive of the true principles of the Constitution, productive of jealousies alone, and fraught with such high ideas of their power, should have manifested itself at so early a period of the Government—If Mr Henry has sufficient boldness to aim the blow at it's existence, which he has threatened, I think he can never meet with a more favourable opportunity; if the assumption should take place on the principles on which it has been contended for; and I understand that tho' lost at present it is to be again brought on[4]—But I doubt much, whether he possesses so adventurous a spirit—It will be the fault of those who are the promoters of such disgustfull measures, if he ever does, or indeed any one else—I believe it has even been considered as a maxim in Governments recently established, and which depend on the affections of the people, that what is rigidly right ought not to be the only standard of conduct with those who govern—Their inclinations & passions too, must be consulted more or less, in order to effict ultimately what is right⟨.⟩ How much more ought this to be do⟨ne⟩ when it rests solely on a construction of their powers, whether a measure in contemplation ought to be carried into execution or not?

A member of the Co⟨un⟩cil, who wrote privately to Mr Henry, to know if he would accept of the office of Senator in Congress, if appointed, shewed me his answer, in which he declines it, and says he was too old to fall into those aukward imitations which were now become fashionable—From this expression, I suspect the old Patriot has heard some extraordinary representations of the Etiquette established at your levees⟨.⟩ Those of his party no doubt think they promote themselves in his good opinion by such high colouring—It may not be amiss therefore to inform you, that Bland is among the dissatisfyed on this score—I am informed by good authority, that he represented, that there was more pomp used there, than at St James's, where he had been, and that your bows were more distant & stiff—This happened at the Governor's table in Richmond—By such accounts, I have no doubt the party think to keep alive the opposition and aversion to the Government, & probably too, to make Proselytes to their opinions.

You have no doubt heard of the number of vessells, we have had this winter at our Ports in this State⟨.⟩ It is mortifying to think how fiew of them have been American—one of the great benefits expected from the operation of the general Government was an encouragement to our own vessells⟨;⟩ and I think Maddison's plan of the last year would have had the desired effect[5]—It seems to give pleasure, that something of that sort is now in contemplation—I mean to the Americans, for it will excite a great clamor among the British factors, as it did before— as I think I must now have fatigued you I will conclude with my best respects to Mrs Washington, and your Family—I am Dr Sir with great respect Your affecte Servt

D:d Stuart

ALS, DLC:GW.

1. The debate over the assumption of state debts in the House of Representatives was interrupted from 16 to 23 Mar. by debate over a response to Quaker antislavery petitions. The unfortunate timing of this latter debate heightened southern fears, already roused by the assumption debate, of federal power (see David Stuart to GW, 15 Mar. 1790, n.4).

2. Probably Thomas Lomax (1746–1811) of Port Tobago, Caroline County, a large plantation on the north bank of the Rappahannock River above Port Royal.

3. The Senate practice of closing its doors to the public was the subject of widespread discontent in Virginia (see David Stuart to GW, 14 July 1789). In accordance with the instructions of the Virginia legislature, Richard Henry Lee made a motion on 29 April 1790 to open the doors of the Senate to the public "when the Senate is sitting in their legislative capacity." The motion was defeated the next day (*DHFC*, 1:296, 298). As Stuart predicted, the Virginia legislature later made a more concerted effort to have the Senate doors opened. On 27 Nov. 1790 it passed a resolution instructing Virginia's senators to "use their utmost endeavors to procure the admission of the citizens of the United States to hear the debates of their House whenever they are exercising their legislative functions" and another requesting other state legislatures to do likewise (*Journal of the House of Delegates,* Oct. 1790 sess., 92). In accordance with their instructions, Lee and James Monroe introduced a resolution to open the doors of the Senate on 24 Feb. 1791. This resolution was defeated the

next day, receiving only nine votes (Bowling and Veit, *Diary of William Maclay,* 388–90). The doors of the Senate were not opened to the public until the Third Congress.

4. On Henry's refusal to serve in the Senate, see also David Stuart to GW, 15 Mar. 1790, especially n.2.

5. In 1789 Madison advocated a policy of commercial discrimination favoring nations that had entered into a commercial treaty with the United States on the basis of reciprocity by imposing higher tonnage and tariff duties on imports from nations that had not concluded such a treaty. The principal target of this policy was Great Britain, which since 1783 had refused to establish mutually acceptable commercial relations with the United States. According to Madison commercial discrimination would encourage the development of native shipping as well as coerce the British into granting American ships access to British ports. See also David Stuart to GW, 14 July 1789.

To the United States Senate

United States [New York]
Gentleman of the Senate,   June 2nd 1790.

The Troops at present in service consisting of one regiment of Infantry and one Battalion of artillery were apportioned by the acts of the former Congress on the States of Massachusetts, Connecticut, New York, New Jersey and Pennsylvania; and as the Officers of said troops are in actual service, I nominate them, as in the list hereunto annexed, according to their ranks respectively, for appointments under the act for regulating the military establishment of the United States, passed the 30th of April 1790.[1] And as the said act requires an additional number of officers for one battalion of Infantry, I nominate, under the head of *"New-Appointments"* in the annexed list, the officers for the same from Maryland, Virginia, North Carolina and Georgia; it being proposed to raise the said battalion in those States.

Go: Washington

Infantry
Officers in Service

Rank	Names	State
Lieutenant colonel commandant.⎫ Josiah Harmer. ⎭		Brigadier General by brevet 31 July 1787 Pennsylvania
Majors	John Palsgrave Wyllys	Connecticut
	John F. Hamtramck	New York
Captains	1 David Zeigler	Pennsylvania
	2 Jonathan Heart	Connecticut

	3 David Strong	ditto
	4 William McCurdy	Pennsylvania
	5 John Mercer	New Jersey
	6 John Smith	New York
	7 Joseph Ashton	Pennsylvania
	8 Erkuries Beatty	ditto
Lieutenants	1 Thomas Doyle	Pennsylvania
	2 John Armstrong	ditto
	3 Ebenezer Frothingham	Connecticut
	4 John Pratt	ditto
	5 William Kersey	New Jersey
	6 William Peters	New York
	7 Jacob Kingsbury	Connecticut
	8 Ebenezer Denny	Pennsylvania
Ensigns	1 Cornelius R. Sedam	New Jersey
	2 Nathan McDowell	Pennsylvania
	3 John Jeffers	Connecticut
	4 Abner Pryor	New York
	5 Asa Hartshorne	Connecticut
	6 Robert Thomson	Pennsylvania
	7 Jacob Melcher	ditto
	8 John Morgan	New Jersey—Vice Francis Luce resigned 1st May 1790.
Surgeon	Richard Allison	Pennsylvania
Mates	John Elliott	New York
	John M. Scott	New Jersey

New Appointments

Major	Alexander Parker	Virginia	
Captains	1 Alexander Trueman	Maryland	
	2 Joseph Monfort	North Carolina	officers
	3 Michael Rudolph	Georgia	who
	4 Ballard Smith	Virginia	served
Lieutenants	1 Thomas Martin	Georgia	in the
	2 Thomas Pasteur	North Carolina	late war
	3 Mark McPherson	Maryland	
	4 John Steel	Virginia	
Ensigns	1 Richard Archer	ditto	
	2 Thomson Seayres	ditto	
[Ensigns]	3 Ezekiel Polke	North Carolina	
	4 James Clay	Georgia	

Artillery
Officers in Service

Major Commandant	John Doughty	New Jersey
Captains	1 William Ferguson	Pennsylvania
	2 James Bradford	New York

	3 Henry Burbeck	Massachusetts
	4 Joseph Savage	ditto
Lieutenants	1 Mahlon Ford	New Jersey
	2 Derick Schuyler	New York
	3 John Pierce	Massachusetts
	4 Moses Porter	ditto
	5 William Moor	ditto
	6 Mathew Ernest	New York
	7 Ebenezer Smith Fowle	Massachusetts
	8 Edward Spear	Pennsylvania
Surgeons Mate	Nathan Hayward	Massachusetts

Go: Washington

LS, DNA: RG 46, First Congress, 1789–91, Records of Executive Proceedings, President's Messages—Executive Nominations; LB, DLC:GW.

1. For the Military Establishment Act, signed into law by GW on 30 April 1790, see *DHFC*, 5:1274–1301. GW's letter and list of nominees were presented to the Senate on 2 June and confirmed the next day (*DHFC*, 2:71–74).

Tobias Lear to Clement Biddle

New York, 3 June 1790. "The Cook arrived and entered upon his duty on the 1st of may; he gives us good dinners, and the Steward says he conducts himself well. We are much obliged by your agency in obtaining him."

ALS, PHi: Washington-Biddle Correspondence; copy, in Lear's writing, ViMtV; LB, DLC:GW.

For the search for a cook for the presidential household, see Tobias Lear to Daniel Grant, 28 Feb. 1790 and notes.

From Robert Crooke

Sir   Newport [R.I.] June 3rd 1790

I had the honor of being appointed by this State, to the office of Collector of Impost for the county of Newport, in the year 1783, and continued in said office with general approbation until the year 1787, and gave full satisfaction to the public; but was removed therefrom by a change in administration, for the sole cause of my disapproving of their opposition, to the new constitution, and their emitting paper money.

I did not think it necessary to trouble your Excellency with any request for an office until the adoption of the constitution by this state—You will herewith have certificates of my former appointment, and my Conduct in said office.

If your Excellency can with propriety confer on me either the office of Collector of Impost or the naval office for this Port, I shall esteem it a great favor. I hope your Excellency will excuse the liberty of my thus addressing You. I am with sincerity and regard your Excellency's Most Obt & very Hume Servt

Robt Crooke

LS, DLC:GW.

Robert Crooke (Crook; c.1717–1802), a Newport merchant and a Federalist, was a member of the Sons of Liberty before the Revolution and served as collecter of impost for Newport in 1783–87 (Crane, *Dependent People,* 129, 146). He was removed from office in 1787 for opposing the emission of paper money. New York businessman Royal Flint described Crooke to Alexander Hamilton as "much respected" (Hunt, *Calendar,* 44). GW appointed him naval officer at Newport on 14 June 1790 (see GW to the U.S. Senate, 14 June 1790).

To Lafayette

My dear Marquis.   New York June 3d 1790.

Your kind letter of the 12th of January is, as your letters always are, extremely acceptable to me. By some chance its arrival had been retarded to this time. Conscious of your friendly dispositions for me and realising the enormous burden of public business with which you was oppressed, I felt no solicitude but that you should progress directly forward and happily effect your great undertakings—How much, how sincerely am I rejoiced, My dear Marquis, to find that things are assuming so favorable an aspect in France! Be assured that you always have my best and most ardent wishes for your success; and that, if I have not troubled you with letters of late, it was because I had nothing which it was very essential to communicate, and because I knew how much better your time was employed than in answering letters merely of a private nature.

You have doubtless been informed from time to time of the happy progress of our affairs. The principal difficulties which opposed themselves in any shape to the prosperous execution of our Government seem in a great measure to have been surmounted. A Good temper prevails among our Citizens. Rhode

Island has just now acceded to the Constitution, and has thus united under the general government all the States of the original Confederacy. Vermont we hope will soon come within the pale of the Union. Two new States exist under the immediate direction of the General Government, Viz. that at the head of which is Genl St Clair, and that which consists of the territory lately ceded by the State of North Carolina.

Our government is now happily carried into operation. Although some thorney questions still remain, it is to be hoped that the wisdom of those concerned in the national Legislature will dispose of them prudently. A funding system is one of the subjects which occasions most anxiety and perplexity. Yet our revenues have been considerably more productive than it was imagined they would be. In the last year, the plentiful crops and great prices of grain, have vastly augmented our remittances— The rate of exchange is also much in our favor. Importations of European goods have been uncommonly extensive, and the duties payable into the public Treasury proportionably so. Our Trade to the East Indies flourishes—The profits to Individuals are so considerable as to induce more persons to engage in it continually; a single vessel just arrived in this Port pays 30,000 Dollars to Government. Two Vessels fitted out for the fur trade to the North West Coast of America have succeeded well.[1] The whole outfits of Vessels and cargoes cost but £7,000: one is returning home loaded with India produce, the other going back to the Coast of America; and they have deposited 100,000 Dollars of their profits in China. I mention this to shew the spirit of enterprize that prevails. I hope and trust our Commerce with the West India Islands belonging to different Nations (which is at present of no great consequence) will shortly be placed upon a better footing. As the People of this Country are sensible of the generous conduct of the French Nation, I can, with great satisfaction, give it as my decided opinion, that the most friendly dispositions prevail on our side the water towards that nation.

Many of your old acquaintances and Friends are concerned with me in the Administration of this Government. By having Mr Jefferson at the Head of the Department of State, Mr Jay of the Judiciary, Hamilton of the Treasury and Knox of that of War, I feel myself supported by able Co-adjutors, who harmonise extremely well together. I believe that these and the other appointments generally have given perfect satisfaction to the Public. Poor Colo. Harrison, who was appointed one of the Judges of the Supreme Court, and declined, is lately dead.[2]

I have, a few days since, had a severe attack of the peripneumony kind: but am now recovered, except in point of strength.[3] My Physicians advise me to more exercise and less application to business. I cannot, however, avoid persuading myself that it is essential to accomplish whatever I have undertaken (though reluctantly) to the best of my abilities. But it is thought Congress will have a recess this summer, in which case, I propose going for a while to Mount Vernon. With sentiments of the sincerest affection I am, My dear Marquis, Yours &c.

George Washington

LB, DLC:GW; Df, DNA: RG 59, Miscellaneous Letters; copy, NNPM; copy, NN: Lafayette Miscellaneous.

1. See Joseph Barrell et al. to GW, 20 Mar. 1790, and notes.

2. See GW to Robert Hanson Harrison, 28 Sept. 1789,and notes.

3. For GW's illness, see William Jackson to Clement Biddle, 12 May 1790, editorial note.

To David Ramsay

Sir,   New York, June 3rd 1790.

A copy of your history of the american Revolution has been presented to me by Mr Allen of this city, in compliance as he informs me with your orders.[1]

I therefore beg, Sir, that you will accept my acknowledgments and best thanks for this mark of polite attention, from which I expect to derive much pleasure and satisfaction in the perusal. with very great esteem, I am Sir, your most obedient humble Servant

G. Washington

LB, DLC:GW.

The historian and physician David Ramsay (1749–1815) was educated at the College of New Jersey and received his medical training at the College of Pennsylvania from which he was given his degree in 1772. In 1773 he began practice in Charleston, S.C., and served in the 1770s and 1780s in the South Carolina legislature and in the Continental Congress in 1782 and 1785. In 1785 Ramsay produced the *History of the Revolution of South Carolina*, criticized for including much verbatim material from the *Annual Register*, a charge that was also levied against his more important work, the *History of the American Revolution,* published in 1789.

1. Thomas Allen, a New York bookseller and a partner in the firm of Hodge, Allen, and Campell, wrote GW on 1 June that "Doctor Ramsay has ordered me to present to you, a Copy of his History of the American Revolution" (DLC:GW). GW's copy of Ramsay's *History* is now in the Collection of Books from Washington's Library at the Boston Athenaeum. Both volumes have GW's signature on the title pages (Griffin, *Boston Athenæum Collection,* 170–71).

To Arthur Fenner

Sir,　　　　　　　　　　　　　　　　N. York June 4th 1790.

In acknowledging the Rect of your Excellency's letter of the 20th of May, I cannot forbear to congratulate you and the people of your State upon the happy event which has since taken place by the adoption and ratification of the Constitution of the United States by the Convention of Rhode Island.

Having now attained the desireable object of uniting under one general Government all those States which were originally confederated, we have a right to expect, with the blessing of a divine providence, that our Country will afford us all those domestic enjoyments of which a free people only can boast—and at the same time secure that respectability abroad which she is entitled to by nature and from circumstances. Since the bond of Union is now compleat, and we once more consider ourselves as one family, it is much to be hoped that reproaches will cease and prejudices be done away; for we should all remember that we are members of that community upon whose general success depends our particular and individual welfare—and, therefore, if we mean to support the Liberty and Independence which it has cost us so much blood & treasure to establish, we must drive far away the dæmon of party spirit and local reproach.

I should be deficient in politeness as well as sensibility was I to close this without acknowledging the impression which the great personal regard & warm wishes for my individual felicity expressed in your Letter—has made upon Your most Obedt Servt.

Copy, DNA: RG 59, Miscellaneous Letters; LB, DLC:GW.

Dominick Lynch to Tobias Lear

Sir   New York 4th June 1790

I hope you will excuse the Liberty I take in addressing you on a subject which my Inclination wou'd lead me not to interfere in, but the wish to serve a most respectable friend induces me to intrude upon you.

Mr John Street of Fyal who in consideration of his services to American Prisoners &c. was by the Portuguese Senate for the western Islands appointed during the war American agent & Consul, at present entertains no pretentions not being a Citizen of the united States, one of his family & a near relation Mr John Street who was sent by him to this Country has been naturalized, & at present resides in Philadelphia. this Gentleman agreeable to the wishes of his Kinsman sollicits the Honor of the appointment & from the respectability of his Connections & family both in Portugal & in the Islands am sure he will at all times act with Integrity.[1]

if not too presumptious request you will be pleased to communicate the purport of this Letter to His Excellency the President. I have the Honor to be with great respect Sir Your most obedient & most humble Servant

Dom. Lynch

ALS, DLC:GW.

For an identification of Dominick Lynch, see Robert Adams to GW, 13 Oct. 1788, n.2.

1. John Street of Fayal (d. 1807) had been appointed by the Portuguese government to act as U.S. consul at Fayal during the Revolution until a consul could be appointed by the U.S. government. On 2 Aug. 1790 John Street (d. 1807) of Fayal rather than John Street of Philadelphia received the appointment as vice-consul of the United States, "for the said Island of Fayal, and for such other of the Azores or Western Islands as shall be nearer to Fayal than to the residence of any other Consul or Vice-Consul of the United States within the same allegiance" (*DHFC*, 2:84).

From John Steele

Sir,   New York June 4th 1790

A sincere desire that the office of district Judge for No. Carolina, may be bestowed upon a worthy character induces me to offer you my opinion at present. I have been told that Colo. Davie's name has been mentioned to you already, he is unquestionably better calculated for the office, than any other man in the State; but acquainted as I am, with his practice as an attorney, his plans, and his prospects, I have reason to believe that he would not relinquish such profitable pursuits for so small a salary.[1] Samuel Spencer Esqr. has been also mentioned, I presume for the same office; he is a good man, at present one of the judges of that state, not remarkable for his abilities, but nevertheless deserves well of his country.[2] Colonel John Stokes, has not been mentioned, but I am authorised to transmit his name to your Excellency as a candidate for the same office.[3]

This Gentleman is a native of Virginia, descended from a very respectable family, was a captain in the Sixth Regiment of that state in the late War, continued in service untill Colo. Beaufort was defeated in So. Carolina, when unfortunately he lost (among⟨st⟩ other wounds) his right hand. He then setled in No. Carolina, has practiced the law ever since, with reputation, and success, has been frequently a member of the State legislature wherein he supported a very respectable, and honorable rank, both as a man of business, and a man of abilities, was a member of the Convention and very instrumental in bringing about the ratification of the Constitution, is at this time Colo. Commandt of a Regt of militia Cavalry, and additional Judge of the supreme Court of Law and Equity in that State. Notwithstanding the loss of his right hand, few men write better than he does with the other, and is extreemely capable of business.

With respect to the Candidates for any other office within that State, or the ceded territory if my opinion, or any information from me, are necessary they shall be given with candor, and impartiality. I have the Honor, to be Your Excellency's Most Humble Servant

Jno. Steele

ALS, DLC:GW.

1. William Richardson Davie (1756–1820) was born in England and was taken to the Waxhaw settlement in western South Carolina, where he was raised by his uncle. After graduating from the College of New Jersey (Princeton) in 1776, he served with distinction as an officer in the southern campaigns, rising to the rank of colonel. After the war he established himself as one of the leading lawyers in North Carolina and served in the legislature

almost continuously from 1786 to 1798. In 1787 he was a delegate to the federal convention and was thereafter a leading advocate of ratification in North Carolina. For other recommendations, see Memorandum of Thomas Jefferson, c.7 June 1790. GW nominated Davie to be district court judge for North Carolina, and the Senate confirmed the appointment on 8 June (see GW to the U.S. Senate, 7 June 1790; *DHFC*, 2:79). Davie declined the office.

2. Samuel Spencer, a North Carolina lawyer and state court judge, was also suggested as a candidate by Timothy Bloodworth (see Bloodworth to GW, 5 June 1790). Spencer received no appointment from GW.

3. John Stokes (1756–1790) was born in Virginia and served as an officer of Virginia troops from 1776 to the close of the war, rising to the rank of captain. After the Revolution he settled in North Carolina, where he established himself as a lawyer. He served in the North Carolina house of commons in 1786–87 and again in 1789 and as a Federalist delegate to the second North Carolina convention called to ratify the federal Constitution in 1789. Stokes was elected a judge of the Morgan District Superior Court in 1788 and assistant judge of the same court in 1789. Steele wrote to GW again on 31 July that Stokes had agreed to serve as district court judge if appointed and that "he would perform the duties of this office with dignity and give general satisfaction, I have not a doubt. His adjudications as additional judge of No. Ca. in several very weighty and intricate causes, have been highly approved" (Steele to GW, 31 July 1790, DLC:GW). Stokes was also suggested for the office by John B. Ashe (see Ashe to GW, 5 June 1790). GW nominated Stokes as district court judge for North Carolina after Davie declined, and his appointment was confirmed by the Senate on 3 Aug. 1790 (see GW to the U.S. Senate, 2 Aug. 1790; *DHFC*, 2:85). Stokes served until his death in October 1790 (Ely and Brown, *Legal Papers of Andrew Jackson*, 388; see also Benjamin Hawkins to GW, 4 Nov. 1790).

To the United States Senate

United States [New York]
Gentlemen of the Senate,   June 4th 1790.

I nominate the following persons to be Consuls and Vice-Consuls of the United States of America for the Ports which are affixed to their names.[1] viz.

Cadiz   Richard Harrison of Virginia to be Consul of the United States of America for the Port of Cadiz in the Kingdom of Spain, and for such parts of the said Kingdom as shall be nearer to the said port than to the residence of any other Consul or Vice-Consul of the United States in the said Kingdom.

Bilboa   Edward Church of Massachusetts to be Consul of the United States of America for the Port of Bilboa in the Kingdom of Spain, and for such parts of the said Kingdom as shall be nearer to the said port than to the residence of any other Consul or Vice-Consul of the United States in the said Kingdom.

Madeira   John Marsden Pintard of New York to be Consul of the United States of America for the Island of Madeira, and such other Islands of the allegiance of her most faithful Majesty as are nearer to the same than to the residence of any other Consul or Vice-Consul of the United States within the same allegiance.

Liverpool   James Maury of Virginia to be Consul of the United States of America for the port of Liverpool in the Kingdom of Great Britain, and for such parts of the said Kingdom as shall be nearer to the said port than to the residence of any other Consul or Vice-Consul of the United States in the said Kingdom.

Cowes   Thomas Auldjo of the Kingdom of Great Britain, to be Vice-Consul of the United States of America for the port of Cowes, and such parts of the same Kingdom as shall be nearer to the said port than to the residence of any other Consul or Vice-Consul of the United States within the said Kingdom.

Dublin   William Knox of New York to be Consul of the United States of America for the port of Dublin in the Kingdom of Ireland, and for such parts of the said Kingdom as shall be nearer to the said port than to the residence of any other Consul or Vice-Consul of the United States in the said Kingdom.

Marseilles   The Sieur Etienne Cathalan the yo[u]nger of the Kingdom of France, Vice-Consul of the United States of America for the port of Marseilles and for such parts of the same Kingdom as shall be nearer to the said port than to the residence of any other Consul or Vice-Consul of the United States within the same Kingdom.

Bordeaux   James Fenwick of Maryland to be Consul of the United States of America for the port of Bordeaux in the Kingdom of France, and for such parts of the same Kingdom as shall be nearer to the said port than to the residence of any other Consul or Vice-Consul of the United States in the same Kingdom.[2]

Nantes   Burrell Carnes of Massachusetts to be Consul of the United States of America for the port of Nantes in the Kingdom of France, and for such parts of the said Kingdom as are nearer to the said port than to the residence of any other Consul or Vice-Consul of the United States in the same Kingdom.

Havre   The Sieur de La Motte of the Kingdom of France, to be Vice-Consul of the United States of America for the port of Havre de grace and such parts of the said Kingdom as shall be nearer to the said port than to the residence of any other Consul or Vice-Consul of the United States within the same Kingdom.

Rouen   Nathaniel Barrett of Massachusetts to be Consul of the United States of America for the port of Rouen in the Kingdom of France, and for such parts of the said Kingdom as shall be nearer to the said port than to the residence of any other Consul or Vice-Consul of the United States in the said Kingdom.

Hispaniola   Sylvanus Bourne of Massachusetts, to be Consul of the United States of America for the Island of Hispaniola, and for such other Islands of the allegiance of his most Christian Majesty as shall be nearer thereto than to the residence of any other Consul or Vice-Consul of the United States within the same allegiance.

Martinique   Fulwar Skipwith of Virginia, to be Consul of the United States of America for the Island of Martinique, and for such other Islands and places of the allegiance of his most Christian Majesty as shall be nearer thereto than to the residence of any other Consul or Vice-Consul of the United States within the same allegiance.

Hamburgh   John Parish, Merchant of Hamburgh, to be Vice-Consul of the United States of America for Hamburgh.

Go: Washington

LS, DNA: RG 46, First Congress, 1789–91, Records of Executive Proceedings, President's Messages—Executive Nominations; LB, DLC:GW.

1. This message was presented to the Senate by Tobias Lear on 4 June. The appointments of Harrison, Pintard, Maury, Knox, Fenwick, Carnes, Barrett, Bourne, and Skipwith as consuls were confirmed on 7 June; consideration of Church as consul for Bilboa and Auldjo, Cathalan, La Motte, and Parish as vice-consuls was postponed, apparently because the nominees for vice-consul were foreigners (*DHFC*, 2:74–78). These nominations were not taken up again until 17 June. On that date the Senate began by considering whether foreigners ought to be permitted to hold consular appointments. The Continental Congress had considered this question in 1784 and had resolved "That it is inconsistent with the interest of the United States to appoint any person not a citizen thereof, to the office of Minister, chargé des affaires, Consul, vice-

consul, or to any other civil department in a foreign country" (*JCC*, 26:144). After considerable debate on 17 June 1790 on what William Maclay called "the grand question," the Senate adopted a resolution, apparently presented by Pierce Butler, "that it may be expedient to advise and consent to the appointment of Foreigners to the Offices of Consuls or Vice-Consuls for the United States." The Senate then voted to approve the appointments of Church, Auldjo, Cathalan, and Parish; final approval of the appointment of La Motte was withheld until 22 June (Bowling and Veit, *Diary of William Maclay*, 295; *DHFC*, 2:80–82). During the weeks that these consular nominations were being considered in the Senate, a conference committee was meeting to reconcile House and Senate versions of the Foreign Intercourse Act, which provided for the salaries of ministers plenipotentiary, their secretaries, and chargés d'affaires. GW was concerned that Congress would use this legislation to encroach on executive authority over foreign affairs, by asserting the right of the Senate to control the grade of diplomatic appointments and the places to which diplomats should be sent (see Thomas Jefferson to GW, 24 April 1790, n.1). These concerns were undoubtedly increased by the Senate resolution of 17 June asserting the authority of the Senate to judge the expediency of appointing foreigners to consular positions. In practice this authority might be used to prevent the establishment of consular posts for which no suitable American candidate could be found, but which the administration considered essential.

2. On 23 June GW informed the Senate that the name James Fenwick had been presented rather than Joseph Fenwick. The change was entered in the Senate record (*DHFC*, 2:82; see GW to the U.S. Senate, 23 June 1790).

From John B. Ashe

Sir   New york 5th June 1790

Having been this evening informd you wish to have the opinion of the No. Carolina Representatives, of Persons, proper to fill the offices of the Government South of the Ohio, also those of the Federal Judiciary in No. Carolina, I beg leave to give mine Sir, and will do so, with candor and disinterest'dness, Colo. William Blount, who I may presume, you are acquainted with, has long and on various occasions had the confidence of the People of that Country, and who in private life has ever conduct'd himself with firmness & independence, and is a man of abilities and business, therefore I think Sir, he wou'd fill the office of Governor with as much dignity, and Satisfaction to the Citizens who he is to preside over, as any one within my knowledge.[1]

Colo. Robert Hayes, an old and valuable officer in our late army, of the rank of Lieutt who has been living in that Country Several years has been a representative from it, in the Legislative body of the State of No. Carolina Several times, I conceive Sir, wou'd fill the office of Secretary of State with propriety;[2] Mr David Campble, a Mr John McNairy, and Mr Howell Tatum,[3] the offices, of Judges, the two former I have no personal knowledge⟨,⟩ of⟨,⟩ they act in those capacities in that Country at present under appointments of No. Carolina—The latter Gentleman, was an old Captain in the late army, and probably may be known to you sir, he now practices the Law in that Country and is consider[ed] clever at his profession, is a man of great application and of a fair and unimpeach'd character. As a States Attorney I wou'd mention a Mr Edward Jones, a young Gentleman, who I [am] not well acquaint'd with, but who I have often heard spoke of as a young Gentleman of Merit and an inlighten'd understanding[.][4] As a Federal Judge, I beg leave to mention Mr John Stokes, who Mr Steel tells me, he express'd his opinion of, to you, this day, and as Federal Attorney Mr John Sitgreaves, a Gentleman who has practi⟨c⟩'d the Law for some years past in No. Carolina, tho' not so brilliant in abilities, Stands as a favorably as to rectitude of mind, as any of his profession[5] in perfect obedience to your Wish sir—I have been more prolix, than I wish'd to have been and which I hope will excuse me to you. With sentiments, of the highest respect sir, I beg leave to conclude myself your Very Obedt And Very hble Servant

John B. Ashe

ALS, DLC:GW.

John Baptista Ashe (1748–1802) served as an officer in the North Carolina Line during the Revolution, rising to the rank of colonel. He was a member of the North Carolina house of commons from 1784 to 1786, serving as speaker in 1786. In 1787 he represented the state in the Continental Congress; he served as chairman of the committee of the whole in the North Carolina convention that ratified the Federal Constitution in 1789. He was elected to the state senate in 1789 and shortly thereafter, to the First Congress.

1. The North Carolina delegation in the House of Representatives was unanimous in recommending Blount for governor of the Territory South of the River Ohio (see Hugh Williamson to GW, 28 May, John Steele to GW, 4 June, and Timothy Bloodworth to GW, 5 June).

2. Robert Hays (1758–1819), an associate of William Blount, settled in the Cumberland Valley about 1784 and by 1790 was one of the principal landowners in the region (Arnow, *Seedtime on the Cumberland*, 330). He represented Davidson County in the North Carolina house of commons in 1787 and was justice of the county court (Ely and Brown, *Legal Papers of Andrew Jackson*, 372). He did not receive an appointment from GW at this time, but in February

1797 GW appointed him U.S. marshal for the district of Tennessee (see GW to the U.S. Senate, 17 Feb. 1797).

3. John McNairy (1762–1837), a North Carolina lawyer, was admitted to the bar in 1784 and elected judge of the superior court of Davidson County by the North Carolina general assembly in December 1787. GW nominated him for judge of the Territory South of the River Ohio on 7 June 1790; the appointment was confirmed by the Senate the next day (see GW to the U.S. Senate, 7 June 1790; *DHFC*, 2:79). McNairy served in this capacity until Tennessee was admitted as a state, when GW appointed him judge of the new federal district court; he served on the federal bench in Tennessee until 1833 (Ely and Brown, *Legal Papers of Andrew Jackson*, 378; see also GW to the U.S. Senate, 17 Feb. 1797). On David Cambell and Howell Tatum, see Hugh Williamson to GW, 28 May 1790.

4. Edward Jones (1762–1841) was born in Ireland and settled in Philadelphia in 1783. In 1786 he moved to Wilmington, N.C., where he studied law and was admitted to the bar in 1788. In that year he was elected to the North Carolina house of commons, serving until 1791. In 1791 he became solicitor general of North Carolina, a post he held until 1827 (Powell, *Dictionary of North Carolina Biography*, 3:317). Jones was recommended for the post of U.S. attorney for the Territory South of the River Ohio by Timothy Bloodworth (see Bloodworth to GW, 5 June 1790). He received no appointment from GW.

5. On John Stokes, see John Steele to GW, 4 June 1790. John Sitgreaves (1757–1802) was born in England, attended Eton College, and settled in New Bern, N.C., where he studied law and was admitted to the bar. During the Revolution he served in the militia and as a clerk to the state senate. He was elected to the North Carolina house of commons in 1784 and again from 1786 to 1788. In 1785 he represented North Carolina in the Confederation Congress (*Biog. Dir. Cong.*, 1818). Sitgreaves was also suggested for the post of U.S. attorney for North Carolina by Timothy Bloodworth (see Bloodworth to GW, 5 June 1790). GW nominated him on 7 June 1790, and the Senate confirmed the appointment the next day (see GW to the U.S. Senate, 7 June 1790; *DHFC*, 2:79). GW appointed Sitgreaves judge of the federal district court for North Carolina in December 1790 after the death of John Stokes (see GW to the U.S. Senate, 17 Dec. 1790).

From Thomas Bird

Portland in the District of Maine
June the 5th 1790

Permit a stranger to inform your Excellency, that about twelve months since, I was apprehended & committed to Goal, in the Town of Portland, within the District of Maine, charged with the murder of Capt. John Conner, of the Sloop Mary, upon the Coast of Africa. That yesterday I was tried & found guilty of the

Crime, & that the District Judge, a few hours since pronounced the fatal sentence, that still rings in my Ears & harrows up my soul, the sentence of Death, which is to be Executed upon me on the 25 day of June Inst., The time is short Great Washington, too short, for a wretch harden'd in Crimes to prepare for that Country, from whose bourn no Traveller e'er return'd. Permit him to intreat your Excellency, in your great Clemency, to grant him a Pardon or Commute the punishment to something, to any thing, short of Death, It is usual for Kings and Emperors, at the Commencement of their Reign to grant such indulgences, Permit me then to beg that the Commencement of your administration may be marked, by Extending mercy to the first Condemned under it, or at least by granting him a Reprieve for a few months longer, your Excellency will be pleas'd to consider that I am at a great distance from the seat of Government, and that the days I have to live are very few, so that my Case demands immediate attention, Hear then and immediately attend to the cries, of a wretch, who unless your Excellency interpose will before Saturday the 26. of this month be beyond the reach of your Excellency's goodness.[1]

his
Thomas X Bird
mark

Signed in presence of John Frothingham

Enoch Preble

L, DNA: RG 59, Miscellaneous Letters.

1. On 5 June 1790 David Sewall, judge of the U.S. District Court wrote GW further details of Bird's case: "That the Supreme Executive of the United States may be duly informed of the Charge, Trial, and Sentence of the district Court of Maine upon *Thomas Bird* for a capital offence, is the intention of my enclosing a Copy of the Process. This Capital Conviction, is probably the first in the Nation since the establishment of the Federal Courts under the new Constitution[.] A Writ or Warrant of Execution will Issue from the district Court to the Marshall, in Consequence of Which the Sentence will be put in force at the Time mentioned in the Judgement, unless the Supreme executive shall deem it expedient to interpose. Should an application be made for Mercy, all I can say on the Occasion [is] that the Charge appeared fully proved" (DNA: RG 59, Miscellaneous Letters). Sewall's enclosure was the proceedings of Bird's trial in the district court on 1 June: "The Jurors for the District of Maine on their oath present, that Thomas Bird, late resident at Bristol in the Kingdom of Great Britain, now confined in the common Gaol in Portland aforesaid, Mariner, not having the fear of God before his eyes, on the twenty-third

day of January, in the year of our Lord, one thousand seven hundred and eighty-nine, upon the High-seas about the latitude of five degrees North, and about four degrees West longitude, off the coast of Africa, within the jurisdiction of the Court aforesaid, the said Thomas Bird, then being a Mariner of a certain Sloop called the Mary, whereof one John Connor was Master, with force and arms piratically, feloniously, wilfully, and of his malice aforethought, in and upon the said John Connor, then in the peace of God and the said United States being, an assault did make, and that the said Thomas Bird, with a hand-gun loaden with gun-powder and leaden ball, which same gun the said Thomas Bird then and there had and held in both his hands, and the same gun thus loaded as aforesaid, piratically, feloniously, wilfully, and of his malice aforethought did discharge in and upon the breast of him the said John Connor thereby giving him the said John Connor a mortal wound, of which mortal wound thus made by the discharge of the same gun in manner as aforesaid, he the said John Connor instantly died; and so the Jurors aforesaid upon their oath aforesaid do say, that the said Thomas Bird, on the High-seas aforesaid, in manner and form aforesaid, the said John Connor piratically, feloniously, wilfully, and of his malice aforethought, did kill and murder.

"And the Jurors aforesaid, upon their oath aforesaid, do further present, that Hans Hanson, late resident at Norway in the Kingdom of Norway, now a prisoner in the Gaol in Portland aforesaid, Mariner on the same twenty-third day of January aforesaid, upon the High seas aforesaid, within the jurisdiction of the Court aforesaid, then being a Mariner on board the same Sloop Mary, was present, and then and there knowingly and willingly did aid, abet and assist the said Thomas Bird, in piratically and feloniously killing and murdering the said John Connor—in manner aforesaid, against the peace of the said United States of America, and the dignity of the same.

"And afterwards on the second day of June instant, the said Thomas Bird, and Hans Hanson, are set to the Bar by the Marshal of this District, and have the Indictment read to them; and it being demanded of them concerning the premises in the said Indictment above specified and charged upon them, how they will acquit themselves thereof, they severally say, they are not guilty, and thereof put themselves upon the Country." The jury, "after fully hearing the evidence produced in behalf of the United States, and also the full defence of the Prisoners, by their Counsel learned in the Law, upon their oath do say, that the said Thomas Bird—is *guilty*—and that the said Hans Hanson is *not guilty*. Whereupon it is ordered by the Court, that the said Hans Hanson be discharged, and go without day. And it is demanded of the said Thomas Bird, wherefore the Court here ought not upon the premises aforesaid to proceed to Judgement and Execution against him. And the said Thomas Bird by his Counsel moved, in arrest of Judgement, the following reasons, viz.

"1. The Bill against the said Bird is not found by the *Jurors of the United States*.

"2. The *place* where the Crime was said to be committed, is *uncertain*.

"3. The Indictment does not conclude, against *the peace and dignity of the United States*, as it ought to do. and is fully heard thereon, which reasons are adjudged insufficient to arrest the Judgement.

"Whereupon all and singular the premises being seen, and by the said Judge fully understood, it is considered by the Court here, that the said Thomas Bird be taken to the Prison from whence he came, and from thence on Friday the twenty-fifth day of June instant, to the place of Execution, and there be hanged by the neck until he be dead. And that a Warrant issue to the Marshal of this District, under the Seal of this Court, to cause Execution to be done upon the said Thomas Bird according to the Judgement, on Friday the twenty-fifth day of June instant, between the hours of three and five in the afternoon" (DNA: RG 59, Miscellanous Letters).

GW evidently requested Jay's opinion of the case in a letter to the chief justice of 13 June, asking "would there be prudence, justice or policy in extending mercy to the Convict mentioned in the enclosed Papers?" Jay found that "There does not appear to be a single Circumstance in the Case of the Murderer in question, to recommend a Pardon—His own Petition contains no averment of Innocence, no Palliative for Guilt, no complaint of Court Jury or witnesses, nor of the want of witnesses" (Jay to GW, 13 June 1790). On 28 June GW wrote Sewall that "No palliating circumstance appeared in the case of this unhappy man to recommend him to mercy for which he applied: I could not therefore have justified it to the laws of my Country, had I, in this instance, exercised that pardoning power which the Constitution vests in the President of the United States" (LB, DLC:GW).

From Timothy Bloodworth

Sir   June 5th 1790
with the utmost defidence I proceed to exercize a priviledge founded in youre indulgence. that of Mentioning Carrecters to fill offices, created by the Adoption of the Constitution, & Ceedure of the Western Country, By North Carolina thiss subject are more irksom, as I consider it out of the line of my Duty, and only warrentable by youre permission. through thiss Chanel I venture to mention Coll⟨l⟩ William Blount, as a Carrecter which I have reason to Believe, would afford satisfaction to the Inhabitants as a Governer. thiss Belief is founded in the attention paid to him by their Members. & the people Electing him a Member for the Last Convention.

for judges David Campble, at present judge in that place also Mr Robert Hays, or Howel Tateham secretary. th⟨esse⟩ are carrecters with whome I have no personal acquaintance for States Attorney in the western Country Mr Edward Jones. with thiss Gentleman I have a personal acquaintance, he supports a good Carrecter, & has been twice return'd for the Town of Wilmington. with respect to Judge for North Carolina, Mr Samuel Spencer one of oure State Judges, has express'd his Desire to fill that station. several Gentlemen have signifyed their Desire to be appointed States Attorney. viz: Mr Arnet, Mr Hambleton, Mr John Hay of Fayettville. & som of my Colliegues have Mentioned Mr John Sitgraves. who is a gentleman of Carrecter & represented the State in Congress in the Year 1785[1] Pleas to excuse the Liberty I have taken. With every sentiment of Esteem Due to Youre exalted Merrit I remain. sir. Youre Devoted Humble Servant

Timothy Bloodworth

ALS, DLC:GW

Timothy Bloodworth (1736–1814) was one of the most conspicuous political leaders in North Carolina during the Revolutionary era. Born in poverty, he received no formal education. At various times in his life Bloodworth was apparently a teacher, tavern keeper, ferry master, preacher, blacksmith, wheelwright, watchmaker, and farmer. He was first elected to the legislature in 1758 and was returned repeatedly in the following thirty-five years. An early supporter of the Revolution in North Carolina, Bloodworth was elected to the Continental Congress in 1784 and 1787. From 1787 to 1789 Bloodworth was one of the leading Antifederalists in the state. An unsuccessful candidate for the Senate in 1789, he was elected to the House of Representatives in 1790 (Powell, *Dictionary of North Carolina Biography*, 1:177).

1. Bloodworth's recommendations for judicial appointments in North Carolina and the Territory South of the River Ohio were similar to those of his North Carolina colleagues in the House of Representatives, Hugh Williamson, John Steele, and John B. Ashe (see Williamson to GW, 28 May 1790, Steele to GW, 4 June 1790, and Ashe to GW, 5 June 1790). Probably at GW's request, Jefferson combined the recommendations of these four, along with those of others, in a single memorandum (see Memorandum of Thomas Jefferson, c.7 June 1790).

From Moses Brown

Providence [R.I.]

Esteemed Friend   6th of 6th Mo. 1790

Having for some years been retired out of Trade, I have had to Contemplate and particularly of late, the consequences of an impartial and faithfull Collection of the Revenue, as on which the prosperity and indeed the happiness of the United States and this in particular much Depends. I therefore as a Citizen desireous of the welfare of the Union, lay before the President some circumstances which appear to me worthy of his attention under our present Divided and peculiarly Unhapy Scituation in this state. To Conciliate contending parties and Restore Harmony within as well as without this State I conceive is an Object for which we may look up to thee as to a Father who desires to Effect the Union and Harmony of his numerous Family. That part of our Difficulties which presents as an Obsticle for Removal, is a Jealousy in the Country part of the state, that the Merchants will Endeavour to Evade the payment of the Duties, this raises their apprehentions of a Land Tax and Lessons their Confidence i⟨n⟩ the General Goverment. This Idea is founded on the former habits in the State of Runing of Good or Makeing false Entr⟨ies⟩ to Evade the payment of Duties, and therefore more Deeply interest them in the appointment of officers who may not be under Mercantile Influence, and suggest the propriety of greater Caution in, and the fullest information to, the Department which make those appointments, that they may be fill'd with those persons who have the Confidence of both the Farmer and the Merchant; as well as to be otherwise Quallified to fill so important a Trust, and altho our Merchants have been much United in the Question of adopting the General Goverment, yet they having their fears of Rival ship in the advantages of Commerce, an additional Reason is thereby Suggested that the persons appointed be as free as may be from influencing Connections or attachments, as there by ocation may be given for False Entries, with all their Train of Evil Consequences affecting not the Revenue only, but allso the Morrals of the Citizens, which is Inseperably involvd in the Transaction and therefore to be avoided as of great Consequence to the future happiness of this Country—the Earliest attention therefore seems Necessary for Us that Men of Coolness Consideration, Candour, Impartialy and Integrity be prefer'd—These General Observations I presume has not Escaped thy Notice yet the Reviving of them to thy attention on the present particular Circumstances of this state may not I hope be tho't wholey impropper. Our present Collector in this Town Ebenezer Thompson, having Long been Unanimusly Chosen the president of the Town Council here, and having there in as well as a Legislature, and a Judge of our Court obtaind the Confidence of all parties, was by the Country Interest Chosen Collector, in which office I am informed on Enquiry, he has given general sattisfaction to the Merchants as well as to the authority which appointd him, and I am of opinion that his appointment to that office by the Federal Goverment will contribute to Consiliating the Great Body of the people thereto and be promotive of Harmony and an increase of Confidence in the different parties in the state, And by his Candour Impartiality and Integrity promote a Ju⟨s⟩t Collection of the Revenue.[1] I therefore Leave the Subject, with my best Wishes that the Lord may preserve thee in his Fear, Guide thee by his Wisdom and Crown thee with the incomes of his Love in thy heart, which concludes thy friend

Moses Brown

ALS, DLC:GW.

1. Ebenezer Thompson wrote to GW to secure his continuance as collector at Providence on 21 May 1790 (see Thompson to GW, 21 May 1790). Thompson's continuance was also recommended by Gov. Arthur Fenner, Deputy Gov. Samuel Potter, and eight of the ten members of the upper house of the legislature (see Arthur Fenner et al. to GW, 9 June 1790, and notes) and by Daniel Owen (Owen to GW, 5 June 1790).

From Henry Hollingsworth

And please your Excellency   Elkton [Md.] June 6th 1790

Encouraged by that well established Maxim that your Excellency does not forget or neglect to reward the Honest Labours of the Virtuous and Industrious, be their Situation and circumstances ever so remote. Strongly Impressed with these Ideas, and encouraged by that condescension which your Excellency has shewn on every occasion that has thrown me in your way, I am Imboldened to offer myself through our worthy Senators as a Candidate for the office of Commissioner for this State, I am the more Induced thereto from the supposition that as great a number of the debts of the United States (in this State) were created by and through me as any other person (for which Certificates were given) and hope I dont flatter myself too much when I conceive that if appointed I could be of some use in giving a Sanction to and Establishing the Loan in this State (being one among the Creditors) should your Excellency think me worthy of such appointment it will confer still higher obligations on—Your Excellencys much obliged & Most obedient Humble Servt

H. Hollingsworth

ALS, DLC:GW.

Henry Hollingsworth (1737–1803) was a merchant, millowner, and manufacturer of gun barrels and bayonets in Cecil County, Maryland. He served as a militia officer in the Revolution and was a member of the lower house of the Maryland legislature from 1789 to 1794 and the upper house from 1801 to 1803. He served as a delegate to the Maryland convention that ratified the federal Constitution in 1788 (*Biographical Dictionary of the Maryland Legislature*, 447–48). He received no appointment from GW.

From Zachariah Rhodes

Pawtuxet State of Rhode Island June 6 1790

May it please your Excellency

When the revenue system was established in this state by the Legislature in September Last, I was appointed surveyor for the Port of Pawtuxet in the district of Providence, and was reappointed at the Late Election—I should be glad to continue to serve the public to the best of my abilities in the same office under the new Constitution. The Port of Pawtuxet is about five miles south of Providence, and it was supposed necessary by the Legislature that a surveyor sho'd be appointed for this place, and I suppose it Probable this office will be continued there after the Organization of the Federal Government in this State for the better security of the collection of the revenue.

Your Excellency may be assured of my faithfull discharge of the Office, and as I can (I hope) Procure a sufficient Recommendation. I beg Leave humbly to solicit that I may under your Excellencies Auspices be continued in the Office, I now hold after the operation of the new constitution shall take effect in this state; and it will greatly oblige him who has the honor to be Your Excellencies most obedient and very hume Servt

Zachariah Rhodes

ALS, DLC:GW.

Zachariah Rhodes (b. 1755) commanded a privateer during the Revolution. In 1789–90 he served as a justice of the peace in Cranston, Rhode Island. To fill the Pawtuxet post, GW initially appointed John Anthony Aborn, who was recommended by Jeremiah Olney (see Memorandum from Jeremiah Olney, 19 June 1790). The president appointed Rhodes in Aborn's place on 2 Aug. 1790 (see GW to the U.S. Senate, 2 Aug. 1790).

Memorandum of Thomas Jefferson

[c.7 June 1790]

North Carolina.

District judge.

Colo. Davie is recommended by Steele.

Hawkins sais he is their first law character.

Brown sais the same.

Samuel Spencer.

Steele sais he is a good man, one of the present judges, not remarkeable for his abilities, but deserves well of his country.

Bloodworth sais Spencer desires the appointment. but sais nothing of him.

John Stokes.

Steele names him at his own request. he is a Virginian, was a Captn in the late war, lost his right hand in Beaufort's defeat. practises law in S. Carolina with reputation & success; has been frequently of the legislature, was a member of the Convention, a federalist, is now a Colo. of militia cavalry, & additional judge of the Supreme court.

Hawkins has understood he is a worthy man.

Ashe names him.

District attorney.

Hamilton. named by Bloodworth.

Hawkins sais he is now under indictment for extortionate fees & will be silenced.

Hay. named by Bloodworth.

Hawkins sais he is an Irishman who came over about the close of the war to see after some confiscated property. he has married in the country.

Arnet. named by Bloodworth. Hawkins sais he is a N. Jersey man of good character.

Sitgreaves. Hawkins sais he lives in Newbern where the courts are held. he is a gentlemanly man, & as good a lawyer as any there. Ashe sais that Sitgreaves is not so brilliant in abilities, but of great rectitude of mind.

Bloodworth sais that Sitgreaves is gentleman of character & represented the state in Congress in 1785.

South-Western government.

Governor

Blount. agreed to be the properest man by Williamson, Hawkins, Bloodworth & Ashe.

Secretary.

Howel Tatham.

Williamson sais he was formerly a Continental officer, is now a lawyer, a man of honor & respectable abilities.

Bloodworth names him, but sais nothing of him.

Brown thinks him illy informed, & more a man of dress than of business.

Robert Hayes.

Bloodworth only mentions his name.

Ashe says he has been a representative several times, & an offic⟨er⟩

Smith. Brown considers him as the ablest & best character there.

Hawkins considers him as a very good & able man. he was a leading character in the opposition to Sevier, and so would not be a very agreeable appointment to Sevier.

Judges.

David Campbell.

Brown thinks him not a well informed lawyer, but honest. he is now judge.

Bloodworth & Ashe name him only.

Williamson sais he is of fair character & respectable abilitie⟨s⟩

Howel Tatham. see what is said of him above for Secretary.

Ashe proposes him as a Judge, and sais he is of great application, fair, unblemished character.

John McNairy. Ashe only names him.

Attorney.

Edward Jones. Ashe proposes him. he has heard that he is a young gentleman of merit & enlightened understanding. Bloodworth sais he is of good character, has been twi⟨ce⟩ returned for the town of Wilmington.

AD, DLC:GW.

Jefferson compiled this list of candidates for judicial offices in North Carolina and the Territory South of the River Ohio, probably at GW's request, from the letters of recommendation submitted by four North Carolina members of the house, John B. Ashe, Timothy Bloodworth, John Steele, and Hugh Williamson (the fifth North Carolina representative, John Sevier, did not take his seat until 16 June) and from the recommendations of Benjamin Hawkins, U.S. senator from North Carolina, and John Brown, the representative from Kentucky in the Virginia delegation in the House and a former law student of Jefferson (see Hugh Williamson to GW, 28 May, John Steele to GW, 4 June, John B. Ashe to GW, 5 June, and Timothy Bloodworth to GW, 5 June). No letter of recommendation from Hawkins or Brown has been found; Jefferson may have received their recommendations in conversation. Jefferson probably drew up the list on 6 June; it was docketed "From the Secretary of State, June 7th 1790." All of the appointees nominated by GW are mentioned in this memorandum (see GW to the U.S. Senate, 7 June 1790).

From Henry Marchant

Highly respected Sir,   Newport [R.I.] June 7th 1790
    whether from a false Delicacy or not, I am unable to say; I have found it a Labour to reconcile to my own Feelings, an Application for an Appointment. My Friends however have told me it was customary: And to Their Judgment and Perswasions I have submitted—I must confess my greatest Reluctance hath arisen from the Apprehension of adding to that Burthen, which a Torrent of Applications must have brought upon Your Excellency—One Thing I sincerely desire; that if Your Excellency finds an Impropriety or Difficulty in gratifying my Wishes, You will dismiss the Application without any Pain on Your Part. I shall remain intirely satisfied in Your better and more impartial Judgment of my Pretensions and the best Good of the Publick.
    After having obtained the Advantage of a liberal Education; and having studied four years and an half under one of the first Law Characters. The Honorable Judge Trowbridge, while Atty Genl of the then Province of Massachusetts; I entered into, and have been in, a very extensive Practice of the Law in this State, for twenty seven years. In 1771 I was honored with an Appointment of Agent for this then Colony to the Court of Great Britain. For about seven Years I held the Office of Atty Genl, and untill I resigned it, upon being appointed a Delegate in the Congress in 1777—My Friends all know I have never made Money by publick Offices, but was continually suffering in my private Business—All the Monies I had at the Commencement of the War, the hard Earnings of a most diligent Exertion in my Profession, I loaned directly to this State, or the United States; and still have the Securities in my own Name, having never bought or sold one—Most of this Money lent was real Gold and Silver—That which was lent to this State is confiscated; what the Continental will be Time may discover. I cannot expect to reallize much of it in my Day—The Pollicy of this State has struck a Blow to Business of every Kind within it. The Profitts arising in my Profession has dwindled nearly to nothing, and I am advanced to the fiftieth Year of my Age.

I would willingly and wishfully, be still serving that Country (in whose Cause I have spent a great Part of my Time, anxious Hours indeed!) in my professional Line; and whereby I might honorably reap some reasonable Advantage to myself—I could wish it may be found consistant with the publick Good to gratify me with the Appointment of District Judge for this State.

I am not entirely unknown to your Excellency, but I wish however if not improper, to refer your Excellency to my Acquaintance in and out of Congress for my political Character, from the Stamp Act of most odious Memory to the present glorious Completion of the Union of the thirteen States by the Adoption of the Constitution by this State, An Event, upon which I most sincerely congratulate your Excellency—Particularly would I wish to refer your Excellency to Mr R. Shearman, Mr Ellsworth, The Honorable Mr Jay Chief Justice, and more especially to the Vice President, with whom, from a Student at Law. I have enjoyed the Pleasure and Honor of an Acquaintance—If this application, or the Manner of it, shall appear improper, I hope your Excellency will excuse it. If your Excellency should grant the Request, I shall endeavour so to discharge my Duty, as that your Excellency may not have Cause to regr⟨e⟩t the Appointment; and a most grateful Sense of the Honor done me will ever be impressed upon my Mind—With the highest Respect, I beg Leave to subscribe myself your Excellencys most obedient and very humble Servt

Henry Marchant

ALS, DLC:GW.

Henry Marchant (1741–1796) was born in Massachusetts and studied at the College of Philadelphia, from which he received a degree in 1762. He studied law with Edmund Trowbridge in Cambridge, Mass., and was admitted to the Rhode Island bar about 1767. Marchant served as attorney general of Rhode Island from 1771 to 1777 and as a member of the Continental Congress from 1777 to 1779. He was a member of the Rhode Island general assembly from 1784 to 1790 and was one of the most outspoken Federalists in the state. Marchant was recommended for district judge by Jabez Bowen (see Bowen to GW, 19 June 1790) and by a group of Newport Federalists including George Hazard, George Champlin, Peleg Clarke, William Tripp, George Sears, William Ellery, George Gibbs, Christopher Champlin, and Samuel Fowler (Newport, R.I., Citizens to GW, 26 June 1790, MHi-A). He was also recommended by William Greene (1731–1809), a lawyer and Federalist leader who had served as governor of Rhode Island from 1778 to 1786 and who had been defeated for reelection in 1786 when he refused to support the emission of paper money advocated by the country party. Greene noted Marchant's "unwearied efforts to accomplish the accession of this State to the Union" (Greene to GW, 16 June 1790, DLC:GW). GW appointed Marchant federal district judge for Rhode Island on 2 July 1790 (see GW to the U.S. Senate, 2 July 1790).

To the United States Senate

United States [New York] June 7th 1790
Gentlemen of the Senate,

In pursuance of the law lately passed for giving effect to an Act entitled "An Act to establish the Judicial Courts of the United States," within the State of North Carolina—I nominate the following persons to fill the Judicial Offices in that district.[1] viz.

William R. Davie	to be Judge—
John Sitgreaves	to be Attorney—and
John Skinner	to be Marshall of the district of North Carolina.

I likewise nominate the following persons to fill offices established by law within the Territory of the United States south of the River Ohio. viz.

William Blount	to be Governor—
David Campbell &	
John McNairy	to be Judges—and
Daniel Smith	to be Secretary of the Territory of the United States south of the River Ohio.

Go: Washington

LS, DNA: R6 46, First Congress, 1789–91, Records of Executive Proceedings, President's Messages—Executive Nominations; LB, DLC:GW.

1. Nominations for these judicial offices were made on the basis of the recommendations of the four members of the House of Representatives from North Carolina then present in New York—John B. Ashe, Timothy Bloodworth, John Steele, and Hugh Williamson—and those of Benjamin Hawkins, senator from North Carolina, and John Brown, representative from the Kentucky district of Virginia. (see Hugh Williamson to GW, 28 May, John Steele to GW, 4 June). Jefferson compiled these recommendations in a single memorandum to GW, from which final selections were apparently made (see Memorandum of Thomas Jefferson, c.7 June).

From William Channing

Sir   Newport [R.I.] June 8th 1790

With deference I beg leave to name my brother Walter Channing, for your consideration as an Officer in the Customs for this Port, and would beg leave most respectfully to refer you, in regard to his qualifications, to those who on this occasion may have kindly interested themselves in his behalf.[1]

Should it please you to honor him with an appointment, I shall consider myself as pledged for his faithful discharge of the trust: Or should another in your wisdom be more eligible I shall from the goodness of your motives cheerfully acquiesce.

If there is any impropriety in this application; I trust Sir that you will consider it as not intentional, but impute it to an ardent wish to promote the Interest of a Brother whom I greatly regard. I have the Honor to be Sir With the greatest Respect Your most Obedt & hble Servt

                                            Willm Channing

ALS, DLC:GW.

William Channing (1751–1793) was born in Newport, graduated from Princeton in 1769, studied law in Providence, and took up practice in Newport in 1771. In 1773 he married Lucy Ellery, daughter of William Ellery, one of Newport's leading citizens. In 1777 he was chosen attorney general of Rhode Island. Channing was a member of the town committee that welcomed GW to Newport in March 1781. GW later wrote Channing in 1783 to introduce his nephew George Augustine Washington who was visiting Newport for his health (see GW to William Channing, 7 June 1783). A hard-money advocate and Federalist, Channing was defeated in the election for attorney general in 1787. GW appointed Channing U.S. attorney on 2 July 1790 (see GW to the U.S. Senate, 2 July 1790). He served until his death from smallpox in 1793 (Harrison, *Princetonians, 1769–1775*, 13–16).

1. Walter Channing (c.1758–1827) served as a lieutenant in the Rhode Island militia during the Revolution and was later clerk of the superior court for the county of Newport (Bartlett, *R.I. Records,* 9:377). Henry Marchant, soliciting Elbridge Gerry's assistance in obtaining the post of naval officer for Channing, described him as "a gentleman of good Sense, Abilities, Strict Honor and Virtue, and from whom the best Information can be had and relied upon" (Marchant to Gerry, 12 June 1790, MHi: Gerry Papers). Channing received no appointment from GW.

From Baron de Périn

at Marebaroux near the Cape. Island of St Domingo
Sir,   8 June 1790.

The Marechal de Castries, then minister of marine, and Monsr de Vergennes minister of foreign affairs, have vainly solicited in 1786, from Congress, the payment of a sum of more than three hundred thousand livres due to me, in capital, since 1779 with interest on that sum to this day—for sugars coming from my habitation in St Domingo, which were laden on board the Ship the Jonathat of Marseilles, which was forced by our enemies and a tempest to put into New London—where this Ship having been condemned, and my sugars, sold and paid for in paper money, have been deposited in the Chancery in Boston, to wait the payment of Congress—and notwithstanding the demands made to this day by our charges des affaires, it has not been possible to obtain any thing.

Permit, Sir, that, on this occasion, I ask of your Excellency the justice that is due to me. I am father of four children, and never has a debt been more sacred than this of mine. it came (issued) from my revenue, charged (laden) at the time of a war which had been brought upon us by the United States, on whose coast (or with whom) the Ship, which carried it, took refuge, as in the port of our true allies; and for the freight of which I have been obliged to pay a considerable sum to the Owner of the said ship—without being able to recur to the Insurers, which would have been the case if the English had captured her, and which I have not been able to recover of them, my sugars having been sold at Boston, and having touched the amount in paper money—it would be therefore doubly distressing for me if I could not recover the amount in some way or other, and this is absolutely at the will of the minister of the finances of the United States, and which is at this day the more sacred as it forms a sacred part of the patrimony of my Children. and I will take on this subject the [   ] which your Excellency shall judge. I have the honor to be, with respect, Sir, your most obedt and most humble Servant

The Baron of Perin
Colonel Commandant of infantry
Governor of St John de Luz

Translation, DNA:RG 59, Miscellaneous Letters; ALS, in French, DNA: RG 59, Miscellaneous Letters. The text is taken from a translation prepared for GW. The original letter may be found in CD-ROM:GW.

1. Périn wrote to GW on 5 Dec. 1783 regarding his claim against the United States for a cargo of sugar seized at New London in 1779: "I here venture to claim, to obtain a reimbursment of more than sixty thousand dollars from the United States, due to me from the sale of sugars, the produce of my estate in St Domingae, that were shipped in a French vessel, the jonathal, of Marseilles; we, after a violent tempest, was obliged to put in, to New London, where, she was condemned, and the cargoe sold—It was paper money the Captain recieved; and by the order, or advice of Monsr de Valnay, who was then French Consul, he put it into the treasury of Boston—I hope Sir, the Congress have too much justice, not to form some arrangements for the liquidation of this paper" (Périn to GW, 5 Dec. 1783). GW received Périn's letter of 8 June in the fall of 1790 while at Mount Vernon and sent it to Hamilton, explaining that "The enclosed letter, addressed to me by the Baron Perin, treating of a subject to which I am a stranger, and the means of information not being within my reach, I have to request that you will cause such enquiry to be made into the circumstances therein stated as may enable you to give him an answer. and I wish you to transmit my letter to him with yours" (GW to Hamilton, 13 Oct. 1790, LB, DLC:GW). GW enclosed a letter to Périn, dated 13 June, explaining that he had received Périn's letter of 8 June on 11 Oct. but that "the subject to which it relates is altogether new to me, and as my absence from the seat of government (being on a visit to my estate in Virginia) denies me the means of obtaining such information as might enable me to make you a reply—I have referred your letter to the Secretary of the Treasury of the United States and requested him to communicate to you the result of his enquiry" (GW to Baron de Périn, 13 Oct. 1790, Df, DNA: RG 59, Miscellaneous Letters). No letter from Hamilton to Périn enclosing GW's letter of 13 Oct. 1790 has been found, but see Hamilton to GW, 26 Oct. 1790.

From Robert Aitken

Sir,   Philadelphia 9. June 1790.

after very Sincere Congratulations upon Your Excellency's Election to the distinguished Office of Chief Magistrate of the United States, I beg leave to Solicit your Excellency's friendship in a Case deeply interesting indeed to me; but in which I conceive, if not mistaken, the Honor and Justice of the Union are also concerned.

Your Excellency, I presume, is uninformed of the large Sums of Continental money I loaned to the United States at an early period of the War, and which I continued to add to, while in my power. I made these loans under a firm belief of being repaid,

according to the pledged faith of Congress; but in this expectation I was disappointed—some of my certificates I converted
into Specie, at an incredible discount; and purchased the House
I now Occupy, for the amount, to the best of my recollection, of
£2700—The great loss I sustained by this Exchange of property,
I felt exceedingly. I doubt not Your Excellency recollects, that I
printed an Edition of the Bible, at a time when the scarcity of
that Valuable book was such, as to claim the attention of Congress, and excite their Solicitude for a Supply; It was done
under the inspection of a Comittee of that Honorable Body,
though at my Sole expence, and the work was highly approved
and recommended to the inhabitants of the United States—"by
the Act of Congress of September 12th 1782." The peace which
took place soon after, removed the Obstructions to importation,
and so glutted the market with Bibles that I was obliged to sell
mine much below prime cost; and in the End, I actually Sunk
above £3000 by the impression. These two circumstances render
my losses exceedingly heavy, and indeed, almost Unsupport-
able: But, Sir, I flatter myself I may hope for some compensation, in a Small Share of Public Favour; especially when it is considered, that the Work was undertaken in a great measure at
the instance, and under the Patronage of Congress—Under this
impression, together with the perfect conviction of Your Excellency's benevolence; and your Sympathy with all the virtuous
feelings of Human Nature; I humbly trust that you will be
pleased to have me appointed Printer & Stationer to Congress;
Or in any other way in which I might be of Public service, in the
Line of my business. I had it in Comtemplation, to petition your
Excellency for an exclusive right, for a term of years, to print the
Bible within the United States, Conceiving that my sufferings, in
Consequence of my former Undertaking would entitle me to a
preference: But a faithful execution of this Work would require,
in Order to carry it on with propriety and good effect, Such
large Sums of Money, as I am utterly incapable of commanding;
and therefore, however pleasing an employment it would be to
me, while I live, I am constrained to relinquish former intentions in this respect, for want of the Means to carry them into
effect.

I would respectfully further inform your Excellency, that the
House I purchased as before Mentioned, is under Mortgage, on

Account of a foreign debt, for about £1400, the payment of which will become due in about 11 Months, and unless I should be so happy as to obtain some steady employment, to improve a valuable Stock in my printing office, I much fear the House must be sold under every possible disadvantage; by which I should be reduced, with a large family, in my old age, after having earned by the industry of many years a handsome little property. It is not my desire to become rich—a moderate Subsistence, in the way of labouring for it, is all I covet.

I now take the liberty of praying Your Excellency's countenance and support—although my feelings might dictate arguments in my favour, I suppress them; in a perfect confidence that they are rendered unnecessary, by Your Excellency's known Benevolence & Love of Justice, (under the *Supreme Being*) I intirely rest my plea.

Happy to hear of Your Excellency's recovery from your late indisposition, and Humbly requesting you to forgive the freedom I have used, I beg leave to Subscribe myself With all Duty and Respect Sir, Your Excellency's Most Obedient Humble Servant

Robt Aitken

N.B. Suffer me to Mention, The Revd Dr Mason, & Dr Rogers of N. York, who have known me for many years—likewise the Honble Robert Morris, Mr Boudinot, Mr Gerry & some others, are perfectly accquainted with my Character.

ALS, DLC:GW.

Robert Aitken (1734–1802), a Philadelphia printer, was born in Scotland. He emigrated to Philadelphia in 1769, where he published the *Pennsylvania Magazine, or American Monthly Museum* in 1775–76. In 1781 Aitken undertook to print the first complete English Bible produced in America and sought the official sanction of Congress for his edition. Congress passed a resolution officially authorizing the edition in September 1782. Known as the "Aitken Bible," this was the first and only edition of the Bible ever authorized by Congress. As Aitken reported to GW, the venture was a financial failure. Lear responded to Aitken on 14 June 1790 that "The President of the U. S. has received your letter of the 9th Instt and directs me to inform you that he is really sorry for the losses which you mention to have sustained by the depreciation of public securities, and the large impression of the Bible which you made in the war; and especially as you observe that this impression was undertaken in conformity to the wishes and under the patronage of the then Congress; But, Sir, however pleasing it would be to the President of the U. S. to see those who have been sufferers in the late revolution retreiving their losses under the auspices of peace & a Good government—and however desireous he may be to yield them assistance; yet it is not in his power to gratify his own feelings by affording relief in every instance; and the request which you make to him to be appointed Printer and Stationer to Congress can only be answered by your application to that Body, in the appointment of whose particular Officers he has no right to interfere" (DNA: RG 59, Miscellaneous Letters). Aitken petitioned Congress for employment as printer on 2 Nov. 1791. The petition was tabled, and Aitken received no appointment from Congress (*Petitions, Memorials, and Other Documents Submitted for the Consideration of Congress*, 131).

From Benjamin Contee

Sr   Tuesday morning ⟨9th⟩ June 90

Being informed you are about to fill up your nominations of Consuls for the United States, I beg leave to mention *Alexander Contee;* who has requested my application in his behalf, for the consulship *at the port of London.* Delicacy forbids my saying much of a Brother, and might restrain me likewise from doing him Justice; But I persuade myself that if your appointment for the above po⟨r⟩t is not allready provided, It will not discredit your choice to place his name in the nomination, as consul for that port.[1] He has resided in London since the year 85 and for the most of the Time at the Head of a mercantile House; He is expected to arrive soon in Maryland, but with intention to return to England in the fall.

forgive me, Sr, for the trouble I occasion you. I thought it best to do it in this mode as it leaves less room for that embarrassment consequent on applications—and places you in a less arduous situation than personal application would.

It does also favor my own deffidence nevertheless if I thought a personal application would be more expressive of respect, I would not hesitate to make it. Having the Honour to be truly, with sentiments of the highest consideration, your very respectful and most Obedient Hble Servant

Ben: Contee

ALS, DLC:GW.

Benjamin Contee (1755–1815) was born near Nottingham, Md., and served briefly as an officer of Maryland troops during the Revolution. He was a member of the Maryland house of delegates from 1785 to 1787 and was elected to the First Congress in 1788. Contee was later a minister in the Episcopal church.

1. Alexander Contee (1752–1810) engaged in mercantile activities and lived near Nottingham, Md. (Bowie, *Prince George's County,* 230). He received no appointment from GW.

From Arthur Fenner et al.

Sir,   State of Rhode Island, Newport June 9th 1790

The exalted Station which your Excellency holds in the Government of the United States, is necessarily attended with the Inconvenience of various Applications for Appointments to Offices in the different Districts in the Union. In consiquence of the Ratification and Adoption of the New National Constitution by the Convention of the People of this State⟨,⟩ on the 29th Ulto, Officers, whose Nomination belongs to your Excellency, must soon be appointed here, for carrying into Execution the Laws of the National Legislature, The People of this State are immediately interested in the Appointment of the Officers in this Part of the Confederacy. We Collectively constitute the upper Branch of the Legislature of th⟨is⟩ State and are under the strongest Obligations to consult and promote the Public Good, that being our only Inducement for the present Application, which wee do not consider as made in our Legislative Capacity, but as coming from Citizens of the Union who have the Good of the whole Confederacy at Heart, and who have the best Means of Information on the Subject we write upon, and we therefore hope the Present Application will appear in a favourable Point of Veiw to your Excellency.

At the last Election held by the General Assembly of this State, on the beginning of the last Month, Ebenezer Thompson Esqr. was appointed Collector of the Revenue Duties, in the District of Providence, Theodore Foster Esqr. was appointed Naval Officer, and William Tyler Esqr. Surveyor.[1] The State at large have Confidence in these Gentlemen, They have all Abilities adequate to the faithful and due Performance of their respective Trusts, They are not concerned in Navigation, or External Commerce, and are not immediately connected, with, or likely to be under the Influence of those who are in the Mercantile Line of Business, Their Vigilance, Industry, Firmness, and Suitable Capacities for their respective Trusts have been experienced and we think their Integrity may be relied on: To these Reasons may be added the weighty Consideration that they are such Persons as wou'd be most likely to appease and soften the spirit of Party in the State as having the General Confidence and good Will of the People, and therefore more likely to conciliate the Affections and Esteem for the National or Federal Government.

We therefore, take the Liberty of recommending to and requesting of your Excellency and the Honorable, the Senate of the United States that those Gentlemen before named may be continued after the Organization of the Federal Government within this State in the Offices which they now respectively hold viz. Ebenezer Thompson Esqr. as Collector, Theodore Foster Esqr. as Naval Officer and William Tyler Esqr. as Surveyor, for the District of Providence.[2] A Compliance with this Request will be in General agreeable, we beleive to all Parties in this State e⟨c⟩cepting the immediate Freinds and Connections of those who have applied or will Apply for Others to be appointed in their Places from Motives of Personal Interest.

That the United States of America may long continue to flourish that they may Experience all the Blessings of Liberty and good Government, and that your Excellency may long live in Health Prosperity (possessing the Hearts and Confidence of the People[)], to enjoy that Glory and National Independence of our Country to which you have so much ⟨contri*illegible*⟩ you[r] Excellency's most Obedient and most humble Servants

> Arthur Fenner.
> Saml J. Potter
> James Arnold
> Thos G. Hazard
> B. Watson
> James Congdon
> Thomas Hoxsie
> John Cook
> John Harris
> Peleg Arnold

LS, DLC:GW. The signers were the governor, deputy governor, and eight of the ten members of upper house of the Rhode Island legislature.

1. Theodore Foster wrote to GW to secure his continuance in February 1790 (see Foster to GW, 18 Feb. 1790). Ebenezer Thompson did likewise in

May (see Ebenezer Thompson to GW, 21 May 1790). Daniel Owen, president of the Rhode Island Ratifying Convention, also wrote to GW recommending the continuance of Thompson, Foster, and Tyler, pointing out that they were not "themselves Immediately concerned in commerce, and not . . . under the undue influence of any of the commercial Houses of the District" (Owen to GW, 5 June 1790, DLC:GW). GW appointed Foster naval officer at Providence after Foster was elected to the Senate on 12 June (see GW to the U.S. Senate, 2 July 1790).

2. GW appointed Daniel Eldridge Updike, Job Comstock, Nathaniel Phillips, Samuel Bosworth, George Stillman, and John Anthony Aborn to be surveyors of the minor Rhode Island ports on 2 July (see GW to the U.S. Senate, 2 July 1790). For other recommendations for these posts, see the Memorandum from Jeremiah Olney, 19 June 1790, and Joseph Stanton and Theodore Foster to GW, 29 June 1790.

From David Olyphant

Sir   [c.9 June 1790]

Being now a Citizen of Newport in the State of Rhode Island, & connected by marriage with a family there, who have suffer'd as well as myself for being firm friends to the late Revolution; I beg leave to Address your Excellency, & offer myself a Candidate for the Office of Collector in the Revenue of that State.

If you, Sir, think this application worthy your Attention, permit me to refer to Mr Izard, Major Butler, Doctr Tucker, & the other Delegates to Congress from the State of So. Carolina, for the propriety of this intrusion; & I flatter myself that a change in times will plead my apology for troubling on th⟨e⟩ occasion. I have the honor to be, with the warmest Attachment for your health & felicity—Your Excellency's Most Obedient & very humble Servant

David Olyphant.

ALS, DLC:GW.

David Olyphant (Oliphant) moved to Rhode Island in the 1780s from South Carolina. See Benjamin Lincoln to GW, 24 Dec. 1789, source note. Newport merchant William Vernon solicited the aid of Connecticut congressman Jeremiah Wadsworth in obtaining the office of collector for Olyphant, writing that "You will doubtless see many applicants for Offices, under the Genl Government⟨,⟩ some that have no pretences either, from their attachment to the Constitution, or their merits: others perhaps, supported by the recommendations of the Merchants and Traders of the state; which in my humble opinion, ought to have little weight or consideration in the appointment; for this well known reason⟨;⟩ that is even proverbial, as to the state of Rhode-Island⟨.⟩ viz. That smuggleing is justifiable, because the Penalty warrants the measure, for the resque by seizure. upon this principle, many instances might be given, where Legislators, that have passed Revenue Laws, have openly, saved more then half their Duties on importation of Goods—Therefore, it cannot be inconsistant with their interest to recommend Persons for Revenue officers that, perhaps may connive at frauds.

"If a firm zealous attachment, a steady uniform perseverance, in the service of the United states, thro' the War. If sustaining the Loss of great property in the cause. If integrity, probity, disinterested, impartial views in serveing the American reve⟨nue⟩ is a rec⟨omme⟩ndation to Office—No Man stands fairer then Doctr David Olyphant; whom the Inhabitants of Newport, can have no objection too—being a respectable Free-holder for some Years" (William Vernon to Jeremiah Wadsworth, 5 June 1790, CtHi: Jeremiah Wadsworth Correspondence). Royal Flint, a New York businessman associated with Wadsworth, wrote to Hamilton on 14 June discouraging Olyphant's appointment, describing him as an old, inactive man (see Hunt, *Calendar,* 44). Olyphant received no appointment from GW.

From the Rhode Island Ratifying Convention

Sir,   Rhode Island, Newport June 9th 1790

I had on the 29th Ulto the Satisfaction of addressing you after the Ratification of the Constitution of the United States of America by the Convention of this State.[1] I have now the Honor of Inclosing the Ratification as then agreed upon by the Convention of the People of this State; the Legislature is now in Session in this Town, an appointment of Senators will undoubtedly take place in the present Week, and from what appears to be the sense of the Legislature, it may be expected that the Gentlemen who may be appointed will Immediately proceed to take their seats in the Senate of the United States.[2] I have the Honor to be with great Respect, Sir, Your obedt humble Servant

Daniel Owen prest

LS, DLC:GW; copy, DNA: RG 46, First Congress, 1789–91, Records of Legislative Proceedings, President's Messages.

1. Owen notified GW of the ratification of the Constitution by the Rhode Island convention on 29 May 1790 but delayed forwarding the formal instrument of ratification until this date (see Daniel Owen to GW, 29 May 1790, n.2). The copy of the ratification enclosed by Owens reads: "(The Constitution of the United States of America precedes the following Ratification.)

"Ratification of the Constitution by the Convention of the State of Rhode Island and Providence Plantations.

"We the Delegates of the people of the State of Rhode Island and Providence Plantations, duly elected and met in Convention, having maturely considered the Constitution for the United States of America, agreed to on the seventeenth day of September in the year one thousand seven hundred and eighty seven, by the Convention then assembled at Philadelphia in the Commonwealth of Pennsylvania (a copy whereof precedes these presents) and having also seriously and deliberately considered the present situation of this State do declare and make known[.]

"1st That there are certain natural rights, of which men, when they form a social compact, cannot deprive or divest their posterity, among which are the enjoyment of Life and Liberty, with the means of acquiring, possessing and protecting property, and pursuing and obtaining happiness and safety.

"2d That all power is naturally vested in, and consequently derived from the people; that Magistrates are therefore their trustees and agents, and at all times amenable to them.

"3d That the powers of government may be reassumed by the people whensoever it shall become necessary to their happiness: That the rights of the States respectively, to nominate and appoint all State Officers, and every other power, Jurisdiction and right which is not by the said Constitution clearly delegated to the Congress of the United States, or to the departments of the Government thereof, remain to the people of the several States, or their respective State-Governments to whom they may have granted the same, and that those clauses in the said Constitution which declare that Congress shall not have or exercise certain powers, do not imply that Congress is entitled to any powers not given by the said Constitution, but such clauses are to be construed as exceptions to certain specified powers, or as inserted merely for greater caution.

"4th That Religion, or the duty which we owe to our Creator, and the manner of discharging it, can be directed only by reason and conviction, and not by force or violence, and therefore, all men have an equal, natural and unalienable right to the free exercise of Religion, according to the dictates of conscience, and that no particular religious sect or society ought to be favoured, or established by law in preference to others.

"5th That the Legislative, Executive and Judiciary powers of Government, should be seperate and distinct, and that the members of the two first may be restrained from oppression by feeling and participating the public burthens, they should at fixed periods be reduced to a private station, return into the mass of the people, and the vacancies be supplied by certain and regular elections, in which all, or any part of the former members; to be eligible or ineligible, as the rules of the constitution of government and the laws shall direct.

"6th That elections of Representatives in legislature ought to be free and frequent, and all men having sufficient evidence of permanent common interest with, and attachment to the community ought to have the right of suffrage, and no aid, charge, tax or fee can be set, rated or levied upon the people without their own consent or that of their representatives so elected, nor can they be bound by any law to which they have not in like manner assented for the public good.

"7th That all power of suspending laws, or the execution of laws, by any authority without the consent of the representatives of the people in the legislature is injurious to their rights, and ought not to be exercised.

"8th That in all capital & criminal prosecutions, a man hath a right to demand the cause and nature of his accusation, to be confronted with the accusers and witnesses, to call for evidence and be allowed counsel in his favour, and to a fair and speedy trial by an impartial jury of his vicinage, without whose unanimous consent he cannot be found guilty; (except in the government of the land & naval forces) nor can he be compelled to give evidence against himself.

"9th That no freeman ought to be taken, imprisoned, or deseized of his freehold, liberties, privileges or franchies, or outlawed, or exiled, or in any manner destroyed or deprived of his life, liberty or property but by the trial by jury, or by the law of the land.

"10th That every freeman restrained of his liberty is entitled to a remedy to inquire into the lawfulness thereof and to remove the same, if unlawful, and that such remedy ought not to be denied or delayed.

"11th That in controversies respecting property, and in suits between man and man the antient trial by Jury, as hath been exercised by us and our ancestors, from the time whereof the memory of man is not to the contrary, is one of the greatest securities to the rights of the people, and ought to remain sacred and inviolable.

"12th That every freeman ought to obtain right and justice freely, and without sale, completely and without denial, promptly and without delay, and that all establishments or regulations contravening these rights are oppressive and unjust.

"13th That excessive bail ought not to be required, nor excessive fines imposed, nor cruel or unusual punishments inflicted.

"14th That every person has a right to be secure from all unreasonable searches and seisures of his person, his papers or his property, and therefore that all warrants to search suspected places, or seize any person, his papers or his property, without information upon oath, or affirmation, of sufficient cause are grevious and oppressive, and that all general warrants (or such in which the place or person suspected, are not particularly designated) are dangerous and ought not to be granted.

"15th That the people have a right peaceably to assemble together, to consult for their common good, or to instruct their representatives; and that every person has a right to petition or apply to the legislature for redress of grievances.

"16th That the people have a right to freedom of speech, and of writing and publishing their Sentiments, that freedom of the press is one of the greatest bulwarks of liberty, and ought not to be violated.

"17th That the people have a right to keep and bear arms, that a well-regulated Militia, including the body of the people capable of bearing arms, is the proper, natural and safe defence of a free state; that the Militia shall not be subject to martial law except in time of war, rebellion or insurrection; that standing armies in time of peace are dangerous to liberty, and ought not to be kept up, except in cases of necessity; and that at all times the military should be under strict subordination to the civil power; that in time of peace no soldier ought to be quartered in any house without the consent of the owner, and in time of war, only by the civil magistrate in such manner as the law directs.

"18th That any person religiously scrupulous of bearing arms, ought to be exempted, upon payment of an equivalent to employ another to bear arms in his stead.

"Under these impressions, and declaring that the rights aforesaid cannot be abridged or violated, and that the explanations aforesaid are consistant with the said constitution, and in confidence that the amendments hereafter mentioned will receive an early and mature consideration, and conformably to the fifth article of said constitution speedily become a part thereof; We the said delegates in the name and in the behalf of the people of the State of Rhode Island and Providence Plantations do, by these presents, assent to and ratify the said Constitution. In full confidence nevertheless, that until the amendments hereafter proposed and under-mentioned shall be agreed to and ratified pursuant to the aforesaid fifth article the Militia of this State will not be continued in service out of this State for a longer term than six weeks without the consent of the legislature thereof, That the Congress will not make or alter any regulation in this State respecting the times, places and manner of holding elections for Senators and Representatives unless the Legislature of this State shall neglect or refuse to make laws or regulations for the purpose, or from any circumstance be incapable of making the same—and that in those cases such power will only be exercised until the Legislature of this state shall make provision in the premises. That the Congress will not lay direct taxes within this State but where the monies arising from the import, tonnage and excise shall be insufficient for the public exigences, nor until Congress shall have first made a requisition upon this State to assess, levy and pay the amount of such requisition made agreeable to the census fixed in the said Constitution in such way and manner as the legislature of this state shall judge best, and that congress will not lay any capitation or poll tax.

"Done in Convention at Newport, in the County of Newport in the state of Rhode Island and Providence Plantations the twenty ninth day of may in the year of our Lord one thousand seven hundred and ninety, and in the fourteenth year of the independence of the United States of America.

By order of the Convention
Daniel Owen President

attest Daniel Updike Secretary.

"And the Convention do in the name and behalf of the people of the state of Rhode Island and Providence Plantations enjoin it upon their Senators and Representative or Representatives which may be elected to represent this state in Congress to exert all their influence, and use all reasonable means to obtain a ratification of the following Amendments to the said Constitution in the manner prescribed therein and in all laws to be passed by the Congress in the mean time to conform to the spirit of the said Amendments as far as the Constitution will admit.

"Amendments.

"1st The United States shall guarantee to each State its sovereignty, freedom and independence, and every power Jurisdiction and right which is not by this constitution expressly delegated to the United States.

"2nd That Congress shall not alter, modify or interfere in the times, places or manner of holding elections for Senators and Representatives or either of them, except when the legislature of any State shall neglect, refuse or be disabled by invasion or rebellion to prescribe the same, or in case when the provision made by the States is so imperfect as that no consequent election is had and then only until the legislature of such State shall make provision in the premises.

"3d It is declared by the Convention that the Judicial power of the United States in cases in which a State may be a party does not extend to criminal prosecutions or to authorize any suit by any person against a State; but to remove all doubts or controversies respecting the same that it be especially expressed as a part of the Constitution of the United States that Congress shall not directly or indirectly either by themselves or through the Judiciary interfere with any one of the States in the redemption of paper money already emitted and now in circulation, or in liquidating or discharging the public securities of any one State. That each and every State shall have the exclusive right of making such laws and regulations for the before mentioned purpose as they shall think proper.

"4th That no Amendments to the Constitution of the United States hereafter to be made pursuant to the fifth article shall take effect or become a part of the Constitution of the United States after the year one thousand seven hundred and ninety three without the consent of eleven of the States heretofore united under one confederation.

"5th That the Judicial powers of the United States shall extend to no possible case where the cause of action shall have originated before the ratification of this constitution except in disputes between States about their territory— disputes between persons claiming lands under grants of different States and debts due to the United States.

"6th That no person shall be compelled to do military duty otherwise than by voluntary inlistment except in cases of general invasion, any thing in the second paragraph of the sixth article of the Constitution, or any law made under the constitution to the contrary notwithstanding.

"7th That no capitation or poll tax shall ever be laid by Congress.

"8th In cases of direct taxes, Congress shall first make requisitions on the several States to assess, levy and pay their respective proportions of such requisitions in such way and manner as the legislatures of the several States shall judge best, and in case any State shall neglect or refuse to pay its proportion pursuant to such requisition, then Congress may assess and levy such State's proportion together with interest at the rate of six per cent per annum from the time prescribed in such requisition.

"9th That Congress shall lay no direct taxes without the consent of the legislatures of three fourths of the States in the Union.

"10th That the Journals of the proceedings of the Senate and House of Representatives shall be published as soon as conveniently may be at least once in every year except such parts thereof relating to treaties, alliances or military operations as in their judgment require secrecy.

"11th That regular statements of the receipts and expenditures of all public monies shall be published at least once a year.

"12th As standing armies in time of peace are dangerous to liberty and ought not to be kept up except in cases of necessity, and as at all times the military should be under strict subordination to the civil power, that therefore no standing army or regular troops shall be raised or kept up in time of peace.

"13th That no monies be borrowed on the credit of the United States without the assent of two thirds of the Senators and Representatives present in each House.

"14th That the Congress shall not declare war without the concurrence of two thirds of the Senators and Representatives present in each House.

"15th That the Words 'without the consent of Congress' in the seventh clause in the ninth section of the first article of the Constitution be expunged.

"16th That no Judge of the supreme Court of the United States shall hold any other office under the United States or any of them, nor shall any officer appointed by Congress or by the President and Senate of the United States be permitted to hold any office under the appointment of any of the States.

"17th As a traffic tending to establish or continue the slavery of any part of the human species is disgraceful to the cause of liberty and humanity. That Congress shall as soon as may be promote and establish such laws and regulations as may effectually prevent the importation of Slaves of every description into the United States.

"18th That the state legislatures have power to recall when they think it expedient their federal Senators and to send others in their stead.

"19th That Congress have power to establish a uniform rule of inhabitancy or settlement of the poor of the different States throughout the United States.

"20th That Congress erect no Company with exclusive advantages of commerce.

"21st That when two members shall move or call for the ayes or Nays, on any question they shall be entered on the Journals of the Houses respectively.

"Done in Convention at Newport in the County of Newport in the State of Rhode Island and Providence Plantations the twenty ninth day of may in the year of our Lord one thousand seven hundred and ninety, and the fourteenth year of the Independence of the United States of America" (DNA: RG 46, First Congress, 1789–91, Records of Legislative Proceedings, President's Messages).

2. The Rhode Island general assembly met in special session in Newport 7–12 June. The assembly elected Joseph Stanton and Theodore Foster to represent the state in the Senate on 12 June; the two took their seats on 25 June (see Theodore Foster to GW, 26 June 1790).

From Michael Jenifer Stone

Sir   June 9th 1790

I have taken the Liberty to enclose a Letter from Major Swan recommending Colonel Barton—I had not the pleasure of being known to that Gentleman untill the present. But I am intimately acquainted with Major Swan and have the fullest confidence in his recommendation of Col. Barton. I have the Honor to be sir your most respectfull and obedient

                                                                    M. J. Stone

ALS, DLC:GW.

1. The enclosed letter was written by John Swan of Baltimore, who served as an officer of dragoons from 1777 until the close of the Revolution, rising to the rank of major. In it Swan introduced William Barton who hoped "to fill One of the Offices under Congress—This Gentmns active Conduct during the revolution Speaks forcibly in his favor" (John Swan to Michael Jenifer Stone, 8 June 1790, DLC:GW). Barton had initially applied for a customs position at Providence in September 1789 (see Barton to GW, 3 Sept. 1789). New York businessman Royal Flint described Barton to Alexander Hamilton as "popular among the lower class of people" (Flint to Hamilton, 14 June 1790, Hamilton Papers, DLC). GW appointed Barton surveyor at Providence on 14 June 1790 (see GW to the U.S. Senate, 14 June 1790).

From William Allen

                                                    Providence [R.I.] 10th June 1790.

May it please your Excellency

The Convention of this State having Ratified the new Constitution by which happy event the Union of the whole is Compleated; and as it is more than Probable that the Laws of the Union will Speedily embrace this State in common with the rest, I beg Leave Sir, with the greatest deference to Present my Self to your Excellency as a Candidate for the Office of Surveyor of the Customs at this Port.

I am aware Sir, that applications for the Same Office may have long Since Reached you, but on my part, till this State had joined the Union I dared not to offer this address, as I was fully persuaded that such application would be considered by your Excellency as Premature.

having had the Honor of Serving through a long and perilous war under your excellencys orders with out censure; Let me hope Sir, so far to engage your Favourable notice, as to induce your excellency to enquire my Character as a Citizen Since the establishment of Peace. I have the Honor, to be Sir with the most lively Sentiments of Respect and esteem you[r] excellencys Most Obt and Humbl. Servant

William Allen

N.B. the Ratification comes on by this Post

ALS, DLC:GW.

William Allen served as an officer in the Continental army from 1776 to 1783, rising from lieutenant to brevet major (Heitman, *Historical Register,* 62). John Brown and John Francis recommended Allen for surveyor as a man "Deserving of the Publick Confidence" (John Brown and John Francis to GW, 11 June 1790, DLC:GW). In the John Carter Brown Library, Providence, R.I., there are unsigned drafts of two letters, one dated 11 June 1790, recommending Allen. The endorsement indicates they were to be sent to the president. Allen received no appointment from GW.

From Arthur Fenner et al.

Sir   State of Rhode Island 10 June 1790

The Public Offices we hold in this State, and our wishes for the Welfare and Happiness of the People induce us to address your Excellency, on the appointment of a Judge for the District Court of this State and to recommend that the Honorable Daniel Owen Esq. late President of the Convention of this State may be appointed to that Office.

He has himself long been employed in Public Trusts which he has discharged with integrity and General Approbation. He is now one of the Justices of the Supreme Court His Established Reputation as a Gentleman of Abilities Virtue and Honour possessing the Confidence and Esteem of the People of this State, who have repeatedly chosen him to the Office of Deputy Governor which he resigned at the late Election lead us to suppose that his Appointment to the Office of District Judge for this State would give very general Satisfaction to the People at large of this

State.[1] We are with great Esteem and affectionate Regard your Excellency Obedient Servants

Arthur Fenner Govr
Thos G. Hazard
Peleg Arnold
Saml J. Potter
Thomas Hoxsie
B. Watson
John Harris

LS, DLC:GW.

    1. Daniel Owen did not receive an appointment from GW.

From Providence, R.I., Citizens

Sir   Providence June 10th 1790

From the change of Sentiment which has gradually taken place in the minds of the Good people of this State, and the Happy Effects of the General Government, which begins to Operate so favorably in the Union, under the Auspices of your Excellency's administration—in Consequence of which the Convention of this State at their late Session were Induced to Adopt the Enlighten'd Policy of confirming and Ratifying the Constitution of the United States A Circumstance highly Important and Interesting to the peace and Happiness of the Nation—permit us therefore, Sir to Congratulat⟨e⟩ your Excellency on this pleasing occasion—in Consequence of our Accession to the Union a Number of Officers will Necessarily be Nominated and Appointed for the Collection of the Revenue within the State—as it will be your Excellency's wish that those Appointments should devolve upon persons of Tried Abilities & Integrity, whose Services and Sacrifices during the late Revolution entitle them to your Excellencys Notice and the favors of their Country—we take the Liberty to Recommend the bearer Colo. Jeremiah Olney (who served with Reputation during the War and since which service he has uniformly Supported a fair Character) as a person worthy to be entrusted with the Office of Collector of Impost for the District of Providence[1]—in him your Excellency and the public will find a Vigilant, faithful Officer, a Good Citizen, a Friend to the Federal Constitution, and, on all occasions a firm Supporter of the principles of a Liberal, Enlighten'd and Just Policy. We have the Honor to be, with profound Defere⟨nce⟩ Your Excellency's Most, Obed: Hble Servts

John Brown
Enos Hitchcock
Clark & Nightingale
Jos. & Wm Russell

LS, RHi: Jeremiah Olney Papers.

1. For Olney's application for the office of collector at Providence, see Olney to GW, 16 Mar. 1789. Olney vigorously pursued the appointment, renewing his application on 31 May and 4 June 1790 and seeking recommendations or assistance from Hamilton and others (see Olney to Hamilton, 7 June 1790, in Syrett, *Hamilton Papers*, 6:458–59). Olney apparently brought the letter from the Providence citizens with him to New York to pursue the appointment in person. GW appointed him collector at Providence on 14 June (see GW to the U.S. Senate, 14 June 1790).

From James Warren

Sir   Plymouth [Mass.] June 10. 1790

The entire confidence I have in your friendship, & the great respect I have for your character, embolden me to hazard an address to you which I never before made to any man; a solicitation for Office. I have long served my country in stations of some distinction & importance; some of those services fell under your own observation during the period you commanded the army in this State;[1] I have the pleasure to retrospect them with satisfaction, because I think they are marked with disinterestedness & fidelity, & though performed at a time when the distress of the country & the novelty of opposition to the power of Britain engaged the passions, have never heard of any imputation on my public character or conduct. I am willing to serve my country again if you should think proper to appoint me to any place suitable to the character I have sustained: I specify no particular object, because I have none in view; the present appearance of public measures makes me suppose that new appointments will be necessary.

Will you, Sir, permit me to add that I have a son Henry Warren who has once taken the liberty to request your notice: he has been educated to business, has activity and abilities, & a character without exception; has been several times chosen by the House of Representatives Collector of Excise in this district, & by the virulence of party against me defeated: if he should be so happy as to meet your notice, I presume to say with confidence, he would never disgrace any appointment you may think proper to give him, or disappoint your expectations from him. My sufferings in the course of the Revolution, & the consequences of them to my family, I hope will be considered as a sufficient apology for this intrusion.[2]

I am very happy to hear of your restoration to health & have the honour to be Sir with perfect Respect & Esteem your Excellency's most obedient & very humble Servant

Jas Warren

LS, DLC:GW.

1. Warren had recently settled his accounts as a member of the Continental Navy Board and had failed in an effort to obtain settlement of a claim against the United States (see Mercy Otis Warren to GW, 18 May 1790, n.3). He received no appointment from GW.

2. Henry Warren (1764–1828) did not receive an appointment from GW, but he apparently served as a clerk to Benjamin Lincoln during the latter's tenure as collector of customs at Boston (see Henry Warren to GW, 1 July 1789) and was appointed collector at Plymouth in 1803 (Whittemore, *Memorials of the Massachusetts Soc. of the Cincinnati,* 665).

From Joseph Anderson

Sir,   New York 11th June 1790

Although I formerly had the Honor, of being personally presented to your Excellency, when an officer of the army of the United States—I apprehend my Charecter was not Sufficiently distinguished; to entitle me to your recollection at this distant period—I must therefore rely on your Benevolence, to pardon the liberty I now take, in offering to introduce myself to your Excellencys notice and Patronage, as a Candidate for the office of the Judge that is yet to be appointed in the new Government lately formed South of the Ohio—as an apology for my present Presumption, I wou'd beg leave to Suggest, that from the Close of the late war until the present period—I have never ask'd any appointment either from the United States or any individual State—Tho my *health* hath been much injured in the Service of my Country—and have Sustain'd *great Losses* from *ill reposed Confidence*—My Peculiar Situation therefore compells me to Obtrude this application upon your Excellency, and that Consideration will I hope, plead my apology—I have long had a Determination to settle in one of the new States—But have for some time past, been ⟨prevented⟩ by sickness—My only Object or defence in that Country was the pursuit of my profession—and as I am at present determined to make the westward my place of permanent residence, the appointment herein Solicited wou'd render my situation there much more Elegible—To give a Sanction thereto I beg leave to offer for your Excellencys persual, Several Certificates relative to my Charecter as an officer—A Certificate of my having gone through a regular Course of Study of the Law—and also Certificates of my admission as an attorney in Several of the Supreme Courts of the United States[1]—I have the honor to be acquainted with Mr Patterson Senator from New Jersey, and also with Mr Read Senator from the State of Delaware, to whom I wou'd beg leave to refer Your Excellency for any further information you may wish on the Subject—My place of residence Since I left the army, has been in the State of Delaware—I mention this for your Excellencys information as a *Local* Circumstance.

Shou'd your Excellency think proper to Honor me with the appointment, I Shall acknowledge it with gratitude—and endeavour to discharge the duty with that Integrity, which I trust, wou'd not disgrace the Honor so Confered. I am with great deference and respect your Excellencys—most obedt & Hble Servt

Jos: Anderson

ALS, DLC:GW.

Joseph Anderson (1757–1837) was born near Philadelphia and joined the 3d New Jersey Regiment in 1776, serving until the close of the war. He was promoted to captain in 1777 and was appointed regimental paymaster. After the war he studied law in New Jersey and was admitted to the bar in Delaware in 1785 and in Pennsylvania in 1787, although he did not practice in either state. GW had appointed John McNairy and David Campbell to be judges in the Territory South of the River Ohio on 7 June 1790, but a third judge still remained to be appointed. GW apparently discussed Anderson's qualifications with senators Paterson and Read, because on 21 June Anderson wrote to GW again, explaining: "some days since I waited, on Mr Patterson, and Mr Read, who acquainted me, that you had Condescended, to take so much notice of my application for the office of a Judge, in the Government South of the Ohio—as to have spoken to them relative to my Charecter." Subsequent delay in making the appointment, Anderson wrote, led him to "fear that your Excellency may not have receiv'd that ample Satisfaction respecting my Legal Knowledge—which you might think requisite, in order to Justify your *nomination* of *me* to *that office.*" Anderson explained that he had moved to Delaware after the war in order to settle the affairs of his late father, and that he had intended to move to western Pennsylvania to begin his legal career. Toward that end he had spent much of his time preparing to join the bar of the supreme court of Pennsylvania, to which he was admitted in 1787, and had declined all opportunities to begin active practice. Neither Paterson nor Read, he wrote, had a substantial knowledge of his legal abilities, since he had not taken up practice in either New Jersey or Delaware. Anderson offered to "submit to any (further) Legal Examination, which you might think requisite, to obtain the fullest information" (Anderson to GW, 21 June 1790, DLC:GW). Two days later Anderson wrote that Paterson had told him that GW had been "inform'd I had a Public account unsetled," and that "you Cou'd not, *Thus Circumstanced, at present,* give me the nomination." Anderson explained that while he was on furlough, his accounts as paymaster of the 3d New Jersey Regiment had been settled by the paymaster general and the paymaster of the 1st New Jersey Regiment. Upon balancing his paybooks against the amount he had received from the general pay office to disburse to the regiment, these officers had found Anderson owed some $180. According to Anderson they had deducted this amount from the pay certificates issued to him. He thus considered the accounts justly settled, "though no entry of settlement appears on the face of the books." If his paybooks could be found, Anderson offered to resettle the accounts in order to put GW's concerns to rest (Anderson to GW, 23 June 1790, DLC:GW). Anderson wrote again the next day, enclosing a letter (not found) that he claimed would "*exculpate* me, from *Voluntary delinquincy* with respect to my Public accounts" (Anderson to GW, 24 June 1790, DLC:GW). Anderson did not receive the appointment at this time; it went instead to William Peery (see GW to the U.S. Senate, 2 Aug. 1790). After Peery declined the appointment, Anderson renewed his application, which initiated another round of correspondence regarding the settlement of his accounts (see Anderson to GW, 7 Jan. 1791). Anderson ultimately received appointment as judge for the Territory South of the Ohio (see GW to the U.S. Senate, 25 Feb. 1791).

1. The enclosed certificates have not been found. In his letter of 21 June Anderson noted that "the two Certificates I presented to your Excellency" were "my admissions in the Court of Delaware and Pennsylvania" (Anderson to GW, 21 June 1790, DLC:GW).

From Samuel Powel

Dear Sir   Philadelphia 11 June 1790

The Bearer hereof Mr Robert Parrish, an Inhabitant of this City, informs me that his Journey to New York is undertaken with a View to obtain Subscriptions to a Work of Mr William Bartram's, containing an account of his Travels thro' Florida &ca & also to obtain Permission to dedicate the Work to you.[1]

From Mr Bartram's character as a Botanist and as a Man, I have no Doubt that his Work is an interesting one & such as will do him Credit. I have seen, tho' I have not had an opportunity of perusing it, The extreme Bashfulness of it's author⟨,⟩ and his little Intercourse with the World, may, possibly have made him choose rather to sollicit the Honor of dedicating it to you thro' the Intervention of a Friend than by a direct Application. This is only Conjecture upon my Part as I am not ascertained of the Fact. Should his present Work meet with Success, I am informed that it will be followed by a second or more volumes.

Mr Parrish, who has requested of me to give him this Introduction to you, is a plain, and I believe, a worthy Citizen possessed of much usefull Information, & who has interested himself deeply in promoting Mr Bartram's Publication.

It gives sincere Pleasure to Mrs Powel & myself to hear that you are likely to be soon restored to Health. Our best good Wishes ever attend you & Mrs Washington.[2] I have the Honor to be dear Sir your most obedt humble Servt

Samuel Powel

ALS, DLC:GW.

1. Parrish may be the Robert Parrish who is listed in the 1790 census as a shopkeeper living on Race Street in Philadelphia (*Heads of Families* [Pennsylvania], 228). Powel is referring to Williams Bartram's *Travels through North and South Carolina, Georgia, East and West Florida, the Cherokee Country, the Extensive Territories of the Muscogulges, or Creek Confederacy, and the Country of the Choctaws; Containing an Account of the Soil and Natural Productions, Together with Observations on the Manners of the Indians.* The volume was published by James & Johnson in Philadelphia in 1791.

2. GW replied to Powel's letter on 20 June: "Your letter of the 11th Inst. was handed to me by Mr Parish, together with proposals for publishing the travels of Mr William Bartram, and requesting permission to dedicate them to me. This request I declined, as I have done many others of a similar nature; not with a view to discourage a work of this kind, which I am pursuaded, if executed by an able hand, may be very useful among us; but to avoid, with propriety, future applications of this nature, unless where some particular circumstances might induce a compliance.

"If affixing my name as a subscriber to this work can promote the Authors good intentions, I am happy in having done it; and I sincerely wish it all the success which its merits may demand. Mrs Washington joins me in compliments to yourself and Mrs Powel" (LS, ViMtV). A copy of the volume, with GW's signature on the title page, was in his library at the time of his death (Griffin, *Boston Athenæum Collection*, 19–20).

To the United States Senate and House of Representatives

United States [New York] June 11th 1790

Gentlemen of the Senate and House of Representatives,

I have directed my Secretary to lay before you a copy of the ratification of the Amendments to the Constitution of the United States by the State of North Carolina; together with an extract from a letter, accompanying said ratification, from the Governor of the State of North Carolina to the President of the United States.[1]

Go: Washington

LS, DNA: RG 46, First Congress, 1789–91, Records of Legislative Proceedings, President's Messages; copy, DNA: RG 233, Journals; LB, DLC:GW.

1. The North Carolina general assembly ratified all twelve proposed amendments to the Constitution on 22 Dec. 1789 (*N.C. State Records*, 25:20–21). Gov. Alexander Martin of North Carolina notified GW of the ratification in a letter dated 25 May 1790, which also acknowledged receipt of GW's letter of 20 Feb. 1790 (Martin to GW, 25 May 1790, Nc-Ar: Governor's Letterbook; see also GW's Circular to the Governors, 20 Feb. 1790). GW's letter to the Senate and House of Representatives reporting the ratification of the amendments was read in both Houses on 11 June (*DHFC*, 1:345–46, 3:457, 591–92).

To the United States Senate

United States [New York]

Gentlemen of the Senate,   June 11th 1790.

I nominate Thomas Bee to be Judge of the South-Carolina district, in the place of William Drayton deceased.[1]

Go: Washington

LS, DNA: RG 46, First Congress, 1789–91, Records of Executive Proceedings, President's Messages—Executive Nominations; LB, DLC:GW.

1. William Drayton died on 18 May 1790. For Thomas Bee's application for the office, see Bee to GW, 23 May 1790.

From Henry Lee

My dear sir   Stratford June 12th 1790

We have been all again made most miserable by the accounts received of the desperate state of your health—True it is that the general gloom has been succeeded by joy in as much as we have just heard that you was safe & likely to be restored to your usual vigor.[1]

But when I recollect that in the course of a few months you have been twice dangerously ill, & am informed by all who have seen you of the unfortunate change which your constitution seems to have undergone, I profess my mind is far from ease & quietude.

Surely sir, either you do not use your accustomed exercise of body, or the air of N. York disagrees with you.

In either or both cases a return to Mt Vernon for a few months might prove highly advantageous. The relaxation from business, as well other concurring causes would probably produce a complete recovery.

The same principles which governed you in your return to public life, commands you to pay every respect to your health.

You engaged in the arduous dutys of your present station from love of country & obedience to the will of the people—To do them permanent good was your sole object—this cannot be done in two years—therefore the conservati⟨on⟩ of your life by every possible means is a duty you owe to the community, a duty which I ardently hope you never will slight, however indifferent the philosophy of your mind may render you to the las⟨t⟩ task of mortals.

Whatever you may do, whether you come once more among us, or determine to run all risks of a life invaluable to your friends & fellow citizens, I beg leave to renew my unabated & sincere zeal for your health & happiness—a zeal which encreases with my knowledge of human nature & my reflexions on those characters whose virtues & labors in different periods of time & different quarters of the globe have stamped with the title of immortality. With the highest ⟨re⟩spect & the warmest affection I am unalterably your most ob. servt

Henry Lee

P.S. My long afflicted Mrs Lee is now very ill & I fear cannot be preserved.[2]

ALS, DLC:GW.

1. On GW's illness, see William Jackson to Clement Biddle, 12 May 1790, editorial note.

2. Henry Lee's first wife, his cousin Matilda Lee (daughter of Philip Ludwell Lee and Elizabeth Steptoe Lee), died in mid-August 1790, perhaps while giving birth to their fifth son (Armes, *Stratford Hall*, 259–60). For GW's letter of consolation, see GW to Henry Lee, 27 Aug. 1790.

From Jabez Bowen

Sir   Newport [R.I.] June 13. 1790

It affoards me the greatest pleasure that I can Congratulate your Excellency on the accession of the State of Rhode-Island to the Federal Union, more especially as it compleats the great Fabrick, and that it has been effected without the sheading of Blood, an Event that must give the greatest pleasure to every Friend to Humanity.

Our General Assembly have been in session for the purpose of Choosing Senators. my Name was made use of for one of them⟨.⟩ but the Antefederal Intrest prevailed Joseph Stanton and Theodore Foster Esqrs. are the two Gentmen Elected the former has been much opposed to the General Government the latter always Friendly.[1] hope they may be able to do good in their stations.

As the Offices for Collecting the Revennue will soon be appointed and that of Navel officer will be vacant by Mr Fosters being Elected a Senator. I have to Request your Excelleny that you will be pleased to appoint my Son⟨,⟩ Oliver Bowen [(]now about Twenty Two Years of Age) to that office I suppose there will be many applicants and therefore put my self much streightned in asking this Favour.[2] Colo. Leonard Member of the Lower House is perfectly acquainted with my son and will be able to give you satisfaction as to his qualifications. Colo. Jereh Olney wishes for the place of Collecter of the district of Providence I need say nothing to Recomme⟨d⟩ him. only that he will be perfect⟨ly⟩ agreable to all our Friends within the same I hartely wish for his obtaining the place.

Colo. Wm Peck also applies for some appointment he is a verry worthy Gentleman and I dare promise will faithfully execute any office that your Excellency may see fit to bestow upon him.

William Tyler has executed the office of Searcher for the port of Providence he has done the same faithfully and should he be Reappointed doubt not will still do the same.

As we are now all one Family hope you Excellency will makes us a Visit in the Recess of Congress ours is a fine Healthy Climate and will tend to Establish your Health and prolong that Life so Dear to us all. With the most perfect Esteem I subscribe your most Obedient and verry Humble Servant

Jabez Bowen

ALS, DLC:GW.

1. Bowen was supported by Federalists in the Rhode Island legislature for a seat in the Senate but was defeated by Joseph Stanton and Theodore Foster (see William Ellery to Benjamin Huntington, 12 June 1790, R-Ar).

2. Oliver Bowen (1767–1804) of Providence, son of Jabez Bowen, graduated from the College of Rhode Island in 1788. He received no appointment from GW (*Representative Men of Rhode Island*, 1011; *Columbian Centinel* [Boston], 19 Dec. 1804). He should not be confused with his uncle, also Oliver Bowen, who was appointed U.S. marshal for Georgia.

To John Jay

Dear Sir,   Sunday Morning 13th June 1790

Would there be prudence, justice or policy in extending mercy to the Convict mentioned in the enclosed Papers?[1]

Under this cover I send you for perusal two letters, just recd, from Mr Gouvr Morris.[2] Yours sincerely and affectionately

Go: Washington[3]

ALS, NNC: John Jay Collection.

1. See Thomas Bird to GW, 5 June 1790, and notes.

2. In a letter to Gouverneur Morris of 7 July 1790, GW acknowledged receipt of Morris's letters of 7 and 13 April and 1 and 2 May "on the business which had been entrusted to you of a public nature." It is uncertain which of these letters GW transmitted to Jay.

3. For Jay's reply, see his letter to GW, this date.

From John Jay

Dear Sir   New York 13 June 1790

There does not appear to be a single Circumstance in the Case of the murderer in question, to recommend a Pardon—His own Petition contains no averment of Innocence, no Palliative for Guilt, no complaint of Court Jury or witnesses, nor of the want of witnesses.

The Silence of the british cabinet on the Subject of Mr Morris's Letters marks their *Indicision*—it may arise from Doubts of what might be the opinion of Parliamt on some of the commercial, and perhaps other Points; and the Expediency of observing the caution and Delay which such Doubts may prescribe. with perfect Respect Esteem & attachment I am Dear Sir your most obt & hble Servant

John Jay

ALS, DNA: RG 59, Miscellaneous Letters.
For background to this letter, see GW to Jay, 13 June 1790.

To John Adams

Monday June 14. 1790

The President of the United States and Mrs Washington request the pleasure of the Vice-Presidents and Mrs Adams's company to dinner on Thursday next at *four* o'clock. an answer is desired.[1]

L, MHi: Adams Family Papers.
1. No reply to this invitation has been found, nor is there a record of the dinner in GW's diary, since he did not resume making entries until 24 June. Social relations between the Washingtons and the Adamses at this time were extremely cordial. Abigail Adams wrote to her sister on 13 June that "I last week accompanied Mrs. Washington to the Jersies to visit the falls of Pasaick. We were absent three days and had a very agreeable Tour" (Abigail Adams to Mary Cranch, 13 June 1790, Mitchell, *New Letters of Abigail Adams,* 51–52).

From Abiel Foster and Benjamin Huntington

Sir   New York June 14th 1790

We hope it's not disagreeable that we mention the Hone William Ellery of Newport as a good man for a Commissioner of loans or a District Judge, or a Collector of the Duties for the Port of Newport in Rhode Island[1] His Character is well known from past services in, & under various appointments from, the late Congress He was commissioner of Loans at the adoption of the Constitution and will doubtless give Satisfaction in any of the abovementioned Offices. We[2] are most Respectfully your most hume Servts

Abiel Foster

Benj. Huntington

ALS, DLC:GW.

Abiel Foster (1735–1806) represented New Hampshire in the First Congress. He graduated from Harvard in 1756 and was a minister from 1761 to 1779. In 1775 he was elected to the New Hampshire Provincial Congress, and he represented that state in the Continental Congress from 1783 to 1785. Benjamin Huntington (1736–1800) was a Norwich, Conn., lawyer and a graduate of Yale. Before his election to the First Congress in 1789, Huntington served in the Massachusetts legislature and the Continental Congress.

1. William Ellery (1727–1820), a prominent Newport lawyer, was one of Rhode Island's leading Federalists. He graduated from Harvard in 1747 and engaged in various activities before taking up the practice of law in 1770. Ellery served as a delegate to the Continental Congress almost continuously from 1776 until 1786, becoming one of the most active members of that body. He was elected chief justice of the Rhode Island Superior Court in 1785 and served as commissioner of loans for Rhode Island from 1786 to 1790. GW appointed him collector at Newport on 14 June 1790. He held the post until his death.

2. In the MS this word reads "were."

From William Turner Miller

Sir   Warren [R.I.] June 14th 1790

I take the Liberty to address your Excellency in the Cause of the most Respectable of the People of this district Respecting the person to be appointed Surveyor of the Customs of the Port of Warren and Barrington, when I mention to you the Name of

Samuel Miller[1] I Speak of the Person who now is in that office and is the Brother to the late Gen. Nathan Miller he hath given good Sattisfaction in that office and done Justice to the Revennue his Connections are of the Most Influential Charracters here who will all find them selves much gratified by your Excellency's being pleased to Reinstate him in Said office I am your Excellencys most obedient Humble Servant

William T. Miller

ALS, DLC:GW.

William Turner Miller of Warren served as lieutenant colonel of Church's Rhode Island Regiment in 1775 and on several committees during the course of the Revolution. He was a member of the Rhode Island general assembly in 1781 and a justice of common pleas for Bristol County from 1782 to 1784 (Bartlett, *R.I. Records*, 8:110, 188, 414, 9:383, 542, 691, 10:22).

1. Samuel Miller, of Warren, served as the surveyor at Warren and Barrington under the state government. He probably shared the Federalist inclinations of his prominent brother, Brig. Gen. Nathan Miller (1743–1790), who served in the Continental Congress, the general assembly, and as a Federalist in the first session of the state ratifying convention in March 1790 (Polishook, *Rhode Island and the Union*, 216; *Biographical Cyclopedia*, 140–41). Samuel Miller did not receive an appointment from GW.

To the United States Senate

United States [New York]
Gentlemen of the Senate, June 14th 1790.
I nominate the following persons to be Collectors, Naval-Officers and Surveyors of the Ports of New Port and Providence in the State of Rhode Island and Providence Plantations—viz.

William Ellery to be Collector,
Robert Crooke to be Naval-Officer, } of New-Port.
Daniel Lyman to be Surveyor
Jeremiah Olney to be Collector,
Theodore Foster to be Naval-
Officer, William Barton to be Sur- } of Providence.
veyor

Go: Washington[1]

LS, DNA: RG 46, First Congress, 1789–91, Records of Executive Proceedings, President's Messages—Executive Nominations; LB, dated 13 June, DLC:GW.

1. This message was delivered to the Senate by Tobias Lear on 14 June. The Senate immediately proceeded to the consideration of the message and on the same day approved the appointment of the persons named by GW (*DHFC*, 2:80).

From Brown & Francis

Dr Sr,   Providence [R.I.] June 15th 1790

We take the Liberty to Inclose you by our Mr Thomas Francis, the Recommendation of a number of Gentlemon in Favour of one of the Best of Citizens and one whome we know to be Truly Desearveing of the most Favorable notice of the Gentlemon of Congress, and had not their have beene a Desided Majority of Anties in both Houses of our Genl Assembly, he Certinly would have beene Elected one of the Senneters,[1] the Gentlemon who was apposed to him and appointed by 16 Majority its True is Reither Fedderal but we are Sorry to have Ocation to Obsearve, that his being Brother in Law to the present Govenour we Fear he will be too much under the Controul of the Anties,[2] we are with the highest Esteeme & Affection Your Obt and Most Humble Servts

Brown & Francis

P.S. the Barer our Mr T. Francis havg Lately Arived from Calcutta ware he was offten in Compy with Lord Corn Wallis perhaps Your Exeleney may if Leasure purmit, wish to have Some Conversation Respecting that Gentlemon, once your prissoner, Mr Francis Stay in New York will be *Very* Short havg not Seen ⟨His⟩ Famely for 19 Months.

LS, DLC:GW.

Brown & Francis was the Providence mercantile house of John Brown and his son-in-law, John Francis (1763–1796).

1. The enclosure was a letter, 15 June 1790, recommending William Bradford (1729–1808) for appointment as district judge for Rhode Island, signed by the Providence mercantile partnerships of Brown & Francis, (John) Clark & (Joseph) Nightingale, Joseph & William Russell, and (Nicholas) Brown & (George) Benson (DLC:GW). Bradford was trained as a physician but abandoned the practice of medicine for the law. He practiced law in Bristol, R.I., served as deputy governor of the state from 1775 to 1778, and was repeatedly a member of the general assembly. As the mercantile party candidate for governor in 1787, he was defeated by John Collins. He received no appointment from GW but was elected to the U.S. Senate in 1792. The enclo-

sure also recommended Benjamin Bourne for appointment as U.S. attorney and John Singer Dexter as U.S. marshal. None of these appointments were made, but Dexter was appointed a supervisor of distilled spirits in 1791 (*DHFC*, 2:128–9).

2. Theodore Foster, elected to the Senate on 12 June, was a nominal Federalist but also the brother-in-law of Rhode Island's Antifederalist governor, Arthur Fenner (see Foster to GW, 26 June 1790, n.1).

From Thomas Jefferson

June 15. 1790.

Th: Jefferson has the honor to inclose for the President's perusal a letter from Mr Gouverneur Morris on the subject of our affairs in Amsterdam; the observations are worthy being known to the President.[1]

Mr Howell of Rhode island has imposed on him the duty also of putting into his hands the letter & papers from him. the printed papers are merely to prove his dispositions enounced in the letter.[2]

Since writing the above, the inclosed letter from mister Short is received.[3]

ALS, DNA: RG 59, Miscellaneous Letters; LB, DLC:GW; copy, DNA: RG 59, GW Correspondence with Secretaries of State.

1. This enclosure was Gouverneur Morris's letter to Jefferson of 10 April 1790. See Boyd, *Jefferson Papers*, 16:328–29.

2. Jefferson enclosed a letter to him from David Howell (1747–1824), 3 June 1790, congratulating Jefferson on his appointment as secretary of state. Howell was a prominent Rhode Island attorney and a graduate of the College of New Jersey (later Princeton). Since 1766 Howell had taught at the College of Rhode Island (Brown) as professor of natural philosophy. He was admitted to the bar in 1768 and from 1790 to 1824 taught jurisprudence at Rhode Island College. Howell served as associate justice of the supreme court of Rhode Island from 1786 to 1787 and as attorney general in 1789. During the 1780s he served in the Confederation Congress. In his letter to Jefferson, Howell also wrote that "Having accidentally heard that the President of the United States did me the honour to enquire into my present political character and flattering myself that he might be prompted by other motives than mere curiosity, I have also enclosed the U. S. Chronicle of February 25. 1790 containing some of my sentiments under the signature of *Solon Junior*. Both the papers in this Town contain other peices under the same signature. As such peices are hastily written and seldom copied, they cannot be correct. In the Providence Gazette of May 22d. Ult. enclosed, you will also see two peices written by me just before our late Election. These may explain to you the reason why I was opposed as attorney General and beat by an Antifederalist

of no abilities." Howell also enclosed "an Oration delivered by my eldest son on his Commencement in the [College] in this Town last September. You will render me as singular satisfaction in putting [this] Oration into the hands of General Washington for his perusal at some leisure moment, explaining to him such parts of this letter as you may think proper" (Boyd, *Jefferson Papers*, 16:451–454). For a description of the enclosures, see ibid.

3. This was probably William Short's letter of 29 Mar. 1790 addressed to John Jay (ibid., 279–81).

From Nathaniel Phillips

Sir,   State of Rhode Island, Warren June 15th 1790

Having served my Country through the late arduous Contest in the Army under the Orders of your Excellency in such a Manner as to secure my Character from being impeached on any Occasion, and being anxious to serve the United States, and support my Family in that Reputation we have heretofore sustained—I am emboldened to request an Appointment to the Office of Surveyor and Searcher for the Ports of Warren and Barrington. The Gentlemen who are elected Senators from this State are possessed of a Recommendation signed by the principal Gentlemen in the Town of which I am an Inhabitant, together with the Members of the late Convention in this State, and the Members to the General Assembly from Barrington.[1] With the highest Respect and Esteem, I have the Honour to be, Your Excellency most Obedient hhble Servt

           Nathl Phillips.

ALS, DLC:GW.

Nathaniel Phillips (1756–1832) served in the army from July 1777 until 1783, reaching the rank of sergeant. Phillips resided at Warren, R.I., and GW appointed him surveyor at Warren and Barrington on 2 July 1790 (see GW to the U.S. Senate, 2 July 1790).

1. Phillips also was recommended to GW by Joseph Stanton and Theodore Foster in their letter of 29 June 1790.

To David Stuart

Dear Sir,   New York June 15th 1790

Your letter of the 2d Instant came duly to hand. If there are any Gazettes among my files at Mount Vernon which can be of use to you they are at your Service.

Your description of the public mind, in Virginia, gives me pain. It seems to be more irritable, sour & discontented than (from the information I receive) it is in any other state in the Union, except Massachusetts; which, from the same causes, but on quite different principles, is tempered like it.

That Congress does not proceed with all that dispatch which people at a distance expect; and which, were they to hurry business, they possibly might; is not to be denied. That measures have been agitated wch are not pleasing to Virginia; and others, pleasing perhaps to her, but not so to some other States; is equally unquestionable. Can it well be otherwise in a Country so extensive, so diversified in its interests? And will not these different interests naturally produce in an assembly of Representatives who are to Legislate for, and to assimilate & reconcile them to the general welfare, long, warm & animated debates? most undoubtedly; and if there was the same propensity in Mankin⟨d to in⟩vestigate the motives, as there is for censuring ⟨the con⟩duct of public characters, it would be found that the censure so freely bestowed is oftentimes unmerited, and uncharitable—for instance, the condemnation of Congress for sitting only four hours in the day. The fact is, by the established rules of the House of Representatives, no Committee can sit whilst the House is sitting; and this is, and has been for a considerable time, from ten o'clock in the forenoon until three, often later, in the afternoon⟨,⟩ before & after which the business is going on in Committees—If this application is not as much as m⟨ost C⟩onstitutions are equal to I am mistaken. Many ⟨othe⟩r things which undergo malignant construct⟨ions⟩ wd be found, upon a candid examination, to we⟨ar oth⟩er faces than are given to them. The misfo⟨rtune⟩ is, that the enemies to the Government—always m⟨ore⟩ active than its friends, and always upon the watch ⟨to give⟩ it a stroke—neglect no opportunity to aim one. If they tell truth, it is not the whole truth; by which means one side only of the picture appears; whereas if both sides were exhibited it might, and probably w⟨oul⟩d assume a different form in the opinions of just ⟨& candid⟩ men who are disposed to measure matters ⟨by a Con⟩tinental Scale. I do not mean however, fr⟨om what⟩ I have here said, to justify the conduct of ⟨Congress⟩ in all its movements; for some of these movements in my opinion, have been injudicious, & others unseasonable, whilst the questions of assumption—Residence—and other matters have been agitated with a warmth & intemperence; with prolixity & threats; which it is to be feared has lessened the dignity of that body, & decreased that respect which was once entertained for it. And this misfortune is encreased by many members, even among those who wish well to the Government, ascribing in letters to their respective States when they are unable to carry a favourite measure, the worst motives for the conduct of their opponants; who, viewing matters through a different medium may, & do retort in their turn; by which means jealousies & distrusts are spread most impolitickly, far & wide; & will, it is to be feared have a most unhappy tendency to injure our public affairs—which, if wisely conducted might make us (as we are now by Europeans thought to be) the happiest people upon Earth. As an evidence of it, our reputation has risen in every part of the Globe; and our credit, especially in Holland, has got higher than that of *any* Nation in Europe (& where our funds are above par) as appears by *Official* advices just received. But the conduct we seem to be pursuing will soon bring us back to our late disreputable condition.

The introductions of the (Quaker) Memorial, respecting Slavery, was to be sure, not only an ill-judged piece of business, but occasioned a great waste of time.[1] The final decision thereon, however, was as favourable as the proprietors of that species of property could well have expected considering the great dereliction to Slavery in a large part of this Union.

The question of assumption has occupied a great deal of time, & no wonder; for it is certainly a very important one; and, under *proper* restrictions, & scrutiny into accounts will be found, I conceive, to be just. The Cause in which the expences of the War was incurred, was a Common Cause. The States (in Congress) declared it so at the beginning⟨,⟩ and pledged themselves to stand by each other. If then⟨,⟩ some States were harder pressed than others, or from particular or local circumstances contracted heavier debts, it is but reasonable when this fact is ascertained (though it is a sentiment I have not made known here) that an allowance ought to be made them when due credit is given to others—Had the invaded, and hard pressed States believed the case would have been other⟨wise;⟩ opposition in them would very soon, I believe, ⟨have⟩ changed to submission; and given a different t⟨er⟩mination to the War.[2]

In a letter of last year to the best of my recollection, I informed you of the motives, which *compelled* me to allot a day for the reception of idle and ceremonious visits (for it never has prevented those of sociability and friendship in the afternoon, or at any other time) but if I am mistaken in this, the history of this business is simply and shortly as follows—Before the custom was established, which now accommodates foreign characters, Strangers, and others who from motives of curiosity, respect, to the Chief Magistrate, or any other cause, are induced to call upon me—I was unable to attend to any business *whatsoever;* for Gentlemen, consulting their own convenience rather than mine, were calling from the time I rose from breakfast—often before—until I sat down to dinner—This, as I resolved not to neglect my public duties, reduced me to the choice of one of these alternatives, either to refuse them *altogether,* or to appropriate a time for the reception of them—The first would, I well knew, be disgusting to many—The latter, *I expected,* would undergo animadversion, and blazoning from those who would find fault, *with,* or *without* cause. To please every body was impossible—I therefore adopted that line of conduct which combined public advantage with private convenience, and which in my judgment was unexceptionable in itself. That I have not been able to make bows to the taste of poor Colonel Bland, (who by the by I believe never saw one of them) is to be regretted especially too as (upon those occasions) they were indiscriminately bestowed, and the best I was master of—would it not have been better to have thrown the veil of charity over them, ascribing their stiffness to the effects of age, or to the unskilfulness of my teacher, than to pride and dignity of office, which God knows has no charms for me? for I can truly say I had rather be at Mount Vernon with a friend or two about me, than to be attended at the Seat of Government by the Officers of State and the Representatives of every Power in Europe—These visits are optional—They are made without invitation—Between the hours of three and four every Tuesday I am prepared to receive them—Gentlemen—often in great numbers—come and go—chat with each other—and act as they please. A Porter shews them into the room, and they retire from it when they please, and without ceremony. At their *first* entrance they salute me, and I them, and as many as I can talk to I do—what pomp there is in all this I am unable to discover—Perhaps it consists in not sitting—To this two reasons are opposed, first it is unusual—secondly, (which is a more substantial one) because I have no room large enough to contain a third of the chairs, which would be sufficient to admit it—If it is supposed that ostentation, or the fashions of courts (which by the by I believe originates oftener in convenience, not to say necessity than is generally imagined) gave rise to this custom, I will boldly affirm that *no* supposition was ever more erroneous; for, if I was to give indulgence to my inclinations, every moment that I could withdraw from the fatigues of my station should be spent in retirement—That they are not proceeds from the sense I entertain of the propriety of giving to every one as free access, as consists with that respect which is due to the chair of government—and that respect I conceive is neither to be acquired or preserved but by observing a just medium between much state and too great familiarity.

Similar to the above, but of a more familiar and sociable kind are the visits every friday afternoon to Mrs Washington where I always am—These public meetings and a dinner once a week to as many as my table will hold with the references *to* and *from* the different Departments of State, and *other* communications with *all* parts of the Union is as much, if not more, than I am able to undergo, for I have already had within less than a year, two *severe* attacks—the last worse than the first—a third more than probable will put me to sleep with my fathers; at what distance this may be I know not.[3] Within the last twelve months I have undergone more, and severer sickness than thirty preceding years afflicted me with, put it altogether—I have abundant reason however to be thankful that I am so well recovered; though I still feel the remains of the violent affection of my lungs—The cough, pain in my breast, and shortness in breathing not having entirely left me. I propose in the recess of Congress to visit Mount Vernon—but when this recess will happen is beyond my ken, or the ken I believe of any of its members. I am dear Sir &ca

G. Washington

ALS (incomplete), ViU; LB, DLC:GW.

1. See Warner Mifflin to GW, 12 Mar. 1790, n.1, GW to David Stuart, 28 Mar. 1790, n.2.

2. At this point the ALS ends. The remainder of the letter is taken from the letter book.

3. For GW's "first" illness, in the summer of 1789, see James McHenry to

GW, 28 June 1789, n.1. For his illness in the spring of 1790, see William Jackson to Clement Biddle, 12 May 1790, editorial note.

From Simeon Thayer

Providence [R.I.] June 15 1790

May it please your Excellency

An Officer in the Fifty third year of his age after much painful service rendered to his Country and Sufferings in her Cause (a brief Sketch whereof is contained in the inclosed paper) finds himself reduced to the necessity of asking for the means of Support for the residue of Life.[1]

The charges of an expensive Family during the period of his service in the War, besides the support of an aged Father and Mother who with three others of his Family are since Dead incumbered him with Debts—these he could not discharge by no other means than by selling his Securities at the rate of three shillings to three shillings and Six pence in the pound.

He begs Leave further to observe that he has now a wife and Six children Dependent on his Industry for their Support the second a Daughter about 17 years of age in a declining State of health.

The Loss of a Right Eye would entitle your Applicant to a compensation on the Invalid Establishment could he have replaced his securities that was out of his power at the Time of passing the order of Congress, and by their enhanced price is rendered still more so.

Your applicant is fully convinced of your Excellency's readiness to attend to the redress of all greivances especially those of a Soldier; and cannot doubt of being taken such notice of as may be practicable. Of this be assured Sir that the reluctance with which this application is made is equal in degree to the chearfulness with which the Service was performed.

It is wholly submitted to your Excellency's Discretion either to provide for your present applicant by giving him a place in the Collection of the Revenue, as Marshal in this State or by recommending his case in any other way that may seem proper and may be calculated to Render the evening of Life comfortable in the enjoyment of a Compentency. With profound veneration and the most cordial attachment, I am your Excellencys most obedient and very Humble Servant

Simeon Thayer

ALS, DLC:GW.

Simeon Thayer (1737–1800) was born in Massachusetts and was apprenticed to a peruke maker in Providence at an early age. He served in the French and Indian War before establishing himself in his trade in Providence. He raised a company of Rhode Island troops in 1775 and participated in Arnold's attack on Quebec, in which he was taken prisoner. He commanded the defense of Fort Mifflin in the Delaware in 1777. He lost an eye at the battle of Monmouth but remained with the army until January 1781, retiring with the rank of major. After the war Thayer kept a public house in Providence and served as brigadier general of the Rhode Island militia (*Collections of the Rhode Island Historical Society*, 6:70–80). He received no appointment from GW.

1. The enclosure was a manuscript diary—"A Journal of the Sufferings and Adventures of Simeon Thayer in the two last Wars in America" (DLC:GW). A transcription is on CD-ROM:GW. Thayer kept a much more extensive journal of experiences on the march on Quebec, published as *The Invasion of Canada in 1775: Including the Journal of Captain Simeon Thayer, Describing the Perils and Sufferings of the Army under Colonel Benedict Arnold, in Its March through the Wilderness to Quebec* in *Collections of the Rhode Island Historical Society*, 6 (Providence, 1867), 1–45.

To the United States Senate and House of Representatives

United States [New York] June 16th 1790.
Gentlemen of the senate and House of Representatives,

The Ratification of the Constitution of the United States of America by the State of Rhode Island and Providence Plantations, was received by me last night, together with a letter to the President of the United States from the President of the Convention, I have directed my secretary to lay before you a copy of each.[1]

Go: Washington

LS, DNA: RG 46, First Congress, 1789–91, Records of Legislative Proceedings, President's Messages; copy, DNA: RG 233, First Congress, 1789–91, Records of Legislative Proceedings, Journals; LB, DLC:GW.

1. GW enclosed a copy of the formal instrument of ratification agreed to by the Rhode Island convention on 29 May 1790 along with a copy of the letter of transmittal from Daniel Owen, president of the Rhode Island convention, dated 9 June 1790. A leader of Rhode Island's Antifederalist country party,

Owen apparently delayed drafting this letter and then delayed longer before sending it, in order to give the Rhode Island legislature time to appoint senators who would rush to New York to urge the continuance of revenue officers appointed by the state. On 9 June Daniel Owen, the president of the Rhode Island convention, sent GW a copy of the state's instrument of ratification (see Rhode Island Ratifying Convention to GW, 9 June 1790). GW did not wait to receive the formal instrument of ratification before nominating candidates for the principal revenue offices in Rhode Island (see GW to the U.S. Senate, 14 June 1790).

From William Floyd

Sir   New York June 17th 1790

Agreable to your Request I wrote for a Machine for gathering Clover Seed, it is now arrived, and is at the Store of Mr David Gelston in front Street, Subject to any orders you may please to give concerning it.

If no opportunity Immediately presents to Send it to Virginia, Mr Winkoop Requests that a Joyner may have it for this Day and tomorrow as a patern to make one by—from Sir your most Obedt and Very humble Servt

Wm Floyd

ALS, PHi: Gratz Collection.

William Floyd (1734–1821) was born in Brookhaven, N.Y., and served as a major general of the New York militia during the Revolution. He was a member of the Continental Congress in 1774–76 and again in 1779–83 and a member of the state senate in 1777–78 and 1784–88. As a representative in the First Congress, Floyd dined with GW on at least two occasions. At one of these dinners—perhaps that of 14 Jan. 1790 when Henry Wynkoop of Pennsylvania was also present—GW may have requested Floyd to procure a machine for gathering clover seed for him (*Diaries*, 6:7).

From James Iredell

Sir,   North Carolina, Wilmington, June 17th 1790.

I had sometime ago the honour of receiving from Mr Jay a copy of the Letter you were pleased to write on the 3d April to him and the other Judges of the Supreme Court I shall not fail, Sir, to do every thing in my power to contribute to the important purpose of it, and shall hope to consult with the other Judges when I have the pleasure of meeting them at New York in order that we may jointly communicate to you the observations which occur to us.[1]

I hope you will excuse, Sir, my taking the liberty, in a letter which perhaps ought to be strictly official, to express the great joy I feel in hearing of your entire recovery from an illness which caused so universal an alarm.[2] May God grant the most melancholy event which America can possibly sustain may long be removed from it, and that you may still enjoy many years of private as well as public happiness! I have the honour to be, with the greatest respect, Sir, Your most faithful and most obedient Servant

Ja. Iredell

ALS, DNA: RG 59, Miscellaneous Letters.

1. On 3 April 1790 GW had written to the justices of the Supreme Court soliciting their thoughts on the organization of the federal judiciary. Iredell was not then present in New York, having been appointed to the court in February (see GW to the U.S. Supreme Court, 3 April 1790, source note). In September 1790 Iredell and the other justices responded to GW's query (see the Supreme Court Justices to GW, c.13 Sept. 1790).

2. On GW's illness, see William Jackson to Clement Biddle, 12 May 1790, editorial note.

From Paul Allen

Sir   Providence [R.I.] June 18th 1790

The happiness Individuals of the United States have in addressing your Excellency, is One of the greatest blessing they enjoy under the present Constitution. Emboldened by the kind reception others have met with from your Excellency in similar circumstances, I have presumed to venture on that ground under the fullest conviction that your Excellency has ever attended to the welfare of those who have suffered in the cause of their Country.

In the beginning of the War⟨,⟩ I took an early and active part being Master of the second vessel that brought warlike stores into this Town. After that I furnished the Army with provisions to the amount of 120,000 Rations, as likewise the sum of £1500 in Ammunition this was nearly all I possessed, and for which I received the public's securities; many of these evidences I have since been under the necessity of parting with at a very low price to supply the wants of a large and growing family who are all of them Minors and depend on me for subsistence, this circumstance with many others has so exhausted my property as to occasion my humbly soliciting your Excellency for the appointment of Naval Officer in this Town, which duty have the confidence to think I could discharge in such a manner as to merit yours and the public approbation, which should I be so happy to have my address handed previous to the choice of that Officer, and your Excellency should be induced to make such enquiry respecting my abilities as a suitable person for that department I would beg leave to mention Theodore Foster Esqr. one of the Senators from this State, who although I presume has previously recommended Ebenr Thompson Esqr. yet will not be wanting to give your Excellency such satisfactory information as the nature of the appointment requires. I have the honor to be with the greatest deference & respect Your Excellency's most Obedient and most Devoted humble Servant

Paul Allen

ALS, DLC:GW.

Paul Allen (c.1741–1800), a Providence ship captain, was involved in the Association movement before the Revolution and was active in supplying the state with military stores during the war. He represented Providence in the Rhode Island general assembly in 1778 and again from 1783 to 1786. Allen's application was supported by a letter of recommendation from Samuel Nightingale, John D. Torrance, Nicholas Powers, and John Spurr, who wrote that "in the late struggle of his Country [Allen] ever discovered a strong attachment to its cause and interest, both of which is manifested by his supplying the Army early in the War with warlike stores and provisions to a very considerable amount" (Samuel Nightingale et al. to GW, 12 June 1790, DLC:GW). Allen did not receive an appointment from GW. In February 1791 a committee of Rhode Islanders, including Jabez Bowen, Enos Hitchcock, John Brown, Jeremiah Olney, James Manning, John James, Samuel Nightingale, and Thomas Smart, recommended Allen for excise collector, also without success (see Jabez Bowen et al. to GW, 14 Feb. 1791, DLC:GW).

1. In 1776 Allen made a voyage to the West Indies on the sloop *Unity*, returning with a cargo of military stores (see Nicholas Brown to Capt. Paul Allen, 31 Dec. 1775, and "Manifest of Cargo Imported in Sloop *Unity* Paul Allen Mr from Curacao," Clark, *Naval Documents*, 3:322–23, 4:593–94).

From Alexander Hamilton

Treasury Department [New York] June 18th 1790

The Secretary of the Treasury has the honor respectfully to submit to the President of the United states for his consideration, a Contract (with the letter that accompanied it) betwen William Allibone Superintendant of the Light-house, Beacons, Buoys & public Piers on the river and Bay of Delaware and Abraham Hargis, Keeper of the Light-house at Cape Henlopen—The yearly Salary of £130. altho' it appeared high, is found, on Examination the same as was allowed to this person by the state of Pennsylvania—The allowance of £13. for the several supplies and services specifyed, does not appear unreasonable.[1]

LB, DLC:GW.

1. GW apparently regarded the salary proposed in the contract as too high and returned it to Hamilton. Although neither the proposed contract nor any reply from GW to Hamilton has been found, on 26 Aug. Hamilton wrote to GW submitting "a new contract made by William Allibone . . . with Abraham Hargis as Keeper of the said ligh[t] house, in lieu of that formerly made, which the President did not think proper to approve" (Hamilton to GW, 26 Aug. 1790 [first letter], DLC:GW). Lear replied to Hamilton on 28 Aug. 1790 that GW approved of the new contract fixing Hargis's salary "at the rate of 266 Dollars 66⅔ Cents per annum" (Lear to Hamilton, 28 Aug. 1790 [first letter], DLC:GW).

From Jabez Bowen

Sir   Providence [R.I.] June 19th 1790

By the arival of Colo. Barton from New York we are informed of the Appointments made in the Revenue Department for this State.[1] I think they will give intire satisfaction to all the Friends of the General Goverment.

some of my Friends inform me that they have wrote to your Excellency Requesting that I may be appointed to the Loan Office. if agreable, should take it as a favour.[2] whoever the person may be he aught to Reside in this Town, as three quarters of the Business will be with the Inhabitants of this County and from the Massachusetts & Connecticutt in this vicinity at the time the

Loans was made the Inhabitants of Rhode Island were under the power of the British.

The Federalists of this State wish that Govr Bradford or Mr Merchant should be appointed District Judge they are both Gentlemen of the Law, and fully equal to the Office, they have been equally good Wiggs and Firm for the Establishing the Federal Government.[3]

It is wished by our Friends that Benjamin Bourne Esqr. may be appointed District Attorney. he is a Gentleman of the verry first abilities and would be the person that we shall Vote for to send as a Representative but at present he can have no chance of succeeding.[4]

I would also Name John S. Dexter as a verry propper Person for Marshall to this District he is well know[n] to your Excellency and cartainly would give good satisfaction to every good man.[5]

I should not have thus Troubled your Excellency but we are informed that Govr Fenner has and will send on the Names of those persons that he and his Friends wish may be put in Office, but the whole of their Conduct having been uniformly oposed to the General Government I cannot think that they will be anxious to promote such persons to Offices as will act for the General weale. Your task Sir is arduous I dont wish to perplex but to give you such information as will make your Administration Honourable and Happy, I Remain with sentements of the highest Esteem & Respect your most Obedient and verry Humle Servant

Jabez Bowen

ALS, DLC:GW.

1. William Barton brought the news of the revenue appointments made by GW on 14 June 1790.

2. Bowen was recommended for commissioner of loans by a committee of Providence merchants (Providence, R.I., Merchants to GW, 14 June 1790, DLC:GW). GW appointed Bowen commissioner of loans on 7 Aug. 1790 (see GW to the U.S. Senate [first letter], 7 Aug. 1790, DNA: RG 46, First Congress, 1789–91, Records of Executive Proceedings, President's Messages—Executive Nominations).

3. GW appointed Henry Marchant district judge for Rhode Island on 2 July 1790 (see GW to the U.S. Senate, 2 July 1790, DNA: RG 46, First Congress 1789–91, Records of Executive Proceedings, President's Messages—Executive Nominations).

4. Benjamin Bourne was elected to the House of Representatives on 31 Aug. 1790 (see DenBoer, *First Federal Elections*, 4:443).

5. John Singer Dexter served as an officer with the Continental army from 1776 to 1783, rising to the rank of major. After the war he lived in Cumberland, R.I., where he was a justice of the peace. He was a member of the Rhode Island general assembly in 1782 and voted for ratification in the Rhode Island convention of May 1790. Jeremiah Olney also recommended Dexter for the post of marshal (see Memorandum from Jeremiah Olney, 19 June 1790). He did not receive a federal appointment at this time, but GW appointed him supervisor of distilled spirits in 1791 (see GW to the U.S. Senate [third letter], 4 Mar. 1791, DNA: RG 46, Second Congress, 1791–93, Records of Executive Proceedings, President's Messages—Executive Nominations).

To Thomas Jefferson

Saturday June 19th 1790

The enclosed Letters & documents from Mr Gouvr Morris are sent for the perusal of the Secretary of State.[1]

The private letters from the Marquis de la Fayette and Mr Payne he also gives Mr Jefferson a sight of; because there are some ideas in the latter which are new—and in the former, geneneral information respecting the affairs of France, which, by being compar'd with other accts may (though not of very late date, but from the respectibility of the authority) enable one to form a better judgment of the situation of things in that Country, than they could do from any single relation of them.

AL, DLC: Jefferson Papers.

1. The enclosures to this letter included Gouverneur Morris to GW, 1 May 1790, with its enclosures, Lafayette to GW, 17 Mar. 1790, and Thomas Paine to GW, 1 May 1790.

Memorandum from Jeremiah Olney

[19 June 1790]

Memo. of Sundry persons Suitable Characters to fill the Offices annexed to their Respective Names—in Rhode Island— Vizt

Towns	Names	Offices
Bristol	William Bradford	
		District Judge
Newport	Henry Marchant	

as to the abilities of these Gentlemen there is but little difference perhaps the Preferance *if any* may be in favour of Mr Marchant but Mr Bradford is the Firmist man of the Two—& has met with great losses of Property during the Revolution—

Providence	Benjamin Bourne	⎱ District attorney
Newport	William Channing	⎰

As to the Abilities of these Gentlemen—Mr Bourne has the Preference—they are However both men of Tallants—

	John S. Dexter	Marshall
Providence	William Peck	Naval officer
	George Olney	Commissioner of Loans
North Kingstown	Danl Updike	Surveyor
East Greenwich	Capt. Tho: Arnold, lost his legg at Monmouth	Surveyor

Warren	I have not a Sufficient knowledge of any gentle-
Bristol	men at these ports to Warrant a Recommendation
Pawcatuck River	to fill these offices.

Pautuxet—John Anthony Aborn—Surveyor Tho I think it most Adviseable to have only an Inspector as there is at most only Two Small Sea Vessells Enter this port a year

Jereh Olney

ADS, DLC:GW.

GW had appointed Olney collector at Providence on 14 June 1790 (see GW to the U.S. Senate, 14 June 1790). Olney apparently traveled to New York to press his application and delivered this memorandum to GW while in the city. His purpose seems to have been to supply GW with a list of reliable Federalists with which to replace Antifederalist state officers. Olney explained to Alexander Hamilton on 7 June that Antifederalist Daniel Owen, president of the ratifying convention, on the advice of Antifederalist Gov. Arthur Fenner, was withholding formal notice of ratification from GW until the legislature could send Antifederalist senators to New York to influence the revenue appointments. Olney explained that "they Wish to have all the *Ante* Revenue officers of the State reappointed & expect the Senators will Influence the President In the nomination of these *Bitter & Uniform* opposers of the Constitution" (Olney to Hamilton, 7 June 1790, in Syrett, *Hamilton Papers*, 6:458–59).

To Daniel Owen

Sir,   United States [New York] June 19th 1790.

I have delayed acknowledging the receipt of your letter of the 29th of may, which contained official information of the adoption and ratification of the Constitution of the United States of America by the State of Rhode Island and Providence Plantations, until the form of the ratification should be received, which, together with your letter accompanying it, got to my hands but a few days ago; and I take this opportunity of offering you my sincere congratulations upon this event, which unites under one general Government all the branches of the great American family; and I doubt not but it will prove as auspicious to the good people of your State as it is pleasing to other parts of the Union.[1] With due consideration, I am, Sir, Your most Obedt Servt

Go: Washington

LS, RPB; LB, DLC:GW.

1. Acting as president of the Rhode Island convention, Owen sent GW notice of the ratification of the Constitution by the state on 29 May 1790 (see GW to the U.S. Senate and House of Representatives, 16 June 1790, n.1). GW did not receive a copy of the formal instrument of ratification from Owen until 15 June. Owen's cover letter to the formal instrument was dated 9 June, but he apparently delayed sending it (see GW to the U.S. Senate and House of Representatives, 16 June 1790, n.1; Memorandum from Jeremiah Olney, 19 June 1790, source note).

From Charles Cotesworth Pinckney

Dear Sr: Charleston June 19. 1790

I am infinitely obliged to you for having favoured me with introductory Letters for my nephew Mr Horry. It will give him an opportunity of travelling with such great advantage that every improvement he may thereby acquire, I shall always with gratitude attribute to your benevolent patronage.[1]

We have lately ratified a new Constitution for this State; you will at once see that it is by no means perfect, but considering the different interests in this State, it is the best we could make, & the representation is calculated to give numbers & wealth their proper influence: By it the poor will be protected in their freedom, & the rich in their property, and it is attended with one great advantage that might not perhaps attend a Constitution theoretically perfect, it gives general satisfaction both to the upper & lower parts of the Country, & was ratified unanimously.[2]

The Convention before they dissolved themselves prepared & directed an address to you⟨;⟩ The Legislature which met last January did not present an address; because as the Convention was to meet in May, it was thought that an address from the Legislature could not so properly or forcibly express the Sentiments & gratitude of South Carolina as the Convention of the People.[3]

Mr Henry Middleton (the Grandson of the deceased Mr Henry Middleton who served with you in the first Congress, and the Son of the deceased Mr Arthur Middleton who you may remember in some subsequent Congresses) will have the honour of delivering you this; he is travelling through the Middle & Northern States for his improvement, and I have desired him to take charge of this letter, that he may have an opportunity of paying his respects to you as he passes through New York.[4] I have the honour to be with great gratitude & respect your much obliged & most obedt hble Sert

Charles Cotesworth Pinckney

ALS, DLC:GW.

1. On Daniel Horry, see Edward Rutledge to GW, 24 Jan. 1790.

2. On the South Carolina constitution, see GW to Charles Pinckney, 8 July 1790.

3. See GW to the People of South Carolina, c.5 July 1790.

4. Henry Middleton (1770–1846), the son of Arthur Middleton, was born in London and educated by tutors in South Carolina and England. He returned to the United States after the death of his father in 1787 and remained until the early 1790s, when he went back to England (Bailey, *Bio. Dir. of the S.C. Senate*, 2:1102–4; see also Edward Rutledge to GW, 20 June 1790).

From David Brown

Sir   New Jersey June the 20 1790

When paynful Necessity Called upon me to utter my greavances to ansure his Demands I wass not Longe Considering at whoss Feet to Lay them for som assistance from your honner I have been a Soldear in this late Contest Duering the whole ware and being Discharged at Newberrey as an Envelede unfitt for dutty in Field or Garrison from Abillity and now finding my Self not able to halp or suport myself without some assistance from your honner For I have Losst the uss of my Right arm by being a Solder lasst Frinch ware and in this Revolution Fithing for Liberty and honner of Amerrica ca[u]s[e] and, suffering a thousend hardship and Callamteys which renders me helples towards montaning my Self Therfore your humble Supplicant Shoold be verry glad of an hearing or of som Releff to Extend your Charryty to him who by Paynfull Nec⟨c⟩essity is obligde to Cr⟨av⟩e. Sir give me Leave to say I honner your Cherrecter and love your person the agreabelness of your mild temper has led me to Com and Se your honner for Relefe. this address Comes from your humble Supplicant David Brown who has been a brother Sufferer in all Lasst war and this late Revolution & that you may Long Live to promote the good of this Common Welth in wich you have so hartyly Engaidged your Self in and that you may Enjoy all the blesings that atend so noble a Case is the Ernest prayers of your humble and affectnet Suplic⟨e⟩nt

David Brown

ALS, DLC:GW.

Brown may be the David Brown of New Jersey who served as a first lieutenant in Spencer's Additional Continental Regiment from 7 Mar. 1777 until his resignation in November of that year.

From Charles Mortimer

Honble Sr   Fredericksburg [Va.] June 20th 1790

When the news of Your Recovery reached this place, it filled us with the greatest joy, and no friend of yours participated more on the occasion than myself, who most ardently prays for a continn⟨uence⟩ of a Life so usefull and necessary for us all.

If the subject of this Address is any wise presumptuous, or inconsistent with your Dignity, I beseech you to forgive me, and only consider the Motive which I will relate in a few words.

I Labored hard for many Years before the war with an unblemished Character, acquired money, lent it out to Gentn *as I thought* in Distress, the greatest part of which was repaid in Depreciated paper in *1780*, I went to Ireland before the war in the begining of *1779*, to sue for my property there, sold from me by an Unfortunate Elder Brother, who had a very considerable paternal Estate, the Loss of time Expenses ⟨&c. &c. &c.⟩ came to more than I Could recover, those matters put it out of my power to have my only son John Educated and brought up to a profession, Therefore bound him to a Merchant in Philada in *1784* where he served his time with good Character and Respect as well as Esteem, as his Moralls and disposition are good.

I have it not in my power to Raise any Capital for him to begin without selling houses and a Bit of Land at under value and injure my family, as I am now unable by gout and Rheumatism often, to labor as formerly.

If it was in your power by any Recommendation of him to any office in this state appointed by Congress or Elswhere as he is a good accountant and a sober young man, who can give the best Security for his Conduct, you would Render me and him very happy, for it grieves me to have him Idle here.[1]

I have not the honor of being acquainted with any gentn in Power or Interest to apply for him, but yourself therefore I pray you forgive the trouble given by your most Sincere and Respectfull Hble Servant

Chs Mortimer

My best wishes attend your Lady and family.

ALS, DLC:GW.

Charles Mortimer, a Fredericksburg doctor, served in the army hospital in Fredericksburg during the Revolution and later attended Mary Ball Washington in her final illness (see Betty Washington Lewis to GW, 11 Oct. 1789; see also Blanton, *Medicine in Virginia*, 358–59). Mortimer served as mayor of Fredericksburg in 1782–83, 1786–87, and 1788–89 (Quinn, *History of Fredericksburg*, 336).

1. John Mortimer did not receive an appointment from GW.

From the National Assembly of France

Paris 20 June 1790.

The national assembly has worn during three days mourning for Benjamin Franklin, your fellow-citizen, your friend, and one of the most useful of your Co-operators in the establishment of american liberty—they charge me to communicate their resolution to the Congress of the United States—in consequence, I have the honor to address to you Mr President the extract from the proceedings of their session of the 11th which contains that deliberation.[1]

The national assembly have not been stopped in their decree by the consideration that Franklin was a Stranger—great men are the Fathers of universal humanity—their loss ought to be felt as a common misfortune by all the Tribes of the great human family, and it belongs without doubt to a nation still affected by all the sentiments which accompany the atchievement of their liberty, and which owes its enfranchisement essentially to the progress of the public reason, to be the first to give the example of the filial gratitude of the people Towards their true Benefactors Besides that these ideas and this example are so proper to disseminate a happy emulation of patriotism, and thus to extend more and more the empire of reason and virtue, which could not fail promptly to determine a Body devoted to the most important legislative combinations—charged with assuring to the french the rights of men and citizens—it has believed without doubt that fruitful and great truths—were likewise numbered among the rights of man.

The name of Benjamin Franklin will be immortal in the records of freedom and philosophy—but it is more particularly dear to a country, where, conducted by the most sublime mission, this venerable man, knew very soon to acquire an infinite number of friends and admirers, as well by the simplicity and sweetness of his manners, as by the purity of his principles, the extent of his knowledge, and the charms of his mind—It will be remembered that every success which he obtained in his important negociation, were applauded and celebrated (so to express it) all over France, as so many crowns conferred on genius and virtue—Even then the sentiment of our rights existed in the bottom of our souls—it was easily perceived that it feelingly mingled in the interest which we took in behalf of america, and in the public vows which we preferred for your liberty. At last the hour of the french has arrived—we love to think that the citizens of the United States have not regarded with indifference our first steps towards Liberty—Twenty six millions of men breaking their chains, and seriously occupied in giving themselves a durable constitution are not unworthy the esteem of a generous people who have preceded them in that noble career. we hope they will learn, with interest, the funeral homage which we have rendered to the nestor of America—may this solemn act of fraternal friendship serve more and more to bind the tie which ought to unite two free nations—may the common enjoyment of liberty shed itself over the whole globe, and become an indissoluble chain of connexion among all the people of the earth—For, ought they not to perceive that they will march more steadfastly, and more certainly to their true happiness in understanding and loving each other, than in being jealous, and fighting—may the Congress of the United States and the national assembly of France be the first to furnish this fine spectacle to the world—and may the individuals of the two nations connect themselves by a mutual affection worthy of the friendship which unites the two men at this day the most illustrious by th⟨eir⟩ exertions for liberty, Washington and la Fayett⟨e⟩.

Permit me, Mr President Sir, to offer on this occasion my particular homage of esteem and admiration. I have the honor to be with respectful consideration Mr President, Your most humble and most obedient Servant[2]

Sieyes President

Translation, DNA: RG 59, Miscellaneous Letters; LS, DNA: RG 59, Communications from Heads of Foreign States, Ceremonial Letters; DNA: RG 46, First Congress, 1789–91, Records of Legislative Proceedings, President's Messages. The text has been taken from a translation made for GW. The original French text may be found on CD-ROM:GW.

1. Benjamin Franklin died on 17 April 1790. The decree, 11 June 1790, concerning mourning for Franklin reads: "The National Assembly decree that their Members shall wear during three days, mourning for Benjamin Franklin, to commence on monday next—that the discourse pronounced on this occasion be printed, and that the President write to the American Congress in the name of the National Assembly" (DNA: RG 46, First Congress, 1789–91, Records of Legislative Proceedings, President's Messages).

2. Washington transmitted the letter from the National Assembly to Congress in January 1791. See GW to the U.S. Senate and House of Representatives, 26 Jan. 1791. For his reply to the French National Assembly, see his letter of 27 Jan. 1791 to that body.

From Edward Rutledge

My dear Sir   Charleston [S.C.] June 20th 1790

The Gentleman who will do himself The Honor of delivering you this Letter, is the Son of my deceased Friend Mr Arthur Middleton, whom you once knew; & who passed his political, as well as his Social Life, without Dishonor, and without Reproach—As his son is about to make the Tour of America, & thro' choice, as well as Duty, will pay his Respects to you, I have taken the Liberty of being his introducer.[1] The Account⟨s⟩ of your severe Indisposition my dear Sir, filled the Hearts of your Friends, with much Anxiety and real Concern;[2] but my Letter of the 25th of May, has in some Measure dispelled the Clouds, tho' our apprehensions are not as yet altogether removed. You will give me leave to assure you what I trust you full well know, that there are few Men who feel more concern at every ill which befalls you, or more Joy, at every Comfort & Honor which affords you, than my dear Sir your very affectionate Friend & devoted Humble Servant

Ed: Rutledge

ALS, DLC:GW.

1. On Henry Middleton, see Charles Cotesworth Pinckney to GW, 19 June 1790.

2. For GW's illness, see William Jackson to Clement Biddle, 12 May 1790, editorial note.

From Jonathan Dayton

Sir,   Elizabeth Town [N.J.] June 21st 1790

I have been informed that the bill for funding the Continental debt which has passed the House of Representatives and is at present under consideration & discussion in the Senate, provides for the appointment of a Commissioner in each state to aid in carrying the system into execution. I take the liberty, sir, of addressing you upon the subject, and of offering myself as a candidate for that appointment in the state of New Jersey.

I have not sought for, nor transmitted, the testimonials of others in my behalf in order to support my application, altho I flatter myself they might have been obtained as fully and extensively as I could have wished. Having had the honor of being personally known to you in the course of the late war, as well as since the establishment of peace and being intimately acquainted with many of the Members of the present Congress with whom I had the pleasure of serving for the two last years under the confederation, I had thought it not necessary to trouble you with recommendatory letters from particular persons. Lest I should intrude too much upon your more important concerns, I shall conclude with adding, that if I should be thought to merit, and should by you be honored with, the appointment in question, I shall zealously endeavour so to discharge the duties which accompany it as to entitle me to your approbation & consequently to that of my country. I have the honor to be sir with the highest respect & regard your most obedt hum. servant

Jona: Dayton

ALS, DLC:GW; ADf, NjR: Jonathan Dayton Papers.

Jonathan Dayton (1760–1824) was born in Elizabethtown, N.J., and graduated from the College of New Jersey in 1776. He served with his father, Elias Dayton, through the Revolution and was a captain at Yorktown. After the war he was admitted to the bar, was a member of the New Jersey legislature, and represented that state at the Federal Convention. He was elected to the House of Representatives in 1788 but declined to serve. In 1789 he was a member of the state council and the next year a member of the assembly. He subsequently served in the House of Representatives and was a prominent Federalist. Dayton did not receive the appointment as a commissioner of loans for New Jersey (for the appointments, see GW to the U.S. Senate, 6 Aug. 1790).

From Alexander Hamilton

Treasury Department [New York] June 21st 1790.

The Secretary of the Treasury has the honor respectfully to submit to the President of the United states, for his approbation, the enclosed contract for timber, boards, Nails and workmanship, for a Beacon to be placed near the Light-house on Sandy-hook; the terms of which, he begs leave to observe, are, in his opinion favourable to the U. States.[1]

LB, DLC:GW.

1. The enclosed contract has not been found. The beacon on Sandy Hook was apparently destroyed in the storm that struck New York City on 25–26 Nov. 1789, causing considerable damage to shipping (*New York Journal,* 3 Dec. 1789; see also Thomas Randall and William Heyer to Alexander Hamilton, 1 Dec. 1789, Syrett, *Hamilton Papers,* 6:2). Hamilton reported the loss of the beacon and the need to replace it in January (see Hamilton to GW, 3 Jan. 1790). Tobias Lear replied on 21 June that GW "directs me to inform you, that he approves of the enclosed contract" (Lear to Hamilton, 21 June 17[90], DLC:GW; Lear erroneously dated this letter 21 June 1789).

From John Eager Howard

Sir   Annapolis [Md.] June 21st 1790

I had the honor to receive your Excellencys letter of the 25th march with a medal ordered to be struck by the late Congress. my only object in the late war was to render any service in my power in the common cause, and my only hope of reward was that my conduct might meet the approbation of my Country; the obliging manner in which you are pleased to communicate this mark of approbation which my Country has expressed of my conduct, affords me the highest satisfaction.

It gives me great pleasure to be informed that you have recovered from your late indisposition, and I indulge the fond hope that your complaints are intirely removed.[1]

Capt. Robert Denny, Auditor General in this State, informs me that he intends making application for the appointment of commissioner of Loans in this State, under the funding system proposed by Congress.[2] If your Excellency should think proper to nominate him for that appointment, I have the highest confidence that he will discharge the duties in the most exact & satisfactory manner, and with the strictest integrity. He is well known to the Gentlemen from this State and I make no doubt they all will give the most satisfactory recommendations in his favour. I have the Honor to be with the highest respect Your · Excellencys Most Obedt Humb⟨le⟩ Servt

J.E. Howard

ALS, DLC:GW.

1. On GW's illness, see William Jackson to Clement Biddle, 12 May 1790, editorial note.

2. Robert Denny (c.1748–1812) served as an officer of Maryland troops from 1778 to the end of the war. He was appointed deputy auditor of Maryland in June 1789 and auditor general in December 1789 (*Md. Archives*, 72:35, 70; *Maryland Gazette* [Baltimore], 29 Oct. 1812). Denny did not receive the appointment as commissioner of loans for Maryland, which went to Joseph Harwood (see GW to the U.S. Senate, 6 Aug. 1790).

To Michael Jenifer Stone

June 21st 1790

The President of the United States requests the pleasure of Mr Stone's company to dinner on Thurs-day next at *4 Oclock*. An answer is requested.[1]

D, DLC: Stone Papers (Maryland), vol. 1730–1863.

1. No reply from Stone has been found. GW recorded in his diary on Thursday, 24 June, that he entertained Stone, along with several other members of the House of Representatives (*Diaries*, 6:77).

Letter not found: From Jonathan Dayton, 22 June 1790. Letter listed in *American Clipper*, January 1943.

From Patrick Dennis

New York June 22d 1790

In order to remove any Objections, to the subscribers Acct of Compe⟨n⟩sation for services renderd during the late War, and for which he has recived any reward, for Services principally undertaken, by the particular Instructions of the Commander in Chief—he hereby humbly begs leave to state some circumstances, which may probably occur to the President—praying that he may be pleased to give a Sanction, to such as may to his Excellency, to have been under his direction—which may enable to the settlment of his Acct by the Auditor of the Treasury.

In the begining of 1776 by a Resolve of Congress was engaged one of the Commps. for building two Frigates in this State.

Being thus in public Service, General Mifflin requested me to fitt out armed Vessels, purcure metearals for fire Ships &c. &c.

The Commander in Chief was pleased, to call on me in Counsal with his Genl Officers, at the same time requested me, to take a survey of the North river Channel, near Fort Washington, with an Acct of the ships in the harbour and make a return thereof, soon after the Commander, in Chief sent for me and gave Positive Orders, that I shol'd take charge of all the Vessels &c. ⟨prepard⟩, and sink them, in order to stop the progress of the enemys Shi⟨pping⟩, going up the North river.

This duty took me from home at a very emportant time as to my privet intrist which fell a Sacerefice, to the enemy.

In 1777 the Commander in Chief directed, my attendence ask'd many questions as to the Coast, and Navigation, desired to know if any persons with us was acquainted—And concluded that he should expect that I w⟨o⟩ld Invarably be at home, hold myself in rediness to his call—in consequence of which order, I could not feel my self at Liberty to attend or engage, in any Buisness but considering myself under the Immediate Command of his Excellency, with a horse kept for the sole purpose waited, for and executed whatever Orders were by him directed to me through the course of the War.

The duty that engaged my greatest attention and most expence was that of securing two pilots, in New York, four times was I at black point, and at Elizabeth town point a grate number of times, expecting to have had an enterveu (on Nightes appointed) but did not succeed.

Made my report to the Commander in Chief, who was pleas'd to tell me he had this buisness much at Heart, and wish'd to have it accomplis'd I then went within the Enemys lines, on Staten Island, where I effected this buisness—All of which caused my unremitted attention, and attendance ever necessary, as the Signals I was to give ware confind to myself. The whole of which he most humbly submits to his Excellency.

AL, DNA: RG 59, Miscellaneous Letters.

Patrick Dennis (died c.1798) served as a merchant ship captain before the Revolution. During the war he was an officer in the independent artillery company formed by the Marine Society and a ship captain in the state service (Clark, *Naval Documents*, 1:822). In 1776 GW employed him to obstruct the Hudson and East rivers (see Council of War, 8 July 1776, in *Papers, Revolutionary War Series*, 5:238–39), and in 1778 he served as pilot for the French fleet under d'Estaing (see Alexander Hamilton to Patrick Dennis, [16 July 1778], Syrett, *Hamilton Papers*, 1:524–25) and apparently obtained other pilots to assist the French. In 1782 he petitioned Congress, seemingly without success, for compensation for securing these pilots (*JCC*, 22:95–96). He was deputy naval officer for eastern New Jersey from about 1786 to 1789. In October 1790 GW appointed him to command of the New York revenue cutter *Vigilant* (Alexander Hamilton to GW, 28 Oct. 1790). No resolution to his claim for compensation for obtaining pilots during the war has been found.

From Wakelin Welch & Son

Sir   London 22d June 1790

Inclosed is copy of the last which we took the Honor of forwarding to your Excellency by the New York Packet.[1]

Since which Mr Morris drew on us for £91. which is all he says that he may want The Balance remaining of £4.16 we suppose will be sufficient to repay Mr Young for any charge he might have been at in sending the Books. We most Respectfully are Your Excellency's Much Hond and Obliged Servts

Wak. Welch & son

LS, DLC:GW.

1. Welch is referring to the letter to GW from the firm of 1 June 1790. The duplicate has not been found.

Tobias Lear to Thomas Jefferson

Wednesday June 23d 1790

By the command of the President of the United States T. Lear has the honor to enclose for Mr Jefferson perusal a Letter from the Count de Estaing to the President which was alluded to by Mr Short in the letter which Mr Jefferson laid before the president at the time when he delivered the above letter from the Ct de Estaing.[1] Likewise two letters a Memorial & a treatise upon establishing a uniformity of Weights & Measures throughout the U.S.—which were written & tran[s]mitted to the President by M. Collignon.[2]

ADf, DNA: RG 59, Miscellaneous Letters; LB, DLC:GW; copy, DNA: RG 59, GW Correspondence with Secretaries of State.

1. See d'Estaing to GW, 20 Mar. 1790. This letter was enclosed in William Short to Acting Secretary of State John Jay (Boyd, *Jefferson Papers,* 16:301–5).

2. For this letter and its enclosures, see Claude-Boniface Collignon to GW, 15 Mar. 1790, and notes. In response to the suggestion made by GW in his annual address to Congress on 8 Jan. that "Uniformity in the Currency, Weights and Measures of the United States, is an object of great importance, and will, I am persuaded, be duly attended to," the House of Representatives on 15 Jan. ordered that the secretary of state should prepare a report dealing with the subject (GW to the U.S. Senate and House of Representatives, 8 Jan. 1790; *DHFC,* 3:264, 265). On his appointment as secretary of state, Jefferson took up the matter and was currently engaged in drafting the report that was

presented to the House on 13 July 1790 (Boyd, *Jefferson Papers*, 16:602–75; *DHFC*, 3:509–10).

To the United States Senate

United States [New York]
Gentlemen of the Senate,   June 23d 1790

In my nomination of persons for Consular appointments on the 4th of the present month, the name of *James* instead of Joseph Fenwick was by mistake laid before you to be Consul for the port of Bourdeaux.[1]

G. Washington

LB, DLC:GW.
1. See GW to the U.S. Senate, 4 June 1790.

From Daniel Jenifer Adams

Sir   Delaware State Wilmington June 25th 1790

With very great diffidence, I beg leave to address your Excellency, on a subject to which I am moved, more from necessity, than either from real inclination, or ambition.

Your Excellency I presume, is not unacquainted, that after near five years perilous & hard Service under your Command (in which I hope I merited your good opinion, in the station I held) I was one of those unfortunate Officers, that laid down my Commission, more for the want of Money to support my rank in the Army, than any other cause; tho' the reasons I assigned to your Excellency, in my resignation, I thought cogent, and perhaps wou'd have acted forcibly with most officers of the Army; yet, the Strong attachment I had to my Country's cause, and the reluctance with which I left its Service, were such strong incentives, that the latter might have been got over, if I had seen a prospect of future support of the former. By a resolution of Congress, which took place about the time of my resignation, excluding officers, who resigned previous to such a date, from any future emoluments arising on their Commissions, which were the only compensations (of any consequence) they were entitled to, for their Services; I was One of those who suffered by this resolution, and I can very safely say, that all the Money I ever rec'd for my Services, was not sufficient to pay my pocket expences whilst I was in the Army.

After ten years close application to business, in which I have been but unfortunate, I have acquired some little property, tho' very inadequate to the support of a large & rising family of Children—I am now advanced to the middle stage of life, with a shattered Constitution, owing to the ⟨*illegible*⟩ & colds, I underwent whilst I was in the Army, which renders me inc⟨a⟩pable of the more rugged, and fatigueing scenes of life, for the better support of my family.

Under a serious impression, of these circumstances, permit me sir, to solicit your Excellency's patronage, and fav'or, to the appointment of such office under the Federal Government, as your Excellency may think suitable to my capacity, and situation—and as it is probable, that a Law will shortly take place in Congress, for Settling the Accompts of the United States, with the individual States, and Commissionors, be appointed for that purpose; shoud your Excellency be pleased to fav'or me, with one of those appointments, I flatter myself, my attention, and fidelity to the trust, will make compensation for the hon'or and fav'or done me, and shou'd it be necessary, I trust, I can come before your Excellency, with such letters of recom⟨me⟩ndation, as will prove satisfactory. With every sence of respect & duty, I have the hon'or to be, Your Excellency's Most Obt & very Hum: Servt

Danl J. Adams

ALS, DLC:GW.

Daniel Jenifer Adams (1751–1796) was born in Port Tobacco, Md., and served as an officer of Maryland troops from January 1776, rising to the rank of major before resigning on 8 June 1779 (Heitman, *Historical Register,* 58). After the war he moved to Delaware, where he served as a militia officer and sheriff of New Castle County (*Delaware Archives,* 1009). He received no appointment from GW. For GW's earlier dealings with Adams, see *Diaries,* 3:120, 240–41, 304.

To John Cannon

Sir,   New-York, June 25th 1790.

Your letter of the 2. instant has reached my hands and in consequence thereof I have applied to Mr Scott for fifty pounds as you desired, who informs me that he did not expect a draught to exceed £15. or £20. and therefore had not made his arrangements for 50. however he says he will pay it if he can make it convenient.[1]

As the rents of my lands under your care were to be paid in wheat, and the demand for, and high price of that article having been very extraordinary the year past, I did not conceive there could have been any difficulty in making payments or in obtaining cash and a good price for the wheat after it was deposited in your hands, for I presume the payment is not commuted from wheat to cash at the customary price, when it would fetch more than double what it does in common years;[2] This would be hardly doing justice to the Landlord, and I always wish for his, and the tenants' interest to be reciprocal.

By a letter which I received from you before I left Mount Vernon,[3] if I recollect the substance of it, the Tenants then upon my lands were to furnish a certain number of rails besides a stipulated quantity of wheat for their rent—and, from that circumstance I thought there might be but little deduction in future on that account—however, I find by your last letter that you expect a considerable portion of the rents will be deducted on that account for the present year—I should wish to have the matter of fences, repairs &ca finished and done away that I might know what net proceeds to calculate upon, which can never be done so long as these annual and uncertain deductions are to be made. I am Sir, with great regard, your most obedient servant

G. Washington

LB, DLC:GW.

1. No letter from Cannon to GW of 2 June 1790 has been found. The "Mr Scott" referred to was probably Thomas Scott, a member of the House of Representatives from western Pennsylvania and the brother of James Scott, a tenant on GW's tract on Millers Run in Washington County, Pennsylvania. GW had employed Cannon as land agent for his Millers Run and Washington's Bottom tracts since 1786 (see GW to John Cannon, 26 Dec. 1788, source note). For a summary of the long history of GW's land investments in Washington County, see Brice McGeehon to GW, 18 Oct. 1788, source note.

2. It has been estimated that the wholesale price of grain in the Philadelphia market, which had been depressed since the end of the war, rose 31.9 percent between 1789 and 1790 (Bezanson, *Wholesale Prices in Philadelphia,* 1:424).

3. No letter from Cannon to GW describing the rents to be received from tenants on Washington's western Pennsylvania lands has been found. GW had written to Cannon requesting this information on 15 Sept. 1788: "As I have

not received a line from you for more than fifteen months, and am altogether in the dark respecting the business which was committed to your care, I would thank you for information respecting the tenements, the Rents &ca of my Lands in Fayette and Washington Counties. And, as the latter, that is the Rents, may have been received in spicific articles I should be glad to know they are disposed off" (LB, DLC:GW). Not receiving a prompt reply, GW wrote again on 26 Dec. 1788 enclosing a duplicate of his September letter (see GW to Cannon, 26 Dec. 1788). Apparently Cannon had made an agreement with the tenants to receive rents in wheat at his mill, with allowances to be made for fence repairs and perhaps for other maintenance and improvement of the property.

To George Clendenin

Sir,   New York, June 25th 1790.

I have upon the great Kanawa and Ohio river, between the two Kanawas several large and valuable tracts of land, which I have been long endeavoring to settle, but without effect. Some three or four years ago I wrote to Colonel Thomas Lewis, who lives in that neighbourhood, requesting his assistance or agency in this business, transmitting to him at the same time instructions expressive of my wishes as to the mode or terms of settlement together with such other papers respecting the lands as were necessary for his information[.]

After a considerable lapse of time Colonel Lewis returned the instructions and papers declining any agency in the business, lest he should not be able to transact it to my satisfaction, as he had lands of his own to settle in that neighbourhood, which might cause a clashing or interfering of interests that would be disagreeable or inconvenient to him. I however returned the same papers to him requesting that he would accept the trust, and at the same time put the matter upon such a footing as I conceived would do away the objections which he had stated.

It is now almost two years since the papers were last deposited in Colonel Lewis's hands, and I have not heard a syllable from him upon the subject, which leads me to believe that he still wishes to decline the trust.[1]

It is therefore necessary for me to place this business in other hands, and your residence in that vicinity with the knowledge which you must have of the Country and the very favorable representations I have received of your character have induced me to request, Sir, that you would assist me in the settlement of these lands, which, if you incline to do, I have requested Colonel Lewis (in the enclosed letter, left open for your perusal, and which, if you accept the trust, you will please to seal and forward to him) to deliver into your hands or to your order, the instructions and other papers respecting my lands which he received from me—These will shew you my *general* ideas on this subject, and give you better information respecting it than I am able to do here, as all my land papers &ca are at Mount Vernon.[2]

I must however add that altho' I may, in my instructions to Colonel Lewis, have mentioned some particular terms upon which I wished to have the lands rented, yet in my letters to him, if my recollection serves me, I desired him to be governed by the custom of the country in this business rather than by my instructions, and to get them settled on the best terms he could, provided the leases were not given for too long a period, and the taxes were paid by the Tenant—This I would repeat to you for my great object at present is to have the lands settled, and be exonerated from the Taxes[.]

I do not expect they will yield me an immediate profit—I would not however wish to have the lands incumbered with long leases—for it is my opinion that property in that country will fast increase in value, and, in that case, long leases upon the terms which they will probably be given to first settlers will be much against the landlord—and they are always considered as an obstacle to the sale of lands.

I will thank you, Sir, for an answer to this letter as soon as it gets to your hands, that I may know upon what ground I stand as to my property in that country. I am Sir, with great esteem, Your most obedient Servant

G. Washington

LB, DLC:GW.

1. For GW's efforts to persuade Lewis to act as his agent, see GW to Thomas Lewis, 25 June 1790, n.1. On Clendenin, see GW to Thomas Lewis, 2 Oct. 1788, n.1.

2. GW had considered using Clendenin as his agent in the area at least as early as November 1788 (see GW to David Stuart, 10 Nov. 1788). Clendenin wrote to GW on 1 Dec. 1790 accepting the agency. See GW to Clendenin, 21 Feb. 1791.

To Thomas Lewis

Sir,   New York, June 25th 1790.

When I returned to your hands the instructions and papers respecting my lands in your neighbourhood, I thought I had sufficiently obviated the reasons which first induced you to decline any agency in that business, by putting it on a footing which might render it perfectly compatible with your own interest and convenience, and I was in a measure confirmed in the opinion that you had accepted the trust, and would comply with my wishes by your not having again returned the papers to me.[1] But near two years have elapsed since that time, and I have not received a line from you, nor heard a syllable respecting the matter. This leads me to believe that it is not convenient for you to serve me in this business—and, as it is necessary for my interest that some person in that country should superintend my lands there, and promote the settlement of them in some way or another I have requested Colonel George Clandenen of Kanawa-county to undertake it, and, if he inclines to do it, he will call upon you for the instructions and papers, which are in your hands, respecting this business, and which I request may be delivered to him or to his order.[2] I am Sir, your most obedient Servant

G. Washington

LB, DLC:GW.

1. GW had asked Lewis to serve as his agent for procuring tenants for his Ohio and Kanawha lands on 25 Dec. 1787 (for a description of the extent of these lands, see GW to Nicholas Dubey, 27 Sept. 1788, n.4). Lewis replied on 27 Aug. 1788 that he was reluctant to act as GW's agent because he was having difficulty obtaining tenants for his own land and returned the papers GW had sent to him. GW responded on 1 Dec. 1788 that he understood Lewis's reservations but that they would "operate, with equal force, upon any other person" he might entrust with the task, and that he did not expect Lewis to "procure tenants for my land in preference to your own." In this letter GW enclosed "my former terms and the plats of the Land." Since Lewis did not return the papers a second time, GW apparently believed he had accepted the agency.

2. See GW to George Clendenin, 25 June 1790.

From "a Sailor"

Sir   George Town [Md.] 25th June 1790.

Of all the different classes of People in this Country Our New Constitution and subsequent laws has provided for the encouragement of all but Sailors, why those people Should be Neglected I cannot Conceive, they certainly are Necessary to every commercial Country, and ought to meet the Patronage of the Government, Our Harbours are crouded with foreign Ships, to carry our produce to Market, and our own Ships are commanded by foreigners there is more than two thirds of the commanders of Ships from this Country foreigners, some of Whom even refuse to do what is Necessary for their being allowed to clear out their Ships themselves, but are under the Necessity of telling their Mates do it for them, this I conceive to be a most Scandalous imposition on Americans and Worthy the Attention of your Excellency, it is well known by all Americans that were they by any Accident to be turned or left on shore in England they would Starve before they could obtain a Birth before the Mast in any British Ship (altho equal in point of Seamanship to any Sailors,) While those people take the bread out of our Mouths, and the⟨n⟩ execrate the Country Which has afforded them an asylum and given them that encouragement they neither need or deserve in their own Country.

I Wish also to observe to your Excellency that I commanded a Ship of 227 Tons Burthen Which for one Voyage to london paid th⟨e⟩ enormous sum of £40 sterling for lights altho ⟨*illegible*⟩ saw more than two, We have no Tax on British Ships equal to this, By a British Act of Parliament an American Ship is not entitled to an entry in any port in Great Britain unless her Command & ⅔ of her Crew are Americans, this Act I conceive ought to have been passed by our legislature, it is evident the British meant to cramp our trade by it, tho if Such a law Was Strictly enforced it would be attended With immense advantages to American Navigators, Who are now Starveing for Want of Bread While those people Who a few years back would have cut our throats are laughing at our credulity, I am pretty certain two thirds of our produce are Shipped from the Southern States in British Bottoms While our Ships always return from England empty and meet with difficulty to procure a frieght even in this Country, People Who are bread to the sea must look to the sea alone for Support, they are incapable of any thing else, and I venture to pronounce no other profession on earth is attend with half the danger and labour as one Who gets his Bread by that profession[.] I humbly request your Excellency to recommend it to Congress to do something in our behalf, hopeing for Your Excellency's pardon for my Presumption I remain Yr Excellencys devoted Servant

a sailor

L, DNA: RG 59, Miscellaneous Letters.

"A sailor" may have been prompted to write by the progress of the Merchant Seamen Act through Congress. Legislation regulating the merchant marine had been presented in the House of Representatives by Thomas Fitzsimons on 3 May 1790 and had been reported out of committee on 17 June, but the House had declined debate on the bill at that time. The act was ultimately passed and signed into law by GW on 20 July (*DHFC*, 5:1261–73) but provided no relief from British discrimination for American seamen.

To David Stuart

Dear Sir   New York June 25th 1790

According to promise, you ought to have received the enclosed at an earlier period; but no inconvenience, I apprehend, will arise from my omitting to do it before now.[1] Our best wishes attend you all and I am—Dear Sir Your Affecte Hble Servt

Go: Washington

ALS, ViHi.

1. The enclosures were probably documents related to the suit brought by Robert Alexander against the estate of John Parke Custis that Stuart had sent to GW in his letter of 2 April 1790 (see Stuart to GW, 2 April 1790). In his reply to Stuart of 11 April 1790, GW wrote that "As this letter will have to travel to Williamsburgh, I shall take another opportunity to forward such original papers as you have transmitted to me" (see GW to Stuart, 11 April 1790).

From Theodore Foster

Sir,   New York June 26th 1790

I have the Honor to inform your Excellency that on the Twelfth Day of the present Month, I was appointed by the Legislature of the State of Rhode Island and Providence Plantations One of the Senators to represent that State, in the National Government. That on the Evening before last I arrived in this City and yesterday had the Honor of being admitted and sworn as a Member of the Senate of the United States.[1]

Be pleased, Sir, to permit Me on the present Occasion to assure you of my most sincere Disposition to promote your personal Honor and private Happiness and to establish the Credit Glory and Prosperity of the Nation at large over which you preside. Your Excellency will ever find Me anxious to render you all the Aid and Support due to the Chief Magistrate in the Administration of the National Government.

Accept my most Sincere Thanks for your Goodness in my Appointment to the Naval office in the District of Providence.[2] At the Time I took the Liberty to write to Your Excellency respecting that office I had no Expectation of the Senatorial Trust I now hold. I undertook the latter not knowing that the former would be confided to Me. As they are incompatible if it would not be deemed presumptuous I would beg leave to request that the Honble Ebenezer Thompson Esqr. of Providence may be appointed to that office. I will pledge myself for his Abilities, his Integrity and for his Fidelity in the Discharge of the Duties of the Office, and I am well assured that his Appointment will give more general Satisfaction to all Parties in the State than that of any other Person.[3]

The Providence Association of Mechanics and Manufacturers consisting of about Two Hundred of the Reputable Citizens of that Town have honored Me with the Care of an Address to your Excellency from their Corporation, a Copy of which I herewith inclose. If it be agreeable to your Excellency to receive it I will do myself the Honor to present it, at such Time as you will be pleased to appoint.[4]

The Honorable Joseph Stanton Esqr. is my Colleague in the Senatorial Representation of Rhode Island. He has Communications which he wishes to make. If your Excellency will be pleased to admit us to an Interview we will wait on you to make our personal Respects, and gratefully acknowledge the Honor done us.[5] I have the Honor to be very respectfully Your Excellency's most obedient and humble Servant.

Theodore Foster.

ALS, DNA: RG 59, Miscellaneous Letters.

1. For Theodore Foster, see Foster to GW, 18 Feb. 1790. Foster served as a Federalist in the Rhode Island Ratifying Convention and was elected to the U.S. Senate through the influence of his brother-in-law, Arthur Fenner. "Mr Foster will do all in his power to promote the Interest of the Union," Henry Sherburne wrote to Henry Knox, "with a proviso, that he does not deviate from any of the determined plans of his Brother Fenner, our present Governor, by whoes Influence he obtained his appointment. This Gentleman possesses a good heart, has genuine Federal Sentiments, a full share of sensibility, and is a man of Liberal Education" (Henry Sherburne to Henry Knox, 17 June 1790, NNGL). Foster and Joseph Stanton were elected to the Senate on 12 June and took their seats on 25 June (DenBoer, *First Federal Elections*, 4:413–35; *DHFC*, 1:371).

2. Foster's election to the Senate left vacant the post of naval officer at Providence, to which he had only recently been appointed (see GW to the U.S. Senate, 14 June 1790).

3. Foster and his Senate colleague Joseph Stanton jointly recommended Ebenezer Thompson for naval officer at Providence in a letter to GW of 29 June (see Stanton and Foster to GW, 29 June 1790). GW appointed Thompson to the post on 2 July 1790 (see GW to the U.S. Senate, 2 July 1790).

4. Foster enclosed the address of the Providence Association of Mechanics and Manufacturers, dated 4 June 1790, and signed by its president, Charles Keen: "The happy period has at length arrived when we can with propriety join our fellow-citizens of the other States, in congratulating you, as Chief Magistrate of United America. Although, the progress of this State to our present situation has been slow and timid, it is some consolation that our accession has compleated the federal-Union.

"Pleased with the establishment of a firm government we are happy in thus having it in our power to express our sentiments of regard and attachment to the President of the Union, and our determination, as far as in us lies, to support the constitution and laws of the United States.

"The mechanics and manufacturers of this Town feel a confidence in the wisdom and patriotism of the Legislature of the United States, that they will do all in their power to promote the manufactures as well as the agriculture and commerce of our Country; this confidence is greatly strengthened by the consideration that you, Sir, are at the head of it.

"In full expectation that under a mild and beneficent administration of the Government, we shall be enabled to lead quiet and peaceable lives, and enjoy the fruits of our honest industry—with grateful hearts for past favors, we join the millions of America in fervent prayers to the Disposer of all events for your health and happiness, and that your important life may long be spared to rule a free, virtuous, and happy nation" (DLC:GW).

Foster probably made a formal presentation of the address when he dined with GW on 1 July. In his undated reply, which may have been presented to Foster at that time, GW wrote: "The accession of the State of Rhode Island to the general Government, which has again completed our union, is indeed, an event that affords me singular satisfaction. For your favorable sentiments respecting myself, as well as for your determination to support the Constitution and Laws of the United States, I return my thanks.

"In full expectation that your confidence in the wisdom and patriotism of the national legislature will not be disappointed; and that they will do all in their power to promote the Manufactures, Agriculture and Commerce of this Country; I assure you, Gentlemen, I shall always heartily concur in all such judicious measures as may seem calculated to enable the good people of the United America to lead quiet and peacable lives, in the enjoyment of the fruits of their honest Industry" (GW to the Providence, R.I., Association of Mechanics and Manufacturers, c.1 July 1790, LS, RHi).

5. Joseph Stanton, Jr. (1739–1807), a farmer from Charlestown, R.I., fought in the French and Indian War and served in the Rhode Island general assembly almost continuously from 1768 to 1790. He was colonel of the Rhode Island state regiment in 1776–77. After the war he became a leader of the Rhode Island country party and was a prominent Antifederalist delegate in the ratifying convention. In 1790 he was also speaker of the general assembly. Federalist William Ellery described Stanton as "a violent paper-money man" and "an obstinate Anti to the last" (Ellery to Benjamin Huntington, 12 June 1790, R-Ar). GW entertained Stanton and Foster at dinner on 1 July (*Diaries*, 6:80).

From Alexander Hamilton

Treasury Department [New York] June 26th 1790
The Secretary of the Treasury has the honor respectfully to inform the President of the United states, that he has received a letter from the Collector of Charleston in South Carolina, from which he learns that some misconception has arisen as to the nature of the qualifications of Mr Thomas Hollingsby, who on the joint recommendation of the Collector & commissioners of Pilotage for that port was appointed Superintendant of the Light-house. These Gentlemen appear to feel much concern, that they shou'd have so expressed themselves, as to promote his appointment to that Duty, and the Collector from his anxiety on the subject has ventur'd to detain the letters directed for Mr Hollingsby 'till the pleasure of the president, after this information, shou'd be Known—Under these circumstances, the Secretary respectfully submits to the President an opinion, that the public interests will be promoted by the appointment of another person as superintendant, who may employ Mr Hollingsby in the station of Keeper, for which the Collector and Commissioners intended to recommend him—He takes the liberty further to add, that Edward Blake Esqr. has been strongly recom-

mended as a suitable person by the Honorable Mr Tucker of the south Carolina Delegation, which is confirmed by the Collector of Charleston.[1]

Alexander Hamilton
Secy of the Treasury

LB, DLC:GW.

1. In his letter to GW of 3 Jan. 1790 regarding appointments in the lighthouse service, Hamilton recommended Thomas Hollingsby, then in charge of the lighthouse, buoys, and beacons in Charleston, as having been "recommended by the Commissioners of Pilotage" of Charleston "as a person perfectly qualified for the business" (Hamilton to GW, 3 Jan. 1790). Hamilton further advised that the conduct of lighthouse superintendent for Charleston be put under the general direction of the collector for that port, George Abbott Hall. Apparently Hall wrote in a letter to Hamilton, not found by the editors of the *Hamilton Papers,* that Hollingsby was unsuited to some of the responsibilities of the office (see Hamilton to GW, 26 June 1790, in Syrett, *Hamilton Papers,* 6:473–74, n.1). Lear replied on 29 June 1790 that "The President of the U. States . . . assents to the removal of Mr Thomas Hollingsby for the office of Superintendant of the Light house of Charleston in south carolina and to the appointment of Edward Blake Esqr. to that place, for the reasons communicated to him by the Secretary of the Treasury on the 26th inst:" (Lear to Hamilton, 29 June 1790, DLC:GW). Edward Blake (d. 1795), a Charleston merchant, served as commissioner of the pilotage in Charleston in 1788–89 and in the South Carolina general assembly in 1779–80, 1782, and 1787–90. In 1788 he was a Federalist delegate to the South Carolina convention that ratified the federal Constitution (*Bio. Dir. of the S.C. House of Representatives,* 3:70–72).

From Alexander Hamilton

Treasury Department [New York] June 26th 1790

The Secretary of the Treasury has the honor respectfully to inform the President of the United states that the collector of Charleston in south Carolina has stated to him, that a proposal has been made by James Robinson of Newport, Rhode Island, to the collector, through the commissioners of Pilotage of that Port, to supply six hundred gallons of spermaceti Oil, for the use of the Light house, at two shillings & six pence, Rhode Island Money, ℔ gallon.

The contract, which appears to the Secretary favourable to the United states, awaits the determination of the President.[1]

Alexander Hamilton
Secy of the Treasury

LB, DLC:GW.

1. Lear replied in his letter of 29 June that "The President of the United states approves of the proposal communicated to him on the 26th Inst: by the Secretary of the Treasury, made by James Robinson to the Collector of Charleston in South Carolina, to supply six hundred Gallons of spermaceti Oil for the use of the Light house at 2/6 per gallon" (Lear to Hamilton, 29 June 1790, DLC:GW).

From William Pike

Sir   Newbury port [Mass.] 26th June 1790

My friends in Congress have been so good as to inform me that the Excise Act will probably pass very soon. Mr Gerry has been so obliging as to write me that he would nominate me to you sir for the appointment of a Collr of Excise for the port of Newbury Port, and such part of Essex County as you may be pleased to annex to it—this State did several Years past divide the County for the purpose of Collecting the Excise, the particular towns annex'd to the Eastern district I take the freedom to enclose. should you be pleased to assign me this district or a less one, or only Newbury port I shall retain a greatfull remembrance of it. for my Abilities to execute the trust I must refer to my friends Mr Gerry, King and Dalton. my connections and nearest friends have all been among the early patriots in the late glorious revolution and they have in general contributed largely & suffer'd much in the cause. with the greatest Respect I have the honour to be sir your most obedt Servt

Willm Pike

ALS, DLC:GW.

William Pike (d. 1794) of Newburyport also sought an appointment from Henry Knox, without success (see Pike to Knox, 24 Aug. 1789, NNGL). He received no appointment from GW.

From Daniel Tillinghast

Sir   Providence, Rhode Island, June 26th 1790

It having been suggested to the Officers and Members composing the United Company of the Train of Artillery in the Town of Providence, which I have the Honor to direct, that some Proceedings had originated in the Department of War, which tended to affect their Charter of Incorporation, I have taken the Liberty to solicit the Interposition of your Excellency in their Behalf.

It may not be improper to intimate to your Excellency the ancient Constitution of this Independent Company, which recieved its Charter of Incorporation from the General Assembly of this State, at so early a period as the Year 1774. During the considerable Interval which has elapsed, this Company has been sustained, with all its Immunities; while other Establishments of a similar Nature sunk under the Pressure of those unavoidable Difficulties which were common to all.

The well known Sentiments of your Excellency will spare me the Necessity of dwelling upon the Utility & Expediency of Military Associations; suffice it, with Respect to this, that in rendering a Duty to our Country, we have the Happiness to superadd your personal approbation. I have only to subjoin the perfect Confidence which we repose in your Excellencys Disposition, should the Organization of the Militia of this State, interfere with those Privilege⟨s⟩ which are annexed to our Charter, and which we have hitherto enjoyed.

Your Excellency will pardon me, if to these Sentiments, I presume to add a Subject of a more private Nature. But it will not fail to occur to your Excellency, that during the late peculiar situation of this State, every Branch of Business was materially obstructed; in the long Catalogue of Sufferers, none within the Compass of my Knowlege, experienced a greater Extremity than that Class of Manufacterers, of which I profess myself a Member.

To evince the Truth of this, I need only remind your Excellency of those invincible Restraints which operated against Distillers, in Consequence of the infatuated policy of this State. But I forbear the Recital of Particulars, which will have long been familiar to your Excellency.

Were it not too importunate, I might here observe to your Excellency, the arduous Capacity which I had the Honor to sustain, during the progress of our Revolution; and the Effects which have resulted to my pecuniary situation, from the Nature & Extent of my private Advances. Although under this Embarrassment, I find a Relief in the Consciousness of having discharged only my Duty, yet the Claims of a numerous Family upon my Indulgence, are too pressing to be totally dispensed with. Thus situated, I leave the Conclusion to be drawn by the humane Consideration of your Excellency; only suggesting an Inclination to avail myself, under the Countenance of your Excellency, of some kind of Employment, which might render me further serviceable to the Community, and at the same Time afford a Compensation for those Losses which I must inevitably experience.

In Addition to my own, I beg Leave to add a Solicitation in Behalf of my Son George Tillinghast; who having qualified himself for the Practice of the Law, under the Tuition of the late General Varnum, is capable of discharging any office connected with the Line of his Profession; and whom, I further mention to your Excellency as a Grandson of the Honble Stephen Hopkins, deceased; a Character which was distinguished, not more by his own Virtues, than the personal Confidence of your Excellency. Should there be any Vacancy in the Gift of your Excellency, which remains to be supplied, either in the Judiciary or other Department, I will pledge myself for the faithful Execution of it, were it consonant to the Inclination and Arrangements of your Excellency to bestow it upon him.[1] I have only to add, the profound Respect, with which, I am, Your Excellency's most obedt & Mo. hbe servant

Daniel Tillinghast

P.S. It appearing from the late Ordinance of Congress that an Appointment will accrue for this State in the Commisi⟨on⟩ers Line, I flatter myself that from my Knowlege & Experience [in] similar Departments, I might execute the Duties of *that* with Ju⟨s⟩tice to the publick & Satisfaction to your Excellency. D.T.

ALS, DLC:GW.

Daniel Tillinghast (1732–1806), a Providence merchant and distiller, was a member of the Rhode Island committee of safety during the Revolution and served as colonel and commander of the Providence United Company of the Train of Artillery (see DenBoer, *First Federal Elections*, 4:386–87). Tillinghast renewed his application for employment on 7 Mar. 1791, requesting an appointment as excise collector, noting his personal knowledge of the distilling trade, and citing the many personal sacrifices he had made and the expenses he had incurred as Continental agent for Rhode Island during the war (DLC:GW). He did not receive an appointment from GW.

1. George Tillinghast did not receive a judicial appointment from GW but was appointed an ensign in the U.S. Infantry in March 1791 (see GW to the

U.S. Senate, 3 Mar. 1791, LS, DNA: RG 46, First Congress, 1789–91, Records of Executive Proceedings, President's Messages—Executive Nominations, enclosing nominations for vacancies, 3 March 1791).

From Alexander White

Sir   New York 26th June 1790

It is with great diffidence I offer the enclosed but having taken that liberty will not add to your trouble by Apologies, I will only state such Facts as may enable you to judge whether th⟨is⟩ institution is like to be useful[1]—the nature of the Country in general, its salubrity and fertility you are well acquainted with—The Academy has been supported several years by private Donations, and the monies arising from Tuition, notwithstanding another Gramm⟨a⟩r School and a number of English and Dutch Schools have been kept up in the Town by private subscriptions—The Assembly of Virginia at their last Session granted to the Trustees a Lot in Winchester, and two Tracts of Land—One on Cedar Creek containing 200 acres the other on Back Creek containing 900 acres—it is proposed to erect the Buildings on the Lot and to rent the Lands, which in the present State of their improvements, may not yield much, but will be very valuable in future—If you think this infant Seminary deserving of any share of your Patronage you will signify it in the manner most agreeable to yourself—I am with the greatest regard and respect Sir Your most Obt Servt

Alex. White

ALS, DLC:GW.

1. The enclosure, probably a circular soliciting support for the Winchester Academy, has not been found. The academy was incorporated by the Virginia assembly in the October 1786 session (12 Hening 388). On 9 Dec. 1789 the assembly passed an amendment of the act of incorporation granting the trustees a lot in the town of Winchester and two escheated tracts outside the town (13 Hening 91–92). No reply from GW has been found.

From Charles Willson Peale

Dr Sir   Philad[elphi]a—June 27 [17]90

I wish to be settled near Congress, and my Museum under their Patronage, having just heard that the office of Post master

General is Vacant, if my abilities may be thought sufficient to do justice to such an appointment, I would use my best endeavours to be a faithful servant.[1]

Excuse me if I have made an improper tender of my service to fill such an office. I would not in the smallest matter be troublesome to you, and I wish also to be grateful for past favors. I will only add that my business in the Portrait line in this City, is not sufficient support for my family. I am obliged now to make journeys into Maryland to seek employment, and the thought of an office which would enable me to ⟨i⟩ncrease the Museum to a National Magnitude, by the many opportunities of obtaining articles of Cur[i]osity from every quarter, without the least expence to Congress would I flatter myself be a public benefit.

The fear of trespassing on your time makes me forbear to say many things that croud on my mind on this subject. My Duty to my family sugested this hasty Petition, but whatever is your pleasure shall be agreable to obliged friend

C.W. Peale

ALS, DLC:GW; ADfS, PPAmP: Charles Willson Peale Papers. The enclosure was a printed letter from Peale, 1 Feb. 1790, regarding his museum (DLC:GW).

Charles Willson Peale (1741–1827), one of the most prominent portrait painters of the Revolutionary era, was born in Maryland and apprenticed to a saddler. He studied painting under Benjamin West in London in 1767–69 and later established himself as the leading portrait painter in Annapolis and Philadelphia. During the Revolution Peale served as an officer in the Trenton and Princeton campaigns and in the defense of Philadelphia. During his military service Peale painted many of the military portraits for which he is known. After the war he established a portrait gallery and natural history museum in Philadelphia.

1. Samuel Osgood did not resign as postmaster general until 11 July 1791, citing "the Inconveniences that would result to me by a Removal to Philadelphia" (see Samuel Osgood to GW, 11 July 1791, DNA: RG 59, Miscellaneous Letters), but he had apparently determined as early as the summer of 1790 not to move with the government to Philadelphia. Timothy Pickering, Osgood's ultimate successor, applied for the post in September 1790, noting that "I am informed that Mr. Osgood is determined to resign" (see Pickering to GW, 3 Sept. 1790). Peale may also have had prior knowledge of Osgood's intentions and probably was prompted to apply for the office by expectations that Congress would soon make Philadelphia the seat of government. On 11 June the House of Representatives passed the Parker Resolution, calling for the next session of Congress to convene in Philadelphia (see *DHFC*, 6:1772, 1780). Peale did not receive an appointment from GW.

From John Rutherfurd

Sir   Morrisania [N.Y.] June 28th 1790

Being informed that a law will shortly pass for appointing two additional commissioners to settle the accounts between the United States and the individual states, and having heard it suggested that one of the commissioners will probably be appointed from New Jersey I take the liberty to intimate to your Excellency that I will be very happy to serve in that capacity, if you should think proper to appoint a person from that state. I have the honor to be with sincere regard and attachment your Excellency's most obedient and devoted humble Servant

John Rutherfurd

ALS, DLC:GW.

John Rutherfurd (1760–1840) was born in New York City and graduated from the College of New Jersey in 1779. He practiced law in New York for a short time before moving to a farm near Allamuchy, N.J., in 1787. In 1788 he was a presidential elector and was elected to the state general assembly, serving from 1789 to 1790, when he was elected to the U.S. Senate. He received no appointment from GW.

From John Wilson

Sire   New York June 28th 1790.

I should be far from troubling you in this occasion, with a detail of my services, & sufferings, but that I have reason to believe myself neglected by my Country, which I served and suffered for, at the time of her adversity. On this day twelve years I had the misfortune to be wounded by a Ball which went thro' my right arm on the plains of Monmouth.

At the time of my being wounded I had the honor of being a Sergeant in your Excellency's Guards, under Capt. Gibbs, I had been in the Capacity from the first raising that Corps at Cambridge in the year 1776. I had the honor also of attending frequently in your Excellency's Family for some time and at may different times previous to my being wounded, and altho' it is a long time since I have no doubt but your Excellency would recognize me, in your Excellencies presence. On being wounded instead of applying for the benefit of an Hospital I went to my Friends and remained among them procuring nourishments that were extraordinary at my own Expense. On being examined by Doctr Shippen Surgeon Genl I was pronounced Incurable by him, I had a Certificate from him to that effect, rendering me Incapable of any longer serving in the Army. In this situation I went to live with my Father in the Northern Country (called Vermont) with him I resided ever since unable to procure an Independant living, being deprived of the use of my right arm so as to prevent me from manual Labour or Husbandry, the mode of business in which I was accustomed previous to my entering into the service of my Country. My Parents being in, but indifferent Circumstances, I conceived it in some measure unreasonable to be dependant on them at my time of Life, and hearing that Pensions were granted to persons of the late Army whose services & Losses entitle them thereto. with the assistance of my Friends I acquired as much as paid my expences to *this City*, where I arrived about three Months past. I was *here* some weeks making application for the bounty of my Country to Individuals, but all in vain, being told that I was too late however I was at length advised to Petition the Hon'ble House of Representatives ⟨in⟩ Congress, which I accordingly did in terms the most humble & supplicating, accompanied by a number of the most unexceptionable Vouchers of my Conduct Fidelity & present situation & circumstances. In that same uncertain situation as when I appealed I am at present. and in a state of suspence the most disagreable to the human mind merely because I have been absent for so long a time & have but few or no Friends in this City to forward & recommend Petition, and I much fear it will be thrown out altogether, or neglected, so as to render my best & most honest endeavours ineffectual. Under these circumstances I am reduced to the necessity of applying to your Excellency, humbly to sollicit the favor of some ordinary, or dependent, Public Employment, or that your Excellency would Patronize & recommend me to some of the Public Officers for an Employment that may be suited to my Capacity & Abilities—for I will candidly acknowledge that I was able to obtain my Livelihood by manual Labour I should be the last that would trouble your Excellency on such an occasion. I shall humbly hope for the countenance & favor of your Excellency, conscious that my services & sufferings merit the encouragement & support of my Country, under this hope I have the honour to be with the most respectfull gratitude, Your ever devoted servant

John Wilson

P.S. As I shall hope for the patronage of your Excell⟨y⟩ I must beg leave to say that my present residence is at Mr James Reeds the corner or Moore street in Little ⟨Water⟩ street.

ALS, DLC:GW.

John Wilson petitioned Congress on 30 April 1790, asking to be placed on the list of invalids. The petition was referred to Knox, who reported on it on 24 May 1790. The report was tabled and apparently no further action was taken to in Wilson's case (*DHFC*, 3:391, 421). No reply to Wilson has been found.

From Joseph Stanton and Theodore Foster

Sir,   New York June 29th 1790.

It being necessary that the Vacancy, in the Naval Office, in the District of Providence, in the State of Rhode Island and Providence Plantations should be filled soon, we beg leave to recommend and request that Ebenezer Thompson Esqr. of Providence may be appointed to that Office.[1] He was educated in the Mercantile Business which he followed till the late War. He is a Good Accountant and well acquainted with Book-Keeping. His Moral Character and his Integrity are every way unimpeachable. He has been intrusted with various public Offices which he has discharged to General Satisfaction. He has been a Representative for the Town of Providence and a Member of the upper House, in the Legislature of that State. He is much esteemed and respected, in the Town of Providence being now the President of the Town Council there, who by the Laws of that State transact the Business of the Probate Courts in the other States. He is not now concerned in Navigation or Mercantile Business, or likely to be under the *undue Influence* of any Gentlemen in that Line, a Recommendation which *every* Candidate ought to have. His Firmness of Character, his Integrity, and his Abilities entitle him to the Confidence of the Public. Recommendations in his Behalf could be procured from respectable Characters of all Parties in Rhode Island and we believe his Appointment would tend to compose and reconcile the Spirit of Party in that State. And we are satisfied that it is the General Wish and hope of the People in the Town of Providence as well as throughout the District that he may be appointed, his Conduct as late Collector for the State having given very general Satisfaction.

We assure you, Sir, that we have no private Veiws to answer in this Recommendation which is made purely from a conviction that the Appointment of Mr Thompson as Naval Officer, in that District will Subserve and promote the Public Good more than that of any other Who we heard has made application for the office. We have the Honor to be, Sir, with the highest Sentiments of Regard and Respect, Your most Obedient and humble Servants

Jos. Stanton Jr ⎫   Senators
          ⎬   of
Theodore Foster ⎭   Rhode ⟨Island⟩

We also beg leave to mention the Names of the following Persons as Surveyors, Viz.,

Zachariah Rhodes for the Port of Pawtuxet, in the District of Providence.

Job Comstock for the Port of East Greenwich in the District of Newport.

Bowen Card for the Port of North Kingstown, in the same District.

George Stillman for Pawcatuck River in the same District.

Nathaniel Phillips for Warren and Barrington in the same District.[2]

LS, DLC:GW.

1. Foster had already recommended Thompson in his letter to GW of 26 June 1790. GW appointed Ebenezer Thompson naval officer at Providence on 2 July 1790 (see GW to the U.S. Senate, 2 July 1790).

2. GW filled the posts of surveyor at these minor Rhode Island ports on 2 July 1790 (see GW to the U.S. Senate, 2 July 1790). Of those recommended for posts, Comstock, Stillman, and Phillips were appointed on 2 July and Rhodes, after the post was declined by John Anthony Aborn, on 3 Aug.; Comstock subsequently declined his appointment (*DHFC*, 2:85).

To the Earl of Buchan

My Lord.   New York June 30th 1790.

I received a few days ago, the letter which your Lordship did me the honour to write to me on the 27th of March last; accompanied with a view of Dr Anderson's proposed periodical publication.[1]

Dr Anderson's plan appears judicious, and if the execution

shall equal the design in goodness (as from your account of the Author we have reason to expect) there can be no doubt but his Journal will be of great utility wherever it may be circulated. For the purpose of promoting the circulation, by bringing its object & importance more generally into notice, some account of this literary undertaking will be published in the Gazette of the United States: a paper which is read extensively in America.[2]

From the multiplicity of business, of different kinds, in which I am involved, I have myself less leisure than I could wish for attending to new publications. I shall, however, be glad to give all the encouragement in my power to the work in question, as well on account of its own merits, as to demonstrate the real respect and esteem, with which I have the honour, to be Your Lordship's Most obedient & very humble Servant

Copy, DNA: RG 59, Miscellaneous Letters; ALS, item 258, sold by Parke-Bernet, 23 Oct. 1962; LB, DLC:GW. The copy is addressed to Buchan at "Dryburgh Abbey in Scotland."

1. See the Earl of Buchan to GW, 27 Mar. 1790.
2. See the *Gazette of the United States* [New York], 14 July 1790.

To Charles-Guillaume-Frédéric Dumas

Sir,   New York June 30th 1790

This late acknowledgement of the receipt of your letter of the 6th of November 1789, and the little box which accompanied it, might require some particular apology had I only my own private concerns to attend to; but when important public duties require my constant attention every allowance must be made for the want of punctuality in those things which regard me individually.

I beg, Sir, that you will accept my best thanks for the polite manner in which you have transmitted to me the poems & epistles which the Society of Leyden for the encouragement of the liberal arts in Holland have done me the honor to send to me; and at the same time, I must ask the favor of you to forward the enclosed letter to that Society which is expressive of the sense I entertain of their polite attention to me. I am Sir, Your most Obedt Servt.

Copy, DNA: RG 59, Miscellaneous Letters; LB, DLC:GW.
For background to the letter, see the Leyden Poetical Society to GW, 29 July 1789, source note.

From Donald Fraser

Sir.   New York [30 June 1790]

I am about publishing a book, entitled the young Gentleman and Lady's Assistant. The manuscript Copy of which, I have submitted to the President and professors of Columbia College, who have been pleased to give their approbation of the same.

The universally and justly establish'd Character, of the President of the United States, for beneficence and affability—and his known desire of promoting the cause Literature, induces me to hope; that he will pardon my presumption, in soliciting the honor, of his patronage to my inten'd publication. With the highest sentiments of respect, I am Sir, your most obedient and most humble Servant

Donald Fraser
School-master

ALS, DNA: RG 59, Miscellaneous Letters.
Donald Fraser (1755–1820), a New York schoolmaster, was the author of *The Young Gentleman and Lady's Assistant; Partly Original, but Chiefly Compiled from the Works of the Most Celebrated Modern Authors; Calculated to Instruct Youth in the Principles of Useful Knowledge* (New York, 1791). He later published other books mostly of a similar didactic nature as well. No reply to this letter, nor any evidence that GW subscribed to the book, has been found.

To Joseph Mandrillon

Sir,   New York June 30th 1790.

In replying to your several letters of the 15th of June and 4th of December 1789, and the 10th of January 1790, I must request you to accept my acknowledgements for the very polite terms in which you express your attachment to me—and my best thanks for the several enclosures which accompanied your letters.[1]

The unremitting attention which my public duties require, will, I am persuaded, sufficiently apologize to *you*, Sir, for the want of punctuallity in my private correspondencies—or for not replying so particularly to the favors of my friends as my inclinations might lead me to do. I am, Sir, Yr most Obedt Servt.

Copy, DNA: RG 59, Miscellaneous Letters; LB, DLC:GW.

1. See Mandrillon to GW, 15 June 1789, 4 Dec. 1789, and 9 Jan. 1790. Mandrillon had also written GW on 1 June 1790, but this letter had not yet arrived.

To the United States Senate and House of Representatives

United States [New York] June 30th 1790.
Gentlemen of the Senate and House of Representatives.

An Act of the Legislature of the State of Rhode Island and Providence Plantations for ratifying certain articles as amendments to the Constitution of the United States, was yesterday put into my hands; and I have directed my Secretary to lay a copy of the same before you.[1]

Go: Washington

LS, DNA: RG 46, First Congress, 1789–91, Records of Legislative Proceedings, President's Messages; LB, DLC:GW; copy, DNA: RG 233, First Congress, 1789–91, Records of Legislative Proceedings, Journals.

1. The enclosures were Arthur Fenner's Certificate, 15 June 1790, and a copy of the ratification of amendments to the federal constitution by Rhode Island. GW had submitted the amendments to the Constitution proposed by Congress to the governors of the states on 2 Oct. 1789. Although Rhode Island had not ratified the Constitution, Congress directed GW to send a copy to Rhode Island governor John Collins (see GW's Circular to the Governors of the States, 2 Oct. 1789; the copy sent to Collins is GW to John Collins, 2 Oct. 1789, R-Ar). The Rhode Island general assembly ratified eleven of these amendments, including the ten amendments that constituted the Bill of Rights during a special session that met in Newport on 7–12 June (Bartlett, *R.I. Records,* 10:380–82). The Rhode Island legislature also ratified the first of the proposed amendments, never ratified by a sufficient number of states, regulating the proportion of representatives in the United States House of Representatives to population in the states. For the text of the amendments, see GW's Circular to the Governors of the States, 2 Oct. 1789, n.1. For Rhode Island's instrument of ratification, see Rhode Island Ratifying Convention to GW, 9 June 1790, n.1. GW's transmittal of the act of the ratification, along with Gov. Arthur Fenner's certification of Henry Ward, the secretary of the Rhode Island general assembly, was delivered to both houses of Congress by Lear on 30 June (*DHFC,* 1:388–89, 3:483).

From Catharine Sawbridge Macaulay Graham

Sir   Bracknal; Berks. [England] June 1790

The sentiments yr Excellency expressed in yr Letter of the 9th of January are worthy of yr exalted character; and must be pleasing to all those who are friends to the happiness of man kind, For when by the success of yr arms, you afforded America the option of a free government; yr task was not so difficult, or more important, than yr present station; as her first Chief Majestrate.

The present system of American Government, contains all those principles which have been regarded as capable of re-sisting every hostile influence arising either from force or seduc-tion. I once thought that such a system of government would be invulnerable; as yr Excellency must have perceived if you have ever read a political tract of mine adressed to Paoli the Corsican General. It is true that in that sketch of a Democratical Govern-ment, I endeavored to keep out corruption by enforcing a gen-eral Rotation; but I must acknowledge to you that the corrup-tions which have crept into our Legislature since the revolution, with the wise caution used by the french patriots in the rules to which they have subjected their National Assembly, have led me to alter my opinion; and this alteration of opinion, incline⟨s⟩ me to fear, that ill consequences may arise from vesting the Legisla-tive body with the power of establishing Offices, of regulating the quantum of their salaries, and of enjoying themselves the emoluments arising from such establishments. I should have thought it safer to have made them incapable of holding at least any Civil Office whilst they were Members of the Legislature. Th⟨ose⟩ who have studied mankind with the greatest attention, find, that there is no depending on their virtue; except where all corrupting motives are put out of their way.

I see also that you have followed the example of the Parent State in dividing yr Legislature into an Upper and a Lower House. I once thought that this was the only method of ob-taining the result of deliberate Counsels; but I at present am of opinion that the French have effectualy secured themselves from the return of Aristocracy in their government, by confining the Legislature to one equal Assembly; and committing the of-fice of approving laws to the King and the people. May not yr

Upper House in length of time, acquire some distinctions which may lay the grounds for political inequality among you? a circumstance which never ought to take place in a Society of free men. The Americans free from every part of the feudal tenure and the unjust distinctions of primo geniture; found it easy when they had shaken of the yoke of England, to form and regulate a popular government; but from the c⟨ir⟩cumstance of always having been exempt from the evils of Aristocracy, they may not have the principle of averssion to such pretenssions planted in their minds, as now happily exist among the French. They may also have regarded wi⟨th⟩ admiration instead of disgust, the splendor of European Society; and mistaken the insolence and ostentation of a few citizens, for National dignity.

But, besides these causes, which appear to form a very important difference in the relative state of things in the two Empires, of France and ⟨of⟩ America; the former Nation has undergone the fiery trial of temptation and come out purified; she has sat an example hitherto unparralled in the annals of humanity, that of emmerging from the depths of frivolous dissipation to the most exalted heigh of National conduct. But as the difficulties which the Americans have to strugle with in the settling a new country, and that mediocrity of wealth which must naturally have attended such difficulties; a good deal enforced a sobriety of manners among them, it is impossible to tell what may be the effects of a change in the internal prosperity of the Country. When the E'ra now so ardently desired by the Americans shall arrive, that commerce pours in wealth on every side, and when they will by this means have it in their power to import all the l⟨uxur⟩ies and copy all the excesses of the Mother Country, and to vye with her Citizens in all the deceitful pleasures of a vicious dissipation; it is more than possible, that the novelty of such seductive enjoyments will overturn all the virtue which at present exists in the Country. That an inattention to public interest will prevail, and nothing be pursued but private gratification and emolument. These do not appear as groundless fears; for the Americans have shewn a greater inclination to the fripperies of Europe, th⟨an⟩ to Classic simplicity.

That these evils may only exist in the imagination of those who like me am tremblingly alive on the subject of human liberty, I most sincerely hope; as also that the future Chief Majestrates of the United States, may in some measure partake of the wisdom, and virtue, of her first Chief Majestrate.

If I have transgressed on yr Excellencies patience by so long a letter; I have been led to it by your condescenssion in giving me some of yr senti⟨me⟩nts and observations, on the present state of things in America; and I hope yr goodness will excuse it.

I have done my self the honor to send yr Excellency a copy of a work I have lately published on education.

Mr Graham joins me in respectful compliments as due, And I am Sir yr Excellency's Most Obliged And Obedt Servt

Cath: Macaulay Graham.

I beg my thanks to Mrs Washington, for the favor of her remembrance.

ALS, DLC:GW.

Letter not found: from Thomas Green, June 1790. On 8 July 1790 Lear wrote Green that: "The President has received your letter of June."[1]

1. In his letter to Green, Lear added: "As it has been contrary to his [GW's] practice to suffer any accounts against him to remain unsatisfied for so long a time he thinks it possible there may be some error in your account that may be rectified by a recurrence to his books or papers at Mount Vernon—As soon as information respecting this matter can be received from thence, whatever may be due to you shall be paid as you desire" (DLC:GW).

Index

NOTE: Identifications of persons in previous volumes of the *Presidential Series* are noted within parentheses.

Iredell, James (*continued*)
pointment, 122; suggested for
office, 184; *letters from*: to GW,
314, 530–31
Ireland: applications for office in,
288–90
Irish Insurance Company for Ships,
Merchandise and Lives (firm),
289
Irvine, William (*see* 1:40): *letters from*:
to GW, 199
Irwin, ——: and American shipping,
378–79
Irwin, Mathew (*see* 3:156), 271
Izard, Ralph: and appointment of
Henry M. Bird, 41; drafts bill,
84; serves on Senate, 84, 410;
and appointment of diplomats,
346; and Thomas Bee, 417; and
David Olyphant, 499

Jackasses, 206
Jackson, ——: and Thomas Ham-
mond, 162
Jackson, George, 94
Jackson, William (*see* 2:75), 71, 394;
and James Manley, 110; de-
scribes GW's illness, 396; secre-
tarial duties, 397; *letters from*: to
Alexander Hamilton, 387; to
Clement Biddle, 393–400; *letters
to*: from chevalier d'Anterroches, 101–2
James (slave), 203; id., 205
James, John: *letters from*: to GW, 532
James & Johnson (firm): publish William Bartram's work, 513
James's Powder, 395
Jarvis, James: and coinage, 335
Jasper, Samuel: appointment of, 362,
420; id., 362; recommended for
office, 362
Jay, John, 28, 468, 523; and northeastern boundary dispute, 117,
118; letters cited, 28, 119, 120,
315; compliments, 242; and Supreme Court meeting, 314; GW
consults, 345; opinion requested
on Thomas Bird case, 481; and
Henry Marchant, 489; *letters

from*: to GW, 481, 518; *letters to*:
from Tobias Lear, 9, 163; from
Elbridge Gerry, 271; from
Thomas Jefferson, 272; from
GW, 517
Jay, Sarah, 395
Jeffers, John: appointment of, 465
Jefferson, Thomas, 101, 302, 305,
370, 403, 468, 490; letters transmitted, 10; and appointment as
secretary of state, 29–31, 138,
164–65, 165; and Nathan Read,
43; and survey of Virginia coast,
176; and Claude-Boniface Collignon, 231; and conferences
with GW, 270–72, 302, 345; and
American captives in Algiers,
271; arrives in New York, 271;
and medals for Revolutionary
War service, 277, 278, 279; circular letter to cabinet, 302–3; description of GW's presidential
procedures, 302–3; description
of John Adams's presidential
procedures, 303; removal from
France, 318; and transmission of
laws to president, 323; compliments, 327; and coinage, 336,
337; opinion on diplomatic appointments, 342–46; comments
on GW's illness, 396, 397; and
North Carolina appointments,
482, 486–88; *letters from*: to GW,
31, 138, 301–3, 315, 342–46,
357–58, 379–81, 381, 522–23; to
Benjamin Franklin, 117–18; to
James Madison, 165; to Adrian
Van der Kemp, 245; to William
Carmichael, 254; to William
Short, 262–63, 358; to John Jay,
272; to Arthur St. Clair, 377; to
Martha Jefferson Randolph,
396; *letters to*: from GW, 29–31,
535; from Benjamin Franklin,
118; from Jacob Vernes, 198;
from William Short, 271, 438;
from James McHenry, 385; from
David Howell, 522–23; from
Tobias Lear, 548–49
Jenckes, John: and Benjamin Stelle,
195; *letters from*: to GW, 195